Communications
in Computer and Information Science 51

T0180977

Zhihua Cai   Zhenhua Li   Zhuo Kang
Yong Liu (Eds.)

Computational Intelligence and Intelligent Systems

4th International Symposium, ISICA 2009
Huangshi, China, October 23-25, 2009
Proceedings

 Springer

Volume Editors

Zhihua Cai
School of Compupter Science, China University of Geosciences, Wuhan, China
E-mail: zhcai@cug.edu.cn

Zhenhua Li
School of Computer Science, China University of Geosciences, Wuhan, China
E-mail: zhli@cug.edu.cn

Zhuo Kang
Computation Center, Wuhan University, Wuhan, China
E-mail: kang_whu@yahoo.com

Yong Liu
School of Computer Science and Engineering, The University of Aizu, Japan
E-mail: yliu@u-aizu.ac.jp

Library of Congress Control Number: 2009936952

CR Subject Classification (1998): I.2, I.2.6, I.5.1, F.1, I.6, J.1

ISSN   1865-0929
ISBN-10   3-642-04961-3 Springer Berlin Heidelberg New York
ISBN-13   978-3-642-04961-3 Springer Berlin Heidelberg New York

springer.com

© Springer-Verlag Berlin Heidelberg 2009
Printed in Germany

Typesetting: Camera-ready by author, data conversion by Scientific Publishing Services, Chennai, India
Printed on acid-free paper   SPIN: 12773022   06/3180   5 4 3 2 1 0

Preface

Volumes of LNCS 5821 and CCIS 51 are the proceedings of the 4th International Symposium on Intelligence Computation and Applications (ISICA 2009) held in Huangshi, China, October 23–25, 2009. These two volumes are in memory of Prof. Lishan Kang, the ISICA 2009 Honorary General Chair, who was a leading figure in the fields of domain decomposition methods and computational intelligence.

ISICA 2009 successfully attracted over 300 submissions. Through rigorous reviews, 58 high-quality papers were included in LNCS 5821, while the other 54 papers were collected in CCIS 51. ISICA conferences are one of the first series of international conferences on computational intelligence that combine elements of learning, adaptation, evolution and fuzzy logic to create programs as alternative solutions to artificial intelligence. The last three ISICA proceedings have been accepted in the Index to Scientific and Technical Proceedings (ISTP) and/or Engineering Information (EI).

Following the success of the past three ISICA events, ISICA 2009 made good progress in the analysis and design of newly developed methods in the field of computational intelligence. ISICA 2009 featured the most up-to-date research in analysis and theory of evolutionary algorithms, neural network architectures and learning, fuzzy logic and control, predictive modeling for robust classification, swarm intelligence, evolutionary system design, evolutionary image analysis and signal processing, and computational intelligence in engineering design. ISICA 2009 provided a venue to foster technical exchanges, renew everlasting friendships, and establish new connections.

On behalf of the Organizing Committee, we would like to thank warmly the sponsors, China University of Geosciences and Hubei Normal University, who helped in one way or another to achieve our goals for the conference. We wish to express our appreciation to Springer for publishing the proceedings of ISICA 2009. We also wish to acknowledge the dedication and commitment of the LNCS and CCIS editorial staff. We would like to thank the authors for submitting their work, as well as the Program Committee members and reviewers for their enthusiasm, time and expertise. The invaluable help of active members from the Organizing Committee, including Jiaoe Jiang, Dajun Rong, Hao Zhang and Xiaowen Jin, in setting up and maintaining the online submission systems, assigning the papers to the reviewers, and preparing the camera-ready version of the proceedings is highly appreciated. We would like to thank them personally for helping make ISICA 2009 a success.

October 2009

Zhihua Cai
Zhenhua Li
Zhuo Kang
Yong Liu

Organization

ISICA 2009 was organized by the School of Computer Science, China University of Geosciences, and Hubei Normal University, and sponsored by China University of Geosciences.

Honorary General Chair

Lishan Kang   China University of Geosciences, China

General Co-chairs

Huiming Tang   China University of Geosciences, China
Boshan Chen   Hubei Normal University, China

Program Co-chairs

Zhihua Cai   China University of Geosciences, China
Shudong Shi   Hubei Normal University, China
Yong Liu   University of Aizu, Japan

Publication Chair

Zhenhua Li   China University of Geosciences, China

Program Committee

Mehdi Hosseinzadeh Aghdam	University of Tabriz, Iran
M. Amiri	Allameh Tabatabaee University, Iran
Sujeevan Aseervatham	University of Grenoble, France
Jeremy Bolton	University of Florida, USA
Hua Cao	Mississippi State University, USA
Jiangtao Cao	University of Portsmouth, UK
Cheng-Hsiung Chiang	Hsuan Chuang University, Taiwan, China
Alessandro Ghio	University of Genova, Italy
Erik D. Goodman	Michigan State University, USA
Peng Guo	University of Science and Technology of China, China
A.S. Hadi	University of Baghdad, Iraq
Fei He	City University of Hong Kong, China
Katsuhiro Honda	Osaka Prefecture University, Japan

Yutana Jewajinda   National Electronics and Computer Technology
                            Center, Bangkok, Thailand
He Jiang   Dalian University of Technology, China
Heli Koskimaki   University of Oulu, Oulu, Finland
Takio Kurita   Neuroscience Research Institute National
                            Institute of Advanced Industrial Science and
                            Technology, Japan
Juan Luis J. Laredo   University of Granada, Spain
Bi Li   Guangdong University of Foreign Studies,
                            China
Yow Tzu Lim   University of York, UK
Xiaojun Lu   University of Electronic Science and
                            Technology of China, China
Wenjian Luo   China Science and Technology
                            University, China
Alejandro Flores Méndez   LaSalle University, Mexico
J.I. Serrano   Universidad de Cantabria, Spain
A.K.M. Khaled   The University of Melbourne, Australia
Ahsan Talukder
H.R. Tizhoosh   University of Waterloo, Canada
Massimiliano Vasile   University of Glasgow, UK
Jun Wang   The Chinese University of Hong Kong, China
Yuxuan Wang   Nanjing University of Posts & Telecom, China
Hongjie Xing   Hebei University, China
Jifeng Xuan   Dalian University of Technology, China
Harry Zhang   University of New Brunswick, Canada

Local Arrangements Chair

Yadong Liu   China University of Geosciences, China

Secretariat

Jiaoe Jiang   China University of Geosciences, China
Dajun Rong   China University of Geosciences, China
Hao Zhang   China University of Geosciences, China
Xiaowen Jin   China University of Geosciences, China

Sponsoring Institutions

China University of Geosciences, Wuhan,China

Table of Contents

Section I: Computational Intelligence Applications

Omnidirectional Motion Control for the Humanoid Soccer Robot 1
    Zhechao Gao, Jia Wu, Hongwu Chen, Bowen Pan, Hao Zheng,
    Dingwen Liang, and Xiaoming Liu

Routing Algorithm Based on Gnutella Model 9
    Feng Ye, Fengmei Zuo, and Sifa Zhang

Sliding-Window Recursive PLS Based Soft Sensing Model and Its
Application to the Quality Control of Rubber Mixing Process 16
    Kejuan Chen, Min He, and Dongzhi Zhang

The Research of Method Based on Complex Multi-task Parallel
Scheduling Problem 25
    Xiang Li, Peng Chen, and Li Zhu

Towards a Bio-inspired Security Framework for Mission-Critical
Wireless Sensor Networks 35
    Wei Ren, Jun Song, Zhao Ma, and Shiyong Huang

Section II: Evolutionary Algorithms

A Cluster-Based Orthogonal Multi-Objective Genetic Algorithm 45
    Jiankai Zhu, Guangming Dai, and Li Mo

An Analysis of Semantic Aware Crossover 56
    Nguyen Quang Uy, Nguyen Xuan Hoai, Michael O'Neill,
    Bob McKay, and Edgar Galván-López

An Artificial Immune Univariate Marginal Distribution Algorithm 66
    Qingbin Zhang, Shuo Kang, Junxiang Gao, Song Wu, and
    Yanping Tian

An Multi-objective Evolutionary Algorithm with Lower-Dimensional
Crossover and Dense Control 76
    Dongdong Zhao, Sanyou Zeng, and Huanhuan Li

Improved Evolutionary Programming and Its Application in Navigation
System 88
    Jianjuan Liu

Multi-objective Emergency Facility Location Problem Based on Genetic
Algorithm 97
    Dan Zhao, Yunsheng Zhao, Zhenhua Li, and Jin Chen

Trigonometric Curve Fitting Based on Genetic Algorithm and the
Application of Data Processing in Geography 104
  Baolei Gu

Section III: Evolutionary Design

A Novel Crossover Operator in Evolutionary Algorithm for Logic
Circuit Design 110
  Guo-liang He, Yuan-xiang Li, and Zhongzhi Shi

Aptasensors Design Considerations 118
  Y.C. Lim, A.Z. Kouzani, and W. Duan

Latent Semantic Analysis of the Languages of Life 128
  Ryan Anthony Rossi

Protein Folding Simulation by Two-Stage Optimization 138
  A. Dayem Ullah, L. Kapsokalivas, M. Mann, and K. Steinhöfel

Search Direction Made Evolution Strategies Faster 146
  Guangming Lin, Xin Lu, and Lishan Kang

Topology Organization in Peer-to-Peer Platform for Genetic Algorithm
Environment 156
  Hong Yao and Linchen Yu

Section IV: Evolutionary Image Analysis and Signal Processing

Almost Periodic Solutions for Shunting Inhibitory Cellular Neural
Networks with Time-Varying and Distributed Delays 162
  Chaojin Fu and Ailong Wu

Applications of Computational Intelligence in Remote Sensing Image
Analysis 171
  Hengjian Tong, Man Zhao, and Xiang Li

Association Relation Mining in Multimedia Data.................... 180
  Wei Wei, Bin Ye, and Qing Li

DSA Image Blood Vessel Skeleton Extraction Based on
Anti-concentration Diffusion and Level Set Method.................. 188
  Jing Xu, Jian Wu, Daming Feng, and Zhiming Cui

Space Camera Focusing Forecast Based on RBF Network 199
  Xingxing Wu, Jinguo Liu, and Da Yu

Wood Defect Identification Based on Artificial Neural Network 207
  Xiao-dong Zhu, Jun Cao, Feng-hu Wang, Jian-ping Sun, and Yu Liu

Section V: Evolutionary Optimization

An Improved Self-adaptive Control Parameter of Differential Evolution
for Global Optimization 215
    Liyuan Jia, Wenyin Gong, and Hongbin Wu

Distributed Evolutionary Algorithms to TSP with Ring Topology 225
    *Shanzhi Huang, Li Zhu, Fang Zhang, Yongxiang He, and
    Haidong Xue*

Self-adaptation in Fast Evolutionary Programming 232
    Yong Liu

Solving SAT Problem Based on Hybrid Differential Evolution
Algorithm.. 240
    Kunqi Liu, Jingmin Zhang, Gang Liu, and Lishan Kang

The Application of Evolution-Branching Algorithm on Earth-Mars
Transfer Trajectory 247
    Jing Liu and Guangming Dai

The Research of Solution to the Problems of Complex Task Scheduling
Based on Self-adaptive Genetic Algorithm.......................... 257
    Li Zhu, Yongxiang He, Haidong Xue, and Leichen Chen

Section VI: Fuzzy Logic Systems

A Novel Approach on Designing Augmented Fuzzy Cognitive Maps
Using Fuzzified Decision Trees 266
    Elpiniki I. Papageorgiou

Computation of Uncertain Parameters by Using Fuzzy Synthetic
Decision and D-S Theory 276
    Lingling Li, Jungang Zhou, Zhigang Li, and Jingzheng Liu

FAHP-Based Fuzzy Comprehensive Evaluation of M&S Credibility 285
    Jing Wu, Xiao-yan Wu, and Zhong-chang Gao

Indirect Dynamic Recurrent Fuzzy Neural Network and Its Application
in Identification and Control of Electro-Hydraulic Servo System........ 295
    Yuan-feng Huang, You-wang Zhang, and Peng Min

Logistics Distribution Center Location Evaluation Based on Genetic
Algorithm and Fuzzy Neural Network 305
    Yuxiang Shao, Qing Chen, and Zhenhua Wei

Mean-VaR Models and Algorithms for Fuzzy Portfolio Selection 313
    Wen Dong and Jin Peng

MOEA-Based Fuzzy Control for Seismically Excited Structures 320
Xiang-liang Ning, Ping Tan, and Fu-lin Zhou

Section VII: Hybrid Methods

A Hybrid E-Institution Model for VOs.............................. 329
Youming Zhou and Ji Gao

An Optimal Class Association Rule Algorithm....................... 344
Turiho Jean Claude, Sheng Yang, Chuang Li, and Kaia Xie

Multiple Sequence Alignment Based on Chaotic PSO 351
Xiu-juan Lei, Jing-jing Sun, and Qian-zhi Ma

Model Checking Algorithm Based on Ant Colony Swarm Intelligence ... 361
Xiangning Wu, Chengyu Hu, and Yuan Wang

QPSO-MD: A Quantum Behaved Particle Swarm Optimization for
Consensus Pattern Identification 369
Souham Meshoul and Tasneem Al-Owaisheq

Section VIII: Neural Network Architectures

Prediction of Hydrocarbon Reservoir Parameter Using a GA-RBF
Neural Network... 379
Jing Chen, Zhenhua Li, and Dan Zhao

Qualitative Simulation of Teachers Group Behaviors Based on BP
Neural Network... 387
Tianyin Liu and Bin Hu

Stabilization of Switched Dynamic Neural Networks with Discrete
Delays... 398
Shiping Wen and Zhigang Zeng

ANN Designing Based on Co-evolutionary Genetic Algorithm with
Degeneration 406
Xianshan Zhou, Bing Luo, and Bing Fu

Research on ACA-BP Neural Network Model 413
Qing Chen, Yuxiang Shao, and Zhifeng Liu

Section IX: Predictive Modeling for Classification

A Text-Independent Speaker Verification System Based on Cross
Entropy 419
Xiaochun Lu and Junxun Yin

An Improved Algorithm of Apriori 427
    Binhua Liao

An Incremental Clustering with Attribute Unbalance Considered for
Categorical Data... 433
    Jize Chen, Zhimin Yang, Jian Yin, Xiaobo Yang, and Li Huang

Decision Tree Classifier for Classification of Plant and Animal Micro
RNA's... 443
    Bhasker Pant, Kumud Pant, and K.R. Pardasani

Embedded Classification Learning for Feature Selection Based on
K-Gravity Clustering 452
    Weizhao Guo, Jize Chen, Zhimin Yang, Jian Yin,
    Xiaobo Yang, and Li Huang

Evaluation Measures of the Classification Performance of Imbalanced
Data Sets 461
    Qiong Gu, Li Zhu, and Zhihua Cai

Hybrid Classification of Pulmonary Nodules 472
    S.L.A. Lee, A.Z. Kouzani, and E.J. Hu

Erratum

Evaluation Measures of the Classification Performance of Imbalanced
Data Sets E1
    Qiong Gu, Li Zhu, and Zhihua Cai

Author Index 483

Omnidirectional Motion Control for the Humanoid Soccer Robot

Zhechao Gao, Jia Wu, Hongwu Chen, Bowen Pan,
Hao Zheng, Dingwen Liang, and Xiaoming Liu

Faculty of Computer Science, China University of Geosciences,
Wuhan 430074, P.R. China
wujiawb@126.com

Abstract. In RoboCup 2008 World Championship, the model of RoboCup 3D simulation has changed from Soccerbot to Nao. A series of parameters have been changed in a Nao model. This has greatly increased the complexity and difficulty of motion controller for Nao. Based on the analysis of Nao's structure, our team G-Star has worked out the quantitative relation of joint angle in motion control and developed a toolkit to calculate the angle of joints accurately. In the experiment on RoboCup 3D server platform, our robots can stand up promptly and walk smoothly, which is fast enough to meet the real-time requirements. In this paper, we will give a detailed description of the architecture in basic motion using Nao model.

Keywords: RoboCup 3D, Humanoid robot, Motion control, Simulation.

1 Introduction

In humanoid robot simulation like RoboCup 3D, the controller of robot motion is prior to the decision system. To make a strategy more flexible and stable, a set of basic actions such as walking, turning, standing up is indispensable. Compared to Soccerbot, Nao, although they are both humanoid robot, has different structure in some joints, which adds joint angle limit and changes some parameters of joints.

Through the analysis of Nao's skeleton structure, we have found a simple principle of basic action under Nao model, which makes our robots walk faster [1] on the field and stand up promptly. In our motion design, the robot can also walk backward [2] as same as walk forward which avoids the time loss of turning and makes the strategy more effective [3].

In this paper, we describe a particular analysis of Nao model and propose a basic motion control approach. Then we give a snapshot of our development toolkit called RoboCup3D-Tool which is helpful to quantitative computing under the motion control of Nao model.

The rest of the paper is organized as follows. In Section 2, we give a formal description of the structure of Nao model and give a preliminary analysis of joint control. In Section 3, we mainly discuss our motion control mechanism. A snapshot of our development tool is presented in Section 4. Section 5 concludes the whole paper and gives some future works.

Z. Cai et al. (Eds.): ISICA 2009, CCIS 51, pp. 1–8, 2009.

2 Preliminaries

2.1 Nao Model

As we can see the Nao's skeleton from Fig. 1, there are five joints [4] can influence the action of leg on one side. Three of them are hinge joints which are most important in controlling forward and backward direction. In the figure, they are joint leg3 which join the robot's body and thigh, joint leg4 which join the robot's thigh and shank and joint leg5 which join the robot's shank and foot. The leg can turn to any configuration with the three joints. What's more, we can achieve more actions in landscape orientation if we use joint leg2 and leg6 which control the offset of transverse.

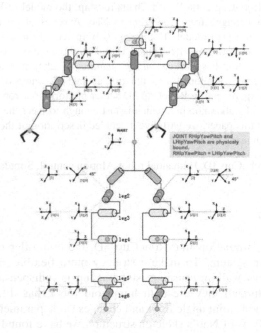

Fig. 1. The joints of Nao robot

2.2 Relations between Joints

According to the joints structure, we choose a suitable initialization angle for the five joints, so that all the other actions can start with this state.

Here, to make the analysis easier to understand, we simply transfer the three-dimensional [5] reference frame into two-dimensional reference frame. We can see the two-dimensional plane in Fig. 2 and Fig. 3, which show the quantitative relationship of the leg and the whole body.

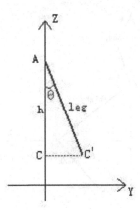

Fig. 2. Quantitative relationship of robot leg

In Fig. 2, we can get the transverse relations of angles and lengths as follows:

$$h = AC' \times \cos\theta. \tag{1}$$

$$dy = CC' = AC' \times \sin\theta. \tag{2}$$

Where h represents the height of the robot's lower body, and dy represents the leg's translation in y direction.

In Fig. 3, we can get the joint angle relations as follows:

$$h = l_{thigh} \times \sin c + l_{shank} \times \sin d. \tag{3}$$

$$dx = l_{thigh} \times \cos c - l_{shank} \times \cos d. \tag{4}$$

$$\angle a + \angle leg3 = 180°. \tag{5}$$

$$\angle c + (-\angle leg4) = 180°. \tag{6}$$

$$\angle e + \angle leg5 = 90°. \tag{7}$$

$$\angle body\_ang = \angle b. \tag{8}$$

$$\angle b + \angle a = 90° + \angle c. \tag{9}$$

$$\angle d = \angle e. \tag{10}$$

Where dx represents the leg's translation in y direction, l_{thigh} and l_{shank} represents the length of the robot thigh and shank respectively, and the $body\_ang$ represents the gradient of the robot body.

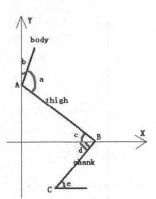

Fig. 3. Quantitative relationship of the whole body

According to the ten equations above, we can figure out the angles of leg2, leg3, leg4, leg5 and leg6 with dx, dy, h. So we can write a function which maps from the inputs dx, dy and h to the outputs all the degrees of the joints above. This is a fundamental function of our motion control system, which keeps the robot body's balance and COM (Center of Mass) smooth. Then, we can use it as a basic control in many action sets.

3 Motion Control

3.1 Moving

Fig. 4 shows the two states in the moving action, the left leg and the right leg. There are two steps in each leg, which hold the legs up and down, stride and stop. The step 1 represents the stride action, while the step 2 is the dropping action. With the move function, we can control actions with the inputs dx, dy, h of each leg.

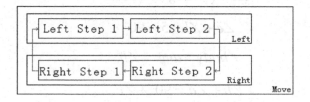

Fig. 4. The process of moving

3.2 Walking

If both of the two legs' dy are 0 and dx are the same, the robot will walk smoothly. Where the positive value leads to forward walk and negative to the backward.

3.3 Turning

3.3.1 Turning When Walking

It's easy to do this job if you add turning while walking straightly. The robot will walk in a roundness path [6]. The relation of step lengths and radius is as follows:

$$2\pi r_1 / 2\pi r_2 = dx_l / dx_r. \tag{11}$$

$$r_2 - r_1 = x. \tag{12}$$

$$r = (r_1 + r_2)/2 = ((dx_l + dx_r) \times x)/(|dx_l - dx_r| \times 2) \tag{13}$$

Where x is the distance between the center of feet, dx_l, dx_r represent the displacement of left and right leg in x direction. Fig. 5 shows the relation which is described above.

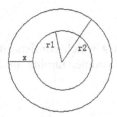

Fig. 5. The relation of turning and walking

3.3.2 Turning without Walking

We can easily get the function from the equations above. That is, if r is zero, the robot stays. So when dx_l plus dx_r equals 0, we will get action of turning without walking.

3.4 Transverse Move

Just if the dy isn't zero, the robot will do transverse moving. You will get more wizardly actions [7] if add other actions.

3.5 Symmetrical Robot Actions

Not a new action but an idea of design. Our robot can do everything with either its face or back. So it will be smarter and faster than ever before. In this way robot saves more time when adjusting [8], which makes our robot easier to get the ball. Also it has advantages in dynamic environments, which has been proved in RoboCup 2008 China Open. Fig. 6 gives a snapshot when using this method.

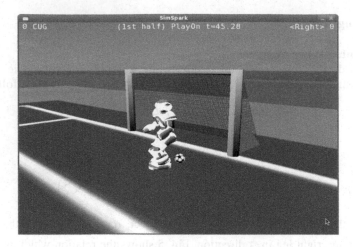

Fig. 6. Walk backward for goal

4   Development Tool

RoboCup3D-Tool is written in C# which consists of four modules: initial module, walk module, transverse move module, turning module. Hera, we will take walk module for presentation.

4.1   Initial Module

Fig. 7 is a snapshot of RoboCup3D-Tool. The picture on the left-top is an initial state of the robot. The other modules are based on the initial state.

The initial state angle is: Leg3 = 35.50, Leg4 = -63.90, Leg5 = 28.40.

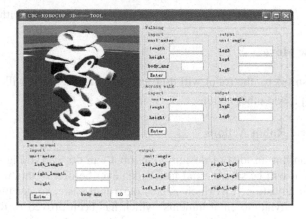

Fig. 7. The main window of RoboCup3D-Tool

4.2 Walk Module

Walk module is the core of the whole action which consists of two sub-window import and output, which can be seen in Fig. 8.

Import:

      Length: the distance between foot and torso (length > 0, forward; length < 0, backward).

      Height: the distance between foot and field.

      Body_ang: the slant angle of torso.

Output:

      Leg3, Leg4, Leg5

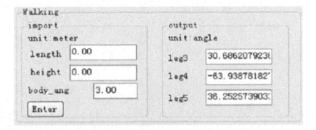

Fig. 8. Walk module

5 Conclusion and Future Works

In experiment, our robots are able to fast walk, and the speed of standing up is also prompt. The principle of walking forward or backward is totally symmetric, so that while robot's direction is against the goal, it can also carry the ball backward quickly. In the future, we will improve our adjusting efficiency between walking and stopping to reduce the time loss in motion transforming.

Acknowledgments

We very thank Mr. Xuesong Yan for his kindly guidance and help.

References

1. Collins, S.H., Wisse, M., Ruina, A.: A 3D Passive — Dynamic Walking Robot with Two Legs and Knees. The International Journal of Robotics Research 20(7), 607–615 (2001)
2. Behnke, S.: Online Trajectory Generation for Omnidirectional BipedWalk. In: Proceeding of the 2006 IEEE International Conference on Robotics and Automation, Orlando, Florida (2006)
3. KÖgler, M.: Simulation and Visualization of Agents in 3D Environments. Diploma Thesis, 13–25 (2003)
4. Kajita, S., Hirukawa, H., Yokoi, K., Harada, K.: Humanoid Robots (Chinese Edition). Tsinghua University Press, Beijing (2007)

5. Lattner, A.D., Rachuy, C., Stahlbock, A., Visser, U., Warden, T.: Virtual Wender 3D team documentation. Technical Report 36, TZI - Center for Computing Technologies, Bremen (2006)
6. Niehaus, C.: Optimierung des omnidirektionalen Laufens eines humanoiden Roboters. Master's thesis, Bremen (2007)
7. Röfer, T., Budelmann, C., Fritsche, M., Laue, T., Müller, J., Niehaus, C., Penquitt, F.: B-Human team description for RoboCup 2007 (2007)
8. Wagner, T., Bogon, T., Elfers, C.: Incremental generation of adductive explanations for tactical behavior. In: Visser, U., Ribeiro, F., Ohashi, T., Dellaert, F. (eds.) RoboCup 2007. LNCS (LNAI), vol. 5001, pp. 401–408. Springer, Heidelberg (2008)

Routing Algorithm Based on Gnutella Model

Feng Ye, Fengmei Zuo, and Sifa Zhang

China University of Geosciences
No.388 Lumo Road Wuhan, P.R. China

Abstract. The traditional Gnutella model can solve the centralized problem of network structure. However, its consumption of a great deal of bandwidth is prone to result in the network congestion and instability. In order to solve this problem, this paper improved the current routing algorithm based on the Ant algorithm. For achieving the optimal routing, the algorithm amended the routing gradually. In the routing search, it also avoided the randomization and blindness of message relay service by adding constrained condition. The test results show that this method can reduce the broadband consumption caused by the flood mechanism of Gnutella network.

Keywords: Gnutella, flood, routing g.

1 Introduction

In recent years, P2P develops rapidly, which attracts thousands up thousands users. The most popular P2P models are centralized, distributed and composite. Especially the research for distributed model such as Gnutella is really extensive.

As it is known to all, traditional Gnutella network model uses the network structure of pure P2P model, which can be known as broadcast P2P model as well. It cancels the central server, every networked computer is both a client and a server, and each client switches in the P2P network randomly, at the same time it makes up a logic overwritten network with the neighborhood node according to connection of port-to-port. The inquiry and share to content between the reciprocal nodes are transmitted through the neighborhood node with broadcast relays, and every node records the search track to prevent search loop. Traditional Gnutella model can solve the centralized problem of network structure with good fault-tolerance [2]. However the search algorithm in Gnutella network works based on flood mode whose control information consumes most broadband, at the same time, brings the network congestion and instability. And it may lead to the Gnutella network fragment. All these things made the entire network poor expansibility and usability. Moreover this kind of network is more likely to be effected by junk information even the malicious attack from virus.

To solve these problems, the paper combined Ant algorithm with routing algorithm, and added constrained condition into the routing search, which is really effective for saving bandwidth. After testing, this method performed well with satisfied results.

Z. Cai et al. (Eds.): ISICA 2009, CCIS 51, pp. 9–15, 2009.
© Springer-Verlag Berlin Heidelberg 2009

2 Improvement of Algorithm

In view of the above question, the new Gnutella model adopts tiered structure such as Figure 1. The idea is that the whole P2P system nodes will be divided into two parts: super node and normal node. One super node manages a few of normal nodes. The super node is in the second layer, the leaf is in the lowest layer [1], the super node acts as the agent for normal node to achieve expansibility and raise network data of availability. However during transmitting process the message still uses flood mode to search for location reciprocal machine which may causes network congestion.

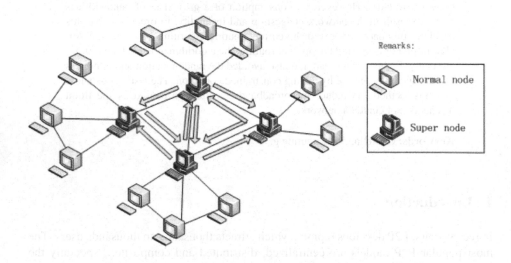

Fig. 1. The layered Gnutella model

In this paper, based on the characteristics of Gnutella, the ways to solve network flow problem brought by flood mode can be shown as follows:

1. Every super node maintains two tables. One is the rout state table of super node (SRT) which records the searching situation between this super node and its neighborhood. The other is the normal node information table (NIT) which connects with it.
2. Every normal node maintains a neighborhood node table (NRT), providing a convenient path for normal node connecting with others, and maintains a resources index table (SIT) to publish local resources information.
3. According to the rout state table of super node (SRT), super node routs its search request to that super node which has close association with it, to overcome blindness of sending request randomly.

For convenience, the following symbols can be described as follows:

Table 1. Symbol Description

Sign	Meaning explain
N	Normal node
S	Super node
C_{suc}	Successful searching number
C_{sum}	Sum searching number
K	Resource
R	Value of the resource information table
m	Flow of transmitting media information
t	Transmit flow media information timing
$\overline{v_i}$	Media flow of the average unit time (an average transmission rate of the media)

2.1 Search Strategy of Normal Node

To control system's flood, it sets up a value ms for every node, which represents the maximum number of nodes to be allowed connecting. When the normal node sends search request to neighborhood node, it sends request to each neighborhood node as a priority through table NRT which has been defined before. After neighborhood node receiving the request, it looks for local resources index table (SIT), if it meets condition return back. When the returned satisfied nodes are more than ms, it will not send request to super node, otherwise send request to super node.

2.2 Search Strategy of Super Node

The advantages of ant algorithm is that, it can keep amending the original line by using the pheromone's principle, which is used in searching food, and then make the line become shorter and shorter. That is, procedures for the implementation of the longer, the more likely the path was close to the optimal path. Therefore, thanks to the Ant algorithm, this target can be achieved by amending the routing gradually in the super-node routing search. Based on the Ant algorithm, the resource information table (RIT) should be established as follows:

Table 2. The resource information table

Query resources	Neighboring nodes		
	B	C	D
K_1	4	7	1
K_2	6	2	3
K_3	1	4	1
K_4	3	3	1

In the table above, Ki refers to the resources waited to be searched. The value of (Ki, B) refers to the number of searching Ki through B. Based on the rules of foraging in the Ant algorithm, (Ki, B) can be looked as pheromones. Apperceive pheromones of neighboring nodes while sending requests, and then send requests to the nodes which have more pheromones. For example, when the resources of K1 need to be searched, find out that C has the most pheromones by observing the table RIT, so send requests to this node, meanwhile plus 1 to the value of (Ki, B). When the nodes maintenance table RIT, they check it periodically. If there is one node which had never been accessed in a week, the corresponding value will minus 1 until it equals 0.

In addition, when there is no pheromone belonging to the neighboring node, or there are several nodes with high pheromone at the same time, for reducing the blindness of random searching and the bandwidth consumption caused by flooding, constrained condition was added. The super-node routing state table (SRT) can be designed as below:

Table 3. The super-node routing state table (SRT)

Super node's routing	Neighboring nodes		
	A	B	C
C_{suc}	12	16	19
C_{sum}	17	18	27
$\overline{v}_i$	24.21	32.05	20.54

Suppose C_{suc} is the number of successful searches, C_{sum} is the number of total searches, $\dfrac{C_{suc}}{C_{sum}}$ represents the rate of successful search through this supper-node. Successful search's rate is just the rate of accuracy through this node. Super node should send request with priority to that node which has higher rate of successful search. However, this rate can not be the only standard, if this node searches with high successful rate but transmits with very low speed, the efficiency of accessing resource will be lower. Therefore, transmission speed also should be one of the standards of sending request. Finally comes up with the following formula:

$$f_i = \frac{C_{suc}}{C_{sum}} * \overline{v}_i \tag{1}$$

$$\overline{v}_i = \frac{1}{n} * \sum_{j=1}^{n} \frac{m_j}{t_j} \quad (其中 : n = c_{suc}) \tag{2}$$

According to the formula (1) and (2), there is:

$$f_i = \frac{1}{c_{sum}} * \sum_{j=1}^{n} \frac{m_j}{t_j} \tag{3}$$

This formula represents the average transmission speed of each node searching, including the successful searching and the unsuccessful.

When the super node sends or transmits the request, calculate fi with the help of data in table SRT and the formula (3), then choose some super nodes with high values to send the requests.

3 Implementation of Algorithm

Based on the above ideas, put forward the improved algorithm, and the designs of this algorithm can be described as follows:

1. Node sends request information to neighborhood nodes as a priority according to table NRT.
2. Compare the number of these nodes returned request (m_r) with the maximum number of pre-set connecting nodes (m_s). If $m_r \geq m_s$, the node will not send request, otherwise it will send request to the super node and transmits request through super node.
3. When super node sends request, it chooses the node which has the highest value in table RIT to send. If there has no such node or its resources information, it calculates according to the formula (3) and the data of SRT, and then chooses the node with the highest value for f_i to be the sending target, at the same time transmits the target node's ID (RDN) with request.
4. When super node receives request, firstly, check if itself meets these requirements, if it meets return request; otherwise sends request to normal node in the same group according to NIT, if meets return request.
5. The super node in step 4, no matter meets the request or not need return to step 3. However before runs the step 3, it gains target node's ID from received request, and compare with the own node' ID from SRT table, if it is the same, it will not need to participate in the calculation of step 3.

The description for this algorithm was shown as follows:

```
Input Query Q, a node N, a SuperNode SN

SendQuery(Q, NRT)

For Match (Q, SIT. key [i])

If Match Successed

Send local answers for Q to N
```

```
mr++
If(mr >= ms)
    return
else
SendQuery(Q, SN, RDN)
        RouteSelectSuperNode(Q, SRT, RDN)
        For Match(Q, SIT.key[i])
RouteSelectSuperNode(Q, SRT, RDN)
If RDN ==
    return
```

4 The Experimental Results

There were some results of the NS2 emulation experiment, which can be shown in Fig.2 and Fig.3 as below. Results in Fig.2 displayed changes of network flow before and after the arithmetic improvement. This fig threw out that the network flow could reduce with time's raising after the algorithm was improved. At last it compared the outcome changes according to the raised searching time which were shown in Fig.3. As the time went ahead, the number of the search results increased very slowly before improvement, but the improved algorithm increased very reposefully. That's because the improved algorithm had higher efficiency for searching information.

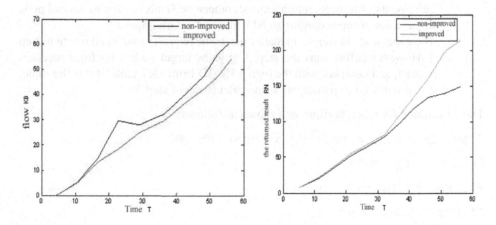

Fig. 2. The network flow and time   Fig. 3. The returned result RN and time

5 Conclusion

The paper introduced the Gnutella network, and gave research to the Gnutella network's deficiency, and improved the algorithm by adding constrained condition to the current routing search algorithm. It overcame blindness form the routing search brought by the primary algorithm. The results of emulation experiment indicated that the network broadband consumption brought by flood mechanism can be reduced.

References

[1] The Annotated Gnutella Protocol Specification v0.4 http://rfc-gnutella sourceforge .net
[2] Yang, B., Hector, G.-M.: Efficient search in peer-to-peer net-works. In: Proc. of ICDCS 2002, Vienna (2002)
[3] Kamrani, A.K., Sferro, P., Handelman, J.: Critical issues in design and evalution of computer aided process planning system. Computers and Eng. 29(1-4), 619–623 (1995)
[4] Huang, D., Li, Z., Zhuang, L.: Research of distributed Peer-to-Peer network Gnutella model. Computer Engineering and Applications (5), 60–61 (2003)
[5] Xiong, Z., Liu, Y., Zhang, Y.: The improved P2P searching algorithm based on the Gnutella protocol. Application Research of Computers (1), 109–111 (2008)
[6] Gkantsidis, C., Mihail, M., Saberi, A.: Hybrid search schemes for unstructured peer-to-peer networks. In: Proc. of IEEE International Conference on Network Protocols (2005)
[7] Pmarkatos, E.: Tracing a larger-scale peer-to-peer system: an hour in the life of Gnutella. In: Proc. of the 2nd IEEE/ACM Interational Symposium on Cluster Computing and the Grid (2002)
[8] Wang, X., Shi, W., Wang, S.: Processing of fuzzy spatial information. Wuhan University Press, Wuhan (2003)
[9] Duan, H.: The theory and application of Ant Algorithm. Science Press, Beijing (2005)
[10] Bhattacharjee, S.: Active Networks: Architectures, Composition, and Applications. Thesis of Georgia Institute of Technology (1999)
[11] Parameswaran, M., Susarla, A.: P2P Networking: An Information Sharing Alternative. IEEE Computing Practices (2001)
[12] Delaney, B.: The Power of P2P. Multimedia at Work (2001)
[13] Mihajlo, A., Jovanovi'c, B.S.: Modeling Large-scale Peer-to-Peer Networks and a Case Strudy of Gnutella. University of Cincinnati (2000)
[14] Karabulut, G.Z., Moura, L., Panario, D., Yongacoglu, A.: Flexible tree-search based crthogonal matching pursuit algorithm. IEEE International Conference on Acoustics, Speech, and Signal Processing 4, iv/673–iv/676 (2005)
[15] Srinivasan, V., Varghese, G.: Fast IP lookups using controlled prefix expansion. ACM Transactions on Computer Systems 17(1), 1–40 (1999)
[16] Xu, C., Zhang, Y., Mao, H.: The routing algorithm of full-text search engine with P2P. Computer Engineering (17), 85–87 (2008)
[17] Zeinalipour, Y.D., Kalogeraki, V., Gunopulos, D.: Information Retrieval Techniques for Peer-to-Peer Networks. Computing in Science & Engineering 6(4), 20–26 (2004)
[18] Wei, Z., Song, O.: An Improved Search Algorithm Based on Unstrured P2P. Comupter Systems and Application (1), 59–61 (2009)

Sliding-Window Recursive PLS Based Soft Sensing Model and Its Application to the Quality Control of Rubber Mixing Process

Kejuan Chen, Min He, and Dongzhi Zhang

School of Mechanical and Automotive Engineering, South China University of Technology, Guangzhou, 510640 Guangdong, China
mmkjchen@scut.edu.cn, hemin0506@163.com, dz.z@mail.scut.edu.cn

Abstract. Rubber industry requires highly the quality control of rubber mixture. In order to overcome the shortage of PLS algorithm in rubber mixing process with complex nonlinearity and time-variance, an adaptive soft sensing model based on sliding-widow recursive PLS (RPLS) is presented to build a prediction model for the Mooney-viscosity of rubber mixture. The improved RPLS model can adaptively adjust the structures and parameters of PLS model according to on-line monitoring data and take characteristics of batch-wise data updated with the process changes and time-variant tracking capabilities. The application results show that the adaptive model has stronger tracking ability and higher precision than the traditional PLS model. The results also verify its effectiveness.

Keywords: rubber mixing process; RPLS algorithm; sliding window; soft sensing model; model simulation.

1 Introduction

The rapid development of rubber industry presents higher requirements to the quality control of rubber mixture. For the present deficient on-line measurement methods, the production quality for rubber mixture is hardly to be on-line real-time monitored by sensors directly [1-2]. Manual sampling and off-line analysis on the viscosity of rubber mixture has been commonly used to monitor the quality of rubber mixture [3]. However, this method has disadvantage of large time-lag and long analysis period, which is not competent for the real-time quality control of rubber mixture and also results in material waste or quality degradation. Therefore, it is significant to improve the on-line measurement accuracy and real-time tracking ability for meeting the demands of practical industrial application in rubber mixing process.

Rubber mixing process is a complex non-linear batch process with strong time-varying and no reliable mechanism model. The Mooney-viscosity of the mixture is the key factor that has great effect on the quality of rubber products. However, The prediction of the Mooney-viscosity of rubber mixture is influenced by multi-factor in the rubber mixing process, such as temperature, rotate speed, filling factor, power, etc., makes the rigorous mixing mechanism is not well developed. In recent years, the

Z. Cai et al. (Eds.): ISICA 2009, CCIS 51, pp. 16–24, 2009.

method of partial least square (PLS) is commonly used in the rubber mixing process as a data-driven method. By virtue of its extraction of hidden variables and space compression technique, PLS captures the relationship between quality variables and process variables under normal operation, and provides error compensation for the impact of process variables on the quality variables [4-5]. However, PLS is a batch process data-driven method using the entire batch of off-line data to determine model parameters, and has no characteristics of time-varying tracking. It would greatly reduce the control accuracy of the rubber mixing quality. Recursive partial least squares [6-8] (RPLS) is attractive for its features of on-line data updating and time-variant tracking, but it is not able to avoid the phenomenon of "data saturation" in practical applications. In order to overcome the shortage of PLS algorithm, an adaptive soft sensing model based on sliding-widow RPLS is proposed to build prediction model of the Mooney-viscosity of rubber mixture. The application results show that the adaptive model has stronger tracking ability and higher precision than the traditional PLS model and its effectiveness is verified.

2 Sliding-Window RPLS Model

2.1 The Prediction Model Based on RPLS

The essence for PLS is statistic regression analysis using the independent principal components extracted from process variables dataset, and eliminate the multicollinearity influence of process variables. Suppose two data matrixes $X \in R_{m \times n}$ (process variables) and $Y \in R_{m \times p}$ (quality variables) meet the linear relationship as follows,

$$Y = XC + V \tag{1}$$

where V and C are the noises and coefficient matrix with the corresponding dimension respectively.

The following model is established by the linear decomposition of X and Y in the PLS regression algorithm,

$$X = \hat{X} + E_k = \sum_{i=1}^{k} t_i p_i^{'} + E_k = TP^{'} + E_k \tag{2}$$

$$Y = \hat{Y} + F_k = \sum_{i=1}^{k} u_i q_i^{'} + F_k = UQ^{'} + F_k \tag{3}$$

Here $\hat{X}$ and $\hat{Y}$ are fitting matrixes for X and Y respectively; Ek and Fk are the corresponding fitting error matrixes; ti and ui are the score vectors for the i th hidden variables of PLS model; p_i and q_i are the corresponding load vectors.

The matrix of regression coefficient for PLS model is

$$C^{PLS} = (X^T X)^{-1} X^T Y \tag{4}$$

After a group new data set $\{X_1, Y_1\}$ is gained, the original PLS model can be updated using the expanded data sets, and the formal expressions are given

$$X_{new} = \begin{bmatrix} X \\ X_1 \end{bmatrix}, \quad Y_{new} = \begin{bmatrix} Y \\ Y_1 \end{bmatrix} \quad (5)$$

The PLS model after update is

$$C^{PLS} = \left(\begin{bmatrix} X \\ X_1 \end{bmatrix}^T \begin{bmatrix} X \\ X_1 \end{bmatrix} \right)^{-1} \begin{bmatrix} X \\ X_1 \end{bmatrix}^T \begin{bmatrix} Y \\ Y_1 \end{bmatrix} \quad (6)$$

Lemma 1[6,9]: if $rank(X) = r \leq n$, then $E_r = E_{r+1} = \cdots = E_n = 0$

If the number k of hidden variables for RPLS meets $r \leq k \leq n$, then has $X = TP' + E_k = TP'$.

Update algorithm for RPLS model: If meets $E_k \leq \varepsilon$, here ε is a any small positive number, we suppose two PLS sub-models $\{X,Y\}\xrightarrow{PLS}\{T,W,P,B,Q\}$ and $\{X_1,Y_1\}\xrightarrow{PLS}$ $\{T_1,W_1,P_1,B_1,Q_1\}$, the models gained by PLS operation of the data sets $\begin{bmatrix} P^T \\ P_1^T \end{bmatrix}, \begin{bmatrix} BQ^T \\ B_1Q_1^T \end{bmatrix}$ and $\begin{bmatrix} X \\ X_1 \end{bmatrix}, \begin{bmatrix} Y \\ Y_1 \end{bmatrix}$ are equipollent. Under the same reason, the principle is competent to the case with s groups data sets, viz. the models acquired by PLS operation of the data set $\{X_i,Y_i\}\xrightarrow{PLS}\{T_i,W_i,P_i,B_i,Q_i\}$, $i=1,2,\cdots,s$ are equipollent, where

$$X_{new} = \begin{bmatrix} P_1^T \\ P_2^T \\ \vdots \\ P_s^T \end{bmatrix}, \quad Y_{new} = \begin{bmatrix} B_1Q_1^T \\ B_2Q_2^T \\ \vdots \\ B_sQ_s^T \end{bmatrix}. \quad (7)$$

The regression coefficient for sliding-window RPLS is

$$C_{new} = \left(X_{new}^T X_{new} \right)^{-1} X_{new}^T Y_{new}$$

$$= \left(\begin{bmatrix} P_1^T \\ P_2^T \\ \vdots \\ P_s^T \end{bmatrix}^T \begin{bmatrix} P_1^T \\ P_2^T \\ \vdots \\ P_s^T \end{bmatrix} \right)^{-1} \begin{bmatrix} P_1^T \\ P_2^T \\ \vdots \\ P_s^T \end{bmatrix}^T \begin{bmatrix} B_1Q_1^T \\ B_2Q_2^T \\ \vdots \\ B_sQ_s^T \end{bmatrix} \quad (8)$$

2.2 Updating Principle of Sliding-Window

In order to avoid the phenomenon of "data saturation" for RPLS algorithm, the method of sliding-window is adopted to determine which condition the model needs to be updated. The width of window should be determined firstly, and then add a new sample into the sliding-window and substitute the oldest data. And then compute the relative root-mean-square error (RRMSE) of all samples using the following formula,

$$RRMSE = \sqrt{\frac{1}{wp}\sum_{i=1}^{w}\sum_{j=1}^{p}\left(\frac{\hat{y}_{ij}-y_{ij}}{y_{ij}}\right)^{2}} \tag{9}$$

Here w is the window width, p is the number of output variables, $\hat{y}_{ij}$ and y_{ij} are the model estimated value and actual value for the jth output out of the ith sample respectively. The model is updated when meeting the following two conditions:

Condition 1: RRMSE is grater than the threshold Th_window.
Condition 2: The proportion of the sample numbers with prediction error which is greater than the threshold Th_single is greater than the threshold ζ .

It illustrates that the model prediction error has exceeded the pre-set threshold when condition1 is met. However, the reasons lead to the prediction error not only includes inaccurate model itself, but also have the incorrect analysis and wrong acquisition from instruments, etc. The condition 2 illustrates that prediction error has remain for a certain time, which shows that the prediction error is not caused by abnormal values. When the two conditions are satisfied simultaneously, the model needs to be updated. The steps for on-line prediction and update for the mode 1 are expressed as follows:

Step 1: Establish the initial PLS model using historical database and preserve the model parameters {T, W, P, B, Q}. Set the threshold Th_window, Th_single and ζ for the condition 1 and 2. The sign Flag is set to update validation for the model, with the initial value Flag=0 for non- update.
Step 2: Online prediction using the RPLS model.
Step 3: When an actual value of output variable is obtained, combine it with the corresponding input variables and is denoted by {x1, y1}. Add the {x1, y1} into the sliding-window and discard the oldest data meanwhile. The new data set after sliding is denoted as {X1, Y1}, and then compute RRMSE by the formula (1). If condition 1 and 2 are both met, Step 4 will be implemented. Otherwise, let the Flag=0 and return to Step 2.
Step 4: model updating,

a) If Flag=0, this shows that the model is not updated by the former steps. Let Flag=1 and use all the data of sliding window {X1, Y1} to update the model.
b) If Flag=1, this shows that the model has been updated when getting the last actual value of output variable. All data has been used for one time besides {x1, y1}, so the model is updated only by {x1, y1}.

After confirming the above parameters, update the model with RPLS algorithm, preserve the model parameters {T, W, P, B, Q} and return to Step 2.

The flowchart of the model updating is expressed in the following Fig.1.

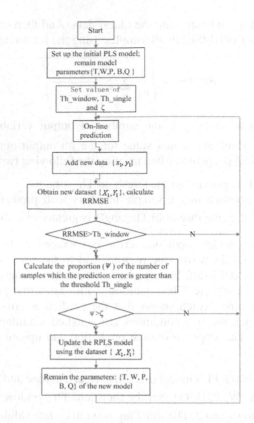

Fig. 1. The flowchart of the model updating

3 Simulation Research

The Banbury oval rotor mixer shown in Fig.2, is used in the rubber mixing process, and the software RMICS of mixer intelligent control system, designed by Guangzhou SCUT Bestry Technology Co., Ltd., is adopted to acquire mixing process data. The Mooney viscometer, designed by GOTECH Testing Machine Inc., is employed to test Mooney viscosity. The 60 experimental samples are divided into 2 groups, 30 samples with rotate speed at 40~60r/ min used to establish the model, and the other 30 samples with rotate speed at 40~80r/min adopted to evaluate the model. The soft-sensing model takes y (viscosity) as the dependent variable and T (temperature), N (rotate speed), P (power), ϕ (filling factor) as independent variables.

3.1 Mooney-Viscosity Prediction Based on PLS Model

The predictive values gained from the PLS model are shown in Fig.3and Fig.4, and also give the actual valves for making a comparison. The abscissa represents sample numbers and the ordinate is Mooney viscosity.

Fig. 2. Sketch of Banbury oval rotor mixer

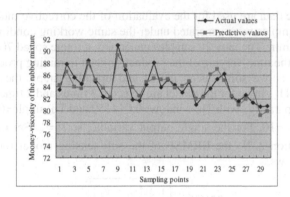

Fig. 3. The comparison of the actual values and the predictive values (Rotate speed: 40~60r/min)

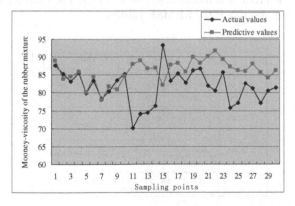

Fig. 4. The comparison of the actual values and the predictive values (Rotate speed: 1~10 samples are40~60r/min; 11~30 samples are70~80r/min)

From Fig.3 and Fig.4, we can see the average error as the follow table1. From the analysis of simulation results, we know that the model has a good prediction for modeling data with stable rotate speed, and becomes unable when the rotate speed takes a sudden change, so it is firmly validate that the PLS model is incompetent for real-time adaptive tracking to the rubber mixing process.

Table 1. The average errors of PLS model

Sample number	Average error (Mooney)	Rotate speed (r/min)
1~10	0.926	40~60
11~30	1.074	
1~10	1.033	40~60
11~30	7.676	70~80

3.2 Mooney-Viscosity Prediction Based on Sliding- Window RPLS Model

30 groups sample data are used for the evaluation of the corrective model one by one. The former 10 samples were generated under the same working conditions with rotate speed at 40~60 r/min. The later 20 samples generated at rotate speed 70~80 r/min were used to simulate the time-varying of the production data in mixing process.

Based on the above soft-sensing model and updating steps, the two thresholds Th_window and Th_single for the model are selected 3 times and 2 times of RRMSE as the initial data separately, with Th_window=0.044159 and Th_single=0.02944. Let the window width W =10. For the single output variable, so P =1. Set the threshold ζ to 60% in condition 2. So the RRMSE of the soft-sensing model for all samples is expressed as follows,

$$RRMSE = \sqrt{\frac{1}{10}\sum_{i=1}^{10}\left(\frac{\hat{y}_{ij} - y_{ij}}{y_{ij}}\right)^2} \qquad (10)$$

The RRMSE for the prediction model is shown in Fig.5. The ordinate represents sample numbers and the abscissa is the RRMSE values.

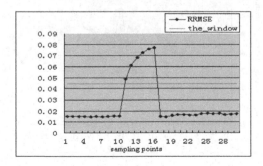

Fig. 5. The graph of RRMSE for the sliding-window RPLS model

From Fig. 5 we can see that the RRMSE for the former 10 samples remains below the threshold Th_window, which illustrates that the model takes satisfactory prediction results. From the 11th sample, the process suddenly changes, and the corresponding RRMSE also becomes larger. But after several samples, the change of the process has been confirmed by the model. And the model based on RPLS algorithm updates itself and adjusts the model parameters adaptively. The RRMSE gets smaller and returns to the threshold range subsequently.

The comparison between the predictive values and the observed values for the on-line updating model of viscosity is shown in Fig.6. The comparison of predictive values between the PLS model and the sliding-window RPLS model is shown in Fig.7. The abscissa represents sample numbers and the ordinate is Mooney viscosity.

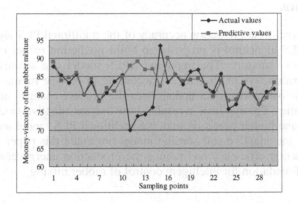

Fig. 6. The comparison of the actual values and the predictive values for the sliding-window RPLS model

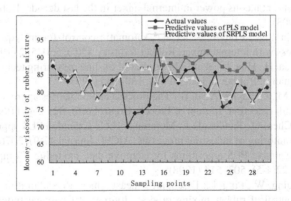

Fig. 7. The comparison of the actual values and predictive values

The average error between the actual values and the predictive values is shown in the Table 2. From the analysis of simulation results, we know that through the on-line sliding-window updating, the performance of model prediction and real-time adaptive tracking is greatly improved. After several interval of sampling, the model adapts to the process change and gives a good prediction results.

Table 2. The average errors of PLS and SRPLS model

Model	Sample numbers	Average error (Mooney)	Rotate speed (r/min)
PLS model	1~10	1.033	40~60
	11~16	11.893	70~80
	17~30	5.869	
SRPLS model	1~10	1.041	40~60
	11~16	12.26	70~80
	17~30	1.3072	

4 Conclusions

To improve the real-time prediction accuracy of the traditional PLS algorithm, a sliding-window RPLS algorithm is proposed to build prediction model of the Mooney-viscosity of rubber mixture. The improved RPLS model can adaptively adjust the structures and parameters of PLS model according to on-line monitoring data, take characteristics of batch-wise data update with the process changes and time-variant tracking capabilities. The application results show that the adaptive model has stronger tracking ability and higher precision than the traditional PLS model and its effectiveness is verified. the adaptive soft sensing model presented this paper benefits to improve the production efficiency and reduce the production energy consumption, and lays a practical foundation for intelligent control of rubber mixing.

References

1. Hai, Z., Tiejun, M., Zhiqiang, Z., et al.: Reviews of rheological theory for rubber mixing and controlling instantaneous power in internal mixer in the last decade. Robber Industry 50(5), 316–319 (2003)
2. Hai, Z., Tiejun, M., Ronglu, S., et al.: Automatic control for mix quality fluctuation in mixing process with internal mixer. Robber Industry 45(9), 550–552 (1998)
3. Hai, Z., Dehua, H., Hua, L., et al.: The studies of on-line measuring technique for the rubber compound quality. Robber Industry 44(3), 160–165 (1997)
4. Wise Barry, M., Gallagher Neal, B.: The process chemometrics approach to process monitoring and fault detection. Journal of Process Control 6(6), 329–348 (1996)
5. Kruger, U., Chen, Q., Sandoz, D.J., Mcfariane, R.C.: Extended PLS approach for enhanced condition monitoring of industrial processes. AIChE Journal 47(9), 2076–2091 (2001)
6. Qin, S.J.: Recursive PLS algorithms for adaptive data modeling. Computers & Chemical Engineering 22(4-5), 503–514 (1998)
7. Kai, S., Haiqing, W., Ping, L.: Discounted-measurement PLS algorithm and its application to quality control of rubber mixing process. Journal of Chemical Industry and Engineering 55(6), 942–946 (2004)
8. Kai, S., Haiqing, W., Ping, L.: RPLS based adaptive statistical quality monitoring of rubber mixing process. Journal of Chemical Industry and Engineering 58(2), 410–416 (2007)
9. Xiaoyong, W., Jun, L., Yuming, L., Wenqing, W.: Recursive PLS based adaptive soft-sensor model and its application. Journal of Zhejiang University (Engineering Science) 39(5), 676–680 (2005)

The Research of Method Based on Complex Multi-task Parallel Scheduling Problem

Xiang Li, Peng Chen, and Li Zhu

China University of Geosciences
No. 388 Lumo Road Wuhan, P.R. China

Abstract. The key point of project management is scheduling problem. While scheduling optimization,which determines the profit of projects, has been one of the hot research spots for domestic and foreign experts or scholars. This paper mainly proposes an optimization method of network planning project by using an improved genetic algorithm for solving complex parallel multi-task scheduling problems. It used a method that gradually increases the number of parallel tasks for increasing the complexity of scheduling algorithm. This paper mainly focuses on the feasibility of the large-scale and complex multi-task parallel scheduling problem in the use of improved genetic algorithm. The experiment results show that using improved genetic algorithm for solving large-scale and complex multi-task parallel scheduling problem is feasible, and meanwhile,produces better results.

Keywords: genetic algorithm, multi-task parallel scheduling problem, scheduling optimization, complexity.

1 Introduction

The key point of scheduling optimization problems is network planning optimization. In the long-term practice of engineering applications, network planning optimization almost uses the network planning skills and mathematical programming skills in the field of operational research, but these methods have many deficiencies in solving complex parallel multi-task scheduling problems in large-scale network planning, they can neither bear the compute complexity nor the optimization effects are very limited. Genetic algorithm has more advantages than others, especially in the field of solving large-scale complex optimization problems; it can gain the better results. In literature from one to four, the author named Xiang Li and others proposed an improved genetic algorithm and hybrid genetical gorithm for solving the multi-task parallel scheduling problem based on resource-constrained project scheduling problems and gained better optimization results. But none of them considered the feasibility of multi-task parallel scheduling problem when the number of tasks and algorithmic complexity are increasingly getting more and more. Thus, this paper proposes an optimization method based on improved genetic algorithm to resolve the problem of large-scale complex multi-task parallel scheduling.

Z. Cai et al. (Eds.): ISICA 2009, CCIS 51, pp. 25–34, 2009.

2 Resource—Constrained Project Scheduling Model

Assuming there are several parallel tasks, and a shared resource pool containing a number of resources that can update (renewable resources), and all our resources which are supplied limitedly. In addition to sharing resources, tasks are independent with each other. To facilitate the description of the problem, the establishment of the mathematical model is as follows: RCPSP has P independent Multi-task scheduling tasks; the task k contains nk+ 1 works. The nk+ 1 task is for terminating work for virtual tasks, and it self occupies no resources and time. P missions' works are to share this kind of M renewable resources; the total for the mth resource is Rm. With Wi expressed the ith misson's work set, Wij expressed in the ith task jth work, its duration is dij, the requirement of the mth resources is rijm, the starting time is Sij, its all tight front duties formed the collection is Pij. The set composed of all tasks on time t is named It. Considering the importance of different tasks, ak is used for the weight k task. Taking these assumptions and symbols, a multi-task scheduling with resource constraints can be described as formula 1 to 6).

$$\min \sum_{k=1}^{P} \partial_k * (S_{k,n_k+1}) \tag{1}$$

$$s.\ t.\quad S_{i,j} \geq S_{i,h} + d_{i,h}\ ,\quad \forall h \in P_{ij}, \forall i,j \tag{2}$$

$$\sum_{w_{i,j} \in I_t} r_{ijm} \leq R_m\ ,\quad \forall m,t. \tag{3}$$

$$I(t) = \{Wkj \in \bigcup_{k=1}^{P} Wk \mid S_{kj} \leq t \leq S_{kj} + d_{kj}\ \} \tag{4}$$

$$r_{ijm} \geq 0 \tag{5}$$

$$\sum_{k=1}^{P} \partial_k = 1 \tag{6}$$

3 Algorithm Design

3.1 RCPSP Problems

As a number of tasks share common resources, so the solution is different form single tasks'. In the way to solve this problem, some documents have proposed a bilevel decision method of multi-resource constraint and multi-task scheduling problem [1]. However, this method has two major flaws. First, the prerequisite is that the duration of shared resource in each task is determined by the distributed resource. The use of shared resources and the allocation of resources were inversely related to working time. Working time = Workload + Resources. In real life, the workload is not an accumulation work. Working time = Workload /Resources. So the tasks do not accumulate in the work of the workload. The model can not be solved. The second defect is that the model adopts the specific resource allocation scheme between tasks. When resources are allocated to a particular task, it will always belong to the task; other tasks can no longer use the resources. This approach would make a larger allocation of resources wasted.

Because such a distribution strategy, There is not exist mutual adjustment of flow of resources between tasks. So when a task in which there is a sort of free resources, other tasks will not use, and it is wasted.

The literature [7] also discussed the multi-task scheduling problem and its solution. However, the solution is to add more tasks network plan to merge into a virtual work of the network plan for the Solution. This method lowers the efficiency and flexibility of the solution.

This paper presents a method based on genetic algorithm to solve tasks of the type of work for more than an accumulation of the task. Between the various tasks and resources are dynamic to the circulation of each other. It will not waste the resources. Various tasks to multi-task and do not plan to conduct any merger of the network. Only needs to input all the tasks, resources and other information, we will be able to carry out all tasks scheduling.

3.2 Data Structure for the Algorithm

Before the generation of initial population, it is first necessary to establish a data structure for storing information of the various tasks.

First, defining a task structure.

```
struct project

{int n;int TP; int TC; int TS;work *w[MAX]; entity
*E[MAX];}*pro;
```

Among them, n is the number of tasks, TP is the task completion time. TC is the calculated completion time of the task, TS is the actual completion time of the task, and work is the definition of the structure. w[MAX] task is working at the point-array. Entity is the definition of the network structure. E[MAX] is the point-array related to the each task. Dynamic information to the importation of various tasks, Cross linked-list node is used store the relationship between the various tasks.

Cross linked-list node of the structure as follows:

```
typedef struct cnode

{int hang;int lie;int value;struct cnode *down;struct
cnode *right;}crossnode;

typedef struct

{int n; crossnode *hc[MAX];}clinknode; clinknode
*Head=new clinknode;
```

'hang' and 'lie' in the structure crossnode mark the position in the linked-list. 'value' is the index of the work, 'down' is the eligible point of it and 'right' is the immediate point. 'In the 'clinknode' hc[MAX]' and 'Head' is the head note of cross linked-list.

In this paper, a key of the multi-task scheduling is for all of tasks using a cross linked-list. And the identification of various tasks is proposed in the linked-list. After the establishment of schedule, the activation of various tasks is based on the linked-list. This is an innovation of this paper.

3.3   The Framework of the Algorithm and the Code of Chromosome

Resource-constrained multi-task scheduling problems can be also considered that the scheduling problem with certain constraints. The key to solving the problem is how to use genetic algorithm to find an appropriate sequencing of multitask. According to a certain sequence of chromosome, we code all of issues on the table. If there are M tasks, each task has n works, then there m*n works. The first expression Vk is Kth chromosome in current population. Suppose Pkij is a gene of chromosome. It expressed a work of the Pkth task at location j of chromosome.

Chromosome can be expressed as follows:

Vk=[P1i1,..., P1ii,...,P1in,...,Pki1,..., Pkii,...Pkin,...,Pmi1,..., Pmii,...,Pmin]
Pkij bound by the random order with the constraint.

3.4   Initialization Population

For the Chromosomes initialization, this paper uses the method that randomly generates various initial chromosomes by the topological scheduling.

Similar with the optimal scheduling method with the shortest Resource Constrained time of the single task, the only difference is that for every work. Firstly judge the task to which it belongs, and then determine the constraint relationship. It is determined the first consider work by a Left to Right approach with a fixed sequence. At each stage of the work order has been maintained and assembled Scheduling can work and completely random from a pool selected to work in the pool. This process is repeated indefinitely until all the work was arranged.

In each iteration of the process all the work at one of the following three conditions:

1. The work has index: Part of the chromosome structure in the work.
2. The work can schedule: All immediate works are ordered.
3. Free work: All of work

v_k^t is a part of chromosome, including t activities. Q_t is in phase t with a corresponding arrangements can be made to the activities set, Pi is all the activities set ,with a corresponding set of arrangements can be made activity set Q_t is defined as formula 7.

$$Q_t = \{ j \mid P_i \subset v_k^t \}$$ (7)

It includes specific arrangements in the end nodes, and it is all competition activity set.

Scheduling changes which may work in the following manner: a. deleted Qt from the work j which has been selected. b. judging if there is work k in all immediate works or not, and its all immediate works are ordered . c. if there is k, it can be added to the scheduling work set Qt.

3.5   Genetic Operators Design

On the base of established cross linked-list, re-number various tasks in the work. Then apply the algorithm described in this paper. All tasks will be mixed with the work. After encoding into a chromosome, the problems become simple. Genetic chromosome operation with the single task is similar to the chromosomal genetic operations.

Participate in the two crossover operator for mothers M and fathers F. We choose a random integer $q, 1 <= q <= J, J$ is chromosome length. M and F through radio spots overlapping operations produced two generations of daughters D and sons S. In the list D work, the former q tasks come from M.

$$j_i^D = j_i^M, i = 1, 2 \ldots q$$

$i = q + 1, \ldots J$, come from the location of the F, And the relative position of the F resurveyed.

$$j_i^D = j_k^F, i = q+1, q+2, \ldots, J$$

Which $k = \min\{k \mid j_k^F \notin \{j_1^D, j_2^D, \cdots, j_{i-1}^D\}, k = 1, 2, \cdots, J\}$

S and D are similar to the formation of the linked-list, not going to repeat here.

Mutation operator adopts centralized search strategy combined with the neighborhood technology to improve the offspring. D genes will not exceed the change in the scheduling of the neighborhood gathered as scheduling x.If x neighborhood than any other solution, then x is called scheduling optimization. Mutation process is shown as follows:

Begin
If (rand () <pmutation)
Take n continuous in a row as the chromosome genes;
Permutations and combinations of the n genes;
Check each gene sequence, the genome sequence will be its discarded if it unreasonable;
Assessing all the neighborhood scheduling;
Neighborhood as the best choice for future generations;
End

In the process of mutation, two consecutive complete gene permutations and combinations. Of course, there has a violation of constrain sequence. Here can directly be discarded, but will not have an impact on the choice of the best neighborhood. This method avoids repairing the chromosome after mutation and improves the efficiency of the procedure.

3.6 Fitness Function

Calculate the shortest duration of tasks, we must first decode chromosome. Calculate the earliest starting time, and then find the earliest completion time for each task. Finally, according to the weight ratio of the various tasks calculate the shortest weighted average duration. Reached the objective function formula 8.

$$\min \sum_{k=1}^{P} \partial_k * (S_{k,n_k} + 1) \tag{8}$$

Since the task is to minimize the total built-constrained Project Scheduling Problem issues. We change the original objective function to ensure that the individual is suited to meet the greatest value. The current population vk is located k chromosome; g (vk) is a fitness function. f (vk) is the original target value. fmax and fmin are the biggest target value and the minimum target value. Conversion methods such as formula 9.

$$g(v_k) = \frac{f_{max} - f(v_k) + \varepsilon}{f_{max} - f_{min} + \varepsilon} \qquad (9)$$

Where ε is a positive number, often limited the open interval (0,1).

3.7 Selection Operator

The operation that winning individuals are chosen from the group and the bad individuals are eliminated is named selection.

Selection is based on the currently popular "breeding pool (Breeding Pool) choice", "To adapt to-value ratio of options", "ranking selection (Ranking Selection)", "Mechanism based on local competitive choices", and so on. Roulette choice (Roulette Wheel Selection) is based on fitness than A choice of the most widely used methods. It is the first calculation of the relative fitness of individual fi/$\sum$fi, named Pi, and then chooses probability {pi. = 1,2,..., N} a disk cut into N copies, 2лPi fan angle of the center of Pi. In making the selection, rotating disk can be assumed that if a reference point to fall into the itch fan, then chose individual i. Generation a random number r in [0, 1], if Po+Pi+... +Pi-1<r<Pl+P2... +Pi, i individual choice, the assumption here Po=0. It is easy to see that this was very similar to roulette choice of trouble. For sector bigger area, it has the greater the probability fall in and it was an opportunity to be chosen.

Thus, the structure of the gene was likely to pass it on to the next generation greater. This paper discusses the use of multi-robin scheduling optimization algorithm choice. Every generation of new groups in the use of optimal preservation strategy that will preserve the best, so far in the contemporary individual and overcome random sampling error.

4 Experiments and Analysis

4.1 Experimental Environment

This paper is to implement the design of optimization algorithm, establishment of optimization algorithm model and the realization of optimization algorithm. The specific experimental environment is shown as table 1.

Table 1. Development environment

Operating System	Windows 2003 server
Programming Tools	Visual C++ 6.0
Processor	Quad-Core AMD Opteron(tm) Processor 2384 2.75GHz
Memory	4G

4.2 Experimental Data

The examples of experimental cases in this paper are based on multi-task parallel scheduling problem. Assuming that every task has a same network structure, the structure is shown as figure 1.Every task has 1202 works and 800 items, the whole 1202 works are to share the whole 20 kinds of resources., the resource have mentioned is single model, every work uses one of the 20 kinds of resources, and has different construction period and requirements, which are shown as table 2.The type and quantity of resource are shown as table 3.

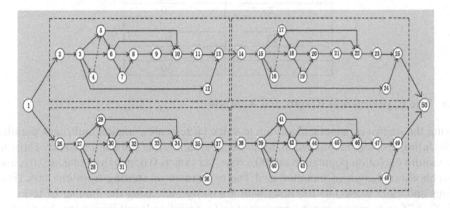

Fig. 1. The map of network structure of project

Table 2. Type and quantity of resource and operation time required by 50 items or 75 works

Serial number	Starting item	Finshing item	Time(s)	Resource type	Quantity
1	1	2	2	1	7
2	1	26	2	1	7
3	2	3	3	2	9
......	......	......	......	......	......
73	47	49	3	11	20
74	48	49	5	8	11
75	49	50	3	16	5

Because each 50 items and 75 works in each task used in this paper based on the examples of experimental cases have same type and quantity of resource, table 1 only make a list of type and quantity of resource required by each 50 items and 75 works in each task. This paper simplify each 50 items and 75 works as one work to operate, simplified network structure is shown as figure 2.

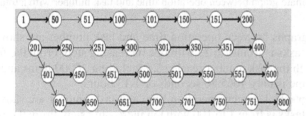

Fig. 2. The brief map of net structure

Table 3. Type and quantity of resource

Serial number	Quantity
0	40
1	50
2	30
......	......
17	40
18	30
19	50

4.3 The Experimental Results and Analysis

Using the improved genetic algorithm to solve large-scale complex multi-task parallel scheduling problem mentioned in this paper, it assumes that population size as 150, the maximum evolution population as 100, crossover rate as 0.8, mutation rate as 0.01, and neighborhood length of mutation as 4.The experiment is starting from one task (800 items and 1202 works) to 100 tasks with gradually increasing the number of tasks. In the first 25 task, increasing the number of tasks with 1 task and increasing the number of tasks with 10 tasks from the 30th to 100th work. In other word, starting from one task including 800 items and 1202 works to 100 tasks including 80000 items and 120200 works. The relationship between operation time and number of tasks are shown as figure 3 and figure 4.

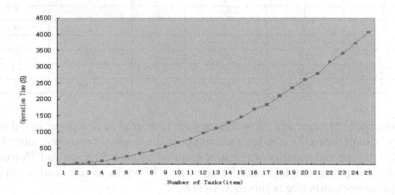

Fig. 3. Coordinate graph between operation time and task number with a total of 25 tasks

Coordinate graphs between operation time and task number are shown as figure 3. The number of tasks is from 1 to 25 with one increasing step. From the figure 3 we can infer even though the task number reaches 25 including 20000 items and 30050 works, the operation time is only 4065.80 seconds or 1.13 hours.

Coordinate graphs between operation time and task number are shown as figure 4. The number of tasks is from 1 to 100 with ten increasing step. From the figure 4 we can infer even though the task number reaches 100 including 80000 items and 120200 works, the operation time is only 65078.28 seconds or 18.07 hours.

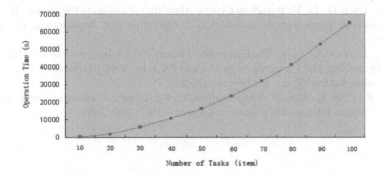

Fig. 4. Coordinate graph between operation time and task number with a total of 100 tasks

From figure 3 and figure 4, we can infer that with the increasement of task number and algorithmic complexity, the operation time obtained by using improved genetic algorithm to solve large-scale complex multi-task parallel scheduling problem mentioned in this paper basically present the trend with increasing linearly. If increasing the number of tasks and algorithmic complexity, it is feasible to solve large-scale complex multi-task parallel scheduling problem using the algorithm mentioned in this paper.

5 Conclusion

This paper proposed a new genetic algorithm to solve large-scale complex multi-task parallel scheduling problem of resource constraints. It mainly studied the feasibility of large-scale complex multi-task parallel scheduling problem. The experimental results show that using improved genetic algorithm to solve large-scale complex multi-task parallel scheduling problem mentioned in this paper linear increased in the basic, and gained better results. It overcame the deficiencies that other algorithms could only solve small-scale and low algorithmic complexity multi-task parallel scheduling problem. Further, it also show that using improved genetic algorithm had more great advantages than others in the field of solving large-scale complex multi-task parallel scheduling problem.

References

1. Li, X., Tan, W., Kan, L.: Research of Resource Equilibrium Optimization Based on Genetic Algorithm. Computer Engineering and Design, 4447–4449 (2008)
2. Li, X., Tong, H., Tan, W.: Network Planning Multi-objective Optimization Based on Genetic Algorithm. In: International Symposium on Intelligence Computation and Applications Progress, pp. 143–147 (2007)
3. Li, X., Tan, W., Tong, H.: A Resource Equilibrium Optimization Method Base on Improved Genetic Algorithm. China Artificial Intelligence Progress 2, 737–743 (2007)
4. Lova, A., Tormos, P., Cervantes, M., Barber, F.: An efcient hybrid genetical gorithm for scheduling projects with resource constraints and mulitiple execution modes. Int. J. Production Economics 117, 302–316 (2009)

5. Li, X., Chen, Q., Li, Y.: Impact on Genetic Algorithm of Different Parameters. In: The 3rd International Symposium on Intelligence Computation and Applications, pp. 479–488 (2008)
6. Xiang, L., Yanli, L., Li, Z.: The Comparative Research of Solving Problems of Equilibrium and Optimizing Multi-resources with GA and PSO. In: 2008 International Conference on Computational Intelligence and Security (2008)
7. Liao, R., Chen, Q., Mao, N.: Genetic algorithm for resource - constrained project scheduling. Computer Integrated Manufacturing Systems 10(7) (July 2004)

Towards a Bio-inspired Security Framework for Mission-Critical Wireless Sensor Networks*

Wei Ren, Jun Song, Zhao Ma, and Shiyong Huang

Department of Information Security, School of Computer Science,
China University of Geosciences (Wuhan), China 430074
weirencs@cug.edu.cn

Abstract. Mission-critical wireless sensor networks (WSNs) have been found in numerous promising applications in civil and military fields. However, the functionality of WSNs extensively relies on its security capability for detecting and defending sophisticated adversaries, such as Sybil, worm hole and mobile adversaries. In this paper, we propose a bio-inspired security framework to provide intelligence-enabled security mechanisms. This scheme is composed of a middleware, multiple agents and mobile agents. The agents monitor the network packets, host activities, make decisions and launch corresponding responses. Middleware performs an infrastructure for the communication between various agents and corresponding mobility. Certain cognitive models and intelligent algorithms such as Layered Reference Model of Brain and Self-Organizing Neural Network with Competitive Learning are explored in the context of sensor networks that have resource constraints. The security framework and implementation are also described in details.

Keywords: Multiple Mobile Agent System, Wireless Sensor Networks, Security, Intelligent Computation Application.

1 Introduction

Wireless Sensor Networks (WSNs) present numerous promising applications in the fields of military (battle field surveillance, nuclear, biological and chemical attack detection and reconnaissance), environment (forest fire detection), and health (telemonitoring of human physiological data), etc. [1]. The security, survivability and availability are crucial to mission-critical WSNs. WSNs encounter some security attacks such as Denial of Service attack (Jamming) [2], the Sybil attack [3], traffic analysis attacks [4], node replication attacks [5], eavesdropping and camouflage [6, 7]. However, few existing works in the researches research extensively on the intelligence of adversaries. For example, the adversaries may dynamically hide themselves, or choose a smart moving path during the intrusion. Especially in mission-critical WSNs, we have to assume adversaries are more sophisticated to achieve higher level security.

---

* Supported by the Science and Research Start-Up Project for the Recruit Talent of China University of Geosciences, Wuhan, under Grant No.20090113.

Z. Cai et al. (Eds.): ISICA 2009, CCIS 51, pp. 35–44, 2009.
© Springer-Verlag Berlin Heidelberg 2009

One promising way to defend the sophisticated adversaries is to detect and defend adversaries in an intelligent manner, called bio-inspired scheme. However, to design a bio-inspired defense schemes in WSNs is not straightforward, because the promising solutions must consider the unique constrains in WSNs. First, sensor devices are limited in their energy, computation, and communication capabilities. Second, unlike traditional networks, sensor nodes are often deployed in accessible areas, presenting the added risk of physical attack. And third, sensor networks interact closely with their physical environments and with people, posing new security problems.

As a basic tool, agent is an important technology to implement intelligent information process. An agent is anything that can be viewed as perceiving its environment through sensors and acting upon that environment through effectors. Multi-agent system consisting of multiple agents can cooperate with each other to reach common objectives, while simultaneously each agent pursues individual objectives. Mobile agent [8] can migrate across the network. The agent system can be implemented by Java, Tcl/Tk or Python. Considering the constraints of the WSNs, the mobile multiple agents system is suitable. Multiple agents can provide the intelligent functionalities, and mobile agents can improve the robustness of the detection and defense in terms of compromise resilience and fault tolerance.

Recently, many researchers explore the implementation of agent (mobile agent or multi-agent) in the WSNs [9], e.g., the intelligent control [10], decision making [11], pattern recognition [12] and autonomic behavior [13], but few works address security issues in WSNs. In this paper, we propose a novel security framework for WSNs based on multiple mobile agents.

Objective of the paper: The goal of this paper is to investigate an intelligence-enabled defense framework against sophisticated adversaries at resource-constraint sensor nodes in mission-critical WSNs.

Contributions: We propose a Multiple Mobile Agent based security framework – MMASec. The advantages of MMASec are as follows: (1) Self-studying: the framework can detect and defend against previously non-presented attacks; (2) Cooperation and robustness: it performs distribute cooperative intrusion or misbehavior detection and defense.

Organization: The remainder of the paper is organized as follows: The related work is presented in Section II. Section III presents proposed scheme. Finally, Section IV concludes the paper.

2 Related Work

Computational Cognitive Modeling (CCM) is one of the most important modeling methods in cognitive models. It provides the methods that produce detailed models of how humans perform complex cognitive tasks that can be run on a computer. Such models can provide a priori performance predictions of how well a certain system by assessing factors such as learning ability, workload, and errors. Software agents that perform tasks in the same way as humans can be used to evaluate proposed systems. The recent advancement of cognitive model is cognitive informatics model of the brain. They propose A Layered Reference Model of Brain (LRMB) [14] for cognitive mechanisms and processes and *Real-Time Process Algebra (RTPA)* [15] to formally and rigorously describe autonomous computing system and cognitive behaviors.

Many intelligence algorithms can be employed in networks such as artificial immune system [16], Evolutionary (Genetic) Algorithms [17] and Cell Biology Based Approaches [18].

At the implementation level, a cognitive architecture specifies the underlying infrastructure for an intelligent system. It is a blueprint for intelligent agents. It proposes artificial computational processes that act like a person, or acts intelligent under some definition. The typical examples of cognitive architecture are SOAR [19-20] and ICARUS [21]. ICARUS focuses on reactive execution of existing skills rather than on problem-space search. Some implementations of middleware for WSNs exist, such as Agilla [22], Deluge [23], SensorWare [24], Impala [25] and BiSNET [26, 27].

3 Proposed Scheme

3.1 Overview of MMASec

The cognitive model and intelligent algorithms should be selected because the WSNs have many constraints. But to maximize the security of WSNs we must try to use more sophisticated algorithms in the system. Hence, the tradeoff between the functionality and resource should be considered in the design.

As an intelligent defense system, the basic design principles of MMASec are as follows:

(1) Distribution: There are no centralized entities in MMASec to control and coordinate agents. Distribution allows the framework to be scalable by avoiding a single point of failures.
(2) Autonomy: Agents sense their local environments, and based on the sensed conditions, they autonomously behave without any intervention from base stations and human administrators.
(3) Natural selection: The abundance or scarcity of stored energy, computation ability, and memory in agents affects their behaviors and triggers natural selection.
(4) Compactness: The system can detect a large set of potentially harmful attacks with a reasonably small number of detectors. This is an essential quality for resource-constrained nodes in sensor networks.
(5) Diverse and Adaptive: The system can detect previously unknown attacks (by some deduction). This ability should be an important feature of the defense framework, as the possible threats cannot be known in advance.
(6) Cooperation. The mobile agents can migrate between different sensor nodes to build a cooperative detection and defense system.

The framework MMASec has major two parts – agents and middleware, constructed over the operating system. The MMASec is shown in Figure 1.

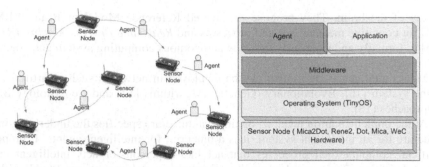

Fig. 1. A Framework for MMASec

3.2 Model and Algorithm Selection

We propose to implement LRMB [14] in mobile agent architecture due to the re-source constraints. The main idea of LRMB is based on the contemporary theories on memory classification, in which memory is commonly described as the sensory mem-ory, short-term memory, and long-term memory. Therefore, the logical architecture of memories in the brain can be classified into the following four categories: (1) The sensory buffer memory (SBM); (2) The short-term memory (STM); (3) The long-term memory (LTM); (4) The action buffer memory (ABM). The different memory is simulated by a thread in the agent process or by a single agent process. SBM is used to store some detection signal, such as message source, message destination, and message length. STM stores some temporary analyzed results. LTM store some ma-ture production rules. STM and LTM can exchange some information. ABM stores some further response, such as alerts, reputation-based voting, log action, or audit for accountable digest.

We employ *Self-Organizing Neural Network with Competitive Learning (SONN)* [28] in the system. One of the main advantages of using SONN is that it does not require a priori knowledge of the phenomenon being monitored, which is like the acquired immune system does not require a priori knowledge of pathogens. Therefore it can be applied to a larger set of sensor network applications than standard statistical approaches. Moreover, some unknown attacks may be detected by the SONN due to its self-organizing properties. It is essential to the detection and defense for the real-world adversaries. The competitive learning network divides a set of input parameters into data clusters and chooses the winning one. The competitive leaning will reserve the best knowledge for the detection and defense. For example, sensor nodes collect sample readings about the environment, such as temperature, humidity et al. Figure 2 shows the architecture of SONN used in our study. For n samples, SONN takes a (nxp) matrix M, a (pxp) weight matrix W as inputs and produces a (pxp) weight matrix W as inputs and produces a (1xp) vector F with its elements equals to the Eucledian distances between W and M.

$$F = \sqrt{\sum (W - M)^2} \tag{1}$$

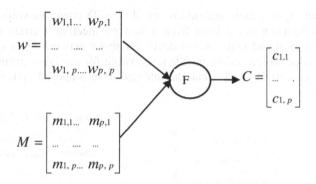

Fig. 2. Self-Organizing Neural Network with Competitive Learning

The competitive layer returns a 1xp vector C, with 0s for all neural inputs except for the closest elements, which corresponds to a winning neuron. The output for the winning neuron is set to one.

$$o_i = \begin{cases} 1 & \parallel w_i(t) - m_i(t) \parallel \leq \parallel w_0(t) - m_i(t) \parallel \forall o \\ 0 & \text{otherwise} \end{cases} \tag{2}$$

The weight of the winning neuron is updated by following a learning rule:

$$w_i(t+1) = w_i(t) + \lambda \times (m_i(t) - w_i(t)) \tag{3}$$

Considering the constraints of the sensor nodes, we set $(\lambda, p) = (0.05, 6)$ and the number of training epochs to 200. Applying this leaning rule, the weight of a winning neuron is updated to approach to the corresponding input column of M, and eventually each cluster will output 1 if a similar vector is presented to SONN and 0 otherwise. This is the way SONN learns to categorize an input vector it witness. Based on the SONN's output, the monitoring node can identify the most frequently winning cluster as the correct sensor readings. The result is a character vector $v = [min_0, max_0]$, where min_0 and max_0 are the values of a winning neuron, which are the minimum and maximum readings learned by this cluster. The vector v of the most frequently winning neuron is sent to the central control agents. Once the training stage is over, the control agents will have the current characters related to sensor readings. These characters will be used to detect abnormal sensor readings.

The proposed agent is a non-monolithic system and employs several types that perform specific functions as follows: (1) Network monitoring: Certain nodes have sensor agents for network packet monitoring, and our design are interested in preserving total computational power and communication overhead. (2) Host monitoring: Every node on the wireless sensor network is monitored internally by a host-monitoring agent. This includes monitoring system-level and application-level activities. System-level activities include current processes, consuming memory, and CPU cycles. Application-level include sensor network functional algorithms, such as routing algorithms, data aggregation algorithms, et al. (3) Decision-making: Every node decides on its intrusion threat level from a host perspective. Certain nodes collect intrusion information and make global decisions about network-level intrusions. (4) Action: Every node has an action module responsible for resolving intrusion situation on a host. The classification of agent and interaction in proposed system is shown in Figure 3.

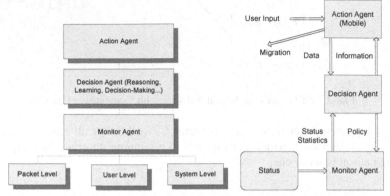

Fig. 3. Layered Agent Classification and Interaction

3.3 Architecture and Functions

The basic architecture and the functions of the middleware for multiple mobile agents are as follows: (1) Automatic fault recognition: The middleware provides basic functions to automatically detect sensor faults or node compromised. Some nodes have abnormal behaviors can be recognized. (2) Adaptive network monitoring: The middleware evolves the monitoring and inference capabilities of the sensor network, so that it can adapt to a wide variety of unknown and unpredictable faults. (3) Cooperative Response: Network entities should coordinate and respond to various types of faults.

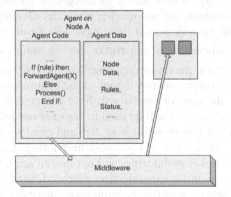

Fig. 4. Architecture and Function for Middleware

Our proposed middleware with multiple mobile agents is shown in Figure 4. In mobile agent, agent code and data that can be transmitted to an arbitrary neighbor node using the pseudo-function ForwardAgent (X). The middleware performs a connection between different agents in one host and mobile agents in different host. The functions of data migration and cognitive networking process can also be provided in middleware. The mobile ability of the agents can help the detection of the failure node or compromised nodes.

3.4 Implementation Issues

We will implement our middleware and test it on Crossbow MICA2 motes [29] running TinyOS or virtual machine, Mate, and in simulation using TOSSIM [30]. The motes have 4kB RAM, 128kB program flash, and a 4 MHz 8-bit Atmel ATmega128L microcontroller.

TinyOS is the most prominent platform for sensor network programming. It also has gained wide acceptance in the research community due to its open-source distribution and ability to suit off-the-shelf hardware. TinyOS employs a component-based architecture that targets resource-constrained nodes by offering only a limited set of services and providing a simple concurrency model. TinyOS applications are typically programmed monolithically with the same program running on every node. The Mate virtual machine, built on top of TinyOS, allows more flexibility in terms of code motion than TinyOS by allowing code to move and update through the network. Mate provides a safe execution environment and permits very compact programs, so we chose to use that platform in the implementation of our agent framework. Mate uses a stack for implicit parameter passing and can be programmed in a simple language called TinyScript. It also provides an efficient framework for global distribution of code, which is utilized to facilitate testing.

Since the real experiments are always none trivial, we develop the simulation codes firstly on TOSSIM to evaluate the scalability performance. TOSSIM is a powerful tool that allows us to test our actual implementation. The code written for TOSSIM can be compiled and run directly on hardware. The simulator provides an empirical radio model that has been found to be representative of real-world performance in many situations.

3.5 Evaluations

We will test the security improvement of our system in mission critical applications. Firstly, the optimization of agent system itself can be evaluated by agent network-usage graph [31]. Network-usage graph can be generated using T_A and η to translate information at the agent layer to the host layer: $K = (H, L_K)$, where

$$L_K = (U_{(a,b) \in LA}(\eta(a), \eta(b))) - (U_{h \in H}(h, h)) .$$ This graph describes which parts of the network are needed to facilitate the agent intended communications. It guides the reduction of the communication overhead of the mobile agents. The agent network-usage weighting w_k , is a function mapping an edge in L_K to the total relative value agents place in that part of the network:

$$w_k(hi, hj) = (\sum_{ai \in \eta^{-1}(hi)} \sum_{aj \in \eta^{-1}(hj)} w_A(ai, aj)) / |A| \tag{4}$$

Secondly, the bio-inspired framework will be compared with the non-intelligence security schemes. The overhead from the intelligence enhancement also need to be evaluated. The parameter tuning of the intelligent algorithms will be compared in the implementation systems. The tradeoff between additional overhead and security increment should be considered to improve the overall performance. For the mission-critical WSNs, the security always occupies the priority comparing with the overhead.

4 Conclusion and Future Work

We presented a bio-inspired security framework - MMASec - by making use of multiple mobile agents to detect and defend sophisticated adversaries in mission-critical WSNs. The cognitive model and intelligent algorithms are selected concerning the constraints of the sensor nodes. The design details are also described for the concrete implementation. The future work is to make extensive evaluation for the implementation components.

References

1. Chong, C.Y., Kumar, S.P.: Sensor Networks: Evolution, Opportunities, and Challenges, Invited Paper. In: Proc. IEEE (August 2003)
2. Wood, A.D., Stankovic, J.A.: Denial of Service in Sensor Networks. Computer 35(10), 54–62 (2002)
3. Newsome, J., Shi, E., Song, D., et al.: The Sybil Attack in Sensor Networks: Analysis & Defenses. In: Proc. of the third International Symposium on Information Processing in Sensor Networks, pp. 259–268. ACM Press, New York (2004)
4. Deng, J., Han, R., Mishra, S.: Countermeasures Against Traffic Analysis in Wireless Sensor Networks. Technical Report CU-CS-987-04, University of Colorado at Boulder (2004)
5. Parno, B., Perrig, A., Gligor, V.: Distributed Detection of Node Replication Attacks in Sensor Networks. In: Proc. of IEEE Symposium on Security and Privacy, SP 2005 (May 2005)
6. Gruteser, M., Schelle, G., Jain, A., et al.: Privacy-aware Location Sensor Networks. In: Proc. of 9th USENIX Workshop on Hot Topics in Operating Systems, HotOS IX (2003)
7. Ozturk, C., Zhang, Y., Trappe, W.: Source-location Privacy in Energy Constrained Sensor Network Routing. In: Proc. of the 2nd ACM workshop on Security of Ad hoc and Sensor Networks (2004)
8. Milojicic, D.: Mobile Agent Applications. IEEE Concurrency 7(3), 80–90 (1999)
9. Tynan, R., O'Hare, G.M.P., Marsh, D., et al.: Intelligent Agents for Wireless Sensor Networks. In: Proc. of the Fourth International Joint Conference on Autonomous Agents and Multi Agent Systems (AAMAS 2005), Netherlands (2005)
10. Singhvi, V., Krause, A., Guestrin, C.: Intelligent Light Control using Sensor Networks. In: Proc. of ACM SenSys 2005, California, USA (2005)

11. Sandhu, J., Agogino, A., Agogino, A.: Wireless Sensor Networks for Commercial Lighting Control: Decision Making with Multi-agent Systems. In: Proc. of AAAI Workshop on Sensor Networks (2004)
12. Khan, A.I., Mihailescu, P.: Parallel Pattern Recognition Computations within a Wireless Sensor Network. In: Proc. of the 17th International Conference on Pattern Recognition, ICPR 2004 (2004)
13. Marsh, D., Tynan, R., O'Kane, D., et al.: Autonomic Wireless Sensor Networks. Engineering Applications of Artificial Intelligence Journal (17), 741–748 (2004)
14. Wang, Y., Wang, Y., Patel, S., Patel, D.: A Layered Reference Model of the Brain (LRMB). IEEE Transactions on Systems, Man, and Cybernetics - Part C: Applications and Reviews 36(2), 124–133 (2006)
15. Wang, Y.: The Real-Time Process Algebra (RTPA). International Journal of Annals of Software Engineering 14, 235–274 (2002)
16. Sarafijanovic, S., Boudec, J.: An Artificial Immune System Approach with Secondary Response for Misbehavior Detection in Mobile Ad-Hoc Networks. IEEE Transactions on Neural Networks, Special Issue on Adaptive Learning Systems in Communication Networks 16(5), 1076–1087 (2005)
17. Das, S.K., Banerjee, N., Roy, A.: Solving Optimization Problems in Wireless Networks using Genetic Algorithms. Handbook of Bioinspired Algorithms (2004)
18. Dressler, F., Krüger, B.: Cell biology as a Key to Computer Networking. In: Proc. of German Conference on Bioinformatics (GCB 2004), Bielefeld, Germany, Abstract and Poster (October 2004)
19. Rosenbloom, P.S., Laird, J.E., Newell, A.: The SOAR Papers: Research on Integrated Intelligence. MIT Press, Cambridge (1992)
20. Gorski, N.A., Laird, J.E.: Experiments in Transfer across Multiple Learning Mechanisms. In: Proc. of the ICML 2006 Workshop on Structural Knowledge Transfer for Machine Learning, Pittsburgh, PA (2006)
21. Shapiro, D., Langley, P.: Controlling Physical Agents through Reactive Logic Programming. In: Proc. of the Third international Conference on Autonomous Agents, pp. 386–387 (1999)
22. Fok, C.-L., Roman, G.C., Lu, C.: Mobile agent middleware for sensor networks: An application case study, Technical Report WUCSE-04-73, Washington University, Department of Computer Science and Engineering, St. Louis (2004)
23. Hui, J., Culler, D.: The Dynamic Behavior of a Data Dissemination Protocol for Network Programming at Scale. In: Proc. of the 2nd International Conference on Embedded Networked Sensor Systems (SenSys 2004), pp. 81–94. ACM Press, New York (2004)
24. Boulis, A., Han, C.C., Srivastava, M.: Design and Implementation of a Framework for Efficient and Programmable Sensor Networks. In: Proc. of the International Conference on Mobile Systems, Applications, and Services, MobiSys 2003 (2003)
25. Liu, T., Martonosi, M.: Impala: A middleware System for Managing Autonomic, Parallel Sensor Systems. In: Proc. of ACM SIGPLAN Symposium on Principles and Practice of Parallel Programming (2003)
26. Boonma, P., Champrasert, P., Suzuki, J.: BiSNET: A Biologically-Inspired Architecture for Wireless Sensor Networks. In: Proc. of the 2nd IEEE International Conference on Autonomic and Autonomous Systems, CA, USA (July 2006)
27. Boonma, P., Champrasert, P., Suzuki, J.: A Biologically-Inspired Architecture for Self-Managing Sensor Networks. In: Proc. of the Third IEEE International Workshop on Wireless Ad hoc and Sensor Networks, New York City, NY (June 2006)

28. Rumelhart, D.E., Zipser, D.: Feature discovery by competitive learning. Cognitive Science 9, 75–112 (1985)
29. Crossbow Inc., http://www.xbow.com/
30. Levis, P., Lee, N., Welsh, M., et al.: TOSSIM: Accurate and Scalable Simulation of Entire TinyOS Applications. In: Proc. of First ACM Conference on Embedded Networked Sensor Systems (ACM SenSys 2003), November 2003, pp. 126–137 (2003)
31. Peysakhov, M., Artz, D., Sultanik, E., et al.: Network Awareness for Mobile Agent on Ad Hoc Networks. In: Proc. of International Joint Conference on Autonomous Agents and Multiagent System (AAMAS 2004), New York, USA (July 2004)

A Cluster-Based Orthogonal Multi-Objective Genetic Algorithm

Jiankai Zhu, Guangming Dai, and Li Mo

Computer Science and Technology,
China Unversity of Geosciences, Wuhan, China
jiankai.cs@gmail.com

Abstract. Multi-objective genetic algorithm is proved to be suitable for solving multi-objective optimization problems. However, it is usually very hard to balance the convergence and diversity of a multi-objective genetic algorithm. This paper introduces a new algorithm, with both good convergence and diversity based on clustering method and multi-parent crossover operator. Meanwhile, an initial population is generated by orthogonal design to enhance the search effort of the algorithm. The experimental results on a number of test problems indicate the good performance of the Cluster-Based Orthogonal Multi-Objective Genetic Algorithm.

Keywords: Multi-objective Optimization Problem, Multi-objective Genetic Algorithm, Orthogonal design, Cluster, Multi-parent Crossover.

1 Introduction

Many optimization problems, in scientific research and engineering areas, belong to multi-objective optimization problems (MOPs). Very often, the objectives of a MOP conflict with each other, and the optimal solutions are a set of solutions. As multi-objective evolutionary algorithms (MOEAs) are based on population and the solutions are a non-dominated solution set. Therefore, they are becoming the most effective approach to solve MOPs. Since the first multi-objective evolutionary algorithm VEGA[1] was proposed by Schaffer in 1985, more and more different MOEAs/ MOGAs have been proposed, such as NSGA, NSGA-II, PAES, SPEA and SPEA2 [2]-[6], etc.

A very important goal in designing a MOEA is that, to improve the convergence rate and maintain the diversity of the solutions simultaneously. Many researches are being done on this. NSGA introduced a niche technology to maintain the diversity. And some techniques such as fitness sharing and crowding distance have been frequently used for maintain the diversity of search [2][7][8]. In 2004, Zheng Jinghua proposed a cluster method which was used to select offspring individuals through their distances [9]. Chan and Ray suggested using two selection operators in MOEAs, one encourages the diversity in the objective space and the other does so in the decision space [10]. Very recently, Aimin Zhou and Qingfu Zhang proposed a Model-Based Multi-Objective Evolutionary Algorithm (MMEA) [11]. At each generation,

Z. Cai et al. (Eds.): ISICA 2009, CCIS 51, pp. 45–55, 2009.

the population was clustered into a number of subpopulations and the PCA technique was used to generate new solutions.

Based on the study and analysis of the above algorithms, this paper proposed a new algorithm, which has the following features: a) The orthogonal design method is used to generate an initial population. It makes the initial individuals scatter evenly in the feasible solution space. b) At every generation, the current population is divided into several clusters in the objective space. Genetic operator is implemented in each cluster. Therefore, the search effort and the population diversity can be promoted. c) The multi-parent crossover operator is used in the algorithm in order to generate offspring individuals. This operator is able to improve the diversity of the population. d) The elitism mechanism for selecting offspring population, which is used in NSGA-II, is employed in this paper.

2 Problem Definition

Generally, continuous multi-objective optimization problem (MOP) can be described as follows:

$$\text{minimize } F(x) = (f_1(x), f_2(x), ..., f_m(x))$$

$$\text{where } x = (x_1, x_2, ..., x_n) \in R^n, \tag{1}$$

$$x_i \in [a_i, b_i], i = 1, 2, ..., n, \ -\infty < a_i < b_i < +\infty.$$

Here, $x = (x_1, x_2, ..., x_n) \in R^n$ is an n-dimension decision variable vector in decision space. $F(x)$ consists of m objective functions is a m-dimension objective variable vector in objective space R^m.

Let $u = (u_1, u_2, ..., u_m)$, $v = (v_1, v_2, ..., v_m) \in R^m$ be two vectors in objective space, if we say u dominates v, denoted by $u \prec v$, only if $u \neq v$ and $u_i \leq v_i$ for all $i = 1, 2, ...m$. A vector $x \in R^n$ is called Pareto optimal if there is no other x' making that $F(x') \prec F(x)$. The set of all the Pareto optimal points is called the Pareto set, denoted by PS. The set of all the Pareto objective vectors is called the Pareto front, denoted by PF, where $PF = \{F(x) \mid x \in PS\}$.

Multi-objective genetic algorithm is designed to construct a set of Pareto optimal solutions to approximate the Pareto front and/or Pareto set in every single run. At last, it gives a most approximate set to decision-maker for making their final choice.

3 Algorithm

3.1 Basic Idea

Multi-objective genetic algorithm begins with an initial population, orthogonal design is used to generate it. The most difference between Cluster-Based Orthogonal

Multi-Objective Genetic Algorithm (COMGA) and traditional MOGAs/MOEAs is that the Clustering method and multi-parent crossover operator. At every generation of the COMGA, we divide the current population based on their distribution, in the objective space, into a number of subpopulations (clusters). There are two benefits from doing this. a) In traditional multi-objective genetic algorithm, genetic operators are usually implemented between individuals chose from the whole population randomly. Hence the operators may be blind, especially when algorithm is approximating to convergence. In contrast, in COMGA, genetic operators are implemented in each cluster individually, therefore the operators will be more efficient and the convergence can be promoted at the same time; b) the population diversity in the objective space can be promoted. After the population was divided into several clusters, we implement multi-parent crossover operator to generate offspring. The multi-parent crossover operator is very effective on improving the diversity of the population. At last, a NDS-selection is used here to generate the offspring population.

3.2 Algorithm Framework

The main framework of COMGA is described as follows:

Step 1 **Initialization:** Set t = 0. Generate an initial population P(0) by orthogonal design. P(t) maintains N individuals.

Step 2 **Clustering:** Partition P(t) into K clusters in the objective space, denoted by C^k, $k = 1, ..., K$.

Step 3 **Offspring Generation:** In each cluster C^k, generate new solutions by multi-parent crossover operator and store them in Q(t).

Step 4 **Selection:** Select P(t+1) from $p(t) \bigcup Q(t)$.

Step 5 **Stopping Condition:** If the stopping condition is met, then stop; otherwise go to Step 2.

3.3 Initialization

Orthogonal design was described systematically in reference [12]. Later in 2001, Leung Y W and Wang Y proposed an orthogonal genetic algorithm with quantization to solve global numerical optimization problem[13]. Orthogonal design is also introduced to solve multi-objective optimization problems[14][15][16][17], the experiment results proved that it can promote the performance of the algorithm.

There are some important properties of orthogonal design. First, it has no two repeat experiments. Second, any two results have no comparability. Thus, it is able to make experiment representatively. More importantly, orthogonal design provides us a set of solutions distributed evenly in feasible solution region, which can make convergence quicker and clustering more efficient.

From (1), $x = (x_1, x_2, ..., x_n) \in R^n$ is a decision variable vector, and x_i, $x_i \in [a_i, b_i]$ is the i-th factor, so there are n factors here. Suppose there are Q (Q is an odd) levels per factor. The orthogonal design works as follows:

Step 1. Set the value of Q, calculate the smallest J by

$$n = \frac{Q^J - 1}{Q - 1}.$$ (2)

Then construct orthogonal array $[z_{i,j}]_{m \times n}$, where $m = Q^J$.

Step 2. Quantize the orthogonal array $[z_{i,j}]_{m \times n}$ by

$$z_{i,j} = \begin{cases} a_i & j = 1 \\ a_i + (j-1)(\dfrac{b_i - a_i}{Q-1}) & 2 \le j \le Q-1. \\ b_i & j = Q \end{cases}$$ (3)

Step 3. Each row in $[z_{i,j}]_{m \times n}$ represents an individual. After Step 2, we get m individuals, m is larger than the population size N. Therefore, we select N optimal individuals as initial population by using the selection operator of NSGA-II.

3.4 Clustering

Typically, the distribution of Pareto front of a continuous MOPs shows a very important regularity. The PF of a m-objective problem is a (m-1)-dimension manifold, which means that the points on PF can be represented in (m-1)-dimension space, as illustrated in Fig.1. This regularity was used to help us partition the population into clusters. The Clustering step works as follows:

Step 1. Build a (m-1)-dimension simplex S in the objective space to represent the current PF.

Step 1.1. For $i = 1, 2, ..., m$ (m is the number of objectives of the MOP), find the non-dominated solution x^i which has the largest f_i objective function value among all the non-dominated solutions in P(t).

Step 1.2. Initialize S with vertexes $F(x^1), ..., F(x^m)$. Then move S along its normal direction to a position such that the points in S dominate all solutions in P(t) and the moved distance should be as short as possible. Let V^i be the vertexes of the moved simplex S. Compute the center O of S, where

$$O = \frac{1}{m} \sum_{i=1}^{m} V^i.$$ (4)

Then enlarge S by moving its vertexes:

$$V^i = V^i + 0.25(V^i - O), i = 1, 2, ..., m.$$ (5)

The main reason to do so is to make sure that the S can represent the latent PF more exactly and to guide the algorithm to extend its search in the objective space.

Step 2. Choose K points $F^1,...,F^k$ which are uniformly spread on simplex S to be K reference points. For each reference point F^i, compute its Euclidian Distance to all the solutions in P(t) in the objective space. And select the $2N/K$ closest solutions to reference point F^i to constitute the cluster C^k. Fig.2 illustrates the procedure when m=2, and S is a one-dimension line segment.

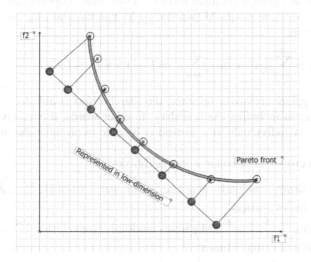

Fig. 1. When m = 2, the points on PF can be represented in one-dimension space

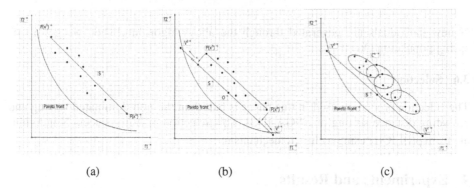

(a)   (b)   (c)

Fig. 2. Build the simplex S when m=2. (a) Find the extreme points. (b) Move the simplex S along its normal direction and enlarge it. (c) Partition the population into several clusters.

We can find that different clusters are associated with different reference points. Therefore, the search effort could be distributed to different reference points of the latent PF in a relatively uniform way. A place needed to pay some attention is that each cluster has $2N / K$ solutions, but the population size is N. Hence different clusters may overlap, which aims at improving the search performance between different reference points and the diversity of the algorithm.

3.5 Offspring Generation

In this paper, offspring solutions are generated by multi-parent crossover operator. Multi-parent crossover operator is a kind of global random search operator based on subspace search and groups climbing method. It has some properties as follows: a) To generate a new solution needs M parents; b) M parents make up of a non-convex linear combination:

$$x = \sum_{i=1}^{M} a_i x^i, where \sum_{i=1}^{M} a_i = 1, -0.5 \le a_i \le 1.5 . \tag{6}$$

Through multi-parent crossover operator, the search effort is able to cover the entire solution space even including the boundary. In other words, it expands the subspace of generating new individuals. It is proved to be able to promote the diversity of the algorithm.

Multi-parent crossover operator works as follows:

Step 1. Uniformly randomly generate an integer k from $\{1, 2, ..., K\}$, K is the number of clusters.

Step 2. Select $x^1, x^2, ..., x^M$, M parents randomly from cluster C^k.

Step 3. Create a new individual x

$$x = a_1 * x^1 + a_2 * x^2 + ... + a_M * x^M, where \sum_{i=1}^{M} a_i = 1.0, -0.5 \le a_i \le 1.5. \tag{7}$$

N new individuals are generated through the above algorithm. Then we get a off-spring population Q(t).

3.6 Selection

The selection procedure used in this paper is based on the non-dominated sorting and crowding distance sorting of NSGA-II [3]. This selection operator selects N individuals from p(t)$\cup$Q(t) using a elitism mechanism.

4 Experiments and Results

4.1 Test Instances and Performance Metrics

In this paper, we chose five test benchmark problems (ZDT1, ZDT2, ZDT3, ZDT4, ZDT6) to evaluate the performance of our algorithm. The details of the test problems can be found in [3]. In order to measure the algorithm numerically, we used two metrics Υ and Δ to evaluate the algorithm. The details can be found in [3].

$$\Upsilon = \sum_{i=1}^{H} \text{mind}(F, F_{i, front}) / n . \tag{8}$$

$$\Delta = \frac{d_f + d_l + \sum_{i=1}^{N-1} |d_i - \overline{d}|}{d_f + d_l + (N-1)\overline{d}} . \tag{9}$$

The first metric Υ measures the extent of convergence to a known set of Pareto optimal solutions. The smaller the value of this metric, the better the convergence toward the Pareto optimal front. The second metric Δ measures the extent of spread achieved among the obtained solutions. The closer to 0 of this metric, the better spread of the solution.

4.2 Experimental Results

In our experiments, we have compared COMGA with several popular algorithms: NSGA-II, SPEA and PAES. The experimental results and parameter setting of NSGA-II, SPEA and PAES can be found in [3]. The population size of each algorithm is 100, and the max generation is 250. The statistical results are based on 10 runs of the algorithm.

Table 1. Mean and variance of the convergence metric Υ and diversity metric Δ in ZDT1 (mean $\pm$ std.)

Algorithm	Convergence metric Υ	Diversity metric Δ
NSGA-II(Real-coded)	0.033482 ± 0.004750	0.390307 ± 0.001875
NSGA-II(Binary-coded)	0.000894 ± 0.000000	0.463292 ± 0.041622
SPEA	0.001799 ± 0.000001	0.784525 ± 0.004440
PAES	0.082085 ± 0.008679	1.229794 ± 0.004839
COMGA	$\mathbf{0.001173 \pm 0.000000}$	$\mathbf{0.163814 \pm 0.000106}$

Table 1-5 shows the mean and variance of the convergence metric Υ and the diversity metric Δ obtained from the five test problems by using five algorithms. From the experimental results, we can see that: a) COMGA is able to converge much better in all problems, especially in ZDT4 and ZDT6. This is because ZDT4 has 21^9 different local Pareto-optimal fronts in the search space and it is usually used to test the ability of the algorithm of solving multi-peak problems. As introduced in Offspring Generation part, a multi-parent crossover operator was used in our algorithm and it is very good at solving the multi-peak problems. ZDT6 doesn't distribute evenly on the global Pareto-optimal front, so the diversity of the solution is very important for a algorithm to maintain. b) In all case with COMGA, the variance of the convergence is very close to 0 (In tables, numbers are just kept to the six places of decimals). c) COMGA performs very well in all test problems in diversity. Because in the algorithm, we have used many measures to maintain the diversity of the population.

In order to demonstrate the working of the algorithm, we also show typical simulation results on the test problems ZDT4, ZDT6 and WFG6. Based on the experiments in [18], WFG6 is hard for NSGA-II to converge. Fig. 3-5 illustrates the results.

Table 2. Mean and variance of the convergence metric Υ and diversity metric Δ in ZDT2 (mean $\pm$ std.)

Algorithm	Convergence metric Υ	Diversity metric Δ
NSGA-II(Real-coded)	0.072391 ± 0.031689	0.430776 ± 0.004721
NSGA-II(Binary-coded)	0.000824 ± 0.000000	0.435112 ± 0.024607
SPEA	0.001399 ± 0.000000	0.755148 ± 0.004521
PAES	0.126276 ± 0.036877	1.165942 ± 0.007682
COMGA	$\mathbf{0.000901 \pm 0.000000}$	$\mathbf{0.171969 \pm 0.000218}$

Table 3. Mean and variance of the convergence metric Υ and diversity metric Δ in ZDT3 (mean $\pm$ std.)

Algorithm	Convergence metric Υ	Diversity metric Δ
NSGA-II(Real-coded)	0.114500 ± 0.007940	0.738540 ± 0.019706
NSGA-II(Binary-coded)	0.043411 ± 0.000042	0.575606 ± 0.005078
SPEA	0.047517 ± 0.000047	0.672938 ± 0.003587
PAES	0.023872 ± 0.000010	0.789920 ± 0.001653
COMGA	$\mathbf{0.001175 \pm 0.000000}$	$\mathbf{0.468940 \pm 0.001264}$

Table 4. Mean and variance of the convergence metric Υ and diversity metric Δ in ZDT4 (mean $\pm$ std.)

Algorithm	Convergence metric Υ	Diversity metric Δ
NSGA-II(Real-coded)	0.513053 ± 0.118460	0.702612 ± 0.064648
NSGA-II(Binary-coded)	3.227636 ± 0.702612	0.479475 ± 0.009841
SPEA	7.340299 ± 6.572516	0.798463 ± 0.014616
PAES	0.854816 ± 0.527238	0.870458 ± 0.101399
COMGA	$\mathbf{0.001049 \pm 0.000000}$	$\mathbf{0.163790 \pm 0.000110}$

Table 5. Mean and variance of the convergence metric Υ and diversity metric Δ in ZDT6 (mean $\pm$ std.)

Algorithm	Convergence metric Υ	Diversity metric Δ
NSGA-II(Real-coded)	0.296564 ± 0.01313	0.668025 ± 0.009923
NSGA-II(Binary-coded)	7.806798 ± 0.001667	0.644477 ± 0.035042
SPEA	0.221138 ± 0.000449	0.849389 ± 0.002713
PAES	0.085469 ± 0.006664	1.153052 ± 0.003916
COMGA	$\mathbf{0.000600 \pm 0.000000}$	$\mathbf{0.151645 \pm 0.000194}$

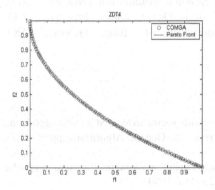

Fig. 3. The Pareto front obtained by COMGA on ZDT4

Fig. 4. The Pareto front obtained by COMGA on ZDT6

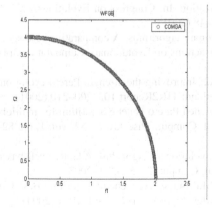
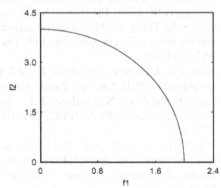

Fig. 5. The Pareto front obtained by COMGA on WFG6. The Pareto front of the WFG6.

5 Conclusion

In this paper, we have introduced a new method to generate an initial population, which can make the solutions scatter evenly in the feasible solutions space. A cluster method was used to partition the population into several subpopulations in order to enhance the search effort and diversity of the algorithm. And, we have used multi-parent crossover operator to generate new offspring individuals and improved the diversity of the algorithm. The new algorithm in this paper shows very good performance on several test problems.

Acknowledgement

This paper is supported by National Natural Science Foundation (NO.60873107), the National High Technology Research and Development Program (NO. 2008AA12A201) and Natural Science Foundation of Hubei Province (NO. 2008CDB348).

References

[1] Schaffer, J.D.: Multiple objective optimization with vector evaluated genetic algorithm. In: Proceedings of the 1st International Conference on Genetic Algorithms, pp. 93–100. Lawrence Erlbaum, Mahwah (1985)

[2] Srinivas, N., Deb, K.: Multiobjective optimization using nondominated sorting in genetic algorithms. Evolutionary Computation 2(3), 221–248 (1994)

[3] Deb, K., Agrawal, S., Pratap, A., Meyarivan, T.: A fast and elitist multiobjective genetic algorithm: NSGA-II. Danpur Genetic Algorit hms Laboratory (kanGAL), Indian Institute of Technology, Kanpur: Technical Report 6(2), 182–197 (2002)

[4] Knowles, J.D., Corne, D.W.: The Pareto archived evolution strategy: A new baseline algorithm for Pareto for multiobjective optimization. In: Congress on Evolutionary Computation (CEC 1999), Piscataway, NJ, pp. 38–48 (2001)

[5] Zitzler, E., Thiele, L.: Multiobjective evolutionary algorithms: A comparative case study and the strength Pareto approach. IEEE Transactions on Evolutionary Computation 3(4), 257–271 (1999)

[6] Zitzler, E., Laumanns, M., Thiele, L.: SPEA2: Improving the strength Pareto evolutionary algorithm. ETH Zent rum, Zurich, Switzerland: TIK2Report 103, 200–210 (2001)

[7] Horn, J., Nafpliotis, N., Goldberg, D.E.: A niched Pareto genetic algorithm for multiobjective optimization. In: 1st IEEE Trans. Evol. Comput., Piscataway, NJ, vol. 1, pp. 82–87 (1994)

[8] Yen, G.G., Lu, H.: Dynamic multiobjective evolutionary algorithm: Adaptive cell-based rank and density estimation. IEEE Trans. Evol. Comput. 7, 253–274 (2003)

[9] Jinghua, Z., Zhongzhi, S., Yong, X.: A Fast Multi-objective Genetic Algorithm Based on Clustering. Journal of computer research and development 41(7), 1081–1087 (2004)

[10] Chan, K.P., Ray, T.: An evolutionary algorithm to maintain diversity in the parametric and the objective space. In: Third International Conference on Computational Intelligence, Robotics and Autonomous Systems, CIRAS 2005 (2005)

[11] Zhou, A., Zhang, Q., Jin, Y.: Approximating the Set of Pareto Optimal Solutions in Both the Decision and Objective Spaces by an Estimation of Distribution Algorithm. Technical Report CES-485

[12] Montgomery, D.C.: Design and Analysis of Experiments (3rd). Wiley, New York (1991)

[13] Leung, Y.W., Wang, Y.: An orthogonal genetic algorithm with quantization for global numerical optimization. IEEE Transactions on Evolutionary Computation 5(1), 41–53 (2001)

[14] Dai, G., Zheng, W., Xie, B.: An Orthogonal and Model Based Multiobjective Genetic Algorithm for LEO Regional Satellite Constellation Optimization. In: Kang, L., Liu, Y., Zeng, S. (eds.) ISICA 2007. LNCS, vol. 4683, pp. 652–660. Springer, Heidelberg (2007)

[15] Zheng, S., Wei, W., Kang, L., et al.: A multi-objective algorithm based on orthogonal design. Chinese Journal of Computers 28(7), 1153–1162 (2005)

[16] Cai, Z., Gong, W., Huang, Y.: A Novel Differential Evolution Algorithm based on epsilon-domination and Orthogonal Design Method for Multiobjective Optimization. In: Obayashi, S., Deb, K., Poloni, C., Hiroyasu, T., Murata, T. (eds.) EMO 2007. LNCS, vol. 4403, pp. 286–301. Springer, Heidelberg (2007)

[17] Gong, W., Cai, Z.: An Improved Multiobjective Differential Evolution based on Pareto-adaptive epsilon-dominance and Orthogonal Design. European Journal of Operational Research 198(2), 576–601 (2009)

[18] Huband, S., Hingston, P., Barone, L., While, L.: A review of multiobjective test problems and a scalable test problem toolkit. IEEE Transactions on Evolutionary Computation 10(5), 477–506 (2006)

An Analysis of Semantic Aware Crossover

Nguyen Quang Uy[1], Nguyen Xuan Hoai[2], Michael O'Neill[1],
Bob McKay[2], and Edgar Galván-López[1]

[1] Natural Computing Research & Applications Group, University College Dublin, Ireland
[2] School of Computer Science and Engineering, Seoul National University, Korea

Abstract. It is well-known that the crossover operator plays an important role in Genetic Programming (GP). In Standard Crossover (SC), semantics are not used to guide the selection of the crossover points, which are generated randomly. This lack of semantic information is the main cause of destructive effects from SC (e.g., children having lower fitness than their parents). Recently, we proposed a new semantic based crossover known GP called *Semantic Aware Crossover* (SAC) [25]. We show that SAC outperforms SC in solving a class of real-value symbolic regression problems. We clarify the effect of SAC on GP search in increasing the semantic diversity of the population, thus helping to reduce the destructive effects of crossover in GP.

Keywords: Semantic Aware Crossover, Semantic, Constructive Effect, Bloat.

1 Introduction

Genetic Programming (GP) is an evolutionary algorithm, inspired by biological evolution, which finds solutions in the form of computer programs for a user-defined task [16]. The program is usually represented in the language of a syntactic formalism such as S-expression trees [16], a linear sequence of instructions, grammar derivation trees, or graphs [23]. The genetic operators in GP are usually designed to guarantee the syntactic closure property, i.e., to produce syntactically valid children from syntactically valid parent(s). In this process, GP evolutionary search is conducted on the syntactic space of programs, with the only semantic guidance coming from the fitnesses of programs. Although GP has shown its effectiveness in evolving programs for solving different problems, this practice is somewhat unusual from the perspective of real programmers. Computer programs are constrained not only by syntax, but also by semantics. In normal practice, any attempt to change to a program should pay heavy attention to the change in semantics. To see how this would play out in GP, we have recently proposed a semantic-based crossover operator called *Semantic Aware Crossover* (SAC) [25]. Our previous results showed that using semantic guidance for the crossover operator in GP improves performance, measured in terms of successful runs in solving a particular problem (in our work, we used real-valued symbolic regression problems). In this paper we extend our previous work by performing a deeper analysis of how SAC affects GP search and reduces the destructive effects of crossover.

The paper is organised as follows. In the following section, we describe previous work on semantic based operators. In Section 3, we briefly describe our approach (i.e.,

Z. Cai et al. (Eds.): ISICA 2009, CCIS 51, pp. 56–65, 2009.

Semantic Aware Crossover). Section 4 provides details on the experimental setup used to conduct our analysis. The results presented in this paper are discussed in Section 5. Finally, conclusions are drawn in Section 6.

2 Previous Work

Using semantic information in GP is not new – there have been a number of related studies in recent years. The use of semantic information in GP can be grouped into three categories, on the basis of their use of: grammars [26,3,4]; formal methods [10,11,12,14,13]; and GP representation [1,19,25].

Attribute grammars have been one of the most popular methods to incorporate semantic information into GP. By using an attribute grammar, and adding attributes to individuals, we can check useful semantic information about individuals during the evolutionary process. This information can be used to remove bad (i.e., less fit) individuals [4] or to prevent generation of invalid individuals [26,3]. However, the attributes are problem dependent, and it may be difficult to design attributes for some problems.

Recently, Johnson has advocated formal methods as a means to incorporate semantic information in the evolutionary process [10,11,12]. In [11], Johnson proposed a number of possible ways to incorporate semantics of programs. In these methods, the semantic information that is extracted by using formal methods, mostly based on Abstract Interpretation and Model Checking, is used as a way of measuring the fitness of individuals for some problems where sampling techniques are difficult to use. Katz and co-workers used model checking to solve a Mutual Exclusion problem [14,13]. In these works, semantics are extracted/calculated and then incorporated into the fitness of an individual.

With expression trees, semantic information has been incorporated mainly by modifying the crossover operator. Early work focused on the syntax and structure of individuals. In [9], the authors modified crossover to take into account the depth of trees. Other work modified crossover to take into account the shape of the individual [24]. More recently, context has been used as extra information for determining GP crossover points [6,17]. However these methods all have to pay the huge time cost of evaluating the context of all subtrees of all individuals.

In [1], the authors investigated the effects of directly using semantic information to guide GP crossover on Boolean domains. The main idea proposed in [1] was to check the semantic equivalence between offspring and parents by transforming the trees to Reduced Ordered Binary Decision Diagrams (ROBDDs). Two trees have the same semantic information if and only if they reduce to the same ROBDD. The semantic equivalence checking is then used to determine which of the individuals participating in crossover will be copied to the next generation. If the offspring are semantically equivalent to their parents, then the parents are copied into the new population. By doing this, the authors argue, there is an increase in the semantic diversity of the evolving population and a consequent improvement in the GP performance.

In our previous work [25], we proposed a new crossover operator (SAC), based on the semantic equivalence checking of subtrees. Our approach was tested on a family of real-value symbolic regression problems (e.g., polynomial functions). Our empirical results showed that SAC improves GP performance. SAC differs from [1] in two ways. Firstly, the test domain is real-valued rather than Boolean. For real-value domains, checking semantic equivalence by reduction to common ROBDDs is not possible. Secondly, the crossover operator is guided not by the semantics of the whole program tree, but by that of subtrees. This is inspired by recent work presented in [19] for calculating subtree semantics.

3   Semantic Aware Crossover

The aim of our previous work [25] was to extend the ideas in [1,19] to real-value domains. For real domains it is not feasible to compute the semantics by reduction to canonical form, as it was for the Boolean domain in [1]. Complete enumeration and comparison of subtree fitness as in [19] is also impossible on real domains. In fact, the problem of determining semantic equivalence between two real-value expressions is known to be complete NP-hard [5]. Therefore, we have to calculate the approximate semantics. In [25], a simple method for measuring and comparing the semantics of two expressions is used. To determine the semantic equivalence of two expressions, we measure them against a random set of points sampled from the domain. If the output of the two trees on the random sample set are close enough (subject to a parameter called *Semantic Sentivity*) then they are semantically equivalent, or in pseudo-code:

If Abs(Value_On_Random_Set(P_1)-Value_On_Random_Set(P_2))<ε then
        Return P_1 is semantically equivalent to P_2.

where *Abs* is the absolute function and ε is a predefined threshold for semantic sensitivity. This method is inspired by the simple technique for simplifying expression trees proposed in [21] known as Equivalence Decision Simplification (EDS), where complicated subtrees are replaced by simpler subtrees if they are semantically equivalent. The semantic equivalence of two subtrees can be used to control the crossover operation by constraining it so that if the corresponding subtrees beneath the crossover point are semantically equivalent, the selection is repeated with two new crossover points. Algorithm 1 shows how SAC works. The motivation behind SAC is to promote GP

Algorithm 1. Semantic Aware Crossover

select Parent 1 P_1;
select Parent 2 P_2;
choose at random crossover points at *Subtree*$_1$ in P_1;
choose at random crossover points at *Subtree*$_2$ in P_2;
if *Subtree*$_1$ *is not equivalent with Subtree*$_2$ **then**
  | execute crossover;
  | add the children to the new population;
  | return true;
else
  | choose at random crossover points at *Subtree*$_1$ in P_1;
  | choose at random crossover points at *Subtree*$_2$ in P_2;
  | execute crossover;
  | return true;

---

to swap subtrees that have different semantics. In [25], SAC had the best performance (compared with SC and other semantic checking operators) on a family of real-value regression problems. The reasons for these good results were not clearly understood. The following sections will aid in understanding how this mechanism affects GP search.

4   Experimental Setup

We used four real-valued symbolic regression problems, of increasing difficulty, to analyse SAC. The underlying functions, from [8], are shown in Table 1, and evolutionary parameters in Table 2.

Table 1. Symbolic Regression Functions

$F_1 = X^3 + X^2 + X$	$F_3 = X^5 + X^4 + X^3 + X^2 + X$
$F_2 = X^4 + X^3 + X^2 + X$	$F_4 = X^6 + X^5 + X^4 + X^3 + X^2 + X$

Table 2. Run and Evolutionary Parameter Values

Parameter	Value	Parameter	Value
Generations	50	Population size	500
Selection	Tournament	Tournament size	3
Crossover probability	0.9	Mutation probability	0.1
Initial Max depth	6	Max depth	15
Non-terminals	+, -, *, /, sin, cos, exp, log (protected versions)		
Terminals	X, 1		
Number of samples	20 random points from $[-1\ldots1]$		
Successful run	sum of absolute error on all fitness cases < 0.1		
Termination	max generations exceeded		
Sensitivities	$0.01, 0.02, 0.04, 0.05, 0.06, 0.08, 0.1$		
Trials per treatment	100 independent runs for each value.		

5   Results and Discussion

5.1   Equivalent Crossovers

Because our crossover operator works by analysing semantics of subtrees, we would like to know how frequently SAC and SC swap equivalent subtrees. We collected statistics of the percentage of such crossover events. Figure 1 shows the percentage of semantically equivalent crossover events with *sensitivity* = 0.01, averaged over 100 runs, for each of the four functions, while Table 3 shows the same further averaged over all generations. We can see that the overall average for SC is around 14.5% whereas for SAC it is around 8 times smaller at about 1.8%. It is clear that SAC is more semantically exploratory than SC on these problems. We also conducted an experiment to test how crossover affects the relative fitness of the offspring compared to their parent when it swaps two semantically equivalent subtrees. The results indicate that in nearly all cases (about 98%), such crossover will result in an unchanged fitness.

Table 3. Average Percentage of Equivalent Crossovers.

Sensitivity		0.01	0.02	0.04	0.05	0.06	0.08	0.1
F_1	SC	14.9%	14.9%	14.9%	14.9%	15.1%	15.1%	15.1%
	SAC	**1.9%**	**1.9%**	**1.9%**	**1.9%**	**1.9%**	**2.0%**	**2.0%**
F_2	SC	14.1%	14.1%	14.1%	14.1%	14.1%	14.2%	14.2%
	SAC	**1.7%**	**1.7%**	**1.7%**	**1.8%**	**1.9%**	**1.9%**	**1.8%**
F_3	SC	14.4%	14.4%	14.4%	14.4%	14.5%	14.5%	14.5%
	SAC	**1.8%**	**1.8%**	**1.8%**	**1.8%**	**1.9%**	**1.9%**	**1.9%**
F_4	SC	14.1%	14.1%	14.1%	14.1%	14.3%	14.3%	14.3%
	SAC	**1.7%**	**1.7%**	**1.8%**	**1.8%**	**1.8%**	**1.8%**	**1.8%**

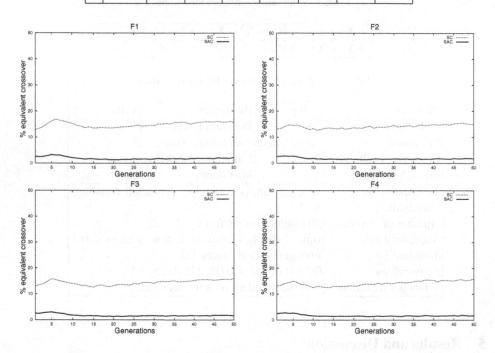

Fig. 1. Average Percentage of Equivalent Crossovers with *sensitivity* = 0.01

5.2 Semantic Diversity

In the previous section, we saw that SAC promotes swapping of semantically different subtrees, encouraging a change in semantics relative to their parents. How well does SAC promote diversity. Population diversity has been long seen as a crucial factor in GP [2]. The search process will be more effective if more diversity in the population is maintained. Two kinds of metrics have been used to measure and control the diversity of a population: genotypic and phenotypic [7]. The former is based on the syntax (i.e., structure) of an individual [22] and the latter on the behavior (i.e., fitness) of an individual [20]. In this paper, we propose a new measure to measure semantic diversity called *Semantic Crossover Diversity* (SCD). SCD works by measuring the difference between

Table 4. Percentage of Children with Different Fitness from their Parents

Sensitivity		0.01	0.02	0.04	0.05	0.06	0.08	0.1
F_1	SC	65.8%	65.8%	65.8%	65.8%	65.8%	65.8%	65.8%
	SAC	**73.4%**	**73.0%**	**72.5%**	**72.1%**	**72.4%**	**72.3%**	**73.1%**
F_2	SC	70.5%	70.5%	70.5%	70.5%	70.5%	70.5%	70.5%
	SAC	**79.0%**	**79.0%**	**78.5%**	**78.3%**	**78.8%**	**78.4%**	**79.1%**
F_3	SC	70.6%	70.6%	70.6%	70.6%	70.6%	70.6%	70.6%
	SAC	**80.6%**	**81.2%**	**81.6%**	**82.0%**	**82.0%**	**81.7%**	**82.2%**
F_4	SC	71.0%	71.0%	71.0%	71.0%	71.0%	71.0%	71.0%
	SAC	**80.2%**	**80.0%**	**80.0%**	**79.8%**	**80.0%**	**80.1%**	**79.7%**

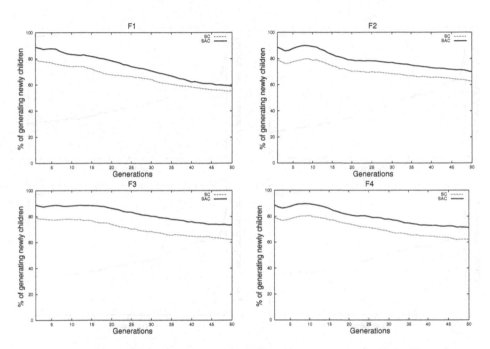

Fig. 2. The percentage of generating newly children with $sensitivity = 0.05$

individuals before and after applying crossover. We used SCD to measure the semantic diversity of SC and SAC by counting the percentage of these crossover events that generated semantically different offspring from their parents. These results are shown in Table 4 and figure 2. We can see that at the beginning of the run, SC generates around 80% of different offspring, while SAC generates about 90%. This is important: the early phase of evolution, is the primary exploration stage, when it is necessary to create semantically new individuals. After a few generations, the percentage decreases in both cases. However SAC still consistently produces about 10% more difference than SC. We note that SAC doest not guarantee to generating semantically new offspring. We believe that there are some fixed semantic subtrees as in the Boolean domain [19].

Table 5. The average percentage of better children than their parent in crossover

Sensitivity		0.01	0.02	0.04	0.05	0.06	0.08	0.1
F_1	SC	11.8%	11.8%	11.8%	11.8%	11.8%	11.8%	11.8%
	SAC	**15.2%**	**15.0%**	**14.7%**	**15.4%**	**15.3%**	**15.5%**	**15.7%**
F_2	SC	13.0%	13.0%	13.0%	13.0%	13.0%	13.0%	13.0%
	SAC	**17.2%**	**16.7%**	**16.9%**	**17.3%**	**17.4%**	**17.3%**	**17.4%**
F_3	SC	12.9%	12.9%	12.9%	12.9%	12.9%	12.9%	12.9%
	SAC	**16.9%**	**16.8%**	**17.0%**	**17.1%**	**17.0%**	**17.2%**	**17.0%**
F_4	SC	12.8%	11.4%	11.4%	11.4%	11.4%	11.4%	11.4%
	SAC	**16.8%**	**16.8%**	**16.7%**	**17.0%**	**17.1%**	**17.0%**	**17.0%**

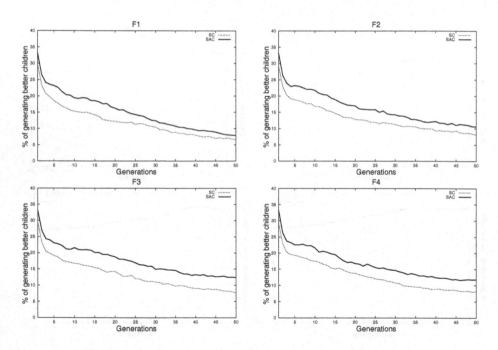

Fig. 3. The percentage of constructive crossover with *sensitivity*= 0.04

5.3   Constructive Effect

If SAC is more semantically productive than SC, then it is interesting to ask whether this helps the crossover operators to breed better children than their parents (more constructive crossover). To answer this, we measured the constructive effect of SAC and SC, using a method similar to that in [18]. The constructive effect is measured by calculating the percentage of events that generate a better child from its parents through crossover. The results are shown in Table 5, figure 3 showing the change over the course of evolution with *sensitivity* 0.04. We can see that SAC is more fitness constructive,

Table 6. The average size of individuals

Sensitivity		0.01	0.02	0.04	0.05	0.06	0.08	0.1
F_1	SC	44.2	44.2	44.2	44.2	44.2	44.2	44.2
	SAC	46.8	46.2	46.7	46.5	46.7	46.9	46.9
F_2	SC	46.1	46.1	46.1	46.1	46.1	46.1	46.1
	SAC	50.0	49.3	49.1	49.8	49.9	49.9	46.7
F_3	SC	44.8	44.8	44.8	44.8	44.8	44.8	44.8
	SAC	49.9	48.7	48.3	48.2	48.3	48.4	48.7
F_4	SC	48.0	48.0	48.0	48.0	48.0	48.0	48.0
	SAC	52.2	51.9	52.4	51.6	51.5	52.0	51.8

Table 7. The average size of subtrees in SAC

Sensitivity	0.01	0.02	0.04	0.05	0.06	0.08	0.1
F_1	4.6	4.3	4.4	4.6	4.8	4.6	4.9
F_2	4.7	4.5	4.6	4.9	5.0	4.7	4.8
F_3	4.7	4.5	4.4	4.6	5.1	4.7	4.9
F_4	4.7	4.5	4.7	4.6	5.0	4.6	5.0

often 5% better, than SC. This strongly suggests why the performance of SAC was better than SC in terms of number of successful runs.

5.4   Code Bloat

The better performance of SAC comes at a cost: it takes time to calculate the subtree semantics. This is reflected in the slightly higher running time of SAC, as compared with SC. How much more expensive are these extra calculations? And is this the sole cause of the extra computational cost, or might code bloat play a role? To determine which is the main source we collected two statistics from the runs. The first is the average size of individuals (number of nodes) over 50 generations, averaged over 100 runs, for SAC versus SC. The second is the average size of subtrees which are semantic equivalence tested in SAC, averaged in the same way. The two statistics are shown in Table 6, and Table 7 respectively.

It is clear that the higher running time of SAC resulted from both causes: the individuals were larger. However it also seems that the overheads are acceptable. From Table 7, we see that the average size of subtrees in SAC is very small in comparison with the average size of individuals. Therefore, the time needed to calculate and compare subtree fitnes is small (in fact, we could reduce this further by using caching to improve the efficiency of subtree semantic calculation as in [15]). The average individual size in SAC was bigger than that of SC but not by a large margin. Nevertheless, we are interested to incorporate the size of subtrees into the selection of crossover points in future work, potentially avoiding this issue.

6 Conclusions

In this paper we have compared Semantic Aware Crossover (SAC) and Standard Crossover (SC) from a number of perspectives. We have shown that about 15% of SC operations exchange semantically equivalent subtrees. As a consequence SC tends to create offspring that are semantically similar to their parents. This weakness can be amended by preventing the swapping of equivalent subtrees. Our approach, Semantic Aware Crossover (SAC), adopts this idea. Secondly, we have shown that SAC helps to promote semantic diversity, so it generates more offspring that are semantically different from their parents. The results also show that SAC is more constructive than SC. Furthermore, we have seen that the additional computation cost of SAC is almost negligible.

Acknowledgements. This research was funded under a Postgraduate Scholarship from the Irish Research Council for Science Engineering and Technology (IRCSET).

References

1. Beadle, L., Johnson, C.: Semantically driven crossover in genetic programming. In: Proc. IEEE WCCI 2008, pp. 111–116. IEEE Press, Los Alamitos (2008)
2. Burke, E.K., Gustafson, S., Kendall, G.: Diversity in genetic programming: An analysis of measures and correlation with fitness. IEEE Transactions on Evolutionary Computation 8(1), 47–62 (2004)
3. Cleary, R., O'Neill, M.: An attribute grammar decoder for the 01 multi-constrained knapsack problem. In: Raidl, G.R., Gottlieb, J. (eds.) EvoCOP 2005. LNCS, vol. 3448, pp. 34–45. Springer, Heidelberg (2005)
4. de la Cruz Echeand'a, M., de la Puente, A.O., Alfonseca, M.: Attribute grammar evolution. In: Mira, J., Álvarez, J.R. (eds.) IWINAC 2005. LNCS, vol. 3562, pp. 182–191. Springer, Heidelberg (2005)
5. Ghodrat, M.A., Givargis, T., Nicolau, A.: Equivalence checking of arithmetic expressions using fast evaluation. In: Proc. of the International Conference on Compilers, Architecture and Synthesis for Embedded Systems – CASES 2005. ACM, New York (2005)
6. Hengpraprohm, S., Chongstitvatana, P.: Selective crossover in genetic programming. In: Proc. of ISCIT International Symposium on Communications and Information Technologies, November 2001, pp. 14–16 (2001)
7. Hien, N.T., Hoai, N.X.: A brief overview of population diversity measures in genetic programming. In: Proc. of 11th Asia-Pacific Workshop on Intelligent and Evolutionary Systems, October 2006, pp. 128–139. Vietnamese Military Technical Academy (2006)
8. Hoai, N.X., McKay, R., Essam, D.: Solving the symbolic regression problem with tree-adjunct grammar guided genetic programming: The comparative results. In: Proc. of CEC 2002, pp. 1326–1331. IEEE Press, Los Alamitos (2002)
9. Ito, T., Iba, H., Sato, S.: Depth-dependent crossover for genetic programming. In: Proc. of IEEE WCCI 1998, pp. 775–780. IEEE Press, Los Alamitos (1998)
10. Johnson, C.: Deriving genetic programming fitness properties by static analysis. In: Foster, J.A., Lutton, E., Miller, J., Ryan, C., Tettamanzi, A.G.B. (eds.) EuroGP 2002. LNCS, vol. 2278, pp. 298–308. Springer, Heidelberg (2002)
11. Johnson, C.: What can automatic programming learn from theoretical computer science. In: Proc. of the UK Workshop on Computational Intelligence. University of Birmingham (2002)

12. Johnson, C.: Genetic programming with fitness based on model checking. In: Ebner, M., O'Neill, M., Ekárt, A., Vanneschi, L., Esparcia-Alcázar, A.I. (eds.) EuroGP 2007. LNCS, vol. 4445, pp. 114–124. Springer, Heidelberg (2007)
13. Katz, G., Peled, D.: Genetic programming and model checking: Synthesizing new mutual exclusion algorithms. In: Cha, S(S.), Choi, J.-Y., Kim, M., Lee, I., Viswanathan, M. (eds.) ATVA 2008. LNCS, vol. 5311, pp. 33–47. Springer, Heidelberg (2008)
14. Katz, G., Peled, D.: Model checking-based genetic programming with an application to mutual exclusion. In: Ramakrishnan, C.R., Rehof, J. (eds.) TACAS 2008. LNCS, vol. 4963, pp. 141–156. Springer, Heidelberg (2008)
15. Keijzer, M.: Alternatives in subtree caching for genetic programming. In: Keijzer, M., O'Reilly, U.-M., Lucas, S., Costa, E., Soule, T. (eds.) EuroGP 2004. LNCS, vol. 3003, pp. 328–337. Springer, Heidelberg (2004)
16. Koza, J.: Genetic Programming: On the Programming of Computers by Natural Selection. MIT Press, MA (1992)
17. Majeed, H., Ryan, C.: A less destructive, context-aware crossover operator for GP. In: Collet, P., Tomassini, M., Ebner, M., Gustafson, S., Ekárt, A. (eds.) EuroGP 2006. LNCS, vol. 3905, pp. 36–48. Springer, Heidelberg (2006)
18. Majeed, H., Ryan, C.: On the constructiveness of context-aware crossover. In: Proc. of GECCO 2007, pp. 1659–1666. ACM Press, New York (2007)
19. McPhee, N., Ohs, B., Hutchison, T.: Semantic building blocks in genetic programming. In: O'Neill, M., Vanneschi, L., Gustafson, S., Esparcia Alcázar, A.I., De Falco, I., Della Cioppa, A., Tarantino, E. (eds.) EuroGP 2008. LNCS, vol. 4971, pp. 134–145. Springer, Heidelberg (2008)
20. Mori, N.: A novel diversity measure of genetic programming. In: Proc. of Randomness and Computation: Joint Workshop "New Horizons in Computing" and "Statistical Mechanical Approach to Probabilistic Information, July 2005, pp. 18–21 (2005)
21. Mori, N., McKay, R., Hoai, N.X., Essam, D.: Equivalent decision simplification: A new method for simplifying algebraic expressions in genetic programming. In: Proc. of 11th Asia-Pacific Workshop on Intelligent and Evolutionary Systems (2007)
22. O'Reilly, U.M.: Using a distance metric on genetic programs to understand genetic operators. In: Proc. of IEEE International Conference on Systems, Man, and Cybernetics, Computational Cybernetics and Simulation, pp. 4092–4097. IEEE, Los Alamitos (1997)
23. Poli, R., Langdon, W., McPhee, N.: A Field Guide to Genetic Programming (2008), http://lulu.com
24. Poli, R., Langdon, W.B.: Genetic programming with one-point crossover. In: Proc. of Soft Computing in Engineering Design and Manufacturing Conference, pp. 180–189. Springer, Heidelberg (1997)
25. Uy, N.Q., Hoai, N.X., O'Neill, M.: Semantic aware crossover for genetic programming: the case for real-valued function regression. In: Vanneschi, L., et al. (eds.) EuroGP 2009. LNCS, vol. 5481, pp. 25–36. Springer, Heidelberg (2009)
26. Wong, M.L., Leung, K.S.: An induction system that learns programs in different programming languages using genetic programming and logic grammars. In: Proc. of the 7th IEEE International Conference on Tools with Artificial Intelligence (1995)

An Artificial Immune Univariate Marginal Distribution Algorithm

Qingbin Zhang[1], Shuo Kang[2], Junxiang Gao[2], Song Wu[1], and Yanping Tian[1]

[1] Shijiazhuang Institute of Railway Technology, Shijiazhuang 050041, China
[2] The Second Hospital of Hebei Medical University, Shijiazhuang 050000, China
zqbin2002@sina.com

Abstract. Hybridization is an extremely effective way of improving the performance of the Univariate Marginal Distribution Algorithm (UMDA). Owing to its diversity and memory mechanisms, artificial immune algorithm has been widely used to construct hybrid algorithms with other optimization algorithms. This paper proposes a hybrid algorithm which combines the UMDA with the principle of general artificial immune algorithm. Experimental results on deceptive function of order 3 show that the proposed hybrid algorithm can get more building blocks (BBs) than the UMDA.

Keywords: UMDA, artificial immune algorithm, hybridization.

1 Introduction

The Univariate Marginal Distribution Algorithm (UMDA)[1] is a simple EDAs which uses the univariate marginal distribution model to estimate the joint probability distribution of the selected promising individuals at each generation. It works very well for the linear problems and problems without many significant dependencies. However, when it encountered problems with strong interactions among variables, the UMDA can not get satisfied solutions.

Hybridization is an extremely effective way of improving the performance of the UMDA. Tang and Lau proposed a hybrid algorithm which combined UMDA with the hill-climbing algorithm [2]. Santana et al. proposed a hybrid UMDA which combined with variable neighborhood search and used in the protein side chain placement problem [3].

Artificial immune algorithm is another novel biological inspired algorithm which has been used in many fields[4,5]. Due to its diversity and memory mechanisms, artificial immune algorithm has also been widely used to integrate with other heuristic optimization algorithms to enhance their performance. A variety of immune genetic algorithms (IGA) have been proposed [4,5]. Hybrid algorithms combined the artificial immune algorithm with ant colony algorithm(ACO)[6] and Particle Swarm Optimization(PSO)[7] have also been proposed.

In this paper, a hybrid algorithm which integrated UMDA with the principle of general artificial immune algorithm is proposed. In the proposed hybrid algorithm, dynamic density regulation mechanism of the artificial immune system is used to

Z. Cai et al. (Eds.): ISICA 2009, CCIS 51, pp. 66–75, 2009.
© Springer-Verlag Berlin Heidelberg 2009

maintain the diversity of the population during the evolution of each generation. Experimental results on deceptive function of order 3 compared with that of the UMDA are reported.

The remainder of this paper is organized as follows: The UMDA is described in section 2. The principle of general artificial immune algorithm is analyzed in section 3. The performance of the proposed hybrid algorithm on deceptive problem of order 3 is shown in section 4. Finally, conclusion is made in section 5.

2 The Univariate Marginal Distribution Algorithm

The UMDA was proposed by Mühlenbein and Paaß[1]. UMDA uses the simplest model to estimate the joint probability distribution of the selected promising individuals at each generation. This joint probability distribution is factorized as a product of independent univariate marginal distributions:

$$p_t(x) = \prod_{i=1}^{n} p_t(x_i) = \prod_{i=1}^{n} p(x_i | D_{t-1}^{se})$$ (1)

Usually each univariate marginal distribution is estimated from marginal frequencies as follows:

$$p(x_i | D_{t-1}^{se}) = \frac{\sum_{j=1}^{N} \delta_j(X_i = x_i | D_{t-1}^{se})}{N}$$ (2)

where

$$\delta_j(X_i = x_i | D_{t-1}^{se}) = \begin{cases} 1, & \text{if in the } j^{th} \text{ case of } D_{t-1}^{se}, X_i = x_i \\ 0, & \text{otherwise} \end{cases}$$ (3)

A pseudo-code for the UMDA can be seen in Figure 1.

```
UMDA

D₀←Generate M individuals to form the initial
population

Repeat for t=1,2,…until the stopping criterion is met

D_{t-1}^{se}←Select N<M individuals from D_{t-1} according to the
selection method

Estimate the joint probability distribution:
```

$$p_t(x) = p(x | D_{t-1}^{se}) = \prod_{i=1}^{n} p_t(x_i) = \prod_{i=1}^{n} \frac{\sum_{j=1}^{N} \delta_j(X_i = x_i | D_{t-1}^{se})}{N}$$

```
D_t←Sample M individuals to form the new population from
p_t(x)
```

Fig. 1. Pseudo-code for the UMDA

3 The Artificial Immune Algorithm

3.1 Principle of the General Artificial Immune Algorithm

The general artificial immune algorithm adopts the basic frame of evolutionary algorithms, it regards the evolution individuals as antibodies, and antigens represent the problem to solve. The algorithm controls the recruitment of antibodies according to the immune density regulation and memory library. The flowchart of the general artificial immune algorithm is shown in Figure 2.

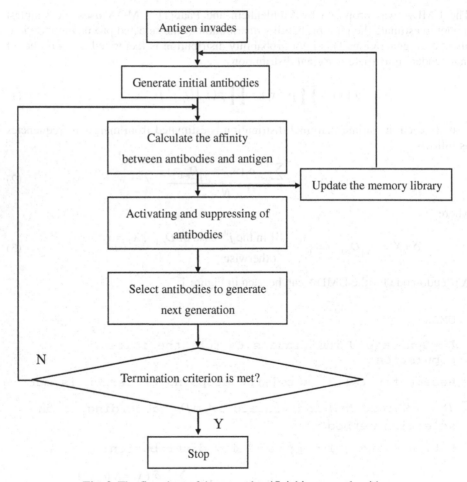

Fig. 2. The flowchart of the general artificial immune algorithm

3.2 Affinity Calculating

There have two types of affinity in the immune algorithm. First, affinity represents the match degree between antigen and antibodies, which means the quality of the solutions just like the fitness in GAs. On the other hand, the affinity can also be used to evaluate the similarity between different antibodies. In this case, it also named as the similarity. Similarity can be measured using Hamming or Euclidean distance and information entropy[4,8]. In this paper, we use the information entropy to evaluate the similarity between antibodies. Supposing there are N antibodies, the coding length of each antibody is l, the size of symbolic aggregate is S, then the information entropy of the antibody gene located at position j can be defined as:

$$H_j(\eta) = -\sum_{i=1}^{s} p_{ij} \log p_{ij} \qquad (4)$$

where p_{ij} is the probability of the ith symbol appearing on the gene location j, η is the number of antibodies. Thus the average entropy $H(\eta)$ can be obtained by:

$$H(\eta) = \frac{1}{l}\sum_{j=1}^{l} H_j(\eta) \qquad (5)$$

The similarity between antibody u and v can be defined as $A_{u,v}$:

$$A_{u,v} = \frac{1}{1+H(2)} \qquad (6)$$

where $H(2)$ is the information entropy between two antibodies u and v.

The similarity of the whole population can be defined as:

$$A(N) = \frac{1}{1+H(N)} \qquad (7)$$

3.3 Activating and Suppressing

As mentioned earlier, the greater similarity value, the greater similarity between antibodies. If the similarity of the population is too high, the search will be focused in some region of the search space which often leads the algorithm to premature and, as a result, to converge to local optimal solutions. Fortunately, the artificial immune algorithm can avoid premature by regulating the similarity of the population through activating the individuals with lower density and suppressing those with higher density.

The density of the antibody i, C_i, can be defined as:

$$C_i = \frac{\text{number of antibodies whose similarity with } i \text{ is higher than } \lambda}{M} \qquad (8)$$

where M is the population size, λ is the similarity parameter often with $0.9 \leq \lambda \leq 1$.

Stimulating operator is often used to evaluate the quality of the individuals (antibodies) after being activated and suppressed. So it can be constructed combined the affinity between antigen and antibodies with the regulation factor based on density of the antibodies. In this paper, stimulating value is defined as:

$$fitness' = fitness * exp(k * C_i) \tag{9}$$

where *fitness'* is the stimulating value, *fitness* is the affinity between antigen and antibodies, C_i is the density, and k is a factor with a negative number.

After the stimulating values have been calculated, selection operation can be applied to select antibodies to construct next generation of population (antibodies). The equation (9) indicates the greater the individual affinity, the higher the selection probability it possesses; while the greater the density of an antibody, the lower the selection probability it possesses. Thus the general artificial immune algorithm can not only maintain the individuals of high affinity, but also guarantee the diversity.

4 The Artificial Immune UMDA

Based on the mechanisms of the aforementioned general artificial immune algorithm, we here propose a hybrid optimization algorithm, named as the Artificial Immune UMDA (AIUMDA). In the AIUMDA, UMDA provides antibodies in each generation for artificial immune algorithm and then the artificial immune algorithm is used to promote and maintain diversity during the evolutional procedures.

The proposed hybrid algorithm can be described as the following steps:

```
AIUMDA
step1. Antigen invades;
step2. Generate initial antibodies;
step3. Calculate the information entropy, affinity and
the similarity;
step4.  If the similarity A<A₀, go to step 7;
step5. Randomly generate p new antibodies and added to
the population;
step6. Calculate the density and stimulating value of
each antibody;
step7. Select the promising individuals according to
the stimulating value and update the memory library;
step8. Estimate the joint probability distribution;
```

Fig. 3. Pseudo-code for the AIUMDA

step9. $D_t\leftarrow$Sample M individuals to form the new population from $p_t(x)$;

step10. If the termination criterion is met, stop and
output the solutions, else go to step3.

Fig. 3. (*continued*)

Apparently, the AIUMDA merges the features of both the UMDA and artificial immune algorithm. Furthermore, it is easy to construct other hybrid EDAs with artificial immune algorithm when we change the procedure in step 8 to building the corresponding probabilistic model and sampling of the probabilistic model in step 9.

5 Simulation Results

In this paper, a GA-hard problem, Deceptive function of order 3 is used to compare the performance of the UMDA and the AIUMDA proposed in this paper. Deceptive function of order 3 is defined as[9]:

$$F_{3deceptive}(x,\pi) = \sum_{i=0}^{\frac{n}{3}-1} f_3(x_\pi(3i) + x_\pi(3i+1) + x_\pi(3i+2)) \tag{10}$$

where x is a bit string, π is any permutation of size n, and f_3 is defined as:

$$f_3(u) = \begin{cases} 0.9 & \text{if } u = 0 \\ 0.8 & \text{if } u = 1 \\ 0 & \text{if } u = 2 \\ 1 & \text{if } u = 3 \end{cases} \tag{11}$$

In the experiments, population size M is set to be 200, 500, and1000, respectively. We use the truncation selection in which the best 50% individuals in the population are selected to be the promising individuals. Memory library size is set to be $0.2*M$, new generated antibodies which used to added to the population is $0.4*M$, similarity threshold $A_0 = 0.9$, $\lambda=0.9$, and $k=-0.8$.

Figure 4 illustrated the performance of the UMDA without elitist when applied to $F_{3deceptive}$ of size $n=30$ with population size is 500. In this case, the building blocks (BBs) UMDA can get decreased to 0 quickly with the evolution generations increasing and the similarity of the population raise to 1 quickly, which means all the individuals have become the same and fall into the local optimal value.

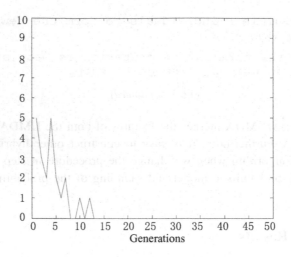

(a) Number of the BBs the UMDA can get

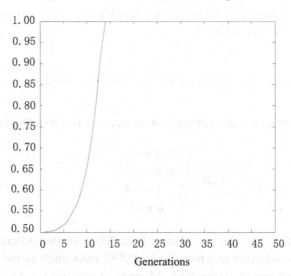

(b) Similarity of the population in the UMDA

Fig. 4. Performance of the UMDA when population size is 500

Figure 5 represents the performance of the UMDA with elitist strategy when applied to the same $F_{3deceptive}$ function. Compared with Figure 4, UMDA with elitist can get some BBs but the similarity of the population is still very high.

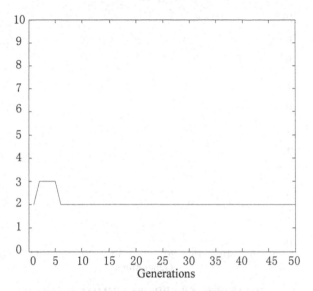

(a) Number of the BBs the UMDA with elitist can get

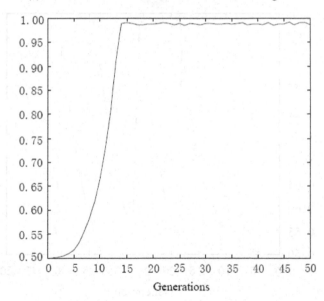

(b) Similarity of the population in the UMDA with elitist

Fig. 5. Performance of the UMDA with elitist when population size is 500

Figure 6 represents the performance of the proposed AIUMDA. It can be observed that the similarity value is dynamic regulated by increasing some randomly generated individuals to the population during the evolution, which can explore more search space to find better solutions. So it can be seen in Figure 6 (b) that the simulating value varied cyclical.

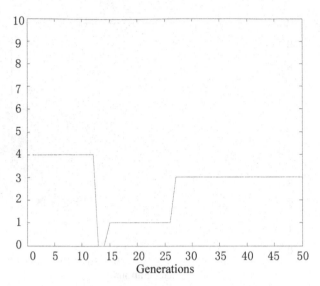

(a) Number of the BBs the AIUMDA can get

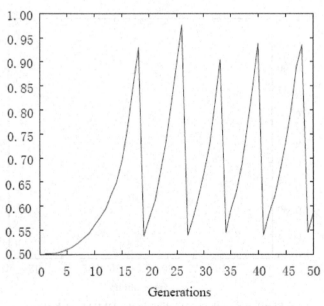

(b) Similarity of the population in the AIUMDA

Fig. 6. Performance of the AIUMDA when population size is 500

Table 1 shows the number of BBs founded by three algorithms with different population size, all the results are averaged by 20 runs. We can conclude that the AIUMDA performs the best among the three algorithms.

Table 1. Average number of the BBs founded by three algorithms

population size	UMDA	UMDA with elitist	AIUMDA
200	0	1.3	2.1
500	0	3.1	3.4
1000	0	3.8	4.5

6 Conclusions

Artificial immune algorithm has been widely used to integrate with other intelligent algorithms to create hybrid algorithms with the benefit of combining different paradigms. In this paper, we proposed a hybrid UMDA which combined the diversity maintain mechanism of the general artificial immune algorithm with the UMDA. Simulation results on deceptive function of order 3 show that the hybrid algorithm performs better than the UMDA and the UMDA with elitist.

Acknowledgments. This work was supported by Nature Science Foundation of Hebei Province (F2008001166) and Mentoring Programs of Scientific and Technological Research & Development in Hebei Province (072135133).

References

1. Mühlenbein, H., Paaß, G.: From Recombination of Genes to the Estimation of Distributions I. Binary Parameters. In: Ebeling, W., Rechenberg, I., Voigt, H.-M., Schwefel, H.-P. (eds.) PPSN 1996. LNCS, vol. 1141, pp. 178–187. Springer, Heidelberg (1996)
2. Tang, M., Lau, R.Y.K.: A Hybrid Estimation of Distribution Algorithm for the Minimal Switching Graph Problem, pp. 708–713. IEEE Computer Society, Washington (2005)
3. Santana, R., Larranaga, P., Lozano, J.A.: Combining variable neighborhood search and estimation of distribution algorithms in the protein side chain placement problem. Journal of Heuristics 14, 519–547 (2008)
4. De Castro, L.N., Timmis, J.I.: Artificial Immune Systems: A New Computational Intelligence Approach. Springer, Heidelberg (2002)
5. De Castro, L.N., Timmis, J.I.: Artificial immune systems as a novel soft computing paradigm. Soft Computing 7, 526–544 (2003)
6. Wang, X., Gao, X.Z., Ovaska, S.J.: A hybrid optimization algorithm based on ant colony and immune principles. IJCSA 4, 30–44 (2007)
7. Afshinmanesh, F., Marandi, A., Rahimi-Kian, A.: A novel binary particle swarm optimization method using artificial immune system. Computer as a Tool. In: The International Conference on EUROCON 2005, vol. 1, pp. 217–220 (2005)
8. Chun, J.S., Kim, M.K., Jung, H.K., Hong, S.K.: Shape optimization of electromagnetic devices using immunealgorithm. IEEE transactions on magnetics 33, 1876–1879 (1997)
9. Pelikan, M., Muehlenbein, H.: Marginal distribution in evolutionary algorithms, vol. 98, pp. 90–95 (1998)

An Multi-objective Evolutionary Algorithm with Lower-Dimensional Crossover and Dense Control

Dongdong Zhao, Sanyou Zeng, and Huanhuan Li

School of Computer Science, Research Centre for Space Science & Technology and The State Key Laboratory of Geological Processes and Mineral Resources, China University of Geosciences, Wuhan, 430074, Hubei, China
`sanyou-zeng@263.net, zhaodongdong1139@yeah.net`

Abstract. As it is hard to control the trade-off between fast convergence and the diversity of the population in designing an EA, this paper proposes an algorithm that can have a good control of both. The algorithm not only adopts the Lowerdimensional Crossover algorithm to accelerate the convergence but also proposes two good methods to keep the wide population distribution for global search. Also a new method is put forward as an algorithm of repulsing mechanism, that every solution repulses other solutions in its neighborhood with a value r_t as its radius. With its control of the wide distribution of solutions and the diversity as well, this algorithm can prevent the solutions from falling into the local optimization and thus prompt global search for the optimal solutions. Then another method is used based on the concept of decomposition for the cutoff operator. As it can choose the solutions better than others in the non-dominated sets, and sort the solutions with well distributed, it is used to keep diversity of the population too.

Keywords: evolutionary algorithms; multi-objective optimization; Pareto optimal set; dense control.

1 Introduction

Almost every real-world problem involves several simultaneous and often competing objectives need to be optimized. Evolutionary algorithm has the ability to find multiple Pareto-optimal solutions in one single run with several objectives simultaneous. So it can be adopt to solve multi-objective problems. Representative evolutionary techniques include vector evaluated genetic algorithm (VEGA)[2], Hajela and Lins genetic algorithm(HLGA) [3], Pareto-based ranking procedure(FFGA) [4], niched Pareto genetic algorithm (NPGA) [5](Non-dominated Sorting Genetic Algorithm (NSGA)(Srinivas and Deb, 1994) and a new effective approach to multi-objective optimization. Recently, some of the proposed methods have made further progress, for instance, NSGAII [6], the strength Pareto evolutionary algorithm SPEA2 [7], rMOGAxs [8], Generalized Regression GA (GRGA) [9] and so on.

In this paper, the algorithm is based on OMOEA-II [10], $DD(\varepsilon; r)EA$ [11] and the algorithm of Song-Gao [12]. The linear crossover operator used in OMOEA-II [10] takes 2 parents. And in the paper of Song Gao, the lower-dimensional crossover operator

Z. Cai et al. (Eds.): ISICA 2009, CCIS 51, pp. 76–87, 2009.

takes 5 parents, but in this paper, 3 parents is taken for the best situation, the experiments tested for this algorithm show that it is more properly to choose 3 parents to control the diversity of population and get much better result. The result also shows the dense control can keep individuals uniform distributed effectively. To have a better diversity of population, more dominant individuals would be created in the offsprings. On the other hand, the copy operation used in the algorithm can preserve the dominant individuals to the next generation, so they can be kept in populations all the time. Doing the cutoff operator with the method based on the concept of decomposition proposed by Q. Zhang and H. Li [1] (See algorithm 8) can choose better solutions in the non-dominated sets, and sort the solutions with well distributed and it can keep diversity of the population.

The rest of this paper is organized as follows: Section II represents the technique of dynamical controlling of diversity. Section III represents the details of algorithm. Section V shows numerical experiment results. Finally, Section IV concludes with a summary of the paper.

2 Introducing Dynamically Controlling Diversity Technique

The diversity of the population may prevent the solutions from falling into the local optimization and it can prompt global search for the optimal solutions. But usually it is a big challenge to control the diversity for a high performance evolutionary agorithm. So a new mechanism is proposed to solve this problem. A repulsing neighborhood with a repulsing radius r_t set in every solution is used to make the them keep a distance from each other, and the a distance matrix D is built to analogue the environment of repulsing mechanism. Every solution repulses the other solutions which are staying in its repulsing neighborhood, and the number of the solutions staying in the repulsing neighborhood is defined as the invaded-degree which may determine the dense of current solution. The dense matrix ρ is built to store the dense of every solution, it is treated as a new objective which is the smaller the better, so that it can influence the evolution of the population. The solution with smaller dense will be hold on the line for longer time. Obviously, the smaller dense represent more independent, and the repulsing operator will make the population widely distributed and with good diversity.

Suppose the repulsing radius is r_t, the invaded-degree of the current solution is defined as the number of the solutions staying in the current repulsing neighborhood.

Definition 1. *Suppose the solutions* $x_i = \{x_{i_1}, x_{i_2}, x_{i_3}, \ldots, x_{i_n}\}$ *and* $x_j = \{x_{j_1}, x_{j_2}, x_{j_3}, \ldots, x_{j_n}\}$, *the distance between* x_i *and* x_j *based on the infinity norm is defined as:*

$$d_{ij} = \| x_i - x_j \|_\infty = max\{| x_{i_1} - x_{j_1} |, | x_{i_2} - x_{j_2} |, | x_{i_3} - x_{j_3} |, \ldots, | x_{i_n} - x_{j_n} |\}$$
(1)

Definition 2. *With the repulsing radius* r_t, *the invaded-degree* Id_{ij} *between solutions* x_i *and* x_j *is defined as :*

$$Id_{ij} = \begin{cases} 1 & if \quad \| x_i - x_j \|_\infty \leq r_t \\ 0 & else \end{cases}$$

Definition 3. *According to the invaded-degree* Id_{ij} *between solutions* x_i *and* x_j, *and the number of the whole solutions* N, *the invaded-degree of the current solution* x_i *is added up as follows:*

$$Id_i = \sum_{j=0 \wedge j \neq i}^{N} Id_{ij}$$

Definition 4. *With the invaded-degree* Id_i *of the current solution* x_i, *its dense* ρ_i *set in the dense matrix is calculated as:*

$$\rho_i = \frac{Id_i}{N}$$

For more, the repulsing radius r_t is dynamically varies with the variable t which accounts for the evolutionary generation. The details are as follows:

$$r_t = e^{-(t/c)^2} \tag{2}$$

Obviously, with the increase of generation, the r_t is quickly decreased, if the generation is large enough, it will satisfied :$r_t \to 0$

3   Algorithm Description

3.1   Framework of Algorithm

1. Randomly create population P_0 with size N_{pop}.
   Let $t = 0$ and initialize neighborhood radius $r_0 = r(0)$(In this paper $r(0) = 1$)
2. Choosing N_{parent} parents(N_{parent} in this paper it is fixed as 3, see Algorithm 1)
3. Crossover, copy and mutate operator and breeding $3 \cdot N_{pop}$ offsprings $Q(t)$. (See Algorithm 2)
4. Unite the offsprings and the population of current generation to be a bigger population R(t): $R(t) = P(t) \cup Q(t)$
5. Calculate distances of each two individuals and the dense of every individual(See Algorithm 3)
6. Calculate $f(x)$, where $x \in R(t)$
7. Select N individuals from $R(t)$ as next population $P(t+1)$. (See Algorithm 4,6,7,8)
8. $r(t) = r(t + 1)$(neighborhood radius varies with the generation), $t = t + 1$(See Algorithm 5)
9. If stopping criterion satisfied goto Step 10, else goto Step 2
10. Output P(t)

3.2   Details of Algorithms

Suppose that the size of the population is N and we consider it as:

$$P(t) = \{X_1, X_2, X_3, X_4, \ldots, X_i, \ldots, X_N\}$$
$$X_i = \{x_{i_1}, x_{i_2}, x_{i_3}, x_{i_4}, \ldots, x_{i_n}\}$$

Breeding offsprings:
Give a critical individual which is expressed as $aParent$ and the index is $(i \bmod N_{pop})$. Under this circle there are two algorithms to be executed as follows (Algorithm 1, Algorithm 2):

FOR $i = 0$ **TO** $nChildren$ (**it is fixed as** $3 \cdot N_{pop}$)

Algorithm 1. *Choosing parents operator*

1. *Exponentially Convert distances(in this paper, c is fixed as -4), make them the larger before the smaller after converting operator, and calculate the sum of the converting distances, store the sum as variable sum_i :*

$$sum_i = \sum_{j=1, j \neq i}^{N_{pop}} e^{c \cdot d_{ij}}$$

2. *Sort N_{parent} individuals which have minimal instances with maximal values after converting operator to the parent set T:*
   (a) If $|T| < N_{parent}$:
   $rand_j = rand(0, sum_i)$
   (b) $sum = \sum_{k=j}^{N_{pop}} e^{c \cdot d_{ik}}$
   (c) IF $sum > rand_j$ (Chose the individual which is more nearby the critical individual aParent, and sort the kth individual to the parents set, break out current circle.)
   (d) $sum_i = sum_i - d_{ik}$(shorten the random dist distance)
   (e) If the number of the chosen parents satisfied the criterion, goto the step1 of the Algorithm 2, else goto step2

   In this algorithm the probability of mutation is 0.05, and the probability of copy is 0.05 too.

Algorithm 2. *Cross,Mutate and copy operator*

1. *Empty $Q(t)$*
2. *Crossover operator:*
   Except the critical individual chosen in the Algorithm 1, the N_{parent} parents : $parent_1, parent_2, parent_3, \ldots, parent_{N_{parent}}$ selected in the algorithm 1 are chosen to be crossed with the critical individual aParent.
   (a) Lower-dimensional   Crossover   operator[12]:   Randomly   create $a_1, a_2, a_3, \ldots, a_M$ in the distance from -1 to M, and make them satisfy: $a_1 + a_2 + a_3 + \ldots + a_M = 1$
   (b) Create a new individual $newI$ satisfy :
   $newI = a_1 \cdot x_{i_1} + a_2 \cdot x_{i_2} + a_3 \cdot x_{i_3} + \ldots + a_M \cdot x_{i_M}.$
3. *Copy operator :*
   $FOR\, j = 1\, TO\, n$
   $newI1_{i_j}$ $= x_{i_j}$ with the probability pc
   $END\, FOR\, j$
4. *mutative operator :*
   $FOR\, j = 0\, TO\, n$
   $newI2_{i_j} = rand(0, 1)$ with the probability pc.
   $(rand(0, 1)$ can give a random value that between 0 and 1)
   $END\, FOR\, j$

Dense control

In this paper, the concept of *repulsing mechanism* is proposed. Obviously, according to the section II, the dense of the individuals is the smaller the better, as the smaller dense is refer to smaller invaded-degree. Suppose that the elements of distance matrix is express as :

$D = [d_{ij}]_{L \times L}(i, j = 0, 1, 2, \ldots, L)$ (L is the current size of the population involved parents and children)

And the elements of the dense matrix is express as:

$\rho = [\rho_i]_{1 \times L}$ (i=0,1,...,L)

The r_t which is determined by the number of evolutions is the dynamic dense control parameter(See algorithm 5)

Algorithm 3. *Set the distance matrix and the dense matrix*

1. *Set the distance matrix:*
   The distance between any two individuals x_i and x_j is set as the infinite norm of vector x ($x = |x_i - x_j|$)
   $$d_{ij} = \|x_i - x_j\|_\infty = max\{(|x_{i_k} - x_{j_k}|) \mid k = 0, 1, \ldots, N_x\};$$
2. *Set the dense matrix (See definition 4):*
   If the number of the individuals whose distance from the current individual x_i is smaller than r_t is m, the dense of x_i is set as:

$$\rho_i = \frac{m}{N_{pop}}$$

While the population is filled with the parents and children, the size of the population is 400 (in this paper, the number of the parents is 100 and the number of the children is 300). In order to make the algorithm convergence fast, we need to find out the non-dominated individuals and add them to the next generation (P(t+1)) for evolution, this operator can select the superior and eliminate the inferior, the details are as follows :

Algorithm 4. *Sort non-dominated sets operator*

1. *Empty $P(t + 1)$ and initialize i=0*
2. *WHILE $|P(t + 1) \cup B_i| < N_{pop}$*
   Perform a non-dominated sorting to R(t) by using the algorithm 6, and identify different non-dominated set : B_i
3. *Move B_i from R(t) to $P(t + 1)$ by using the sorting order :*
   $P(t + 1) = P(t + 1) \cup B_i$
4. *$i = i + 1$*
5. *IF $|P(t + 1)| > N$Execute the cutoff operator(see Algorithm 8).*
6. *Output P(t+1)*

It is the last operator in evolution, according to the equation (2), the constant dense parameter r_t varies with the generation of population, and is determine by two other parameters, in this paper, we give one basic parameter c is fixed as 500, t is equal to the generation of the current population, and we make a little change to the equation(2) in order to adjust to this algorithm. We take the other dynamic control integral parameter as d_t. And dt is changed with t but not equal to t, but it also varies with the evolutionary generation. Another more exactitude control is used to do better control of the diversity, the concept is that when the number of independent solution is checked to be in less than the tenth of the size of the population, we consider the diversity of the population is not good enough, so we will slow down the speed of increase the dynamic control parameter d_t, and else keep the normal speed. The details is as follows:

Algorithm 5. *Dynamic control*

While evolution once the follow operators are taken one by one:

1. *Count the number of the solutions whose dense is equal to zero and store in the variable 'nzero'.*
2. *Change the value of d_t with the situation of the population:*

$$IF \; nzero < \frac{N_{pop}}{10}$$
$$d_t = d_t + 2$$
$$END \; IF$$
$$ELSE$$
$$d_t = d_t + 3$$
$$END \; ELSE$$

3. *Calculate the r_t:* $\qquad\qquad r_t = e^{-(d_t/c)^2}$

As the number of the evaluation in once evolution is about 300 and the total times is demanded to be 300000, so the r_t will decrease to the dist distance arrange from $e^{-(\frac{\frac{300000}{300} \cdot 2}{500})^2} = e^{-16}$ to $e^{-(\frac{\frac{300000}{300} \cdot 3}{500})^2} = e^{-36}$. So, if we demand the precision is 10^{-6}, the convergence is proper to get the optimal solutions.

Algorithm 6. *Non-dominated operator*
How to sorting the non-dominated sets from P(t) to R(t) is introduced in this part. Suppose the index of the whole population is from 0 to L.

1. *a=0*
2. *WHILE ($|R(t)| < N_{pop}$), goto step3*
3. $\qquad$ *FOR i = a TO N_{pop}*
   $\qquad\qquad$ *Add it to the non-dominated set B_k. and delete it from the set $P(t)$*
   $\qquad\qquad$ *when ith individual satisfy :*
   $\qquad\qquad$ $\forall j \in (0, L) satisfied : (\rho_i, f_i(x)) \geq (\rho_j, f_j(x))$ *(See equation (3))*
   $\qquad$ *END FOR i*
4. $\qquad$ $R(t) = R(t) \cup B_k$
   $\qquad$ $a = i$*(Distinguish the non-dominated sets and the dominated sets)*
   $\qquad$ $k = k + 1$
   $\qquad$ *Goto step2.*

Suppose that: $f_i = f_i(x) = \{f_{i_1}, f_{i_2}, \ldots, f_{i_k}\}$, and k is the number of the objectives, $x = \{x_1, x_2, \ldots, x_n\}$, and n is the dimension of vector

$$(\rho_i, f_i) \geq (\rho_j, f_j) = (\rho_i \geq \rho_j, f_{i_1} \geq f_{j_1}, f_{i_2} \geq f_{j_2}, \ldots, f_{i_k} \geq f_{j_k}) \qquad (3)$$

Method based on the concept of decomposition proposed in [1]

The number of the non-dominate individuals is not equal to the number we demand (In this paper, the demanded number is 100). So if the number is more than N_{pop}, the cutoff operator is needed to done and make it proper(Reduce to N_{pop} or increase to N_{pop}). (Suppose the original population is $P(t)$, and the final population is $P(t+1)$).

In this part we set up a random matrix of λ with N_{pop} rows and $nv(nv = nf + ng + nh)$columns(nf is the number of the objectives and ng is the number of the inequality constraints and nh is the number of the equation constraints), we use the elements in this matrix to be the weights of the objectives when do the cutoff operator to select N_{pop} better solutions. We make the elements in this matrix to be random created, and make the elements in each row satisfied equation (4) and (5).

For the the test problems, some problems have two objectives and some have more. If the problem is a constraint problem, the constraint conditions may be regarded as new objectives to be compared in the population. λ_{ij} is the element at the situation of ith row and jth column, it is set as the weight of the jth objective of the solution whose index is i, the sequence of the column for objectives from 0 to nv ranges from original objectives to inequality constraints to equation constraints.

If we choose the different rows to the weights of the objectives when comparing, we would get the different Paroto-optimal solutions, and these solutions may be well distributed. The related algorithm called MOEA/D[1] was ever proposed to select optimal solutions. The method is used in algorithm 7, 8.

Algorithm 7. *Set λ matrix*

1. *Make the front nv rows with nv columns to be an identity matrix.*
2. *Make the elements of the remanent part under identity matrix produced in Step1 in the whole dense matrix to be randomly created, and satisfy that:*
   (s_i is the sum of the elements in ith crow, and s is the set of s_i)

$$s = \{s_i \mid i = 0, 1, \ldots, N_{pop}\} \tag{4}$$

$$s_i = \sum_{j=0}^{nv} \lambda_{ij} \equiv 1 \tag{5}$$

In this algorithm the inequality constraints and the equation constraints are regard as new objectives, and they are both stored in the vector v with the original objectives.

Algorithm 8. *Cutoff operator*

1. *Empty $P(t+1)$*
2. *WHILE $\mid P(t+1) \mid < N_{pop}$ goto Step3*
3. *Calculate the maximal value of the product of the values of objectives and the weights (in λ matrix)for every solution (It is represented as Max_i or Max_j down), then chose the solution with the minimal value of the maximal value Max_i or Max_j in the population,and the index of the solution chosen to $P(t+1)$ stores in variable 'mini':*

$FOR\ i = 0\ TO\ N_{pop}$

    Random create a index r in the solutions between i and $(N_{pop} - 1))$

    $Max_i = max\{\lambda_{rk} \cdot v_{ik} \mid k = 0, 1, 2, \dots, nv\}$

    $min = Max_i$

    $mini = i$

    $FOR\ j = i + 1\ TO\ N_{pop}$

        $Max_j = max\{\lambda_{rk} \cdot v_{jk} \mid k = 0, 1, 2, \dots, nv\}$

        IF $Max_j < min$

            $min = Max_j$

            $mini = j$

        END IF

    END FOR j

    Sorting the solution whose index is $mini$ *to* $P(t + 1)$

  END FOR i

4. *If stopping criterion satisfied goto Step 5,else goto Step 2*

5. *Output* $P(t + 1)$

4 Numerical Experiments and Discussion

4.1 Test Problems

10 Unconstrained multi-objective optimization test instances for the CEC 2009 Special Session and Competition are taken to test the algorithm. All the problems are required to take 30 decision variables. Seven of the test problems have 2 objectives to be minimized and the rest three problems have 3 objectives. All the test problems are treated as black-box problems.

4.2 Testing Environment

Parameter setting

For all test instances, parameter settings are the same as follows:

Population size	100
Number of parent in linear crossover	3
Mutation probability	0.05
Copy probability	0.05
The dense basic control parameter	500
Maximal number of function evaluations	300,000

PC Configuration

CPU Intel T2300 ,	1.8 GHz
RAM 1 GB,	667MHz
Operating System Windows xp with SP3	
Computer Language Visual C++	

Testing method. We use a performance metric[13] to assess the final solutions:

Let P^* be a set of uniformly distributed points along the PF (in the objective space). Let A be an approximate set to the PF, the average distance from P^* to A is defined as:

$$IGD(A, P^*) = \frac{\sum_{v \in P^*} d(v, A)}{|P^*|}$$

where d(v,A) is the minimum Euclidean distance between v and the points in A. If $|P^*|$ is large enough to represent the PF very well, IGD(A, P^*) could measure both the diversity and convergence of A in a sense. To have a low value of IGD(A, P^*), the set A must be very close to the PF and cannot miss any part of the whole PF.

Due to the population size, 400 final solutions will be produced. We use the same algorithm as selection operator (Algorithm 4,5,6)and cutoff operator(Algorithm 7,8) to reduce them. To meet the requirement of the contest, the numbers of solutions are reduced to 100 for 2-objective problems, and 100 for 3-objective problem. Then the metric above is used to assess the 100 solutions.

For each test problem, the algorithm is set to be run independently 30 times. The average IGD value of 30 test results is the assessed value for a test instance.

4.3   Results

Distribution of obtained solutions (Figure 1(b),1(c),1(d),...,1(k) For each test problem, we draw a figure of obtained solutions from the test instance who has the best IGD value. The points for solutions are represented by blue $'\cdot'$s. For contrast, the true Pareto Front represented by red $'\cdot'$s are drawn in the same figure. The distribution figures show the diversity and how close the obtained solution set is close to the true Pareto Front.

Comparing with the results of the algorithm proposed by Song Gao [12], for five problems (problem 1,2,3,4,8)the results got in this algorithm are much better than Song Gao's, it proves that this algorithm is really effective for solving multi-objective problems. The details of IGD values is shown as follows :

Table 1. Means and Standard Deviations of IGD values

Problem	IGD Values			
	Best	Average	Worst	St. Deviation
Problem 1	**0.027623525127422**	**0.037784160813627**	0.054128891555132	0.001272705416217
Problem 2	**0.021278985975676**	**0.024849918816937**	0.037602200952890	0.0005359050255922899
Problem 3	**0.027927926018305**	**0.195107258323758**	0.475298068314582	0.027745499793497
Problem 4	**0.043252508287933**	**0.044647658050600**	0.046253239174811	0.0001617610309870773
Problem 5	0.136459554896640	0.190560516299306	0.204109016453496	0.002116911140209
Problem 6	0.250544433773948	0.288961167481612	0.331121052594927	0.004983837325385
Problem 7	0.013866116969479	0.248626499251028	0.311281906249458	0.012030515069999
Problem 8	**0.090892845201290**	**0.117769278556657**	0.213558207387047	0.006168931269290
Problem 9	0.087061492579827	0.244258875974435	0.337257241192212	0.013141605299859
Problem 10	0.243232224316801	0.536013743394762	0.658868876332530	0.012976365345059

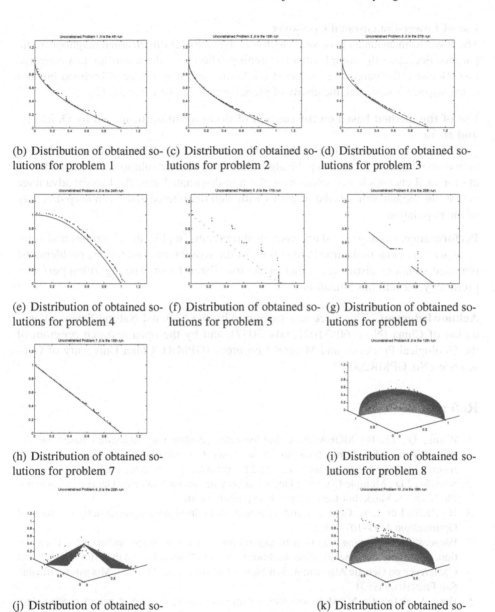

(b) Distribution of obtained solutions for problem 1

(c) Distribution of obtained solutions for problem 2

(d) Distribution of obtained solutions for problem 3

(e) Distribution of obtained solutions for problem 4

(f) Distribution of obtained solutions for problem 5

(g) Distribution of obtained solutions for problem 6

(h) Distribution of obtained solutions for problem 7

(i) Distribution of obtained solutions for problem 8

(j) Distribution of obtained solutions for problem 9

(k) Distribution of obtained solutions for problem 10

5   Conclusions

Use of dense control
The *mechanism of repulsing*, which can repulse neighborhood of the solution regarding a value 'r' as its radius, so that it can make the solutions keep widely distributed and keep diversity, then the solutions will not falls into the local optimization and prompt global search for the optimal solutions.

Use of Lower-dimensional Crossover
The lower-dimensional crossover, which searches a lower dimensional neighbor of the parents, decreases the complexity of searching. Therefore, the algorithm can converge fast. Because the parents are selected randomly, and it is the neighborhood but not convex space is searched, the ability of global search can be ensured [12].

Use of the method based on the concept of decomposition proposed by Q. Zhang and H. Li
Use the method to cutoff the population when the number of non-dominated solutions is over the demand. It may keep the algorithm to sort better solutions for the next generation,as it chooses better solutions in the non-dominated sets, the biggest advantage is that this method can sort the solutions with well distributed and it can keep diversity of the population.

Performance. Among the 10 unconstrained problems in [13], the algorithm find solutions are very close to the true Pareo Front for three problems, and for one problem, the obtained solutions distribute on part of the true Pareo Front. The algorithm performs preferably, but still has limitations.

Acknowledgment. This work was supported by the National Natural Science Foundation of China (No.s: 60871021, 60473037), and by the open research program of the Geological Processes and Mineral Resources (GPMR), China University of Geosciences(No. GPMR200618).

References

1. Zhang, Q., Li, H.: MOEA/D: A multiobjective evolutionary algorithm based on decomposition. IEEE Transactions on Evolutionary Computation, 11(6), 712–731 (2007), http://cswww.essex.ac.uk/staff/qzhang/papers/moead.pdf
2. Schaffer, J.D.: Multiple Objective Optimization with Vector Evaluated Genetic Algorithms. Ph. D. thesis, Vanderbilt University (1984) (unpublished)
3. Hajela, P., Lin, C.Y.: Genetic search strategies in multicriterion optimal design. Structural Optimization 4, 99–107 (1992)
4. Fonseca, C.M., Fleming, P.J.: Genetic algorithms for multiobjective optimization: Formulation, discussion and generalization. In: Forrest, S. (ed.) Proceedings of the Fifth International Conference on Genetic Algorithms, San Mateo, California, pp. 416–423. Morgan Kaufmann, San Francisco (1993)
5. Horn, J., Nafpliotis, N.: Multiobjective optimization using the niched pareto genetic algorithm. IlliGAL Report 93005, Illinois Genetic Algorithms Laboratory, University of Illinois, Urbana, Champaign (1993)
6. Deb, K., Pratap, A., Agarwal, S., Meyarivan, T.: A Fast and Elitist Multiobjective Genetic Algorithm: NSGA-II. IEEE Transactions on Evolutionary Computation 6(2), 182–197 (2002)
7. Zitzler, E., Laumanns, M., Thiele, L.: SPEA2: Improving the Strength. Pareto Evolutionary Algorithm for Multiobjective Optimization. In: Giannakoglou, K.C., et al. (eds.) Proceedings of the EUROGEN 2001 Conference, Barcelona, Spain, CIMNE, pp. 95–100 (2002)
8. Purshouse, R.C., Fleming, P.J.: The Multi-objective Genetic Algorithm Applied to Benchmark Problems Can Analysis. Research Report No. 796. Department of Automatic Control and Systems Engineering, University of Sheffield, Sheffield, S1 3JD, UK (2001)

9. Tiwari, A., Roy, R.: Generalised Regression GA for Handling Inseparable Function Interaction: Algorithm and Applications. In: Guervós, J.J.M., Adamidis, P.A., Beyer, H.-G., Fernández-Villacañas, J.-L., Schwefel, H.-P. (eds.) PPSN 2002. LNCS, vol. 2439, p. 452. Springer, Heidelberg (2002)

10. Zeng, S., Yao, S., Kang, L., Liu, Y.: An Efficient Multi-objective Evolutionary Algorithm: OMOEA-II, pp. 108–119. Springer, Heidelberg (2005)

11. Zeng, S., Zhou, A., Jia, L., Liu, Y., Kang, L.: $DD(\varepsilon; r)$ EA: An Evolutionary Algorithm Based on Dynamic Dominance$(\varepsilon; r)$ for Constrained Optimization, School of Computer Science, Research Centre for Space Science & Technology, China University of GeoSciences, 430074 Wuhan, Hubei, P.R.China (2008)

12. Gao, S., Zeng, S., Xiao, B., Zhang, L., Shi, Y., Tian, X., Yang, Y., Long, H., Yang, X., Yu, D., Yan, Z.: An Orthogonal Multi-objective Evolutionary Algorithm with Lower-dimensional Crossover. In: Proceedings of the CEC 2009 Conference, WuHan, China (2008) (accepted)

13. Zhang, Q., Zhou, A., Zhao, S., Suganthan, P.N., Liu, W., Tiwari, S.: Multiobjective optimization Test Instances for the CEC 2009 Special Session and Competition, http://cswww.essex.ac.uk/staff/qzhang/MOEAcompetition/report081203.pdf

Improved Evolutionary Programming and Its Application in Navigation System

Jianjuan Liu

Department of Electrical Engineering, Henan University of Technology,
Zhengzhou 450007, China

Abstract. In designing BP neural network, it is difficult to determine the network parameters and weights, or to achieve the best effect under random perturbation, and impossible to satisfy the real-time requirement of system. To solve these problems, this paper introduces an evolutionary neural network and puts forward some improvements on conventional evolutionary programming. This algorithm is then used in the integrated navigation system. Experiment results indicate that BP neural network based on evolutionary programming can not only overcome the shortcomings of BP artificial neural network, but also avoid problems of genetic algorithms caused by binary-coded and cross operation. Also the navigation system based on this algorithm can get rid of the problems of kalman filter when the outside observation data are unreliable. Finally, the normal operation of kalman filter is ensured with a higher accuracy.

Keywords: evolutionary programming; evolutionary neural network; inertial navigation; kalman filter; niche technology.

1 Introduction

Applications of BP neural network in navigation system have achieved certain effect. However, there are problems when designing BP neural network. Such as, difficult to determine the network parameters and the weights, can not achieve the best effect under random perturbation, and can not meet the real-time requirement of system. Researchers at home and abroad have put forward a number of improved algorithms. But these improvements have obvious signs of tinkering, and there are no fundamental difference and breakthroughs.

Evolutionary programming is a random search algorithm, which is put forward by Fogel. It simulates survival of the fittest and organic evolution mechanism, and searches the optimum point in solution space through population search strategy. BP neural network optimized by evolutionary programming can not only overcome easy enter into local minimum, long training time and other shortcomings of conventional BP neural network, but also avoid problems of genetic algorithm caused by binary-coded and cross operation.

Z. Cai et al. (Eds.): ISICA 2009, CCIS 51, pp. 88–96, 2009.

In this paper, evolutionary programming is used for automatic design of BP neural network. Evolutionary programming uses mutation as the only operation for genetic recombination. It overcomes the difficulties caused by cross-operation. And it directly uses the feasible solution of question to represent the individuals. So it is no longer needed to encode on individuals. It not only can avoid expressions in double space, but also can naturally express the question. This is the advantage of evolutionary programming. So it is more appropriate to design neural network.

2 Improvements of Evolutionary Programming

According to characteristics of navigation system, improvements carried on evolutionary programming are as following.

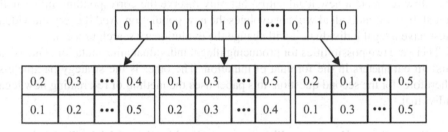

Fig. 1. Structure of hierarchical gene

2.1 Encoding Improvements-Hierarchical Evolutionary Programming

In Biology, genes of all kinds of biological individuals interact with each other. In some cases, some genes are active, while others are dormant. And genes in first-class control genes in second-class. Simulation of the biological characteristics and in accordance with the characteristics of design evolutionary neural network, genetic structure in this paper to design the chromosomes has two classes. And genes in first-class control and affect genes in second-class. The specific structures shown in Fig.1.The first-class genes use the binary "0"and"1"encoding. "0"indicates that the second-class associated gene is in dormant state, and the output is zero. While "1"indicates that the second-class associated gene is in active and bringing result in an effective output. The second-class genes use decimal encoding. Each expresses a corresponding weight of network. So the chromosome in this structure contains more information. Substituting optimization using evolutionary programming can directly find the optimal network topology and network parameters.

2.2 Mutation Improvements-Evolutionary Programming Based on Legal
Individual

Found in the experimental process that even if individuals of initial population uniformly distributed in the solution space, evolutionary programming can not guarantee that the new individual in it. Especially in the initial stages of evolution search, even more individuals outside the solution space, which are called illegal individuals. The existence of such illegal solutions will reduce the rate of evolution.

There are two basic ways to curb illegal solutions. One is to improve the mutation in EP to ensure that no illegal solution. The other is to determine the legality of the new individuals after mutation, and exclude illegal solutions. Here, mainly discuss the second solution.

In typical EP algorithm, the legality of the new individual is inspected immediately after mutation. If the new individual is not legally, it will be removed. There are two points worthy of discussion. First, after new illegal individual removed from population, whether to allow re-create a new legal individual? Second ,how to re-create a new legal individual?

On the first question, combination of typical EP algorithm, it is not difficult to see, if not allow re-create a new legal entity, but only reserve the corresponding father individual, then the individual will not evolutes the new population. And if every individual must have a legal individual, it will change the evolutionary search process.

There are two possibilities for producing illegal individual after mutation. One is the random parameters in the formula of mutation. The other is the strategy parameters. Therefore, for the second question, this paper uses the method of re-creating new legal individual.

2.3 Prevention of Premature Phenomenon-Combination of Niche Technology and EP Selection

From analysis of the premature phenomenon of EP, we can see that, during evolution, maintain the diversity of the target vector population can also guarantee that step vector not attenuate too quickly. And it is a effective method to prevent the premature phenomenon. Niche technology is more mature and effective means to maintain diversity. It can be used to get more than one optimal solution at the same time. Representations of it are the sharing function technology and the exclusion technology. However, there are shortcomings when applying these technologies separately. Such as too much additional calculation, no obvious effect, etc.

According to characteristics of EP algorithm, integrate niche technology into the selection mechanism of EP. New selection process is proposed to maintain the diversity, and prevent premature.

First, for any two individuals, expressed as x_1 and x_2, the definition of their standardized Euclidean distance is as following.

$$\text{neud}(x_1, x_2) = \sqrt{\frac{1}{n} \sum_{k=1}^{n} \left[\frac{x_1(k) - x_2(k)}{b_k - a_k} \right]^2} . \tag{1}$$

Of which, b and a are the maximum and minimum values respectively.

Improvement of competitive selection of EP is as follows. In EP algorithm, for a selected individual in it to compete with other individuals, if its standardized European distance with one of the individuals less than a predetermined constant, then these two individuals do not compare, Then individual will lose a potential opportunity to win.

After adoption of this measure to reduce the number of individuals who win the competition for those relative dense individuals in population, there is less possibility of surviving in the next generation for these individuals. While there are virtually no impact on the other individuals. In this way, can maintain the existence of a number of niches, and maintain the diversity of population. So as to achieve the purpose of the prevention of premature.

Using this method, there are $\mu \bullet q$ times of calculation of the standardization Euclidean distance in each generation. And it increases the additional calculation amount. However, with comparing with sharing function method which needs $\mu \bullet (\mu - 1)/2$ times of calculation of the standardization Euclidean distance in each generation, this increased calculation is very small. Because q normally take for five to ten percents of μ.

3 Design of BP Neural Network Based on Evolutionary Programming

Using above improved evolutionary programming algorithm to design BP neural network. According to the navigation system, design of BP neural network aims at design the network weights and the structure (that is, the number of neurons in hidden layer) of neural network. Assumed that the number of input nodes is n, the number of output nodes is p, and the number of hidden nodes is m (to be confirmed).

3.1 Population Initialization

Use encoding method described above to encode. The genetic structure to design the chromosomes has two classes. And genes in first-class control and affect genes in second-class. The first-class genes use the binary encoding. Each bit represents a hidden node. "0"indicates that the corresponding hidden node is in dormant state. And "1"indicates that the corresponding hidden node is in active. The second-class genes use decimal encoding. The first dimension on behalf of the weights between the input nodes and hidden nodes, and the second dimension represent the weights between the output nodes and hidden nodes.

Select appropriate population has a very important influence on evolutionary programming. The size of the population is often taken as ten to one hundred and fifty.

3.2 Learning Algorithm

New individual after initialization or mutation may not have suitable parameters. If use this kind of network calculate the fitness and select individuals, there may miss the best network structure. Therefore, before calculating the fitness, it is necessary to carry out certain number network trainings. Here, use BP algorithm.

3.3 Fitness Calculation

Since algorithm used in this paper can automatically simplify the structure, the fitness function therefore only considers the learning error of the network. And the formula for calculating the individual fitness is as following.

$$f = \frac{1}{E}. \tag{2}$$

Of which, E is the learning error of individual. And it expressed as following.

$$E = \frac{\sum_{t=1}^{N_s} \sum_{k=1}^{p} (d_k^t - o_k^t)^2 / 2}{p \cdot N_s}. \tag{3}$$

Of which, N_s is the number of training samples, p is the number of the output nodes, and $d_k^t - o_k^t$ is the margin between the desired output and actual output of the node k when training the sample t. In order to not be affected by the number of output nodes and samples in learning collection, error is divided by these two parameters.

Taking into account that, with same error, network with simples structure should has a higher fitness, the final formula of error is expressed as following.

$$f = \frac{1}{E} \times 10^6 - N_h. \tag{4}$$

Of which, N_h is the number of hidden nodes, $-N_h$ can ensure that network with simpler structure has greater fitness. In order to ensure the influence of error is far greater than the influence of the complexity of structure, $\frac{1}{E}$ is multiplied by 10^6 to ensure $\frac{1}{E} \times 10^6$ is far larger than N_h.

3.4 Mutation Operator

Individuals are randomly varied by mutation rate, which is always between 0.001 and 0.010.The mutation method for control-class is: if one bit of individual is "0", then into "1", otherwise into "0".The mutation method for parameters is the Cauchy mutation operator. Then check the legalization of the new individual. If it is legal, then continue. Otherwise, re-mutation using other methods. Here, the condition for checking the legalization of individuals are as: $f_k' \geq f_k$.

3.5 Select Operator

Using q -competitive select method, select μ individuals which have higher scores in the collection composed of the parent and offspring individuals. Choice is based on the scores of individuals, and the score is the result of competing with the random selection competitors. Therefore, the q random selection competitors have a great impact on the selection results. Here, uniform random selection method is the q selection method, and q is selected as the 0.1 times of the size of population. In order to prevent premature in evolutionary programming, introduce niche technology which is described in 2.3.

Unless meet the requirement, improved evolutionary programming algorithm repeated in accordance with above process.

3.6 Hybrid Algorithm Design

Improved evolutionary programming algorithm can converge to the global optimum. But it can not effectively make use of local information. So it can not be applied to fine-tune the solution, and can not determine their precise location. Therefore, convergence to the global optimal solution may be required a very long time. Here, combine the global search capability of evolutionary programming and the local search capability of BP algorithm.

Adopting the network structure and parameters optimized by evolutionary programming as the initial parameters of the network, optimize the neural network using BP algorithm until meeting the requirement.

4 Application of Improved Evolutionary Neural Network in Navigation System

In engineering practice, kalman filter is widely used in navigation system. For the system, one of the necessary conditions for the normal operation is having reliable outside observation data. However, the actual operating environment is extremely poor. So the condition is not easy to meet. This may leads to decrease in navigation precision and even leads to divergence. Improved evolutionary neural network is introduced to solve this problem.

Navigation system based on improved evolutionary neural network is shown in Fig.2.When observation data is available and reliable, using the navigation parameters of SINS as the input variables of the improved evolutionary neural networks, and using the errors between parameters of SINS and observation data as the reference output. At this time, improved evolutionary neural network at learning sate, and in Fig.2, (1) is connected, and (2) is broken. When observation data is unavailable or unreliably, improved evolutionary neural network at forecasting state, forecasts the observation errors of Kalman filter, thereby ensuring the normal operation of kalman filter, even overcome the problem of accuracy slipping. And in Fig.2, (1) is broken, and (2) is connected.

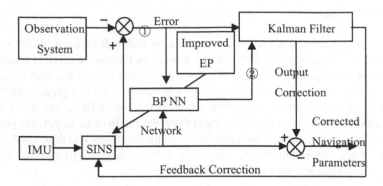

Fig. 2. Navigation system based on evolutionary neural networks

5 Simulation Results and Conclusions

Improved evolutionary neural network is applied to the navigation system, and the simulation experiments are made. In this simulation, the system has two-hour running time. In order to verify the effects of improved evolutionary neural network, supposed that the observation data is unavailable during the running time from 1.0 to 1.5.When the observation data is unavailable, some person keep the forward data, and some person set the observation error to zero. To compare the effects of improved evolutionary neural network, this paper also set the observation error to zero, then navigation system at pure inertial navigation state. The reliability of the outside observation data is determined by the margins between the outside observation data and the navigation parameters.

Based on experience, as well as the observability of the navigation system, the output parameters of SINS are selected as the input variables. That is, V_E, V_N, ϕ_E, ϕ_N, ϕ_U . So the number of neurons in input layer is five. And the outside observation errors are selected as the reference output variables. That is, ΔV_E, ΔV_N, $\Delta \phi_U$. So the number of neurons in output layer is three. The initial parameters of improved evolutionary programming are as following: neural network are as, $N_{EP} = 50$, $E = 1e - 4$, $\mu = 20$, $q = 10$. And the initial parameters of BP neural network are as, $n = 0$, $E = 0$, $\eta = 0.01$, $E_{\min} = 1e - 6$, $N = 100$.

Convergence results of neural network based on BP algorithm and improved algorithm shown in Fig.3 As can be seen from the chart, improved evolutionary algorithm in this paper can increase the convergence rate of neural network, and achieve the desired object.

Simulations results with improved evolutionary neural network when the observation data is unavailable shown in Fig.4 As can be seen from the chart, BP neural network based on evolutionary programming can not only overcome the shortcomings of conventional artificial neural network, but also avoid problems of genetic algorithms caused by binary-coded and cross operation. And the navigation system based on this algorithm can overcome the problems of kalman filter when the outside observation data is unreliable. Then ensuring the normal operation of kalman filter with a higher accuracy.

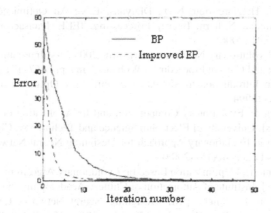

Fig. 3. Convergence results of neural network based on BP algorithm and improved algorithm

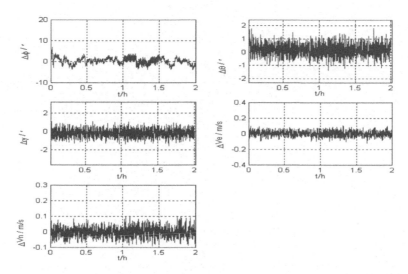

Fig. 4. Simulations results with improved evolutionary neural networks when the observation data is unavailable

Acknowledgments. The work was supported by the Natural Science Research Foundation of Education Department of Henan Province (No.2008B120003), the Dr. Foundation of Henan University of Technology (No.2007BS049),and the National Natural Science Foundation of China(No.50575042).

References

1. Yu, L., Baolin, L., Yong, L., et al.: Study of the Application of Improved BP Neural Networks to Development Cost Prediction in Missle. Tactical Missile Technology (2), 48–53 (2006)
2. Yang, Z.R.: A Novel Radial Basis Function Neural Network for Discriminant Analysis. IEEE Transactions on Neural Networks 17(3), 604–612 (2006)

3. Tsekouras, G.J., Hatziargyriou, N.D., Dialynas, E.N.: An Optimized Adaptive Neural Network for Annual Nidterm Energy Forecasting. IEEE Transactions on Power System 21(1), 385–391 (2006)
4. Gao, W.: New Evolutionary Neural Networks. In: 2005 First International Conference on Neural Interface and Control Proceedings, Wuhan, China, pp. 167–171 (2005)
5. Fogel, D.B.: An Introduction to Simulated Evolutionary Optimization. IEEE Trans. on Neural Networks (1994)
6. Jie, Z.: Research on Evolutionary Computation and Its Application in Adaptive Filtering. [Master's Thesis]. University of Electronin Science and Technology, Chengdu (2005)
7. Tan, Z.-H.: Hybrid Evolutionary Approach for Designing Neural Networks for Classification. Electronics Letters 40(15) (2004)
8. Yunwei, S.: Numerical Optimization Based on Evolutionary Algorithm and Its Application. [Doctoral Thesis]. Institute of Automation of Chinese Academy of Science, Beijing (2004)
9. Fang, L., Renhou, L., Shichun, M.: Designing Neural Networks Ensembles Based on Evolutionary(Programming). Control and Decision 19(8), 877–880 (2004)

Multi-objective Emergency Facility Location Problem Based on Genetic Algorithm

Dan Zhao[1,2], Yunsheng Zhao[2], Zhenhua Li[1], and Jin Chen[1]

[1] School of Computer, China of University, Wuhan, 430074
[2] School of Engineering, China of University, Wuhan, 430074
xinjiezhao@cug.edu.cn

Abstract. Recent years, emergent disasters have occurred frequently. This has attracted more attention on emergency management, especially the multi-objective emergency facility location problem (EFLP), a NP problem. However, few algorithms are efficient to solve the probleme and so the application of genetic algorithm (GA) can be a good choice. This paper first introduces the mathematical models for this problem and transforms it from complex constraints into simple constraints by punishment function. The solutions to the experiments are obtained by applying GA. The experiment results show that GA could solve the problems effectively.

Keywords: Multi-objective, Emergency Facility Location Problem, Genetic Algorithm, Punishment Function.

1 Introduction

Review in 2008 in China, heavy snow disaster in January and 5.12 seismic in Wenchuan. Such as emergent disasters lead to enormous human and property loss. Emergent disasters are large intractable problems that test the ability of communities and nations to effectively protect their populations and infrastructure, to reduce both human and property loss, and to rapidly recover. The most important task in emergency management is transport goods and materials from emergency facility locations to emergency sites as soon as possible. So, the emergency facility location problem influent the emergency management greatly.Since1994, many high level study results arise continuously in this research field from international academic. Such as J.L.Wybo[1], Suleyman Tufekei[2], Luis[3], WLodzimierz[4], C.Subramania[5], and our country Hejianmin, Fanglei etc did many significant works in emergence field. Literature [6] discussed emergency facility location problem with a definite time, only proposed a greedy heuristic method, which can not assure reliability of the solution.

In this paper, we use genetic algorithm to solve multi-objective emergency facility location problem. Emergency facility location problem can be modeled as integer programming question and have NP-hardness. Evolutionary algorithm is effective method in solving NP problems, so here we choose genetic algorithm [7,8] to search

Z. Cai et al. (Eds.): ISICA 2009, CCIS 51, pp. 97–103, 2009.
© Springer-Verlag Berlin Heidelberg 2009

for the solution. The rest of this paper is organized as follows: in section 2, we give a mathematical model and discuss how to evaluate a solver for emergency facility location problem; in section 3, we propose an evolutionary algorithm to solve emergency facility location problem; At last, the conclusions and future work are given in section 4.

2   Mathematical Model of EFLP

Give some emergency sites and possible emergency facility locations, the time from emergency facility location to emergency site we call emergency time, description of multi-objective emergency facility location problem as: how to build any emergency facility locations with lowest expense and can transport goods and materials from emergency facility location to emergency sites in time, when the emergency occurred. Generally speaking, there are two objectives in this problem, one is building an emergency facility location with the lowest expense, the other is emergency time must achieve minimum. So, this is a multi-objective problem.

We suppose that $S=\{S_1, S_2, ...S_m\}$ is the set of possible emergency facility locations, $E=\{E_1, E_2, ...E_n\}$ is the set of emergency sites. t_{ij} denotes the shortest time from emergency facility location S_j to emergency site E_i. Considering the characteristics of emergency site E_i, we set t_i as the time restriction of E_i when there is an emergency. For any $E_i \in E$, $N_i = \{j \mid t_{ij} < t_i, j = 1,2,...n\}$ denotes the set of possible emergency facilities for E_i. C_i represents the expense of building an emergency, so the model [9] of above problem is:

$$Min\ f_1(x) = \sum_{j=1}^{n} c_j x_j$$

$$Min\ f_2(x) = \max\{x_j t_{ij}\}\quad (i = 1,2,...,m)$$

$$s.t. \sum_{j \in N}^{n} x_j \geq 1 \tag{1}$$

$$x_j \in \{0,1\}\quad (j = 1,2,...,n)$$

Here, $x_j =$
$$\begin{cases} 1 \text{ if build an emergency facility at } S_j \\ \\ 0 \text{ otherwise} \end{cases}$$

In order to solve the problem, we define a matrix $A=\{a_{ij}\}_{m*n}$, here,

$$a_{ij} = \begin{cases} 1 & \text{if } t_{ij} \leq t_i \\ 0 & \text{otherwise} \end{cases}$$

The above model can be transformed into the model as follows:

$$Min \ f_1(x) = \sum_{j=1}^{n} c_j x_j$$

$$Min \ f_2(x) = \max\{x_j t_{ij}\}$$

(2)

$$s.t. \sum_{j \in N}^{n} a_{ij} x_j \geq 1 \quad (i = 1,2,...,m)$$

$$x_j \in \{0,1\} \quad (j = 1,2,...,n)$$

The solution of this model can be expressed as $X = x_1 x_2 ... x_m$, in which, x_j ($j = 1,2,...,n$) assume 0 or 1, stand for the jth site is selected as emergency facility locations or not Model (2) is a multi-constraints optimization problem, it is very complex to solve it directly. So we use punishment function to transform it into simple constraints. Punishment function [10] is a kind of method of solving constraints in optimization theory, which is very effective to deal with inequality constraints in GA.

Make $g_j(x) = 1 - \sum_{i=1}^{m} a_{ij} x_i$, $j = 1,...,n$. Take punishment function as

$p(x) = M \sum_{j=1}^{n} \max\{g_j(x),0\}$, in which M is punishment factor. In the course of solving,

we can reflect satisfaction degree of model (2)'s constraints using by the value of punishment function, the value is bigger, the solution's feasibility is worse, on the contrary, the solution's feasibility is better. When $p(x) = 0$, which illustrate the solution is real good, if punishment factor M has suitable value, model (2) can be transformed into simple constraints multi-objective problem as follows:

$$Min \ f_1(x) = \sum_{j=1}^{n} c_j x_j$$

$$Min \ f_2(x) = \max\{x_j t_{ij}\}$$

(3)

$$Min \ p(x)$$

s.t. $x_i \in \{0,1\} \quad i = 1,2,...,m$

When X meets the constraints of model (2), $g_j(x) \leq 0$ ($j = 1,2,...,n$) then punishment function $p(x) = 0$, that is, we can ignore the third objective of model (2), which is show that model (2) and (3) have the same optimal solution and optimal value in feasible region, on the contrary, there must exist $j \in \{1,2,...,n\}$, makes $g_j(x) > 0$, this time sufficiently large punishment factor M makes punishment function $p(x)$ become very large other than the optimal solution, so, optimization process can go on.

3   How to Solve EFLP by GA

3.1   The Choice of Original Individuals

Produce L original individuals and two weights w_1, w_2 randomly ($w_1 + w_2 = 1$, $w_1 \geq 0$, $w_2 \geq 0$). Define integrated objective function correspond to original solutions as follows:

$$F(x) = w_1 f_1(x) + w_2 f_2(x) + p(x) \tag{4}$$

3.2   Fitness Function

Fitness function is very important in constrained optimization of genetic algorithm, a good fitness function can make our algorithm convergent more quickly. Considering the constraints of the problem, so we choose the fitness function as follows.

$$F(x) = \frac{1}{w_1 f_1(x) + w_2 f_2(x) + p(x)} \tag{5}$$

3.3   GA Operators

Here, we only expound the two most important operators in our algorithm: crossover operator and mutation operator.

1)   Crossover operator: We choose the single point across method, for example, a: 5 2 4 1 3; b: 1 3 2 4 5, randomly generate a point, if it is n1, exchange the right part of the 1st gene between two chromosomes, and get a: 5 2 4 1 5; b: 1 3 2 4 3.

2)   Mutation operator: mutation operation can make our algorithm obtain better diversification, using changeable mutation probability, when the individual's fitness value is larger than its generation's average fitness value 0.1 times, which show that the individual is excellent, using Pm=0.001,otherwise choosing large mutation probability Pm=0.5. In this way, we ensure that the best individual is not damaged, meanwhile, maintain the diversity of population.

3.4   Stopping Criteria

We consider combining "maximum generation" and "checking fitness value change" as the stopping criteria. After the calculation, the chromosome which has the largest fitness value is the final solution.

4   Experiments and Results

Assuming $S = \{S_1, S_2, S_3, S_4, S_5\}$ is the set of possible emergency facility locations, $E = \{E_1, E_2, E_3, E_4, E_5\}$ is the set of emergency sites. Ti is the time restriction of E_i

when there is an emergency $Ti = 11$ ($i = 1,2,...,5$), $C = \{9,11,13,8,15\}$. the shortest times from emergency facilities S to sites E are as follows:

$$\begin{bmatrix} 11 & 10 & 14 & 4 & 8 \\ 25 & 7 & 5 & 13 & 14 \\ 9 & 13 & 18 & 10 & 6 \\ 15 & 6 & 12 & 11 & 24 \\ 10 & 11 & 11 & 7 & 9 \end{bmatrix}$$

After conversion, we obtain the matrix A as follows :

$$\begin{bmatrix} 1 & 1 & 0 & 1 & 1 \\ 0 & 1 & 1 & 0 & 0 \\ 1 & 0 & 0 & 1 & 1 \\ 0 & 1 & 1 & 1 & 0 \\ 1 & 1 & 1 & 1 & 1 \end{bmatrix}$$

The parameters of GA are set as follows: the mutation probability Pm=0.001, the cross probability Pm=0.5 or 0.001 for different fitness value, and the population P=50. We did five times 01emulation experiments on this example. Table1 shows the emulation results.

From table1, we can see that when w_1 is 0.892, w_2 is 0.108, our objective function have minimum 17.944 and we obtain that the solution to the problem is to build emergency facilities at S_1, S_2, S_4, and the total expense is 28.

Table 1. Results of Emulation

Emulation times	w_1	w_2	x_1	x_2	x_3	x_4	x_5	Optimal Objective Value
1	0.696	0.304	0	1	0	1	1	21.472
2	0.245	0.755	1	1	0	1	0	25.795
3	0.065	0.935	1	1	0	1	0	27.415
4	0.500	0.500	1	1	0	1	0	23.500
5	0.892	0.108	0	1	0	1	1	17.944

From Figure 1, we can see that, when w_1 and w_2 have the same value that is 0.500, the objective function, total rescue time and expenses are distributed as follows:

The two functions have consistent change tendency, which show that our algorithm can balance the two optimization aims well and approach the approximate optimal objective solution to the problem after about the 30th generation. This point is very obviously showed from Figure 2, and the best fitness value is 0.042.

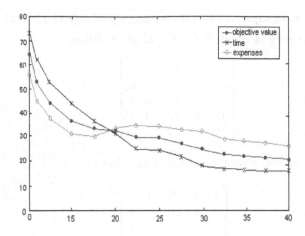

Fig. 1. The Change of the Objective Function Value

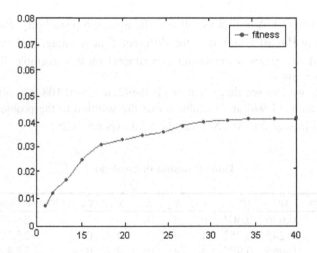

Fig. 2. The Change of the Fitness Function Value

5 Conclusions

In this paper, we first give a mathematical model of multi-objective emergency facility location problem, then propose this model with complex constraints is transformed into simple constraints using by punishment function. Subsequently, describe how to solve EFLP using by GA, at last after many times emulation experiments, results showed that we can obtain the optimal solution to objective function, that is to say, our algorithm is effective and efficient for solving this problem. In the future work, we will do more experiments in multi-objective emergency facility location problem by the application of genetic algorithms.

References

1. Jean –Luc, W.: FMIS: a decision support system for forest fire prevent and fighting. IEEE Transaction on Engeering 45(2), 127–131 (1998)
2. Suleyman, T.: An integrated emergency management decision support system for hurricanes emergencies. Safety Science 20, 39–48 (1995)
3. Luis, G., Acosta, E., Roberto, D.G.: Dual-based heuristics for a hierarchical covering Location Problem. Computer &Operations research 30, 65–180 (2003)
4. WLodzimierz, O.: On the distribution approach to Location Problem. Computers &Industrial Engineering 37, 595–612 (1999)
5. Chandran, S.: Dissemination of weather information to emergency managers: A decision support tool. IEEE Transaction on Engineering Management 45(2), 106–114 (1998)
6. Fang, L., He, J.: Emergency system model based on AHP method and Objective Mehtod. System Engieering Theory and Practice (12), 116–120 (2003)
7. Deb, K.: Multi-objective genetic algorithms: Problem difficulties and construction of test functions. Evolutionary Computation 7(3), 205 (1999)
8. Srinivas, N., Deb, K.: Multi-Objective Function Optimization Using Non-Dominated Sorting Genetical Algorithms. Evolutionary Computation 2(3), 221–248 (1995)
9. He, J., Liu, C.: Emergency management and Emergency system-Location and Algorithm. Science Publishment, Beijing (2005)
10. Noeedal, J., Wright, S.J.: Numerical optimization, pp. 490–527. Springer Science+Business Media lac, Berlin (1999)

Trigonometric Curve Fitting Based on Genetic Algorithm and the Application of Data Processing in Geography

Baolei Gu

Baolei Gu, School of Computer Science, China University of Geosciences,
Lumo Road 388, Wuhan 430074, China

Abstract. Based on the characteristics of genetic algorithm, the paper provides a method of curve-fitting of trigonometric functions on genetic algorithm. It also takes geological data as an example to explain the application of the algorithm. At the same time, it improves and optimizes some shortcomings existing in the simple genetic algorithm in curve fitting trigonometric functions and the convergence speed as well.

Keywords: genetic algorithm; trigonometric curve fitting; Optimization.

1 Introduction

The principle of least squares can be used in fitting linear and simple nonlinear equations, but there is not often the strict relationship between the relevant variables and the independent variables of function. The more basic functions are given in the fitting function, the more closer to the true function, and the better the effects of fitting.

GA (genetic algorithm) refers to a kind of evolved randomized search method which draws from the laws of Darwin's natural selection and biological evolution regularities (genetic mechanism of survival of the fittest). Compared with the traditional search strategy, genetic algorithm uses the group search strategy, and the random function which efficiently searches the encoded parameter space. It is independent on the problem of model, the complexity of issues, the inherent implicit parallelism, the strong ability of searching for probability and overall situation, and the characteristics that can automatically gain, guide, and optimize the searching space, and adaptively adjust the searching direction.

Influenced by such factors as topography, geomorphology, environment, etc, geographical data have the characteristics, such as huge data, collection difficulties, non-interval sampling, etc. For the relatively complicated data processing like this, the using of principle of least squares fitting would not be very good. But the using of genetic algorithms could be better to deal with complex nonlinear problems that can not be solved by the traditional search strategies.

In the genetic algorithm, a set of values of unsettled coefficients is encoded as a set of binary strings called chromosome. Each string contains a number of sub-strings. Each sub-string is coefficients' binary-coded of the goal fitting function; sub-string's a one or several combinations are called a gene. Each group of string stands for the

Z. Cai et al. (Eds.): ISICA 2009, CCIS 51, pp. 104–109, 2009.
© Springer-Verlag Berlin Heidelberg 2009

value of the coefficient of objectives of fitting function, which is called an individual, a collection of individuals groups.

Trigonometric functions in general form can be written:

f(x)=A$_1$*Sin (B$_1$* x+C$_1$)+ A$_2$*Sin (B$_2$* x+C$_2$)+......+ A$_i$ *Sin (B$_i$ * x+C$_i$)+......+D
(i=1,2,......,n)   (1)

As a function approximately describing the data, in which R=(A$_1$,B$_1$, C$_1$, A$_2$, B$_2$, C$_2$,......, A$_i$,B$_i$,C$_i$......,D) ^{T} is the (3n +1) unsettled coefficients, which can be converted to binary .i.e., chromosome in the genetic algorithm. Obviously, it requires of more basic function in the fitting function to achieve better fitting effects. So, the more parameters to be determined, the length of the longer chromosomes.

Set Y$_i$ is the measured value at the point x$_i$ (i = 1,2, ..., n), Y'$_i$ is the results of the calculation by the fitting function at point x$_i$, the mean square error of the n data points is $\delta = \sqrt{\sum_{i=1}^{n}(Y_i - Y'_i)^2}$, Obviously, the smaller the value of this function, the better the results are.

Before it constitutes the initial group in the process of random initialization, given individuals set the scope of their value. Under general circumstances, according to the characteristics of boundary of trigonometric functions, the relationship between the maximum pure trigonometric function (A), the maximum (max) and minimum (min) of data is: A ≤ (max + min) / 2; as the periodic characteristics of the trigonometric function (period 2π), the B$_i$ * x + C$_i$ data will repeat every 2π, every π positive and negative values will be changed. So, C$_i$ and Bi * x 's absolutely value should be less than π; considering the accuracy, the minimum spacing between numerical as X is determined to be the maximum absolute value of B$_i$ for the π / X; D range of value : min ≤ D ≤ max; to determine the size of group is determined by the unsettled numbers of coefficients.

The using of the fitting Trigonometric functions on each individual, by selecting, leaves a given number of individuals. Selection means the random selection of individual in accordance with the fit value of individual. The individual with the larger adapted value is more likely to be chosen. The remaining is made with the process of the genetic variation and gene hybridization. Hybridization is a pair of matching chosen randomly based on a certain probability, and then the two chromosomes randomly exchange part of the chromosome to form a new gene. Variation refers to the random change of the value of certain individuals as a certain degree, that is, the negation operator, which prevents the group from the evolution and entering some local area of the search space.

2   The Improvement of Genetic Algorithm in the Trigonometric Functions in Curve Fitting

Starting from various initial points, the genetic algorithm quickly identifies the areas where the most advantages lie in as a greater probability of the overall situation, free from the interference of the most advantages in the other part. So, the genetic algorithm has the characteristics of the rapid development approaching better individuals in the early searching stage. The fixed population size are undergone a series of optimal operations. Once some good individuals have absolute advantages in the population, and genetic algorithm will strengthen the advantage, and groups began to converge, which has been referred to be the premature convergence of genetic algorithms. Premature convergence has such defects as: there is low efficiency in the latter of a global search evolution; the results may not be such as the global optimal solution. The algorithm using binary coding and a fixed probability and mutation probability of hybrid will have a slow convergence, premature convergences or no convergences will result the failure of optimization.

In order to improve shortcomings, mentioned above, maintain the competitive mechanism of population and improve the performance of genetic algorithm, the efficiency of solving and accuracy, real-coded should be used in the process of trigonometric function fitting, i.e. the chromosome composed of coefficients directly, not by any coding; At the same time, dynamic adjustment probability of adaptive selection, hybridization, mutation, and the scope of hybridization and mutation, thereby it can give the best unsettled curve fitting coefficients while improving the convergence rate.

(1) Compared with the binary coding, the real coding can not only easily denotes the number of large range and accuracy, which is easy to be searched in a larger space; but also reduces the complexity of the genetic algorithm and increases the efficiency of the computing and accuracy of the reconciliation.

(2) In order to ensure the convergence of the genetic algorithm in the whole area, a sufficient number of groups of different individuals must be maintained by dynamic adaptive adjustment of probability and scope of hybridization and so on, in the whole process of evolution convergence. However, in order to speed up the algorithm convergence rate, as well as to approach the optimal direction made by the individuals in the population, it will be inevitable to reduce the diversity of the population. Therefore, the dynamic choice of a reasonable probability and the extent of hybridization is essential.

3   The Application of Trigonometric Function Fitting Based on Genetic Algorithm in Geological Data

In the fitting function, it is necessary to make curve fitting infinitely close to a series of measured data points. But these discrete data often have some errors because of various influences. Geographical data are hard to be collected for the effects of topographical features so that the data of sampling are often between right and wrong, etc., which make data processing more difficult, after the sampling in generally, it will making the sampling interval from unequidistant to equidistant by the calculating the distance or interpolation to estimate of man-made , and then use some of the standard Matlab function to deal with, so after several treatments, not only make the operate more complex, also more man-made, which will also make the error become more greater. Using trigonometric function fitting based on Genetic algorithm, whether it is for equidistant or not, can be one-off best fitting for all the data, a great reduction of errors arising.

Table 1. Collected Data to Be Processed

spacing	element	spacing	element	spacing	element	spacing	element	spacing	element	spacing	element
0	7.425135	354	4.845237	731	7.255245	1278	7.428311	1917.5	5.875899	2227	6.699579
45	4.56738	362.5	3.787804	787	7.182292	1306.5	6.993034	1954	2.604043	2256	7.092707
86	3.747561	371.5	5.499566	859.5	2.618023	1317.5	5.522241	1975	2.56139	2267.5	3.621778
109	6.462044	382	5.880725	878.5	6.410883	1332.5	2.598815	1985	4.022218	2280.5	7.400677
131.5	5.361465	455	6.692531	896	5.842771	1357	2.974677	1991.5	6.367731	2304.5	6.140991
158	4.748363	487	7.266216	914	7.022973	1389	2.581055	1996.5	2.791186	2321	2.561775
181	5.022002	507.5	4.936225	950.5	5.061488	1419	7.402134	2031.5	2.548389	2330.5	5.848638
199	3.587373	514	2.898583	997	2.857306	1462	6.426699	2074.5	3.827813	2340.5	7.40747
226	7.454931	518.5	6.589987	1060	4.737873	1497	7.250375	2083.5	5.475366	2370.5	2.581541
257	5.448854	544	7.09111	1095	6.009997	1556	5.486433	2109.5	2.888993	2405	4.245001
268.5	7.369434	554.5	7.288058	1139	3.520794	1612.5	5.580929	2120	2.722976	2457.5	6.159428
280	4.297244	579	7.447335	1154	6.943517	1841	2.58011	2126.5	2.995164	2471	7.443093
286.5	6.586145	593	7.410319	1176	6.689479	1853.5	7.264314	2149.5	7.130201	2493.5	3.312651
309.5	3.588563	619	3.7829	1212	3.863907	1877	4.526973	2190.5	2.61219	2505.5	5.309909
314	7.209861	679	3.822699	1248	2.594626	1894	2.621175	2203	7.194683	2526	2.840769
334	2.952888	717	7.025411	1265.5	2.573351	1903.5	5.367431	2219	3.067411	2554	2.549043

Table 2. Dynamic Adaptive Adjust Probability (%) and Scope of Hybrid and So On

	adaptability	probability of selection	probability of hybridization	probability of variation	scope of hybridization	scope of variation
	well	10	10	10	6.905	6.905
$\delta>10$	medium	5	20	5	6.905	6.905
	worse	2	26	2	6.905	6.905
	well	12	6	12	4	4
$10>\delta>1$	medium	6	18	6	4	4
	worse	3	24	3	4	4
	well	14	2	14	2	2
$1>\delta>0.1$	medium	7	16	7	2	2
	worse	3	24	3	2	2
	well	16	0	14	1	1
$0.1>\delta$	medium	8	14	8	1	1
	worse	4	22	4	1	1

On the function (1) take n = 2, that is, f (x) = A_1 * Sin (B_1 * x + C_1) + A_2 * Sin (B_2 * x + C_2) + D, the length of chromosome is 7 in algorithm. The range of value should be determined before the initial group is composed in the process of the random initialization. Under the general circumstances, the characteristics of boundary of trigonometric functions determines , A ≤ (max + min) / 2 = (7.454931+ 2.548389) /2 = 5.00166; as the periodic (period 2π) characteristics of the trigonometric function, so C ≤ π, B * x ≤ π, considering the question of accuracy, the value of the minimum spacing 4.5 as X, determine the maximum absolute value of B is π / 4.5 = 0.698132; D range is: 7.454931≤D≤2.548389.

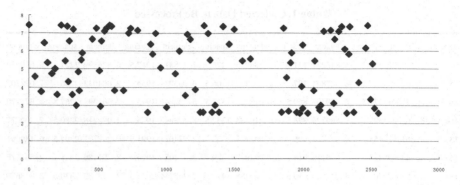

Fig. 1. Collected data to be processed

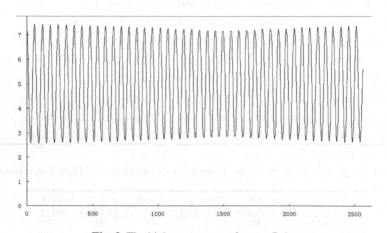

Fig. 2. The higher accuracy of curve fitting

Set Y_i is the measured value at the point x_i (i = 1,2, ..., n), Y'_i is the results of the calculation at point x_i with the fitting function. Therefore ,the mean square error of the n data points is $\delta= \sqrt{\sum_{i=1}^{n}(Y_i - Y'_i)^2}$, Obviously, the smaller the value of this function, the result is better. Fitness function can be set to f = 1 / (δ +0.0001).

The result is the higher accuracy of curve fitting after the evolution 200,000 about the population.

4 Conclusion

Instead of such information as the differential coefficient of the objective function, it only requires of the direct value of function and variable, which is easy to use. Curve fitting is made only one time in the overall framework, which can greatly reduce the error, and be in accordance with the actual situation. Because genetic algorithm is random in the process of initialization group, genetic recombination and gene mutation, and it dynamically adaptive adjusts the probability and the extent of hybridization, the local optimum can be avoided by the random process when the searching of optimum encounters local optimum, so that the global optimum can be reached; at the same time, the use of real-coded can be easily signified the data with the wide range and high precision. Therefore, it is feasible to adopt the method the genetic algorithm the method using carrying trigonometric function curve fitting of is feasible, enough in the search number of circumstances, can work. In the enough searching circumstances, a better fitting curve can be reached.

References

1. Luger, G.F.: Artificial Intelligence: Structures and Strategies for Complex Problem Solving, 5th edn. Addison Wesley, Reading (2004)
2. Dai, W.: Based on Genetic Algorithm for Text Categorization and Clustering. Science Press, Beijing (2008)
3. Negnevitsky, M.: Artificial Intelligence A Guide to Intelligent Systems, 2nd edn. Addison Wesley, Reading (2004)
4. Yu, R.: Principle and Technology of artificial intelligence. Zhejiang University Press (2007)
5. Winston, P.H.: Artificial Intelligence, 3rd edn. Addison Wesley/Pearson (2008)
6. Shang, F.: Artificial Intelligence and Its Applications. Petroleum Industry Press, Beijing (2006)
7. Gen, M., Cheng, R.: Genetic Algorithms and Engineering Optimization, Hardcover (1999)

A Novel Crossover Operator in Evolutionary Algorithm for Logic Circuit Design

Guo-liang He[1,2], Yuan-xiang Li[1], and Zhongzhi Shi[2]

[1] State Key Laboratory of Software Engineering, Wuhan University, Wuhan, China
[2] Key Laboratory of Intelligent Information Process, Institute of Computing Technology,
The Chinese Academy of Sciences, Beijing, China
glhe@whu.edu.cn, yxli@whu.edu.cn, shizz@ics.ict.ac.cn

Abstract. In recent years the evolution of digital circuits has been intensively studied. This paper proposes an elitist pool evolutionary algorithm based on novel approach in order to improve evolutionary design of logic circuits in efficiency and capability of optimization. In the process of evolution, a novel sub-circuit crossover strategy can improve the local optimization by inheriting the better parts of two parental circuits, and an adaptive mutation strategy based on importance of gene-position can maintain the diversity of a population. Experiments show that the proposed method is able to design logic circuits efficiently.

Keywords: Evolvable hardware, evolutionary algorithm, logic circuit.

1 Introduction

In 1990s, Hugo de Gairs advanced a new hardware design method, *evolvable hardware (EHW)*, based on the method of evolutionary computation (EC) and the reconfigurable characteristics of FPGA. By simulating the evolution process in nature, EHW is used to design physical circuits, especially electronic circuits. As a new multi-discipline research field involved in computer science, electronic engineering and biology, EHW provides a feasible method for automation design and improving intelligence of hardware systems, such as adaptive filter, intelligent controller, intelligent antenna systems, etc [1-3].

Currently, the research of EHW is mainly on the auto-design of electronic and analog circuits. And a great number of algorithms for EHW have been proposed with encouraging results. For instance, Koza designed a single uniform approach using genetic programming for the automatic synthesis of both the topology and sizing of different prototypical analog circuits, including a lowpass filter, a source identification circuit, an amplifier, etc [4]. Emanuele Stomeo et al. proposed generalized disjunction decomposition (GDD) [5] based on rewriting the truth table in such a way that the inputs needed to describe the system were decomposed in a lower-level circuit and a multiplexer. It is beneficial for solving more complex logic circuits, not obtaining optimized logic circuits. Meanwhile, other intelligent approaches such as multi-objective

Z. Cai et al. (Eds.): ISICA 2009, CCIS 51, pp. 110–117, 2009.

approaches [6-7], variable length chromosome GA [8], and incremental development evolution [9-10], were also proposed for automated design of logic circuit.

In this paper, we investigated a novel elitist pool evolutionary algorithm (EPEA) for designing logic circuits. It employs evolutionary strategies to quicken the local optimization and maintain the diversity of a population in terms of the characteristics of logic circuits. In section 2, we briefly describe the encoding method of logic circuits. Section 3 presents a novel elitist pool evolutionary algorithm, including a novel evolutionary operator, an adaptive mutation strategy and an evaluation strategy. Section 4 gives some examples to analyze the performance of the proposed approach. Finally, we discuss conclusive remarks in Section 5.

2   Representation of Individual

We use a matrix structure to represent digital circuits as shown in Fig. 1. The inputs of each cell are the original inputs or other cells' outputs, and the outputs of last column are the circuit's outputs. In order to represent combinational logic circuits fully, definitions of the function types of cells and the connectivity among cells are required for the matrix. In this matrix, each cell represents a logic gate, and some function types of gates are shown in Table 1. For the connectivity, we define that only previous cells connect to next cells to avoid a circle. The outputs of the cells of the last column in the matrix are the outputs of the encoded circuit respectively and the remaining cells of the last column are redundant.

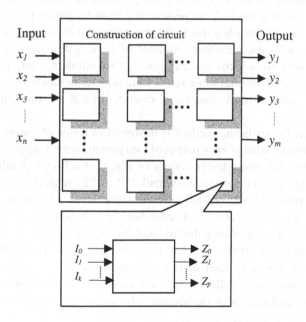

Fig. 1. The matrix encoding representation for digital circuits

Table 1. Function types of basal logic gates

	Function type		Function type
0	A*	3	A + B
1	!A	4	A $\oplus$ B
2	A $\bullet$ B	5	A $\bullet$!C + B $\bullet$ C

* This function type means the first input of a cell is directly connected to its output, without employing any logic operators.

3 Elitist Pool Evolutionary Algorithm

In general, local search optimization and the population diversity are two basic principles in evolutionary algorithm. Based on the principles and characteristics of logic circuits, an elitist pool evolutionary algorithm with a new crossover operator and an adaptive mutation strategy is introduced as follows.

3.1 Sub-circuit Crossover Operator

The evolution design of logic circuits is a multi-objective optimization problem when every output of the circuit is considered as an objective which is a sub-circuit containing some cells and their connections. Therefore, the structure of a circuit can be formed by the fusion of all sub-circuits of outputs. Based on the local optimization, a sub-circuit of a new individual can be selected from the better parental sub-circuits corresponding to the same objective in the process of the crossover. In order to obtain correct circuits with the minimized number of logic gates, sharing cells must be widely used while all sub-circuits are fused into a whole circuit. Therefore, some cells of these selected parental sub-circuits should be implemented by some replacing approaches to form a new integrated circuit instead of the collection of all sub-circuits.

In this paper, the replacing method is designed in terms of outputs location. For example, the fitness value of each output of two parents with 3 inputs and 2 outputs is 7/8, 4/8 and 5/8, 6/8 respectively shown in Fig. 2. Each cell is labeled to which sub-circuit it belongs. For instance, symbol "1" or "2" respectively denotes that it belongs to the first or the second sub-circuit, and symbol "-1" denotes this cell does not belong to any sub-circuits but a redundant cell. A cell noted "1,2" means this cell is a shared logic gate of both the first and the second sub-circuit. The sub-circuit of the first output is firstly selected from the better corresponding sub-circuit of parent I, and the sub-circuit of the second output is selected from parent II. At the same time, some cells of the first sub-circuit should be replaced when these cells are conflicted with the second sub-circuit in the same positions of this matrix.

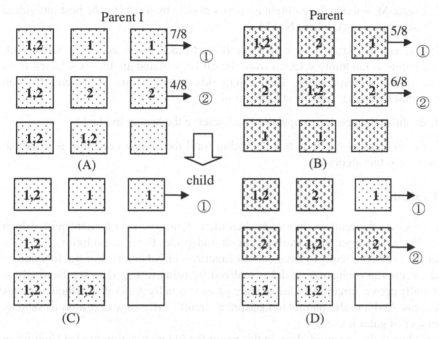

Fig. 2. The process of sub-circuit crossover from parents: (A) and (B) are the parents; (C) the first sub-circuit of a new individual from parent 1, which is better than parent 2; (D) an new integrated individual is produced after the fusion of the three sub-circuits from parents.

3.2 Adaptive Mutation Strategy

According to the importance of gene-position in the chromosome, the important genes are mutated with a lower rate to enhance the convergence of the algorithm, and the less important genes are mutated with a high rate to maintain the diversity of population. In terms of the encoding scheme used here, each cell of the rectangular array corresponds to a section of genes, and its sharing degree determines its importance. The higher the sharing degree is, the lower the rate is. At the same time, considering the function of each circuit, the mutation rate of a cell will be increased if its corresponding function of a sub-circuit including this cell does not completely match the truth table; otherwise, it will be decreased.

This is essential for the evolution of circuits. It has a bigger chance for the better part of the circuit to be reserved while the worse part may be possible to be changed drastically.

3.3 Framework of Elitist Pool Evolutionary Algorithm

The main process of elitist pool evolutionary algorithm is as follow:

Step1: Initialize a host population A and its scale is N. And evaluate each individual of this population.

Step2: Create M individuals to obtain an elitist pool B by mutating the best individual in the host population A, where N>>M.

Step3: The sub-circuit crossover operator is performed to create a new individual, where a parent is randomly selected from the elitist pool and another is selected from the host population respectively. Then mutate this new individual. Repeating this step N times until obtaining a new host population A.

Step4: Evaluate the new host population and reserve the best individual.

Step5: Go to step2 to continue this algorithm until the ending condition is satisfied; otherwise, end this algorithm.

3.4 Evaluation

In the process of circuit evolution, evaluation criterion is an important part, which reflects the performance of an evolved circuit and guides the next evolution. Firstly, it is vital for evolved circuits to have correct functions or behaviors. For the function of digital circuit, the evaluation model is realized by using testing data set. Secondly, a functionally correct circuit with fewer logic gates is usually preferable, which occupies fewer areas. And it is also natural to measure a circuit's efficiency of resource usage by the number of gates it uses.

According to the proposed ideas, in this paper the fitness function $F(x_i)$ evaluating an encoded circuit x_i is defined as follows:

$$F_t(x_i) = H(x_i) + w*V(x_i)$$

Here, $H(x_i)$ is defined as the matching degree by comparing the function of all output with the truth table; $V(x_i)$ is the number of cells whose function type are *wires* in the circuit x_i and the redundant cells in the matrix; w is a weight coefficient, which changes in the different phases.

4 Experiment

Three case studies including 2-bit adder, 2-bit multiplier and 2-bit comparator are carried out using EPEA and its parameters are as follow: the population size N=100, maximum of number of generations T=20000; the mutation rate is initialized as 0.08 and the crossover rate is 0.8. Here we use gate-level and function-level evolution to design these arithmetic circuits. In order to simplify the function type, in this paper the function types of basic gates are shown in Table 1, and the function blocks include these basic gates and 2-multiplexers.

For the 2-bit adder, by function-level method, EPEA could obtain an optimized 2-bit adder circuit at 100 percent by evolving about 2800 generations when the size of the encoding matrix is 3×3, and its circuit is shown in Fig. 3. However, it could not get a correct circuit with the same size of the encoding matrix by gate-level method. When the size of the encoding matrix increases to 4×4, EPEA could get an optimized 2-bit adder circuit as follow in Fig.4.

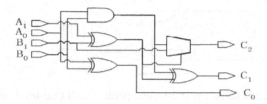

Fig. 3. Circuit design of 2-bit adder with function-level approach

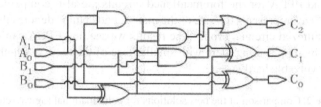

Fig. 4. Circuit design of 2-bit adder with gate-level approach

For the 2-bit multiplier, the size of the encoding matrix is 4×4, EPEA could get the same optimized 2-bit multiplier circuit with 7 gates by gate-level and function-level approaches and one of these optimized circuits is shown in Fig.5.

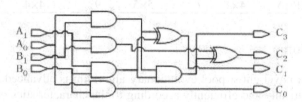

Fig. 5. Circuit design of 2-bit multiplier

For the 2-bit comparator, the size of the encoding matrix is 5×5. By function-level method, EPEA could obtain an optimized 2-bit comparator circuit with 7 gates as shown in Fig. 6 while an optimized 2-bit comparator circuit with 9 gates by gate-level evolution is shown in Fig.7.

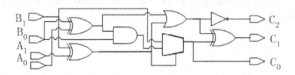

Fig. 6. Circuit design of 2-bit comparator with function-level approach

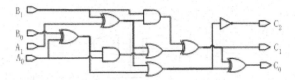

Fig. 7. Circuit design of 2-bit comparator with gate-level approach

On the other hand, the best solutions obtained by NGA [11], MGA [12], KM [13], QM [14-15] and EPEA for the forementioned circuits are also compared in Table 2 (The symbol "Size" represents the size of the matrix, and "Num" denotes the number of gates in the optimized circuit). From these results we see that EPEA can similar optimized circuits by representing them with smaller size of the matrix, which is adaptive for designing evolvable hardware.

Table 2. Comparison of the best solutions for combinational logic circuits

Method	2×2 multiplier		2-bit comparator		2-bit adder	
	Size	Num	Size	Num	Size	Num
KM	—	8	—	19	—	12
QM	—	12	—	13	—	—
NGA	5×5	9	6×7	12	5×5	7
MGA	5×5	7	6×7	9	5×5	7
EPEA	4×4	7	5×5	9	4×4	7

5 Conclusion

In this paper, a novel elitist pool evolutionary algorithm is advanced to design logic circuits automatically and efficiently according to the characteristics of logic circuits. Experiments on auto-design of some combinational logic circuits show the proposed evolutionary strategies can be extraordinarily encouraging in efficiency and capability of optimization, and some of evolved circuits can be used as basic macro-blocks to design larger logic circuits automatically.

Acknowledgments

This project was supported by National Natural Science Foundation of China (under grants No. 60773009) and National High-Tech Research and Development of China (No. 2007AA01Z290).

References

1. Linden, D.S.: Optimizing signal strength in-situ using an evolvable antenna system. In: 2002 NASA/DoD Conference on Evolvable Hardware, pp. 147–151 (2002)
2. Vinger, K.A., Torresen, J.: Implementing evolution of FIR-filters efficiently in an FPGA. In: 2003 NASA/DoD Conference on Evolvable Hardware, pp. 26–29 (2003)

3. Glette, K., Torresen, J., Gruber, T., Sick, B., Kaufmann, P., Platzner, M.: Comparing Evolvable Hardware to Conventional Classifiers for Electromyographic Prosthetic Hand Control. In: NASA/ESA conference on adaptive hardware and systems, Noordwijk, the Netherlands, June 2008, pp. 32–39 (2008)
4. Koza, J.R., Bennett, F.H., Andre, D., Keane, M.A., Dunlap, F.: Automated Synthesis of Analog Electrical Circuits by Means of Genetic Programming. IEEE Transactions on Evolutionary Computation 1(2), 109–128 (1997)
5. Stomeo, E., Kalganova, T., Lambert, C.: Generalized Disjunction Decomposition for Evolvable Hardware. IEEE Transactions on, Systems, Man and Cybernetics (Part B) 36(5), 1024–1043 (2006)
6. Ishida, Y., Nosato, H., Takahashi, E., Murakawa, M., Kajitani, I., Furuya, T., Higuchi, T.: Proposal for LDPC Code Design System Using Multi-Objective Optimization and FPGA-Based Emulation. In: The 8th international Conference on Evolvable Systems: From Biology to Hardware, Prague, Czech Republic, September 2008, pp. 237–248 (2008)
7. Coello, C.A.C., Aguirre, A.H.: Design of combinational logic circuits through an evolutionary multiobjective optimization approach. Ai Edam-Artificial Intelligence for Engineering Design Analysis and Manufacturing, 16(1), 39–53 (2002)
8. Kalganova, T., Miller, J.F.: Circuit layout evolution: An evolvable hardware approach. In: IEE Colloquium (Digest), pp. 11–14 (1999)
9. Miller, J.F., Job, D., Vassilev, V.K.: Principles in the evolutionary design of digital circuits—part II. In: Genetic Programming and Evolvable Machines, vol. 1, pp. 259–288 (2000)
10. Bidlo, M., Vasicek, Z.: Gate-Level Evolutionary Development Using Cellular Automata. In: NASA/ESA conference on adaptive hardware and systems, Noordwijk, the Netherlands, pp 11–18 (June 2008)
11. Coello Coello, C.A., Christiansen, A.D., Aguirre, A.H.: Use of Evolutionary Techniques to Automate the Design of Combinational Circuits. International Journal of Smart Engineering System Design 2, 299–314 (2000)
12. Coello Coello, C.A., Aguirre, A.H.: Design of combinational logic circuits through an evolutionary multiobjective optimization approach. Artificial Intelligence for Engineering, Design, Analysis and Manufacture 16(1), 39–53 (2002)
13. Karnaugh, M.: A Map Method for Synthesis of Combinational Logic Circuits. Transaction of the AIEE, Communications and Electronic 72(I), 593–599 (1953)
14. Quine, W.V.: A Way to Simplify Truth Function. American Mathematical Monthly 62(9), 627–631 (1955)
15. McCluskey, E.J.: Minimization of Boolean Function. Bell Systems Technical Journal 35(5), 1417–1444 (1956)

Aptasensors Design Considerations

Y.C. Lim[1], A.Z. Kouzani[1], and W. Duan[2]

[1] School of Engineering, Deakin University, Geelong, Victoria 3217, Australia
[2] School of Medicine, Deakin University, Geelong, Victoria 3217, Australia
{yangchoo,kouzani,wduan}@deakin.edu.au

Abstract. With the advancement of biotechnology, aptamer-based sensors have received intense attention in both research and commercial worlds. This is driven by the advantages of small molecule size, chemical stability, and cost effectiveness of aptamers over the conventional analyte detection using antibodies. This paper explores the aptasensors from a designer perspective and discusses the aptasensor design considerations by giving an overview of surface functionalization techniques and the existing mechanisms used to detect biomolecular interactions. It also expounds the factors that influence the accuracy and sensitivity of aptasensors

Keywords: aptamer, immobilization, aptasensor.

1 Introduction

Aptamers are synthetic nucleic acid isolated from large combinatorial libraries of oligonucleotides via an iterative in-vitro selection and amplification. This process is known as systematic evolution of ligands by exponential enrichment (SELEX). Aptamers are gaining popularity among molecular biologists due to their inherent advantage of superior specificity in binding a wide variety of protein and non-protein targets. Aptamers are smaller in size and have better physicochemical stability compared to antibodies. Furthermore, they are less prone to denaturation and can be easily modified to facilitate surface functionalization with long storage life. These advantages qualify them as an excellent biorecognition element in biosensors. A biosensor comprises of two main parts: a biorecognition element and a transducer that translates biorecognition event into measurable electrical, optical, or mechanical signals. Biosensors that employ aptamer as their biorecognition element are known as aptasensors.

To date, there exist a few excellent review papers [1, 2] that discuss aptasensors from different perspective. In this paper, the common surface immobilization techniques as well as the existing methods used to convert the aptamer-binding event into measurable signals are described. Factors that influence the analytical performance of an aptasensor are also addressed.

2 Surface Modification

Modification of the biosensor chip surface is a crucial first step that determines the specificity of a biosensor in detecting any analyte of interest. There are various

Z. Cai et al. (Eds.): ISICA 2009, CCIS 51, pp. 118–127, 2009.
© Springer-Verlag Berlin Heidelberg 2009

immobilization techniques available, but the self-assembly technique is the most commonly employed method by many researchers. Self-assembled monolayer (SAM) involves dipping the substrate into a solution to allow adsorption of molecules on the surface. Physisorption involves non-covalent interactions between molecules such as electrostatic interactions, van der Walls forces and hydrophobic interactions. Surface immobilization on gold is usually performed via chemisorptions of three-segment thiol-terminated aptamers [3, 4]. The first segment, thiolalkane hydrocarbon, promotes formation of a monolayer on surface. Aptamer is extended from the monolayer surface via the second segment, a linker, to enable easy accessibility of aptamer binding site to target. The third element is the aptamer molecular probe that recognizes the target protein. To ensure proper orientation of surface immobilization onto thiol-functionalized silicon oxynitride waveguide, Johnson et al [5] used a cysteine-terminated STM scaffold protein.

Besides thiol, other functional group such as amine, biotin or carboxyl can be used to modify the terminus of an aptamer. Amine-terminated thrombin aptamers is implemented by Lee et al [6] to functionalize pyrolyzed carbon working electrode. Phosphate buffer saline (PBS) with Triton X-100 is used to remove unreacted functional groups. Non-specific binding of thrombin on the surface is prevented by blocking with 1% bovine serum albumin. Meanwhile, Bini et al [7] employed the layer-by-layer (LBL) approach. LBL is another form of self-assembly technique whereby multi-layers of biomolecules with opposite charged groups bond uniformly on the chemically modified surface. C-reactive protein (CRP) aptamer is immobilized via N-hydroxysuccinimide (NHS)-mediated chemical reaction and specific interaction between biotin and avidin.

3 Transduction Approach

Integration of a transducer in aptasensor is essential to convert the biorecognition event into measurable signals. This section will provide an overview of various transduction methods including reporters that assist the detection of aptamer-target binding event.

3.1 Electrochemical

Aptasensors that implements electrochemical detection consist of three electrodes: working, auxiliary, and reference. Detection of analyte of interest is achieved by measuring current or voltage changes generated by aptamer-target interactions at the electrode. Reporters such as catalytic labels, inorganic or organic catalysts, and nanoparticles are integrated in this type of detection system.

Commonly used electroactive labels are ferricyanide $[Fe(CN)_6]^{4-/3-}$ [8-10], ferrocene [11, 12], methylene blue (MB) [13, 14], and bis-anthraquinone-modified propanediol [15]. This type of detection technique exploits the conformational change of aptamer structure upon binding to its target. As shown in Fig. 1(a), in the signal "on" architecture, the electroactive end is distant from the electrode surface, limiting the electron transfer. Electron transfer increases upon target binding due to the conformational change of aptamer bringing the label to the surface. On the other hand, the signal "off" architecture (Fig. 1(b)) yields a lower electron transfer upon target binding as the addition of a target disassociates the initially attached redox-tag.

In the work presented by Li et al. [8], small molecule such as adenosine is detected using part of the complementary aptamer strand in electrochemical impedance spectroscopy. This approach eliminates the dependence on conformational change of aptamers. Negatively charged adenosine-binding aptamer attached on the surface repels the negatively charged probe ($[Fe(CN)_6]^{4-/3-}$ anions. This causes high impedance that hinders the interfacial electron-transfer kinetics of redox probes. Impedance is reduced upon adenosine binding by releasing its negatively charged aptamer-target strand. The sensitivity of electrochemical detection can be amplified by incorporating polymerase chain reaction [16].

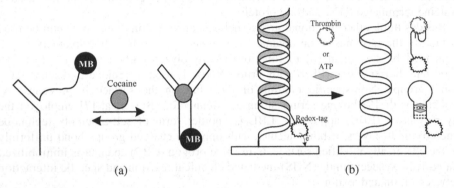

Fig. 1. Schematic representation of electrochemical detection based on (a) signal "on" (Adapted from [13]), and (b) signal "off" (Adapted from [15]) architectures

3.2 Electrical

Ion-sensitive field effect transistors (ISFETs) initially used for measuring pH has extended their usage in biomolecular interactions detection. This is due to their inherent advantage of robustness, small size, and cost effectiveness. Electrical sensing using field-effect transistor is a label-free approach. In this system, a reference electrode is exposed to the analyte solution. The source and drain deposited on silicon layer is separated by a thin insulating layer. The interfacial electron transfer resistance is controlled by the formation of target-aptamer complex. Hence, target molecules are identified by measuring the gate potential variations. Fig. 2 illustrates an example of ISFET-based aptasensor employed in adenosine detection [17].

Instead of using external reference electrode in ISFET-based transducer , Cid and co-workers [18] employed a network of single-walled carbon nanotube (CNT) as the transduction layer. The use of CNT in FET fabrication is favorable because it exhibits superior performance in terms of transconductance and subthreshold slope. An aptasensor based on aptamer-modified CNT-FETs for immunoglobulin E (IgE) detection has been developed by Maehashi et al [19]. Linker molecules are used to covalently bind 5'-amino-modified IgE aptamers to CNT. Alternately, So et al [20] modified the side wall of CNT with carbodiimidazole (CDI)-Tween for thrombin detection.

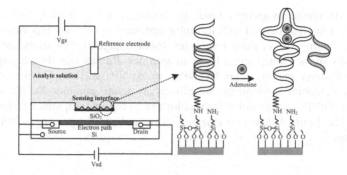

Fig. 2. Schematic diagram of an ISFET-based sensor (Adapted from [17])

Hydrophobic interactions bring Tween to the side walls while 3'-amine group of the thrombin aptamer is covalently bound to CDI moiety. The formation of aptamer-target complex shields the negative charges of aptamer, producing an increased height of Schottky barrier between the metal electrodes and CNT channel and thus leading to a decrease in the electrical response.

3.3 Optical

The most popular optical transduction method is the fluorescence detection. Fluoro-phore-quencher label pair is incorporated into DNA aptamer to detect the presence of L-argininamide in the work presented by Ozaki et al [21]. The structure of the DNA aptamer employed in this work is of a random shape without the addition of a target. As illustrated in Fig. 3 (a), when L-argininamide is injected, the binding of the target to the aptamer stabilizes the stem loop structure and subsequently quenches the fluo-rescence. Quantum dots have been implemented as an alternative to the fluorophore-quencher due to their robustness, stability, and the ability to tune via size variations [22]. Other optical transduction methods include the surface enhanced Raman scatter-ing (SERS) [23] and colorimetric detection by Wang et al [24]. In the SERS method

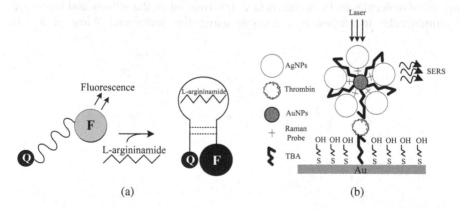

(a)   (b)

Fig. 3. Schematic representation of: (a) Fluorescent-quencher pair (Adapted from [21]), and (b) SERS transduction method (Adapted from [23])

(see Fig. 3(b)), thrombin-aptamer binds to thrombin at one binding site while gold nanoparticles (AuNPs) labeled with thrombin aptamer and Raman reporters are bound to the other binding site of thrombin target. Electromagnetic hot spots are generated on the AuNPs surface when target binds to aptamer. Raman signals are amplified via deposition of silver nanoparticles (AgNPs) on AuNPs surface. On the other hand, colorimetric detection implements dot-blot assay using aptamer-AuNPs conjugates whereby the AuNPs change color from colorless to red upon aptamer-target complex formation. The limit of detection can be further enhanced by using silver enhancement solution.

3.4 Mass

Formation of aptamer-target complex on the sensor surface generates changes in mass on the surface. Acoustics-based sensors measure the changes in mass for the target detection. This type of transduction method is also another form of label-free approaches. They operate based on piezoelectric effect and are effective in determining protein affinity on functionalized surfaces. An example of acoustic aptasensor is the quartz crystal microbalance (QCM) devised by Yao et al [25] to detect IgE. An electrical potential difference is generated between deformed piezoelectric surfaces when a pressure is exerted on a small piece of quartz. A detection limit of 2.5µg/l IgE in 5 min is achieved. To improve sensor's sensitivity, Lee et al [26] increased the amount of analyte molecules bound to the surface by implementing zinc oxide nanorod-grown QCM.

Surface acoustic wave (SAW) is another type of acoustic-based sensors. Interdigital transducers are employed to produce and detect acoustic waves at the guiding layer at the surface of the substrate. Detection of biomolecular binding is performed by measuring the frequency or phase change that corresponds to the mass on the surface. SAW love-wave sensor implements shear horizontal waves guided in a layer on the sensor surface to reduce energy dissipation of the acoustic wave in order to increase surface sensitivity. This detection method is employed in the detection of thrombin binding [27].

Surface plasmon resonance (SPR) spectroscopy [7, 28-30] is a surface-sensitive label-free technique. This method measures the variations in reflective angle upon adsorption of molecules on the metal surface. Information on the affinity and kinematics of biomolecular interaction is obtainable using this technique. Wang et al [31]

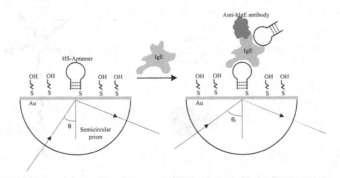

Fig. 4. Schematic of SPR detection. (Adapted from [31]).

implemented curvette-based SPR to characterize the interaction between IgE and aptamer (see Fig. 4) . Streptavidin and anti-IgE antibody are introduced during sensing to amplify the SPR signals. Eight-channel SPR sensor based on spectral modulation and wavelength division multiplexing is developed by Ostatná et al [29]. These sensing channels are formed by combining the wavelength division multiplexing of pairs of sensing channels with four parallel light beams.

Microcantilever provides a simple and label-free sensing mechanism. When molecules adsorb on to the surface, a difference in surface stress between the upper and lower surfaces causes the cantilever to bend [32, 33]. In static microcantilever sensing, this deflection is measured and it can be either positive (bend upwards) or negative (bend downwards) depending on the interaction between molecules [34]. As illustrated in Fig. 5, attraction between molecules will produce a positive deflection while repulsion interaction between molecules generates a negative deflection. Shu et al [35] demonstrated a V-shaped microcantilever detection using optical method to measure the deflection. This has been employed for the detection of human CDK2 in yeast cell lysate.

Dynamic microcantilever detects the presence of target protein by measuring frequency variations in an oscillating beam. Lu et al [36] incorporated a PZT actuator in their microcantilever. Sensitivity of the sensor is improved by separating the PZT actuator from the resonant structure to suppress energy dissipation. Q factor tends to decrease when cantilevers operate in liquid environment. To overcome this limitation, Li et al [37] introduced a new active magnetostrictive cantilever actuated by a time-varying magnetic field which exhibits a high Q value in liquid environment.

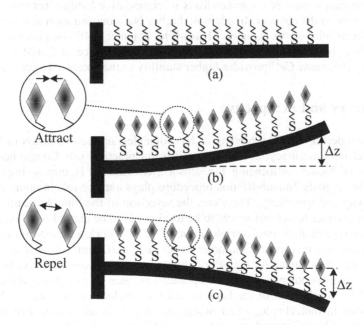

Fig. 5. (a) Before immobilization of target. (b) Attraction interaction between molecules causes the upward bending of cantilever. (c) Repulsion between molecules causes the downward bending of cantilever.

4 Sensor Performance

The immobilization procedure will determine the orientation of aptamers on the surface. These procedures directly affect selectivity and binding affinity of aptamers. The surface immobilization method is dependent on the functional groups (thiol, amine, or biotin) linked to the aptamers. Immobilization procedure that utilizes a linker such as avidin-biotin technique produces sensor with a higher sensitivity [38]. With the presence of linker, the binding site of aptamer is easily accessible to the target. The disassociation constant can be improved by integrating a spacer in between the binding moiety and aptamer. Liss et al. [39] achieved an improvement of disassociation constant from 8.4 nM to 3.6 nM. Regeneration of sensor surface is possible in aptamer-based biosensors because aptamers are less susceptible to denaturation compared to its antibody counterpart. This is a valuable characteristic as it allows the aptamer biosensor to be reused by removing target analytes using HCl without affecting its binding efficiency [12].

The structure of aptamer binding site is affected by pH. Effect of pH sensing solution on aptamer binding affinity was investigated using thrombin as the system model in [38] and [40]. The pH ranging from 4.7 to 8.5 has been tested. Denaturation of some biocomponents under extreme pH generates lower signal and higher background. The optimum pH for the thrombin model is found to be at pH 7.5. Binding affinity of aptamer is also influenced by ionic strength in the solution. Under nonoptimal conditions, the presence of K^+ facilitates the maintenance of structural integrity in thrombin aptasensor [40]. Increased concentration of Na^+ in solution shields the negative charge on DNA aptamer leads to competitive binding between Na^+ and methylene blue to the aptamer. In addition, higher Na^+ concentration also contributed to the lower affinity of the aptamer. Meanwhile, aptamer-CRP complex presented in [7] exhibits a lower disassociation constant with the presence of 2 mM Ca^{2+} in the buffer. This is because Ca^{2+} provides higher stability to the aptamer-target complex.

5 Summary and Perspective

For effective detection of the binding of biomolecules, aptasensor needs to have excellent selectivity, accuracy, as well as stability for practical use. Comprehensive investigation of factors influencing the sensor performance is utmost important in achieving these goals. Immobilization procedure plays a major role in optimizing sensor sensitivity and specificity. Therefore, the selection of the immobilization method and type of aptamer linker and spacer to be used needs to be carried out with care and take surface regeneration into considerations. Optimal working condition is another factor that requires investigation in order to produce maximum sensor response. It is envisioned that the demand for high-throughput analysis and cost-effective biosensors will drive the development of label-free aptasensors since they circumvent the need to understand the mechanism of the binding and the labeling of the aptamer. With the advancements in biotechnology and bioengineering, it is anticipated that in future, aptasensors will be an integral part of lab-on-a-chip that will make instantaneous output results for quick decision-making. This will significantly advance point-of-care diagnosis.

References

1. Song, S., Wang, L., Li, J., Fan, C., Zhao, J.: Aptamer-based biosensors. Trends in Analytical Chemistry 27, 108–117 (2008)
2. Strehlitz, B., Nikolaus, N., Stoltenburg, R.: Protein Detection with Apatmer Biosensors. Sensors 8, 4296–4307 (2008)
3. Huang, Y.-F., Chang, H.-T., Tan, W.: Cancer Cell Targeting Using Multiple Aptamers Conjugated on Nanorods. Analytical Chemistry 80, 567–572 (2008)
4. Min, K., Cho, M., Han, S.-Y., Shim, Y.-B., Ku, J., Ban, C.: A simple and direct electrochemical detection of interferon-γ using its RNA and DNA aptamers. Biosensors and Bioelectronics 23, 1819–1824 (2008)
5. Johnson, S., Evans, D., Laurenson, S., Paul, D., Davies, A.G., Ko Ferrigno, P., Walti, C.: Surface-Immobilized Peptide Aptamers as Probe Molecules for Protein Detection. Analytical Chemistry 80, 978–983 (2008)
6. Lee, J.A., Hwang, S., Kwak, J., Park, S.I., Lee, S.S., Lee, K.-C.: An electrochemical impedance biosensor with aptamer-modified pyrolyzed carbon electrode for label-free protein detection. Sensors and Actuators B: Chemical 129, 372–379 (2008)
7. Bini, A., Centi, S., Tombelli, S., Minunni, M., Mascini, M.: Development of an optical RNA-based aptasensor for C-reactive protein. Analytical and Bioanalytical Chemistry 390, 1077–1086 (2008)
8. Li, B., Du, Y., Wei, H., Dong, S.: Reusable, label-free electrochemical aptasensor for sensitive detection of small molecules. Chemical Communications, 3780–3782 (2007)
9. Estrela, P., Paul, D., Migliorato, P., Ferrigno, P.K., Ling, W., Huq, E.: Potentiometric detection of protein interactions with peptide aptamers. In: 2008 IEEE Sensors, pp. 646–649 (2008)
10. Kim, Y.S., Jung, H.S., Matsuura, T., Lee, H.Y., Kawai, T., Gu, M.B.: Electrochemical detection of 17β-estradiol using DNA aptamer immobilized gold electrode chip. Biosensors and Bioelectronics 22, 2525–2531 (2007)
11. Mir, M.n., Katakis, I.: Aptamers as elements of bioelectronic devices. Molecular BioSystems 3, 620–622 (2007)
12. Radi, A.-E., Snchez, J.L.A., Baldrich, E., O'Sullivan, C.K.: Reagentless, Reusable, Ultrasensitive Electrochemical Molecular Beacon Aptasensor. Journal of the American Chemical Society 128, 117–124 (2006)
13. Baker, B.R., Lai, R.Y., Wood, M.S., Doctor, E.H., Heeger, A.J., Plaxco, K.W.: An Electronic, Aptamer-Based Small-Molecule Sensor for the Rapid, Label-Free Detection of Cocaine in Adulterated Samples and Biological Fluids. Journal of the American Chemical Society 128, 3138–3139 (2006)
14. Cash, K.J., Heeger, A.J., Plaxco, K.W., Xiao, Y.: Optimization of a Reusable, DNA Pseudoknot-Based Electrochemical Sensor for Sequence-Specific DNA Detection in Blood Serum. Analytical Chemistry 81, 656–661 (2009)
15. Yoshizumi, J., Kumamoto, S., Nakamura, M., Yamana, K.: Target-induced strand release (TISR) from aptamer-DNA duplex: A general strategy for electronic detection of biomolecules ranging from a small molecule to a large protein. The Analyst 133, 323–325 (2008)
16. Xiang, Y., Xie, M., Bash, R., Chen, J.J.L., Wang, J.: Ultrasensitive Label-Free Aptamer-Based Electronic Detection. Angewandte Chemie 119, 9212–9214 (2007)
17. Zayats, M., Huang, Y., Gill, R., Ma, C.-a., Willner, I.: Label-Free and Reagentless Aptamer-Based Sensors for Small Molecules. Journal of the American Chemical Society 128, 13666–13667 (2006)

18. Cid, C.C., Riu, J., Maroto, A., Rius, F.X.: Ion-sensitive field effect transistors using carbon nanotubes as the transducing layer. The Analyst 133, 1001–1004 (2008)
19. Maehashi, K., Katsura, T., Kerman, K., Takamura, Y., Matsumoto, K., Tamiya, E.: Label-Free Protein Biosensor Based on Aptamer-Modified Carbon Nanotube Field-Effect Transistors. Analytical Chemistry 79, 782–787 (2007)
20. So, H.-M., Won, K., Kim, Y.H., Kim, B.-K., Ryu, B.H., Na, P.S., Kim, H., Lee, J.-O.: Single-Walled Carbon Nanotube Biosensors Using Aptamers as Molecular Recognition Elements. Journal of the American Chemical Society 127, 11906–11907 (2005)
21. Ozaki, H., Nishihira, A., Wakabayashi, M., Kuwahara, M., Sawai, H.: Biomolecular sensor based on fluorescence-labeled aptamer. Bioorganic & Medicinal Chemistry Letters 16, 4381–4384 (2006)
22. Alivisatos, P.: The use of nanocrystals in biological detection. Nature Biotechnology 22, 47–52 (2004)
23. Wang, Y., Wei, H., Li, B., Ren, W., Guo, S., Dong, S., Wang, E.: SERS opens a new way in aptasensor for protein recognition with high sensitivity and selectivity. Chemical Communications, 5220–5222 (2007)
24. Wang, Y., Li, D., Ren, W., Liu, Z., Dong, S., Wang, E.: Ultrasensitive colorimetric detection of protein by aptamer-Au nanoparticles conjugates based on a dot-blot assay. Chemical Communications, 2520–2522 (2008)
25. Yao, C., Qi, Y., Zhao, Y., Xiang, Y., Chen, Q., Fu, W.: Aptamer-based piezoelectric quartz crystal microbalance biosensor array for the quantification of IgE. Biosensors and Bioelectronics 24, 2499–2503 (2009)
26. Lee, D., Yoo, M., Seo, H., Tak, Y., Kim, W.-G., Yong, K., Rhee, S.-W., Jeon, S.: Enhanced mass sensitivity of ZnO nanorod-grown quartz crystal microbalances. Sensors and Actuators B: Chemical 135, 444–448 (2009)
27. Schlensog, M.D., Gronewold, T.M.A., Tewes, M., Famulok, M., Quandt, E.: A Love-wave biosensor using nucleic acids as ligands. Sensors and Actuators B: Chemical 101, 308–315 (2004)
28. Lee, S.J., Youn, B.-S., Park, J.W., Niazi, J.H., Kim, Y.S., Gu, M.B.: ssDNA Aptamer-Based Surface Plasmon Resonance Biosensor for the Detection of Retinol Binding Protein 4 for the Early Diagnosis of Type 2 Diabetes. Analytical Chemistry 80, 2867–2873 (2008)
29. Ostatná, V., Vaisocherová, H., Homola, J., Hianik, T.: Effect of the immobilisation of DNA aptamers on the detection of thrombin by means of surface plasmon resonance. Analytical and Bioanalytical Chemistry 391, 1861–1869 (2008)
30. de-los-Santos-Álvarez, N., Lobo-Castañón, M.J., Miranda-Ordieres, A.J., Tuñón-Blanco, P.: SPR sensing of small molecules with modified RNA aptamers: Detection of neomycin B. Biosensors and Bioelectronics 24, 2547–2553 (2009)
31. Wang, J., Lv, R., Xu, J., Xu, D., Chen, H.: Characterizing the interaction between aptamers and human IgE by use of surface plasmon resonance. Analytical and Bioanalytical Chemistry 390, 1059–1065 (2008)
32. Ndieyira, J.W., Watari, M., Barrera, A.D., Zhou, D., Vogtli, M., Batchelor, M., Cooper, M.A., Strunz, T., Horton, M.A., Abell, C., Rayment, T., Aeppli, G., McKendry, R.A.: Nanomechanical detection of antibiotic-mucopeptide binding in a model for superbug drug resistance. Nat. Nano. 3, 691–696 (2008)
33. Ji, H.-F., Gao, H., Buchapudi, K.R., Yang, X., Xu, X., Schulte, M.K.: Microcantilever biosensors based on conformational change of proteins. The Analyst 133, 434–443 (2008)
34. Vashist, S.K.: A Review of Microcantilevers for Sensing Applications. Journal of Nanotechnology Online 3, 1–15 (2007)

35. Shu, W., Laurenson, S., Knowles, T.P.J., Ko Ferrigno, P., Seshia, A.A.: Highly specific label-free protein detection from lysed cells using internally referenced microcantilever sensors. Biosensors and Bioelectronics 24, 233–237 (2008)
36. Lu, J., Ikehara, T., Zhang, Y., Mihara, T., Itoh, T., Maeda, R.: High Quality Factor Silicon Cantilever Driven by PZT Actuator for Resonant Based Mass Detection. In: Symposium on DTIP of MEMS & MOEMS, pp. 60–65. EDA Publishing (2008)
37. Li, S., Fu, L., Barbaree, J.M., Cheng, Z.Y.: Resonance behavior of magnetostrictive micro/milli-cantilever and its application as a biosensor. Sensors and Actuators B: Chemical 137, 692–699 (2009)
38. Hianik, T., Ostatná, V., Sonlajtnerova, M., Grman, I.: Influence of ionic strength, pH and aptamer configuration for binding affinity to thrombin. Bioelectrochemistry 70, 127–133 (2007)
39. Liss, M., Petersen, B., Wolf, H., Prohaska, E.: An Aptamer-Based Quartz Crystal Protein Biosensor. Analytical Chemistry 74, 4488–4495 (2002)
40. Baldrich, E., Restrepo, A., O'Sullivan, C.K.: Aptasensor Development: Elucidation of Critical Parameters for Optimal Aptamer Performance. Analytical Chemistry (2004)

Latent Semantic Analysis of the Languages of Life

Ryan Anthony Rossi[*]

Jet Propulsion Laboratory,
California Institute of Technology,
Pasadena, CA 91106, U.S.A.
ryan.a.rossi@jpl.nasa.gov

Abstract. We use Latent Semantic Analysis as a basis to study the languages of life. Using this approach we derive techniques to discover latent relationships between organisms such as significant motifs and evolutionary features. Doubly Singular Value Decomposition is defined and the significance of this adaptation is demonstrated by finding a phylogeny of twenty prokaryotes. Minimal Killer Words are used to define families of organisms from negative information. The application of these words makes it possible to automatically retrieve the coding frame of a sequence from any organism.

Keywords: Languages of Life, Motifs, Phylogeny, Minimal Killer Words, Doubly Singular Value Decomposition, Latent Semantic Analysis, Cross Language Information Retrieval, Knowledge Discovery, Data Mining.

1 Introduction

Latent Semantic Analysis (LSA) has been successfully used in applications such as natural language processing, speech recognition, cognitive modeling, document classification, search engines, and more recently security [1-8]. A significant application is in Cross Language Information Retrieval where direct matching of words is unlikely. A set of documents are used to create a reduced dimension space representation in which words that occur in similar contexts are near one another. This allows a query to retrieve relevant documents even if they have no words in common. LSA uses the Singular Value Decomposition (SVD) to model relationships between words that appear in similar contexts [2-4]. Cross Language LSA has been used to retrieve documents in different languages without having to translate the query [2]. From this method, queries in one language can retrieve documents in the same language and in different languages.

In this work we use techniques based on LSA to study the languages of life. In the second section we briefly describe the mathematical framework. In the third section we use cross language information retrieval of the languages of life to extract evolutionary features. The results validate the cross language information retrieval technique using unnatural languages. The algorithm proposed could be used for several applications such as studying the biological relationships between words and genes

---

[*] Work supported by NSF Grant ATM-0521002.

Z. Cai et al. (Eds.): ISICA 2009, CCIS 51, pp. 128–137, 2009.
© Springer-Verlag Berlin Heidelberg 2009

from various organisms. It is shown how these techniques can be applied to model an arbitrary organism's language. In the fourth section, we validate the Cross Language of Life results using a method to extract the most significant motifs in an organism. We propose a technique called Doubly SVD to generate a phylogeny of twenty pro- karyotes and show how this method can be extended to an arbitrary set of organisms. Finally we define Minimal Killer Words and describe how they can be used to auto- matically retrieve the frame of a coding sequence from an organism.

2 Mathematical Framework

The rows in our data set represent words and the columns represent gene sequences. If $M \in \Re^{nxm}$ then we decompose M into three matrices using the Singular Value Decomposition:

$$M = U S V^T \tag{1}$$

where $U \in \Re^{nxm}$, $S \in \Re^{mxm}$ and $V^T \in \Re^{mxm}$. The matrix S contains the singular values located in $[i, i]_{1...n}$ cells in descending order of magnitude and all other cells contain zero. The eigenvectors of MM^T make up the columns of U and the eigenvec- tors of M^TM make up the columns of V. As a consequence, the singular values are the square roots of the eigenvalues of MM^T and M^TM. The matrices U and V are or- thogonal, unitary and span vector spaces of dimension n and m, respectively. The inverses of U and V are their transposes.

$$
\begin{bmatrix} | & | & & | \\ d_1^g & d_2^g & \cdots & d_k^g \\ | & | & & | \end{bmatrix}
\begin{bmatrix} s_1 & 0 & 0 & 0 \\ 0 & s_2 & 0 & 0 \\ 0 & 0 & \ddots & 0 \\ 0 & 0 & 0 & s_k \end{bmatrix}
\begin{bmatrix} - d_1^w - \\ - d_2^w - \\ \vdots \\ - d_k^w - \end{bmatrix}
$$

$$\qquad U \qquad\qquad\qquad S \qquad\qquad\qquad V^T$$

The columns of U are the *principal directions of the genes* and the rows of V^T are the *principal directions of the words*. In a reduced space the rows of U are the coordi- nates of the words and the columns of V^T are the coordinates of the genes. The princi- pal directions are ranked according to the singular values and therefore according to importance.

An important theorem by Eckart and Young [9] demonstrates that the error in ap- proximating M by M_k is given by:

$$\left\| M - M_k \right\|_F = \min_{rank(B) \le k} \left\| M - B \right\|_F = \sqrt{\sigma_{k+1}^2 + .. + \sigma_{rM}^2} \tag{2}$$

Where,

$$M_k = U_k S_k V_k^T \tag{3}$$

and is the closest rank-k least squares approximation of M. This theorem can be used in two ways. To reduce noise by setting insignificant singular values to zero or by setting the majority of the singular values to zero and keeping only the few influential singular values. The latter approach allows us to create a reduced space from which words used in the same context with one another are represented close together.

3 Cross Language of Life

As our training corpus or dual language semantic space we have selected 4000 gene sequences from Escherichia coli K12. From the training corpus, we construct a word by gene sequence matrix for DNA and Protein languages. The protein language has an alphabet of 20 amino acids,

$$\alpha_p = \{A, R, N, D, C, E, Q, G, H, I, L, K, M, F, P, S, T, W, Y, V\}$$

and the DNA language has an alphabet of 4 nucleotides,

$$\alpha_d = \{A, C, G, T\}$$

We select an arbitrary gene in both amino acids and nucleotides. We have to consider that one trinucleotide codes an amino acid. Therefore, we construct words of length three in amino acids and length nine in nucleotides. We use overlapping words. We check to see if the word w exists in our lexicon. If it does not, we add this word to our lexicon and add a 1 to the cell corresponding to the word and gene. We do this for 4000 Escherichia coli K12 genes which we use as our training corpus.

Let D be a word by gene matrix of m DNA sequences and n^d nucleotide words and P be a word by gene matrix of m protein sequences and n^p amino acid words.

$$M = \left\{ \begin{matrix} D \\ P \end{matrix} \right\} \tag{4}$$

Such that M is of size $(n^d + n^p) \times m$ where column i is a vector representing amino acid and nucleotide words appearing in the union of sequence i expressed in the two languages. After we have constructed our word by gene training corpus, we apply the Singular Value Decomposition:

$$M_k = \begin{bmatrix} U_k^d \\ U_k^p \end{bmatrix} S_k V_k \tag{5}$$

Where U_k^d and U_k^p are k-dimensional vector lexicons for DNA and Protein sequences from Escherichia coli K12. In this example, we chose k to be 210. In this space, similar DNA and Protein words are given similar definitions, so this vector lexicon can be used for cross-language information retrieval.

	g_1	g_2	g_3	$\cdots$	g_k		T_1^d		T_1^p
d_1	—	—	—	—	—	d_1	—	d_1	0
d_2	—	—	—	—	—	d_2	—	d_2	0
d_3	—	—	—	—	—	d_3	—	d_3	0
$\cdots$	—	—	—	—	—	$\cdots$	—	$\cdots$	0
d_n	—	—	—	—	—	d_n	—	d_n	0
p_1	—	—	—	—	—	p_1	0	p_1	—
p_2	—	—	—	—	—	p_2	0	p_2	—
$\cdots$	—	—	—	—	—	$\cdots$	0	$\cdots$	—
p_n	—	—	—	—	—	p_n	0	p_n	—

$$US^{-1}$$

If we have two sets of sequences in both languages denoted T^d for DNA sequences and T^p for Protein sequences, we can retrieve sequences in either languages. As an example, we have a query in DNA and want to retrieve similar protein sequences. We find the similarity between the DNA query T_1^d and the protein database T^p using:

$$sim\langle US^{-1}T_1^D, \; US^{-1}T^P \rangle \tag{6}$$

Where,

$$sim\langle d_1, \; p_1 \rangle = \frac{d_1^T p_1}{\left\| d_1^T \right\|_2 \left\| p_1 \right\|_2} \tag{7}$$

This gives us a ranking of the relevant protein sequences.

3.1 Empirical Results

In the experiments below we use 4000 genes from Escherichia coli K12 as our dual-language semantic space. We use a technique called cross-language mate retrieval [2] to test the significance of our dual-language semantic space. We extract at random 1000 nucleotide sequences and their corresponding translated sequences in amino acids from Escherichia coli HS. These two strains of Escherichia coli are considered very similar. We use Escherichia coli HS as a starting point to see if our choice of k = 210 is at all reasonable for our dual-language semantic space.

The cross-language mate retrieval technique works by considering each of the 1000 nucleotide gene sequences as queries that have only one relevant 'mate' sequence in the corresponding amino acid language and conversely. We compute the accuracy by strictly testing if the cross language mate returned as the most relevant.

From the 1000 Escherichia coli HS gene sequences the cross-language mate is retrieved 94.8% of the time using the nucleotide sequences as queries against the amino acid sequences. Similarly, the cross-language mate is retrieved 94.4% of the time using the amino acid sequences as queries against the nucleotide sequences. We find

Table 1. Results using Escherichia coli K12 as our semantic space where we have genes from Escherichia coli HS as queries and sequences in both amino acids and nucleotides

Semantic Space	Query	Sequences	Accuracy
Escherichia coli K12	Escherichia coli HS Nucleotide	Escherichia coli HS Amino Acid	94.8%
	Escherichia coli HS Amino Acid	Escherichia coli HS Nucleotide	94.4%

that most of the sequences where the mate was not returned as the most significant are very short sequences (around 30-40 amino acids or 90-120 nucleotides). From this analysis we find that these two strains of Escherichia coli strongly share the same set of words of length three and are considered very similar.

In the experiment below we use the same Escherichia coli K12 dual-language semantic space. As our testing set we select 1000 genes from Shigella sonnei in both nucleotides and amino acids.

The same phenomenon is seen using Shigella sonnei and Yersinia pestis KIM.

We decided to do an experiment using genes from a wide range of organisms as our testing set. We picked up 2800 genes from 34 prokaryotes, 12 eukaryotes and 13 archaea. From each of these organisms we randomly selected on average 50 genes.

The cross-language mate is retrieved as the most relevant 59.57% of the time using the nucleotide sequences as queries against the amino acid sequences. Similarly, the cross-language mate is retrieved as the most relevant 57.78% of the time using the amino acid sequences as queries against the nucleotide sequences. Nevertheless, these results provide evidence that there exists a structure and similarity in the language that defines all organisms. A more systematic study is warranted to find this universal structure [11].

Table 2. Results using Escherichia coli K12 as our semantic space where we have genes from Shigella sonnei as queries and sequences in both amino acids and nucleotides

Semantic Space	Query	Sequences	Accuracy
Escherichia coli K12	Shigella sonnei Nucleotide	Shigella sonnei Amino Acid	92.00%
	Shigella sonnei Amino Acid	Shigella sonnei Nucleotide	93.30%

Table 3. Results using Escherichia coli K12 as our semantic space where we have genes from Yersinia pestis KIM as queries and sequences in both amino acids and nucleotides

Semantic Space	Query	Sequences	Accuracy
Escherichia coli K12	Yersinia pestis KIM Nucleotide	Yersinia pestis KIM Amino Acid	88.80%
	Yersinia pestis KIM Amino Acid	Yersinia pestis KIM Nucleotide	88.10%

Table 4. Results using Escherichia coli K12 as our semantic space where we have genes from a wide range of organisms as queries and sequences in both amino acids and nucleotides

Semantic Space	Query	Sequences	Accuracy
Escherichia coli K12	Variety of genes Nucleotide	Variety of genes Amino Acid	59.57%
	Variety of genes Amino Acid	Variety of genes Nucleotide	57.78%

4 Organism Motifs and Profiles

We start with a word by protein sequence matrix and compute the Singular Value Decomposition. The first few principal directions of U can be interpreted as containing the most significant characteristics or motifs of a particular organism [8]. As an example, the most significant value in the first principal direction provides an indication of the 'most important' motif of length three in that organism. The first few principal directions are viewed as a profile for an arbitrary organism. This can also be used to model a particular organism's language.

In the table below we select the first principal direction of several organisms including a dataset with 59 organisms from the three domains. We extract the ten most significant motifs for each organism/dataset.

Table 5. Ranking of motifs of length three in various organisms

Organism	Top 10 Motifs From Different Organisms
Escherichia coli K12	KLL, FFA, GAL, GLA, NAA, TAI, TRL, LAA, HLA, TAA
Shigella sonnei	KLL, FFA, GAL, GLA, NAA, TRL, VLL, LAA, PKE, HLA
Yersinia pestis KIM	VVG, IAL, QLA, CLA, MLL, LLA, CLL, SNL, QLE, MSL
59 Organisms	NVT, GEI, NTI, GRL, MAM, DHK, DIN, PGD, NKQ, HLH

Escherichia coli K12 and Shigella sonnei share most of the significant motifs with the exception of a few. Using the dataset with 59 organisms from the 3 domains we extract Universal Motifs. These are motifs that can be found in all organisms. A more systematic study of the Universal Motifs is needed to find biological meaning.

5 Phylogeny Using Doubly Singular Value Decomposition

We start with 20 prokaryotes. From each of these organisms we extract 1000 genes in amino acids and construct a word by gene matrix for each organism. We use overlapping words of length three.

We compute the Singular Value Decomposition for each word by gene matrix (corresponding to a prokaryote) and extract the first principal direction of the genes (of U) and the first principal direction of the words (of V^T) from each organism. From these principal directions, we derive two matrices:

	p_1^g	p_2^g	p_3^g	...	p_{20}^g		c_1^g	c_2^g	c_3^g	...	c_{1000}^g
c_1^w	—	—	—	—	—	p_1^w	—	—	—	—	—
c_2^w	—	—	—	—	—	p_2^w	—	—	—	—	—
c_3^w	—	—	—	—	—	p_3^w	—	—	—	—	—
c_4^w	—	—	—	—	—	p_4^w	—	—	—	—	—
c_5^w	—	—	—	—	—	p_5^w	—	—	—	—	—
c_6^w	—	—	—	—	—	p_6^w	—	—	—	—	—
c_7^w	—	—	—	—	—	p_7^w	—	—	—	—	—
...	—	—	—	—	—	...	—	—	—	—	—
c_{8000}^w	—	—	—	—	—	p_{20}^w	—	—	—	—	—

Computing the SVD of the matrix on the left; we find that the columns of U are the **principal directions of prokaryotes** and the highest absolute value of the principal direction of prokaryotes represents the **most influential word**. The rows of V^T are the **principal directions of words** for prokaryotes and the highest absolute value of the principal direction of words for prokaryotes represents the **most influential prokaryote**. Similarly, taking the SVD of the matrix on the right; we find that the columns of U are the **principal directions of genes** for prokaryotes and the highest absolute value of the principal direction of genes for prokaryotes represents the **most influential prokaryote**. The rows of V^T are the **principal directions of prokaryotes** and the highest absolute value of the principal direction of prokaryotes represents the **most influential gene**.

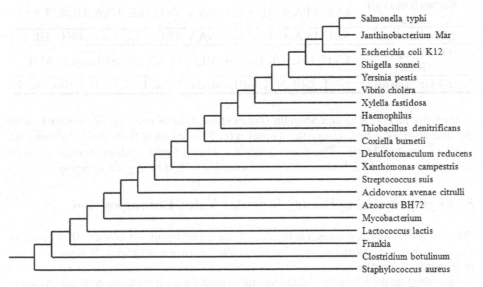

Fig. 1. Phylogeny of 20 prokaryotes using the principal direction of words

Our technique uses the principal directions of the words to build a comparatively accurate phylogenetic tree. We call this method doubly singular value decomposition (DSVD). These results are fairly strong. The influence values are close together with the exception of Staphyloccoccus aureus. The majority of the organisms are represented in the first principal direction, while Staphylococcus aureus is more accurately represented in the second direction which is orthogonal to the first. This could be due to major evolutionary differences between Staphylococcus aureus and the other prokaryotes.

6 Minimal Killer Words

Let A be a finite alphabet with the symbols {A, C, G, T} and A* be the set of words drawn from the alphabet A.

Let $L \subseteq A*$ be a language consisting of all factors of its words from a given organism. Let F_0, F_1 and F_2 be sets containing all factors of its words from the frames of an organism. A word $w \in A*$ is called a Minimal Killer Word for L if $w \notin F_0$ and $w \in F_2$ and all proper factors of w do not belong to M K (L). We denote by M K (L) the language of Minimal Killer Words for L.

Consider the subsequence AGGCTAGCT. We derive F_0, F_1 and F_2.

F_0 = {AGG, CTA, GCT, AGGCTA, AGGCTAGCT}
F_1 = {GGC, TAG, GGCTAG}
F_2 = {GCT, AGC, GCTAGC}

Therefore, M K (L) = {AGC}. The word GCTAGC is not minimal because a proper factor is in the set M K (L).

The following circular codes $\mathbf{X_0}$, $\mathbf{X_1}$, and $\mathbf{X_2}$ have been found as subsets of the genetic code [11-12].

$\mathbf{X_0}$ = {AAC, AAT, ACC, ATC, ATT, CAG, CTC, CTG, GAA, GAC, GAG, GAT, GCC, GGC, GGT, GTA, GTC, GTT, TAC, TTC}

$\mathbf{X_1}$ = {ACA, ATA, CCA, TCA, TTA, AGC, TCC, TGC, AAG, ACG, AGG, ATG, CCG, GCG, GTG, TAG, TCG, TTG, ACT, TCT}

$\mathbf{X_2}$ = {CAA, TAA, CAC, CAT, TAT, GCA, CCT, GCT, AGA, CGA, GGA, TGA, CGC, CGG, TGG, AGT, CGT, TGT, CTA, CTT}

However, it is the codes

$$T_0 = X_0 \cup \{AAA, TTT\}, \quad T_1 = X_1 \cup \{CCC\} \quad and \quad T_2 = X_2 \cup \{GGG\}$$

that we will consider as their union forms the entire genetic code. These codes have remarkable properties and have been used to find a universal coding frame [11]. We associate three T-Representations to any coding sequence u:

The first representation, T, is obtained by replacing each codon by 0 if it belongs to T_0, 1 if it belongs to T_1 and 2 if it belongs to T_2. This representation corresponds to the coding frame, while the two others represent the shifted frames. The second representation T^+ is obtained by elimination of the first letter of u and applying the preceding construction. Finally, the third representation T^{++} is obtained by eliminating a second letter from u and again applying the same construction.

We find the Minimal Killer Words of an organism using the representations T, T^+ and T^{++}. We arbitrarily selected Escherichia coli K12 and Shigella sonnei to use as a starting point. The set of Minimal Killer Words of length nine for Escherichia coli K12 and Shigella sonnei are shown below.

M K$_9$ (E) = { 122121222, 122222121, 211222122, 212221112, 212221221,
          221221121, 221222121, 222121221, 222122211 }

M K$_9$ (S) = { 122222121, 211222122, 221222121, 222122211 }

Interestingly, the Minimal Killer Words of length nine for Escherichia coli K12 and Shigella sonnei are formed from strictly T_1 and T_2. These words highlight evolutionary features in the organisms. As an example, M K$_9$(S) is a subset of M K$_9$ (E) indicating similarity. The Minimal Killer Words provide a way to define families of organisms using negative information.

The Minimal Killer Words allow us to automatically retrieve the coding frame of a sequence from an organism. This is a direct consequence of the definition and is a very powerful property. As an example, consider the set L of coding sequences where μ belongs to the set M K (L). Therefore, if μ appears in a coding sequence of L we can infer the coding frame of that sequence.

7 Conclusion

We describe techniques based on Latent Semantic Analysis to study the languages of life. Latent relationships between organisms such as motifs and evolutionary features are identified. Using DSVD we build a phylogeny of twenty prokaryotes. The definition of Minimal Killer Words allows for the retrieval of the coding frame from an organism. A more systematic study is warranted to find biological meaning of the motifs and Minimal Killer Words. A natural future direction will be to define more precisely this universal structure in the language of life.

Acknowledgments. We thank Jean-Louis Lassez for his help in clarifying our ideas as well as the many insightful discussions. This work was partly supported by a research fellowship through the National Aeronautics and Space Administration.

References

1. Landauer, T.K., Foltz, P.W., Laham, D.: Introduction to Latent Semantic Analysis. Discourse Processes 25, 259–284 (1998)
2. Landauer, T.K., Littman, M.L.: Fully automatic cross language document retrieval using latent semantic indexing. In: Cross Language Information Retrieval. Kluwer, Dordrecht (1998)
3. Deerwester, S., Dumais, S.T., Landauer, T.K., Furnas, G.W., Harshman, R.A.: Indexing by latent semantic analysis. JSIS 41(6), 391–407 (1990)
4. Lemaire, B.: Tutoring Systems Based on LSA. AIED, 527–534 (1999)

5. Alter, O., Brown, P.O., Botstein, D.: Singular value decomposition for genome-wide expression data processing and modeling. PNAS 97, 10101–10106 (2000)

6. Kintsch, W.: Comprehension: A Paradigm for Cognition. Cambridge University Press, Cambridge (1998)

7. Lassez, J.-L., Rossi, R., Jeev, K.: Ranking Links on the Web: Search and Surf Engines. In: Nguyen, N.T., Borzemski, L., Grzech, A., Ali, M. (eds.) IEA/AIE 2008. LNCS (LNAI), vol. 5027, pp. 199–208. Springer, Heidelberg (2008)

8. Lassez, J.-L., Rossi, R., Sheel, S., Mukkamala, S.: Signature Based Intrusion Detection System using Latent Semantic Analysis. IJCNN, 1068–1074 (2008)

9. Eckart, C., Young, G.: The approximation of one matrix by another of lower rank. Psychometrika 1, 211–218 (1936)

10. Berry, M., Browne, M.: Understanding Search Engines: Mathematical Modeling and Text Retrieval. SIAM, Philadelphia (1999)

11. Lassez, J.-L., Rossi, R.A., Bernal, A.E.: Crick's Hypothesis Revisited: The Existence of a Universal Coding Frame. AINA/BLSC, 745–751 (2007)

12. Lassez, J.-L.: Circular Codes and Synchronization. IJCIS 5, 201–208 (1976)

Protein Folding Simulation by Two-Stage Optimization[*]

A. Dayem Ullah[1], L. Kapsokalivas[1], M. Mann[2], and K. Steinhöfel[1]

[1] King's College London, Department of Computer Science, London WC2R 2LS, UK
[2] Bioinformatics Group, University of Freiburg, Georges-Köhler-Allee 106, 79016 Freiburg, Germany

Abstract. This paper proposes a two-stage optimization approach for protein folding simulation in the FCC lattice, inspired from the phenomenon of hydrophobic collapse. Given a protein sequence, the first stage of the approach produces compact protein structures with the maximal number of contacts among hydrophobic monomers, using the CPSP tools for optimal structure prediction in the HP model. The second stage uses those compact structures as starting points to further optimize the protein structure for the input sequence by employing simulated annealing local search and a 20 amino acid pairwise interactions energy function. Experiment results with PDB sequences show that compact structures produced by the CPSP tools are up to two orders of magnitude better, in terms of the pairwise energy function, than randomly generated ones. Also, initializing simulated annealing with these compact structures, yields better structures in fewer iterations than initializing with random structures. Hence, the proposed two-stage optimization outperforms a local search procedure based on simulated annealing alone.

1 Introduction

The question of how proteins fold and whether we can efficiently predict their structure remain the most challenging open problems in modern science. Proteins regulate almost all cellular functions in an organism. They are composed of amino acids connected in a linear chain. These chains fold in three-dimensional space. The 3D structure of proteins, also referred to as tertiary structure, plays a key role in their functionality. According to Anfinsen's thermodynamic hypothesis, proteins fold into states of minimum free energy and their tertiary structure can be predicted from the linear sequence of amino acids [2]. In nature, proteins fold very rapidly, despite the enormous number of possible configurations. This observation is known as the Levinthal paradox and implies that protein folding can not be a random search for the global minimum [20].

One of the driving forces of folding, mainly in globular proteins, is the hydrophobic interaction, which tends to pack hydrophobic amino acids in the center of the protein. This effect can be captured by the HP model, a coarse

---

[*] Research partially supported by EPSRC Grant No. EP/D062012/1.

Z. Cai et al. (Eds.): ISICA 2009, CCIS 51, pp. 138–145, 2009.

grained model, where the twenty different amino acids are classified into two classes, namely hydrophobic and polar [13]. Protein structure prediction is an NP-complete problem in the HP model [9]. Consequently, one can resort to constraint programming and stochastic local search to tackle this problem. Both techniques are commonly used to approach NP-complete problems.

Previous approaches using local search methods for protein structure prediction include tabu search [19,6], simulated annealing [3], and a population-based local search method [16]. Constraint programming techniques have been successfully applied to the protein structure prediction [4,11] as well as to resolve protein structures from NMR data [18].

The constraint programming approach, employed in [4], predicts the optimal structure of a protein in the HP model in very short computational time. Nevertheless, it is computationally intractable for more elaborate energy functions such as a 20 amino acid pairwise interactions energy function. Local search approaches, on the other hand, work well in practice for elaborate energy functions, despite the large number of iterations required. In this paper we aim to combine the advantages of both approaches.

We introduce a protein folding simulation procedure that employs two stages of optimization in order to find structures of minimum energy. The input protein sequence first collapses to a compact structure and then a slower annealing procedure follows to find the minimum energy structure. Specifically we employ the Constraint-based Protein Structure Prediction (CPSP) tools introduced in [22] to obtain an HP model conformation with maximal number of contacts among hydrophobic monomers in the FCC lattice. Then the CPSP output is given as input to a simulated annealing-based local search procedure which employs the pairwise energy function introduced in [7]. The choice of the FCC lattice is motivated by the fact that it was shown to yield very good approximations of real protein structures [23]. Also it does not suffer from the bipartiteness of the cubic lattice, which allows interactions only between amino acids of opposite parity in the chain. The two-stage optimization introduced in this paper, produces better conformations with less computational cost than local search alone that starts with randomly generated initial structures.

This paper is organized as follows. In Section 2 we first give the outline of the two-stage optimization as well as useful definitions for the detailed illustration of the method. In Section 3 we present experimental results for benchmarks along with a discussion. Finally, Section 4 contains the concluding remarks.

2   The Two-Stage Optimization

The approach works in three phases, namely, the sequence conversion, the constraint programming and the local search. The sequence conversion phase takes as input a protein sequence in the 20 letter amino acid alphabet and returns a converted sequence in the HP model. The resulting sequence consists of two kinds of amino acids, namely, hydrophobic and polar. Let us denote the input sequence as S_{orig} and the resulting sequence as S_{HP}. The constraint programming

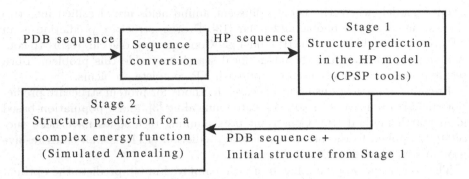

Fig. 1. An outline of the two-stage optimization

phase is the first stage of optimization and utilizes the CPSP tool *HPstruct* for optimal protein structure prediction in the HP model, introduced in [22]. The input to this tool is a sequence S_{HP}. For each sequence S_{HP}, the tool provides a set of structures in the FCC lattice with maximal number of H-monomer contacts. Let us denote this set of structures as $\mathcal{L}_{HP}$ to distinguish it from a set of randomly generated structures $\mathcal{L}_{rand}$. The final phase is the local search, which is also the second stage of optimization. It employs the simulated annealing algorithm with the pull-moves for triangular lattices and optimizes a more complex energy function. During this phase, each sequence S_{HP} is converted back to its original composition S_{orig}, first. Then, the local search is executed for a number of iterations with an initial structure from $\mathcal{L}_{HP}$. In the subsections below we analyze each phase of the approach.

2.1 Sequence Conversion

The conversion of a 20 letter amino acid sequence into an HP sequence utilizes the approach in [10]. This approach establishes a classification of the 20 amino acids into hydrophobic and polar as the result of a hierarchical clustering applied to the Miyazawa-Jernigan [21] pairwise contact values. In Table 1 we give the classification of amino acids used in the sequence conversion phase.

Table 1. Amino acid classification for sequence conversion

Hydrophobic	Polar	
C - Cysteine	H - Histidine	N - Asparagine
F - Phenylalanine	A - Alanine	D - Aspartic Acid
I - Isoleucine	T - Threonine	E - Glutamic acid
L - Leucine	G - Glycine	K - Lysine
M - Methionine	P - Proline	
V - Valine	S - Serine	
W - Trytophan	Q - Glutamine	
Y - Tyrosine	R - Arginine	

2.2 Constraint-Based Optimal Structure Prediction in HP-Models

The Constraint-based Protein Structure Prediction (CPSP) approach enables the calculation of optimal structures in 3D HP-models [22]. Using its implementation *HPstruct* [22], we enumerate for a given sequence S_{HP} a representing set of optimal structures $\mathcal{L}_{HP}$, all showing a compact hydrophobic core and shape.

The CPSP approach utilizes a database of precalculated (sub)optimal H-monomer placements (H-cores) [5]. These are sequence independent, defined by the number of H-monomers and the lattice. For a sequence S_{HP}, a self-avoiding walk describing constraint satisfaction problem is formulated that in addition constrains the H-monomers of the sequence to a given H-core. Any solution yields an optimal solution of the optimal structure prediction problem [4]. A screen through all appropriate H-cores enables the prediction of all optimal structures. For details on the CPSP approach see [4].

2.3 Local Search

Simulated annealing was introduced as an optimization tool independently in [17,8] (see also [1]). The algorithm traverses the space of conformations employing the pull-move neighborhood relation in triangular lattices [6]. The objective function to be optimized is the empirical contact potential described in [7], which is a 20 amino acid pairwise interactions energy function. A logarithmic cooling schedule is employed which was shown to converge to optimal solutions [14].

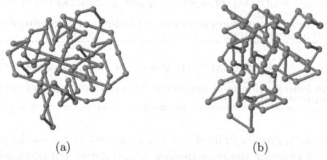

(a)   (b)

Fig. 2. 1CTF: (a) Structure produced by CPSP tool. (b) Predicted structure by two-stage optimization.

3   Experiments

Let us now describe the benchmark selection and the protocol we followed in our experiments. The protocol serves the purpose of a fair performance comparison between the two-stage optimization presented above and an optimization procedure, based on local search alone. Although the new approach involves the CPSP tool in addition to local search, in practice the CPSP tool's runtime is very short and can be neglected [22]. Thus, the performance of each method depends on

Table 2. Benchmark sequences from Protein Data Base (PDB) and the derived HP-sequences

PDB id: 4RXN	
length:	54
S_{orig}:	MKKYTCTVCGYIYDPEDGDPDDGVNPGTDFKDIPDDWVCPL CGVGKDEFEEVEE
S_{HP}:	HPPHPHPHHHPHHHPPPPPPPPPPHPPPPPHPPHPPPHHHP HHPHPPPPHPPHPP
PDB id: 1ENH	
length:	54
S_{orig}:	RPRTAFSSEQLARLKREFNENRYLTERRRQQLSSELGLNEA QIKIWFQNKRAKI
S_{HP}:	PPPPPHPPPPHPPHPPPHPPPPHHPPPPPPPHPPPHPHPPP PHPHHHPPPPPPH
PDB id: 4PTI	
length:	58
S_{orig}:	RPDFCLEPPYTGPCKARIIRYFYNAKAGLCQTFVYGGCRAKRNNF KSAEDCMRTCGGA
S_{HP}:	PPPHHHPPPHPPPHPPPHHPHHHPPPPPHHPPHHHHPHPPPPPPH PPPPPHHPPHPPP
PDB id: 2IGD	
length:	61
S_{orig}:	MTPAVTTYKLVINGKTLKGETTTKAVDAETAEKAFKQYANDNGVDGVW TYDDATKTFTVTE
S_{HP}:	HPPPHPPHPHHHPPPPHPPPPPPPPHPPPPPPPPHPPHPPPPPHPPHH PHPPPPPPHPHPP
PDB id: 1YPA	
length:	64
S_{orig}:	MKTEWPELVGKAVAAAKKVILQDKPEAQIIVLPVGTIVTMEYRIDRVRLFVD KLDNIAQVPRVG
S_{HP}:	HPPPHPPHHPPPHPPPPPHHHPPPPPPPHHHHPHPPHHHPHPHPHPPPHPHHHP PHPPHPPHPPHP
PDB id: 1R69	
length:	69
S_{orig}:	SISSRVKSKRIQLGLNQAELAQKVGTTQQSIEQLENGKTKRPRFLPELASALG VSVDWLLNGTSDSNVR
S_{HP}:	PHPPPHPPPPHPHPHPPPHPPPHPPPPPPHPPHPPPPPPPPPHHPPHPPPH PHPHPHHHPPPPPPPHP
PDB id: 1CTF	
length:	74
S_{orig}:	AAEEKTEFDVILKAAGANKVAVIKAVRGATGLGLKEAKDLVESAPAALKEGVSK DDAEALKKALEEAGAEVEVK
S_{HP}:	PPPPPPHPHHHHPPPPPPHPHHPPHPPPPPHPHPPPPPHHPPPPPPHPPPHPP PPPPPHPPPHPPPPPPHPHP

the energy reached, given a limited number of iterations for the local search. In other words, we examine the performance of simulated annealing with $\mathcal{L}_{HP}$ as the set of initial structures versus its performance with a randomly generated set of initial structures $\mathcal{L}_{rand}$.

Table 2 shows the benchmark sequences that we used for our experiments and their corresponding derived HP sequences. Benchmarks 4RXN, 4PTI, 1R69 and 1CTF are taken from [7]. In [7], the authors show that the empirical contact potential we employ in our approach, is able to discriminate the native structures of these 4 benchmarks. Benchmarks 1ENH, 2IGD and 1YPA are taken from [11].

For each protein sequence we performed 10 independent local search runs starting with random initial structures ($\mathcal{L}_{rand}$). Then we performed 10 independent runs for the two-stage approach where the initial structures for the local search phase are taken from the CPSP tool *HPstruct*, namely, the set of

Table 3. Comparison between the two-stage optimization and the local search alone

PDB id.	Length	Method	Avg S.E.	Avg F.E.	B.E.	Avg It.
4RXN	54	SA-only	-2.405	-161.625	-165.401	1,019,588
		2-stage	-140.377	-164.483	-167.781	816,844
1ENH	54	SA-only	-2.395	-149.456	-152.747	926,785
		2-stage	-127.347	-151.36	-153.098	904,368
4PTI	58	SA-only	-3.4799	-208.969	-215.698	1,056,287
		2-stage	-179.196	-210.357	-212.500	652,600
2IGD	61	SA-only	-2.5611	-178.941	-180.893	1,160,557
		2-stage	-163.201	-182.564	-183.205	706,773
1YPA	64	SA-only	-3.1447	-252.556	-256.017	1,004,750
		2-stage	-236.895	-256.504	-257.81	1,142,827
1R69	69	SA-only	-3.055	-202.338	-215.166	1,073,051
		2-stage	-188.966	-216.708	-219.402	1,001,264
1CTF	74	SA-only	-1.804	-221.713	-228.921	1,176,490
		2-stage	-176.088	-231.225	-233.86	1,043,517

Avg S.E. - Average Start Energy
Avg F.E. - Average Final Energy
B.E. - Best Energy Observed
Avg It. - Average Iterations

structures $\mathcal{L}_{HP}$. The number of initial structures in $\mathcal{L}_{HP}$ per benchmark was limited to 10 by setting approprietly the argument -maxSol for HPstruct. Each structure was used to initialize an independent run of simulated annealing for the two-stage approach. The initial temperature for simulated annealing in both approaches was set equal to $D * \ln(2)$, where D is an estimation for the maximum depth of local minima of the underlying energy landscape. In a similar fashion to [3], D was set equal to $n^{2/3}/c$, where n is the sequence length and c was chosen to be 1.5. Moreover, the maximum number of iterations of each run in local search phase was limited to 1,500,000 for both approaches.

In Table 3, for each protein sequence, the first row corresponds to the results observed from local search alone, whereas the second row corresponds to the results observed from the two-stage optimization. Figure 2 shows the best initial structure provided by the CPSP tools and the best structure obtained by the two-stage optimization for benchmark 1CTF.

As we can see in Table 3, the average energy of $\mathcal{L}_{HP}$ structures for the empirical contact potential is up to two orders of magnitude lower than the average energy of $\mathcal{L}_{rand}$ structures. We observe that, given the same maximum iteration limit to both approaches, the two-stage optimization always leads to conformations of lower energy on average compared to simulated annealing alone. Also, the two-stage optimization reached lower best energy conformations within the time limit for all benchmarks except 4PTI. Moreover, it requires on average less number of iterations to produce conformations within the average final energy level, except for benchmark 1YPA. In general, the two-stage optimization approach outperforms simulated annealing alone, since it reaches better final conformations in fewer iterations for the majority of benchmarks.

4   Conclusions

In this paper we introduced a two-stage optimization approach for protein folding simulation which combines the advantages of Constraint-based Protein Structure Prediction (CPSP) and local search. CPSP is very efficient for the HP model but computationally infeasible for a 20 amino acid pairwise interactions energy function. At the same time, local search methods are applicable to the problem, despite the considerable amount of computational effort required. Experimental results with PDB sequences show that the CPSP tool *HPstruct* produces compact structures, whose energy for the pairwise energy function is up to two orders of magnitude better than the energy of a randomly generated structure. Further experimentation with a simulated annealing-based local search procedure starting from these compact structures, shows that better structures are obtained in fewer iterations compared to simulated annealing with a random initialization. Hence, the proposed two-stage optimization outperforms a local search procedure based on simulated annealing alone.

References

1. Aarts, E.H.L.: Local search in combinatorial optimization. Wiley, New York (1998)
2. Anfinsen, C.B.: Principles that govern the folding of protein chains. Science 181, 223–230 (1973)
3. Albrecht, A.A., Skaliotis, A., Steinhöfel, K.: Stochastic protein folding simulation in the three-dimensional HP-model. Computational Biology and Chemistry 32(4), 248–255 (2008)
4. Backofen, R., Will, S.: A Constraint-Based Approach to Fast and Exact Structure Prediction in Three-Dimensional Protein Models. Constraints 11(1), 5–30 (2006)
5. Backofen, R., Will, S.: Optimally Compact Finite Sphere Packings - Hydrophobic Cores in the FCC. In: Amir, A., Landau, G.M. (eds.) CPM 2001. LNCS, vol. 2089, pp. 257–272. Springer, Heidelberg (2001)
6. Böckenhauer, H.-J., Dayem Ullah, A.Z.M., Kapsokalivas, L., Steinhöfel, K.: A Local Move Set for Protein Folding in Triangular Lattice Models. In: Crandall, K.A., Lagergren, J. (eds.) WABI 2008. LNCS (LNBI), vol. 5251, pp. 369–381. Springer, Heidelberg (2008)
7. Berrera, M., Molinari, H., Fogolari, F.: Amino acid empirical contact energy definitions for fold recognition in the space of contact maps. BMC Bioinformatics 4, 8 (2003)
8. Cerny, V.: A thermodynamical approach to the travelling salesman problem: an efficient simulation algorithm. Journal of Optimization Theory and Applications 45, 41–51 (1985)
9. Crescenzi, P., Goldman, D., Papadimitriou, C., et al.: On the complexity of protein folding. Journal of Computational Biology 5, 423–465 (1998)
10. Cheon, M., Chang, I.: Clustering of the Protein Design Alphabets by Using Hierarchical Self-Organizing Map. Journal of the Korean Physical Society 44, 1577–1580 (2004)

11. Dal Palú, A., Dovier, A., Fogolari, F.: Constraint Logic Programming approach to protein structure prediction. BMC Bioinformatics 5(1) (2004)
12. DeLano, W.L.: The PyMOL Molecular Graphics System. DeLano Scientific, Palo Alto, CA, USA (2002), http://www.pymol.org
13. Dill, K.A., Bromberg, S., Yue, K., et al.: Principles of protein folding - A perspective from simple exact models. Protein Sci. 4, 561–602 (1995)
14. Hajek, B.: Cooling schedules for optimal annealing. Mathem. Oper. Res. 13, 311–329 (1988)
15. Herráez, A.: Biomolecules in the Computer: Jmol to the rescue. Biochem. Educ. 34(4), 255–261 (2006)
16. Kapsokalivas, L., Gan, X., Albrecht, A.A., Steinhöfel, K.: Two Local Search Methods for Protein Folding Simulation in the HP and the MJ Lattice Models. In: Proc. BIRD 2008. CCIS, vol. 13, pp. 167–179. Springer, Heidelberg (2008)
17. Kirkpatrick, S., Gelatt Jr., C., Vecchi, M.P.: Optimization by simulated annealing. Science 220, 671–680 (1983)
18. Krippahl, L., Barahona, P.: PSICO: Solving Protein Structures with Constraint Programming and Optimization. Constraints 7(4-3), 317–331 (2002)
19. Lesh, N., Mitzenmacher, M., Whitesides, S.: A complete and effective move set for simplified protein folding. In: Proc. 7th Annual International Conference on Computational Biology, pp. 188–195. ACM Press, New York (2003)
20. Levinthal, C.: Are there pathways for protein folding? J. de Chimie Physique et de Physico-Chimie Biologique 65, 44–45 (1968)
21. Miyazawa, S., Jernigan, R.L.: Estimation of effective interresidue contact energies from protein crystal structures: quasi-chemical approximation. Macromolecules 18, 534–552 (1985)
22. Mann, M., Will, S., Backofen, R.: CPSP-tools - Exact and Complete Algorithms for High-throughput 3D Lattice Protein Studies. BMC Bioinformatics 9 (2008)
23. Park, B.H., Levitt, M.: The complexity and accuracy of discrete state models of protein structure. Journal of Molecular Biology 249(2), 493–507 (1995)

Search Direction Made Evolution Strategies Faster

Guangming Lin[1], Xin Lu[1], and Lishan Kang[2]

[1] Shenzhen Insititute of Information Technology, Shenzhen, China
[2] School of Computer Science, China University Geoscience, Wuhan, China

Abstract. Genetic operators are primarily search operators in Evolution Strategies (ES). In fact, there are two important issues in the evolution process of the genetic search: exploration and exploitation. The analysis of the impact of the genetic operators in ES shows that the Classical Evolution Strategies (CES) relies on Gaussian mutation, whereas Fast Evolution Strategies (FES) selects Cauchy distribution as the primary mutation operator. With the analysis of the basic genetic operators of ES as well as their performances on a number of benchmark problems, this paper proposes an Improved Fast ES (IFES) which applies the search direction of global optimization into mutation operation to guide evolution process convergence, thus making the process quicker.

Extensive empirical studies have been carried out to evaluate the performances of IFES, FES and CES. The experimental results obtained from four widely used test functions show that IFES outperforms both FES and CES. It is therefore concluded that it is important to strike a balance between exploration and exploitation.

Keywords: Search Direction Mutations, Evolution Strategies, Exploration and Exploitation.

1 Introduction

Evolutionary Algorithms (EAs) are a powerful stochastic search and optimization technique based on the mechanism of natural evolution. It is applicable to a wide range of problems for which little prior knowledge is available. Genetic operators play an important role in EAs. In general, an abstract task which is to be accomplished by EAs can be perceived as a search through a space of potential solution. Since usually we are following "the best" solution, we can view this task as an optimization process. For large search spaces, the methods of EAs are more sufficient than the classical exhaustive methods; they are stochastic algorithms whose search methods model some natural phenomena: genetic inheritance and Darwinian strife for survival [9]. The best known techniques in the class of EAs are Genetic Algorithms (GAs), Evolution Strategies (ESs), Evolutionary Programming (EP), and Genetic Programming (GP).

The Classical ES and Classical EP fist use a Gaussian mutation to generate new offspring and then use the deterministic selection to test them. There has been lots of work on different selection schemes for ES [1]. However work on mutations has been concentrated on self adaptation [2, 3] rather than new operators. Gaussian mutations

Z. Cai et al. (Eds.): ISICA 2009, CCIS 51, pp. 146–155, 2009.

seemed to be the only choice [2, 3]. Recently, Cauchy mutation has been proposed as a very promising search operator due to its higher probability of making long jumps [4, 5, 6]. However in [4, 5, 7] a fast EP and a fast ES based on Cauchy mutation were proposed.

It seems that there are two important issues in the evolution process of the genetic search: exploration and exploitation. Exploration is the creation of population diversity by exploring the search space; exploitation is the reduction of the diversity by focusing on the individuals of higher fitness, in other words, exploiting the fitness information (or knowledge) represented within the population. These factors are strongly related: an increase in the exploitation decreases the diversity of the population or the exploration, and vice versa. In other words, strong exploitation "supports" the premature convergence of the genetic search, but has excellent ability to tune solutions when they are near optima; a weak exploitation can make the genetic search ineffective, because exploration is lack of the power to improve the solution quality.

Based on the optimization theory, there are two important factors: search direction and search step size to affect the performance of the search algorithms. When the search points are far away from the global optimum in the initial search stages, increasing the search step size will increase the probability of escaping from a local optimum, and if the search direction is correct, it also has higher probability to reach the global optimum. On the other hand, with the progress of search, the current search points are likely to move closer and closer towards a global optimum. So it is necessary to restrict the step size in the later stages. However, it is hard to know in advance whether the search points are far from the global optimum. Unfortunately, the probability that a randomly generated initial population is very close to a global optimum is quite small in practice. It certainly worth enlarging the search step size in the early stages when we use EAs. In the final stages, the population of EAs tends to converge, and the step size tends to be reduced.

The rest of this paper is organized as follows. Section 2 formulates the global function optimization problem considered in this paper and describes the implementation of CES and FES. Section 3 analyzes the impact of the genetic operators on the exploration-exploitation tradeoff. Section 4 describes the implementation of VFES. Section 5 presents some discusses the experimental results. Finally, section 6 concludes with some discussions.

2   Function Optimization by Classical and Fast Evolution Strategies

A global minimization problem can be formalized as a pair (S, f), where $S \subseteq R^n$ is a bounded set on R^n and f: $S \mapsto R$ is an n-dimensional real-valued function. The problem is to find a point $x^{min} \in S$ such that $f(x^{min})$ is a global minimum on S. More specifically, it is required to find an $x^{min} \in S$ such that $\forall x \in S : f(x_{min}) \leq f(x)$, Where f does not need to be continuous but, it must be bounded. This paper only considers unconstrained function optimization.

2.1 Classical Evolution Strategies

According to the description by Bäck and Schwefel [7], in this study (μ,λ)-CES is implemented as follows:

1. Generate the initial population of μ individuals, and set k=1. Each individual is taken as a pair of real-valued vectors, $(x_i,\eta_i), \forall i \in \{1,2,...,\mu\}$, where x_i's are variables and η_i's are standard deviations for Gaussian mutations (also known as strategy parameters in self-adaptive evolutionary algorithms).

2. Evaluate the fitness score for each individual $(x_i,\eta_i), \forall i \in \{1,2,...,\mu\}$, of the population based on the objective function, $f(x_i)$.

3. Each parent $(x_i,\eta_i), \forall i \in \{1,2,...,\mu\}$, creates λ/μ offspring on average, so that a total λ offspring are generated: for i=1,..., μ, j=1,...,n, and k=1,..., λ,

$$x_k'(j) = x_i(j) + \eta_i(j) \, N(0,1) \tag{2.1}$$

$$\eta_k'(j) = \eta_i(j) \exp(\tau' N(0,1) + \tau N_j(0,1)) \tag{2.2}$$

Where $x_i(j)$, $x_k'(j)$, $\eta_i(j)$ and $\eta_k'(j)$ denote the j-th component of the vectors x_i, x_k', η_i and η_k', respectively. N(0,1) denote a normally distributed one-dimensional random number with mean 0 and standard deviation 1. $N_j(0,1)$ indicates that a new random number is generated for each value of j. The τ and τ' are commonly set to $\left(\sqrt{2\sqrt{n}}\right)^{-1}$ and $\left(\sqrt{2n}\right)^{-1}$ [7,8].

4. Calculate the fitness of each offspring $\left(x_i',\eta_i'\right), \forall i \in \{1,2,..., \lambda\}$.

5. Sort offspring $\left(x_i',\eta_i'\right), \forall i \in \{1,2,..., \lambda\}$ in a non-descending order according to their fitness values, and selection the μ best offspring out of λ to be parents of the next generation.

6. Stop if the stopping criterion is satisfied; otherwise, k=k+1 and go to Step 3.

2.2 Fast Evolution Strategies

The one-dimensional Cauchy density function centered at the origin is defined by:

$$f_t(x) = \frac{1}{\pi} \frac{t}{t^2 + x}, \qquad -\infty < x < \infty \tag{2.3}$$

where t>0 is a scale parameter. The corresponding distribution function is

$$F_t(x) = \frac{1}{2} + \frac{1}{\pi} \arctan(\frac{x}{t}).$$

The FES studied in this paper is exactly the same as CES described in last section except for Eq. (2.1) which is replace by the following [6]:

$$x_i{}'(j)= x_i(j)+ \eta_i(j) \; \sigma_j \tag{2.4}$$

Where σ_j is a Cauchy random variable with the scale parameter t=1, and is generated anew for each value of j. It is worth indicating that we leave Eq.(2.2) unchanged in FES in order to keep our modification of CES to a minimum. It is also easy to investigate the impact of the Cauchy mutation on ES when other parameters are kept the same.

3 Analysis the Impact of the Genetic Operators in ES

Evolution Algorithms (EAs) is a class of direct probabilistic search algorithm based on the model of organic evolution. In general, all EAs are characterized by the fact that they work on a population of individuals, each of which represents a search point in the space of potential solutions to a given optimization problem. The population undergoes subsequent modification steps by means of randomized genetic operators that are intended to model recombination (or crossover in GAs), mutation, and selection. The allocation of responsibilities to the genetic operators is relatively well understood: Mutation introduces innovations into the population, recombination changes the context of already available, useful information, and selection directs the search towards promising regions of the search space. Acting together, mutation and recombination *explore* the search space while selection *exploits* the information represented within the population. Next we will analyze the impact of these different genetic operators or various designs of any genetic operator on the balance between exploration and exploitation.

3.1 The Impact of Selection Operators

The selection operator uses the fitness information to favor individuals of higher quality to transfer their information to the next generation of the evolution process. It provides a mechanism to affect this balance towards exploitation—by increasing emphasis on the better individuals; or towards exploration—by providing similar chances to survive even for worse individuals. Informally, the term *selective pressure* is widely used to characterize the strong (high selective pressure) or the weak (small selective pressure) emphasis of selection on the best individuals. Selection operators guide individuals towards the better solutions according to the better search directions.

3.2 The Impact of Crossover Operators

The crossover operator usually destroys the links between parents and children. In other words, this operator focuses more on exploration but less on exploitation. When the population is almost with the same pattern, the crossover operator is lack of the power to improve the solution quality. The different crossover operators are analyzed in terms of *crossover point*. Under certain conditions a multi-point crossover is better in exploration than a one-point one, because increasing the number of crossover point will increase crossover's search step size.

3.3 The Impact of Mutation Operators

Like crossover, the term *step size* is used to characterize the different mutation operators. This is probably due to the fact that the large search step size mutation operator can more easily generate offspring that are quite distant from their parents occasionally, and thus more easily escape from local minima as compared with the small search step size mutation operator. On the other hand, the small search step size mutation operator could lead to finer local search.

4   An Improved Fast Evolution Strategies

Generally, Cauchy mutation performs better when the current search point is away from the global minimum, while Gaussian mutation is better at finding a local optimum in a given region. It would be ideal if Cauchy mutation is used when search points are far away from the global optimum and Gaussian mutation is adopted when search points are in the neighborhood of the global optimum. Unfortunately, the global optimum is usually unknown in practice, making the ideal switch from Cauchy to Gaussian mutation very difficult. Self-adaptive Gaussian mutation [7,2,9,15,16] is an excellent technique to partially address the problem. That is, the evolutionary algorithm itself will learn when to "switch" from one step size to another. However, there is room for further improvement to self-adaptive algorithms like CES or even FES.

In this section, we propose an improved FES (IFES) base on *mixing* (rather than switching) different mutation operators. The idea is to mix different search biases of Cauchy and Gaussian mutation. The implementation of IFES is very simple. It differs from FES and CES only in Step 3 of the algorithm described in Section 2.1. Instead of using Eq. (2.1) (for CES) or Eq. (2.4) (for FES) alone, IFES generates two offspring from each parent, one by Cauchy mutation and the other by Gaussian. The better one is then chosen as the offspring. The rest of the algorithm is exactly the same as FES and CES. Chellapilla [10] has presented some more results on comparing different mutation operators in EP.

We define a Boolean function *"better"* as:

$$
better\ (X_1, X_2) = \begin{cases} W(X_1) < W(X_2) & \text{TRUE} \\ W(X_1) > W(X_2) & \text{FALSE} \\ (W(X_1) = W(X_2)) \wedge (f(X_1) \le f(X_2)) & \text{TRUE} \\ (W(X_1) = W(X_2)) \wedge (f(X_1) > f(X_2)) & \text{FALSE} \end{cases}
$$

If *better* (X_1, X_2) is TRUE, this means that the individual X_1 is "better" than the individual X_2.

The new algorithm can now be described as follows:

Begin

        initialize $P = \{Z_1, Z_2, \ldots, Z_N\}$; $Z_i \in D^*$;

        $t := 0$;

        $Z_{best} = \arg \underset{1 \le i \le N}{Min} f(Z_i)$;

        $Z_{worst} = \arg \underset{1 \le i \le N}{Max} f(Z_i)$;

        while not abs $(F(Z_{best}) - F(Z_{worst})) \le \varepsilon$ **do**

            select randomly M points $Z_1', Z_2', \ldots, Z_M'$ from P to form the subspace V;

            select s points *randomly* $Z_1^*, Z_2^* \ldots Z_s^*$ from V;

            for i=1,…s **do**

                for j=1,…p+q **do**

                $Z_{Gi}^*(j) := Z_i^*(j) + \sigma_i(j) N_j(0, 1)$

                $Z_{Ci}^*(j) := Z_i^*(j) + \sigma_i(j) C_j(1)$

                $\sigma_i(j) := \sigma_i(j) \exp(\tau N(0,1) + \tau' N_j(0,1))$

                endfor

              if *better*(Z_{Gi}^*, Z_{Ci}^*)

                then $Z_i^{'*} := Z_{Gi}^*$ **else** $Z_i^{'*} := Z_{Ci}^*$;

            endfor

            $Z' = \arg \underset{1 \le i \le N}{Min} f(Z_i)$;

            if *better*(Z', Z_{worst}) **then** $Z_{worst} := Z'$;

            $t := t + 1$;

            $Z_{best} = \arg \underset{1 \le i \le N}{Min} f(Z_i)$;

            $Z_{worst} = \arg \underset{1 \le i \le N}{Max} f(Z_i)$;

            if abs $(f(Z_{best}) - f(Z_{worst})) \le \eta$ **.and.** $M \ge 3$ **then**

                $M := M - 1$;

        endwhile

        output t, Z_{best}, $f(Z_{best})$;

end

Where $Z_{Gi}^*(j)$, $Z_{Ci}^*(j)$ and $\sigma_i(j)$ denote the j-th component of the vectors Z_{Gi}^*, Z_{Ci}^* and σ_i, respectively. N(0,1) denotes a normally distributed one-dimensional random number with mean zero and standard deviation one. $N_j(0, 1)$ indicates that the Gaussian random number is generated anew for each value of j. $C_j(1)$ denotes a Cauchy distributed one-dimensional random number with $t=1$.

The factors τ and τ' have commonly set to $\left(\sqrt{2\sqrt{(p+q)}}\right)^{-1}$ and $\left(\sqrt{2(p+q)}\right)^{-1}$.

The new algorithm has the two important features:

(1) This algorithm is an ergodicity search. During the random search of the sub-space, we employ a "non-convex combination" approach, that is, the coefficients a_i of $Z' = \sum_{i=1}^{m} a_i Z_i$ are random numbers in the interval [-0.5, 1.5]. This ensures a non-zero probability that any point in the solution space is searched. This ergodicity of the algorithm ensures that the optimum is not ignored.

(2) The monotonic fitness decrease of the population (when the minimum is required). Each iteration $(t \rightarrow t+1)$ of the algorithm discards only the individual having the worst fitness in the population. This ensures a monotonically decreasing trend of the values of objective function of the population, which ensures that each individual of the population will reach the optimum.

5 Experimental Studies

In order to further explain the impact, we have studied some functions by our research on ESs.

Also we drew some conclusions from the results of the comparison of the different genetic operators. The following sets of functions were studied:

(Corridor) $F_1(x) = -\sum_{i=1}^{n} x_i$, $n = 3$

Constraints:

$$G_j(x) = \begin{cases} -x_j + 100 \geq 0, \ j = 1(1)n \\ x_{j-n+1} - \dfrac{1}{j-n} \sum_{i=1}^{j-n} x_i + \sqrt{\dfrac{j-n+1}{j-n}} \geq 0, \ n+1 \leq j \leq 2n-1 \\ -x_{j-2n+2} + \dfrac{1}{j-2n+1} \sum_{i=1}^{j-2n+1} x_i + \sqrt{\dfrac{j-2n+2}{j-2n+1}} \geq 0, 2n \leq j \leq 3n-2 \end{cases}$$

Minimum: $x_i^* = 100$, $F(x^*) = -300$, $i = 1(1)n$

Start: $x_i^{(0)} = 0$, $F(x^{(0)}) = 0$, $i = 1(1)n$

(Hyper banana) $F_2(x) = \sum_{i=2}^{n} \left[(x_1 - x_i^2)^2 + (x_i - 1)^2\right]$ $n = 5$

Minimum: $x_i^* = 1$, $F(x^*) = 0$, $i = 1(1)n$

Start: $x_i^{(0)} = 10$, $F(x^{(0)}) = 32724$, $i = 1(1)n$

(Sphere) $F_3(x) = \sum_{i=1}^{n} x_i^2$, $n = 5$

Minimum: $x_i^* = 0$, $F(x^*) = 0$, $i = 1(1)n$

Start: $x_i^{(0)} = 10$, $F(x^{(0)}) = 500$, $i = 1(1)n$

(Schwefel) $F_4(x) = \sum_{i=1}^{n} (\sum_{j=1}^{i} x_j)^2$, $n = 5$

Minimum: $x_i^* = 0$, $F(x^*) = 0$, $i = 1(1)n$

Start: $x_i^{(0)} = 10$, $F(x^{(0)}) = 5500$, $i = 1(1)n$

A typical ES utilizes Guassian mutation as the primary search operator. That means the variance is generated by normal (Gaussian) distribution. In order to compare, we adopt another mutation operator: Cauchy mutation. That mutation operator means the variance is generated by Cauchy distribution (obtained by a variable of normal distribution divided by another variable of normal distribution). Clearly, the search step size of Cauchy mutation is larger than the one of Gaussian mutation. In order to avoid the above case of F_2, we design an improved algorithm called the improved FES(IFES) and the original ESs with Gaussian mutation is called GES. IFES generates two offspring from each parent, one by Cauchy mutation and the other by Gaussian mutation. The better one is then chosen as the offspring. In this study, the number of parent is 10, the number of descendants is 100, the selection operator is (μ, λ) selection, the recombination operator is discrete recombination of pairs of parents. The following table shows the results of the studies, taken over 20 trials for each function respectively.

Table 1. Comparison between IFES and FES on F_1 - F_4. All results have been averaged over 20 runs, where "Mean Best" indicates the mean best function values found in the last generation.

Function	No. of Gen.	IFES Mean Best	FES Mean Best
F_1	50	-295.43	-290.35
F_2	50	2.43239e-06	0.362848
F_3	50	2.73408e-12	8.78729e-12
F_4	50	1.72527e-11	5.13986e-10

From above table, we can see that the improved algorithm (IFES) can gain efficiencies for every function somewhat, especially for F_2.

6 Conclusion

Except genetic operators, there are other strategy parameters to impact on the balance. For example, the population size also has impact on the diversity of the population, so it can impact the balance as well. Also we can change the object function by increasing or decreasing penalty coefficients for violated constraints to strike the tradeoff.

As EAs implement the idea of evolution, and as evolution itself must have evolved to reach its current state of sophistication, it is natural to expect adaptation to be used in not only for finding solutions to a problem, but also for tuning the algorithm to strike the balance for efficiency. In EAs, not only do we need to choose the algorithm, representation and operators for the problem, but we also need to choose parameter values and operator probabilities for the evolutionary algorithm, so that the algorithm will find the solution finally and, what is also important, find it efficiently. Researchers have used various ways of finding good values for the strategy parameters to strike the balance between exploration and exploitation, as these can significantly affect the performance of the algorithm. They tried to modify the values of strategy parameters during the run of the algorithm; it is possible to do this by using some (possibly heuristic) rule (deterministic) [11], by taking feedback from the current state of the search (adaptive), for example, Rechenberg's '1/5 success rule', or by employing some self-adaptive mechanism [12]. Clearly, by changing these values while the algorithm is searching for the solution of the problem, further efficiencies can be gained.

Evolutionary Computation can solve many large search space problems that the traditional methods cannot handle. But if we want to make the Evolutionary Algorithms more efficient, we must handle this problem from the main part of EC: Genetic Search. By analyzing the evolution progress of genetic search, we find two factors that impact the behavior or the performance of EAs: Exploration and Exploitation. Through the analysis of genetic operators and discussion of implementation, we can conclude that in the early stage of the EA, we'd better focus on exploration, because it can avoid the local optimum and premature convergence; in the later stage of the EA, we have to emphasize on exploitation, for its ability to improve the solution quality. Once the balance between the two factors is struck, further efficiencies of EAs can be gained.

Acknowledgements. This work was supported by the National Natural Science Foundation of China (No.60772163) and the Shenzhen Scientific Technology Project (No. SY200806300270A). Thanks especially give to the anonymous reviewers for their valuable comments.

References

1. Baeck, T.: Evolutionary Algorithms in Theory and Practice. Oxford University Press, New York (1996)
2. Fogel, D.B.: An Introduction to Simulated Evolutionary Optimization. IEEE Trans. on Neural Networks 5(1), 3–4 (1994)
3. Baeck, T., Schwefel, H.-P.: Evolutionary Computation: An Overview. In: Proc. of the 1996 IEEE Int'l. Conf. on Evolutionary Computation (ICEC 1996), Nagoya, Japan, pp. 20–29. IEEE Press, New York (1996)
4. Yao, X., Liu, Y.: Fast Evolutionary Programming. In: Fogel, L.J., Angeline, P.J., Baeck, T. (eds.) Evolutionary Programming V: Proc. of the Fifth Annual Conference on Evolutionary Programming, pp. 257–266. The MIT Press, Cambridge (1996)
5. Yao, X., Lin, G., Liu, Y.: An Analysis of Evolutionary Algorithms Base on Neighborhood and Step Sizes. In: Angeline, P.J., McDonnell, J.R., Reynolds, R.G., Eberhart, R. (eds.) EP 1997. LNCS, vol. 1213, pp. 297–307. Springer, Heidelberg (1997)

6. Kappler, C.: Are Evolutionary Algorithms Improved by Large Mutations? In: Ebeling, W., Rechenberg, I., Voigt, H.-M., Schwefel, H.-P. (eds.) PPSN 1996. LNCS, vol. 1141, pp. 346–355. Springer, Heidelberg (1996)
7. Yao, X., Liu, Y.: Fast Evolutiona Strategies. Control and Cybernetics 26(3), 467–496 (1997)
8. Baeck, T., Gudolph, G., Schwefel, H.-P.: Evolutionary Programming and Evolution Strategies: Similarities and Differences. In: Fogel, D.B., Atmar, W. (eds.) Proc. of the Second Ann. Conf. on Evol. Prog., pp. 11–22. Evolutionary Programming Society, La Jolla
9. Davis, L.: Genetic Algorithms and Simulated Annealing, pp. 1–11. Morgan Kaufmann Publishers, Los Altos (1987)
10. Chellapilla, K.: Combining mutation operators in evolutionary programming. IEEE Trans. on Evolutionary Computation 2(3), 91–96 (1996)
11. Michalewicz, Z.: Genetic Algorithms + Data Structures = Evolution Programs, 3rd edn. Springer, Heidelberg (1996)
12. Schwefel, H.-P.: Evolution and Optimum Seeking. Sixth Generation Computer Technology Series. Wiley, Chichester (1995)
13. Guo, T.: Evolutionary Computation and Optimization. PhD thesis, Wuhan University, Wuhan (1999)
14. Guo, T., Kang, L.: A New Evolutionary Algorithm for Function Optimization. Wuhan University Journal of Natural Sciences 4(4), 404–419 (1999)
15. Lin, G., Kang, L., Chen, Y., McKay, B., Sarker, R.: A Self-adaptive Mutations with Multi-parent Crossover Evolutionary Algorithm for Solving Function Optimization Problems. In: Kang, L., Liu, Y., Zeng, S. (eds.) ISICA 2007. LNCS, vol. 4683, pp. 157–168. Springer, Heidelberg (2007)
16. Lin, G., Kang, L., Chen, Y., McKay, B., Sarker, R.: Comparing the Selective Pressure of Different Selection Operators Progress in Intelligence Computation and Applications, pp. 41–45 (2007)

Topology Organization in Peer-to-Peer Platform for Genetic Algorithm Environment

Hong Yao and Linchen Yu

School of Computer Science and Technology
China University of Geosciences
Wuhan, 430074, China
yaohong@cug.edu.cn

Abstract. Genetic algorithms (GAs) have the inherent nature of parallel search. With the advantage of the computing power of PCs, GA computing environment can be shifted from a single machine to Internet. Topology, the organization of the peers, as well as their dynamic change and maintaining mechanisms, is important to organize an efficient and stable topological structure. A new topology is proposed in this paper to create a hybrid structure for large scale of peers. The whole structure is divided into two layers. The upper part is composed by super nodes, while the lower part is composed by the ordinary nodes. Testing shows that it is good for maintaining the platform stable and scalable.

Keywords: peer-to-peer network, topology, super node, ordinary node.

1 Introduction

Genetic algorithms (GAs) have been demonstrated to be an effective problem-solving tool. The evolutionary process has the inherent nature of parallel search. There is an approach of reducing computational workload is to develop a GA computing platform, which is running in many PCs over network. Paper [1] brings forward a layered architecture for this job by K.C. Tan and M.L. Wang, etc. However, how to organize the topology is not clearly defined.

For the advantages of non-centralization, scalability, robustness, load balancing, and etc, P2P [2] technology has become more and more popular. With the advancement of hardware and network, end nodes which are considered at the edge of Internet have better performance and bigger bandwidth. As end nodes wish and have ability to share resources, the traditional *Client/Server* (C/S) model is challenged by the *Peer-to-Peer* (P2P) model. End nodes are organized in application layer of Internet, which forms the overlay network.

1.1 Related Works

We can divide P2P overlay network into four modules according to their topology, which are centralized topology, decentralized unstructured topology, decentralized structured topology, and partially decentralized topology.

Z. Cai et al. (Eds.): ISICA 2009, CCIS 51, pp. 156–161, 2009.

The biggest advantage of centralized topology is simple maintaining and efficient discovery. Because resources discovery depends on centralized catalog system, the algorithm is effective and supporting complex inquiry. The most major problem is similar to the traditional client/server structure, which is easy to result in the server breakdown, situation of visiting hotspot.

The distributed unstructured model distributes the resources in each peer. There is no centralized server, and every peer in the network is equally. Its disadvantage is that in order to search some resources, the request packets may pass through the entire network or at least a very great scope.

Distributed Hash Table, called DHT [3] for short, is actually an enormous hash table maintained by a large number of peers in a wide area. Peers will dynamic join and leave DHT structure adaptively, and it has the advantages of scalability, robustness, uniform distribution of node ID, and self-organizing capacity. The biggest problem is that maintenance of DHT is complex, especially when peers join and leave frequently, it will greatly increase the cost of maintenance. Another problem is that DHT only supports precise search, but not complex enquiries based on content or semantic.

Hybrid topology [4], is also called partially decentralized topology, is a balance of centralized structure and distributed structure, utilizing both of their merit. The advantages of this model is that compared to distributed model, it will reduce inquiry packets from dissemination, and compared to centralized model, it will reduce the influence of failure in the centre node. The main disadvantage is that it is difficult to partition super peer and ordinary peer [5]. Besides, the two kinds of peers are not easy to manage.

1.2 Contribution of This Work

Even though the hybrid model is popular currently, it also faces the following drawback: 1. How to judge peers' service ability and partition SN and ON rationally; 2. How to manage peers on upper layer, locating near neighbors fast, and avoiding isolated peers; 3. How to reduce churning of peers on lower layer when peers leaving on upper layer; 4. How to reduce searching packets from flooding in the network, improving search efficiency.

This paper introduces a novel hybrid topology, which is as follows: 1. Ring based topology of super peers, providing fast search of neighbors and avoiding isolated peers; 2. Ordinary peers will maintain backup father nodes, reducing churning when some father nodes leave; 3. Based on peers' value of relative ability, partitioning SN and ON according to the size of peers' number, balancing the system's load as far as possible.

2 Design of Overlay

2.1 System Overview

The overall topology adopts the popular two-tier structure, as shown in Figure 1. The upper layer is composed by those peers with strong power, called super node (SN for short), while the lower layer is composed by the others, called ordinary node (ON for short). The hierarchical structure not only reduces the size of distributed peers on upper tier, but also disperses pressure of the central peers. It integrates the advantages of central and distributed structure.

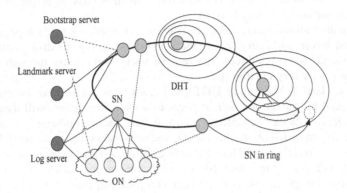

Fig. 1. Overlay Topology

Neighbor peers of super node are organized as a serial of rings based on delay. On the one hand, it is used for searching low delay neighbors, and on the other hand it avoids isolated node group from keeping sampling neighbor peers of delay in every interval.

Besides, there is also a distributed hash table (called DHT for short) for managing all super nodes. It is used for searching precise resources. It can find the specified resource within Log(n) hops in a DHT network of n nodes. This mechanism is a supplement of the searching strategy. It not only avoids the searching packets from flooding over the entire network, but also ensures scarce resources to be found with high probability.

The management of ONs is like centralized approach. Every ON should connect to a SN, and only keeps the relation with its father nodes. This structure will take low overhead of ONs, because they need neither maintain neighbor peers, nor manage resources, and most of this work is done by their father SNs.

2.2 Super Node Structure

Each SN will maintain a certain number of neighbor nodes, and each node is placed in a specified ring according to the delay, as is shown in Figure 2.

Peer A will randomly select some neighbors such as peer B from each ring periodically. Then A will send B a packet containing some other peers from its rings.

When peer B receives the packet from peer A, it will measure the delay with A and all the peers in the packet, and then add new peers in its rings, or update the old peers' delay.

This ring structure is different from former methods that only maintaining the near neighbor. It improves the coverage of each node. In the search process, it reduces the frequency of communication between peers effectively, reducing system load too. On neighbor's discovery mechanism, we use Gossip protocol [6].

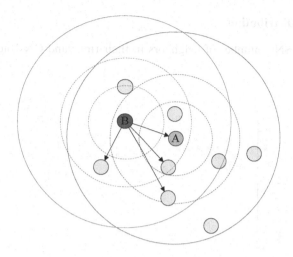

Fig. 2. Maintenance of ring structure

2.3 Ordinary Node Organization

ONs are on the lower layer of the system, because of their weak service capability, they only maintain their own resources, and don't transmit packets for other peers. This will not only reduce the radius of the entire network, increase search coverage, but also balance performance of all peers, improve efficiency of the whole system.

Every ON must connect to a SN, taking the SN as its father node, and the SN will process most of its request, including searching for neighboring nodes, publishing resources, searching resources, and so on. Therefore, the upper SN nodes are important to the lower ONs. If father node leaves, and the ON can't quickly find another father node to replace the former one, it will make the ON instability. So how to manage the ONs effectively is very important for the users on this layer.

3   Performance Evaluations

Test environment is shown in Table 1. The network environment is LAN. There is one Bootstrap server, one Landmark server, and 120 client peers.

Table 1. Test Environment

Node	OS	CPU	Memory	Bandwidth
Bootstrap server	Red Hat9.0	P4 2.4G Hz	1GB	100Mbps
Landmark server	Windows XP	Celeron(R) 1.70G Hz	256MB	100Mbps
Client peer	Windows XP	Athlon(tm) XP 2500+	512MB	100Mbps
...	...	...	...	...

3.1 Neighbor Distribution

Figure 3 shows SNs' number of neighbors in their rings and ONs' number of father nodes.

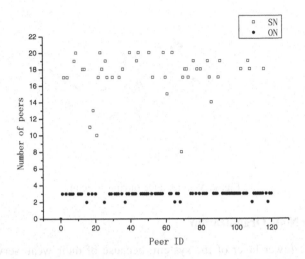

Fig. 3. Distribution of neighbor/father nodes

Because we limit the maximum number of SN's neighbors is 20, we can see from the figure that they are almost between 17 and 20, indicating the efficient and stable structure of neighbor peers in the system.

In addition, as can be seen from the figure, almost all the number of ONs' father nodes is 3, because we assign a primary father node and two backup father nodes to an ON. When an ON logins successfully, it will fetch information of other SNs from its primary father node. So the peers on the lower layer will not be jittering by the departure of peers on the upper layer.

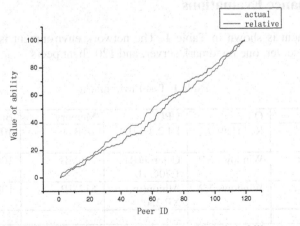

Fig. 4. Distribution of value of actual/relative ability

3.2 SN/ON Partition

The partition of SN and ON is according to their service ability. Our goal is that those peers with high value of ability act as SN, and those with low value of ability act as ON. Besides, the proportion of SN and ON should be controllable, avoiding imbalance for peers dynamic joining and leaving.

Figure 4 shows the distribution of peers' value of actual ability and value of relative ability namely random number.

4 Conclusion

This paper proposes a new P2P topology based on current existing mode for GA distributed computing environment. The whole structure is divided into two layers, and the upper part is composed by those peers with strong power, called super nodes, while the lower part is composed by the others, called ordinary nodes. Testing shows that it is good for maintaining the platform stable and scalable, as well as processing joining and leaving of the peers. Besides, it improves the system's load balancing.

However, there are still some thorough problems to be solved. For example, how to figure out the upper limit of neighbors on SN is a question that should be solved according to actual network environment. Moreover, the choice of Landmark servers in large-scale environment is also difficult to determine.

In the near future, we will shift some implementation of GA, such as TSP problem, to this overlay network.

References

[1] Tan, K.C., Wang, M.L., Peng, W.: A P2P Genetic Algorithm Environment for the Internet. Communications of the ACM 48(4), 113–116 (2005)

[2] Kant, K., Iyer, R., Tewari, V.: A Framework for classifying peer-to-peer technologies. In: Proceedings of the 2nd IEEE/ACM International Symposium on Cluster Computing and the Grid (CCGRID 2002), pp. 368–379. ACM Press, USA (2002)

[3] Jain, S., Mahajan, R., Wetherall, D.: A study of the performance potential of DHT-based overlays. In: Proceedings of the 4th conference on USENIX Symposium on Internet Technologies and Systems, Seattle, WA. USENIX Association, USA (March 2003)

[4] Xiao, L., Zhuang, Z., Liu, Y.: Dynamic Layer Management in Superpeer Architectures. IEEE Transactions on Parallel and Distributed Systems 16(11), 1078–1091 (2005)

[5] Garbacki, P., Epema, D.H.J., van Steen, M.: Optimizing Peer Relationships in a Super-Peer Network. In: Proceedings of the 27th International Conference on Distributed Computing Systems, pp. 31–42. IEEE Computer Society, USA (2007)

[6] Baset, S.A., Schuizrinne, H.G.: An Analysis of the Skype Peer-to-Peer Internet Telephony Protocol. In: Proceedings of 25th IEEE International Conference on Computer Communications, Barcelona, Spain, pp. 1–11. IEEE Computer Society, Los Alamitos (2006)

Almost Periodic Solutions for Shunting Inhibitory Cellular Neural Networks with Time-Varying and Distributed Delays

Chaojin Fu and Ailong Wu

Department of Mathematics, Hubei Normal University,
Huangshi 435002, China
chaojinfu@126.com, alequ@126.com

Abstract. This paper discusses shunting inhibitory cellular neural networks (SICNNs) with time-varying and distributed delays. It introduces the establishment of some new suffcient conditions for the existence and exponential stability of the almost periodic solutions without assuming the global Lipschitz conditions of activation functions. Finally, it presents a numerical example to demonstrate the effectiveness of the obtained result.

Keywords: Almost periodic, Shunting inhibitory cellular neural networks, Stability.

1 Introduction

Recently, the dynamical behaviors of almost periodic solutions for shunting inhibitory cellular neural networks (SICNNs) have been extensively studied (see $[1-11]$), due to SICNNs have been extensively applied in psychophysics, speech, perception, robotics, adaptive pattern recognition, vision, and image processing. Many important results have been established and successfully applied to signal processing, pattern recognition, associative memories, and so on. However, in the existing literatures (see $[1-3, 5-9]$), almost all results on the stability of almost periodic solutions for SICNNs are obtained under global Lipschitz neuron activations. When neuron activation functions do not satisfy global Lipschitz conditions, people want to know whether the SICNNs is stable. In practical engineering applications, people also need to present new neural networks. Therefore, developing a new class of SICNNs without global Lipschitz neuron activation functions and giving the conditions of the stability of new SICNNs are very interesting and valuable.

Consider the following SICNNs with time-varying and distributed delays:

$$x'_{ij}(t) = -a_{ij}(t)x_{ij}(t) - \sum_{C_{kl} \in N_r(i,j)} C_{ij}^{kl}(t)f(x_{kl}(t - \tau(t)))x_{ij}(t)$$

$$- \sum_{C_{kl} \in N_q(i,j)} B_{ij}^{kl}(t) \int_0^\infty K_{ij}(u)f(x_{kl}(t - u))du\,x_{ij}(t) + L_{ij}(t), \quad (1.1)$$

Z. Cai et al. (Eds.): ISICA 2009, CCIS 51, pp. 162–170, 2009.
© Springer-Verlag Berlin Heidelberg 2009

where $i = 1, \cdots, m$, $j = 1, \cdots, n$, C_{ij} is the cell at the (i, j) position of the lattice, the r-neighborhood $N_r(i, j)$ of C_{ij} is

$$N_r(i, j) = \{C_{kl} : \max(|k - i|, |l - j|) \leq r, 1 \leq k \leq m, 1 \leq l \leq n\},$$

$N_q(i, j)$ is similarly specified. x_{ij} is the activity of the cell C_{ij}, $L_{ij}(t)$ is the external input to C_{ij}, $a_{ij}(t) > 0$ is the passive decay rate of the cell activity, $C_{ij}^{kl}(t) \geq 0$ and $B_{ij}^{kl}(t) \geq 0$ are the connections or coupling strengths of postsynaptic activity of the cells in $N_r(i, j)$ and $N_q(i, j)$ transmitted to the cell C_{ij}, respectively. The activity function $f(x_{kl})$ is a continuous function representing the output or firing rate of cell C_{kl}, and $\tau(t) \geq 0$ is the transmission delay.

Throughout this paper, we will assume that $\tau(t) : R \to R$ is an almost periodic function, and $0 \leq \tau(t) \leq \bar{\tau}$, where $\bar{\tau} \geq 0$ is a constant.

Set $\{x_{ij}(t)\} = (x_{11}(t), \cdots, x_{1n}(t), \cdots, x_{m1}(t), \cdots, x_{mn}(t))$, for $\forall x = \{x_{ij}(t)\} \in R^{m \times n}$, we define the norm $\|x\| = \max_{(i,j)} \{|x_{ij}(t)|\}$.

Set $B = \{\varphi \mid \varphi = \{\varphi_{ij}(t)\} = (\varphi_{11}(t), \cdots, \varphi_{1n}(t), \cdots, \varphi_{m1}(t), \cdots, \varphi_{mn}(t))\}$, where φ is is an almost periodic function on R. For $\forall \varphi \in B$, we define the norm $\|\varphi\|_B = \sup_{t \in R} \|\varphi(t)\|$, then B is a Banach space.

The initial conditions associated with system (1.1) are of the form

$$x_{ij}(s) = \varphi_{ij}(s), s \in (-\infty, 0], i = 1, \cdots, m, j = 1, \cdots, n, \qquad (1.2)$$

where $\varphi = \{\varphi_{ij}(t)\} \in C((-\infty, 0], R^{m \times n})$.

Definition 1.1. Let $k \in Z^+$. A continuous function $u : R \to R^k$ is called almost periodic if for each $\varepsilon > 0$ there exists a constant $l(\varepsilon) > 0$ such that every interval of length $l(\varepsilon)$ contains a number δ with the property that

$$\|u(t + \delta) - u(t)\| < \varepsilon \quad \text{for all} \quad t \in R.$$

Definition 1.2. Let $x \in R^n$ and $Q(t)$ be a $n \times n$ continuous matrix defined on R. The linear system

$$x'(t) = Q(t)x(t) \qquad (1.3)$$

is said to admit an exponential dichotomy on R if there exist positive constants k, α, projection P and the fundamental solution matrix $X(t)$ of (1.3) satisfying

$$\|X(t)PX^{-1}(s)\| \leq ke^{-\alpha(t-s)} \quad \text{for} \quad t \geq s,$$

$$\|X(t)(I - P)X^{-1}(s)\| \leq ke^{-\alpha(s-t)} \quad \text{for} \quad t \leq s.$$

Lemma 1.1[12]. If the linear system (1.3) admits an exponential dichotomy, then almost periodic system

$$x'(t) = Q(t)x(t) + g(t) \qquad (1.4)$$

has a unique almost periodic solution $x(t)$, and

$$x(t) = \int_{-\infty}^{t} X(t)PX^{-1}(s)g(s)\mathrm{d}s - \int_{t}^{+\infty} X(t)(I - P)X^{-1}(s)g(s)\mathrm{d}s.$$

Lemma 1.2[12]. Let $c_i(t)$ be an almost periodic function on R and

$$M[c_i] = \lim_{T \to +\infty} \frac{1}{T} \int_t^{t+T} c_i(s)ds > 0, \quad i = 1, \cdots, n.$$

Then the linear system $x'(t) = diag(-c_1(t), \cdots, -c_n(t))x(t)$ admits an exponential dichotomy on R.

2   Existence of Almost Periodic Solutions

Theorem 2.1. Assume that
(H_1) For $i = 1, \cdots, m$, $j = 1, \cdots, n$, the delay kernels $K_{ij} : [0, \infty) \to R$ are continuous and integrable, $a_{ij}, C_{ij}^{kl}, B_{ij}^{kl}, L_{ij} \in B$;
(H_2) there exists a continuous function $L : R^+ \to R^+$ such that for each $r > 0$,

$$|f(u) - f(v)| \le L(r)|u - v|, \quad |u|, |v| \le r.$$

(H_3) there exists a constant $r_0 > 0$ such that

$$D[|f(0)|r_0 + L(r_0)r_0^2] + L \le r_0, \quad D|f(0)| + 2DL(r_0)r_0 < 1,$$

where $D = \max\limits_{(i,j)}\{\dfrac{\sum\limits_{C_{kl} \in N_r(i,j)} \overline{C}_{ij}^{kl} + \sum\limits_{C_{kl} \in N_q(i,j)} \overline{B}_{ij}^{kl} \int_0^\infty |K_{ij}(u)|\,du}{\underline{a}_{ij}}\} > 0$, $L = \max\limits_{(i,j)} \dfrac{\overline{L}_{ij}}{\underline{a}_{ij}}$,

$\overline{L}_{ij} = \sup\limits_{t \in R} |L_{ij}(t)|$, $\overline{C}_{ij}^{kl} = \sup\limits_{t \in R} C_{ij}^{kl}(t)$, $\overline{B}_{ij}^{kl} = \sup\limits_{t \in R} B_{ij}^{kl}(t)$, $\underline{a}_{ij} = \inf\limits_{t \in R} a_{ij}(t) > 0$.

Then SICNNs (1.1) has a unique almost periodic solution in the region $E := \{\varphi \in B : \|\varphi\|_B \le r_0\}$.

Proof. For any given $\varphi \in B$, we consider the following almost periodic differential equation:

$$x'_{ij}(t) = -a_{ij}(t)x_{ij}(t) - \sum_{C_{kl} \in N_r(i,j)} C_{ij}^{kl}(t)f(\varphi_{kl}(t - \tau(t)))\varphi_{ij}(t)$$

$$- \sum_{C_{kl} \in N_q(i,j)} B_{ij}^{kl}(t) \int_0^\infty K_{ij}(u)f(\varphi_{kl}(t - u))du\varphi_{ij}(t) + L_{ij}(t). \quad (2.1)$$

Then, notice that $M[a_{ij}] > 0$, from Lemma 1.2, the linear system

$$x'_{ij}(t) = -a_{ij}(t)x_{ij}(t), \quad i = 1, \cdots, m, j = 1, \cdots, n, \quad (2.2)$$

admits an exponential dichotomy on R. Thus, by Lemma 1.1, we obtain that the system (2.1) has exactly one almost periodic solution:

$$x_\varphi(t) = \int_{-\infty}^t e^{-\int_s^t a_{ij}(u)du}\left(-\sum_{C_{kl} \in N_r(i,j)} C_{ij}^{kl}(s)f(\varphi_{kl}(s - \tau(s)))\varphi_{ij}(s)\right.$$

$$\left. - \sum_{C_{kl} \in N_q(i,j)} B_{ij}^{kl}(s) \int_0^\infty K_{ij}(u)f(\varphi_{kl}(s - u))du\varphi_{ij}(s) + L_{ij}(s)\right)ds.$$

Now, we define a nonlinear operator on B by $T(\varphi)(t) = x_\varphi(t), \forall \varphi \in B$. Next, we will prove $T(E) \subset E$. For any given $\varphi \in E$, it suffices to prove that $\|T(\varphi)\|_B \leq r_0$. By (H_2) and (H_3), we have

$$\|T(\varphi)\|_B = \sup_{t \in R} \max_{(i,j)} \{| \int_{-\infty}^{t} e^{-\int_s^t a_{ij}(u)du} \Big(- \sum_{C_{kl} \in N_r(i,j)} C_{ij}^{kl}(s) f(\varphi_{kl}(s - \tau(s))) \varphi_{ij}(s)$$

$$- \sum_{C_{kl} \in N_q(i,j)} B_{ij}^{kl}(s) \int_0^\infty K_{ij}(u) f(\varphi_{kl}(s - u)) du \varphi_{ij}(s) + L_{ij}(s) \Big) ds |\}$$

$$\leq \sup_{t \in R} \max_{(i,j)} \{| \int_{-\infty}^{t} e^{-\underline{a}_{ij}(t-s)} \Big(\sum_{C_{kl} \in N_r(i,j)} \overline{C}_{ij}^{kl} f(\varphi_{kl}(s - \tau(s))) \varphi_{ij}(s) ds$$

$$+ \sum_{C_{kl} \in N_q(i,j)} \overline{B}_{ij}^{kl} \int_0^\infty K_{ij}(u) f(\varphi_{kl}(s - u)) du \varphi_{ij}(s) ds \Big) |\} + \max_{(i,j)} \frac{\overline{L}_{ij}}{\underline{a}_{ij}}$$

$$\leq \sup_{t \in R} \max_{(i,j)} \{| \int_{-\infty}^{t} e^{-\underline{a}_{ij}(t-s)} \Big(\sum_{C_{kl} \in N_r(i,j)} \overline{C}_{ij}^{kl}(|f(0)| + L(r_0) | \varphi_{kl}(s$$

$$- \tau(s)) |) |\varphi_{ij}(s)| ds + \sum_{C_{kl} \in N_q(i,j)} \overline{B}_{ij}^{kl}(|f(0)| + L(r_0) |\varphi_{kl}(s - \tau(s))|) \cdot$$

$$\int_0^\infty |K_{ij}(u)| du |\varphi_{ij}(s)| ds \Big) |\} + L$$

$$\leq \sup_{t \in R} \max_{(i,j)} \{| \int_{-\infty}^{t} e^{-\underline{a}_{ij}(t-s)} \Big(\sum_{C_{kl} \in N_r(i,j)} \overline{C}_{ij}^{kl}(|f(0)| + L(r_0)r_0)r_0 ds$$

$$+ \sum_{C_{kl} \in N_q(i,j)} \overline{B}_{ij}^{kl}(|f(0)| + L(r_0)r_0)r_0 \int_0^\infty |K_{ij}(u)| du ds \Big) |\} + L$$

$$\leq D[|f(0)| r_0 + L(r_0)r_0^2] + L \leq r_0.$$

Therefore, $T(E) \subset E$.

Taking $\varphi, \psi \in E$, combining (H_2) and (H_3), we deduce that

$$\|T(\varphi) - T(\psi)\|_B = \sup_{t \in R} \|T(\varphi)(t) - T(\psi)(t)\|$$

$$= \sup_{t \in R} \max_{(i,j)} \{| \int_{-\infty}^{t} e^{-\int_s^t a_{ij}(u)du} \sum_{C_{kl} \in N_r(i,j)} -C_{ij}^{kl}(s) \Big(f(\varphi_{kl}(s - \tau(s))) \varphi_{ij}(s)$$

$$- f(\psi_{kl}(s - \tau(s))) \psi_{ij}(s) \Big) ds | + | \int_{-\infty}^{t} e^{-\int_s^t a_{ij}(u)du} \sum_{C_{kl} \in N_q(i,j)} -B_{ij}^{kl}(s) \cdot$$

$$\int_0^\infty K_{ij}(u) \Big(f(\varphi_{kl}(s - u)) du \varphi_{ij}(s) - f(\psi_{kl}(s - u)) du \psi_{ij}(s) \Big) ds |\}$$

$$\leq \sup_{t \in R} \max_{(i,j)} \{ \int_{-\infty}^{t} e^{-\underline{a}_{ij}(t-s)} \sum_{C_{kl} \in N_r(i,j)} \overline{C}_{ij}^{kl} |f(\varphi_{kl}(s - \tau(s)))| | \varphi_{ij}(s) - \psi_{ij}(s) | ds\}$$

$$+ \sup_{t\in R} \max_{(i,j)} \{ \int_{-\infty}^{t} e^{-\underline{a}_{ij}(t-s)} \sum_{C_{kl}\in N_r(i,j)} \overline{C}_{ij}^{kl} \mid f(\varphi_{kl}(s-\tau(s))) - f(\psi_{kl}(s}$$

$$- \tau(s))) \mid \cdot \mid \psi_{ij}(s) \mid ds\} + \sup_{t\in R} \max_{(i,j)} \{ \int_{-\infty}^{t} e^{-\underline{a}_{ij}(t-s)} \sum_{C_{kl}\in N_q(i,j)} \overline{B}_{ij}^{kl}\cdot$$

$$\int_{0}^{\infty} \mid K_{ij}(u)f(\varphi_{kl}(s-u))du \mid \cdot \mid \varphi_{ij}(s) - \psi_{ij}(s) \mid ds\}$$

$$+ \sup_{t\in R} \max_{(i,j)} \{ \int_{-\infty}^{t} e^{-\underline{a}_{ij}(t-s)} \sum_{C_{kl}\in N_q(i,j)} \overline{B}_{ij}^{kl} \int_{0}^{\infty} \mid K_{ij}(u)\Big(f(\varphi_{kl}(s-u))$$

$$- f(\psi_{kl}(s-u))\Big)du \mid \cdot \mid \psi_{ij}(s) \mid ds\}$$

$$\leq \sup_{t\in R} \max_{(i,j)} \{ \int_{-\infty}^{t} e^{-\underline{a}_{ij}(t-s)} \sum_{C_{kl}\in N_r(i,j)} \overline{C}_{ij}^{kl}(\mid f(0)\mid + L(r_0)r_0)ds\} \cdot \|\varphi - \psi\|_B$$

$$+ \sup_{t\in R} \max_{(i,j)} \{ \int_{-\infty}^{t} e^{-\underline{a}_{ij}(t-s)} \sum_{C_{kl}\in N_r(i,j)} \overline{C}_{ij}^{kl} L(r_0)r_0 ds\} \cdot \|\varphi - \psi\|_B$$

$$+ \sup_{t\in R} \max_{(i,j)} \{ \int_{-\infty}^{t} e^{-\underline{a}_{ij}(t-s)} \sum_{C_{kl}\in N_q(i,j)} \overline{B}_{ij}^{kl}(\mid f(0)\mid + L(r_0)r_0) \int_{0}^{\infty} |K_{ij}(u)| du ds\}$$

$$\cdot \|\varphi - \psi\|_B$$

$$+ \sup_{t\in R} \max_{(i,j)} \{ \int_{-\infty}^{t} e^{-\underline{a}_{ij}(t-s)} \sum_{C_{kl}\in N_q(i,j)} \overline{B}_{ij}^{kl} L(r_0)r_0 \int_{0}^{\infty} |K_{ij}(u)| du ds\} \cdot \|\varphi - \psi\|_B$$

$$\leq D(|f(0)| + L(r_0)r_0) \cdot \|\varphi - \psi\|_B + DL(r_0)r_0 \cdot \|\varphi - \psi\|_B$$

$$\leq [D|f(0)| + 2DL(r_0)r_0] \cdot \|\varphi - \psi\|_B < \|\varphi - \psi\|_B$$

So T is a contraction from E to E. Since E is a closed subset of B, T has a unique fixed point in E, which means system (1.1) has a unique almost periodic solution in E.

3   Exponential Stability of the Almost Periodic Solution

Theorem 3.1. Suppose $(H_1) - (H_3)$ hold, let $x^*(t) = \{x^*_{ij}(t)\}$ be the unique almost periodic solution of SICNNs (1.1) in the region $\|\varphi\|_B \leq r_0$. Further we assume that
(H_4) there exists a constant $r_1 \geq r_0$ such that

$$|f(0)| + L(r_0)r_0 + L(r_1)r_1 < \frac{1}{D};$$

(H_5) For $i = 1, \cdots, m, j = 1, \cdots, n$, there exists a constant $\lambda_0 > 0$ such that

$$\int_{0}^{\infty} |K_{ij}(s)| e^{\lambda_0 s} ds < +\infty.$$

Then there exists a constant $\lambda > 0$ such that for any solution $x(t) = \{x_{ij}(t)\}$ of SICNNs (1.1) with initial value $\sup\limits_{t \in (-\infty,0]} \|\varphi(t)\| \leq r_1$,

$$\|x(t) - x^*(t)\| \leq Me^{-\lambda t}, \quad \forall t > 0,$$

where $M = \sup\limits_{t \in (-\infty,0]} \|\varphi(t) - x^*(t)\|$.

Proof. Set

$$\Gamma_{ij}(\alpha) = \alpha - \underline{a}_{ij} + \sum_{C_{kl} \in N_r(i,j)} \overline{C}_{ij}^{kl}(|f(0)| + L(r_0)r_0 + L(r_1)r_1 e^{\alpha \overline{\tau}}) + \sum_{C_{kl} \in N_q(i,j)} \overline{B}_{ij}^{kl}.$$

$$\left[(|f(0)| + L(r_0)r_0) \int_0^\infty |K_{ij}(s)|\,ds + L(r_1)r_1 \int_0^\infty |K_{ij}(s)| e^{\alpha s} ds \right]$$

where $i = 1, \cdots, m$, $j = 1, \cdots, n$. It is easy to prove that Γ_{ij} are continuous functions on $[0, \lambda_0]$. Moreover, by (H_4) and (H_5), we have

$$\Gamma_{ij}(0) = -\underline{a}_{ij} + \sum_{C_{kl} \in N_r(i,j)} \overline{C}_{ij}^{kl}\big(|f(0)| + L(r_0)r_0 + L(r_1)r_1\big)$$

$$+ \sum_{C_{kl} \in N_q(i,j)} \overline{B}_{ij}^{kl}\big[|f(0)| + L(r_0)r_0 + L(r_1)r_1\big] \int_0^\infty |K_{ij}(s)|\,ds < 0.$$

Thus, there exists a sufficiently small constant $\lambda > 0$ such that

$$\Gamma_{ij}(\lambda) < 0, \quad i = 1, \cdots, m, j = 1, \cdots, n. \tag{3.1}$$

Take $\varepsilon > 0$. Set $Z_{ij}(t) = |x_{ij}(t) - x_{ij}^*(t)| e^{\lambda t}$, $i = 1, \cdots, m$, $j = 1, \cdots, n$. It follows that: $Z_{ij}(t) \leq M < M + \varepsilon, \forall t \in (-\infty, 0]$, $i = 1, \cdots, m$, $j = 1, \cdots, n$. In the following, we will prove that

$$Z_{ij}(t) \leq M + \varepsilon, \forall t > 0, i = 1, \cdots, m, j = 1, \cdots, n. \tag{3.2}$$

If this is not true, then there exist $i_0 \in \{1, \cdots, m\}$ and $j_0 \in \{1, \cdots, n\}$ such that

$$\{t > 0 \mid Z_{i_0 j_0}(t) > M + \varepsilon\} \neq \emptyset. \tag{3.3}$$

Let

$$t_{ij} = \begin{cases} \inf \{t > 0 \mid Z_{ij}(t) > M + \varepsilon\}, & \{t > 0 \mid Z_{ij}(t) > M + \varepsilon\} \neq \emptyset, \\ +\infty, & \{t > 0 \mid Z_{ij}(t) > M + \varepsilon\} = \emptyset. \end{cases}$$

Then $t_{ij} > 0$ and

$$Z_{ij}(t) \leq M + \varepsilon, \forall t \in (-\infty, t_{ij}], i = 1, \cdots, m, j = 1, \cdots, n. \tag{3.4}$$

We denote $t_{ph} = \min\limits_{(i,j)} t_{ij}$, where $p \in \{1, \cdots, m\}$ and $h \in \{1, \cdots, n\}$. From (3.3), we have $0 < t_{ph} < +\infty$. It follows from (3.4), we have

$$Z_{ij}(t) \leq M + \varepsilon, \forall t \in (-\infty, t_{ph}], i = 1, \cdots, m, j = 1, \cdots, n. \tag{3.5}$$

In addition, noticing that $t_{ph} = \inf\{t > 0 \mid Z_{ph}(t) > M + \varepsilon\}$, we obtain

$$Z_{ph}(t_{ph}) = M + \varepsilon, \quad \text{and} \quad D^+ Z_{ph}(t_{ph}) \geq 0. \tag{3.6}$$

Since $x(t)$ and $x^*(t)$ are solutions of Eq.(1.1), combining with (3.5)-(3.6), (H_2) and (H_3), we have

$$0 \leq D^+ Z_{ph}(t_{ph}) = D^+[\,|x_{ph}(t) - x_{ph}^*(t)|\,e^{\lambda t}]\,|_{t=t_{ph}}$$

$$\leq |x_{ph}(t_{ph}) - x_{ph}^*(t_{ph})|\,\lambda e^{\lambda t_{ph}} - \underline{a}_{ph}\,|x_{ph}(t_{ph}) - x_{ph}^*(t_{ph})|\,e^{\lambda t_{ph}}$$

$$+ \sum_{C_{kl} \in N_r(p,h)} \overline{C}_{ph}^{kl}\,|\,f(x_{kl}(t_{ph} - \tau(t_{ph})))x_{ph}(t_{ph}) - f(x_{kl}^*(t_{ph} - \tau(t_{ph})))x_{ph}^*(t_{ph})|\,\cdot$$

$$e^{\lambda t_{ph}} + \sum_{C_{kl} \in N_q(p,h)} \overline{B}_{ph}^{kl}\,|\int_0^\infty K_{ij}(u) f(x_{kl}(t_{ph} - u))\mathrm{d}u\,x_{ph}(t_{ph})$$

$$- \int_0^\infty K_{ij}(u) f(x_{kl}^*(t_{ph} - u))\mathrm{d}u\,x_{ph}^*(t_{ph})|\,e^{\lambda t_{ph}}$$

$$\leq (\lambda - \underline{a}_{ph}) Z_{ph}(t_{ph}) + \sum_{C_{kl} \in N_r(p,h)} \overline{C}_{ph}^{kl}\,|\,f(x_{kl}^*(t_{ph} - \tau(t_{ph})))|\cdot|\,x_{ph}(t_{ph})$$

$$- x_{ph}^*(t_{ph})|\,e^{\lambda t_{ph}} + \sum_{C_{kl} \in N_r(p,h)} \overline{C}_{ph}^{kl}\,|\,f(x_{kl}(t_{ph} - \tau(t_{ph})))$$

$$- f(x_{kl}^*(t_{ph} - \tau(t_{ph})))|\cdot|\,x_{ph}(t_{ph})|\,e^{\lambda t_{ph}} + \sum_{C_{kl} \in N_q(p,h)} \overline{B}_{ph}^{kl} \int_0^\infty |K_{ij}(u)|\cdot$$

$$|f(x_{kl}^*(t_{ph} - u))|\,\mathrm{d}u\cdot|\,x_{ph}(t_{ph}) - x_{ph}^*(t_{ph})|\,e^{\lambda t_{ph}} + \sum_{C_{kl} \in N_q(p,h)} \overline{B}_{ph}^{kl}\cdot$$

$$\int_0^\infty |K_{ij}(u)|\cdot|\,f(x_{kl}(t_{ph} - u)) - f(x_{kl}^*(t_{ph} - u))|\,\mathrm{d}u\cdot|\,x_{ph}(t_{ph})|\,e^{\lambda t_{ph}}$$

$$\leq (\lambda - \underline{a}_{ph})(M + \varepsilon) + \sum_{C_{kl} \in N_r(p,h)} \overline{C}_{ph}^{kl}(|f(0)| + L(r_0)r_0)\cdot Z_{ph}(t_{ph})$$

$$+ \sum_{C_{kl} \in N_r(p,h)} \overline{C}_{ph}^{kl} L(r_1)\,|x_{kl}(t_{ph} - \tau(t_{ph})) - x_{kl}^*(t_{ph} - \tau(t_{ph}))|\cdot$$

$$e^{\lambda(t_{ph} - \tau(t_{ph}))} e^{\lambda \tau(t_{ph})}\cdot r_1 + \sum_{C_{kl} \in N_q(p,h)} \overline{B}_{ph}^{kl}(|f(0)| + L(r_0)r_0)\cdot$$

$$\int_0^\infty |K_{ij}(u)|\,\mathrm{d}u\cdot Z_{ph}(t_{ph}) + \sum_{C_{kl} \in N_q(p,h)} \overline{B}_{ph}^{kl} L(r_1) \int_0^\infty |K_{ij}(u)|\cdot$$

$$|x_{kl}(t_{ph} - u) - x_{kl}^*(t_{ph} - u)|\,e^{\lambda(t_{ph} - u)} e^{\lambda u}\,\mathrm{d}u\cdot r_1$$

$$\leq (\lambda - \underline{a}_{ph})(M + \varepsilon) + \sum_{C_{kl} \in N_r(p,h)} \overline{C}_{ph}^{kl}(|f(0)| + L(r_0)r_0) \cdot (M + \varepsilon)$$

$$+ \sum_{C_{kl} \in N_r(p,h)} \overline{C}_{ph}^{kl} L(r_1)r_1 e^{\lambda \overline{\tau}} \cdot (M + \varepsilon) + \sum_{C_{kl} \in N_q(p,h)} \overline{B}_{ph}^{kl}(|f(0)|$$

$$+ L(r_0)r_0) \cdot \int_0^\infty |K_{ij}(u)| \, du \cdot (M + \varepsilon)$$

$$+ \sum_{C_{kl} \in N_q(p,h)} \overline{B}_{ph}^{kl} L(r_1)r_1 \int_0^\infty |K_{ij}(u)| e^{\lambda u} du \cdot (M + \varepsilon)$$

It follows that:

$$\lambda - \underline{a}_{ph} + \sum_{C_{kl} \in N_r(p,h)} \overline{C}_{ph}^{kl}(|f(0)| + L(r_0)r_0 + L(r_1)r_1 e^{\lambda \overline{\tau}}) + \sum_{C_{kl} \in N_q(p,h)} \overline{B}_{ph}^{kl} \cdot$$

$$\left[(|f(0)| + L(r_0)r_0) \int_0^\infty |K_{ij}(u)| \, du + L(r_1)r_1 \int_0^\infty |K_{ij}(u)| e^{\lambda u} du \right] \geq 0,$$

that is $\Gamma_{ph}(\lambda) \geq 0$. This contradicts with (3.1). Hence, (3.2) holds, i.e.,

$$\left| x_{ij}(t) - x_{ij}^*(t) \right| e^{\lambda t} = Z_{ij}(t) \leq M + \varepsilon, \forall t > 0, i = 1, \cdots, m, j = 1, \cdots, n.$$

Therefore,

$$\|x(t) - x^*(t)\| = \max_{(i,j)} \left| x_{ij}(t) - x_{ij}^*(t) \right| \leq (M + \varepsilon)e^{-\lambda t}, \forall t > 0.$$

Let $\varepsilon \to 0$, we get

$$\|x(t) - x^*(t)\| \leq M e^{-\lambda t}, \forall t > 0.$$

4 Illustrative Example

Consider SICNNs (1.1) descried by $i, j = 1, 2, 3$, $\tau(t) = \cos^2 t$, $f(x) = \frac{x^4+1}{6}$,

$$K_{ij}(u) = e^{-u} \sin u, \quad a_{ij}(t) = \begin{pmatrix} 5 + |\sin t| & 5 + |\sin \sqrt{2}t| & 9 + |\sin t| \\ 6 + |\sin t| & 6 + |\sin t| & 7 + |\sin t| \\ 8 + |\sin t| & 8 + |\sin t| & 5 + |\sin \sqrt{3}t| \end{pmatrix}, \quad C_{ij}(t) =$$

$$B_{ij}(t) = |\sin \sqrt{3}t| \begin{pmatrix} \frac{1}{10} & \frac{3}{10} & \frac{1}{2} \\ \frac{1}{5} & \frac{1}{10} & \frac{1}{5} \\ \frac{1}{10} & \frac{1}{5} & \frac{1}{10} \end{pmatrix}, \quad L_{ij}(t) = \begin{pmatrix} \sin t & \sin t & \cos t \\ \frac{\sin t + \sin \sqrt{2}t}{2} & \cos t & \cos t \\ \cos t & \frac{\cos t + \cos \sqrt{3}t}{2} & \sin t \end{pmatrix}.$$

Obviously , let $L(r) = \frac{2}{3}r^3$ and $r_0 = 1$, then we get $D \leq 0.6, L = 0.2$, so $D[|f(0)| r_0 + L(r_0)r_0^2] + L \leq 0.7 < 1 = r_0, D|f(0)| + 2DL(r_0)r_0 \leq 0.81 < 1$. From Theorem 2.1, the system in example has a unique almost periodic solution in the region $\|\varphi\|_B \leq 1$.

Take $r_1 = \sqrt[4]{\frac{51}{50}}$, then $D[|f(0)| + L(r_0)r_0 + L(r_1)r_1] < 1$. From Theorem 3.1, all the solutions with initial value $\sup_{t \in [-1,0]} \|\varphi(t)\| \leq r_1$ converge exponentially to the unique almost periodic solution in the region $\|\varphi\|_B \leq 1$ as $t \to +\infty$.

5   Conclusion

In this paper, some new sufficient conditions are established to ensure the existence and exponential stability of almost periodic solutions for SICNNs with time-varying and distributed delays. Since we do not need the neuron activations to satisfy global Lipschitz conditions, the result in this paper is new, and it is also valuable in the design of neural networks which is used to solve efficiently problems arising in practical engineering applications.

Acknowledgements. The work is supported by Key Science Foundation of Educational Department of Hubei Province under Grant D20082201 and Innovation Teams of Hubei Normal University.

References

1. Liu, B., Huang, L.: Existence and Stability of Almost Periodic Solutions for Shunting Inhibitory Cellular Neural Networks with Continuously Distributed Delays. Physics Letters A 349, 177–186 (2006)
2. Xia, Y., Cao, J., Huang, Z.: Existence and Exponential Stability of Almost Periodic Solution for Shunting Inhibitory Cellular Neural Networks with Impulses. Chaos, Solitons and Fractals 34, 1599–1607 (2007)
3. Zhou, Q., Xiao, B., Yu, Y., Peng, L.: Existence and Exponential Stability of Almost Periodic Solutions for Shunting Inhibitory Cellular Neural Networks with Continuously Distributed Delays. Chaos, Solitons and Fractals 34, 860–866 (2007)
4. Liu, B.: Almost Periodic Solutions for Shunting Inhibitory Cellular Neural Networks without Global Lipschitz Activation Functions. Journal of Computational and Applied Mathematics 203, 159–168 (2007)
5. Liu, B., Huang, L.: Existence and Stability of Almost Periodic Solutions for Shunting Inhibitory Cellular Neural Networks with Time-Varying Delays. Chaos, Solitons and Fractals 31, 211–217 (2007)
6. Liu, Y., You, Z., Cao, L.: Almost Periodic Solution of Shunting Inhibitory Cellular Neural Networks with Time-Varying and Continuously Distributed Delays. Physics Letters A 364, 17–28 (2007)
7. Zhao, W., Zhang, H.: On Almost Periodic Solution of Shunting Inhibitory Cellular Neural Networks with Variable Coefficients and Time-Varying Delays. Nonlinear Analysis: Real World Applications 9, 2326–2336 (2008)
8. Ding, H., Liang, J., Xiao, T.: Existence of Almost Periodic Solutions for SICNNs with Time-Varying Delays. Physics Letters A 372, 5411–5416 (2008)
9. Cai, M., Zhang, H., Yuan, Z.: Positive Almost Periodic Solutions for Shunting Inhibitory Cellular Neural Networks with Time-Varying Delays. Mathematics and Computers in Simulation 78, 548–558 (2008)
10. Chen, L., Zhao, H.: Global Stability of Almost Periodic Solution of Shunting Inhibitory Cellular Neural Networks with Variable Coefficients. Chaos, Solitons and Fractals 35, 351–357 (2008)
11. Shao, J., Wang, L., Ou, C.: Almost Periodic Solutions for Shunting Inhibitory Cellular Neural Networks without Global Lipschitz Activaty Functions. Applied Mathematical Modelling 33, 2575–2581 (2009)
12. Fink, A.: Almost Periodic Differential Equations. Springer, Berlin (1974)

Applications of Computational Intelligence in Remote Sensing Image Analysis

Hengjian Tong, Man Zhao, and Xiang Li

Computer Science School, China University of Geosciences(Wuhan)
{thj26,zhaoman,lixiang}@cug.edu.cn

Abstract. Remote sensing image analysis, such as image segmentation, image classification and feature extraction, is a very hard task because there are many uncertainties in remote sensing and there is not a definite mathematical model in remote sensing image data. It is difficult for traditional methods to deal with this problem. Therefore, many scholars try to solve the problem by introducing computational intelligence techniques to remote sensing image analysis. This paper surveys the applications of some computational intelligence techniques in remote sensing image analysis, including neural networks, fuzzy systems, evolutionary computation, swarm intelligence, artificial immune systems.

Keywords: Computational Intelligence, remote sensing image analysis, neural networks, fuzzy systems, evolutionary computation, swarm intelligence, artificial immune systems.

1 Introduction

With the rapid development of aerospace technologies, remote sensing sensor technologies, communication technologies and information technologies, images of the earth surface have been obtained more frequently and quickly than before. Therefore, remote sensing images have significant applications in different areas such as land use/land cover, soil investigations, surveys and mapping, crop inventory, detection of crop injury, crop residue evaluation and yield prediction, vegetation change, climate studies, assessment of forest resources, examining marine environments etc. Remote sensing image analysis, especially image segmentation and image classification and feature extraction, is a very important task in the applications of remote sensing images. It is very difficult to develop detailed analytical models for solving the problems because of complexities and uncertainties in remote sensing images analysis. Therefore, it is necessary to use computational intelligence techniques in remote sensing image analysis.

IEEE Computational Intelligence Society defines its subjects of interest as neural networks, fuzzy systems and evolutionary computation, including swarm intelligence. The book *Computational Intelligence: An Introduction* [1] defines computational intelligence as "the study of adaptive mechanisms to enable or facilitate intelligence behavior in complex and changing environments. As such, the author thinks that computational intelligence includes artificial neural networks, evolutionary computing, swarm intelligence and fuzzy systems". Wlodzislaw Duch [2] thinks that

Z. Cai et al. (Eds.): ISICA 2009, CCIS 51, pp. 171–179, 2009.

computational intelligence studies problems for which there are no effective algorithms, either because it is not possible to formulate them or because they are NP-hard and thus not effective in real life applications. The objective of this paper is to introduce the applications of computational intelligence in remote sensing images analysis for those experts in remote sensing fields.

The remainder of the paper is organized as follows: Section 2 introduces the application of neural networks in remote sensing image analysis. Section 3 introduces the application of fuzzy systems in remote sensing image analysis. Section 4 introduces the application of evolutionary computation in remote sensing image analysis. Section 5 introduces the application of swarm intelligence in remote sensing image analysis. Section 6 introduces the application of artificial immune systems in remote sensing image analysis. Finally, the conclusion is given in section 7.

2   Neural Networks

About the applications of Neural Networks in remote sensing image, there are a very good summary in the literature [3] and [4]. Traditional parametric statistical approaches, such as Parallelepiped, Minimum Distance and Maximum Likelihood, depend on the assumption of a multivariate Gaussian distribution for data to be classified. However, remote sensing image data may not follow the assumed model. One of the main advantages of neural networks for classification is that they don't depend on any specific distribution. Neural networks are applied widely in remote sensing image because it has the following four abilities [3]: (1) perform more accurately than other techniques such as statistical classifiers, particularly when the feature space is complex and the source data has different statistical distributions; (2) perform more rapidly than other techniques such as statistical classifiers; (3) incorporate a priori knowledge and realistic physical constraints into the analysis; (4) incorporate different types of data (include those from different sensors) into the analysis, thus facilitating synergistic studies. There are some problems in Neural Networks that impact its application in remote sensing image analysis. Firstly, it needs large computation time, because the "learning process" of the Neural Networks is some sort of "try and error". Secondly, it is not easy to find a good working architecture of the Neural Networks for an application, such as which type Neural Networks to choose? How much neuron? How many layers? Thirdly, Convergence to the global minimum of the risk function (squared error) can not be guaranteed. That is to say, it may be trapped a local minima. Neural network is a black-box system. It may be seen as data transformers. It will produce a corresponding output results when you give it any input. But it can not explain why this decision is reached and how reliable it is. Although Neural Networks models have some shortcomings, because it can implicitly detect complex nonlinear relationships between variables, it is still studied by many scholars and is applied in different fields.

3   Fuzzy Systems

There are many uncertainties in remote sensing. Uncertainty starts with noisy sensor measurements with limited accuracy, degrading signal processing methods for data compression and filtering, ambiguous feature extraction and classification and ends with imprecise concepts of land cover and land use classes [5]. Uncertainties involve uncertainties of the sensor, uncertainties of image generation, uncertainties of image understanding, uncertainties of parameters, uncertainties of model, etc [5] [6]. It is natural to apply the principles of fuzzy systems theory in remote sensing image analysis because of these uncertainties in remote sensing. A famous algorithm, Fuzzy C Means (FCM) clustering algorithm [7] was proposed in 1984. The FCM algorithm can generate fuzzy partitions for any set of numerical data. These partitions are useful for corroborating known substructures or suggesting substructure in unexplored data. The clustering criterion used to aggregate subsets is a generalized least-squares objective function. Features of this algorithm include a choice of three norms (Euclidean, Diagonal, or Mahalonobis), an adjustable weighting factor that essentially controls sensitivity to noise, acceptance of variable numbers of clusters, and outputs that include several measures of cluster validity. In the paper [8], NEFCLASS, a neuro-fuzzy system for the classification of data was presented. NEFCLASS combines Neural Networks and Fuzzy Systems. NEFCLASS uses a supervised learning algorithm based on fuzzy error back propagation. It can derive fuzzy rules from data to classify patterns into a number of classes. In the paper [9], authors used the NEFCLASS algorithm to classify remote sensing images landsat7 ETM+ in the field of land cover. In the paper [10], authors did image mining based on the idea of neuro-fuzzy system for accident prediction in two vehicles scenario. In the paper [11], author presented a fuzzy supervised classification algorithm for Landsat MSS remote sensing images. The algorithm consists of two major steps: the estimate of fuzzy parameters from fuzzy training data, and a fuzzy partition of spectral space. Partial membership of pixels allows component cover classes of mixed pixels to be identified and more accurate statistical parameters to be generated, resulting in higher classification accuracy. In the paper [12], authors presented an improved edge detection algorithm of remote sensing images based on fuzzy logic theory and conventional Pal. King Algorithm. A hierarchical fuzzy expert system was developed for the remote sensing image classification in the paper [13]. In the paper [14], author presented a method for improving remote sensing image analysis through fuzzy information representation. In the paper [15], authors presented several spatial fuzzy relationships based on fuzzy set theory and suggested some potential applications in image segmentation and image retrieval. In the paper [16], authors introduced the application of fuzzy theory in remote sensing image classification, including classification methods (unsupervised classification, supervised classification, and fuzzy convolution), definition and verification of the training areas and classification procedure. In the paper [17], authors compared three fuzzy knowledge acquisition methods and evaluated their classification performances. In the paper [18], authors proposed an object-based image classification procedure which is based on fuzzy image-regions instead of crisp image-objects. The approach includes three stages: (1) fuzzification in which fuzzy image-regions were developed, resulting in a set of images whose digital values express the degree of membership of each pixel to target land-cover classes; (2) feature analysis in which contextual properties of fuzzy image-regions were quantified; and (3) defuzzification in which fuzzy image-regions were allocated to target land-cover classes. In summary, Fuzzy Systems techniques have obtained great successes in the applications of remote sensing image analysis. The commercial software (eCognition) based on the idea of fuzzy systems techniques has been developed [5] and had many successful applications.

4 Evolutionary Computation

Evolutionary computation comprises genetic algorithms, evolutionary programming, evolution strategy, genetic programming, etc. Genetic algorithms are one of the most important techniques in the applications of remote sensing images analysis. Genetic algorithms are search and optimization algorithms based on natural selection and natural genetics [19]. Genetic algorithm is a population-based method, which operates on a population of individuals called chromosomes. Each chromosome represents a solution to the given problem. Each chromosome is associated with a "fitness" value that evaluates the performance of a possible solution the chromosome represents. Instead of a single point, genetic algorithms usually keep a set of pints as a population, which is then evolved repeatedly toward a better overall fitness value. The chromosomes evolve through successive generations and two genetic operators are used to produce offspring: crossover and mutation. The resulting offspring update the population according to a fittest function. In the paper [20], authors used a genetic algorithm to improve an unsupervised MRF-based (Markov Random Field) segmentation approach for multi-spectral textured images. The proposed hybrid approach has the advantage that combines the fast convergence of the MRF-based iterative algorithm and the powerful global exploration of the genetic algorithms. In the paper [21], authors used genetic algorithms to handle larger search spaces for finding the optimal configuration of the sub-pixels. There are two reasons: (1) It will produce the fraction values with a random configuration for every pixel. (2) It is very difficult to enumerate all possible configurations for larger search spaces. In the paper [22], authors used a genetic algorithm to do image feature extraction for remote sensing applications. Authors described their basis set of primitive image operators, presented their chromosomal representation of a complete algorithm and discussed the choice of evolutionary control parameters. In the paper [23], a genetic-algorithm-based selective principal component analysis (GA-SPCA) method was proposed and tested using hyperspectral remote sensing data and ground reference data collected within an agricultural field. The proposed method used a global optimizer, the genetic algorithms, to select a subset of the original image bands, which first reduced the data dimension. A principal component transformation was subsequently applied to the selected bands. By extracting features from the resulting eigenimage, the remote sensing data, originally high in dimension, would be further reduced to a feature space with one to several principal component bands. Subsequent image processing on the reduced feature space could thus be performed with improved accuracy. In the paper [24], authors used genetic algorithms to obtain the best representative feature for each group band, in the sense of maximizing the separability among clusters. In the paper [25], supervised color image segmentation using a binary-coded genetic algorithm identifying a region in Hue-Saturation-Intensity color space for outdoor field weed sensing was successfully implemented. In the paper [26], authors used variable string genetic algorithms with chromosome differentiation to design a nonparametric classifier. The classifier is able to evolve automatically the appropriate number of hyperplanes efficiently for modeling any kind of class boundaries optimally. It implemented a partition for different land cover regions with complex class boundaries. In the paper [27], real-coded variable string length genetic fuzzy clustering with automatic evolution of clusters was used for pixel classification. The cluster centers were encoded in the chromosomes, and the Xie–Beni index was used as a measure of the validity of the corresponding partition. In the paper [28], a multiobjective optimization algorithm was utilized to tackle the problem of fuzzy partitioning where a number of fuzzy cluster validity indices were simultaneously optimized. The resultant set of near-Pareto-optimal solutions contains a number of non-dominated solutions, which the user can judge relatively and pick up the most promising one according to the problem requirements. Real-coded encoding of the cluster centers was used for this purpose.

5 Swarm Intelligence

Swarm intelligence comprises particle swarm optimization and ant colony optimization. J. Kennedy and R. C. Eberhart brought forward particle swarm optimization (PSO) inspired by the choreography of a bird flock in 1995 [29]. Unlike conventional evolutionary algorithms, PSO possesses the following characteristics: (1) Each individual (or particle) is given a random speed and flows in the decision space; (2) each individual has its own memory; (3) the evolutionary of each individual is composed of the cooperation and competition among these particles. Since the PSO was proposed, it has been of great concern and become a new research field. PSO has shown a high convergence speed in single objective optimization, and it is also particularly suitable for multi-objective optimization. In this paper [30], a new coarse-to-fine registration framework is proposed. In coarse registration step, Quantum Particle Swarm Optimization (QPSO) was used as optimizer to find best rigid parameters. The similarity measure is the Mutual Information of whole images. In this paper [31], firstly, authors selected the road's extremities. Secondly, authors calculated the each pixel's road membership value using local road detector in the original SAR images. Thirdly, authors used particle swarm optimization to obtain the optimal B-spline control points from the result of road detection. Finally, according to the optimal B-spline control points, authors obtained the B-spline curve that is the result of road extraction. In this paper [32], a new method which combines the feature texture knowledge with BP neural network trained by PSO was presented. In the paper [33], an image classification algorithm based on PSO was proposed. The algorithm finds the centroids of a user specified number of clusters, where each cluster groups together similar pixels. The image classifier has been applied successfully to three types of images to illustrate its wide applicability. In the paper [34], authors presented a framework to hybridize the rough set theory with PSO. Authors treated image segmentation as a clustering problem. Each cluster was modeled with a rough set. PSO was employed to tune the threshold and relative importance of upper and lower approximations of the rough sets. Davies–Bouldin clustering validity index was used as the fitness function, which was minimized while arriving at an optimal partitioning. Ant Colony Optimization (ACO) algorithm [35] is based on the following model [36]:

(1)An ant runs more or less at random around the colony;

(2)If it discovers a food source, it returns more or less directly to the nest, leaving in its path a trail of pheromone;

(3)These pheromones are attractive, nearby ants will be inclined to follow, more or less directly, the track;

(4)Returning to the colony, these ants will strengthen the route;

(5)If two routes are possible to reach the same food source, the shorter one will be, in the same time, traveled by more ants than the long route will

(6)The short route will be increasingly enhanced, and therefore become more attractive;

(7)The long route will eventually disappear, pheromones are volatile;

(8)Eventually, all the ants have determined and therefore "chosen" the shortest route.

In the paper [37], authors applied ACO algorithm to generate the optimal mask for texture classification. In the paper [38], authors used a colony of artificial ant search for an optimal labeling of image pixels that maximizes a posteriori probability estimate of the labeling space, then implemented discrete optimization in MRF-based image segmentation. In the paper [39] [40], authors proposed an ACO scheme which jointly estimates the regularized classification map and the optimal nonstationary neighborhood. The ants collect information through the image, from one pixel to the others. The choice of the path is a function of the pixel label, favoring paths within the same image segment. In the paper [41], authors presented a method based on ACO for remote sensing image classification. In the method, authors combined gray feature and texture feature to construct feature vector.

6   Artificial Immune Systems

The human immune system, which is a complex system of cells, molecules, and organs, symbolizes an identification mechanism capable of perceiving and combating dysfunction from our own cells and the action of exogenous infectious microorganisms. This immune system protects the body from infectious agents such as viruses, bacteria, fungi, and other parasites. Any molecule that can be recognized by the adaptive immune system is known as an antigen. The gamma globulin proteins that are used by the immune system to identify and neutralize foreign objects, such as bacteria and viruses, are known as antibodies. Antibodies are found in blood or other bodily fluids of vertebrates. Artificial immune systems (AIS) are computational systems inspired by the principles and processes of the vertebrate immune system. The algorithms typically exploit the immune system's characteristics of learning and memory to solve a problem. There are some applications based on AIS in remote sensing image analysis. In the paper [42], AIS was used for aerial image segmentation. In the paper [43], an unsupervised artificial immune classifier was proposed and was successfully applied for the classification of remote-sensing imagery. In the paper [44], an unsupervised classification algorithm based on the paradigm of the nature immune systems was designed and implemented. The algorithm was successfully applied for classification of multi/hyperspectral remote sensing images. In the paper [45], a supervised classification algorithm based on a multiple-valued immune network was presented and was successfully applied for classification of remote sensing images. In the paper [46], a supervised classification algorithm based on AIS was presented and was successfully applied for classification of land cover. In the paper [47], a supervised classification algorithm for remote sensing image classification based on artificial immune B-Cell network was proposed.

7 Conclusions

This paper overviews the applications of some computational intelligence techniques (neural networks, fuzzy systems, evolutionary computation, swarm intelligence, artificial immune systems) in remote sensing image analysis, There are two characteristics in these applications: (1) The combination of computational intelligence techniques and traditional techniques (statistics methods). (2) The combination of various computational intelligence techniques.

Acknowledgments. This paper is sponsored by the GPMR200717, the Research Foundation for Outstanding Young Teachers, China University of Geosciences (Wuhan, No.CUGQNL0506) and the I2I program of the Natural Science and Engineering Research Council (NSERC), Canada.

References

1. Engelbrecht, A.P.: Computational Intelligence: An Introduction. Wiley, Chichester (2003)
2. Duch, W.: What is Computational Intelligence and what could it become? Technical Report, Department of Informatics, Nicolaus Copernicus University and School of Computer Engineering, Nanyang Technological University, Singapore (2007)
3. Atkinson, P.M., Tatnall, A.R.L.: Neural networks in remote sensing–Introduction. International Journal of Remote Sensing 18(4), 699–709 (1997)
4. Egmont-Petersen, M., de Ridder, D., Handels, H.: Image processing with neural networks-a review. Pattern Recognition 35, 2279–2301 (2002)
5. Benz, U.C., Hofmann, P., Willhauck, G., Lingenfelder, I., Heynen, M.: Multi-resolution, object-oriented fuzzy analysis of remote sensing data for GIS-ready information. ISPRS Journal of Photogrammetry and Remote Sensing 58(3-4), 239–258 (2004)
6. Foody, G.M., Atkinson, P.M.: Uncertainty in Remote Sensing and GIS. Wiley, Chichester (2003)
7. Bezdek, J.C., Ehrlich, R., Full, W.: FCM: The fuzzy c-means clustering algorithm. Comp. GEOSCI. 10(2-3), 191–203 (1984)
8. Nauck, D., Kruse, R.: NEFCLASS a neuro-fuzzy approach for the classification of data. In: Proc. of the 1995 ACM Symposium on Applied Computing, Nashville, February 26-28, pp. 461–465. ACM Press, New York (1995)
9. Wei, W., Guanglai, G.: An application of neuro-fuzzy system in remote sensing image classification. In: International Conference on Computer Science and Software Engineering, Wuhan, China, December 2008, pp. 1069–1072 (2008)
10. Maghooli, K., Eftekhari Moghadam, A.M.: Development of Neuro-fuzzy System for Image Mining. In: Bloch, I., Petrosino, A., Tettamanzi, A.G.B. (eds.) WILF 2005. LNCS (LNAI), vol. 3849, pp. 32–39. Springer, Heidelberg (2006)
11. Wang, F.: Fuzzy supervised classification of remote sensing images. IEEE Transactions on Geoscience and Remote Sensing 28(2), 194–201 (1990)

12. Yi, L., Xue-quan, C.: An Edge Detection Algorithm of Remote Sensing Images Based on Fuzzy Sets. In: International Conference on Communications, Circuits and Systems, ICCCAS 2004, Chengdou, China (2004)
13. Wang, Y., Jamshidi, M.: Fuzzy logic applied in remote sensing image classification. In: IEEE International Conference on Systems, Man and Cybernetics, pp. 6378–6382 (2004)
14. Wang, F.: Improving remote sensing image analysis through fuzzy information representation. Photogramm. Eng. Remote Sens. 56(8), 1163–1169 (1990)
15. Zhige, J., Xiaoli, L.: Modeling Spatial Relationships for Remote Sensing Image Processing Based on Fuzzy Set Theory. In: International Conference on Computer Science and Software Engineering, Wuhan, China, pp. 1101–1104 (2008)
16. Droj, G.: The applicability of fuzzy theory in remote sensing image classification. Studia Univ. Babes-Bolyai, Informatica LII(1) (2007)
17. Martinez, E., Gonzalo, C., Arquero, A., Gordo, O.: Evaluation of different fuzzy knowledge acquisition methods for remote sensing image classification. In: IEEE International Geoscience and Remote Sensing Symposium, IGARSS 1999, pp. 2489–2491 (1999)
18. Lizarazo, I., Elsner, P.: Fuzzy segmentation for object-based image classification. International Journal of Remote Sensing 30(6), 1643–1649 (2009)
19. Goldberg, D.E.: Genetic Algorithms in Search, Optimization, and Machine Learning. Addison-Wesley Longman, Reading (1989)
20. Tseng, D.-C., Lai, C.-C.: A genetic algorithm for MRF-based segmentation of multispectral textured images. Pattern Recognition Letters 20(14), 1499–1510 (1999)
21. Mertens, K.C., Verbeke, L.P.C., Ducheyne, E.I., De Wulf, R.R.: Using genetic algorithms in sub-pixel mapping. International Journal of Remote Sensing 24(21), 4241–4247 (2003)
22. Brumby, S.P., Theiler, J.P., Perkins, S.J., et al.: Investigation of image feature extraction by a genetic algorithm. In: Fogel, D.B., Bezdek, J.C. (eds.) Proc. SPIE. Applications and Science of Neural Networks, Fuzzy Systems, and Evolutionary Computation II, Bruno Bosacchi, vol. 3812, pp. 24–31
23. Yao, H., Tian, L.: A genetic-algorithm-based selective principal component analysis (GA-SPCA) method for high-dimensional data feature extraction. IEEE Transactions on Geoscience and Remote Sensing 41(6), 1469–1478 (2003)
24. Viana, R., Malpica, J.A.: Genetic algorithm for accomplishing feature extraction of hyperspectral data using texture information. In: Serpico, S.B. (ed.) Image and Signal Processing for Remote Sensing V, The International Society for Optical Engineering. SPIE, December 1999, vol. 3871, pp. 367–372 (1999)
25. Tang, L., Tian, L., Steward, B.L.: Color image segmentation with genetic algorithm for infield weed sensing. Trans. ASAE 43(4), 1019–1027 (2000)
26. Bandyopadhyay, S., Pal, S.K.: Pixel classification using variable string genetic algorithms with chromosome differentiation. IEEE Transactions on Geoscience and Remote Sensing 39(2), 303–308 (2001)
27. Maulik, U., Bandyopadhyay, S.: Fuzzy partitioning using a real coded variable-length genetic algorithm for pixel classification. IEEE Transactions on Geoscience and Remote Sensing 41(5), 1075–1081 (2003)
28. Bandyopadhyay, S., Maulik, U., Mukhopadhyay, A.: Multiobjective genetic clustering for pixel classification in remote sensing imagery. IEEE Trans. Geosci. Remote Sensing 45, 1506–1511 (2007)
29. Kennedy, J., Eberhart, R.C.: Particle swarm optimization. In: Proc. IEEE Int. Conf. Neural Networks, December 1995, vol. 4, pp. 1942–1948 (1995)

30. Lu, Y., Liao, Z.W., Chen, W.F.: An automatic registration framework using quantum particle swarm optimization for remote sensing images, November 2007, vol. 2, pp. 484–488 (2007)
31. Xu, G., Sun, H., Yang, W.: Particle Swarm Optimization for Road Extraction in SAR Images. LNCIS, vol. 345, pp. 392–401. Springer, Heidelberg (2006)
32. Yu, J., Zhang, Z., Guo, P.: Multispectral Remote Sensing Image Classification Considering Texture Based on PSO-BP. In: Proceeding of the 7th World Congress on Intelligent Control and Automation, Chongqing, June 2008, pp. 6807–6810 (2008)
33. Omran, M., Salman, A., Engelbrecht, A.P.: Image Classification using Particle Swarm Optimization. In: Proceedings of the 4th Asia-Pacific Conference on Simulated Evolution and Learning, Singapore (2002)
34. Das, S., Abraham, A., Sarkar, S.: A hybrid rough set-particle swarm algorithm for image pixel classification. In: The Sixth International Conference on Hybrid Intelligent Systems, pp. 26–30 (2006)
35. Dorigo, M., Colomi, A., Maniezzo, V.: The Ant System: Optimization by a colony of co-operating agents. IEEE Transactions on Systems, Man, and Cybemetics-Part B 26, 1–13 (1996)
36. http://en.wikipedia.org/wiki/Ant_colony_optimization (June 2009)
37. Zheng, H., Zheng, Z., Xiang, Y.: The application of ant colony system to image texture classification. In: Proceedings of the 2nd International Conference on Machine Learning and Cybernetics, Xi'an, China, vol. 3, pp. 1491–1495 (2003)
38. Ouadfel, S., Batouche, M.: MRF-based image segmentation using ant colony system. Electronic Letters on Computer Vision and Image Analysis 2(2), 12–24 (2003)
39. Le Hegarat-Mascle, S., Kallel, A., Descombes, X.: Ant Colony Optimization for Image Regularization Based on a Nonstationary Markov Modeling. IEEE Trans. Image Processing 16(3), 865–879 (2007)
40. Le Hegarat-Mascle, S., Kalel, A., Descombes, X.: Application of ant colony optimization to image classification using a Markov model with non-stationary neighborhoods. In: Image and Signal Proceeding for Remote Sensing XI, Proceedings of the SPIE, Brugge, September 2005, vol. 5982, 59820C1–10 (2005)
41. Song, Q., Guo, P., Jia, Y.: Ant colony optimization algorithm for remote sensing image classification using combined features. In: International Conference on Machine Learning and Cybernetics, July 2008, pp. 3478–3483 (2008)
42. McCoy, D., Devarajan, V.: Artificial Immune Systems and Aerial Image Segmentation. In: IEEE International Conference on System Systems, Mans, and Cybernetics and Stimulation, vol. 1, pp. 867–872 (1997)
43. Zhang, L., Zhong, Y., Li, P.: Applications of artificial immune systems in remote sensing image classification. In: Proc. 20th Congr. Int. Soc. Photogrammetry Remote Sens., Istanbul, Turkey, July 2004, vol. 35, pp. 397–401 (2004)
44. Zhong, Y., Zhang, L., Huang, B., Li, P.: An unsupervised artificial immune classifier for multi/hyperspectral remote sensing imagery. IEEE Trans. Geosci. Remote Sens. 44(2), 420–431 (2006)
45. Zhong, Y., Zhang, L., Gong, J., Li, P.: A Supervised Artificial Immune Classifier for Remote-Sensing Imagery. IEEE Trans. Geosci. Remote Sens. 45(12), 3957–3966 (2007)
46. Pal, M.: Artificial immune-based supervised classifier for land-cover classification. International Journal of Remote Sensing 29(8), 2273–2291 (2008)
47. Xua, S., Wu, Y.: The International Archives of the Photogrammetry. In: Remote Sensing and Spatial Information Sciences, Beijing, vol. XXXVII, Part B6b, pp. 107–112 (2008)

Association Relation Mining in Multimedia Data

Wei Wei, Bin Ye, and Qing Li

Department of Computer Science and Technology
Chengdu University of Information Technology
Chengdu, China
weiwei@cuit.edu.cn, yebin@cuit.edu.cn, liqing@cuit.edu.cn

Abstract. In media content analysis, the semantic concepts are often treated as a separate class label. However, many visual semantic concepts are semantically related and so class labels are correlated. This paper presents a mining method for media semantic concept. Semantic frequent label set are selected when their occurrence frequency of several labels in one shot is greater than or equal to the support threshold. Then, semantic frequent item sets are used to generate association dependency relation. The correlations of more than two concepts could be directly obtained by this method. Finally, the mining results of association relation are applied to improve classification performance for concepts. Experiments on real-world media data show that the method can effectively extract potential association and dependency relations among semantic concepts.

Keywords: association relations mining, multimedia concept, media content analysis, semantic content.

1 Introduction

Often, the concepts, including high-level video concept and middle-level video concept, in one shot have strong correlation and dependence each other. The co-occurrence of concepts is positive correlations and vice versa. To improve the performance of individually video concept classifier is very difficult. But, making use of the correlations and dependence between concepts is a relatively easy way to increase the detection performance. For instance, *sky* and *ocean* concept are resemble in visual feature. Thus, it is very difficult to distinguish these two concept based on visual features alone. If there is one region is blue in color. It is not easy to class it to *sky* or *ocean* class. It is common sense that the grass and sky are usually simultaneity appear in landscape video. Therefore, grass and sky have strong correlation because of the co-appearance of them. However, if we are confident the appearance of grass concept in the same shot, then it is more likely that a region of blue in the frame should be annotated as "sky" rather than "ocean".

Many media content applications, such as video content analysis and image understanding, regard the semantic concept category as mutually exclusive class. Although some encouraging progresses have been made with the development of association mine in web mining, the methods suiting for media concept association and dependency

Z. Cai et al. (Eds.): ISICA 2009, CCIS 51, pp. 180–187, 2009.

relation mining are very few. The typical method for video concept in multimedia content analysis is *Correlative Multi-Label* (CML) [1]. CML method could directly extract the correlations mutual information between each pair concepts. But, the correlation relations of three or more concepts could not be indirectly extracted, which must be indirectly got from pair concepts correlation.

More researchers focus on the intensive study in individual video concept classification and learning technique. Few researchers consider the inter correlations and dependence relation between video concepts. In this paper, the strong correlation and dependence between concepts will be mining. Although some previous work such as method in paper [1] shares similar spirit of using inter-concept correlations relationship to improve multi-label video concept detection, most of them integrated such ideas into their framework only using pair concept correlation. Whereas, the distinctly difference is the correlations of more than two video concepts could be directly got by compound label in this paper. This correlation among classes can be helpful for predicting class labels of test concept examples.

The remaining paper is arranged as follows: Section 2 explores mining method of association and dependence relation. Section 3 is about the mining example for video concept. Section 4 reports about the experiment.

2 Association and Dependence Mining

Video data has typical structure. Frame is the base unit. Several or more frames consist of shot. Scene is composed of one or more shots. Thus, one video data must be decompressed and segmented. Before the video content understanding, video must be segmented into shot, decompressed into key-frames. In multimedia understanding, Shots are the basic semantic units for annotation and concept extraction. To extraction semantic concept, the train shot set must be are annotated by people.

Let *Concept*= $\{c_1, c_2, ..., c_m\}$ is the set of video concepts. Sometimes, *C* is called video concept items. In the set, the subscript m means the concept number that the system attempts to extract. Let *Shot* = $\{s_1, s_2,... s_i, ..., s_n\}$ be the train samples of n video shot. In the *Shot* set, s_i is the i-th shot in the train set. Each shot have an id, which is denoted as SID. *Label*= $\{l_1, l_2,... l_i, ..., l_n\}$ is a set of semantic concept labels, in which l_i is the annotation label corresponding to s_i shot. In video analysis, it is common that several concepts will appear in one shot. Thus, the annotated label l_i is a subset of *Concept* ($l_i \subseteq C$). $X \rightarrow Y$ means the strong association and dependency relation among concept X and Y, . Where, $X \subseteq C$, $Y \subseteq C$, $X \cap Y = \varnothing$. The support of $X \rightarrow Y$ is the percentage of shots that containt contain X also contain Y. The confidence of $X \rightarrow Y$ is the percentage of annotations containing X that also contain Y. A set of items is referred to as semantic label itemset. In this paprer, labels to each shot means itemset. An itemset containing k items is called k-itemset. An itemset can also be seen as a conjunction of items (or a predicate) Suppose *min_sup* is the minimum support threshold. An itemset satisfies minimum support if the occurrence frequency of the itemset is greater than or equal to *min_sup*. If an itemset satisfies minimum support, then it is a frequent itemset. Any subset of frequent itemset must be frequent. In this paper, the frequent itemsets is used to generate strong association and dependency relation of video concepts.

182   W. Wei, B. Ye, and Q. Li

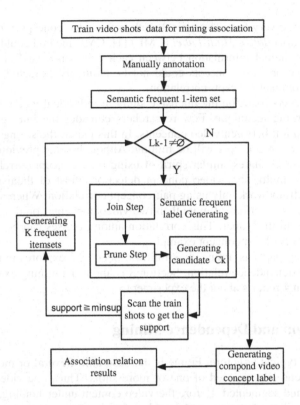

Fig. 1. Mining of association relation

The relations that satisfy both a minimum support threshold and a minimum confidence threshold are called strong association and dependency. Frequent itemsets is used to generate association dependency relation. The *frequent itemsets* have minimum support. A subset of a semantic frequent itemset must also be a frequent itemset. For example, if the video semantic label $\{L_1, L_2\}$ is a frequent itemset, both concept $\{L_1\}$ and concept $\{L_2\}$ should be a frequent itemset.

To find semantic frequent itemsets is an iterative process, which have cardinality from 1 to k (k-itemset). The iterative process of extraction strong association and dependency relation for video semantic have Join and prune steps [2, 3], illustrating in Figure 1.

(1) Join Operation: To find L_k, a set of candidate k-itemsets is generated by joining L_{k-1} with itself.

(2) Prune Step: Any (k-1)-itemset that is not frequent cannot be a subset of a frequent k-itemset

Given the train video shot set **Shot** = $\{s_1, s_2, ... s_i, ..., s_n\}$ and the minimum support threshold *min_sup*, the strong association and dependency relation $S_{assoc.}$ is extracted by the above method.

3   Mining Instance of Video Strong Association and Dependence Relation

Table 1 is a train shot set of video concept, annotated semantic label. $L_i(i=1,...,4)$ is annotation label set. The following will shows the process of relation extraction. Support threshold is 50%.

Table 1. Train video shot set

Shot	Semantic label(video concept)
S_1	$L_1=$ { ocean, ship, beach, sky }
S_2	$L_2=$ { ship, sky }
S_3	$L_3=$ { ocean, beach, mountain }
S_4	$L_4=$ { ship, beach, mountain }

For the concision of extraction, A= *ocean*, B= *ship*, C= *beach*, D= *mountain* and E= *sky*. The set of frequent 1-itemsets, L_1, consists of the candidate 1-itemsets satisfying minimum support 3, illustrated in Table 2.

Table 2. Frequent 1-itemsets L1

Semantic Item set	{ *ocean* }	{ *ship* }	{ *beach* }	{ *sky* }
Support count	2	3	3	3

$$L_1=\{ ocean, ship, beach, sky \}$$

The process of generating 2-itemset frequent is illustrated by Figure 2.

Join step is used to generate a candidate se C_k. Pseudo code of Join step is:

Insert into Ck
  Select *p*.item*1* , *p*.item*2* , ... , *p*.item*k-1*,*q*.item*k-1*
Form L_{k-1} *p* , L_{k-1} *q*
  Where *p*.item*1* = *q*.item*1* , ... , *p*.item*k-2* = *q*.item*k-2* , *p*.item*k-1* < *q*.item*k-1*;

Prune step helps to avoid heavy computation due to large C_k. Pseudo code of prune step is:

for itemsets *c* $\in$ *Ck* do
  forall (*k*-1)-subsets *s* of *c* do
    if (*s* $\in$ L_{k-1}) **then**
      delecte *c* form C_k;

To discover the set of frequent 2-itemsets, L_2, the algorithm uses L_1 *Join* L_1 to generate a candidate set of 2-itemsets, C_2. Next, the transactions in D are scanned and the support count for each candidate itemset in C_2 is accumulated. The set of frequent 2-itemsets, L_2, is then determined, consisting of those candidate 2-itemsets in C_2 having minimum support.

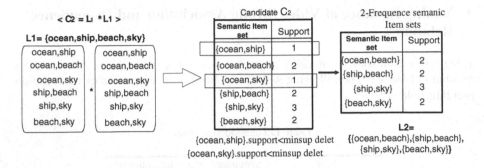

Fig. 2. Generating 2-frequence semantic itemset

L_2= {{ocean,beach},{ship,beach},{ship,sky},{beach,sky}}

{ship,beach} is the sub set of L_3 delete
{ship,sky} is the sub set of L_3 delete $\longrightarrow$ $L = \{ship,beach,sky\}$
{beach,sky} is the sub set of L_3 delete   , $L_2' = \{ocean,beach\}$

$\downarrow$ Scan

$S_{assoc.} = \{\{ocean,beach\},\{ship,beach,sky\}\}$

Fig. 3. Generating of S_{assoc}

The generation of the set of candidate 3-itemsets, C_3, involves use of the Apriori Property. In order to find C_3, we compute L_2 *Join* L_2. After join step, prune step will be used to reduce the size of C_3. Prune step helps to avoid heavy computation due to large C_k.

Figure 3 is the generating of strong association and dependency compound label $S_{assoc.}$. the final strong association and dependency compound label is $S_{assoc.} = \{ocean \wedge beach, ship \wedge beach \wedge sky\}$. To illuminate the semantic association and dependency relation in video shot, the confidence of video concept *ocean* and *beach* is:

$$c(ocean \rightarrow beach) = \frac{s(beach/ocean)}{s(beach)} = \frac{2}{2} = 100\% \qquad (1)$$

$$c(beach \rightarrow ocean) = \frac{s(ocean/beach)}{s(ocean)} = \frac{2}{3} = 67\% \qquad (2)$$

The relation *ocean* $\rightarrow$ *beach* means the co-occurrence of *ocean* concepts in a shot implies the presence of *beach* concepts in that shot. From (1), we could draw that 100% of the shots whose annotations contain *ocean* also contain *beach*. Equation (2) shows that 67% of the shots whose annotations contain *beach* concept also contain *ocean* concept in the train data. Therefore, the semantic concept *ocean* and *beach* have strong association and dependence relation. The method in this paper will re-gards the *ocean* and *beach* as one compound label *ocean* $\wedge$ *beach* in the process of learning, which will improve the performance of classifier. From the deduce, we could get:

$$c(ocean \rightarrow beach) \neq c(beach \rightarrow ocean) \tag{3}$$

BCE= $ship \wedge beach \wedge sky$, the relation of each other as follow:

$$c(ship \rightarrow beach, sky) = \frac{s(beach, sky/ship)}{s(ship)} = 67\% \tag{4}$$

$$c(ship, beach \rightarrow sky) = \frac{s(sky/ship, beach)}{s(ship, beach)} = 100\% \tag{5}$$

$$c(beach, sky \rightarrow ship) = \frac{s(ship/ship, sky)}{s(beach, sky)} = 100\% \tag{6}$$

Equation (4) are the percents of the shots whose annotations contain one of the three concepts also contain another two concepts in the train data. Equation (5)-(6) illustrate the percents of shots in train set that contain two compound concepts (such as *ship* and *beach*) among the three concepts also contain another concept.

4 Experiment

The experimental data is *MediaMill* [5].The *MediaMill* video data have 101 concept lexicon evaluated in the TRECVID benchmark. The items vary from pure format like a detected *split screen*, or a style like an *interview*, or an object like a *horse*, or an event like an *airplane take off*. Any one of those brings an understanding of the current content. At present, the researchers are trying to extend to a thesaurus of 500 concepts. *MediaMill* data scene are available at http://www.csie.ntu.edu.tw/~cjlin/libsvmtools/. Another attributes of *mediamil* are showed in Table 3. For all samples, 3039 are trained and 12941 are testing sample. The features number is 120. Different data set have different attribution. The attribution between the number of labels of each example and the total semantic category number will be represented by *label cardinality* and *label density* [4].

Association mining is very important for media content analysis. In this experiment, the method proposed in this paper is applied to multi-label classification. Association and dependency relation mining method presented above will be used in the process of multi-label classification in video data. Let $X = R^d$ denote the input space and $L = \{L_1, L_2, \cdots, L_{|L|}\}$ denote the finite set of possible video semantic labels. Given a multi-label training set $\{(x_1, L_1), (x_2, L_2), \cdots, (x_m, L_m)\}$, where $x_i \in X$ is a single instance and $L_i = (l_1^{(i)}, l_2^{(i)}, \cdots, l_{l_i}^{(i)})$ is the label set associated with x_i, the goal of multi-label learning is to learn a function $h: X \rightarrow 2^L$, which can predicts a set of labels for an unseen example.The most common problem transformation method learns $|Y|$ binary classifiers $h: \chi \rightarrow \{y, \neg y\}$, one for each different label y in Y [4], which denotes as PT Method for short. It transforms the original data set into $|Y|$ data sets D_y that contain all examples of the original data set, labelled as y if the labels of the original example contained y and as $\neg y$ otherwise.

Table 3. Another Attributes of mediamill

Data name	Density	Distinct	Labels num.	Cardinality
Mediamill	0.043	6555	101	4.376

In the experiment, the method presented above be applied to multi-label semantic concept analysis. Firstly, multi-labels with strong association and dependency relation are extraction. Then multi-labels will be looked as a single compound label. Finally, PT method is used to the compound multi-label learning. Comparing with the method in this paper, ML-kNN [6] is used to directly multi-label semantic concept learning.

Table 4. Experimental results between the compared method and the method in this paper

Evaluation metrics	Method in this paper	Direct PT method
Hammloss ↓	0.139	0.141
One-error ↓	0.211	0.215
Ranking loss ↓	0.186	0.189
Average precision ↑	0.793	0.781
Coverage ↓	7.680	7.683

Supposing the minimum support threshold is 50%. Strong association and dependency compound label $S_{assoc.}$ are generated. The final labels include strong association and dependency compound label $S_{assoc.}$ and the labels which are not in $S_{assoc.}$. To compare the performance of directly multi-label semantic concept classification and the multi-label classification method in this paper, the experiment results are showed in Table 4. Contrast data of two methods directly using ML-kNN[6], the performance of multi-label learning using the presented method are better.

The evaluation metrics in this experiment are hammloss, one-error, ranking loss, average precision and coverage [7, 8]. For each evaluation criterion, ↓ indicates "the smaller the better" while ↑ indicates the bigger the better. Because more media semantic concepts have strong association and dependency relation in each other, the proposing method can improve the performance. That is the fundamentality of the method.

5 Conclusion

Semantic concepts in media present a context, which are latent association and dependence. The relations can be used to infer the presence of a concept based on the presence of other associated semantic concepts.

In this paper, one association relation mining method for media is proposed. Semantic frequent label set are selected and used to generate association dependency relation.It makes use of the rich correlations between the semantic concepts. Experiment results shows that the mining method could effectively extracted the association among media concepts.

Acknowledgment

This paper is supported by Project (CSRF200803) Supported by the Scientific Research Foundation of CUIT and Development Found of Chengdu University of Information Technology under Grant No.KYTZ200914.

References

1. Agrawal, R., Imielinski, T., Swami, A.: Mining Association Rules between Sets of Items in Large Databases. In: Proc. of the 1993 ACM on M anagement of Data, Washington, DC, pp. 207–216 (1993)
2. Schapire, E., Singer, Y.: BoosTexter:A Boosting-based System for Text CategorizationA Boosting-based System for Text Categorization. Machine Learning 39(2/3), 135–168 (2000)
3. Godbole, S., Sarawagi, S.: Discriminative methods for multi-labeled classification. In: Dai, H., Srikant, R., Zhang, C. (eds.) PAKDD 2004. LNCS (LNAI), vol. 3056, pp. 22–30. Springer, Heidelberg (2004)
4. Liu, K.-H., Weng, M.-F., Tseng, C.-Y., Chuang, Y.-Y., Chen, M.-S.: Association and Temporal Rule Mining for Post-Filtering of Semantic Concept Detection in Video. IEEE Transactions on Multimedia 10(2), 240–251 (2008)
5. Qi, G.-J., Hua, X.-S., Rui, Y., Tang, J., Mei, T., Zhang, H.-J.: Correlative Multi-Label Video Annotation. In: Proc. ACM International Conference on Multimedia (ACM MM 2007), Augsburg, Germany, pp. 17–26 (2007)
6. Snoek, C.G.M., Worring, M., van Gemert, J.C., Geusebroek, J., Smeulders, A.W.M.: The Challenge Problem for Automated Detection of 101 Semantic Concepts in Multimedia. In: Proc. Proceedings of ACM Multimedia, Santa Barbara, USA, pp. 421–430 (2006)
7. Tsoumakas, G., Katakis, I.: Multi-label classification: An overview. International Journal of Data Warehousing and Mining 3(3), 1–13 (2007)
8. Zhang, M.-L., Zhou, Z.-H.: Ml-knn: A Lazy Learning Approach to Multi-Label Learning. Pattern Recognition 40(7), 2038–2048 (2007)

DSA Image Blood Vessel Skeleton Extraction Based on Anti-concentration Diffusion and Level Set Method

Jing Xu, Jian Wu, Daming Feng, and Zhiming Cui

The Institute of Intelligent Information Processing and Application,
Soochow University, JS China 215006
pargejessie@163.com
http://www.springer.com/lncs

Abstract. Serious types of vascular diseases such as carotid stenosis, aneurysm and vascular malformation may lead to brain stroke, which are the third leading cause of death and the number one cause of disability. In the clinical practice of diagnosis and treatment of cerebral vascular diseases, how to do effective detection and description of the vascular structure of two-dimensional angiography sequence image that is blood vessel skeleton extraction has been a difficult study for a long time. This paper mainly discussed two-dimensional image of blood vessel skeleton extraction based on the level set method, first do the preprocessing to the DSA image, namely uses anti-concentration diffusion model for the effective enhancement and uses improved Otsu local threshold segmentation technology based on regional division for the image binarization, then vascular skeleton extraction based on GMM (Group marching method) with fast sweeping theory was actualized. Experiments show that our approach not only improved the time complexity, but also make a good extraction results.

Keywords: medical DSA image, vessel skeleton extraction, anti-concentration diffusion, level set method, threshold segmentation.

1 Introduction

The human cerebrovascular system is a complex 3-D anatomical structure. Serious types of vascular diseases such as carotid stenosis, aneurysm and vascular malformation may lead to brain stroke, which are the third leading cause of death and the number one cause of disability. An accurate model of the vascular system from DSA data set is needed to detect these diseases at early stages and hence may prevent invasive treatments. Over the years, three-dimensional reconstruction of blood vessels by digital subtraction has been a very active research direction, with the goal of using computer vision method to describe three-dimensional vascular qualitative or quantitative. This process is basically composed of the following four steps [1]: (1) Accession and correction of digital subtracted images; (2) Segmentation of vascular and structural description

Z. Cai et al. (Eds.): ISICA 2009, CCIS 51, pp. 188–198, 2009.

in image (skeleton extraction); (3) The matching between a sequence (different time) of subtracted images; (4) Three-dimensional reconstruction and display. The key step is the matching between the subtracted images, but the strategy to be taken and its realization depend on the second step of a great extent. The overall framework of vascular structure three-dimensional reconstruction relies heavily on the effective detection and structure description of the vascular between the images.

Skeleton (or axis) has very important applications in many areas, such as objects expression, data compression, computer vision and animation. Use skeleton express the original image, the original image can be retained in the topology and shape characteristics, under the premise of reducing redundant information. Skeletons extraction algorithm can generally be divided into three categories: First one is the topology thinning algorithm, which detects topology relativity to the objects data rather than the shape of geometric features. The second method is looking the axis as the geometry bisectrix, calculating using Voronoi diagram, but the calculation is fairly complex. The third method is the distance transform for calculating objects borders.

Distance transform can be calculated by the Fast Marching Method (FMM) [2], FMM evolution meets the distance transform by a fixed rate along the normal direction of border. Then as the axis for the transformation from singular point, the singular point of distance transformation can be detected. But how to detect the distance transform singular point is a major difficulty. Singular point direct calculation is unstable; there is usually a row of discrete points. Siddiqi [3], who is tracking the marked point on the evolution interface, skeleton point is the point which conservation of energy had been destroyed, although this method are more stable than direct detection to the singular point, there is a great amount of caculation. Martin [4] detected skeleton use the moment analysis by the distance transformation obtained from the FMM, there is also a great amount of computation.

In this paper, blood vessel skeleton extraction based on the level set model and anti-concentration diffusion model is proposed. Anti-concentration diffusion model enhances the blood vessels effectively, and after using improved Otsu local threshold segmentation technology based on regional division for the image binarization, we get the purpose of vascular skeleton accurate extraction based on GMM (Group marching method) with fast sweeping theory.

2   Anti-concentration Diffusion to Enhance the Blood Vessels

As the differences between vessel diameters, and different contrast agent thickness in the blood vessels, the DSA images shows the thicker the vessel is, the higher the gray value , while the more exiguous the vessels is, the lower the gray value. Gray-scale inconsistency and the impact of noise, making it difficult to extract blood vessels skeleton better from the DSA images, such as missing part of the skeleton and serious burr phenomenon. In order to segment the capillaries, see the gray image information as the concentration information, Pixels with high gray value represent the high concentration regions, Pixels with low gray value represent the low concentration regions, anti-concentration diffusion model is as followed [5]: 1)Diffuse from low concentration regions to high concentration regions; 2)The shorter the distance is, the greater the diffuse quantity is in a certain period of time; 3)The higher the concentration difference is, the greater the diffuse quantity is in a certain period of time; 4)The lower the concentration is the greater diffuse outside in a certain period of time; 5)After the diffusion, the regional concentration of high become higher, regional concentration of low become lower; 6)Regional material increase of high concentration in the total is equal to regional material decrease of lower concentration in the sum equivalent; 7)regional differences in concentrations are larger final for the diffusion. Model formula is as follows:

$$F = EXP(\frac{-\varepsilon u_0(x,y)}{u_0(x,y) - u_0(\bar{x},\bar{y})}) \times EXP(\frac{-d^2}{2\sigma^2}) \tag{1}$$

F is the anti-concentration diffusion quantity, ε is the control coefficient, $u_0(x,y)$ is the gray value as the current pixels, $u_0(\bar{x},\bar{y})$ is the gray value as the diffuse pixels, and$u_0(x,y) < u_0(\bar{x},\bar{y})$. $EXP(\frac{-d^2}{2\sigma^2})$ is the Gaussian function, for d is the distance between the two pixels, σ is the standard deviation. Expression (1) shows the relationship of anti-concentration diffusion quantity F, concentration difference, $|u_0(x,y) - u_0(\bar{x},\bar{y})|$ distance d and the gray value of the current pixels $u_0(x,y)$: 1)The greater the concentration difference is, the bigger the F; 1)The greater the distance is, the smaller F ; 2)The greater the current pixels gray value is, the smaller F. Please always cancel any superfluous definitions that are not actually used in your text. If you do not, these may conflict with the definitions of the macro package, causing changes in the structure of the text and leading to numerous mistakes in the proofs.

3   Otsu Local Threshold Segmentation Based on Regional Division

Otsu [6] brought forward the OTSU method in 1979 (also known as the Dajin method) has been considered as the best practices in the method of threshold selected automatically. OTSU method is simple, under certain conditions, not be influenced by image contrast and brightness changes, which has been widely applied in image processing. However, due to uneven illumination, more information is losing while using OTSU method. We hope that we can make some improvements on this basis to gain better results.

First of all, we use the standard Mallat DWT algorithm to decompose image [7], which radix wavelet is three B-shape wavelet [8]. The original image is A_1, the j-1 layer of sub-image as A_{j-1}, wavelet decomposition followed along the line and row direction using low-pass filter or high-pass filter to sub-image A_{j-1}, we will get four sub-images: detail sub- images D_j^1, D_j^2, D_j^3 and a similar sub-image A_j (j = 2,3, J), only on the top-level (the Jth layer) using the complete form of Mallat multi-resolution analysis, geting similar sub-images and detail sub-images at the same time, while other layers simply through the low pass filter, geting the similar corresponding sub-images of A_j.

We divide image domain Ω into M target sub-regions Ω_i (i=1, 2M, M N) and a background sub-region Ω_b, that is $\Omega = \sum_{i=1}^{M} \Omega_i + \Omega_b$. The target sub-region includes a target in the sub-region, sub-regionΩ_s meet:$\Omega_s \cap \Omega_i \neq \phi$, $\Omega_s \cap \Omega_j = \phi$ (i=1,2...N, j=1,2...N, M$\geq$N, i$\neq$j); Background sub-region is not including any target, sub-region$\Omega_s$meet: $\Omega_s \cap \Omega_i = \phi$(i=1,2...N). Sub-region division is in the layer J. First along the horizontal, vertical and 45° direction detect the details sub-images (D_j^1, D_j^2, D_j^3) to determine the edge pixels, and then through the connectivity of edge pixels gain the sub-regions.

Select the best threshold r, make the best separability between different types [9]. First get the division of probability of all segment characteristic based on the histogram, and divide segment characteristic into two categories by the threshold r, and then seek the type of variance and covariance of each category, select r as the best threshold making the type of variance largest between the categories and the variance smallest inside categories. Namely:

$$\sigma_T^2 = \sigma_B^2 + \sigma_W^2 \tag{2}$$

$$\eta(t) = \frac{\sigma_B^2}{\sigma_T^2} \tag{3}$$

$$t = Arg \max_{0 \leq t \leq L-1} \eta(t) \tag{4}$$

σ_w^2 is the variance inside categories,σ_B^2 is the variance between categories, σ_T^2 is the overall variance, L is the gray levels of original gray images. The judgment criteria based on the gray histogram of the first order statistics, so it gains high computing speed. The whole image of Ostu threshold is r_1, one of the regional Ostu threshold is r_2, then the regional binarization used by the threshold $r' = k_1 r_1 + k_2 r_2$, $(k_1 + k_2 = 1)$. The weight k meets: 1)The smaller the inside category variance is, the greater the weight is; 2)The change of regional edge threshold can not be too much.

4   Vascular Skeleton Extraction Based on GMM and Fast Sweeping Method

FMM algorithm is used to calculate T, the distance from border, the human visual will be able to distinguish the skeleton we need easily. But in fact, if this process completed by computer simulation, get precise and rational framework exists considerable difficulties [10]. We hope bypassed this complex work, using a relatively fast GMM combine fast sweeping method to get the cerebrovascular skeleton.

We discusse how to improved algorithm on the basis of GMM, combined the spirit of fast sweeping method, using relatively simple calculation get the cerebrovascular skeleton directly. By document [11] we know that, skeleton is the compact boundary line, the points disappear in the course of dissemination

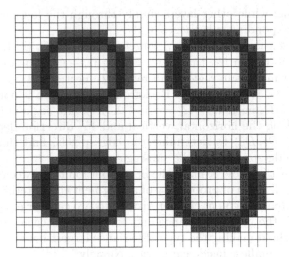

Fig. 1. Initialization sketch map of W_m

of the interface. In other words, all the spread points on interface are from the border, each point inside the border has a source point on the border. Therefore, we need only ascertain each point on the evolution curve from which points on the border.

Given object border Φ, distance transform defined as:

$$DISTANT(x) = \min_{y \in \Phi}(dist(x, y)) \tag{5}$$

The distance distribution for each point x from the nearest point y on the border, $dist(x, y) = ||x - y||_2$. By calculating the distance value DISTANT by GMM, FDT is introduced in the DISTANT of two parameters each point and get this value's boundary points y.

$$FDT(x) = \{DISTANT(x), \{y\}\}, y = arg\min_{y \in \Phi}(dist(x, y)) \tag{6}$$

We recorded the distance between any two points x and y as $PDF_0(y\text{-}x)$, the distance equation for each point PDF_0: $\delta_2 - \delta$.

We introduce a boundary parameters W: $W_m(0 < m < n + 1)$, initially, only select an arbitrary point at the border of the T = 0, from the point $W_m = 1$, we along the boundary line to increase 1 monotonously, as shown in Figure 1.

After initialization of W_m on the border, we get W of the whole image from W_m with iteration by GMM.

With the evolution of surface, the spread of W_m marked the initial border of the W_m arrived each grid point inside the region surrounded by the initial border, therefore the whole image will have a W.

If the current point of the four neighborhood points greater than $\sqrt{2}$, that means they do not come from neighboring points, because the largest value W_m

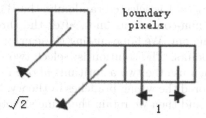

Fig. 2. Largest margin of Wm of adjacent pixels

of adjacent two points is $\sqrt{2}$, as shown in Figure 2. We only have to promote the neighborhood of current points' W_m to further place.

Once all grid points' W are computed out, S is the skeleton of the image:

$$S(\Phi, W) = \{(i,j)|max(|W_m(i+1,j) - W_m(i,j)|, |W_m(i,j+1) - W_m(i,j)|) > s\} \tag{7}$$

$$wp = W_m(i+1,j) - W_m(i,j) \tag{8}$$

$$wq = W_m(i,j+1) - W_m(i,j) \tag{9}$$

$$v = max(|wp|, |wq|) \tag{10}$$

We chose the skeleton threshold s for filtering, the retain points is the skeleton points. Practice has proved that the skeleton operator v is very strong, and we can get the consecutive skeleton points. In fact, if the margin value W_m1 and W_m2 of the adjacent point p_1, p_2 over a given threshold s, it must have the margin value of W_m of adjacent point y of point p_1 or p_2 and its adjacent points more than the value of s. Intuitive to say that is because as each grid T value is calculated to meet the time equation. If there is a hole in the image: initialize W_m from different directions, and there are W_m1 and W_m2. Skeleton function is:

$$min(S(\Phi, W_m1), S(\Phi, W_m2)) \tag{11}$$

Algorithm can be summarized as follows:

1 initialize DISTANT to max_value
2 initialize W_m on boundary
3 for all boundary points x
4 for every point y
5 if $(PDF_0(y-x) < DISTANT(y))$
6 $DISTANT(y) = PDF_0(y-x)$
7 $W_m(y) = W_m(x)$
8 if there is a hole $S(\Phi, W) = min(S(\Phi, W_m1), S(\Phi, W_m2))$
  else

$$S(\Phi, W) = \{(i,j)|max(|W_m(i+1,j) - W_m(i,j)|, |W_m(i,j+1) - W_m(i,j)|) > s\}$$
The skeletons which are filtered out through the threshold appear branch we do not need (we can call it Burr). In the initialization of the border point of the

W_m, border point at $W_m = 1$ is selected randomly, the W_m we have received all will have a number of non-continuous lines, after the threshold filtering, these branches are not filtering out. We hope cutting these error branches of the skeleton caused by initial points. The solution is: select two different initial points which $W_m = 1$, and then use the two algorithms above respectively, we can get same skeleton after ignored the wrong branches in theory, but wrong branches in the different positions, and then we retain the same skeleton, cut different ones.

5   Experiment and Analysis

5.1   Enhancement Effect of Vessel Using Anti-concentration Diffusion

Figure 3 is the original image of the vessel to be enhanced, Figure 4 is the result using Sobel arithmetic operators, Figure 5 is the result using anti-concentration diffusion and the parameters are: $\sigma=10$, $\varepsilon=0.125$, w=5, $\lambda=10$, k=5. Compared to Figure 3, Figure 4, Figure 5, we can find that adopting anti-concentration diffusion model gets a good enhancement effect and has an obvious advantage than Sobel method.

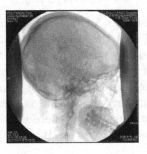

Fig. 3. DSA original image

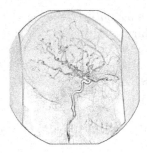

Fig. 4. Enhancement effect by Sobel method

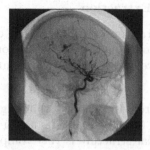

Fig. 5. Enhancement effect using anti-concentration diffusion model

5.2   Effect of Regional Division Otsu Local Threshold Segmentation

Using local threshold segmentation method based on Otsu, we can see that smaller the divided regions are, better the effect should be in theory, but the amount of computation will be larger and the speed will be slower. Compared to the overall threshold segmentation effect in Figure 6, we can see that: 1) little information is lost at the end of the vessels and maintain its basic integrity, 2) the small vessels and the big ones are not confusing with each other in the middle region, and the basic structures of big vessels are not damaged. As shown in Figure 7.

Fig. 6. Overall threshold segmentation effect

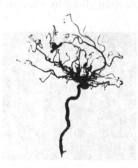

Fig. 7. Regional division Otsu local threshold segmentation effect

5.3 Effect of Skeleton Extraction

The effects of skeleton extraction of the two DSA cerebrovascular images are shown in Figure 8 is the effect using the thinning algorithm, Figure 9 is the effect using our method. Compared to thinning algorithm, our method has obvious advantages:

1) The axis result gotten from the classical thinning algorithm is influenced by border noise obviously, the axis level of smooth is not good and has more burr. The axis of vascular structure is very complex;
2) Improved GMM algorithm can set a different filter width and extract frameworks fitting with different requirements can ignore the capillary vessels.

Figure 10, Figure 11, Figure 12 is the results of the comparison of the main artery of the brain blood vessels adding salt and pepper noise, fine lines and broad-brush noise interference.

Figure 10 are the extraction results of the thinning algorithm and our algorithm after adding salt and pepper noise in the original image.

Figure 11 are the extraction results of the thinning algorithm and our algorithm after adding fine lines noise interference in the original image.

Figure 12 are the extraction results of the thinning algorithm and our algorithm after adding broad-brush noise interference in the original image.

The results show that in dealing with salt and pepper noise, the traditional thinning method has the similar effect with our algorithm. By adding fine line

Fig. 8. Extraction effect by thinning algorithm

Fig. 9. Extraction effect by our method

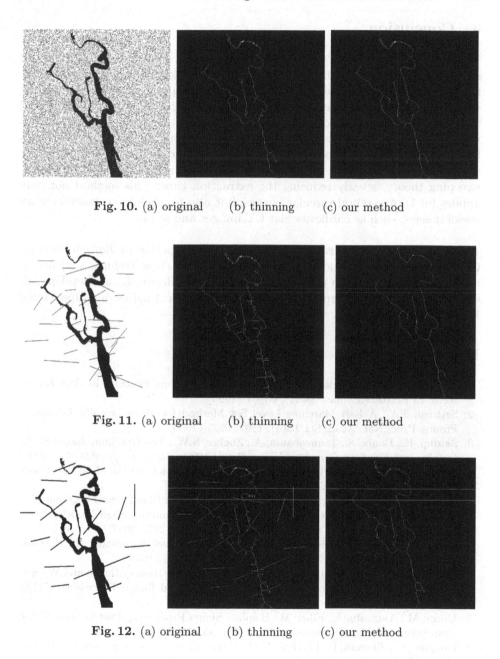

Fig. 10. (a) original   (b) thinning   (c) our method

Fig. 11. (a) original   (b) thinning   (c) our method

Fig. 12. (a) original   (b) thinning   (c) our method

interference noise, our algorithm is superior to thinning algorithm apparently at the aspect of the assurance of skeleton topology and integrity. By adding broad-brush noise interference, only use this paper's algorithm can eliminate the broad-brush noise interference, and the skeleton remains good integrity, but the thinning algorithm was interfered obviously, can not achieve the ideal extraction of the skeleton basically, and our algorithm's advantage is reflected obviously.

6 Conclusion

This paper proposes blood vessel skeleton extraction based on the level set model and anti-concentration diffusion model has the following advantages: (1)Due to the anti-concentration diffusion model to do the preprocessing, enhance the vascular information in the DSA image effectively; (2) Use improved Otsu local threshold technology based on regional division for the image segmentation to vascular DSA images, makes blood vessels information loss less, divide the small blood vessels from large blood vessels well, and not undermine the basic structure of the large vessels. (3) Then extract vascular skeleton based on GMM with fast sweeping theory, greatly reducing the extraction time. This method not only applies for DSA cerebral vascular images, but also for skeleton extraction of all vessel images, such as cardiovascular CT images and so on.

Acknowledgments. This research was partially supported by Jiangsu Province Colleges Industry Promotion Project (JHB06-26), Soochow Technological Breakthrough Project (Industry) (SGR0703) and Jiangsu Research and Development Center for Modern Enterprise I nformation Software Engineering Open Fund Project (SX200803).

References

1. Fei, M., Limin, L., Xudong, B.: Extraction of Structure Features in DSA Image. Acta. El Ectronica Sinica 23(11), 60–64 (1995)
2. Sethian, J.A.: A Fast Marching Level Set Method for Monotonically Advancing Fronts. Proc. Nat. Acad. Sci. 93(4), 1591–1595 (1996)
3. Siddiqi, K., Bouix, S., Tannenbaum, A., Zucker, S.W.: The Hamilton-Jacobi Skeleton. In: Intl. Conf. on Computer Vision ICCV 1999, vol. 22(1), pp. 828–834 (1999)
4. Rumpf, M., Telea, A.: A Continuous Skeletonization Method Based on Level Sets. In: IEEE TCVG Symposium on Visualization (2002)
5. Haiyong, Q., Weiping, Z., Xudong, B., Limin, L.: MRA Blood Vessel Segmentation Based on Anti-concentration Difusion Method and Mumford-Shah Model relating to Grayscale Histogram. Signal Processing 23(2), 273–277 (2007)
6. Otsu, N.: A Threshold Selection Method from Gray-Level Histograms. IEEE Transactions on Systems, Man, and Cybernetics 9(1), 62–66 (1979)
7. Mallat, S.G., et al.: Multifrequency Channel Decomposition of Image and Wavelet Models. IEEE Transactions on Acoustics, Speech and Signal Processing 37(12), 2091–2110 (1989)
8. Unser, M., Aldroubi, A., Eden, M.: B-spline Signal Processing: Part I-theory. IEEE Transaction on Signal Processing 41(2), 821–833 (1993)
9. Donglan, C., Jingnan, L., Lingling, Y.: Comparison of Image Segmentation Thresholding Method. Machine Building and Automation 43(1), 77–80 (2003)
10. Rumpf, M., Telea, A.: A Continuous Skeletonization Method Based on Level Sets. In: IEEE TCVG Symposium on Visualization (2002)
11. Kimmel, R., Shaked, D., Kiryati, N., Bruckstein, A.M.: Skeletonization vis Distance Maps and Level Sets. Computer Vision and Image Understanding 62(3), 382–391 (1995)

Space Camera Focusing Forecast Based on RBF Network

Xingxing Wu, Jinguo Liu, and Da Yu

Changchun Institute of Optics, Fine Mechanics and Physics, Chinese Academy of Sciences,
Changchun, Jilin 130033, China
starglare@126.com

Abstract. As circumstance temperature of space camera changes, flex of structural components and distortion of optical components lead to change of focal length and image quality. Radial Basis Function (RBF) network is used to approximate the complex nonlinear relation between focalization quantity, image quality, temperature level and axial temperature difference of space camera. After the RBF Network is trained with thermo-optical experiment data, temperature level and axial temperature difference could be input to the network to obtain colder value of best image position. In this way focusing forecast under different temperatures can be realized. Results of focusing forecast experiment validate this method.

Keywords: Space camera, Neural network, Radial basis function, Focusing.

1 Introduction

Space cameras for earth observation usually work on circular orbits and stay at a fixed altitude, which is different from cameras used in other fields. Circumstance temperature of space camera changes according to position relative to sun and other celestial bodies. As temperature changes, deformation of structural components lead to change of distance between Optical components. Distortion of optical component surface and change of refractive index bring on aberration. All these result in change of focal length and image quality. In addition to temperature level, axial temperature difference is another important factor that influences image quality of optical system[1-3].So image quality of space camera has a complex nonlinear function relationship with image plane position, temperature level and axial temperature difference.

Generally on-orbit focusing was performed according to people's experience and analyses of on-ground thermo-optical experiments data, which is rather subjective and inefficient. Radial basis function (RBF) networks are capable of approximating any function with a finite number of discontinuities. As far as function approximation ability and learning speed are concerned, RBF networks are superior to BP networks and have been successfully applied in many fields [4-5]. In this paper RBF network was used to approximate the complex nonlinear function relations among image quality, image plane position, temperature level and axial temperature difference. Consequently the ideal image position with best image quality at a specific temperature level and axial temperature difference could be acquired as the output of Radial basis network. In this way space camera focusing forecast can be realized.

Z. Cai et al. (Eds.): ISICA 2009, CCIS 51, pp. 199–206, 2009.

2 Analysis of Network Model

Image quality of space camera can be measured by Modular Transfer Function (MTF) at Nyquist space frequency f_n. MTF is the modulus of optical transfer function (OTF), which represents response function of space camera to space frequency[6-7]. Coder installed on focus control indicated current position of image plane. As instructions were sent to camera controller, step motor drove focus control to move image plane and coder recorded current image position. Thermistors attached to different sections of space camera measured current temperature level and axial temperature difference. From above analysis MTF of space camera at Nyquist space frequency MTF_n can be described as formula (1).

$$MTF_n = F(C_i, T_m, T_{ad})$$ (1)

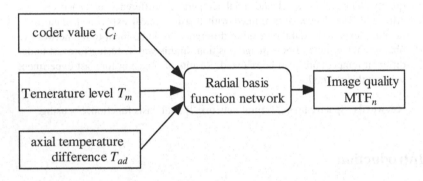

Fig. 1. RBF network for space camera focusing forecast

RBF network for space camera focusing forecast is as Fig.1 shows. Code value C_i, temperature level T_m and axial temperature difference are inputs of the network, while MTF_n serves as output of the network. After having been trained, if only current temperature level and axial temperature difference are known, MTF_n at each image position inside focusing range can be calculated. In result best image position with highest MTF_n can be acquired by scanning focusing range.

Swatch data for training RBF network were acquired from thermo-optical experiments.Fig.2 is sketch of thermo-optical experiments. Space circumstance simulator provided vacuum and thermal circumstance for space camera. Temperature of space camera could be adjusted by the simulator. Remote control and test system sent instructions to camera controller and acquired camera temperatures. Collimator produced parallel light to simulate target at infinity. Camera data acquisition and monitor system gathered output of charge couple device (CCD) and formed image of reticle.

Reticle was designed to meet the Nyquist space frequency f_n, which is determined by pixel size of CCD and could be calculated by formula (2). Fig.3 shows structure of reticle .Width of black stripe D should meet formula (3).

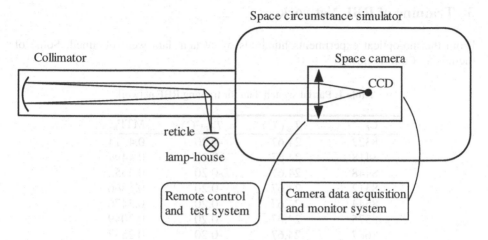

Fig. 2. Sketch of thermo-optical experiments

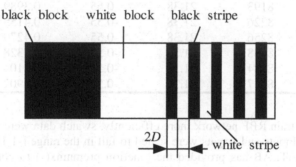

Fig. 3. Structure of reticle

$$f_n = \frac{1}{2a} \tag{2}$$

$$D = \frac{f_p \cdot a}{f_s} = \frac{f_p}{2f_s \cdot f_n} \tag{3}$$

Where a is pixel size of CCD. f_p and f_s is respectively focal length of collimator and space camera. MTF_n can be calculated from image of reticle by formula (4).

$$MTF_n = \frac{\pi}{4} \cdot \frac{(I_{ws} - I_{bs})}{(I_{ws} + I_{bs})} \cdot \frac{(I_{wb} + I_{bb})}{(I_{wb} - I_{bb})} \tag{4}$$

I_{ws} and I_{bs} are respectively gray scale value of white stripe and black stripe. I_{wb} and I_{bb} are respectively gray scale value of white block and black block.

3 Training of RBF Network

From thermo-optical experiments hundreds of swatch data were obtained. Some of them is as Table 1 shows.

Table 1. Partial swatch data for training RBF network

C_i	T_m (℃)	T_{ad} (℃)	MTF_n
8322	24.67	-0.20	0.4314
8418	24.67	-0.20	0.4494
8448	24.67	-0.20	0.4552
8512	24.67	-0.20	0.3866
8544	24.67	-0.20	0.3476
8575	24.67	-0.20	0.3049
8607	24.67	-0.20	0.2587
8640	24.67	-0.20	0.2189
8130	21.38	-0.55	0.3519
8193	21.38	-0.55	0.3989
8226	21.38	-0.55	0.4155
8256	21.38	-0.55	0.4270
8288	21.38	-0.55	0.4328
8384	21.38	-0.55	0.4104
8417	21.38	-0.55	0.3902

In order to train RBF network more efficiently, swatch data were preprocessed before training. Inputs and targets were scaled to fall in the range [-1,1].Neural network toolbox in MATLAB has provided the function premnmx( ) to complete such preprocess[8]. Two design functions of RBF network can be used in neural network toolbox. Function newrbe( ) produces a network with as many hidden neurons as there are input vectors and does not return an acceptable solution when many input vectors are needed to properly define a network. Function newrb( ) creates neurons one at a time and is more efficient than function newrbe( ). At each iteration the input vector that results in lowering the network error the most, is used to create a neuron. Function newrb( ) was used in this paper as there were many input vectors to train the network.

Fig.4 and Fig.5 are respectively training curve without preprocess and training curve without preprocess as SPREAD =1. Obviously the RBF network converged more quickly with preprocess than without preprocess.It's very important to select the spread constant SPREAD for the radial basis layer in training of RBF networks. SPREAD should be large enough so that the active input regions of the radbas neurons overlap enough, which makes the network function smoother and results in better generalization for new input vectors occurring between input vectors used in the training. Whereas if SPREAD is too large the radial basis neurons will output large values for all the inputs used to training the network and any information presented to the network becomes lost.

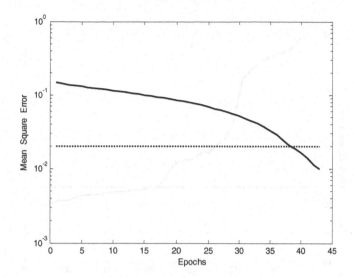

Fig. 4. Training curve without preprocess as spread=1

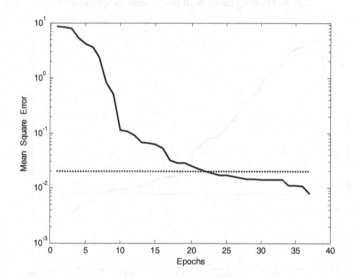

Fig. 5. Training curve with preprocess as spread=1

Fig.6 and Fig.7 are respectively training curve with preprocess as SPREAD=0.8 and training curve with preprocess as SPREAD=0.4.As SPREAD=1 it took 22 epochs for Mean square Error(MSE) to reach the goal 0.02 and the network has 22 neurons. When SPREAD=0.4 it took 23 epochs for Mean square Error(MSE) to reach the goal 0.02 and the network has 23 neurons. However it took only 19 epochs for Mean square Error(MSE) to reach the goal 0.02 as SPREAD=0.8. So SPREAD=0.8 was used in this paper.

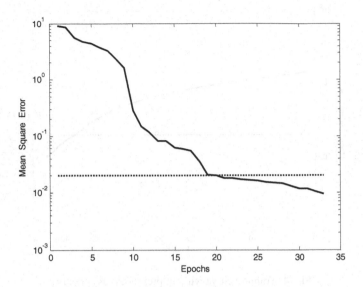

Fig. 6. Training curve with preprocess as spread=0.8

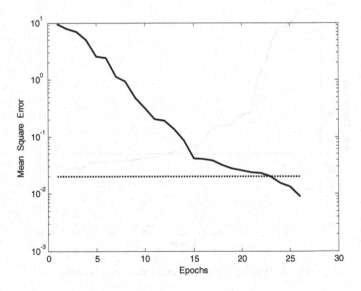

Fig. 7. Training curve with preprocess as spread=0.4

4 Result of Focusing Forecast Experiments

In order to validate the RBF network having been trained, focusing forecast experiments were made. Experiment circumstance was similar to that of thermo-optical experiments. Firstly space circumstance simulator was adjusted to make the space camera reach a certain temperature level. Then the temperature level and axial temperature difference were input to the RBF network. While various coder value during focusing range was input to the network to find the max output MTF_n. At last image plane was moved to the position of coder value corresponding to max RBF network output. Real MTF_n was measured by camera data acquisition and monitor system at that position. The RBF network can be validated by checking if Real MTF_n is coincide with output MTF_n. As the swatch data had been preprocessed before the RBF network was trained. It's required that inputs to the network in focusing forecast experiments be preprocessed in the same way as swatch data for training. Because outputs in swatch data had been preprocessed, outputs of the RBF network in focusing forecast experiments should be postprocessed before used.

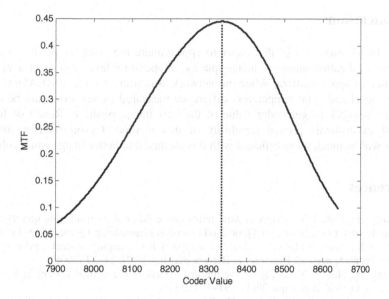

Fig. 8. MTF-Coder value curve at 22.09℃

For example, when temperature level of space camera was adjusted to 22.09℃ and axial temperature Was -0.12℃.MTF-Coder value curve could be drawn as Fig.8 by scanning focusing range with the RBF network. According to the curve Best image position was at 8335 coder value and MTF_n reached 0.4448. Then the camera was focused to 8335 coder value. Real MTF_n was measured to be 0.4473 by image, which is coinciding with the output of the RBF network.

Test Result of focusing forecast experiments is as Table.2 shows. T_a and T_{adf} are respectively temperature level and axial temperature difference of space camera in focusing forecast experiments. C_f is coder value searched to be best image position. MTF_f is output of the RBF network while MTF_r is real MTF_n measured at C_f .It can be concluded that output of the RBF network is coincide with real value. Space camera focusing forecast based on radial basis network is valid. With this method efficiency of on-bit focusing will be improved and better remote sensing image will be obtained.

Table 2. Result of focusing forecast experiments

T_a (℃)	T_{adf} (℃)	C_f	MTF$_f$	MTF$_r$
22.09	-0.12	8335	0.4448	0.4473
23.52	-0.06	8366	0.4631	0.4589
20.60	-0.29	8268	0.4278	0.4254
19.04	-0.14	8208	0.4312	0.4302
18.55	-0.11	8195	0.4323	0.4361
17.03	-0.36	8154	0.4285	0.4321
16.49	-0.23	8135	0.4255	0.4298
14.03	-0.17	8038	0.4273	0.4235

5   Conclusions

RBF network was used in this paper to approximate the complex nonlinear relation between focalization quantity, image quality, temperature level and axial temperature difference of space camera. After the network was trained with SPREAD=0.8, temperature level and axial temperature difference measured by sensors could be input to the RBF network to get coder value of the best image position. Result of focusing forecast experiments proved feasibility of this method. On-bit focusing of space camera will be much more efficient with this method and better image can be obtained.

References

1. Wang, H., Tian, T.Y.: Effect of axial temperature difference on imaging quality of space remote sensor optical system. Optics and Precision Engineering 15(10), 1489–1494 (2007)
2. Lin, Z.R.: Thermo-Optical analysis of a typical R-C imaging system's primary optical equipment. Spacecraft Recovery & Remote Sensing 27(2), 23–27 (2006)
3. Wang, H., Han, C.Y.: Study on the thermal effects of the optical system in a aerospace camera. Optical Technique 29(4), 451–457 (2003)
4. Krzyzak, A., Linder, T., Lugosi, G.: Nonparametric Estimation and Classification Using Radial Basis Function Nets and Empirical Risk Minimization. IEEE Trans. on Neural Networks 2(7), 475–487 (1996)
5. Esposito, A., Marinaro, M., Oricchio, D., Scarpetta, S.: Approximation of Continuous and Discontinuous Mapping by a Growing Neural RBF-based Algorithm. Neural Networks 13(6), 651–665 (2000)
6. Gostik, R.W.: OTF-based optimization criteria for automatic optical design. Optical and Quantum Electronics 1(8), 31–37 (1976)
7. Fantone, S.D., Imrie, D.A., Orband, D.: MTF testing algorithms for sampled thermal imaging systems. In: Proceedings of SPIE, vol. 6835, p. 683510 (2007)
8. Demuth, H., Beale, M., Hagan, M.: Neural Network Toolbox for use with MATLAB User's Guide, 6th edn. The MathWorks Inc., Natick (2008)

Wood Defect Identification Based on Artificial Neural Network

Xiao-dong Zhu, Jun Cao, Feng-hu Wang, Jian-ping Sun, and Yu Liu

Key laboratory of Bio-Based Material Science and Technology of Ministry of Education,
Northeast Forestry University, Harbin, China
pse4646@126.com

Abstract. Defects in wooden material reduce the value of timber. In order to save and improve the utilization of the timber, many studies are carried out on the ways to detect defects in wood. The recent development of computer technology, data processing technology and signal processing technology provides researchers with more damage identification problem solution ideas and methods. This article studies the vibration characteristics of wood. With an exploration of the wavelet analysis and artificial neural network for the wood composite material defects based on non-destructive testing, an artificial neural network model is established for wood-based composite materials non-destructive testing technology.

Keywords: neural network; wood; non-destructive; vibration frequency.

1 Introduction

Defects in wood materials including natural defects, drying defects, machining defects, biological hazards defects[1]. These defects affect the wood material, reducing the value of timber[2-3]. In order to save and improve the utilization rate of timber, it has been studying ways to detect defects in wood. In recent years, computer technology, data processing technology and signal processing technology, providing researchers with more damage identification problem solution ideas and methods, such as modal analysis, wavelet theory, neural network and genetic algorithm[4-5]. Despite the damage identification in the field of theoretical study of these has just launched, but these methods have their unique advantages, their applications to address the structural damage identification of a number of new solutions[6-10].

This article research the vibration characteristics of wood. Explore the wavelet analysis and artificial neural network for the wood composite material defects based on non-destructive testing, build an artificial neural network model for wood-based composite materials non-destructive testing technology.

2 Material and Method

Specimen used for Larix. In the bending vibration of the nodes (0.224L) the specimen with string hanging. The use of percussion hammer one end of the sample to produce

Z. Cai et al. (Eds.): ISICA 2009, CCIS 51, pp. 207–214, 2009.

vibration, the other side of the sample by measuring the vibration microphone signal, convert it to electricity signal; signal processing circuit to power the microphone signal shaping, conversion, filter processing into the standard signal; data acquisition card acquisition signal of the voltage signal processing circuit, and converted to a computer can handle the digital signal; through device drivers, digital signal into the industrial machine;in the LabVIEW platform, the call signal processing sub-templates, vibration signals acquisition and FFT analysis of vibration signals obtained spectrum, the sample can be the resonant frequency. Sampling frequency of the tests for 10KHz, for the 2048 sampling points.

3   Artificial Neural Network Damage Detection

3.1 Damage Detection Based on Wavelet Packet Energy Changes in the Artificial Neural Network

The sample is divided into three modules. A total of 260 vibration signal acquisition, which left 30 group of defects, defects in the middle of the 200 groups, 30 group of defects in the right side. Use of wavelet packet signal in this group of 260 three-wavelet packet transform, the signal in the high-frequency and low frequency components of 8 and 8 to calculate this component in various energy band occupied by the ratio of the energy rate to be as a neural network input samples. In this set of data in 260, out of 16 sets of data (left-3 group, the middle of 10 groups, the right end of the 3 groups), as a test to promote the ability of neural network simulation samples. Another group of 244 samples as the training network. Optional four-BP network, neural network input layer nodes is 8, the corresponding signal after wavelet packet decomposition of the 8-band energy ratio, the output layer nodes is 3, corresponding to defects in the extreme left, the right end of the defects and deficiencies in the middle of the three models. The first node of hidden layer neurons is set to 10,12,15,18,20, and the second hidden layer nodes is 6 for training. Analysis of these five characteristics of the network of training and promotion of performance, in order to identify the best network structure. Network training, the left defects in the middle of the right end of the defects and deficiencies in the target output of the three models, respectively [1 0 0], [0 1 0], [0 0 1]. Network Sigmoid transfer function for the tangent function, the output layer transfer function for the pure linear function, learning algorithm for the Levenberg-Marquarat back-propagation algorithm. Network training, simulation of the neural network output and target output to do linear regression analysis, three different locations on the simulation of bubble defects, such as the correlation coefficient Table 1.

As can be seen from the table, the central defect of the test results very satisfactory, with the goal of their output in the correlation coefficient above 0.9, the detection of defects in the results of the extreme left and the target output of the correlation coefficient is also high in between 0.859-0.983. Defects in the right side of the test results with the target output in the correlation coefficient between 0.676-0.784 is not very

Table 1. Correlation coefs of five networks with different hidden nodes

The first hidden layer node	The second hidden layer nodes	Actual output and target output of the regression correlation coefficient		
		Left	Middle	Right
10	6	0.983	0.934	0.676
12	6	0.929	0.990	0.784
15	6	0.881	0.991	0.726
18	6	0.859	0.901	0.683
20	6	0.904	0.938	0.678

satisfactory. From 16 groups (3 groups left, the middle of 10 groups, the right end of the 3 groups) of the sample did not participate in training to promote the performance of the network authentication. According to the actual network output and target output of the contrast from 0.6 to the experience of identification to determine whether the value of the actual output for the correct identification of greater than 0.6, less than 0.6 can not correctly identify.Figure 1,2,3,4,5 in the black solid line is the ability to correctly identify the standard line defects.

The first hidden layer node 10, the network structure of the 8 × 10 × 6 × 3, the network output after training on their simulation results and the target output for linear regression analysis. The promotion of a performance test network in Figure 1. As can be seen from the figure, there is a middle and a right side of the defect can not be identified defects, accounting for a total of 16 samples of 12.5%.

The first hidden layer node 12, the network structure of the 8 × 12 × 6 × 3, the network output after training on their simulation results and the target output for linear regression analysis. The promotion of a performance test network in Figure 2. From the figure we can see that there is only one defect in the right side can not be identified, accounting for a total of 16 samples of 6.25%.

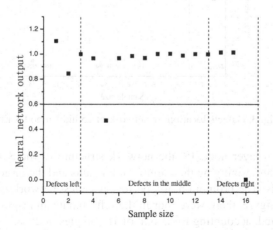

Fig. 1. Defects location by network of 10 hidden nodes first

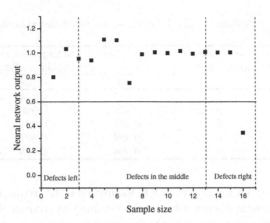

Fig. 2. Defects location by network of 12 hidden nodes first

The first hidden layer node 15, the network structure of the $8 \times 15 \times 6 \times 3$, the network output after training on their simulation results and the target output for linear regression analysis. The promotion of a performance test network in Figure 3. As can be seen from the figure, there were two defects in the left and right side can not be identified, accounting for a total of 16 samples of 12.5%.

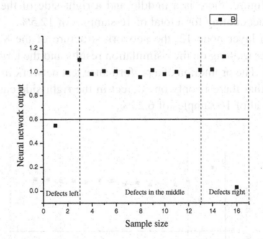

Fig. 3. Defects location by network of 15 hidden nodes first

The first hidden layer node 18, the network structure of the $8 \times 18 \times 6 \times 3$, the network output after training on their simulation results and the target output for linear regression analysis. The promotion of a performance test network in Figure 4. As can be seen from the figure, there were four in the left, middle and right side of the defect can not be identified, accounting for a total of 16 samples of 25%.

Based on wavelet packet energy changes in the neural network found a comparative analysis of different hidden layer nodes, Tangent Sigmoid transfer function for four of

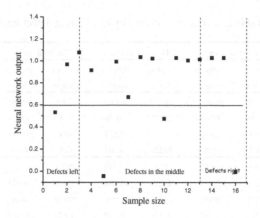

Fig. 4. Defects location by network of 18 hidden nodes first

five BP network in different locations to identify deficiencies in the training bubble characteristics and the promotion of performance has the following characteristics.

The defects in the middle of five network simulation best, the correlation coefficient above 0.9, the simulation of the extreme left coefficient between 0.859-0.983. Defects in the right side of the test results with the target output in the correlation coefficient between 0.676-0.784 is not very satisfactory.

The wavelet packet decomposition to extract the rate of signal energy in different frequency bands eigenvectors as input samples of neural network for training and learning network, training the BP network model can be achieved at different positions of the automatic recognition of bubble defects. Defects of the middle of the recognition rate of over 90% of the extreme left and the right side of the recognition rate in more than 80%.

Characteristics of network training, and promotion of performance considerations and other factors, defects of different automatic identification of the optimal location of network model for the first hidden layer of 12, the second hidden layer nodes is 6, the transfer function of Tangent Sigmoid function, the output layer transfer function for the pure linear function, learning algorithm for the Levenberg-Marquarat back-propagation algorithm, the network of defects in the recognition rate reached 93.75 percent.

3.2 Based on the Frequency of Types of Structural Damage Detection Indicators

Larix for a sample divided into three defect unit, the extent of defect were 30%, 50%, 70% and 90% respectively. Table 2 for the various modules of different degrees of defect changes in modal frequency values. As can be seen from the table Larix defective beam, the modal frequency decreases. Frequency changes from the absolute and relative changes can be seen that the changes in modal frequencies with the degree of injury increases, but the modal frequency of the different bands of different changes in the sensitivity of the location of injury are not the same, without the same laws. From the frequency shift can easily determine the existence of defects, but if no further analysis could not determine the location and size of defects.

Table 2. Variance of frequency of different defect level

Defect unit	Defect extent	The first-order		The second-order		The third-order		The fourth-order	
		Absolute change	Relative change	Absolute change	Relative change	Absolute change	Relative change	Absolute change	Relative change
1	30%	83.75	0.077	175	0.063	312.5	0.062	362.5	0.048
	50%	93.75	0.083	218.75	0.076	375	0.073	425	0.055
	70%	150	0.128	362.5	0.124	475	0.099	512.5	0.075
	90%	281.25	0.243	562.5	0.202	625	0.131	906.25	0.132
2	30%	62.5	0.053	125	0.043	187.5	0.038	287.5	0.041
	50%	125	0.128	212.5	0.084	337.5	0.073	437.5	0.063
	70%	156.25	0.135	287.5	0.099	406.25	0.083	468.75	0.066
	90%	250	0.216	312.5	0.110	781.25	0.157	812.5	0.113
3	30%	62.5	0.053	218.75	0.075	312.5	0.062	406.25	0.056
	50%	112.5	0.096	256.25	0.088	331.25	0.063	531.25	0.068
	70%	158.75	0.141	343.75	0.120	425	0.082	625	0.083
	90%	212.5	0.201	412.5	0.140	612.5	0.128	812.5	0.113

The square of the frequency change is related to deficiencies in more than just the location of the volume and frequency of changes in structural damage of the monotone function can be a direct reflection of the extent of injury. But it is very difficult relationship with a function to defective expression and function of the location and extent of the relationship between changes. And neural networks to solve a collection to another collection of non-linear mapping relationship between an effective way. Neural network through the learning and memory to simulate one of the working principle of neurons, found between the input and output of the internal relations and with the approximation function to be a powerful tool. Considering the above factors, the following structure to identify indicators of the frequency of injury as a neural network vector of input parameters, the location of the defects and deficiencies in the level of recognition at the same time. From the data in Table 2 can be constructed neural network training and testing samples.

3.3 Damage Detection Based on the Frequency in the Neural Network

The sample which 1,2,3 units to 30%, 50%, 90% of 10 at the time of defect indicators as the frequency of defect in the importation of samples of neural network, neural network input layer nodes is 10. Corresponding neural network output of the ideal vector is defined as (y1, y2, y3), one of y1 on behalf of a unit of the injury situation, y2 on behalf of units of the two injuries, y3 unit 3 on behalf of the injuries. For example, the network output for the (0.3,0,0), on behalf of modules there is a degree of 30% of the damage occurred; (0,0.5,0), on behalf of modules there are two of the 50 percent level of injury, we can see the output of neural network nodes 9. This constitutes a neural network input and output, the network training. The use of three neural networks, neurons in hidden layer nodes were selected as training 6,8,10,12,14,16,18,20, in order to find the best network structure.

Network training, simulation of the neural network output and target output to do linear regression analysis, the location of different defects and deficiencies in the simulation of the degree of correlation coefficient as shown in Table 4. As can be seen from the table, hidden layer nodes for the 16 test results are satisfactory, with the target output of the correlation coefficient in the more than 0.979, the training step 21. More than 16 nodes network training, the results changed little.

Table 3. Correlation coefs and training epochs of five networks with different hidden nodes

Neurons in hidden layer nodes	The actual network output and target output of the correlation coefficient			Training step
	Left	Middle	Right	
6	0.863	0.937	0.786	27
8	0.792	0.884	0.779	24
10	0.816	0.951	0.880	15
12	0.846	0.951	0.852	17
14	0.995	0.996	0.966	38
16	0.979	0.999	0.984	21
18	0.942	0.989	0.940	20
20	0.906	0.944	0.931	20

After training the neural network simulation analysis and promotion test, 10,12,14,16 hidden layer nodes for the neural network simulation results and the actual output of the linear regression between the target value analysis. when the network training, the network after the success of network simulation to be the actual output and the target coefficient of linear regression between the hidden layer nodes with increases in the hidden layer nodes is 16, the linear regression correlation coefficient of 0.98, the best training effect.

Nodes of the neural network for the 16 simulation results shown in Table 5. Judging from the table of the sample to identify the location of injury, resulting in entirely correct, of varying degrees of damage identification results are correct, the network to

Table 4. Identify result of network with 16 hidden nodes

Samples	Ideal output of network			actual output of network			Error
	0.3	0	0	0.2801	-0.0067	-0.0249	3.32%
Unit 1	0.5	0	0	0.5193	-0.0278	0.0071	1.93%
	0.9	0	0	0.9842	0.0103	-0.1952	9.35%
	0	0.3	0	0.0212	0.3079	-0.1776	2.63%
Unit 2	0	0.5	0	0.0045	0.4988	-0.0037	0.24%
	0	0.9	0	-0.0038	0.9009	0.0031	0.1%
	0	0	0.3	0.0211	-0.0060	0.2827	5.77%
Unit3	0	0	0.5	-0.0088	0.0074	0.5023	0.46%
	0	0	0.9	0.0849	-0.0186	0.8304	7.73%
Average identification error							3.5%

214 X.-d. Zhu et al.

identify the average error is 3.5%. The degree of cell injury in the first 90% of the time, 9.35 percent maximum error. Based on the frequency of changes in the rate of injury indicators to identify defects in neural network is feasible, but two or more samples to determine the defects, but also the need to further improve the structure of neural network.

4 Conclusion

(1)The use of artificial neural network can detect the location of defects. Five kinds of network simulation of defects in the middle of the best.

(2)The frequency and mode shape parameters of the neural network as input, using BP neural network to achieve the degree of damage and damage location identification.

(3)Based on the frequency of changes in the rate of defect indicators to identify defects in neural network is feasible, but two or more samples to determine the defects need to further improve the structure of neural network.

Acknowledgments. This paper is supported by national natural science foundation of China (30571457 and 30700629).

References

1. Wang, J., Biernacki, J.M., Lam, F.: Nondestructive evaluation of veneer quality using acoustic wave measurements. Wood science and technology (34), 505–516 (2001)
2. Tiitta, M.E., Beall, F.C., Biernacki, J.M.: Classification study for using acoustic-ultrasonics to detect internal decay in glulam beams. Wood science and technology (35), 85–96 (2001)
3. Teixeira, D.E., Moslemi, A.L.: Assessing modulus of elasticity of wood-fiber c-ement(WFC) sheets using nondestructive evaluation(NDE). Bioresource Technology (79), 193–198 (2001)
4. Tsuchikawa, S., Inoue, K.: Application of near-infrared spectroscopy to wood discrimination. The Japan Wood Research Society (49), 29–35 (2003)
5. Passialis, C., Adamopoulos, S.: A comparison of three NDT methods for determining the modulus of elasticity in flexure of fir and black locust small clear wood specimens. Holz als Roh-und Werkstoff (60), 323–324 (2002)
6. Zou, G.P., Naghipour, M.: A nondestructive method for evaluatiing natural frequency of glued-laminated beams reinforced with GRP. Nondestructive Testing and Evaluation 19(1), 53–65 (2003)
7. Zou, G.P., Naghipour, M.: A nondestructive method for evaluatiing natural frequency of glued-laminated beams reinforced with GRP. Nondestructive Testing and Evaluation 19(1), 53–65 (2003)
8. siqun, W.: An optical technique for determination of layer thickness swell of MDF and OSB. Forest Products Journal 53(9), 64–66 (2003)
9. Ross, R.J., Willits, S.W.: A Stress wave based approach to NDE of logs for as-sessing potential veneer quality. Forest Products Journal 49(11), 60–62 (1999)
10. Salawu, O.S.: Detection of structural damage through changes in frequency: A review. Engineering Structure 9(9), 718–723 (1997)

An Improved Self-adaptive Control Parameter of Differential Evolution for Global Optimization

Liyuan Jia[1], Wenyin Gong[2], and Hongbin Wu[1]

[1] Department of Computer Science,
Hunan City University, Yiyang Hunan 413000, P.R. China,
jia_4211003@126.com
[2] School of Computer Science,
China University of Geosciences, Wuhan 430074, P.R. China
cug11100304@yahoo.com.cn

Abstract. Differential evolution (DE), a fast and robust evolutionary algorithm for global optimization, has been widely used in many areas. However, the success of DE for solving different problems mainly depends on properly choosing the control parameter values. On the other hand, DE is good at exploring the search space and locating the region of global minimum, but it is slow at exploiting the solution. In order to alleviate these drawbacks of DE, this paper proposes an improved self-adaptive control parameter of DE, referred to as ISADE, for global numerical optimization. The proposed approach employs the individual fitness information to adapt the parameter settings. Hence, it can exploit the information of the individual and generate the promising offspring efficiently. To verify the viability of the proposed ISADE, 10 high-dimensional benchmark problems are chosen from literature. Experiment results indicate that this approach is efficient and effective. It is proved that this approach performs better than the original DE in terms of the convergence rate and the quality of the final solutions. Moreover, ISADE obtains faster convergence than the original self-adaptive control parameter of DE (SADE).

Keywords: Multiobjective optimization, Immune algorithm, Similar individuals, Evolutionary algorithm.

1 Introduction

Differential Evolution (DE) [1] is a simple yet powerful population-based, direct search algorithm with the generation-and-test feature for global optimization problems using real-valued parameters. DE uses the distance and direction information from the current population to guide the further search. It won the third place at the first International Contest on Evolutionary Computation on a real-valued function test-suite [2]. Among DE's advantages are its simple structure, ease of use, speed and robustness. Price and Storn [1] gave the working principle of DE with single scheme. Later on, they suggested ten different schemes of DE [2], [3]. However, DE has been shown to have certain weaknesses, especially if the global optimum should be located using a limited number of fitness function evaluations (NFFEs). In addition, DE is good at exploring the search space and locating the region of global minimum, but it is slow at exploitation of the

Z. Cai et al. (Eds.): ISICA 2009, CCIS 51, pp. 215–224, 2009.
© Springer-Verlag Berlin Heidelberg 2009

solution [4]. Moreover, the parameters of DE are problem dependent and the choice of them is often critical for the performance of DE [5].

In order to remedy these drawbacks of DE, in this paper, we propose an improved self-adaptive control parameter of DE, referred to as ISADE, for global optimization. Our work is an extension of the self-adaptive control parameter of DE (SADE) [6]. First, the self-adaptive control parameter is adopted to alleviate to choose appropriately control parameter values for different problems. Second, our approach employs the individual fitness information to adapt the parameter settings. And hence, it can exploit the information of the individual and generate the promising offspring efficiently. To verify the viability of the proposed ISADE, 10 high-dimensional benchmark problems are chosen from literature. Experimental results indicate that our approach is efficient and effective. Our approach performs better than the original DE in terms of both the convergence rate and the quality of the final solutions. Moreover, ISADE obtains faster convergence rate than the original self-adaptive control parameter of DE (SADE).

The rest of this paper is organized as follows. Section 2 briefly introduces the DE algorithm and the related work in control parameter of DE. In Section 3 presents our proposed approach in detail. Followed by the experimental results and the analysis shown in Section 4. In the last section, Section 5, we denote the conclusion and our future work.

2   Differential Evolution

Consider the following optimization problem:

$$\text{Minimize} \quad f(X), \quad X \in S \tag{1}$$

where $S \subseteq \Re^D$ is a compact set, and D is the dimension of the decision variables.

The DE algorithm [1] is a simple EA that creates new candidate solutions by combining the parent individual and several other individuals of the same population. A candidate replaces the parent only if it has better fitness. This is a rather greedy selection scheme that often outperforms the traditional EAs. In addition, DE is a simple yet powerful population-based, direct search algorithm with the generation-and-test feature for globally optimizing functions using real-valued parameters. Among DE's advantages are its simple structure, ease of use, speed and robustness. Due to these advantages, it has many real-world applications, such as data mining [7], [8], pattern recognition, digital filter design, neural network training, etc. [3], [9].

The DE algorithm in pseudo-code is shown in Algorithm 1. D is the number of decision variables, NP is the size of the parent population P; F is the mutation scaling factor; CR is the probability of crossover operator; U^i is the offspring; rndint$(1, D)$ is a uniformly distributed random integer number between 1 and D; $X_j^{r_1}$ is the j-th variable of solution X^{r_1}; and rnd$_j[0, 1)$ is a uniformly distributed random real number in $[0, 1)$. Many schemes of creation of a candidate are possible. We use the DE/rand/1/bin scheme (see lines 6 - 13 of Algorithm 1) described in Algorithm 1 (more details on DE/rand/1/bin and other DE schemes can be found in [2] and [3]).

Algorithm 1. DE algorithm with DE/rand/1/bin

1: Generate the initial population P
2: Evaluate the fitness for each individual in P
3: **while** The halting criterion is not satisfied **do**
4:      **for** $i = 1$ to NP **do**
5:          Select uniform randomly $r_1 \neq r_2 \neq r_3 \neq i$
6:          $j_{rand} = \text{rndint}(1, D)$
7:          **for** $j = 1$ to D **do**
8:              **if** $\text{rnd}_j[0, 1) > CR$ or $j == j_{rand}$ **then**
9:                  $U_j^i = X_j^{r_1} + F \times (X_j^{r_2} - X_j^{r_3})$
10:             **else**
11:                 $U_j^i = X_j^i$
12:             **end if**
13:         **end for**
14:         Evaluate the offspring U^i
15:         **if** U^i is better than P^i **then**
16:             $P^i = U^i$
17:         **end if**
18:     **end for**
19: **end while**

From Algorithm 1, we can see that there are only three control parameters in this algorithm. These are NP, F and CR. As for the terminal conditions, one can either fix the maximum NFFEs *Max_NFFEs* or the precision of a desired solution *VTR* (value to reach).

Since the parameters of DE are problem dependent and the choice of them is often critical for the performance of DE [5], [10]. Adapting the DE's control parameters is one possible improvement. Liu and Lampinen [10] proposed a Fuzzy Adaptive DE (FADE), which employs fuzzy logic controllers to adapt the mutation and crossover control parameters. Brest *et al.* [6] proposed self-adapting control parameter settings. Their proposed approach encodes the F and CR parameters into the chromosome and uses a self-adaptive control mechanism to change them. Salman *et al.* [11] proposed a self-adaptive DE (SDE) algorithm that eliminates the need for manual tuning of control parameters. In SDE, the mutation weighting factor F is self-adapted by a mutation strategy similar to the mutation operator of DE. Nobakhti and Wang [12] proposed a Randomized Adaptive Differential Evolution (RADE) method, where a simple randomized self-adaptive scheme was proposed for the mutation weighting factor F. Das *et al.* [13] proposed two variants of DE, DERSF and DETVSF, that use varying scale factors. They concluded that those variants outperform the original DE. Teo [14] presented a dynamic self-adaptive populations DE, where the population size is self-adapting. Through five De Jong's test functions, they showed that DE with self-adaptive populations produced highly competitive results. Brest and Maučec [15] proposed an improved DE method, where the population size is gradually reduced. They concluded that their approach improved efficiency and robustness of DE.

3 Our Approach: ISADE

As mentioned above, there are many works for adapting the control parameters of DE. Despite its simplicity, the SADE method [6] seems to have good performance for a various set of test problems. However, the performance of this self-adaptive control parameter strategy proposed in [6] can be further improved to obtain faster convergence rate. Based on this consideration, in this work, we propose an improved self-adaptive control parameter method for the DE algorithm. Inspired by the ideas in [16], in our approach the fitness information of each individual is considered to adapt the CR and F values. Thus, it can exploit the information of the individual and generate the promising offspring efficiently. Our approach, referred to as ISADE, is presented in detail as follows.

3.1 Improved Self-adaptive Control Parameter

Similar to [6], the individual is represented by a D-dimensional vector in the following way:

$$X^i = (X_1^i, X_2^i, \cdots, X_j^i, \cdots, X_D^i, CR^i, F^i)^T \tag{2}$$

where X_j^i is the j-th variable of the i-th individual; and the values of scaling factor F^i and crossover probability CR^i are initially randomly generated between 0 and 1.

In our proposed improved self-adaptive parameter control, the fitness information of each individual is considered. It is introduced as follows:

$$F^i = \begin{cases} 0.1 + (F^i - 0.1) \times \frac{f(X^i) - f_{min}}{f_{avg} - f_{min}}, & \text{rnd}[0,1] < \tau_1 \text{ and } f(X^i) < f_{avg} \\ \text{rnd}[0.1, 1], & \text{rnd}[0,1] < \tau_1 \text{ and } f(X^i) \geq f_{avg} \\ F^i, & \text{otherwise} \end{cases} \tag{3}$$

$$CR^i = \begin{cases} CR^i \times \frac{f(X^i) - f_{min}}{f_{avg} - f_{min}}, & \text{rnd}[0,1] < \tau_2 \text{ and } f(X^i) < f_{avg} \\ \text{rnd}[0, 1], & \text{rnd}[0,1] < \tau_2 \text{ and } f(X^i) \geq f_{avg} \\ CR^i, & \text{otherwise} \end{cases} \tag{4}$$

where $\text{rnd}[a, b]$ is the uniform random variable between a and b. τ_1 and τ_2 indicate probabilities to adjust factors F^i and CR^i. f_{avg} and f_{min} are the average fitness and the minimal fitness of the current population, respectively.

The main idea of the modification is that when the fitness of the individual is lower than the average fitness in the current population, its CR and F values are shrunken occasionally. The offspring generated by the CR and F is located in the neighborhood of its parent. And hence, the offspring can exploit the useful information of the good parent and accelerate the convergence rate. Compared with SADE [6], our method does not add any additional parameters. To maintain the diversity of the population [17], the lower bound of F^i is 0.1, which is the same as used in SADE.

3.2 Handling the Boundary Constraint of Variables

After using the DE/rand/1/bin scheme to generate a new solution, if one or more of the variables in the new solution are outside their boundaries, i.e., $X_j \notin [l_j, u_j]$, the following repair rule is applied:

$$X_j = \begin{cases} l_j + \text{rnd}_j[0,1] \times (u_j - l_j) & \text{if } X_j < l_j \\ u_j - \text{rnd}_j[0,1] \times (u_j - l_j) & \text{if } X_j > u_j \end{cases} \tag{5}$$

where $\text{rnd}_j[0,1]$ is the uniform random variable from [0,1] in each dimension j. And l_j and u_j are the lower bound and upper bound of the j-th variable, respectively.

4 Experimental Results

In order to evaluate the performance of our method 10 benchmark functions ($f_{01} - f_{10}$) were used. The test functions are described in Table 1. All of the functions are minimization problems with $D = 30$. Functions $f_{01} - f_{04}$ are high-dimensional and unimodal problems. Also function f_{04} is a noisy quartic function, where *random* [0,1) is a uniformly distributed random variable in [0,1). Functions $f_{05} - f_{10}$ are high-dimensional and multimodal problems with many local minima, where the number of local minima increases exponentially with the problem dimension. They appear to be the most difficult class of problems for many optimization algorithms.

Table 1. The 10 benchmark functions used in our experimental study, where D is the number of variables, "optimal" is the minimum value of the function, and $S \subseteq \Re^D$. A detail description of all functions can be found in [18].

Test Functions	D	S	optimal
$f_{01} = \sum\limits_{i=1}^{D} x_i^2$	30	$[-100, 100]^D$	0
$f_{02} = \sum\limits_{i=1}^{D} \|x_i\| + \prod\limits_{i=1}^{D} \|x_i\|$	30	$[-10, 10]^D$	0
$f_{03} = \sum\limits_{i=1}^{D-1} (\lfloor x_i + 0.5 \rfloor)^2$	30	$[-100, 100]^D$	0
$f_{04} = \sum\limits_{i=1}^{D} x_i^4 + random[0, 1)$	30	$[-1.28, 1.28]^D$	0
$f_{05} = \sum\limits_{i=1}^{D} (-x_i \sin(\sqrt{\|x_i\|}))$	30	$[-500, 500]^D$	-12569.48662
$f_{06} = \sum\limits_{i=1}^{D} (x_i^2 - 10\cos(2\pi x_i) + 10)$	30	$[-5.12, 5.12]^D$	0
$f_{07} = -20\exp(-0.2\sqrt{\frac{1}{D}\sum\limits_{i=1}^{D} x_i^2})$ $- \exp(\frac{1}{D}\sum\limits_{i=1}^{D} \cos(2\pi x_i)) + 20 + \exp(1)$	30	$[-32, 32]^D$	0
$f_{08} = \frac{1}{4000}\sum\limits_{i=1}^{D} x_i^2 - \prod\limits_{i=1}^{D} \cos(\frac{x_i}{\sqrt{i}}) + 1$	30	$[-600, 600]^D$	0
$f_{09} = \frac{\pi}{D}\{10\sin^2(\pi y_i)$ $+ \sum\limits_{i=1}^{D-1} (y_i - 1)^2 \cdot [1 + 10\sin^2(\pi y_{i+1})] + (y_D - 1)^2\}$ $+ \sum\limits_{i=1}^{D} u(x_i, 10, 100, 4)$	30	$[-50, 50]^D$	0
$f_{10} = \frac{1}{10}\{\sin^2(3\pi x_1)$ $+ \sum\limits_{i=1}^{D-1} (x_i - 1)^2[1 + \sin^2(3\pi x_{i+1})] + (x_D - 1)^2[1 + \sin^2(2\pi x_D)]\}$ $+ \sum\limits_{i=1}^{D} u(x_i, 5, 100, 4)$	30	$[-50, 50]^D$	0

Table 2. Best error values of DE, SADE, and ISADE on all test functions with $D = 30$ after $300,000$ NFFEs. Where "Mean" indicates the mean best error values found in the last generation; "Std Dev" stands for the standard deviation.

F	DE			SADE			ISADE		
	Mean	Std Dev	SR	Mean	Std Dev	SR	Mean	Std Dev	SR
f_{01}	2.03E-33	5.48E-33	50	**0.00E+00**	0.00E+00	50	**0.00E+00**	0.00E+00	50
f_{02}	0.00E+00	0.00E+00	50	0.00E+00	0.00E+00	50	0.00E+00	0.00E+00	50
f_{03}	0.00E+00	0.00E+00	50	0.00E+00	0.00E+00	50	0.00E+00	0.00E+00	50
f_{04}	3.54E-03	9.40E-04	50	3.31E-03	9.00E-04	50	**3.20E-03**	7.25E-04	50
f_{05}	3.81E+02	6.51E+02	3	**0.00E+00**	0.00E+00	50	**0.00E+00**	0.00E+00	50
f_{06}	1.54E+01	1.05E+01	0	**0.00E+00**	0.00E+00	50	**0.00E+00**	0.00E+00	50
f_{07}	4.14E-15	0.00E+00	50	4.14E-15	0.00E+00	50	4.14E-15	0.00E+00	50
f_{08}	1.87E-03	4.03E-03	40	**0.00E+00**	0.00E+00	50	**0.00E+00**	0.00E+00	50
f_{09}	1.04E-02	6.02E-02	48	**1.57E-32**	0.00E+00	50	**1.57E-32**	0.00E+00	50
f_{10}	3.89E-03	1.93E-02	48	**1.35E-32**	0.00E+00	50	**1.35E-32**	0.00E+00	50

4.1 Experimental Setup

For all experiments, we use the following parameters unless a change is mentioned.

- Population size: $NP = 100$;
- $\tau_1 = \tau_2 = 0.1$;
- DE scheme: DE/rand/1/bin;
- Value to reach: VTR $= 10^{-8}$, except for f_{04} of VTR $= 10^{-2}$;
- Maximum NFFEs: Max_NFFEs $= 300,000$.

Moreover, in our experiments, each function is optimized over 50 independent runs. We also use the same set of initial random populations to evaluate different algorithms in a similar way done in [4]. All the algorithms are implemented in standard C++.

4.2 Performance Criteria

Five performance criteria are selected from the literature [19], [20] to evaluate the performance of the algorithms. These criteria are described as follows.

- **Error** [20]: The error of a solution X is defined as $f(X) - f(X^*)$, where X^* is the global optimum of the function. The minimum error is recorded when the Max_NFFEs is reached in 50 runs. Also the average and standard deviation of the error values are calculated.
- **NFFEs** [20]: The number of fitness function evaluations (NFFEs) is also recorded when the VTR is reached. The average and standard deviation of the NFFEs values are calculated.
- **Number of successful runs (SR)** [20]: The number of successful runs is recorded when the VTR is reached before the max_NFFEs condition terminates the trial.
- **Convergence graphs** [20]: The convergence graphs show the mean error performance of the total runs, in the respective experiments.

- **Acceleration rate (AR)** [19]: This criterion is used to compare the convergence speeds between ISADE and other algorithms. It is defined as follows: $AR = \frac{\text{NFFEs}_{\text{other}}}{\text{NFFEs}_{\text{ISADE}}}$, where $AR > 1$ indicates ISADE is faster than its competitor.

4.3 General Performance of ISADE

In order to show the superiority of our proposed ISADE approach, we compare it with the original DE algorithm and the SADE algorithm. The parameters used for DE, SADE, and ISADE are the same as described in Section 4.1. The control parameters of DE are set as $F = 0.5$ and $CR = 0.9$. All functions are conducted for 50 independent runs. Table 2 shows the best error values of DE, SADE, and ISADE on all test functions. The average and standard deviation of NFFEs are shown in Table 3. The best results are highlighted in **Bold** face. In addition, some representative convergence graphs of DE, SADE, and ISADE are shown in Fig. 1.

When compared with DE: From Table 2 it can be seen that ISADE can obtain the optimal or close-to-optimal solutions for all test functions. And the standard deviations for all functions are very small, which means that our proposed ISADE method is very robust. It can solve these functions over all 50 runs. However, for DE it fails to solve two functions (f_{05} and f_{06}). For three functions (f_{08}, f_{09}, and f_{10}), DE locates the local minima some times. Table 3 shows that ISADE is able to achieve faster convergence rate for all test functions. Additionally, it is apparent that ISADE obtains higher convergence velocity than DE according to Fig. 1.

When compared with SADE: Table 2 shows that both SADE and ISADE can solve these functions over 50 runs. Nevertheless, from Table 3 and Fig. 1 we can see that ISADE converges faster than SADE. It needs less NFFEs to reach the *VTR* for all test functions.

In summary, our proposed ISADE approach can achieve better performance than DE in terms of both the convergence rate and the quality of the final solutions. Both SADE

Table 3. NFFEs Required to obtain accuracy levels less than VTR. "NA" indicates the accuracy level is not obtained after $300,000$ NFFEs. Where "1 vs 3" means "DE vs ISADE" and "2 vs 3" indicates "SADE vs ISADE".

F	DE		SADE		ISADE		AR	AR
	Mean	Std Dev	Mean	Std Dev	Mean	Std Dev	1 vs 3	2 vs 3
f_{01}	6.92E+04	1.55E+03	5.43E+04	1.03E+03	**4.90E+04**	9.73E+02	1.41	1.11
f_{02}	1.04E+05	1.98E+03	7.56E+04	1.44E+03	**6.46E+04**	1.12E+03	1.62	1.17
f_{03}	2.54E+04	1.86E+03	2.06E+04	7.84E+02	**1.89E+04**	7.43E+02	1.35	1.09
f_{04}	1.07E+05	3.16E+04	1.11E+05	2.01E+04	**1.02E+05**	2.34E+04	1.04	1.09
f_{05}	2.72E+05	1.55E+04	8.94E+04	2.27E+03	**7.77E+04**	1.98E+03	3.50	1.15
f_{06}	NA	NA	1.14E+05	3.59E+03	**8.62E+04**	2.61E+03	NA	1.32
f_{07}	1.07E+05	1.85E+03	8.26E+04	1.73E+03	**7.36E+04**	1.22E+03	1.45	1.12
f_{08}	7.22E+04	2.79E+03	5.74E+04	2.84E+03	**5.13E+04**	1.97E+03	1.41	1.12
f_{09}	6.32E+04	3.34E+03	5.00E+04	1.26E+03	**4.65E+04**	1.25E+03	1.36	1.07
f_{10}	8.03E+04	2.09E+04	6.03E+04	1.79E+03	**5.58E+04**	1.49E+03	1.44	1.08

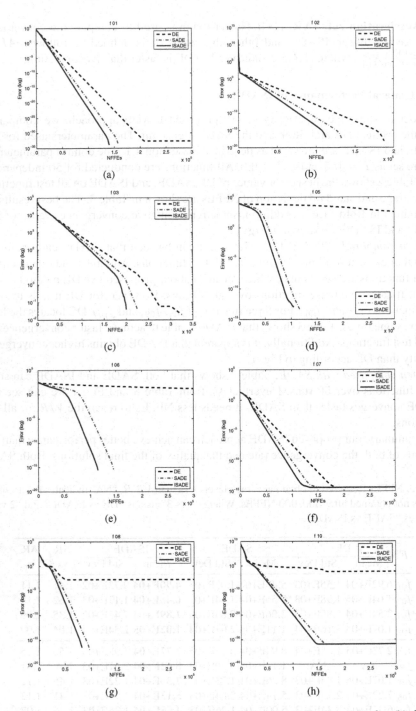

Fig. 1. Mean error curves of DE, SADE, and ISADE for 8 selected functions. (a) f_{01}. (b) f_{02}. (c) f_{03}. (d) f_{05}. (e) f_{06}. (f) f_{07}. (g) f_{08}. (h) f_{10}. Log-scale of Y axis is to make the comparison more clearly for all functions.

and ISADE obtain similar results with respect to the best error values. While ISADE is able to converge faster than SADE. The experimental results confirm that our proposed improved self-adaptive control parameter can exploit the fitness information of each individual efficiently. It can enhance the performance of the original DE algorithm.

5 Conclusion and Future Work

In this paper, we propose an improved self-adaptive control parameter for the DE algorithm. Our proposed method is an extension of SADE. In our approach the fitness information of each individual is used to adapt the CR and F values of DE. In this manner, our proposed approach can exploit the useful information of its parent, and hence, it can accelerate the convergence rate compared with the original SADE method.

In order to verify the viability of our proposed ISADE method, 10 high-dimensional benchmark functions are chosen from literature. Moreover, five performance criteria are employed to compare the performance of ISADE with those of DE and SADE. Experimental results indicate that ISADE can achieve better performance than DE in terms of both the convergence rate and the quality of the final solutions. Both SADE and ISADE obtain similar results with respect to the best error values. While ISADE is able to converge faster than SADE.

Our future work will test our approach on more various functions. In addition, using ISADE for the constrained optimization is another direction in our future work.

Acknowledgments

The authors would like to thank Prof. Brest for providing the SADE code.

References

1. Storn, R., Price, K.: Differential evolution - a simple and efficient heuristic for global optimization over continuous spaces. Journal of Global Optimization 11(4), 341–359 (1997)
2. Storn, R., Price, K.: Home page of differential evolution (2008)
3. Price, K., Storn, R., Lampinen, J.: Differential Evolution: A Practical Approach to Global Optimization. Springer, Berlin (2005)
4. Noman, N., Iba, H.: Accelerating differential evolution using an adaptive local search. IEEE Transactions on Evolutionary Computation 12(1), 107–125 (2008)
5. Gäperle, R., Müler, S., Koumoutsakos, P.: A parameter study for differential evolution. In: Proc. WSEAS Int. Conf. Advances Intell. Syst., Fuzzy Syst., Evol. Comput., pp. 293–298 (2002)
6. Brest, J., Greiner, S., Bošković, B., Mernik, M., Žumer, V.: Self-Adapting Control Parameters in Differential Evolution: A Comparative Study on Numerical Benchmark Problems. IEEE Transactions on Evolutionary Computation 10(6), 646–657 (2006)
7. Alatas, B., Akin, E., Karci, A.: Modenar: Multi-objective differential evolution algorithm for mining numeric association rules. Applied Soft Computing 8(1), 646–656 (2008)
8. Das, S., Abraham, A., Konar, A.: Automatic clustering using an improved differential evolution algorithm. IEEE Transaction on Systems Man and Cybernetics: Part A 38(1), 218–237 (2008)

9. Chakraborty, U.: Advances in Differential Evolution. Springer, Berlin (2008)
10. Liu, J., Lampinen, J.: A fuzzy adaptive differential evolution algorithm. Soft Comput. 9(6), 448–462 (2005)
11. Salman, A., Engelbrecht, A.P., Omran, M.G.H.: Empirical analysis of self-adaptive differential evolution. European Journal of Operational Research 183(2), 785–804 (2007)
12. Nobakhti, A., Wang, H.: A simple self-adaptive differential evolution algorithm with application on the ALSTOM gasifier. Appl. Soft Comput 8(1), 350–370 (2008)
13. Das, S., Konar, A., Chakraborty, U.K.: Two improved differential evolution schemes for faster global search. In: Beyer, H.G., O'Reilly, U.M. (eds.) Genetic and Evolutionary Computation Conference, GECCO 2005, Proceedings, Washington DC, USA, June 25-29, pp. 991–998. ACM, New York (2005)
14. Teo, J.: Exploring dynamic self-adaptive populations in differential evolution. Soft Comput. 10(8), 673–686 (2006)
15. Brest, J., Maučec, M.S.: Population size reduction for the differential evolution algorithm. Appl. Intell. 29(3), 228–247 (2008)
16. Srinivas, M., Patnaik, L.M.: Adaptive probabilities of crossover and mutation in genetic algorithms. IEEE Transactions on Systems, Man, and Cybernetics 24(4), 656–667 (1994)
17. Zaharie, D.: Critical values for the control parameters of differential evolution algorithms. In: Matoušek, R., Ošmera, P. (eds.) MENDEL 2002, 8th International Mendel Conference on Soft Computing, June 5-7, pp. 62–67 (2002)
18. Yao, X., Liu, Y., Lin, G.: Evolutionary programming made faster. IEEE Transactions on Evolutionary Computation 3(2), 82–102 (1999)
19. Rahnamayan, S., Tizhoosh, H., Salama, M.: Opposition-based differential evolution. IEEE Transactions on Evolutionary Computation 12(1), 64–79 (2008)
20. Suganthan, P., Hansen, N., Liang, J.: Problem definitions and evaluation criteria for the cec2005 special session on real-parameter optimization (2005)

Distributed Evolutionary Algorithms to TSP with Ring Topology

Shanzhi Huang, Li Zhu, Fang Zhang, Yongxiang He, and Haidong Xue

Faculty of Computer Science, China University of Geosciences
Wuhan, Hubei, P.R. China, 430074
huangshanzhi@gmail.com

Abstract. Distributed Evolutionary Algorithms (dEAs) are stochastic search methods applied successfully in many searches, optimization, and machine learning problems. This paper proposes a dEA based on IGT. The dEA uses a ring topology ,with each population choosing a random individual from it in a migration interval. The individual will be sent to next population and replace the worst individual of the population. It can be seen from the experiment that dEA with Ring transmission can produce better solutions when the population size of a TSP problem is large enough. The numerical results show the utility, versatility, efficiency and potential value of the proposed distributed evolutionary algorithm.

Keywords: TSP; distributed evolutionary algorithms; PVM; cluster computing; ring topologies.

1 Introductin

The Traveling Salesman Problem (TSP)[2] is a problem in combinatorial optimization studied in operations research and theoretical computer science. Given a list of cities and their pair wise distances, the task is to find a shortest possible tour that visits each city exactly once.

In the theory of computational complexity, the decision version of TSP belongs to the class of NP-complete problems. Thus, it is assumed that there is no efficient algorithm for solving TSP problems. A variety of algorithms have been proposed for TSP problem, such as exhaustive search, greedy method, dynamic programming, Branch and Bound Algorithm, minimum Spanning Tree. All of these algorithms have a common problem. TSP is used as a paradigm for a wide class of problems having complexity due to the combinatorial explosion. TSP has become a target for the Evolutionary Algorithms(EAs) [1] community, because it is probably the central problem in combinatorial optimization and many new ideas in combinatorial optimization have been tested on the TSP.

Because of the large population size, the serial EA needs more individuals to carry out more genetic and evolutionary operations. The computing process of evolution will be slow which hard achieve on the requirements of computing speed. Otherwise we should note that the EAs use individual collection for computing objects and all various genetic manipulations have some mutual independence, so the EAs have an

Z. Cai et al. (Eds.): ISICA 2009, CCIS 51, pp. 225–231, 2009.

inherent parallelism. Therefore, developing a DEA is an effective way to improve the performance of EAs.

The goal of this paper is to give a DEA to TSP based on cluster of PC. We do the experiments by PVM using a distributed environment of PC cluster. The numerical results show that compared with serial evolutionary algorithms which use some chromosomes, hybridization and mutation and local optimization methods the algorithm achieves near linear speedup performance at a certain range.

2 Distributed Evolutionary Algorithms

2.1 PVM

The PVM [3] is a software system that supports the message-passing paradigm and permits the utilization of a heterogeneous network of parallel and serial computers as a single general and flexible concurrent computational resource. PVM offers a suite of user interface primitives for communication and other chores. Application programs are composed of components that are subtasks at a moderately large level of granularity. The advantages of PVM are its wide acceptability and its heterogeneous computing facilities, including fault-tolerance issues and interoperability. Managing a dynamic collection of potentially heterogeneous computational resources as a single parallel computer is the real appealing treat of PVM.

2.2 Algorithm Model of dEAs

A dEA is a island model performing sparse exchanges of individuals among the elementary populations[4]. This model can be readily implemented in distributed memory MIMD computers, which provides one main reason for its popularity. A migration policy controls the kind of dEA being used. The migration policy must define the island topology, when migration occurs, which individuals are being exchanged, the synchronization among the subpopulations, and the kind of integration of exchanged individuals within the target subpopulations.

2.3 Ring Topology

A ring topology is a network topology in which each node connects to exactly two other nodes, forming a single continuous pathway for signals through each node - a ring. Data travels from node to node, with each node along the way handling every packet.

2.4 Master-Slave Model

Based on PVM technology and island model, we design the parallel algorithm by a master-slave model[5]. This computing model has a control process which called master process. The master process is responsible for the process of generation, initialization, and collection and displays the results. The others are called sub process which does the real calculation. The load of sub process is distributed by either master process or the distribution process itself.

In the mode, the sub processes evolve independently in a species island and the master process is responsible to change information in the islands.

The procedure of the DEA for solving the TSP problem is described as follows:

Master Process:

Step1. Initialize each sub processes.

Step2. Block and wait for the messages of the sub process.

Step3. Process the messages received from sub processes and then send the result to the sub processes.

Step4. Block and wait for the messages of the sub process. If the message is an end message then go to step 5, otherwise go to step 2.

Step5. Send an end message to each sub progress.

Sub process:

Step1. Evolve independently.

Step2. If the condition sent to the master process meets the master process then sent a message to master process, otherwise block and wait for the messages of the master process.

Step3. Put the message received from master process in the population.

Step4. If the condition meets the end condition then send a end message to master process, otherwise go to step 1.

Step5. Wait for the end massage of master process.

2.5 Migration Strategy

Each population which evolves on their own islands forms a ring topology. Each population should choose a random individual from it in a migration interval. The individual will be sent to next population and replace the worst individual of the population.

The rule of information transmission is described as follows:

1. Conditions of submission: Each process evolves independently in a species island and submits the immigration at same time in a migration interval.

2. Choose an individual at random in each population of islands.

3. Information processing way:

a. The master process sends the individual of a sub process to the next sub process after it receives all the random individual of sub process.

b. Each sub process put the individual received from the master process in a right position of the population. Because chromosomes are arranged in accordance with good and bad at the same generation, the individual is inserted into the appropriate place. Following chromosomes are moved to one backward and worst will be eliminated.

2.6 Load Balancing

LAN consisting of PC cluster with star topology is used under current experiment condition. Under this condition, each PC is the same, their performances are similar and network communication speed is relatively high, assigning processes to every host averagely seems a reasonable distribution strategy. Obviously, in such a distribution strategy, each PC which runs PVM has difference, and can also has the processes which are nothing to do with the calculation, so it will cause the unbalance between different hosts. Then the PC which has a faster process has to wait the PC which runs the slower process. We have to solve the load unbalancing problem in our algorithm in case increasing unnecessary time cost. At the beginning of the calculation, the scale of the population of each sub-process is equal. When the immigration time arrives, each sub-process submits the individuals and the cost of time it consumes. Main process compares the consuming time of each sub-processes. If the difference between Maximum and minimum value has surpassed threshold level D, we punish the worst a% advancement, simultaneously rewards the best a% advancement. The method is that the master process reduces the subpopulation size of the process which punished, migrates these individuals to another process which rewarded.

The number of migration individuals Pt is decided by the following formula:

$$P_t = P_{t-1}[1- (b\% - nb/Na)] \tag{1}$$

Pt is the number of individuals after sub-process are punished or rewarded and Pt-1 is the number of individuals before sub-process are punished or rewarded. N is the total of processes. a% is percentages of rewards and punishment processes. b% is the biggest percentage of rewards and punishment processes. The worst Na% processes (taking N = 0, 1, 2, 3......) sort by the time consumed, and then the individuals are received in turn by the best Na% processes. The threshold level can not be too small or too large and we must choose the balance point between the Load Balancing and the overall load[5].

3 Experiments and Outcome Analysis

IGT [6](Improved Guo Tao algorithm) uses a new genetic operator basis on GI(Guo Tao algorithm).IGT makes some changes of GI [7] in order to improve the convergence rate of algorithm. Because IGT is capable of attaining the best answer in small scale of TSP, the larger scales from ad198 to fl1577 problems are introduced to compare the performance of IGT and two kinds of parallel IGT. This paper proposes a dEA based on IGT.

Paper [5] mentioned a star topology migration strategy. The subpopulations send their best individual to the master process and the master process also sends a best individual in all the individual have been received to the subpopulations. The best individual replaces the worst individual of the population. According to the strategy, the best individual has submitted to the master process and returned to the subpopulations are similar or even near the same. This way reduces the evolved advancement greatly. The best individual of whole population is copied to every subpopulation and population multiplicity reduces rapidly. The evolved computation advancement becomes slow even bogs down and cannot get a better solution. In the paper, the dEA use a ring topology and each population chooses a random individual from it in a migration interval. The individual will be sent to next population and replace the worst individual of the population. This way reduces the evolved advancement slowly and gets a better solution.

Experiment 1. Evolutionary parameters: Population Size=100, Edge Speed=50, Mutation Probability=0.02, Mapping Probability =0.05.Parallel parameters: Process Quantity=10, Migration Interval=5000.

Table 1. Result of ad198 (10 times running)

Algorithm/ Process Quantity	Worst Outcome	Best Outcome	Average	Standard Deviation	T-test of Ring/ Traditional
IGT /1	15776.911963	15754.002036	15756.293029	6.872978	
Traditional/20	15754.002036	15754.002036	15754.002036	0.0	0.000000
Ring/20	15754.002036	15754.002036	15754.002036	0.0	

Experiment 2. Evolutionary parameters: Population Size=100, Edge Speed=50, Mutation Probability=0.02, Mapping Probability =0.05.Parallel parameters: Process Quantity=20, Migration Interval=40000.

Table 2. Result of lin318 (10 times running)

Algorithm/ Process Quantity	Worst outcome	Best outcome	Average	Standard deviation	T-test of Ring / Traditional
IGT /1	42574.776257	42062.478575	42233.313253	167.878322	
Traditional/20	42042.535089	42042.535089	42042.535089	0.0	0.000000
Ring/20	42042.535089	42042.535089	42042.535089	0.0	

Experiment 3. Evolutionary parameters: Population Size=300, Edge Speed=50, Mutation Probability=0.02, Mapping Probability =0.05.Parallel parameters: Process Quantity=20, Migration Interval=100000.

Table 3. Result of pcb442 (10 times running)

Algorithm/ Process quantity	Worst outcome	Best outcome	Average	Standard deviation	T-test of Ring / Traditional
IGT /1	51548.695651	50831.233207	51029.757875	200.665507	
Traditional/20	50933.869965	50787.381005	50872.182607	50.581691	-1.781147
Ring/20	50921.280677	50787.381005	50835.179522	41.921837	

Experiment 4. Evolutionary parameters: Population Size=300, Edge Speed=10, Mutation Probability=0.02, Mapping Probability =0.05.Parallel parameters: Process Quantity=20, Migration Interval=80000.

Table 4. Result of rat783 (10 times running)

Algorithm/ Process quantity	Worst outcome	Best outcome	Average	Standard deviation	T-test of Ring / Traditional
IGT /1	8969.611595	8857.736489	8883.102277	33.818643	
Traditional/20	8857.637994	8845.033817	8850.944948	4.128772	-4.846211
Ring/20	8846.773936	8842.994960	8844.413300	1.057577	

Experiment 5. Evolutionary parameters: Population Size=100, Edge Speed=30, Mutation Probability=0.02, Mapping Probability =0.05.Parallel parameters: Process Quantity=20, Migration Interval=500000.

Table 5. Result of vm1084 (10 times running)

Algorithm/ Process quantity	Worst outcome	Best outcome	Average	Standard deviation	T-test of Ring / Traditional
IGT /1	245490.040923	239483.378193	241902.217199	1748.515757	
Traditional/20	239059.947755	238774.054341	238908.848844	85.861968	-2.498043
Ring/20	238967.144098	238751.225126	238807.154679	78.955034	

Experiment 6. Evolutionary parameters: Population Size=100,Edge Speed=100, Mutation Probability=0.02, Mapping Probability =0.05.Parallel parameters: Process Quantity=20, Migration Interval=2000000.

Table 6. Result of fl1577 (5 times running)

Algorithm/ Process quantity	Worst outcome	Best outcome	Average	Standard deviation	T-test of Ring / Traditional
IGT /1	22542.542350	22446.638561	22471.335115	36.140533	
Traditional/20	22422.312092	22406.834538	22415.817560	5.450847	-1.676670
Ring/20	22412.780630	22402.795325	22408.684660	3.241397	

It can be seen from the experiment that distributed EA with Ring transmission can get better answers when the parameters are the same when the scale of a problem is large enough. Furthermore, the standard deviation shows that the answers of new algorithm fluctuates little comparing with that of the traditional one. Of course, this new algorithm needs more generations to achieve final convergence. The experiment shows, to solve above problems, the needful generations in new algorithm are about 40% more than traditional distributed EA.

4 Conclusions

In this Paper, we proposed new distributed evolutionary algorithm to solve the Traveling Salesman Problem. As we know EAs need to solve the problems of the slow computation and the low success rate. With the development of network technology, designing a efficient dEA by using a cluster in the same local area network under the PVM environment becomes possible.

Because the LAN have a faster transfer rate and the algorithm is compute-intensive, the communication holding time will not increase along with the host machine obviously increases in some ration interval, but is paused in the some order of magnitude. Therefore this algorithm may obtain the close linear acceleration ratio in certain expansion scope. In the paper, each population chooses a individual randomly and the individual is sent to next population and replace the worst individual of the population. This way will reduce similar or the same individual in the subpopulation greatly. The computation convergence rate also greatly reduces, so we can get a better solution.

The next most urgent work is optimizes some parameters such as transport ratio, migration strategy and further enhance the algorithm efficiency.

References

[1]   Alba, E., Tomassini, M.: Parallelism and Evolutionary Algorithms. IEEE Transactions on Evolutionary Computation 6(5) (October 2002)
[2]   Tsujimura, Y., Gen, M.: Entropy-based genetic algorithm for solving TSP. In: Proceedings of the 1998 2nd International Conference on knowledge-Based Intelligent Electronic Systems (KES 1998), April 21-23 (1998)
[3]   Michalewicz, Z.: Genetic algorithms + data structure = evolution programs. Springer, Heidelberg (1996)
[4]   Sun, J., Zhang, L., Chi, X., Wang, D.: Network parallel computing and distributed programming environment. Science Press, Beijing (1997)
[5]   Xiong, S., Li, C.: Distributed Evolutionary Algorithms to TSP Based on Cluster of PC. Mini-Micro Systems 24(6) (June 2003)
[6]   Cai, Z., Guo, P., Gao, W., Wei, W., Kang, L.: An Improved Evolutionary Algorithm for theTraveling Salesman Problem. Chinese journal of Computers 28(5) (May 2005)
[7]   Tao, G., Michalewicz, Z.: Inver-over operator for the TSP. In: Eiben, A.E., Bäck, T., Schoenauer, M., Schwefel, H.-P. (eds.) PPSN 1998. LNCS, vol. 1498, p. 803. Springer, Heidelberg (1998)

Self-adaptation in Fast Evolutionary Programming

Yong Liu

The University of Aizu
Aizu-Wakamatsu, Fukushima 965-8580, Japan
yliu@u-aizu.ac.jp

Abstract. It had been discovered that the same self-adaptation used in fast evolutionary programming (FEP) and classical evolutionary programming (CEP) had shown quite different behaviors on optimizing the same test functions from the same initial populations. The experimental results presented in this paper suggest that the strategy parameters in FEP generally could not rise as high as their values in CEP in the rising stage, but dropped faster than their values in CEP in the falling stage. Such different behaviors were led by the strong correlation existing between mutations and self-adaptation in CEP and FEP.

1 Introduction

The step size is crucial for the performance of a search operator in evolutionary programming (EP) [1,2,3]. Different search operators often have different step sizes, and thus are appropriate for different problems as well as different evolutionary search stages for a single problem [1,4,5,6]. Since the global optimum is generally unknown in real world applications, it is impossible to know a priori what step sizes should be applied in an EP. Self-adaptation was therefore adopted in Gaussian mutation in which the strategy parameters are encoded and evolved together with each individual in EP [7,8,9]. Through evolving the strategy parameters, step sizes could therefore be controlled in EP. For an one-dimensional Gaussian mutation, its step size is actually a product of a strategy parameter and the absolute value of a random number generated from a Gaussian distribution used in the mutation. Step sizes of mutations are therefore also controlled by the distributions of random numbers besides the strategy parameters. Different random distributions lead to the different step sizes of mutations. For example, for Gaussian mutations using Gaussian random number with standard deviation 1 and Cauchy mutations applying Cauchy random number with the scale parameter 1 [10], Cauchy mutations would tend to generate larger step sizes than Gaussian mutations on average if the values of the strategy parameters used in the two mutations were the same [1].

It was assumed in [1] that the different performance between fast evolutionary programming (FEP) and classical evolutionary programming (CEP) was merely caused by Cauchy mutations and Gaussian mutations when no any explicit change

Z. Cai et al. (Eds.): ISICA 2009, CCIS 51, pp. 232–239, 2009.

has been made in self-adaptation. However, such an assumption turned out not to be true. The observation results from the evolution of self-adaptation explored another discovery that there existed a strong correlation between mutations and self-adaptation [11]. Self-adaptation had been found to show quite different behaviors in CEP and FEP in which the strategy parameters in FEP had often had much smaller values than those in CEP. The smaller strategy parameters in Cauchy mutations had made it possible that effective Cauchy mutations in FEP could have the smaller step sizes than effective Gaussian mutations in CEP.

The rest of this paper is organized as follows. Section 2 describes the major steps of CEP and FEP discussed in this paper. Section 3 describes the experimental setup, and presents the explanations of different behaviors of strategy parameters in both CEP and FEP with self-adaptation. Finally, Section 4 concludes with some remarks and future research directions.

2   Function Optimization by Classical Evolutionary Programming

A global minimization problem can be formalized as a pair (S, f), where $S \subseteq R^n$ is a bounded set on R^n and $f : S \mapsto R$ is an n-dimensional real-valued function [12]. The problem is to find a point $\mathbf{x}_{min} \in S$ such that $f(\mathbf{x}_{min})$ is a global minimum on S. More specifically, it is required to find an $\mathbf{x}_{min} \in S$ such that

$$\forall \mathbf{x} \in S : f(\mathbf{x}_{min}) \leq f(\mathbf{x}),$$

where f does not need to be continuous but it must be bounded. This paper only considers unconstrained function optimization.

According to the description by Bäck and Schwefel [7,1], CEP with self-adaptation for function optimization is implemented as follows:

1. Generate the initial population of μ individuals, and set $k = 1$. Each individual is taken as a pair of real-valued vectors, $(\mathbf{x}_i, \eta_i)$, $\forall i \in \{1, \cdots, \mu\}$, where $\mathbf{x}_i$'s are objective variables, and η_i's are standard deviations for Gaussian mutations, which is known as strategy parameters in self-adaptive evolutionary algorithms.
2. Evaluate the fitness score for each individual $(\mathbf{x}_i, \eta_i)$, $\forall i \in \{1, \cdots, \mu\}$, of the population based on the objective function, $f(\mathbf{x}_i)$.
3. Each parent $(\mathbf{x}_i, \eta_i)$, $i = 1, \cdots, \mu$, creates a single offspring $(\mathbf{x}_i', \eta_i')$ by: for $j = 1, \cdots, n$,

$$\eta_i'(j) = \eta_i(j) \exp(\tau' N(0, 1) + \tau N_j(0, 1)) \qquad (1)$$
$$x_i'(j) = x_i(j) + \eta_i(j) N_j(0, 1), \qquad (2)$$

   where $x_i(j)$, $x_i'(j)$, $\eta_i(j)$ and $\eta_i'(j)$ denote the j-th component of the vectors $\mathbf{x}_i$, $\mathbf{x}_i'$, η_i and η_i', respectively. $N(0, 1)$ denotes a normally distributed one-dimensional random number with mean 0 and standard deviation 1. $N_j(0, 1)$ indicates that the random number is generated anew for each value of j. The factors τ and τ' are commonly set to $\left(\sqrt{2\sqrt{n}}\right)^{-1}$ and $\left(\sqrt{2n}\right)^{-1}$ [7].
4. Calculate the fitness of each offspring $(\mathbf{x}_i', \eta_i')$, $\forall i \in \{1, \cdots, \mu\}$.

5. Conduct pairwise comparison over the union of parents $(\mathbf{x}_i, \eta_i)$ and offspring $(\mathbf{x}_i', \eta_i')$, $\forall i \in \{1, \cdots, \mu\}$. For each individual, q opponents are chosen uniformly at random from all the parents and offspring. For each comparison, if the individual's fitness is no larger than the opponent's, it receives a "win."
6. Select the μ individuals out of $(\mathbf{x}_i, \eta_i)$ and $(\mathbf{x}_i', \eta_i')$, $\forall i \in \{1, \cdots, \mu\}$, that have the most wins to be parents of the next generation.
7. Stop if the halting criterion is satisfied; otherwise, $k = k+1$ and go to Step 3.

FEP discussed in this paper is exactly the same as CEP except for Eq.(2) which is replaced by the following [1]:

$$x_i'(j) = x_i(j) + \eta_i(j)\delta_j, \tag{3}$$

where δ_j is a Cauchy random variable with the scale parameter $t = 1$ [10], and is generated anew for each value of j. It is worth indicating that self-adaptation defined in Eq.(1) was left unchanged in FEP in order to keep the modification of CEP to a minimum.

3   Experimental Studies

3.1   Benchmark Functions and Experimental Setup

Twenty-three benchmark functions used in [1,7,13] were tested in our experimental studies. Among the twenty-three benchmark functions, there are unimodal functions f_1 to f_7, multimodal functions f_8 to f_{13} with many local minima, and low-dimensional multimodal functions f_{14} to f_{23} with a few local minima.

In all experiments, the same self-adaptive method (i.e., Eq.(1)), the same population size $\mu = 100$, the same tournament size $q = 10$ for selection, the same initial $\eta = 3.0$, the same lower bound 0.001 for η, and the same initial population was used in both CEP and FEP. In each run of CEP and FEP, the initial population was generated uniformly at random in the specified ranges for each test function in Table 1.

3.2   Self-adaptation of Strategy Parameters

Figures 1 and 2 display the evolution of the mean of the average values of η defined by Eq. 1 from each individual in the population at each generation from 50 runs for both CEP and FEP. η had grown very quickly at the beginning in both CEP and FEP for most of the test functions except for f_2 and f_9. Since the offspring after mutation should stay in the search domain, the mutation steps cannot be too large if the search domain is small. Correspondingly, η cannot be too large either on target functions with small domains, such as f_2 in $[-10, 10]^n$ and f_9 in $[-5.12, 5.12]^n$. It is the reason that η did not rise much at the beginning of evolution in both CEP and FEP on f_2 and f_9.

The initial solutions in the populations are normally rather different, in which some are much better than others. No matter what mutations had been taken, the offspring from the better individuals were often better than other poor

Table 1. The 23 benchmark functions used in our experimental study, where n is the dimension of the function, f_{min} is the minimum value of the function, and $S \subseteq R^n$.

Test function	n	S	f_{min}
$f_1(x) = \sum_{i=1}^{n} x_i^2$	30	$[-100, 100]^n$	0
$f_2(x) = \sum_{i=1}^{n} |x_i| + \prod_{i=1}^{n} |x_i|$	30	$[-10, 10]^n$	0
$f_3(x) = \sum_{i=1}^{n} \left(\sum_{j=1}^{i} x_j\right)^2$	30	$[-100, 100]^n$	0
$f_4(x) = \max_i \{|x_i|, 1 \le i \le n\}$	30	$[-100, 100]^n$	0
$f_5(x) = \sum_{i=1}^{n-1} [100(x_{i+1} - x_i^2)^2 + (x_i - 1)^2]$	30	$[-30, 30]^n$	0
$f_6(x) = \sum_{i=1}^{n} (\lfloor x_i + 0.5 \rfloor)^2$	30	$[-100, 100]^n$	0
$f_7(x) = \sum_{i=1}^{n} i x_i^4 + random[0, 1)$	30	$[-1.28, 1.28]^n$	0
$f_8(x) = \sum_{i=1}^{n} -x_i \sin(\sqrt{|x_i|})$	30	$[-500, 500]^n$	-12569.5
$f_9(x) = \sum_{i=1}^{n} [x_i^2 - 10\cos(2\pi x_i) + 10)]$	30	$[-5.12, 5.12]^n$	0
$f_{10}(x) = -20\exp\left(-0.2\sqrt{\frac{1}{n}\sum_{i=1}^{n} x_i^2}\right) - \exp\left(\frac{1}{n}\sum_{i=1}^{n} \cos 2\pi x_i\right)$ $+20 + e$	30	$[-32, 32]^n$	0
$f_{11}(x) = \frac{1}{4000}\sum_{i=1}^{n} x_i^2 - \prod_{i=1}^{n} \cos\left(\frac{x_i}{\sqrt{i}}\right) + 1$	30	$[-600, 600]^n$	0
$f_{12}(x) = \frac{\pi}{n}\{10\sin^2(\pi y_i) + \sum_{i=1}^{n-1}(y_i - 1)^2[1 + 10\sin^2(\pi y_{i+1})]$ $+(y_n - 1)^2\} + \sum_{i=1}^{n} u(x_i, 10, 100, 4),$ $y_i = 1 + \frac{1}{4}(x_i + 1)$ $u(x_i, a, k, m) = \begin{cases} k(x_i - a)^m, & x_i > a, \\ 0, & -a \le x_i \le a, \\ k(-x_i - a)^m, & x_i < -a. \end{cases}$	30	$[-50, 50]^n$	0
$f_{13}(x) = 0.1\{\sin^2(3\pi x_1) + \sum_{i=1}^{n-1}(x_i - 1)^2[1 + \sin^2(3\pi x_{i+1})]$ $+(x_n - 1)[1 + \sin^2(2\pi x_n)]\} + \sum_{i=1}^{n} u(x_i, 5, 100, 4)$	30	$[-50, 50]^n$	0
$f_{14}(x) = \left[\frac{1}{500} + \sum_{j=1}^{25}\frac{1}{j + \sum_{i=1}^{2}(x_i - a_{ij})^6}\right]^{-1}$	2	$[-65.536, 65.536]^n$	1
$f_{15}(x) = \sum_{i=1}^{11}\left[a_i - \frac{x_1(b_i^2 + b_i x_2)}{b_i^2 + b_i x_3 + x_4}\right]^2$	4	$[-5, 5]^n$	0.0003075
$f_{16}(x) = 4x_1^2 - 2.1x_1^4 + \frac{1}{3}x_1^6 + x_1 x_2 - 4x_2^2 + 4x_2^4$	2	$[-5, 5]^n$	-1.0316285
$f_{17}(x) = \left(x_2 - \frac{5.1}{4\pi^2}x_1^2 + \frac{5}{\pi}x_1 - 6\right)^2 + 10\left(1 - \frac{1}{8\pi}\right)\cos x_1 + 10$	2	$[-5, 10] \times [0, 15]$	0.398
$f_{18}(x) = [1 + (x_1 + x_2 + 1)^2(19 - 14x_1 + 3x_1^2 - 14x_2$ $+6x_1 x_2 + 3x_2^2)] \times [30 + (2x_1 - 3x_2)^2(18 - 32x_1$ $+12x_1^2 + 48x_2 - 36x_1 x_2 + 27x_2^2)]$	2	$[-2, 2]^n$	3
$f_{19}(x) = -\sum_{i=1}^{4} c_i \exp\left[-\sum_{j=1}^{4} a_{ij}(x_j - p_{ij})^2\right]$	4	$[0, 1]^n$	-3.86
$f_{20}(x) = -\sum_{i=1}^{4} c_i \exp\left[-\sum_{j=1}^{6} a_{ij}(x_j - p_{ij})^2\right]$	6	$[0, 1]^n$	-3.32
$f_{21}(x) = -\sum_{i=1}^{5}[(x - a_i)(x - a_i)^T + c_i]^{-1}$	4	$[0, 10]^n$	-10
$f_{22}(x) = -\sum_{i=1}^{7}[(x - a_i)(x - a_i)^T + c_i]^{-1}$	4	$[0, 10]^n$	-10
$f_{23}(x) = -\sum_{i=1}^{10}[(x - a_i)(x - a_i)^T + c_i]^{-1}$	4	$[0, 10]^n$	-10

individuals and their offspring. When offspring by mutations with large step sizes could survive, η was allowed to become larger at the beginning of evolution. After the fast rise at the beginning, η turned to decrease quickly in the early evolution. The reason for the η's fast declining is that offspring by large mutations only had some chances to survive at the beginning when there are some poor solutions in the population. When the whole population became a little better after a few generations, offspring by mutations with large step sizes could hardly survive because large mutations could rarely generate better offspring. Therefore, η was forced to be smaller through self-adaptation in order to make the mutation step size smaller. At the late evolution, η became rather stable when its value was smaller. Because of lower bound 0.001 was set for η in the experiments, the average values of η did not decrease further in the late evolution.

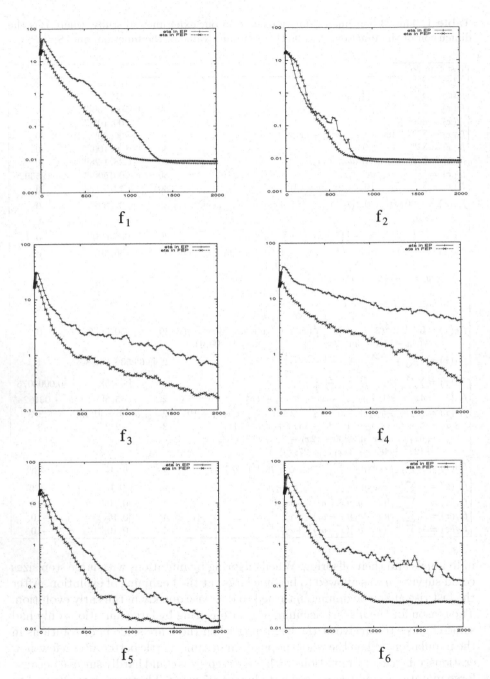

Fig. 1. Comparison between EP and FEP on the mean of the average values of η over all individuals in the population at each generation from 50 runs on unimodal functions f_1 to f_6. The vertical axis is the value of η, and the horizontal axis is the number of generations.

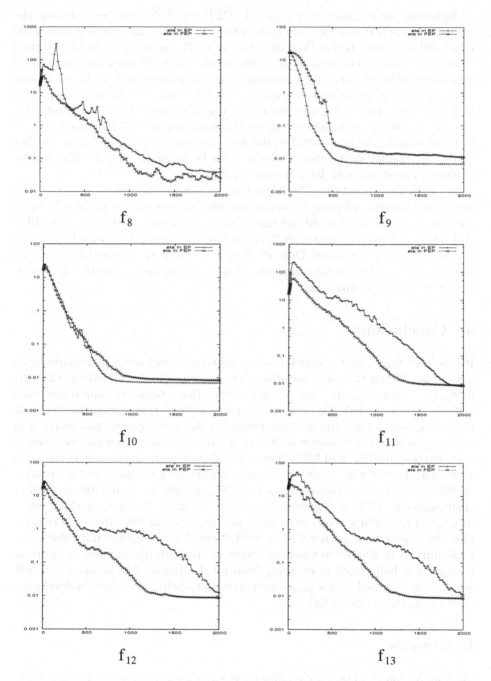

Fig. 2. Comparison between EP and FEP on the average of the values of η from 50 runs on multimodal functions f_8 to f_{13}. The vertical axis is the value of η, and the horizontal axis is the number of generations.

Although the evolution trends of η in CEP and FEP had been similar, the values of η in CEP and FEP are quite different. For the most of test functions, η in CEP was much bigger than its values in FEP. Especially, η in CEP turned to be very large at its initial rising period, while η in FEP could only manage to increase a little bit. The larger random values generated by Cauchy mutations were the driving force that prevented η in FEP from being very large. If η had been very large in Cauchy mutations, the step sizes would be too large for Cauchy mutations to generate either valid solutions within the search ranges or good offspring to be selected to the next generation. Meanwhile, the smaller Gaussian random values would permit η to be large as long as offspring by Gaussian mutations with large η could survive.

In the falling period of η, the larger Cauchy random numbers pushed η to be even lower because offspring by mutations with smaller step sizes were likely to survive. It should be pointed out that Cauchy mutations with lower η in FEP still had larger average step sizes than the Gaussian mutations with higher η in nearly all the test functions. Only effective Cauchy mutations had hold smaller step sizes than effective Gaussian mutations with the help of smaller η in FEP for the most of test functions.

4   Conclusions

It has been found that effective Cauchy mutations had often had shorter step sizes than effective Gaussian mutations. The force on the shorter effective Cauchy mutations came from the strong correlation between mutations and self-adaptation in EP. There were normally a brief rising stage in the early evolution, and a long falling stage thereafter for the strategy parameter η in self-adaptation. It had long been assumed that self-adaptation had behaved in a similar way in CEP and FEP. However, different mutations, such as Gaussian mutations and Cauchy mutations, could actually alter the same self-adaptation so differently that the parameters η in FEP generally could not rise as high as their values in CEP in the rising stage, but dropped faster than their values in CEP in the falling stage. Very small parameters η at the later evolution are also the reason that neither CEP nor FEP could likely escape from the found local minimum. Simple methods of trying to dynamically increase or decrease η might not help much in escaping from local minima. The behaviors of self-adaptation explored in this paper are expected to help researchers in developing better self-adaptation in EP.

References

1. Yao, X., Liu, Y., Lin, G.: Evolutionary programming made faster. IEEE Transactions on Evolutionary Computation 3(2), 82–102 (1999)
2. Lee, C.Y., Yao, X.: Evolutionary programming using the mutations based on the Lévy probability distribution. IEEE Transactions on Evolutionary Computation 8(1), 1–13 (2004)

3. Liu, Y., Yao, X.: How to control search step size in fast evolutionary programming. In: Proceedings of the 2002 Congress on Evolutionary Computation (CEC 2002), pp. 652–656. IEEE Press, Los Alamitos (2002)
4. Yao, X., Liu, Y.: Scaling up evolutionary programming algorithms. In: Porto, V.W., Waagen, D. (eds.) EP 1998. LNCS, vol. 1447, pp. 103–112. Springer, Heidelberg (1998)
5. Yao, X., Lin, G., Liu, Y.: An analysis of evolutionary algorithms based on neighbourhood and step sizes. In: Angeline, P.J., McDonnell, J.R., Reynolds, R.G., Eberhart, R. (eds.) EP 1997. LNCS, vol. 1213, pp. 297–307. Springer, Heidelberg (1997)
6. Liu, Y., Yao, X., Zhao, Q., Higuchi, T.: Scaling up fast evolutionary programming with cooperative coevolution. In: Proc. of the 2001 Conference on Evolutionary Computation, pp. 1101–1108. IEEE Press, Los Alamitos (2001)
7. Bäck, T., Schwefel, H.-P.: An overview of evolutionary algorithms for parameter optimization. Evolutionary Computation 1(1), 1–23 (1993)
8. Angeline, P.J.: Adaptive and Self-Adaptive Evolutionary Computations. In: Palaniswami, M., Attikiouzel, Y. (eds.) Computational Intelligence: A Dynamic Systems Perspective, pp. 152–163. IEEE Press, Los Alamitos (1995)
9. Beyer, H.-G., Melkozerov, A.: Mutative η-self-adaptation can beat cumulative step size adaptation when using weighted recombination. In: Proceedings of the 10th Annual Conference on Genetic and Evolutionary Computation, pp. 487–494. ACM, New York (2008)
10. Feller, W.: An Introduction to Probability Theory and Its Applications, 2nd edn., vol. 2. John Wiley & Sons, Chichester (1971)
11. Liu, Y.: Correlation between mutations and self-adaptation in evolutionary programming. In: Kang, L., Cai, Z., Yan, X., Liu, Y. (eds.) ISICA 2008. LNCS, vol. 5370, pp. 58–66. Springer, Heidelberg (2008)
12. Törn, A., Žilinskas, A.: Global Optimisation. In: Törn, A., Žilinskas, A. (eds.) Global Optimization. LNCS, vol. 350. Springer, Heidelberg (1989)
13. Schwefel, H.-P.: Evolution and Optimum Seeking. John Wiley & Sons, New York (1995)
14. Liu, Y.: Operator adaptation in evolutionary programming. In: Kang, L., Liu, Y., Zeng, S. (eds.) ISICA 2007. LNCS, vol. 4683, pp. 90–99. Springer, Heidelberg (2007)

Solving SAT Problem Based on Hybrid Differential Evolution Algorithm

Kunqi Liu[1,2], Jingmin Zhang[2], Gang Liu[3], Lishan Kang[1,4]

[1] School of Computer, China University of Geosciences, Wuhan, 430074
[2] Department of Computer Science, Shijiazhuang University of Economics,
Shijiazhuang, 050031
[3] Faculty of Earth Resources, China University of Geosciences, Wuhan 430074, China
[4] State Key Laboratory of Software Engineering, Wuhan University, Wuhan 430072, China
Liu_kq@126.com

Abstract. Satisfiability (SAT) problem is an NP-complete problem. Based on the analysis about it, SAT problem is translated equally into an optimization problem on the minimum of objective function. A hybrid differential evolution algorithm is proposed to solve the Satisfiability problem. It makes full use of strong local search capacity of hill-climbing algorithm and strong global search capability of differential evolution algorithm, which makes up their disadvantages, improves the efficiency of algorithm and avoids the stagnation phenomenon. The experiment results show that the hybrid algorithm is efficient in solving SAT problem.

Keywords: SAT Problem; Differential Evolution Algorithm; Hill-climbing algorithm; Hybrid differential evolution algorithm.

1 Introduction

Satisfiability problem (SAT) is not only the very important central issue of the computer science, but also the first NP-complete problem [1] to be proved. Many problems in many research fields such as artificial intelligence, database retrieval, computer network system design, VLSI design, computer-aided design problems are transferred to the SAT problem. Therefore improving the method of solving the SAT question has important theoretical and practical significance. At present the methods of solving SAT problem is divided into two classes: the complete algorithm and the incomplete algorithm [2]. The complete algorithm can guarantee to find the solution absolutely, but its efficiency is very low, the average computing time is the multinomial, the worst situation is an exponential. So it does not suit to solve the large-scale SAT problem. The advantage of the incomplete algorithm [3,4] is that it has quicker speed than the complete algorithm, but it can not assured to find the solution in few cases. Because the efficiency of complete algorithm is low, finding an efficient and practical incomplete algorithm has become a research focus.

In this paper, the SAT problem is translated into an optimization problem of solving the minimum of polynomial in binary coded space. A hybrid differential evolution algorithm is proposed to solve the Satisfiability problem. It makes full use of strong

Z. Cai et al. (Eds.): ISICA 2009, CCIS 51, pp. 240–246, 2009.

global search capacity of hill-climbing algorithm and strong local search capability of differential evolution algorithm, which makes up their disadvantages, improves the efficiency of algorithm and avoids the stagnation phenomenon. The experiment results show that the hybrid algorithm is efficient in solving SAT problem.

2 SAT Problem and Its Transformation

2.1 SAT Problem

The basic elements of SAT problem contains the true value, text, clause, conjunctive normal form[5].

Let $U=\{u_1,u_2,\cdots,u_P\}$ be the boolean variable set.

(1) True Value

The truth assignment on the U is a function: $t: U \rightarrow \{T, F\}$. If $t(u) = T$, then u gets the true value under the assignment t. If $t(u) = F$, then u gets the false value under the assignment t. The truth assignment may be denoted simply by a boolean variable group.

(2) Text

If u is a variable of U, then u and $\neg$ u are text. Text u takes the true value under assignment t if and only if variable u takes true value under assignment t. Text $\neg$ u takes the true value under assignment t if and only if variable u takes false value under assignment t.

(3) Clause

The clause on U is the disjunction of some text of U. The clause takes the true value under assignment t if and only if at least one text of the clause takes the true value under assignment t. The k-clause expresses that the clause contains k texts.

(4) Conjunctive Normal Form (CNF)

CNF on the U is the conjunction of some clauses on U. CNF takes the true value under assignment t (also called that CNF is satisfiability under assignment t) if and only if all the clauses of CNF take the true value under assignment t.

The SAT problem is defined as follows:

Given variable set U and CNF C on the U, if there exists assignment t which satisfies C, then SAT problem is called satisfiability, else it is called unsatisfiability.

If the length of every clause in CNF C is k, then the SAT problem is called the K-SAT problem.

2.2 SAT Problem Is Translated into an Optimization Problem Based on {0,1}

Regarding a concrete evaluation based on U, assume the evaluation function of CNF $C= c_1 \wedge c_2 \wedge \cdots \wedge c_n$ is as follows:

$$f=\prod_{i=1}^{n} f(c_i)$$

Where $f(c_i)$ expresses the value of clause c_i. If all the c_i are true, then $f = 1$. If there exists at least a c_i is false, then $f = 0$.

Take the opposite value for each u_{ij} of each clause c_i. If we regard the "and" operation as plus operation, regard the "or" operation as multiplication operation, regard $\neg u_i$ as real parameter x_i of a function, then the SAT problem is translated into an optimization problem on sloving the minimum of corresponding real function [6]. The function T expresses the transformation, which definition is as follows:

$$T(A)=T(c_1 \wedge \cdots \wedge c_i \cdots \wedge c_n)= T(c_1)+ \cdots\cdots+ T(c_i)+ \cdots\cdots+ T(c_n)$$
$$T(c_i)=T(u_{i,1} \vee u_{i,2} \vee \cdots u_{i,k} \vee \cdots\cdots u_{i,j})$$
$$=T(u_{i,1}) T(u_{i,2}) \cdots\cdots T(u_{i,k}) \cdots\cdots T(u_{i,j})$$
$$T(u_i)=1- x_i \quad T(\neg u_i)= x_i \ (x_i \in [0,1] \ 1 \leqslant i \leqslant n)$$
$$T(T)=1 \quad T(F)=0$$

For example, let CNF $B=c_1 \wedge c_2$, where $c_1 = u_1 \vee \neg u_2 \quad c_2 = \neg u_1 \vee \neg u_2$.

The SAT problem of CNF B will be transformed into the minimum optimization problem of function T (B) , the transformation process is as follows:

$$T(B)=T(c_1 \wedge c_2)$$
$$=T(c_1)+ T(c_2)$$
$$=T(u_1 \vee \neg u_2)+T(\neg u_1 \vee \neg u_2)$$
$$=T(u_1)T(\neg u_2)+T(\neg u_1)T(\neg u_2)$$
$$=(1- x_1) x_2 + x_1 x_2$$

3 Solving SAT Problem with Hybrid Differential Evolution Algorithm

3.1 Chromosome Structure

It is convenient to use binary code to describe the SAT problem. In this paper, a chromosome is equivalent to the truth assignment of p logical variables.

3.2 Differential Evolution Algorithm

Differential Evolution Algorithm(DEA) [7] is a kind of evolutionary algorithm based on real encoding. Its integral structure is similar to the genetic algorithm. The main difference between them is mutation operation. The mutation operation of DEA is based on differences vectors of chromosome. The rest genetic operations are similar to the genetic algorithm's. And there are also several critical parameters must be determined in advance. In the following DEA is introduced to solve SAT problem.

3.2.1 Parameters

DEA mainly involves four parameters: ① population scale, ② individual (also called variable) dimension, ③ mutation factor, ④ crossover probability. The Literature [7] indicated that the general population size ranged from 5 to 10(the dimension of variable is determined by the actual issues). The mutation factor is between 0 and 2 and we take 0.5 generally. Crossover probability is between 0 and 1. In general, the greater the crossover probability is, the faster the convergence is, but it is easy to premature, easy to fall into local optimum and the worse the stability of algorithm is. We believe the better choice is 0.3. Of course, these are just the experience and it is not rigorously proved. For some specific issues it may have better results if we take other parameter values. Initial Population is generated randomly with size N.

3.2.2 Mutation Operation

Mutation Operation of DEA is the main feature to differ with other evolutionary algorithms. Its mutation operation is based on differences vectors of chromosome. Its main idea is to use the differences between individual information to narrow the differences between the various entities. In general, the differences among individuals are larger in early time, but with the evolution generation increasing, the differences between individuals gradually reduce duo to the addition of noises, which can guarantee the convergence of algorithm. DEA has several evolution patterns. In this paper we choose the most powerful mutation mode DE/rand/1/bin with global search capability. The concrete mutation operation is to add noise to every individual of the current generation. Firstly, randomly select three individuals X_a, X_b, X_c, where $i \neq a \neq b \neq c$, then we get the noise for $H_{ij}(t+1)=[x_{aj}(t)+F(x_{bj}(t)-x_{cj}(t))]$ mod 2, where H_{ij} is the new individual after mutation, $x_{bj}(t)-x_{cj}(t)$ is difference vector, F is the scalling factor and it can control the speed of convergence, mod is operation of complement computation. Because the encoding form of individual is binary mode, it is need to ask-odd through molding 2.

3.2.3 Crossover Operator

The crossover operation is to increase the diversity of population. The specific operations are as follows:

If $rand_{ij}$ CR or j=rand(i), then the value of $V_{ij}(t+1)$ is $h_{ij}(t+1)$. If $rand_{ij}$>CR or j≠ rand(i), then the value of $V_{ij}(t+1)$ is $X_{ij}(t)$. $rand_{ij}$ is the random decimal between 0 and 1. CR is crossover probability where $CR \in [0,1]$. rand(i) is random integer between 1 and n. This strategy will ensure that at least one component of $X_i(t+1)$ is dedicated by corresponding component of $X_i(t)$.

3.2.4 Selection Operator

Let $X_i(t+1)$ and $X_i(t)$ respectively be the individuals of t+1 generation and t generation, $V_i(t+1)$ be the ith individual of t+1 population. The selection operator is defined as follows:

$$X_i(t+1) = \begin{cases} V_i(t+1) & f(V_i(t+1)) < f(X_i(t)) \\ X_i(t) & f(V_i(t+1)) \geq f(X_i(t)) \end{cases}$$

3.3 The Hill-Climbing Algorithm

Hill-climbing algorithm is a heuristic searching method of artificial intelligence[8] which is commonly used to find the local optimal solution. It has better versatility for solving various optimization problems, simply and nimbly. When using DEA to solve SAT problem, the speed of convergence in early stage is fast, however, it is easy to fall into local optimum in late stage. Thus, hill-climbing algorithm is introduced in later period. The specific steps of hill-climbing algorithm are as follows:

Step1 To randomly assign for variables which cause the SAT function value stagnate;

Step2 Calculating function value of the SAT after randomly assignment for variables which cause the SAT function value stagnated;

Step3 If the new function value <the best individual fitness value, then update the best fitness value of individual.

3.4 Hybrid Differential Evolution Algorithm

When we use differential evolution algorithm to solve SAT problems, in the evolution later period, the diversity of population gradually reduces, the similarity between individual increases and the successfully effective gene's reorganization probability obviously reduces. Thus the improvement speed of optimal solution drops much and falls into the status of a local optimum. And hill-climbing algorithm is commonly used to seek for the local optimal solution. So in the paper we integrate hill-climbing algorithm with DEA. We call it Hybrid differential evolution algorithm(HEDA). The HEDA has strong global search capability of differential evolution algorithm, enhances the capability of local optimization and the calculating efficiency of the latter. Its robustness is stronger than the difference evolution algorithm. The specific steps of HDEA are as follows:

Step1 Determine population size N, mutation factor F and crossover rate CR;

Step2 Initial Population is generated randomly with size N;

Step3 Carry out Mutation, crossover and selection operation according to section 3.2.2 --3.2.4;

Step4 Judge whether the termination condition is satisfied, that is to determine whether the SAT function value is 0, and if so, then output the result and the algorithm ends;

Step5 Determine whether SAT function optimum value is bogging down in some value and to determine whether the optimization number exceeds the maximum of the termination, and if so, then switch to step6 and carry out local climbing optimize, otherwise switch to step3;

Step6 Find all the individuals ($Y_i,1 \leqslant i \leqslant N$) which cause algorithm optimization result bogging down. Let j=1;

Step7 Circulation: when j<=k and there is no optimum value, then repeat Step7.1, Step7.2; 6 Liu KunqiP1,2P Zhang JingminP2 PLiu GangP3P P PKang LishanP1,4

Step7.1 For individual Y_j, carry on the climbing optimization operation according to Step1~Step3 of section 2.3. If the SAT function value achieves the optimum value, then climbing is successful, then output the result, the algorithm ends;
Step7.2 j=j+1;
Step8 If j>k, then climbing is fail, else switch to step2.

4 Experiment

In order to test the computation effect of HDEA, we use the randomly generated 3-SAT model(the length of each of the words L = 3, and the variables of the words is different each other) as an example. HDEA and DEA are all programed by C language and run in Intel (R) Celeron (R) CPU 1.7GHZ computer. The run time is 300 (s), sample number of each test example is 20. In order to obtain the good experimental performance, the parameters of each algorithm have been optimized. The analysis and comparison are carried by the average execution time of the calculation and the number of satisfied sample. The result is shown in Table 1 and it should be comprehensive and convincing.

From Table 1 we know when the number of clauses increase, computing speed of HDEA is quicker than that of DEA(we can see it from average execution time of sat-isfied examples of 20 examples). Therefore HDEA is better than DEA in the optimi-zation results, computational efficiency and robustness. Therefore, it is feasible and highly effective to solve the large-scale SAT question with the HDEA algorithm.

Table 1. Comparison of HDEA and DEA

CNF			Average execution time (s)		the number of satisfied	
m	n	L	HDEA	DEA	HDEA	DEA
100	200	3	0.2	0.6	20	20
100	250	3	1.41	1.6	20	20
100	300	3	4.36	5.47	20	19
100	350	3	13.2	21.4	15	14
100	380	3	10.3	12.3	7	7
100	400	3	11.3	14.0	6	5
100	410	3	19.3	22.3	4	3

5 Conclusion

In the paper a hybrid differential evolution algorithm is proposed. It integrates hill-climbing algorithm with DEA. The experimental results indicate the HDEA could find the globally optimal solution quickly in a short time. It can avoid premature and the stagnation in later period of DEA, and enhance reliability and speed. The HDEA can quickly and easily find the optimal solution of the SAT problem. However, further proof of the theory and experiment of other problem are needed in order to guarantee the general effectiveness of HDEA .

Acknowledgments

This research is supported by National Natural Science Foundation of China (Grant No. 40772196).

References

[1] qiang, L.M., song, K.J., Dan, L., Shu-quan, L.: The basic theory of genetic algorithms and applications, pp. 247–248. Science Press, Beijing (2002)

[2] Wei, L., Xiong, H.: The Analysis of Algorithms for the Propositional Logic Satisfiability Problem Propositional. Computer Science 26(3), 1–9 (1999)

[3] Selman, B., Kautz, H., Cohen, B.: Noise strategies for improving local search. In: Proc 12th National Conference on AL, American Association for Artificial Intelligence, pp. 337–343 (1994)

[4] Wei, L., qi, H.W.: A Mathematical and Physical Method for Solving CNF Satisfiability Problem. Science in China Series A 25(11), 1208–1217 (1994)

[5] Ji, Y.J., Le Su, K.: Improvement of Local Research in SAT Problem. Journal of Computer Research and Development 42(1), 60–65 (2005)

[6] Storn, R., price, K.: Minimizing the real functions of the ICEC 1996 contest by differential evolution. In: Proceedings of the IEEE Conference on Evolutionary ComPutation, ICEC, pp. 842–844 (1996)

[7] Storn, R., price, K.: Differential evolution-a simple and efficient heuristic for global optimization over continuous spaces. Journal of Global Optimization 11(4), 341–359 (1995)

[8] you, L.S.: Introduction to Artificial Intelligence Techniques. Xidian University Press, Xi'an (2002)

The Application of Evolution-Branching Algorithm on Earth-Mars Transfer Trajectory

Jing Liu and Guangming Dai

China University of Geosciences, Wuhan 430074, China
191043121j@gmail.com, gmdai@cug.edu.cn

Abstract. In this paper, a novel algorithm which combines a deterministic and random algorithm is used to optimize Earth to Mars double impulse orbit optimization function. While the deterministic algorithm uses branching technique and the stochastic algorithm takes advantage of evolution programming. Based on the analysis of Evolution-Branching Algorithm, we propose an improved algorithm (OEBA). The OEBA is a new branching technology: the standard bisection method. It generates the initial population with orthogonal design so that the individuals yield a more representative distribution of the feasible solutions. The experiment results show that the novel algorithm is very effective for Earth to Mars double impulse orbit optimization. At the same time, it provides a possibility for solving more complex optimization problems.

Keywords: evolution programming, branching technique, orthogonal design, global optimization.

1 Introduction

In an ecliptic reference frame centered into the Sun and considering the gravity action of the Sun only, the dynamic of a spacecraft is governed by the following differential system[1]:

$$\bar{r} = v$$

$$\bar{v} = -\frac{\mu}{r^3} r \tag{1}$$

Where μ is the gravity constant of the Sun, γ is the position vector of the spacecraft and v is its velocity vector. Now in the hypothesis of Keplerian motion taking two points in space and fixed a time of flight (TOF) T, Lambert's problem[2][3][4] consists of finding the transfer arc from one point to the other in the given time. If this is applied to the problem of finding the optimal transfer trajectory from Earth to Mars, an infinite number of trajectories can be generated, each one characterized by a different departure date from the Earth t_0, a different time of flight T. Therefore the following objective function can be defined:

$$f = \Delta V_E + \Delta V_M \tag{2}$$

Z. Cai et al. (Eds.): ISICA 2009, CCIS 51, pp. 247–256, 2009.

Where Δv_E is departure velocity from the Earth and Δv_M is arrival velocity at Mars. f is the cost in terms of propellant to transfer a spacecraft from the Earth to Mars, which must be minimized with respect to the departure time and transfer time.

If we defined t_0 in the interval [3000, 6000] expressed in Modified Julian Day (i.e. number of days from 1st January 2000) while the TOF is defined in the interval [100,400] expressed in days, then the objective function f can be showed in Fig.1 and Fig.2.

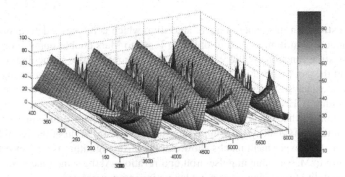

Fig. 1. Three-dimensional plot of the objective function f

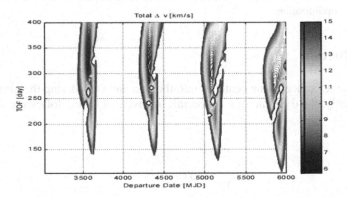

Fig. 2. Two-dimensional plot of the objective function f

The less the function f value is, the less cost we spend. Therefore, it is very significance to find the global minimum. Since the problem is generally highly nonlinear and not necessary differentiable in all the solution space, it is a very difficult optimization problems.

In this paper, a mixed approach combining a branching technique and a particular implementation of evolution programming (EP) is proposed to solve Earth to Mars double impulse orbit. EP is used to explore local information, to select promising branches.

2 Evolution Programming

The present evolution programming simulates the action of people migrating from one region to the other region. When its implement is based on four fundamental operators: mutation, migration, mating and filtering.

2.1 Generate an Initial Population by Orthogonal Design

In reference[5], Yiu-Wing leung proposed an orthogonal genetic algorithm with quantization to solve numerical optimization for continuous variables. Some researchers introduced the orthogonal design to multi-objective optimization problems[6][7][8][9]; the experiment results proved that it can improve the performance of the algorithm.

Orthogonal design has some properties. First, it has no two repeat experiments. Second, any two results have no comparability. Thus, orthogonal design is able to guarantee the representativeness of experiment.

2.2 Migration

A person in one region has a active region. In the active region, he (or she) wants to find a better life-style. So his (or her) active trend is to find the best-style.

The implement of the active region is migration region. The migration process [8] generates a subpopulation in a neighborhood of an individual y . If the best individual in the subpopulation is better than the parent y , survives to the next generation instead of the parent. The subpopulation is generated using mutation and mating.

If f_k^i is the fitness value associated to and individual i at generation k and f_{k+1}^i the fitness value associated to the same individual at generation k+1, the differential improvement as:

$$df^i = f_{k+1}^i - f_k^i \tag{3}$$

The migration radius is defined as:

$$\rho_j^i = \frac{len(y_j^i)}{len(D^i)} \tag{4}$$

Where ρ_j^i is the j-th dimensional radius of individual i, $len(y_j^i)$ is the j-th dimensional length of individual i, and $len(D_j)$ is the j-th dimensional length of the whole domain.

During convergence the change of migration radius depend on the fitness of the individuals inside the migration region and the differential improvement of the individual from one generation to another:

If none of the children of the subpopulation is better than the parent the radius is reduced.

$$\rho_j = \begin{cases} max([le-8, \delta y_{min}]) & if\ \delta y_{min} \geq \varepsilon \rho_j^i \\ \varepsilon \rho_j & if\ \delta y_{min} < \varepsilon \rho_j \end{cases} \tag{5}$$

Where ε has been set to 0.5 and δy_{min} is the distance of the best child y^*, among the ones in the migration, from the parent i, normalized with respect to the dimensions of the migration region:

$$\delta y_{min} = \sqrt{\sum_{j=1}^{n} (\frac{y_j^* - y_j^i}{S_j^i})} \tag{6}$$

Where S_j^i is the difference between the value of the upper bound and of the lower bound.

If from generation k to generation k+1 the differential improvement increases, then the migration radius is recomputed according to the prediction:

$$\rho_{k+1}^i = \rho_k^i \eta log(e + \sqrt{i-1}) \tag{7}$$

Where η is equal to 2 in this implementation.

2.3 Mutation

Mutation operates [10] in three different ways:

①. Generate a random number, taken form a Gaussian distribution

②. Exchanges a random component of the individual with one of the bounds.

③. Generate a symmetric perturbation of a selected component y_i with respect to its original value within an interval in a neighborhood of y

2.4 Mating

The mating procedure takes two individuals and generates one or two children mixing the genotypes of the two parents. Three schemes are used to mate individuals:

①. Single point crossover which simply exchange part of the genes between the two parents

②. Arithmetic crossover, which generate a new individual with an interpolation of the two parents: chosen two individual y^1 and y^2 and a random number α, the resulting child will be given by:

$$y^3 = \alpha y^2 + (1 - \alpha) y^1 \tag{8}$$

③. Extrapolation generates a new individual on the side of the best individual between the two parents at a distance from the best parents equal to the vector connecting the two parents:

$$y^3 = \alpha(y^2 - y^1) + y^2 \tag{9}$$

2.5 Filtering

If a person in one region don't satisfy his life (or live in the lowest level), he may migrate to another region. Or after his efforts, he may access to the higher level.

The implement of the action is the filtering operator. Different from traditional selection mechanisms based on fitness, the filtering operator allow each individual to survive from one generation to another provided that it remains inside the filter. The filter ranks all the individuals on the basis of their fitness from the best to the worst. All the individuals with fitness worse than a given threshold will mutate to another place, while migration is applied to all individuals within the filter.

3 Branching Technique

Because of the stochastic nature of evolution algorithm, we can not guarantee to find the global optimal solution when the algorithm converges. Therefore, a deterministic technology, branching technique[11][12], is taken on the basis of the output of the evolution algorithm.

3.1 Branching Procedure

Step 1: Initialization

Let $F = \{D\}$

Step 2: Node selection

Let θ be a function which associates a value to each node $H \in F$. Then, select a node $\overline{H} \in F$ such that

$$\overline{H} \in \arg\min_{H \in F} \theta(H)$$

Step 3: Evaluation

Evaluate the selected node $\overline{H}$ through evolution programming described above.

Step 4: Node branching

Subdivide $\overline{H}$ into η nodes H_i , $i = 1,...,\eta$ for some integer $\eta \geq 2$, and update F as follows:

$$F = (F \setminus \{\overline{H}\}) \cup \{H_1,...,H_\eta\} \tag{10}$$

Step 5: Node deletion

Delete nodes from F according to some rule.

Step 6: Stopping rule

If $F = \emptyset$, then stop. Otherwise, go back to Step 1.

Note that in the scheme above each node corresponds to a subdomain.

3.2 Node Branching

First we call that each subdomain is a hyper rectangle. Branching can be done through many different methods, such as standard bisection, divided through the worst individual which is out of filter.

In this paper, we use the standard bisection method: the (relative) largest edge of the domain to be subdivided is selected and two new subdomains (i.e., $\eta = 2$) are obtained by splitting with respect to its midpoint. More formally, let

$$H = [a_1, b_1] * ... * [a_n, b_n] \tag{11}$$

Be the domain to be subdivided. Let

$$j \in \arg \max_{i=1,...,n} \frac{b_i - a_i}{D_i - d_i}$$

Where d_i and D_i denote respectively the lower and upper bounds for variable x_i in the original domain D. Let

$$\bar{x}_j = \frac{a_j + b_j}{2}$$

be the midpoint of edge $[a_j, b_j]$. Then, we define the two subdomains:

$$H_1 = [a_1, b_1] * ... * [a_j, \bar{x}_j] * ... * [a_n, b_n]$$
$$H_2 = [a_1, b_1] * ... * [\bar{x}_j, b_j] * ... * [a_n, b_n] \tag{12}$$

3.3 Node Evaluate

Before defining the node evaluate function θ, we need to introduce two other functions ω and φ. Let H be a given subdomain and $\overline{H}$ be its father. Function ω is defined as follows for H :

$$\omega(H) = \frac{\max\{N(H), 1\}}{N} \frac{\ell(D)}{\ell(H)} \tag{13}$$

Where $N(H)$ is the number of individuals in the node H , N is the size of population. Function ℓ is defined as follow:

$$\ell(D) = (Vol(D))^{\frac{1}{n}} \tag{14}$$

As can be seen from the formula definition, the function ω is similar to the density of node H. Small values for ω means a low density of node H, so it has more chance to be explored.

Function φ is defined as follows for H:

$$\varphi(H) = \begin{cases} \dfrac{f_{best}^H - f_{best}}{f_{worst} - f_{best}} & \textit{if } N(H) > 0 \\ 1 & \textit{otherwise} \end{cases} \tag{15}$$

Where f_{best} and f_{worst} are respectively the best (lowest) and worst (highest) function values observed up to now by the EP within the feasible region, and f_{best}^H are the best function values within H. For $N(H) > 0$, φ returns a value between 0 and 1, while for $N(H) = 0$ the φ value is simply set to 1.

Now, we are ready to define the function θ:

$$\theta(H) = \sigma\omega(H) + (1 - \sigma)\varphi(H) \tag{16}$$

Where $\sigma \in [0,1]$ is a parameter which controls the relative weights of ω and φ. That the choice of σ allows us to balance global and local exploration of the algorithm. If σ is close to 0, φ has a higher weight and nodes where good function values have been observed are favored (local exploration), while when σ is close to 1, ω has the higher weight and nodes with low density are favored (global exploration).

The procedure is shown as follow(Fig. 3):

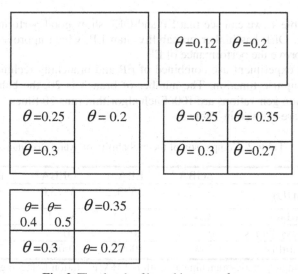

Fig. 3. The sketch of branching procedure

3.4 Node Deletion

In this paper, a simply rule is used to delete node: all nodes are deleted at the same time when the number of explored subdomains reaches a predefined number, then algorithm stop.

4 Experiments

At first, only the EP algorithm without branching technique is tested to verify the effectiveness and efficiency of the new operators. The problem is solved by running the EP several times, with no branching step.

Because the EP algorithm will be combined with the branching technology in the next, the size of initial population of EP should not be too large. In this experiment, the initial population is set to 10 individuals, while the size of filter is 7. So the population should be good diversity with more local information. Thus, an orthogonal design is used to generate the initial population.

Since the nature of the method is stochastic, 20 runs have been performed and evolution generations are 200 in each run. The results are showed in Table 1.

Table 1. Comparison of the probability of finding the global minimum

Value	SGA[13]	EP	OEP
f(km/s)	5.6695	5.6695	5.6695
t_0 (MJD)	3573.5	3573.2	3573.0
TOF(day)	324.0	324.2	324.1
Success Times	1	12	14
probability	5%	60%	80%

(SGA: simple Genetic algorithm, OEP: orthogonal design EP).

From the table 1, we can see that EP and OEP show good performance on finding the global one. OEP has higher probability than EP, which approve that orthogonal design can improve the performance of EP.

The second experiment use combined of EP and branching technique to solve the E-M double impulse function. The number of branch is 20, the balance factor σ is 0.5 and evolution generations are 100. Each algorithm runs 20 times.

The results are showed in Table 2.

Table 2. Comparison of the probability of hybrid algorithms

Value	SGBA	EBA	OEBA	EPIC[11]
t_0 (MJD)	3573.5	3573.2	3573.0	3573.5
TOF(day)	324.0	324.2	324.1	324.3
Success Times	4	20	20	------
probability	20%	100%	100%	75%

(SGBA: simple genetic-branching algorithm, EBA: evolution-branching algorithm
OEBA: orthogonal design EBA, EPIC: Evolution Programming and Interval Computation).

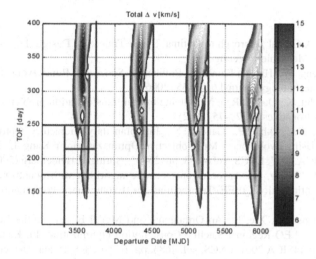

Fig. 4. Characterization of one of the OEBA branch result

It can be seen that the algorithm combining of EP and branching technique have higher probability than pure EP algorithm. The bisection method combined with EP has higher probability than EPIC, which result in the table 2 is from reference [11].

5 Conclusions

Earth to Mars double impulse thrust optimization function is generally highly non-linear and not necessary differentiable in all the solution space. And it is very significance to find the global minimum. In this paper, a novel algorithm combining EP and branching technique is used to solve the hard and significative problem. Base on the study and analysis of Evolution-Branching Algorithm, we introduced a new method to generate an initial population: orthogonal design, which can make the initial population scatter evenly in the feasible solutions space. At the same time, a new branching technique, bisection method, is used to combine with OEP. The experiments show OEBA has better performance than EPIC.

Although the hybrid algorithm is quite effective as a general tool for Earth to Mars double impulse transfer trajectory, an extension to treat more complex constraints is under development.

Acknowledgement

This paper is supported by National Natural Science Foundation(NO.60873107), the National High Technology Research and Development Program(NO.2008AA12A201) and Natural Science Foundation of Hubei Province(NO.2008CDB348).

References

1. Vasile, M.: A Global Approach to Optimal Space Trajectory Design. In: 13th AAS/AIAA Space Flight Mechanics Meeting
2. Zhu, R., Meng, W., Hu, X.: Lambert's Problem in Spacecraft Rendezvous. Chinese Space science and technology, journal 6, 49–55 (2006)
3. Wang, S., Zhu, K., Dai, J., Ren, X.: Solving orbital transformation problems based on EA. Journal of astronautics 23, 73–75 (2002)
4. Kalyanmoy, D., Nikhil, P., Ganesh, N.: Interplanettary Trajectory Optimization with Swing-Bys Using Evolutionary Multi-objective Optimazation. In: Kang, L., Liu, Y., Zeng, S. (eds.) ISICA 2007. LNCS, vol. 4683, pp. 26–35. Springer, Heidelberg (2007)
5. Leung, Y.W., Wang, Y.: An orthogonal genetic algorithm with quantization for global numerical optimization. IEEE Transactions on Evolutionary computation 5(1), 41–53 (2001)
6. Dai, G., Zheng, W., Xie, B.: An Orthogonal and Model Based Multiobjective Genetic Algorithm for LEO Regional Satellite Constellation Optimization. In: Kang, L., Liu, Y., Zeng, S. (eds.) ISICA 2007. LNCS, vol. 4683, pp. 652–660. Springer, Heidelberg (2007)
7. Zeng, S., Wei, W., Kang, L., et al.: A multi-objective algorithm based on orthogonal design. Chinese Journal of Computers 28(7), 1153–1162 (2005)
8. wang, J., Dai, G., Zheng, W.: An Improved Regularity Model-Based Multi-objective Estimation of Distribution Algorithm. In: ISICA 2008 (2008)
9. Xie, B., Dai, G., Xie, C., Chen, L.: Orthogonal scatter search algorithm. Computer Engineering and Design (May 2008)
10. Michaelewicz, Z.: Genetic Algorithms + Data Structures = Evolution Programs, 3rd edn. Springer, Telos (1996)
11. Vasile, M.: A Systematic-Heuristic Approach for space Trajectory. Design. Astrodynamics, Space Missions, and Chaos. In: Annals of the New York Academy of Sciences, vol. 1017
12. Vasile, M., Locateli, M.: A hybrid multiagent approach for global trajectory optimization. Journal of Global Optimization 41(3) (2008) ISSN 1573-2916
13. Wang, X., Cao, L.: Genetic Algorithm– Theory and Software Applications. Xi'an Jiaotong University Press, Xi'an

The Research of Solution to the Problems of Complex Task Scheduling Based on Self-adaptive Genetic Algorithm

Li Zhu, Yongxiang He, Haidong Xue, and Leichen Chen

Faculty of Computer Science, China University of Geosciences
Wuhan, Hubei, P.R. China, 430074
xiang816@gmail.com

Abstract. Traditional genetic algorithms (GA) displays a disadvantage of early-constringency in dealing with scheduling problem. To improve the crossover operators and mutation operators self-adaptively, this paper proposes a self-adaptive GA at the target of multitask scheduling optimization under limited resources. The experiment results show that the proposed algorithm outperforms the traditional GA in evolutive ability to deal with complex task scheduling optimization.

Keywords: self-adaptive, genetic algorithm, Complex Task Scheduling, optimization of network planning.

1 Introduction

The key point of project management is scheduling problems. Optimization of scheduling has been a hot research topic that domestic and foreign experts and scholars focus on. It determines the profit of the project. Feng[1], Li and Love[2] were the first to use genetic algorithm to solve the scheduling optimization problem. And in Bibliography[3-6], Xiang Li gained better results, using an improved genetic algorithm and a hybrid genetic algorithm to solve the multi-task scheduling problem. But the quantities of data in those experiments are small, and network planning is assumed to be relatively simple, therefore it impacts little to the optimization when the algorithm converges early. However, when the number of works increases to a large scale, the shortcoming of the algorithm will be showed out, and causes unsatisfactory optimization of scheduling. Therefore, this paper presents a self-adaptive genetic algorithm to solve the complex multi-task scheduling.

2 Resource-Constrained Project Scheduling Model

Suppose there are some parallel projects and a shared resource library, including some kinds of renewable resources. All resources have only limited supply, and projects are independent with each other in addition to shared resources. In order to facilitate the descriptions of problems, now a mathematical model is established as follows: the

Z. Cai et al. (Eds.): ISICA 2009, CCIS 51, pp. 257–265, 2009.
© Springer-Verlag Berlin Heidelberg 2009

multi-task scheduling problem have P independent tasks, and No.k task contains nk+1 works, among which No.nk+1 work is the virtual termination working of the task, occupying no resource and time. The all tasks share M kinds of renewable resources, among which the total volume of the No.m resource is R_m. W_i stands for working sets of the No.i task, W_{ij} stands for the No.j working of the No.i task, whose working period is d_{ij}, r_{ijm} stands for demand for the No.m resource, $S_{i,j}$ marks the start time of the task, and P_{ij} marks the collection formed by all pre-tasks. In time of t all ongoing tasks are marked as $I(t)$. In view of different importance degree of different projects, ∂_k represents weight of the No.k task. Given the above assumptions and symbols adopted, the multi-task scheduling problem agianst the background of resource constraint can be described as:

$$\min\sum_{k=1}^{P}\partial_k *(S_{k,n_k+1}) \tag{1}$$

$$s.\, t. \quad S_{i,j} \geq S_{i,h}+d_{i,h} \,, \quad \forall h \in P_{ij}\,, \forall i,j \tag{2}$$

$$\sum_{w_{i,j}\in I_t}r_{ijm}\leq R_m \,, \quad \forall m,t. \tag{3}$$

$$I(t)=\{Wkj\in\bigcup_{k=1}^{P}Wk \,|\, S_{kj} \leq t \leq S_{kj}+d_{kj} \} \tag{4}$$

$$r_{ijm}\geq 0 \tag{5}$$

$$\sum_{k=1}^{P}\partial_k = 1 \tag{6}$$

3   Using Self-adaptive Genetic Algorithm to Solve the Problems of Complex Task Scheduling

3.1   RCPSP Problems

As it is a sharing of common resources among the work of multiple projects, its solution is different from that of solving the sharing of common resources among the work of individual projects. Of the solutions to solve this problem, there is a bi-level decision-making method for Multi-Resource Constrained Multi-task Scheduling put forward in literature [3], however, the method has two major flaws.

First, the assumption prerequisite of the method is that the duration of work of shared resources in each task is decided by the allocated resource volume. The duration of work of shared resources is inversely proportional to the volume of resource allocation(such as 2 machines work for 6 days, 4 machines works for 3 days), that is, the duration of the work = work capacity ÷ resources volume. But in real life, the work capacity is not cumulative, that is, the duration of the work ≠ Work capacity ÷ resources volume, so the model is unable to solve the problems of non-cumulative work capacity in project.

Second, the model adopts a specific resource-allocation strategy among tasks. The resources will always belong to the project after they are allocated to it, and other projects can no longer use this part of the resources. This resource-allocation method results in a great waste of resources as resources among projects cannot exchange. When a project has some idle resources which cannot be used by any other projects, it is wasted.

The method in Literature [8] finally is combining the multi-project network plans into one network plan to solve. And it reduces the solving efficiency and flexibility.

And the method proposed in this paper is now able to solve the multi-task problems of non-cumulative work capacity; and as the resources among projects are dynamic and exchangeable, the method will not waste idle resources and is able to dispatch each task and makes all tasks completed in the shortest possible period according to the weight of each task. Not the combination of each task network plan but only the information like duration of time and resources of each task is needed for the completion.

3.2 Self-adaptive Genetic Algorithm Design

The Fig.1 shows the flowchart of the self-adaptive genetic Algorithm. And this paper will solve the Resource-constrained multi-task scheduling problems as the process of the flowchart.

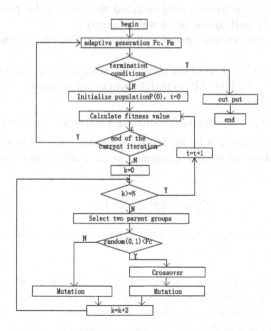

Fig. 1. Flowchart of the self-adaptive genetic Algorithm

(1) Structure of chromosome
The problem of multi-project scheduling under resource constraints can also be seen as the scheduling problem subject to certain constraints. The key to solve this problem is how to find a suitable order for all the work of multi-projects with genetic algorithm. Here we ranked all work lists according to a certain order for chromosome encoding the issues. With m projects and n works in each project, there will be m * n work, that is, the length of the chromosome is m * n. Make V_k stands for the NO.K chromosomes in current population and P_{kij} a gene for the chromosome that stands for the work of NO.pk task in j chromosome location. The chromosome can be expressed as follows:

$$Vk = [P_{1i1}, ..., P_{1ii}, ..., P_{1in}, ..., P_{ki1}, ..., P_{kii}, ... P_{kin}, ..., P_{mi1}, ..., P_{mii}, ..., P_{min}]$$

The P_{kij} can be arbitrarily ordered in the premise of meeting constraints.

(2) Initialization population
For the Chromosomes initialization, this paper is divided into two parts. One is randomly generating various chromosomes by the topological scheduling, the other is generating chromosome through a variety of heuristic methods.

Method 1: Randomly generated initial chromosome
Similar with the optimal scheduling method with the shortest Resource Constrained time of the single task, the only difference is that for every work. Firstly judge the task to which it belongs, and then determine the constraint relationship. It is determined the first consider work by a Left to Right approach with a fixed sequence. At each stage of the work order has been maintained and assembled Scheduling can work and completely random from a pool selected to work in the pool. This process is repeated indefinitely until all the work was arranged.

In each iteration of the process all the work at one of the following three conditions:
1. The work has index: Part of the chromosome structure in the work.
2. The work can schedule: All immediate works are ordered.
3. Free work: All of work

Where, v_k^t is a part of chromosome, including t activities. Q_t is in phase t with a corresponding arrangements can be made to the activities set, Pi is all the activities set, with a corresponding set of arrangements can be made activity set Q_t is defined as formula 7.

$$Q_t = \{j \mid P_i \subset v_k^t\} \tag{7}$$

It includes specific arrangements in the end nodes, and it is all competition activity set.

Method 2: Initializing chromosome through various heuristic methods:
Bai Sijun listed 31[7] heuristic methods. Based on the resources 11 more effective heuristic ones are picked out here. Application of these 11 heuristic methods generates a good number of chromosomes of relatively activation effects.

The 11 heuristic criteria are as follows:

(1) Minimum total time difference priority standard (MinTS), according to the earliest starting time if they are same.

(2) Maximum total time difference priority standard (MinTS), according to the earliest starting time if they are same.

(3) Minimum criteria for priority period (SOF), according to the numbers of work if they are same.

(4) Maximum criteria for priority period (SOF), according to the numbers of work if they are same.

(5) LS priority minimum standard (MinLS), according to the numbers of work if they are same.

(6) EF priority minimum standard (MinEF), according to the numbers of work if they are same.

(7) LF priority minimum standard (MinLF), according to the numbers of work if they are same.

(8) ACTIM standard, the different between the length of the critical path and the latest starting time, the greater the value has the priority.

(9) Maximum priority greatest resource requirements standard (MaxR).

(10) Minimum priority greatest resource requirements standard (MinR).

(11) Most intended tight works priority criterion (MostIS).

The literature [9] also makes some heuristic criteria considered: First considering the work on the critical path. If there are conflicts among several key tasks, considering the following programs:

(1) The smallest total time priority.
(2) First start priority.
(3) First completion priorities.
(4) Priority for the most intense work, the remaining processing time and delivery time ratio is smaller becomes tenser.

(3) Self-adaptive crossover and mutation

Standard GA exists the shortcoming of constringing optimal value partially, which is hard to get over. The selection of crossover probability Pc and mutation probability Pm is the key to capability of GA and influences the constringency directly. Srinvivas present a self-adaptive GA that automatically adjusts Pc and Pm with fitness function. Self-adaptive parameter formula as follows:

$$P_C = \begin{cases} P_{C\max} & (f < f_{avg}) \\ P_{C\max} - \dfrac{(P_{C\max} - P_{C\min})(f' - f_{avg})}{f_{\max} - f_{avg}} & (f \geq f_{avg}) \end{cases} \tag{8}$$

$$P_M = \begin{cases} P_{M\max} & (f < f_{avg}) \\ P_{M\max} - \dfrac{(P_{M\max} - P_{M\min})(f - f_{avg})}{f_{\max} - f_{avg}} & (f \geq f_{avg}) \end{cases} \tag{9}$$

Where, $P_{C\max}$ is max value of the crossover probability; $P_{C\min}$ is min value of the crossover probability; $P_{M\max}$ is max value of the mutation probability; $P_{M\min}$ is min value of the mutation probability; $f_{\max}$ is The largest population fitness value; f_{avg} is the average fitness value in each generation; f' is the larger of the two individual fitness value; f is individual fitness value.

(4) Fitness function
Requiring the minimum period of a number of tasks, first we will decode the chromosome and calculate the possible earliest time to start all work, and then we calculate the earliest completion time and afterwards the earliest completion time of each project. Finally we calculate the shortest average duration in accordance with the ratio of the weight. We come to the objective function as follows:

$$\min\sum_{k=1}^{P}\partial_k *(S_{k,n_k}+1) \tag{10}$$

Since the RCPSP problem is to minimize total task duration, it is needed to convert the original objective function to ensure that appropriate individuals have the greatest fitness. Make v_k the NO.K chromosome in current population, $g(v_k)$ the fitness function, $f(v_k)$ the original target, $f_{\max}$ and $f_{\min}$ the biggest and the smallest target of the current population respectively conversion method:

$$g(v_k)=\frac{f_{\max}-f(v_k)+\varepsilon}{f_{\max}-f_{\min}+\varepsilon} \tag{11}$$

Of which ε is arithmetic number which is usually limited in open interval (0,1).

(5) Selection Operator
The operation that winning individuals are chosen from the group and the bad individuals are eliminated is named selection.

4 Experiments and Analysis

4.1 Experimental Description

The experiment in this paper is to solve complex multi-task scheduling problem through self-adaptive genetic algorithms. It assumes that each task shares the same flowchart structure, and each task has 800 items and 1202 works, Fig.2 only shows one part of the flowchart structure of the task; It also assumes all tasks in one experiment share the same resource distribution as shown in Table.2 with the total resource capacity unchanged. The resource here mentioned is single-patterned, which is to say, each task uses one type of resource. The period, resource type and quantity of the all works in one task are showed in Table 1.

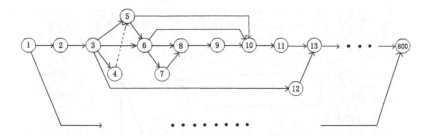

Fig. 2. One part of the network flowchart in this experiment

Table 1. Period, resource type and quantity

Serial number	Starting Item	Finishing Item	Period	Resource type	Resource quantity
1	1	2	2	1	7
2	2	3	3	2	9
3	3	4	2	3	3
......	......	......	......	......	......
1200	797	799	3	11	20
1201	798	799	5	8	11
1202	799	800	3	16	5

Table 2. Type and quantity of resource

type	Quantity
1	42
2	50
3	36
......	......
29	32
30	48

This paper designs the optimization algorithm through the Visual C++6.0, under Windows 2003 server operating system. The type of processor is Quad-Core AMD Opteron(tm) Processor 2.75GHz, and the memory size is 4G.

4.2 The Experimental Results and Analysis

The experiments compared the results between the traditional GA with the self-adaptive GA in this paper, on solving the problems of complex task scheduling. Both of the population sizes are 150, the max evolution algebras are 100, and the lengths of the neighborhood in mutation operation are 4. The differences are that the Crossover probability and mutation probability are set as 0.8 and 0.01 in traditional GA, but in self-adaptive GA we adopt an adaptive approach. It is calculated form 1 task which includes 800 items and 1202 works, to 15 tasks gradually, in this experiment. Fig.3 shows the comparison of the average periods between traditional GA and self-adaptive GA on solving the Resource-constrained multi-task scheduling problem.

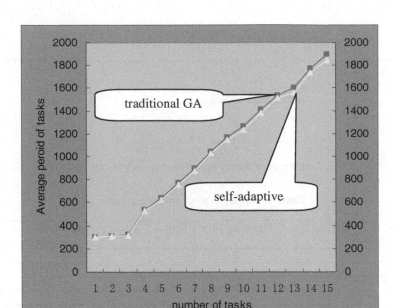

Fig. 3. The comparison of the average periods between traditional GA and self-adaptive GA

When the number of tasks is from 1 to 3, resources can be better allocated to all works. This means the average periods of these tasks differs little. But when the number grows, the average periods show a linear growth. When the number is 15, the periods of the tasks from task 1 to task 15 after optimized by traditional GA are: 1890, 1890, 1892, 1895, 1895, 1897, 1900, 1900, 1902, 1905, 1905, 1907, 1910, 1910, 1912, and the average period is 1900. The periods of the tasks from task 1 to task 15 after optimized by self-adaptive GA are: 1823, 1836, 1836, 1837, 1840, 1839, 1854, 1852, 1849, 1862, 1863, 1855, 1868, 1863, 1870, and the average period is 1850. Therefore, the self-adaptive GA can gain a better result than traditional GA on solving the problems of complex task scheduling.

5   Conclusion

Traditional GA has the weakness of converging partial optimal value too early. Proposed self-adaptive GA automatically adjust crossover probability Pc and mutation probability Pm, and ensure the community diversity and convergence. The results of experiment demonstrate that the self-adaptive GA is preferable to traditional GA on large scale complex multitask scheduling problems with limited resources. The proposed method overcomes the shortcomings of other algorithms, such as dealing only with small scale task and early constringency, which indicates its feasibility.

References

1. Burns, S., Liu, L., Feng, C.: The LP/IP Hybrid Method for Construction Time-cost Trade-of Analysis. Construction Management and Economics 24, 265–267 (1996)
2. Li, H., Love, P.: Using Improved Genetic Algorithms to Facilitate Time-Cost Optimization. Journal of Construction Engineering and Management 123(3), 233–237 (1997)
3. Li, X., Tan, W., Kan, L.: Research of Resource Equilibrium Optimization Based on Genetic Algorithm. Computer Engineering and Design, 4447–4449 (2008)
4. Li, X., Tong, H., Tan, W.: Network Planning Multi-objective Optimization Based on Genetic Algorithm. In: International Symposium on Intelligence Computation and Applications Progress, pp. 143–147 (2007)
5. Li, X., Tan, W., Tong, H.: A Resource Equilibrium Optimization Method Base on Improved Genetic Algorithm. In: China Artificial Intelligence Progress, vol. 2, pp. 737–743 (2007)
6. Lova, A., Tormos, P., Cervantes, M., Barber, F.: An efcient hybrid genetical gorithm for scheduling projects with resource constraints and mulitiple execution modes. Int. J. Production Economics, 117302–117316 (2009)
7. Li, X., Chen, Q., Li, Y.: Impact on Genetic Algorithm of Different Parameters. In: The 3rd International Symposium on Intelligence Computation and Applications, pp. 479–488 (2008)
8. Xiang, L., Yanli, L., Li, Z.: The Comparative Research of Solving Problems of Equilibrium and Optimizing Multi-resources with GA and PSO. In: 2008 International Conference on Computational Intelligence and Security (2008)
9. Sijun, B.: Heuristic Method for Multiple Resource-Constrained in the Network. Systems Engineering Theory and Practice 7 (2004)
10. Liao, R., Chen, Q., Mao, N.: Genetic algorithm for resource - constrained project scheduling. Computer Integrated Manufacturing Systems 10(7) (July 2004)
11. Sijun, B.: Evaluating Heuristics for Re source-constrained Activity Network(III) 8(4) (December 1999)
12. Guangnan, X., Zunwei, C.: Genetic Algorithm and Engineering Design. Science publishing company, Ithaca (2000)

A Novel Approach on Designing Augmented Fuzzy Cognitive Maps Using Fuzzified Decision Trees

Elpiniki I. Papageorgiou

Department of Informatics & Computer Technology, Technological Educational Institute of
Lamia, 3rd Km PEO Lamia-Athens, 35100 Lamia, Greece
epapageorgiou@teilam.gr

Abstract. This paper proposes a new methodology for designing Fuzzy Cognitive Maps using crisp decision trees that have been fuzzified. Fuzzy cognitive map is a knowledge-based technique that works as an artificial cognitive network inheriting the main aspects of cognitive maps and artificial neural networks. Decision trees, in the other hand, are well known intelligent techniques that extract rules from both symbolic and numeric data. Fuzzy theoretical techniques are used to fuzzify crisp decision trees in order to soften decision boundaries at decision nodes inherent in this type of trees. Comparisons between crisp decision trees and the fuzzified decision trees suggest that the later fuzzy tree is significantly more robust and produces a more balanced decision making. The approach proposed in this paper could incorporate any type of fuzzy decision trees. Through this methodology, new linguistic weights were determined in FCM model, thus producing augmented FCM tool. The framework is consisted of a new fuzzy algorithm to generate linguistic weights that describe the cause-effect relationships among the concepts of the FCM model, from induced fuzzy decision trees.

1 Introduction

Nowadays, the knowledge acquisition and representation constitutes a major knowledge engineering bottleneck. A large number of techniques in the field of artificial intelligence used to represent knowledge: production rules, decision trees, rule-based architectures semantic nets, frameworks, fuzzy logic, causal cognitive maps, among others. The decision trees gained popularity because of their conceptual transparency. The well-developed design methodology comes with efficient design techniques supporting their construction, cf. [1-3]. The decision trees generated by these methods were found useful in building knowledge-based expert systems. Due to the character of continuous attributes as well as various facets of uncertainty one has to take into consideration, there has been a visible trend to cope with the factor of fuzziness when carrying out learning from examples in the case of tree induction. In a nutshell, this trend gave rise to the name of fuzzy decision trees and has resulted in a series of development alternatives; cf. [4-6]. The incorporation of fuzzy sets [7-10] into decision trees enables us to combine the uncertainty handling and approximate reasoning capabilities of the former with the comprehensibility and ease of application of the latter. Fuzzy decision trees [10,11] assume that all domain attributes or linguistic

Z. Cai et al. (Eds.): ISICA 2009, CCIS 51, pp. 266–275, 2009.
© Springer-Verlag Berlin Heidelberg 2009

variables have pre-defined fuzzy terms for each fuzzy attribute. Those could be determined in a data driven manner. The information gain measure, used for splitting a node, is modified for fuzzy representation and a pattern can have nonzero degree of matching to one or more leaves [12,13].

Fuzzy logic and causal cognitive maps, in the other hand, are some of the main topics of artificial intelligence on representation of knowledge and approximation of reasoning with uncertainty [14]. The choice of a particular technique is based on two main factors: the nature of the application and the user's skills. The fuzzy logic theory, based on representation of knowledge and approximation of reasoning with uncertainty, is very close to the expert's reasoning, and it is well known as artificial intelligence-based method, especially in the field of medical decision making. An outcome of this theory is fuzzy cognitive maps [15,16]. Fuzzy cognitive maps are diagrams used as causal representations between knowledge/data to represent events relations. They are modeling methods based on knowledge and experience for describing particular domains using concepts (variables, states, inputs, outputs) and the relationships between them. FCM can describe any system using a model having signed causality (that indicates positive or negative relationship), strengths of the causal relationships (that take fuzzy values), and causal links that are dynamic (i.e. the effect of a change in one concept/node affects other nodes, which in turn may affect other nodes).

Most decision tree induction methods used for extracting knowledge in classification problems do not deal with cognitive uncertainties such as vagueness and ambiguity associated with human thinking and perception. Fuzzy decision trees represent classification knowledge more naturally to the way of human thinking and are more robust in tolerating imprecise, conflict, and missing information.

In this work, a new algorithm for constructing fuzzy cognitive maps by using pre-generated fuzzy decision trees is proposed. The methodology is partly data driven and knowledge driven so some expert knowledge of the domain is required.

The fuzzy decision tree approach is used to implement the fuzzy algorithmic methodology in order to assign new linguistic weights among the FCM nodes as well as new paths between FCM nodes that enhance their structure and improve their operational ability to handle with complex modeling processes. This naturally enhances the representative power of FCMs with the knowledge component inherent in fuzzy decision trees rule induction.

2 Main Aspects of Fuzzy Decision Trees

Fuzzy decision trees are an extension of the classical artificial intelligence concept of decision trees. The main fundamental difference between fuzzy and crisp trees is that with fuzzy trees, gradual transitions exist between attribute values [7]. The reasoning process within the tree allows all rules to be fired to some degree, with the final crisp classification being the result of combining all membership grades. Recent approaches to developing such trees were through modifications to the ID3 algorithm [3,5,6,8,18]. Sison and Chong [3] proposed a fuzzy version of ID3 which automatically generated a fuzzy rule base for a plant controller from a set of input–output data.

Umano et al. [5] also proposed a new fuzzy ID3 algorithm. This algorithm generates an understandable fuzzy decision tree using fuzzy sets defined by the user. The fuzzy tree methodologies proposed by [3,5] require the data to have been pre-fuzzified before the fuzzy decision trees are induced.

More recent work by Janikow involves the induction of fuzzy decision trees directly from data sets by the FID algorithm [10,11]. The [10] takes a detailed introduction about the non fuzzy rules and the different kind of fuzzy rules.

In this point it is essential to refer that the data (real values) are partitioned into fuzzy sets by experts.

This approach consists on the following steps:

Step 1: A fuzzy clustering algorithm is used for input domain partition. The supervised method takes into account the class labels during the clustering. Therefore the resulted partitions, the fuzzy membership functions (fuzzy sets) represent not only the distribution of data, but the distribution of the classes too.

Step 2: During a pre-pruning method the resulted partitions could analyze and combine the unduly overlapped fuzzy sets.

Step 3: The results of the pre-pruning step are input parameters (beside data) for the tree induction algorithm. The applied tree induction method is the FID (Fuzzy Induction on Decision Tree) algorithm by C. Z. Janikow.

Step 4: The fuzzy ID3 is used to extract rules which are then used for generating fuzzy rule base.

Step 5: While the FID algorithm could generate larger and complex decision tree as it is necessary, therefore a post pruning method is applied. The rule which yields the maximal fulfillment degree in the least number of cases is deleted.

This method provides compact fuzzy rule base that can be used for building FCM-DSS.

2.1 Fuzzy Cognitive Mapping Causal Algebra

Fuzzy cognitive maps are an intelligent modeling methodology for complex decision systems, which originated from the combination of Fuzzy Logic and Neural Networks [14]. An FCM describes the behavior of an intelligent system in terms of concepts; each concept represents an entity, a state, a variable, or a characteristic of the system [15]. FCM nodes are named by such concepts forming the set of concepts $C = \{C1,C2, \ldots ,Cn\}$. Arcs (Cj,Ci) are oriented and represent causal links between concepts; that is how concept Cj causes concept Ci Weights of arcs are associated with a weight value matrix $Wn \cdot n$, where each element of the matrix wji taking values in $[-1, \ldots ,1]$. Kosko has developed a fuzzy causal algebra that describes the causal propagation and combination of concepts in an FCM. The algebra depends only on the partial ordering P, the range set of the fuzzy causal edge function e, and on general fuzzy-graph properties (e.g., path connectivity). Kosko notes that this algebra can be used on any digraph knowledge representation scheme.

A causal path from some concept node Ci to concept node Cj, say $Ci\text{-}\text{-}\sim Ck1$, $Ckl\text{-}\text{-}\sim\ldots Ckn$, $Ckn \text{-}\text{-}\sim Cj$, can be indicated by the sequence $(i, k, \ldots \ldots kn,j)$. Then the indirect effect of *Ci* on *Cj* is the causality *C~I* imparts to *Cj* via the path *(i, kl . . . . . . kn,j)*. The total effect of *Ci* on *Cj* is the composite of all the indirect-effect causalities *C~* imparts to *Cj*. If there is only one causal path from *Ci* to *Cj*, the total effect C~ imparts to *Cj* reduces to the indirect effect.

The indeterminacy can be removed with a numeric weighting scheme. A fuzzy causal algebra, and hence FCMs, bypasses the knowledge acquisition processing tradeoff.

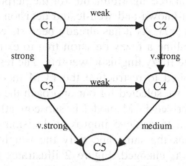

Fig. 1. A cognitive map with fuzzy labels at the edges

A simple fuzzy causal algebra is created by interpreting the indirect effect operator *I* as the minimum operator (min) and the total effect operator *T* as the maximum operator (max) on a partially ordered set P of causal values. Formally, let ~ be a causal concept space, and let e: ~ × ~ P be a fuzzy causal edge function, and assume that there are m-many causal paths from *Ci* to *Cj*: (i, k~ ..... k~, j) for 1 ~< r ~< m. Then let *Ir(Ci, Cj)* denote the indirect effect of concept *Ci* on concept *Cj* via the rth causal path, and let *T(i, Cj)* denote the total effect of *Ci* on *Cj* over all m causal paths. Then

$I\sim(Ci,Cj)=min\{e(Cp,Cp+,):(p,p+\ 1)\sim(i,k\sim\ .\ .\ .\ .\ .\ k,\sim,j)\ \}$
$T(Ci,Cj)=\ max(\ Ir(Ci,Cj))\ ,\ where\ l<\sim r<\sim m$

where p and p + 1 are contiguous left-to right path indices.

The indirect effect operation amounts to specifying the weakest causal link in a path and the total effect operation amounts to specifying the strongest of the weakest links. For example, suppose the causal values are given by P = *{none, weak, medium, strong, v.strong}* and the FCM is defined as in Figure 1. There are three causal paths from C1 to C5: *(C1, C3, C5)*, (C1, C3, C4, C5) , (C1, C2, C4, C5).

The three indirect effects of C1 on C5 are:

I1(C1,C5) = min {el3 , e35) = min *{strong, v.strong}* = *strong*
I2 (C1 ,C5) = min{e13,e34,e45}= *weak,*
I3(C1,C5) = min{e12,e24,e45}= *weak.*

Hence, the total effect of C 1 on C5 is:

T(C1,C5) = max {I1,(C1,C5), I2(C1,C5), I3(C1,C5) }
= *max {strong, weak, weak} = strong.*

In words, C1 can be said to impart *strong* causality to C5.

3 Novel Approach on Designing Augmented Fuzzy Cognitive Maps

There is a necessity to develop a framework extracting fuzzy interconnections among attributes from available data using knowledge extraction techniques and then insert these fuzzy linguistic interconnections to restructure the fuzzy cognitive map model producing a new augmented FCM tool for medical decision making. The framework can incorporate any decision tree algorithm, but for the purpose of this work C4.5 has been chosen as it is a well-known and well-tested decision tree induction algorithm for classification problems [17]. As it has already been stated, the central idea of the proposed method is to combine a fuzzy decision tree to extract the available knowledge of data and to generate fuzzy linguistic weights. The resulted fuzzy relationships among leaf nodes are applied to restructure the FCM model. Among the different fuzzy inference techniques we selected for our approach the Zadeh's union and intersection parameters. The derived FCM model is subsequently trained using an unsupervised learning algorithm to achieve improved decision accuracy. The inference algorithm of FCMs remains the same and only the weight matrix multiplied with previous concept values was changed. Figure 2 illustrates the proposed framework with the corresponding steps and final decision.

The algorithmic approach for the restructure of FCM using fuzzy decision trees is consisting of the following steps:

Step 1: For all the M experts, set credibility weight $b_k = 1$

Step 2: Each of the M experts is asked to suggest and describe each of the N concepts that comprise the FCM.

Step 3: For all the ordered pair of concepts (Ci and Cj) each kth of the M experts is asked to make the following statement (using an if-then rule):

IF the value of concept Ci {increases, decreases,is stable} **THEN** causes value of concept Cj to {increase, decrease, nothing} **THUS** the influence of concept Ci on concept Cj is $T(influence)$

Through this step a number of linguistic weights have been assigned by experts.

Step 4: If quantitative data (numeric or symbolic) are available, the approach of using fuzzified crisp decision trees (presented in above section 2.1) is implemented into the data set to derive the available structure of fuzzy decision trees and the fuzzy labels in the branches Di.

Step 5: From the created fuzzy decision trees, a number of causal paths among the branches i, connecting leaf nodes Di to Dj, is determined. These causal paths transferred in FCM model as causal paths interconnecting concepts Ci to Cj, through a number of direct positive relationships.

Step 6: Using the fuzzy causal algebra, an indirect effect operator I used as the minimum operator (min) on an ordered set P of causal values. The simple fuzzy causal algebra is created by interpreting the indirect effect operator I as the minimum operator (min) on the set P of fuzzy values, corresponding to the above designed causal paths among the FCM concepts. Then the max operator T is applied to the resulted effect operators I, and a new linguistic weight produced among Ci and Cj. The overall linguistic weight is the sum of the path products. Thus a new linguistic weight is assigned between the concepts Ci and Cj.

Step 7: IF for one interconnection between the concepts Ci and Cj, more than 3M/4 different linguistic weights are suggested THEN ask experts to reassign weights for this particular interconnection and go to step 3.

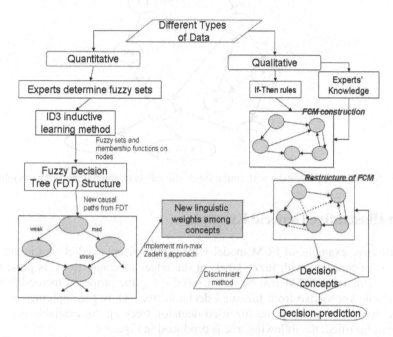

Fig. 2. Framework for constructing augmented FCMs by complementary use of fuzzy decision trees

Step 8: Aggregate all the linguistic weights proposed for every interconnection using the SUM method where the membership function μ suggested by kth expert is multiplied by the corresponding credibility weight b_k. Use the COG defuzzification method to calculate the numerical weight Wij for every interconnection.

Step 9: IF there is an ordered concept pair not examined go to step 3,
    ELSE construct the weight matrix W whose are the defuzzified weights Wij
    END.

Using the above algorithm, someone could use fuzzy decision trees to pass available knowledge into FCM reconstructed them by paths. Experts construct fuzzy sets and fuzzy membership functions for each problem and these fuzzy sets are used into the fuzzy decision tree algorithm due to compatibility reasons. This happens in the case of FCMs to derive the respective linguistic variables and then make the necessary comparisons.

The causal paths of the leaf nodes used to determine new causal paths in the FCM model. Thus the FCM model was augmented as new direct and indirect relationships among concepts determined.

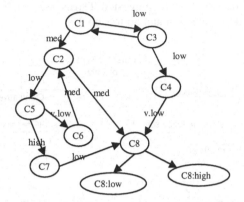

Fig. 3. Example FCM model with initial linguistic labels on interconnections (weights)

4   An Illustrative Generic Example

An illustrative example, of FCM model with eight concepts and eleven interconnections among concepts, with fuzzy labels at the edges of connections, is presented in Figure 3. This initial FCM will be restructured using the proposed methodology and the available knowledge from fuzzified decision trees. Only for implementation reason, we consider that using the fuzzified decision trees on the available data which have been fuzzified, the following tree is produced in Figure 4.

The produced tree has a number of three paths for C1 to C8, two paths for C2 to C8, and one path of each one of the other concepts to C8, thus defining new interconnections and/or update the initial ones of the FCM model.

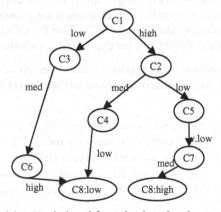

Fig. 4. Example Fuzzy decision tree induced from the data showing membership grades at each branch

Here, the causal effect of C1 to C8 is determined by taking the minimum of the attached labels of the individual paths. Let I1, I2 and I3 denote the effect of C1 to C8 through the paths 1 to 3 respectively, and e_{ij} be the label attached with edge from node i^{th} to node j^{th}. Then, to determine the total effect of C1 to C8, we take the maximum of paths I1 through I3 causal paths.

Path 1 from C1 to C8: c1→c3→ c6→ c8
I1(C1 to C8)=min(low, med, high)=low
Path 2 from C1 to C8:c1→c2→ c5→ c7 →c8
I2(C1 to C8)=min(high, low, v.low, med)=v.low
Path 3 from C1 to C8: c1→c2→ c4 →c8
I3(C1 to C8)=min(high, med, low)=low

Thus total effect of C1 to C8, denoted by T(C1,C8) is computed below:

   T(c1,c8)=max{I1,I2,I3}=max{low,v. low,low}=*low*

In words, c1 imparts *low* causality to c8.

To determine the total effect of C2 to C8, we take the maximum of paths I4 through I5.

Path 4 from C2 to C8: c2→ c5→ c7 →c8
I4(C2 to C8)=min(low, v.low, med)=v. low
Path 5 from C2 to C8: c2→ c4 →c8
I5(C2 to C8)=min(med, low)=low

Thus total effect of C2 to C8, denoted by T(C2,C8) is: T(c2,c8)=max{I4,I5}=max{low, v. low}=*low*

In words, c2 imparts *low* causality to c8.

Path 6 from C6 to C8: c6 →c8: I6=high

To determine the total effect of C6 to C8, we take the maximum of path I6.

In words, c6 imparts *high* causality to c8.

Path 7 from C4 to C8: c4 →c8: I7=low

The total effect of C4 to C8 is determined by taking the maximum of path I7.

In words, c4 imparts *low* causality to c8.

To determine the total effect of C5 to C8, we take the maximum of path I8.

Path 8 from C5 to C8: C5→ C7 →C8: I8(C5 to C8)=min(v.low, med)=v.low

Thus total effect of C5 to C8, denoted by T(C5,C8) is computed: T(C5,C8)=max{I8}=v. low

In words, C5 imparts *v.low* causality to C8.

Summarizing, new causal paths describing the interconnections among concepts as well as some interconnections have updated their initial values due to the above paths.

After the implementation of the investigating methodology, the FCM model was restructured and a new FCM model was produced illustrated in Figure 5. Where each branch has fuzzy labels, fuzzy values derived from corresponding fuzzy sets as they have been initially prescribed by experts.

Some of the important points in the proposed approach are:

➢ Each attribute is represented by a fuzzy set.
➢ All branches will fire to some degree.
➢ Multiple input-single output fuzzy if-then rules.
➢ Each case passes through the tree fires all rules to some degree.

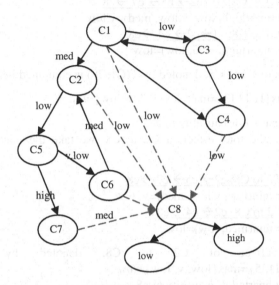

Fig. 5. The new restructured FCM model using the proposed framework

Some of the limitations of the proposed approach are the way of data fuzzification which has to be done automatically from data and without the experts' intervention.

The proposed algorithm and the methodology for constructing FCMs using complementary the fuzzy decision trees as knowledge extraction methods can be used for decision making tasks especially in the medical field. In medical decision making there is enough knowledge hidden in data and the experts-physicians have difficulty to recognize and suggest this knowledge. Thus though the complementary use of fuzzy decision trees as knowledge extraction algorithm and the knowledge representation model of FCMs, an advanced decision making tool with sufficient accuracy and interpretability can be produced. This tool keeps the advantages of FCMs and FDTs coming to a promising task.

5 Conclusion

In this study, it was shown the role of the fuzzy decision tree framework in the design and analysis of augmented fuzzy cognitive maps. We discussed the role of the fuzzy decision tree in the determination of fuzzy linguistic weights and causal paths of FCM. It was stressed that this technique takes advantage of the available experimental data. We proposed a detailed design algorithm producing augmented FCMs that offer a comprehensive interpretation of the cognitive model. In particular, the formalism of fuzzified crisp decision trees helped us come up with endowing the medical decision making results with meaningful models.

References

1. Quinlan, J.: Induction of Decision Trees, Machine Learning, vol. 1, pp. 81–106. Kluwer Academic Press, Dordrecht (1986)
2. Sestino, S., Dillon, T.: Using single-layered neural networks for the extraction of conjunctive rules and hierarchical classifications. J. Appl. Intell. 1, 157–173 (1991)
3. Sison, L., Chong, E.: Fuzzy modeling by induction and pruning of decision trees. In: IEEE Symposium on Intelligent Control U.S.A., pp. 166–171 (1994)
4. Mitra, S., Konwar, K.M., Sankar, K.P.: Fuzzy decision tree, linguistic rules and fuzzy knowledge-based network: generation and evaluation. IEEE Trans. Syst. Man Cybern. Part C: Appl. Rev. 32(4), 328–339 (2002)
5. Umano, M., Okamoto, H., Hatono, I., Tamura, H.: Generation of fuzzy decision trees by fuzzy ID3 algorithm and its application to diagnosis by gas in oil, Japan–U.S.A. Symposium, pp. 1445–1450 (1994)
6. Olaru, C.W.: A complete fuzzy decision tree technique. Fuzzy Sets and Systems 138, 221–254 (2003)
7. Pedrycz, W., Sosnowski, A.: Designing decision trees with the use of fuzzy granulation. IEEE Trans. Syst. Man Cybern. A 30, 151–159 (2000)
8. Crockett, K., Bandar, Z., Mclean, D., O'Shea, J.: On constructing a fuzzy inference framework using crisp decision trees. Fuzzy Sets and Systems 157, 2809–2832 (2006)
9. Ishibuchi, H., Nozaki, K., Yamamoto, N., Tanaka, N.: Selecting fuzzy if–then rules for classification problems using genetic algorithms. IEEE Trans. Fuzzy Systems 3(3), 260–270 (1995)
10. Janikow, C.Z.: Fuzzy decision trees: issues and methods. IEEE Trans. Systems Man and Cybernetics 28(1), 1–14 (1998)
11. Janikow, C.Z.: Fuzzy partitioning with FID3.1. In: Proceedings of the 18th International Conference of the North American Fuzzy Information Society, pp. 467–471 (1999)
12. Yuan, Y., Shaw, M.J.: Induction of fuzzy decision trees. Fuzzy Sets Systems 69, 125–139 (1995)
13. Weber, R.: Fuzzy ID3: a class of methods for automatic knowledge acquisition. In: Second International Conference on Fuzzy Logic and Neural Networks, Iizuka, Japan, pp. 265–268 (1992)
14. Kosko, B.: Neural Networks and Fuzzy Systems: A Dynamical Systems Approach to Machine Intelligence. Prentice-Hall, New Jersey (1992)
15. Kosko, B.: Fuzzy Cognitive Maps. International Journal of Man-Machine Studies, 24, 65–75 (1986)
16. Papageorgiou, E.I., Stylios, C.D., Groumpos, P.: An Integrated Two-Level Hierarchical Decision Making System based on Fuzzy Cognitive Maps (FCMs). IEEE Trans. Biomed. Engin. 50(12), 1326–1339 (2003)
17. Quinlan, J.R.: Is C5.0 better than C4.5 (2002), http://www.rulequest.com/see5-comparison.html
18. Hayashi, I., Maeda, T., Bastian, A., Jain, L.C.: Generation of fuzzy decision trees by fuzzy ID3 with adjusting mechanism of and/or operators. In: Proc. Int. Conf. Fuzzy Syst., pp. 681–685 (1998)

Computation of Uncertain Parameters by Using Fuzzy Synthetic Decision and D-S Theory

Lingling Li, Jungang Zhou, Zhigang Li, and Jingzheng Liu

Electrical apparatus institute, Hebei University of Technology, 300130 Tianjin, China
haohaohao@eyou.com, jungang1983@126.com,
zgli@hebut.edu.cn, loojz@126.com

Abstract. In the course of design, decision making and other problems alike being settled, parameter, whose value is limited to a Real-interval, can often be found. Such parameters are named Uncertain Parameters in this paper. The value of such a parameter is usually determined by several factors, which are named Decisive Factors of the parameter. The research in this paper aims at how to specify an uncertain parameter if it fails to get a function about the Uncertain Parameter and its decisive factors, it can only get a group of production rules expressing the restrictive relationship between the decisive factors and the uncertain parameter. To settle this problem, a method based on Fuzzy Comprehensive Decision is proposed in this study. Another method based on the Combination Rule in Dempster-Shafer Theory of Evidence (called "D-S Rule" for short) is also proposed to solve the problem. Usually, the results of the two methods are similar to each other. Relatively, the former one is simpler and with less calculation work.

Keywords: uncertain parameter, the limit of real-interval, fuzzy comprehensive decision, D-S Rule.

1 Introduction

There was a specific problem in the design process of rotary subminiature electromagnetic relay.

The resistance of contact point on relay, which was denoted as R^*, was an index about reliability. And its value was calculated by the equation as follows.

$$R^* = f(p, \Delta u, I)$$

It was an uncertain parameter for p, where $p \in [0.5, 0.8]$. It was voltage drop of contact point for Δu. It was rated current for I. It was the restrictive relation between R_C and p, Δu and I for f.

But it could not be expressed by specific mathematical function expression for f, so it only could be abstracted a group of production rule as follows.

R_1: If the value of I is lager, then p is smaller; otherwise p is lager.

R_2: If the value of Δu is lager, then p is smaller; otherwise p is lager.

Z. Cai et al. (Eds.): ISICA 2009, CCIS 51, pp. 276–284, 2009.

They were production rules for R_1 and R_2. They were fuzzy language for "larger" and "smaller".

In the actual design, the expression of I and Δu wasn't always fuzzy languages such as "larger" and "smaller", but it was a numeric value, for example, a real number. Therefore the numeric values must be translated into fuzzy language values. In that process, established the corresponding fuzzy sets of fuzzy language values.

The characteristic of the above-mentioned problem was that p was an uncertain parameter in a certain real interval, as p could be evaluated by domain knowledge of a group of production rules. These problems in design, decision, control and other fields were very common. So the method based on fuzzy comprehensive decision and the Combination Rule could be proposed to research further in this paper.

2 The Solution Method of Uncertain Parameter p Based on Fuzzy Comprehensive Decision

2.1 The Instruction of Principle

In order to describe the method conveniently, there were some terms that were described as follows.

It was called uncertain parameter for p and its limited interval was defined $[\,p_a\,,p_b\,]$. For example, it was defined as $[\,p_a\,,p_b\,]$=[0.5, 0.8] in rotary subminiature electromagnetic relay.

The factor called decisive factor had a decisive role for p, such as Δu and I. The set of decisive factor of p was recorded as Z={ $z_j \big| j = 1,2,\cdots,m$ }.

The status of "larger" and "smaller" all were fuzzy, and the set of fuzzy status was denoted as $Y = \{Y_i \big| i = 1,2,\cdots,n\}$. Y was also called domain of fuzzy status, and Y_i was a fuzzy status and it also represented a subset of a fuzzy status.

The value of uncertain parameter p was calculated as follows.

Step 1: completed the preparatory work as follows.

Determined the decisive factor set Z for p and the weight set $W =$ { $w_j \big| j = 1,2,\cdots,m$ } for Z, where $w_j > 0$ and $\sum_{j=1}^{m} w_j = 1$, established the memebership functions the fuzzy status set Y for p and each factor in Z, acquired a group of production rules, R_1, R_2, $\cdots$, R_m describing the relationship of p and Z.

Most of the above works have relationship with the domain knowledge. The knowledge could be provided by experts and could also be acquired by using technology of data mining and knowledge discovery. For example, Z could be determined based on attribute reduction [1,2]; W could be acquired based on the methods such as mathematical statistics [3], entropy [4], neural network [5], rough set theory [6], and so on; the production rule R_j could be acquired based on computational intelligence methods such as fuzzy logic, neural network, genetic algorithm [7,8], rough set [9,10].

Step 2: chosed $c-1$ real numbers from interval $[\ p_a\ ,\ p_b\ ]$ which devided $[\ p_a, p_b\ ]$ into c subintervals. Subsequently, a real number set could be established as follows.

$$\Theta = \{\theta_k | k = 0,1,2,\cdots,c\}\ .$$

$$\theta_k = p_a + (p_b - p_a)\frac{k}{c}\ . \tag{1}$$

The intent using the above equation was to disperse the infinite set $[\ p_a, p_b]$ as the finite set Θ.

Step 3: established the membership function of each fuzzy status for p, so as to obtain a series of fuzzy distributions over Y for the members belonging to Θ.

$Y = \{Y_i | i = 1,2,\cdots,n\}$. The membership function of Y_i was denoded as $\mu_{Y_i(p)}(x)$. The fuzzy distribution of $\theta_k \in \Theta$ over Y was as follows.

$$\boldsymbol{D}_{\theta_k} = \left(d_1(\theta_k), d_2(\theta_k), \cdots, d_n(\theta_k)\right)\ .$$

$$d_i(\theta_k) = \mu_{Y_i(p)}(x)|_{x=\theta_k} \tag{2}$$

where, $d_i(\theta_k)$ was the membership degree that θ_k belongs to fuzzy set Y_i.

Step 4: constructed a matrix to describe the fuzzy status of all the elements in $\Theta = \{\theta_k | k = 0,1,2,\cdots,c\}$, and denoted the matrix as $\Re_{n\times(c+1)}$ whose elements located at No. $k+1$ line were constructed by $\boldsymbol{D}_{\theta_k}{}^T$.

$$\Re_{n\times(c+1)} = \begin{bmatrix} \boldsymbol{D}_{\theta_0}{}^T & \boldsymbol{D}_{\theta_1}{}^T & \boldsymbol{D}_{\theta_2}{}^T & \cdots & \boldsymbol{D}_{\theta_C}{}^T \end{bmatrix} = \left(d_i(\theta_k)\right)_{n\times(c+1)}\ . \tag{3}$$

Where $i = 1,2,\cdots,n$, $k = 0,1,2,\cdots c$. The transpose of matrix and vector was denoted as "T".

Step 5: established the membership functions of various fuzzy status for each decisive factor, and determined the current status of each decisive factor according to its characteristic value, represented the status of each factor as a fuzzy distribution over Y as well.

Where, $Z = \{\ z_j | j = 1,2,\cdots,m\ \}$, denoted membership function of z_j about fuzzy status Y_i as $\mu_{Y_i(z_j)}(x)$, characteristic value of z_j as v_{z_j}. The fuzzy distribution of v_{z_j} over Y was as follows.

$$\boldsymbol{D}_{z_j} = \left(d_1(z_j), d_2(z_j), \cdots, d_n(z_j)\right). \tag{4}$$

If v_{z_j} was a real number, then $d_i(z_j)$ was the membership degree of v_{z_j} to $\mu_{Y_i(z_j)}(x)$, on the other hand, if v_{z_j} was a fuzzy number, then $d_i(z_j)$ was the closeness degree of v_{z_j} and $\mu_{Y_i(z_j)}(x)$.

Step 6: determined the impaction of z_j to the status of p according to the production rule R_j, and constructed a matrix according to D_{z_j} which described the fuzzy status of various decisive factors. Denoted the matrix as $\mathfrak{R}'_{m\times n}$.

According to the impaction of z_j to p, the group of rules could be divided into two classes. The first class of rules could be expressed as "if the value of z_j is larger, then p is larger", its meaning is that "if the status of z_j is Y_i, then the value of p is Y_i", as well the second class of rules could be expressed as "if the value of z_j is larder, then p is smaller", its meaning is that "if the status of z_j is Y_i, then the value of p is Y_{n+1-i}".

The construction principle of $\mathfrak{R}'_{m\times n}$ was that the row j of $\mathfrak{R}'_{m\times n}$ was constructed by all the components of D_{z_j} in equation (4), but the order of elements of D_{z_j} in $\mathfrak{R}'_{m\times n}$ was different for the two classes of rules.

The component $d_i(z_j)$ of $D_{z_j} = \big(d_1(z_j), d_2(z_j), \cdots, d_n(z_j)\big)$ was used as an element of $\mathfrak{R}'_{m\times n}$, which located at No. j row, No. i line in $\mathfrak{R}'_{m\times n}$, $i = 1, 2, \cdots, n$ and $j = 1, 2, \cdots, m$, if the rule relating with z_j belong to the first class.

The component $d_i(z_j)$ was used as the element of $\mathfrak{R}'_{m\times n}$ which located at No. j row, No. $n+1-i$ line, if the rule relating with z_j belong to the second class.

Step7: denoted the weight vector of Z as $W = (w_1, w_2, \cdots, w_m)$, the subsequent algorithm was as follows.

$$\mathfrak{R}^* = [r_0^* \quad r_1^* \quad r_2^* \quad \cdots \quad r_c^*] = W \circ \big(\mathfrak{R}'_{m\times n} \circ \mathfrak{R}_{n\times(c+1)}\big). \tag{5}$$

Where r_k^* is nonnegative real number, $k = 0, 1, 2, \cdots c$; "$\circ$" was the composite operator of matrixs and the Sum-product model was selected here.

Step8: determined the parameter p according to $\mathfrak{R}^*$ and the relational algorithm was as follows.

Let

$$A = (a_0, a_1, a_2, \cdots, a_c).$$

$$a_k = \frac{r_k^*}{\sum_{k=0}^{c} r_k^*}, \quad k = 0, 1, 2, \cdots, c. \tag{6}$$

Simultaneously, transformed the finite set $\Theta = \{\theta_k | k = 0,1,2,\cdots,c\}$ acquired by discreting $[\,p_a\,,p_b\,]$ as vector $\boldsymbol{\Theta}'$, as follows.

$$\boldsymbol{\Theta}' = (\boldsymbol{\theta_0},\boldsymbol{\theta_1},\boldsymbol{\theta_2},\cdots,\boldsymbol{\theta_c})\,.$$

$$\theta_k = p_a + (p_b - p_a)\frac{k}{c}\,.$$

Therefore

$$p = A \circ \boldsymbol{\Theta}' = \sum_{k=0}^{c} \frac{r_k^*}{\sum\limits_{k=0}^{c} r_k^*} \left[p_a + (p_b - p_a)\frac{k}{c} \right]. \tag{7}$$

2.2 An Example of Application

The processing results of knowledge and information for the problem in the design of electromagnetic relay were as follows according to the above 8 steps.

(1) the available knowledge and information included: $p \in [0.5,\ 0.8]$, $Z = \{\,z_1, z_2\,\} = \{\,I\,,\ \Delta u\,\}$, R_1 and R_2, but it was not enough to solve p. So the necessary information was supplied as follows. The weight set of Z was $W = \{\,w_1\,,\ w_2\,\} = \{0.6,\ 0.4\}$ and the set of fuzzy status was $Y = \{Y_i | i = 1,2,\cdots,5\}$ = {small, smaller, slight small, general, slight large, larger, large}.

(2) divided the limited interval [0.5, 0.8] of p into 10 subintervals, which was denoted as $\Theta = \{\theta_k | k = 0,1,2,\cdots,10\}$, where $\theta_k = 0.5 + 0.03\,k$

(3) the membership functions of fuzzy status for p were illustrated in Figure 1. The fuzzy distribution of θ_k over Y was as follows, $k = 0,1,2,\cdots,10$.

$\boldsymbol{D}_{\theta_0} = (1,0,0,0,0,0,0)$; $\boldsymbol{D}_{\theta_1} = (0.4,0.6,0,0,0,0,0)$; $\boldsymbol{D}_{\theta_2} = (0,0.8,0.2,0,0,0,0)$;

$\boldsymbol{D}_{\theta_3} = (0,0.2,0.8,0,0,0,0)$; $\boldsymbol{D}_{\theta_4} = (0,0,0.6,0.4,0,0,0)$; $\boldsymbol{D}_{\theta_5} = (0,0,0,1,0,0,0)$;

$\boldsymbol{D}_{\theta_6} = (0,0,0,0.4,0.6,0,0)$; $\boldsymbol{D}_{\theta_7} = (0,0,0,0,0.8,0.2,0)$; $\boldsymbol{D}_{\theta_8} = (0,0,0,0,0.2,0.8,0)$;

$\boldsymbol{D}_{\theta_9} = (0,0,0,0,0,0.6,0.4)$; $\boldsymbol{D}_{\theta_{10}} = (0,0,0,0,0,0,1)$

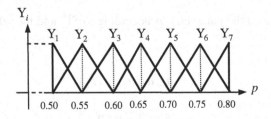

Fig. 1. The membership function of p with respect to each fuzzy status

(4) acquired the matrix $\mathfrak{R}_{7\times11}$ as follows.

$$\mathfrak{R}_{7\times11} = \begin{bmatrix} D_{\theta_0}^{\text{T}} & D_{\theta_1}^{\text{T}} & D_{\theta_2}^{\text{T}} & \cdots & D_{\theta_{10}}^{\text{T}} \end{bmatrix}$$

$$= \begin{bmatrix} 1 & 0.4 & 0 & 0 & 0 & 0 & 0 & 0 & 0 & 0 & 0 \\ 0 & 0.6 & 0.8 & 0.2 & 0 & 0 & 0 & 0 & 0 & 0 & 0 \\ 0 & 0 & 0.2 & 0.8 & 0.6 & 0 & 0 & 0 & 0 & 0 & 0 \\ 0 & 0 & 0 & 0 & 0.4 & 1 & 0.4 & 0 & 0 & 0 & 0 \\ 0 & 0 & 0 & 0 & 0 & 0 & 0.6 & 0.8 & 0.2 & 0 & 0 \\ 0 & 0 & 0 & 0 & 0 & 0 & 0 & 0.2 & 0.8 & 0.6 & 0 \\ 0 & 0 & 0 & 0 & 0 & 0 & 0 & 0 & 0 & 0.4 & 1 \end{bmatrix}.$$

(5) according to the characteristic value of z_1 and z_2, the fuzzy distribution D_{z_1} and D_{z_2} over Y could be calculated.

here, assumed $D_{z_1} = (0.5,1,0.4,0,0,0,0)$; $D_{z_2} = (0,0,0.1,0.8,0.3,0.05,0)$.

(6) according to rule R_1 and R_2, the matrix describing the fuzzy status of z_1 and z_2 was as follows.

$$\mathfrak{R}'_{2\times7} = \begin{bmatrix} 0.5 & 1 & 0.4 & 0 & 0 & 0 & 0 \\ 0 & 0.05 & 0.3 & 0.8 & 0.1 & 0 & 0 \end{bmatrix}$$

(7) according to the above calculated results and the weight vector $W = (0.6, 0.4)$ of Z, $\mathfrak{R}^*$ could be acquired as follows.

$$\mathfrak{R}^* = W \circ \left(\mathfrak{R}'_{2\times7} \circ \mathfrak{R}_{7\times11} \right)$$

$$= (0.300, 0.492, 0.568, 0.412, 0.344, 0.320, 0.152, 0.032, 0.008, 0, 0).$$

(8) The normalization vector of $\mathfrak{R}^*$ was as follows.

$$A = (0.114, 0.187, 0.216, 0.157, 0.131, 0.122, 0.058, 0.012, 0.003, 0, 0).$$

The result of p was as follows.

$$p = A \circ \mathbf{\Theta}'^{\text{T}} = 0.114\times0.5 + 0.187\times0.53 + 0.216\times0.56 + 0.157\times0.59 + 0.131\times0.62$$

$$+ 0.122\times0.65 + 0.058\times0.68 + 0.012\times0.71 + 0.003\times0.74 + 0\times0.77 + 0\times0.80$$
$$= 0.580.$$

3   The Solution Method of Uncertain Parameter Based on D-S Rule

The basic theory of this method was that: firstly a group of mass-functions, based on the knowledge and information with determinant factors in $Z = \{ z_j | j = 1,2,\cdots,m \}$, were established over frame of discernment, and then the group of mass-functions were combined based on D-S Rule. So the uncertain parameter p could be calculated.

The frame of discernment and mass-function were the basic concept based on D-S Rule. The discernment frame of a problem was defined as the finite set of all "alternative answer". The frame of discernment was defined as follows.

$$\Theta = \{\theta_k | k = 0,1,2,\cdots,c\}, \text{ where } \theta_k = p_a + (p_b - p_a)\frac{k}{c}, \ p \in [\ p_a, p_b].$$

Assumed that

$$\forall \theta' \subseteq \Theta, \text{ if it satisfied } \sum_{\theta' \subseteq \Theta} m(\theta') = 1, \ m(\Phi) = 0,$$

then it was a mass-function for $m : 2^\Theta \to [0,1]$ over Θ, that was rewrote m for short.

It was used to combine mass-function by D-S Rule. So the rule is argued about the problem in this paper.

Assumed that m_1 and m_2 were two mass-functions over Θ.

Where

$$m_1 : (m_1(\theta_0), m_1(\theta_1), \cdots, m_1(\theta_c), m_1(\Theta)).$$
$$m_2 : (m_2(\theta_0), m_2(\theta_1), \cdots, m_2(\theta_c), m_2(\Theta)).$$

Then D-S Rule was described as follows.

$$m_* = m_1 \oplus m_2$$
$$m_* : (m_*(\theta_0), m_*(\theta_1), \cdots, m_*(\theta_c), m_*(\Theta))$$
$$m_*(\theta_k) = Km_1(\theta_k)m_2(\theta_k) + K \sum_{\substack{i,j=1,2 \\ i \neq j}} m_i(\theta_k)m_j(\Theta)$$
$$m_*(\Theta) = Km_1(\Theta)m_2(\Theta). \tag{8}$$

Where $k = 0,1,2,\cdots,c$; It was an orthogonal sum operator to combine these two mass-functions for $\oplus$; it was normalization factor for K, so

$$m_*(\Theta) + \sum_{k=0}^{c} m_*(\theta_k) = 1.$$

The uncertain parameter p could also be calculated by the method of Step1~ Step6 in part 2 based on D-S Rule. The next calculation steps were as follows.

(1) Let

$$\mathfrak{R}'_{m \times n} \circ \mathfrak{R}_{n \times (c+1)} = \mathfrak{R}'^*_{m \times (c+1)}.$$
$$\mathfrak{R}'^*_{m \times (c+1)} = [D_1 \quad D_2 \quad \cdots \quad D_m]^{\mathrm{T}}.$$
$$D_j = (d_0, d_1, d_2, \cdots, d_c), \ j = 1,2,\cdots,m. \tag{9}$$

(2) A mass-function was constructed over Θ by D_j and recorded as m_j. The equation was described as follows.

$$m_j : \left(m_j(\theta_0), m_j(\theta_1), \cdots, m_j(\theta_c), m_j(\Theta) \right).$$

$$m_j(\theta_k) = \frac{w_j d_k}{\sum_{k=0}^{c} d_k}, \quad j = 1,2,\cdots,m \ . \ k = 0,1,2,\cdots,c \ .$$

$$m_j(\Theta) = 1 - w_j . \tag{10}$$

(3) The above mass-function was constructed based on D-S Rule and the value of p was acquired by the combined result, so they were recorded as follows.

$$m = m_1 \oplus m_2 \oplus \cdots \oplus m_m .$$
$$m : \left(m(\theta_0), m(\theta_1), \cdots, m(\theta_c), m(\Theta) \right) .$$

$$p = \sum_{k=0}^{c} \left(\theta_k m(\theta_k) \Big/ \sum_{k=0}^{c} m(\theta_k) \right)$$

$$= \sum_{k=0}^{c} \left[\left(p_a + (p_b - p_a)\frac{k}{c} \right) m(\theta_k) \Big/ \sum_{k=0}^{c} m(\theta_k) \right] . \tag{11}$$

For the example in part 2 of this paper, the uncertain parameter p was calculated under the same preconditions so the result was $p = 0.572$ by equation (8) ~ (11).

4 Conclusion

Two methods of calculating uncertain parameter were proposed respectively based on fuzzy comprehensive decision and D-S Rule in this paper. The reasonable result was acquired by the method when the function relationship couldn't be acquired between uncertain parameter and its decisive factor and only a group of production rule of fuzzy status could be acquired. The example in this paper was effectively tested by the method.

Two methods are compared as follows. The method based on fuzzy comprehensive decision is simple and has small computational amount, but it is absent for D-S Rule. The method based on fuzzy comprehensive decision could process the fuzziness of related knowledge and information, but it couldn't process the other uncertainty so that is its limitation.

It is an effective uncertain reasoning model for D-S theory, its character is that randomness, fuzziness and other uncertainties can be processed by it. The fuzziness of the uncertain parameter solving was processed by the Combination Rule in D-S theory. In fact, the potential superior of D-S theory could be reflected in some more complicated situations such as some kinds of uncertainty existed at the same time.

Acknowledgement. This work was supported by the National Natural Science Foundation (No. 60771069) and the Hebei Province Natural Science Foundation (No. F2007000115 and No. 602069).

References

[1] Jinhai, L., Yuejin, L.: Relation Matrix-based Algorithm for Reduction of Attribute in Information Systems. Computer Engineering and Applications. 44(9), 147–149 (2008)

[2] Xuesong, X., Jing, Z., Qing, H., et al.: Attribute Reduction Method of Rough Sets Based on Bacterin Extraction and Immune Optimum. Control and Decision 23(5), 497–502 (2008)

[3] Lingling, L., Zhigang, L., Chunlai, Z., et al.: A New Method of Conceptual Design Based on the Theory of Fuzzy Sets Pattern Recognition and Its Application in the Electrical Apparatus Design Expert System. In: Proc. of Fifth World Congress on Intelligent Control and Automation, pp. 4092–4096 (2004)

[4] Kun, Z., Deyun, Z.: TOPSIS Method Based on Entropy in Evaluating the Air Multi-target Threat. Systems Engineering and Electronics 29(9), 1493–1495 (2007)

[5] Jinye, W., Xunyin, B., Yingjian, L., et al.: Fuzzy Comprehensive Evaluation of Friction Coefficient of Mine Hoist Lining Based on Neural Network. Journal of Shandong University of Science and Technology 25(3), 85–87 (2006)

[6] Zhaohui, G.: The Study on Uncertain Information Processing in Electrical Apparatus. In: Intelligent Design and Reliability Metric [Ph.D dissertation]. Hebei University of Technology, Tianjin (2008)

[7] Gómez-Skarmeta Antonio, F., Mercedes, V., Fernando, J., et al.: Approximative fuzzy rules approaches for classification with hybrid-GA techniques. Information Sciences 136(1-4), 193–214 (2001)

[8] Wong, S.V., Hamouda, A.M.S.: Optimization of fuzzy rules design using genetic algorithm. Advances in Engineering Software 31(4), 251–262 (2000)

[9] Xiaobin, L., Dongyi, Y.: A Rule Acquisition Method Based on Extended Discernibility Matrix. Computer Science 35(3), 231–233 (2008)

[10] Kun, S., Yanhui, Z., Kaishe, Q.: New certainty degree of decision rule based on local attribute sets. Journal of Computer Applications 28(11), 2970–2971 (2008)

FAHP-Based Fuzzy Comprehensive Evaluation of M&S Credibility

Jing Wu*, Xiao-yan Wu, and Zhong-chang Gao

Missile Institute, Air Force Engineering University, Sanyuan, Shaanxi, 713800, China
Ken1983414@126.com

Abstract. Credibility evaluation of modeling and simulation (M&S) applications is becoming increasingly important as M&S applications get larger and more complex currently. To perform the M&S credibility evaluation efficiently, cost-effectively and successfully, this research establishes a hierarchical evaluation model of M&S credibility and proposes a methodology of FAHP-based fuzzy comprehensive evaluation (FCE). Aslo a hierarchical evaluation model of M&S credibility is built up based on a detailed discussion of credibility evaluation indicators. Meanwhile a methodology of FAHP-based FCE model is introduced to reduce the effect of individual subjective judgment and favoritism on the evaluation results,. Finally, a case study is presented to prove the feasibility and validity of the proposed approach.

Keywords: credibility evaluation; verification and validation; fuzzy comprehensive evaluation.

1 Introduction

Credibility evaluation of M&S applications is becoming increasingly more important as M&S applications are used more and more for complex system design evaluation, M&S-based acquisition, problem solving, military training, and critical decision making [1]. However, both the size and complexity of M&S application are growing; the domains of application continue to expand; the larger M&S projects are requiring increased levels of involvement of people with diverse capabilities and background; the expected lifetime of M&S application is continually increasing [2]. All these changes introduce more uncertainties and complexities into M&S credibility evaluation, which make credibility evaluation more difficult and intractable.

Therefore, in order to proper execute M&S credibility evaluation, we should rethink the following problems in the simulation community: what is M&S credibility? how to establish a generic hierarchical evaluation model of M&S credibility? aiming at the uncertainties and fuzziness involved in credibility evaluation, which evaluation method could be selected to properly perform the M&S credibility evaluation.

---

* Jing Wu is a Ph.D. student. He studies in Missile Institute, Air Force Engineering University, Sanyuan, Shaanxi, China. His current research interests include M&S credibility evaluation and VV&A. His email address is < ken1983414@126.com >.

Z. Cai et al. (Eds.): ISICA 2009, CCIS 51, pp. 285–294, 2009.

Aiming at the problems stated above, on one hand, some existing related standards, guidelines, and views about M&S credibility are presented as follows: Balci and Saadi [3] present the M&S development life cycle evaluation processes for certification to help engineers, analysts, and managers to formulate a certification decision for a large-scale complex M&S application. Brade [4] proposes a phase-wise credibility building process and presents the dependencies between verification and validation (V&V) related terms. The decision to use the simulation1 will depend on the simulation's capabilities and correctness, the accuracy of its results, and its usability in the specified application [5]. Liu et al. [6] present that at least five metrics contribute to the evaluation of simulation credibility, which are validity, correctness, reliability, usability and interoperability, and proposes a credibility metrics driven verification, validation and accreditation (VV&A) process. However, how to integrate existing related standards, guidelines, and views and set up a generic hierarchical evaluation model of M&S credibility is an important problem for current credibility evaluation.

On the other hand, M&S credibility evaluation is a very complex process, involves the measurement and evaluation of hundreds of qualitative and quantitative elements, mandates subject matter expert evaluation, and requires the integration of disparate measurements and evaluations [3]. Fuzzy analytic hierarchy process (FAHP)-based fuzzy comprehensive evaluation (FCE) is a combination of qualitative and quantitative evaluation method. And it is an effective method especially to the complex simulation system involving multi-hierarchies and fuzzy factors. Therefore, this paper explores the credibility evaluation of M&S applications based on the method.

The remainder of this paper is organized as follows: Section 2 describes the hierarchical evaluation model of M&S credibility; a brief introduction of FAHP-based FCE model is provided in Section 3; Section 4 gives a case study; and Section 5 gives the conclusions and future work perspectives.

2   Hierarchical Evaluation Model of M&S Credibility

2.1 M&S Credibility

Proper execution of M&S credibility evaluation is on the basis of comprehending the M&S credibility systematically and thoroughly. The credibility of a model or simulation is an expression of the degree to which one is convinced that a particular model or simulation is suitable for an intended purpose. The M&S credibility is established stage by stage in the entire M&S development process. Influencing factors, V&V process, and credibility evaluation indicators all play an important role in building the M&S credibility. Therefore, the concept of M&S credibility is established, as depicted in Fig. 1.

M&S credibility depends on the four primary influencing factors, namely as follows: credibility of the data, credibility of the model, credibility of the model operation,

Fig. 1. M&S credibility

and credibility of the simulation results. Those influencing factors have a certain effect on each other and couldn't be separate from each other.

V&V process is a process of applying incremental review, analysis, evaluation, and testing to M&S products for the purpose of improving credibility. It includes five process, namely as M&S requirements verification, conceptual model validation, system design verification, implementation verification, and simulation results validation. The primary purpose of the V&V effort is to establish the credibility of the model or simulation [7]. Therefore, M&S credibility has a close relationship with V&V process.

The credibility of a model or simulation is an expression of the degree to which one is convinced that a particular model or simulation is suitable for an intended purpose. The degree of confidence in the model or simulation is only based on some indicators that reflect the property of the model or simulation [6].

2.2 Hierarchical Evaluation Model of M&S Credibility

The hierarchical evaluation model of M&S credibility is the synthetic representation of influencing factors, V&V process and credibility characteristics. In order to perform credibility evaluation efficiently and successfully, based on the V&V process, combined with credibility evaluation indicators, the hierarchical evaluation model of M&S credibility is set up (see Fig. 2).

The dependencies between V&V process and credibility evaluation indicators are also depicted in Fig. 2. Validation activities in V&V process mainly deal with the examination of validity fidelity and accuracy. Verification activities in V&V process mainly deal with the examination of completeness consistency traceability and interoperability. System operation activities mainly deal with the examination of reliability, maintainability and usability.

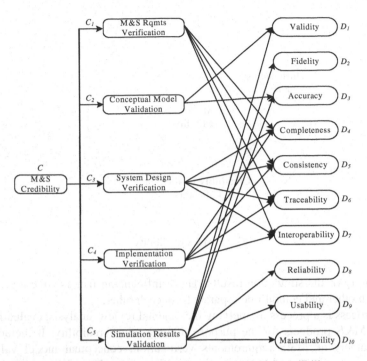

Fig. 2. Hierarchical evaluation model of M&S credibility

3   FAHP-Based FCE Model

The traditional AHP method usually constructs the judgment matrix based on one-to-nine scale method, which could not describe the fuzziness and ambiguity of human judgments validly. Therefore, Van proposes a method based on the triangular fuzzy number to construct the judgment matrix and extend the AHP method to FAHP method [9]. In this section, based on a brief introduction of triangular fuzzy number and its operation laws, a methodology of FAHP-based FCE is proposed.

3.1   Triangular Fuzzy Number and Its Operation Laws

A triangular fuzzy number, a special case of a trapezoidal fuzzy number, is very popular in fuzzy applications. The triangular fuzzy number M represented by (l, m, u) is often used to represent the fuzzy relative importance and the membership function of triangular fuzzy numbers can be described as [10]:

$$\mu_M(x) = \begin{cases} \dfrac{x-l}{m-l} & l \leq x \leq m \\ 0 & otherwise \\ \dfrac{u-x}{u-m} & m \leq x \leq u \end{cases} \tag{1}$$

with $-\infty < l \leq m \leq u < \infty$.

The main operation laws for two triangle fuzzy numbers $M_1 = (l_1, m_1, u_1)$ and $M_2 = (l_2, m_2, u_2)$ are as follows:

$$M_1 \oplus M_2 = (l_1, m_1, u_1) \oplus (l_2, m_2, u_2) = (l_1 + l_2, m_1 + m_2, u_1 + u_2) \tag{2}$$

$$M_1 \otimes M_2 = (l_1, m_1, u_1) \otimes (l_2, m_2, u_2) = (l_1 l_2, m_1 m_2, u_1 u_2) \tag{3}$$

$$\lambda M = \lambda(l, m, u) = (\lambda l, \lambda m, \lambda u) \tag{4}$$

where $\lambda \in R$

$$\frac{1}{M} = \left(\frac{1}{u}, \frac{1}{m}, \frac{1}{l} \right) \tag{5}$$

The possible degree of $M_1 \geq M_2$ is defined as follows:

$$V(M_1 \geq M_2) = \begin{cases} 1 & m_1 \geq m_2 \\ \dfrac{l_2 - u_1}{(m_1 - u_1) - (m_2 - l_2)} & m_1 < m_2, l_2 \leq u_1 \\ 0 & otherwise \end{cases} \tag{6}$$

3.2 FAHP-Based FCE Model

To reduce the effect of individual subjective judgment and favoritism on the evaluation results and integrate disparate measurements and evaluations, a methodology of FAHP-based FCE is proposed. The detailed steps are as follows:

a). Confirm the factors set (evaluation indicators) of the evaluation object $U = \{u_1, u_2, \cdots, u_n\}$ and the remark set $V = \{v_1, v_2, \cdots, v_m\}$.

b). Execute single factor evaluation and confirm the fuzzy evaluation matrix. The fuzzy relation between factor sets and remark sets can be described by the evaluation matrix

$$R = \begin{bmatrix} r_{11} & r_{12} & \cdots & r_{1m} \\ r_{21} & r_{22} & \cdots & r_{2m} \\ \vdots & \vdots & \vdots & \vdots \\ r_{n1} & r_{n2} & \cdots & r_{nm} \end{bmatrix}$$

Where r_{ij} representing the grade of membership of factor u_i aiming at remark v_j.

c). Confirmation of evaluation weight $A = \{a_1, a_2, \cdots, a_n\}$. Based on the definition and operation laws of the triangular fuzzy number, the detailed steps of FAHP are as follows:

Step1: construct fuzzy judgment matrix $A = \left(a_{ij}\right)_{n \times n}$ using the triangular fuzzy number.

Step2: calculate the fuzzy synthesis degree S_i of each element in every fuzzy judgment matrix. Let M_{Ei}^{j} be the synthesis degree which the ith object corresponding to the jth target, thus the synthesis degree which the ith object corresponding to m targets could be obtained from the follow formula:

$$S_i = \sum_{j=1}^{m} M_{Ei}^{j} \otimes \left[\sum_{i=1}^{m} \sum_{j=1}^{m} M_{Ei}^{j} \right]^{-1} \tag{7}$$

Step3: calculate the weight allocation. As to each fuzzy judgment matrix, the possibility degree of A_i is important than others is calculated by the follow formula:

$$d'(A_i) = \min_{j=1,2,\cdots,n, j \neq i} V(S_i \geq S_j), (i = 1, 2, \cdots, n) \tag{8}$$

Thus the weight allocation $W = \left(d(A_1), d(A_2), \cdots, d(A_n)\right)^{T}$, where $d(A_i)$ is the normalization of $d'(A_i)$.

d). Single level fuzzy comprehensive evaluation result is obtained from the following equation:

$$B = W \circ R = \{b_1, b_2, \cdots, b_m\} \tag{9}$$

The symbol ' $\circ$ ' expresses the fuzzy operator. Different definitions of fuzzy operator will lead to different fuzzy comprehensive evaluation models. In this paper, we use the fuzzy operator $M(\wedge, \vee)$, and its formula is given below:

$$b_j = \bigvee_{i=1}^{n} \left(a_i \wedge r_{ij}\right) = \max \left[\min\left(a_1, r_{1j}\right), \min\left(a_2, r_{2j}\right), \cdots, \min\left(a_n, r_{nj}\right) \right] \tag{10}$$

e). Multi-level fuzzy comprehensive evaluation. For example, evaluate the advanced layer. Normalize B to B', the overall evaluation result C is that $C = W' \circ B'$ (W' is the weight set of the advanced layer).

4   Case Study

Based on the hierarchical evaluation model of M&S credibility, we apply the proposed method to credibility evaluation of a steering flight visual simulation system (SFVSS) [11]. In order to improve the development quality of the M&S program and ensure the M&S credibility, we integrate V&V with credibility evaluation in the entire M&S development process.

First of all, we should confirm the weight allocation based on FAHP method. Taking the 1st layer indicators of the hierarchical evaluation model of M&S credibility (see Fig. 2) for example, the fuzzy judgment matrix A is constructed (see Table 1).

Table 1. Fuzzy judgment matrix of the 1st layer indicators

	C_1	C_2	C_3	C_4	C_5
C_1	(1,1,1)	(1/2,1,2)	(2/5,1/2,2/3)	(2/7,1/3,2/5)	(2/9,1/4,2/7)
C_2	(1/2,1,2)	(1,1,1)	(2/3,1,2)	(1/3,1, 2/3)	(1/4,1/3,2/5)
C_3	(3/2,2,5/2)	(1/2,1,3/2)	(1,1,1)	(2/3,1,2)	(1/3,1/2,2/3)
C_4	(5/2,3,7/2)	(3/2,2,3)	(1/2,1,3/2)	(1,1,1)	(1/2,1,7/4)
C_5	(7/2,4,9/2)	(5/2,3,4)	(3/2,2,3)	(4/7,1,2)	(1,1,1)

Calculating the fuzzy synthesis degree S_i of each element in the fuzzy judgment matrix according to formula (7):

S_1 =(2.4079, 3.0833, 4.3524) $\otimes$ (43.3357, 31.4167, 24.2294)=(0.0556, 0.0981, 0.1796); S_2 =(0.0635, 0.1220, 0.2504); S_3 =(0.0923, 0.1751, 0.3164); S_4 =(0.1385, 0.2546, 0.4437); S_5 =(0.2093, 0.3501, 0.5984).

According to formula (8), $d'(A_1) = \min_{j=1,2,\cdots,n, j\neq 1} V(S_1 \geq S_j)$ =min(0.8295, 0.5317, 0.2083, 0.5429)= 0.2083.

Thus, $W' = (d'(A_1), d'(A_2), \cdots, d'(A_7))$ =(0.2083, 0.1525, 0.3795, 0.7105, 1). Normalize W' to W, the weight allocation is obtained: W =(0.0850, 0.0622, 0.1549, 0.2899, 0.4080).

Similarly, the rest weight allocation can be deduced (see Table 2).

Table 2. The rest weight allocation

Indicator	Sub-indicators	Weight
C_1	D_4, D_5, D_6, D_7	W_1 =(0.3548, 0.2849, 0.2131, 0.1471)
C_2	D_1, D_3	W_2 =(0.6299, 0.3701)
C_3	D_4, D_5, D_6, D_7	W_3 =(0.5090, 0.3048, 0.0786, 0.1077)
C_4	D_4, D_5, D_6, D_7	W_4 =(0.4563, 0.2482, 0.1746, 0.1210)
C_5	$D_1, D_2, D_3, D_8, D_9, D_{10}$	W_5 =(0.2994, 0.0560, 0.2994, 0.1943, 0.1352, 0.0158)

Confirm the remark set, as shown in Table 3.

Table 3. Confirmation of remark set

Remark set	v_1	v_2	v_3	v_4	v_5
Score	0.85–1	0.70–0.85	0.55–0.70	0.40–0.55	0–0.40
Credibility level	Highest	Higher	Medium	Lower	Lowest

Invite subject matter experts (SMEs) to measure and evaluate the single factor based on Table 2. Thus, the single level normalized judgment matrix is confirmed respectively as follows:

$$R_1 = \begin{bmatrix} 0.51 & 0.23 & 0.19 & 0.05 & 0.02 \\ 0.45 & 0.18 & 0.23 & 0.09 & 0.05 \\ 0.53 & 0.13 & 0.26 & 0.07 & 0.01 \\ 0.44 & 0.24 & 0.20 & 0.08 & 0.04 \end{bmatrix}, R_2 = \begin{bmatrix} 0.45 & 0.35 & 0.15 & 0.03 & 0.02 \\ 0.48 & 0.25 & 0.15 & 0.08 & 0.04 \end{bmatrix},$$

$$R_3 = \begin{bmatrix} 0.50 & 0.23 & 0.20 & 0.03 & 0.04 \\ 0.45 & 0.20 & 0.21 & 0.06 & 0.08 \\ 0.50 & 0.16 & 0.26 & 0.06 & 0.02 \\ 0.44 & 0.24 & 0.20 & 0.08 & 0.04 \end{bmatrix}, R_4 = \begin{bmatrix} 0.50 & 0.27 & 0.17 & 0.04 & 0.02 \\ 0.52 & 0.22 & 0.23 & 0.02 & 0.01 \\ 0.53 & 0.15 & 0.23 & 0.08 & 0.01 \\ 0.60 & 0.24 & 0.10 & 0.05 & 0.01 \end{bmatrix},$$

$$R_5 = \begin{bmatrix} 0.45 & 0.30 & 0.20 & 0.03 & 0.02 \\ 0.48 & 0.25 & 0.15 & 0.08 & 0.04 \\ 0.60 & 0.24 & 0.10 & 0.05 & 0.01 \\ 0.56 & 0.30 & 0.10 & 0.01 & 0.03 \\ 0.54 & 0.30 & 0.10 & 0.05 & 0.01 \\ 0.44 & 0.24 & 0.20 & 0.08 & 0.04 \end{bmatrix}$$

The comprehensive evaluation result of B_1 based on formula (9) is $B_1 = W_1 \circ R_1$ =(0.3548, 0.2300, 0.2300, 0.0900, 0.0500). Similarly, we can obtain $B_2 - B_5$ respectively. Normalize $B_i (i = 1, 2, \cdots, 7)$ and establish the overall evaluation transfer matrix

$$B' = \begin{bmatrix} 0.3716 & 0.2409 & 0.2409 & 0.0943 & 0.0524 \\ 0.4206 & 0.3271 & 0.1402 & 0.0748 & 0.0374 \\ 0.4545 & 0.2091 & 0.1909 & 0.0727 & 0.0727 \\ 0.4320 & 0.2556 & 0.2177 & 0.0757 & 0.0189 \\ 0.3346 & 0.3346 & 0.2235 & 0.0626 & 0.0447 \end{bmatrix}$$

Then, execute credibility evaluation of the top layer. The overall evaluation result C is obtained as follows:

$C = W \circ B' = (0.3346, 0.3346, 0.2235, 0.0850, 0.0727)$

The credibility quantitative vector is constructed by Table 3 as follows: V =(1, 0.85, 0.70, 0.55, 0.40). Thus, the final credibility score is that $F = CV^T$ =0.851, which means that the credibility level of SFVSS is the highest according to Table 3.

5 Conclusions

A credibility evaluation effort must be cost-effective, responsive, and sufficient to succeed. Establishing a generic M&S credibility evaluation model with a valid evaluation method is essential to credibility evaluation. Based on a detailed discussion of credibility evaluation indicators, a hierarchical evaluation model of M&S credibility is established. In order to integrate disparate measurements and evaluations from SMEs, this paper explores the credibility evaluation of M&S applications based on FAHP-based FCE method.

To maintain a balance between application requirements and real-world constraints, the M&S credibility evaluation model should be tailored to fit the purpose of the application and the type(s) of simulation(s) involved. M&S credibility evaluation based on FAHP-based FCE is a very complex process, and it is perceived as taking too long and costing too much. Therefore, to improve the efficiency of it, the next step would be to develop an automated support tool of credibility evaluation.

Acknowledgments

This paper is supported by the Nature Science Foundation of Shaanxi, China (NO. 2007F40).

References

1. Balci, O., Adams, R.J., Myers, D.S., Nance, R.E.: A collaborative evaluation environment for credibility assessment of modeling and simulation applications. In: Yücesan, E., Chen, C.-H., Snowdon, J.L., Charnes, J.M. (eds.) Proceedings of the 2002 Winter Simulation Conference, pp. 214–220. IEEE, Piscataway (2002a)
2. Arthur, J.D., Sargent, R.G., Dbney, J.B., Law, A.M., Morrison, J.D.: Verification and validation: what impact should project size and complexity have on attendant V&V activities and supporting infrastructure. In: Farrington, P.A., Nembhard, H.B., Sturrock, D.T., Evans, G.W. (eds.) Proceedings of the 1999 Winter Simulation Conference, pp. 148–155. IEEE, Phoenix (1999)
3. Balci, O., Saadi, S.D.: Proposed standard processes for certification of modeling and simulation applications. In: Yücesan, E., Chen, C.-H., Snowdon, J.L., Charnes, J.M. (eds.) Proceedings of the 2002 Winter Simulation Conference, pp. 1622–1627. IEEE, Piscataway (2002b)
4. Brade, D.: A generalized process for the verification and validation of models and simulation results. Phd dissertation, Universität Der Bundeswehr, München (2003)
5. DMSO.: DoD Verification, Validation, and Accreditation Recommended Practices Guide, millennium ed. Defense Modeling and Simulation Office, Alexandria (2000)
6. Fei, L., Yang, M., Wang, Z.: Study on simulation credibility metrics. In: Kuhl, M.E., Steiger, N.M., Armstrong, F.B., Joines, J.A. (eds.) Proceedings of the 2005 Winter Simulation Conference, pp. 2554–2560. IEEE, Orlando (2005)
7. DMSO.: Department of Defense Verification, Validation and Accreditation (VV&A) Recommended Practices Guide. Defense Modeling and Simulation Office, Alexandria (1996)
8. Yujiong, G., Kunliang, C., Kun, Y.: Fuzzy comprehensive evaluation method based on analytic hierarchy process for fault risk analysis of power plant equipment. In: Fifth International Conference on Fuzzy Systems and Knowledge Discovery, pp. 443–448. IEEE, Jinan (2008)

9. Van, P.J., Laargoven, M., Pedrycz, W.: A fuzzy extension of saaty's priority theory 11(3), 229 (1993)

10. Yang, J.: Integrative Performance Evaluation for Strategic Supplier's under Supply Chain Management based on Logarithm Triangular Fuzzy Number- AHP Method. In: Fifth International Conference on Fuzzy Systems and Knowledge Discovery, pp. 311–316 (2008)

11. Jing, W., Xiaoyan, W., Yanyan, Z.: Research on Design and Realization of Steering Flight Visual Simulation System. In: Asia Simulation Conference 2008/the 7th International Conference on System Simulation and Scientific Computing, pp. 1567–1570. IEEE, Beijing (2008)

Indirect Dynamic Recurrent Fuzzy Neural Network and Its Application in Identification and Control of Electro-Hydraulic Servo System

Yuan-feng Huang[1], You-wang Zhang[2], and Peng Min[3]

[1] School of Electrical and Electronic Engineering, Wuhan Institute of Technology, Wuhan, Hubei Province, P.R. C
[2] College of Mechanical and Electrical Engineering, Central South University, Changsha, Hunan Province, P.R. C
[3] JingzhouTelevision University, Jingzhou, Hubei Province, P.R. C

Abstract. As the affine nonlinear system is characterized by differential relations between the states, an adaptive dynamic recurrent fuzzy neural network (ADRFNN) taking only the measurable states as its inputs and describing the system's inner dynamic relation by its feedback matrix is proposed to evaluate the unknown dynamic nonlinear functions including nonlinearity, parameter uncertainty and load disturbance. The adaptive laws of the adjustable parameters and the evaluation errors' bounds of ADRFNN are formulated based on lyapunov stability theory. Also the stable indirect ADRFNN controller (ADRFNNC) with gain adaptive VSC (GAVSC) for the estimation errors by ADRFNN and the load disturbance are synthesized. It can overcome the short-comings of the structural expansion caused by larger number of inputs in traditional adaptive fuzzy neural networks (TAFNN) taking all states as its inputs. The application in electro-hydraulic position tracking system (EHPTS) shows that it has an advantage over the TAFNN controller (TAFNNC) in steady characteristics of system. Furthermore, the chattering of the system's control effort is weakened and so the system possesses greater robustness.

Keywords: Indirect ADRFNN; EHPTS; GAVSC; secondary uncertainty.

1 Introduction

Fuzzy system, neural network and VSC are widely used in the solution of uncertainty and nonlinearity's affect on the performance of the EHPTS. The adaptive fuzzy neural networks are widely used to identify the primary uncertainties including structural and parameter uncertainty, unmodeled dynamics, nonlinearity and load disturbance caused by variations of working point and environment. The stability and robustness of the whole system can hardly be guaranteed if the networks are adjusted by the traditional BP methods. So Lyapunov stability theory were extensively adopted [1,2] And the identification errors, called secondary uncertainty here, exist. VSC [3-5] or adding an additional VSC term [6] can suppress the secondary uncertainty, but its bound used to determine the correction term's gain of the VSC must be known. In practice, the correction term's gain is conservative to guarantee the robustness of system. This may

Z. Cai et al. (Eds.): ISICA 2009, CCIS 51, pp. 295–304, 2009.

make the chattering of system become serious. So estimating the gain online was proposed [7], but all the state variables of the system must be measurable and it is hard to be realized. High gain state estimator based on variable structure was proposed [8] to solve the unrealization, but its estimation errors may transfer into the neural networks and make the identification errors bigger. In fact, the chattering caused by VSC is related closely to the correction term's gain of the VSC determined by the bound of the secondary uncertainty, so it is necessary to adopt high accurate identification tool for the primary uncertainties to obtain smaller secondary uncertainties, and evaluate the bound of the secondary uncertainties online to determine the gain of VSC. Although the fuzzy systems and neural networks were adopted in many researches [2], [9-10], but they are static and not suitable for identification for dynamic system. On the other hand, the static fuzzy system or neural network takes all states as its inputs; it is unrealizable in systems having immeasurable states. So ADRFNN only taking measurable states as its inputs and the dynamic relations between the immeasurable and measurable states are represented by its inner feedback matrix, is proposed, and the indirect adaptive controller in which the primary uncertainty identified by ADRFNN with high accuracy was designed, so the secondary uncertainty become smaller and the system become realizable. On the other hand, GAVSC may weaken the system's chattering. The application in EHPTS shows system's robustness is strengthened, the system's steady error is improved and the chattering of the control effort is weakened concurrently.

2 ADRFNN

Many systems can be described by affine nonlinear system whose states have differential relations between each other if the states are selected suitably. So the states can be described by each other through differentiating operator. Based on this, ADRFNN shown in Fig.1 is proposed, it has dynamic recurrent characteristics and describes the system's inner dynamic between the states by its feedback relations between the inner neurons, and takes the measurable variables as its inputs and overcome the shortcoming of structural expansion caused by larger number of inputs. So it is suitable for identifying such affine nonlinear system as above. And its model was described in [11] in detail.

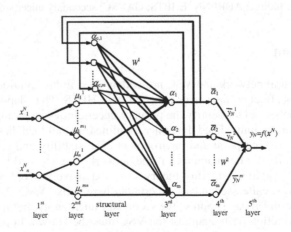

Fig. 1. Structure of ADRFNN

3 Indirect ADRFNNC

3.1 Design of Indirect ADRFNNC

For the following system

$$x^{(n)} = f_0(x) + f_\Delta(x) + [\, g_0(x) + g_\Delta(x)\,]u + d(t) \quad y = x_1 \tag{1}$$

$f(x)=f_0(x)$ and $g(x)=g_0(x)$ if the parameter values in $f(x)$ and $g(x)$ in (1) are nominal, and the variations of $f(x)$ and $g(x)$ are defined as $f_\Delta(x)$ and $g_\Delta(x)$ respectively, which are caused by the variations of the parameters, nonlinearities and other uncertainties, the system (1) can be described in the following form.

The design of indirect ADRFNNC is to obtain the control $u=u(x|\theta_{f\Delta}, \theta_{g\Delta})$ and the adaptive laws for $\theta_{f\Delta}$ and $\theta_{g\Delta}$ including adjustable parameters to satisfy $\lim\limits_{t\to\infty} E = 0$.

Two ADRFNN systems $\hat{f}_\Delta(x_1 | \theta_{f\Delta})$ and $\hat{g}_\Delta(x_1 | \theta_{g\Delta})$ are used to evaluate the unknown functions $f_\Delta(x)$ and $g_\Delta(x)$ respectively, where $\hat{f}_\Delta(x_1 | \theta_{f\Delta})$ is described as

$$s(l) = \sum_{j=1}^{m} w_{f,jl}^1 \alpha_{c,j}^f(k) + \exp[-(\frac{x - \bar{x}_f^l}{\sigma_f^l})^2] \tag{2}$$

$$\alpha_{c,l}^f(k) = \alpha_l^f(k-1) \tag{3}$$

$$\alpha_l^f(k) = h[s(l)] = \frac{1}{1 + e^{-\mu[s(l)-0.5]}} \tag{4}$$

$$\hat{f}_\Delta(x_1 | \theta_{f\Delta}) = \sum_{l=1}^{m} \bar{y}_f^l \alpha_l^f(k) / \sum_{l=1}^{m} \alpha_l^f(k) \tag{5}$$

replace f in (2)~(5) by g, $\hat{g}_\Delta(x_1 | \theta_{g\Delta})$ yields. Take only x_1 as the input of ADRFNN and fix the center $\bar{x}_\# = [\bar{x}_\#^1, \bar{x}_\#^2, \cdots, \bar{x}_\#^m]^T$, then $\theta_{\#\Delta}$ is $2m+m^2$ dimension vector including the adjustable parameters $\sigma_\# = [\sigma_\#^1, \sigma_\#^2, \cdots, \sigma_\#^m]^T$ representing the width of the membership function, weights $\bar{y}_\# = [\bar{y}_\#^1, \bar{y}_\#^2, \cdots \bar{y}_\#^m]^T$ from hidden layer to output layer, and $\mathbf{w}_\#^1 = [w_{\#,11}^1\ w_{\#,12}^1\ \cdots\ w_{\#,1m}^1;\ w_{\#,21}^1\ w_{\#,22}^2\ \cdots\ w_{\#,2m}^1;\ \cdots;\ w_{\#,m1}^1\ w_{\#,m2}^1\ \cdots\ w_{\#,mm}^1]^T$ in structural layer et al. # stands for f or g. the following control effort can be synthesized from feedback linearization of nonlinear system.

$$u_c = [-f_0(\mathbf{x}) - \hat{f}_\Delta(x_1 | \theta_{f\Delta}) + y_m^{(n)} + \mathbf{C}^T\mathbf{E}] / g_0(\mathbf{x}) + \hat{g}(x_1 | \theta_{g\Delta}) \tag{6}$$

$C=[c_n,\ldots,c_1]^T$, C is chosen such that polynomial $s^n+c_1 s^{n-1}+\ldots+ c_n$ is Hurwitz. In order to compensate the evaluation errors and strengthen the system robustness, VSC control term $u_s = \hat{K}_{vsc}^T \varphi\, \mathrm{sgn}(E^T PB) / \beta$ is adopted. Then

$$u = u_c + u_s \tag{7}$$

where $\hat{K}_{vsc}$ is the evaluation for K_{vsc}^*, φ, P, B and β are defined in the next section.

3.2 Analysis on Stability of Indirect ADRFNNC

Lemma 1. For the affine nonlinear system (1), if the control effort is determined by (7) and the adaptive laws for the adjustable parameter vectors in ADRFNN and the gain of the variable structure is adopted as follows

$$\dot{\theta}_{f\Delta} = -\Gamma_{f\Delta} E^T PB \frac{\partial \hat{f}_\Delta}{\partial \theta_{f\Delta}} \tag{8}$$

$$\dot{\theta}_{g\Delta} = -\Gamma_{g\Delta} E^T PB \frac{\partial \hat{g}_\Delta}{\partial \theta_{g\Delta}} u_c \tag{9}$$

$$\dot{\hat{K}}_{vsc} = \Gamma_{Kvsc} \mid E^T PB \mid \varphi \tag{10}$$

Then system (1) is asymptotically stable. Where $\Gamma_{f\Delta}$, $\Gamma_{g\Delta}$ and Γ_{Kvsc} are positive adaptive gain matrices, and $\Gamma_{f\Delta}^{ij} = 0$, $\Gamma_{g\Delta}^{ij} = 0$ and $\Gamma_{Kvsc}^{ij} = 0$ hold if $i \neq j$.

Proof: From $\dot{e}_n = y_d^{(n)} - \dot{x}_n$, control term (7) and affine nonlinear system (1), the following error dynamic equation can be obtained.

$$\dot{E} = \Lambda E + B\{(\hat{f}_\Delta - f_\Delta^*) + (f_\Delta^* - f_\Delta) + [(\hat{g}_\Delta - g_\Delta^*) + (g_\Delta^* - g_\Delta)]u_c - (g_0 + g_\Delta)u_s\} \tag{11}$$

Where $\Lambda = \begin{bmatrix} 0 & 1 & 0 & \cdots & 0 \\ 0 & 0 & 1 & \cdots & 0 \\ \vdots & \vdots & \vdots & & \vdots \\ 0 & 0 & 0 & \cdots & 1 \\ -c_n & -c_{n-1} & -c_{n-2} & \cdots & -c_1 \end{bmatrix}$, $B = \begin{bmatrix} 0 \\ 0 \\ \vdots \\ 0 \\ 1 \end{bmatrix}$, f_Δ^* and g_Δ^* are the optimal ap-

proximation for functions $f_\Delta(x)$ and $g_\Delta(x)$.

Known from the selection principle of C, Λ is a stable matrix, so there exits a positive-definite symmetric matrix Q make Lyapunov equation $\Lambda^T P + P\Lambda = -Q$ have a unique solution P. Consider the candidate Lyapunov function

$$V = \frac{1}{2} E^T PE + \frac{1}{2} \Phi_{f\Delta}^T \Gamma_{f\Delta}^{-1} \Phi_{f\Delta} + \frac{1}{2} \Phi_{g\Delta}^T \Gamma_{g\Delta}^{-1} \Phi_{g\Delta} + \frac{1}{2} \tilde{K}_{vsc}^T \Gamma_{Kvsc}^{-1} \tilde{K}_{vsc} \tag{12}$$

where $\Phi_{f\Delta} = \hat{\theta}_{f\Delta} - \theta_{f\Delta}^*$, $\Phi_{g\Delta} = \hat{\theta}_{g\Delta} - \theta_{g\Delta}^*$, $\tilde{K}_{vsc} = \hat{K}_{vsc} - K_{vsc}^*$, $\dot{\Phi}_{f\Delta} = \dot{\hat{\theta}}_{f\Delta}$, $\dot{\Phi}_{g\Delta} = \dot{\hat{\theta}}_{g\Delta}$ and $\dot{\tilde{K}}_{vsc} = \dot{\hat{K}}_{vsc}$ hold.

Consider $\hat{f}_\Delta - f_\Delta^* = \Phi_{f\Delta}^T \frac{\partial \hat{f}_\Delta}{\partial \theta_{f\Delta}} + o(\Phi_{f\Delta}^2)$, $\mid f_\Delta^* - f_\Delta \mid \leq w_f$, $\varepsilon_{fd} = \mid o(\Phi_{f\Delta}^2) \mid + w_f$,

$\hat{g}_\Delta - g_\Delta^* = \Phi_{g\Delta}^T \frac{\partial \hat{g}_\Delta}{\partial \theta_{g\Delta}} + o(\Phi_{g\Delta}^2)$, $\mid g_\Delta^* - g_\Delta \mid \leq w_g$, $\varepsilon_g = \mid o(\Phi_g^2) \mid + w_g$, let $g = g_0 + g_\Delta$,

then the time derivative along (11) of V is

$$\dot{V} = \frac{1}{2}\dot{E}^{T}PE + \frac{1}{2}E^{T}P\dot{E} + \Phi_{f\Delta}^{T}\Gamma_{f\Delta}^{-1}\dot{\Phi}_{f\Delta} + \Phi_{g\Delta}^{T}\Gamma_{g\Delta}^{-1}\dot{\Phi}_{g\Delta} + \tilde{K}_{vsc}^{-1}\Gamma_{Kvsc}^{-1}\dot{\tilde{K}}_{vsc}$$

$$\le -\frac{1}{2}E^{T}QE + E^{T}PB(\varepsilon_{fd} + \varepsilon_{g} \mid u_{c}\mid -gu_{s}) + E^{T}PB(\Phi_{f\Delta}^{T}\frac{\partial \hat{f}_{\Delta}}{\partial \theta_{f\Delta}} \tag{13}$$

$$+ \Phi_{g\Delta}^{T}\frac{\partial \hat{g}_{\Delta}}{\partial \theta_{g\Delta}}u_{c}) + \Phi_{f\Delta}^{T}\Gamma_{f\Delta}^{-1}\dot{\theta}_{f\Delta} + \Phi_{g\Delta}^{T}\Gamma_{g\Delta}^{-1}\dot{\theta}_{g\Delta} + \tilde{K}_{vsc}^{T}\Gamma_{Kvsc}^{-1}\dot{\tilde{K}}_{vsc}$$

Define $K^{*}=[\varepsilon_{fd}, \ \varepsilon_{g}\ ]^{T}$ and $\varphi=[1,\mid u_{c}\mid]^{T}$, after substituting (8) and (9) into (13), the following inequality yields.

$$\dot{V} \le -\frac{1}{2}E^{T}QE + E^{T}PB[K^{*T}\varphi - gu_{s}] + \tilde{K}_{vsc}^{T}\Gamma_{Kvsc}^{-1}\hat{K}_{vsc} \tag{14}$$

Assume $g\ge\beta>0$, define $u_{s} = \hat{K}_{vsc}^{T}\varphi\mathrm{sgn}(E^{T}PB)/\beta$, and substitute (10) into (14), the following inequality yields.

$$\dot{V} \le -\frac{1}{2}E^{T}QE \tag{15}$$

By Lyapunov stability theory, system (1) is asymptotically stable.

3.3 Modified Algorithm Preventing Parameters from Drifting

The physical meaning of the weights in the structural layer is unclear and it is difficult to determine its reasonable range, so parameter adaptive laws with projection are adopted to constrain the m^{2} dimension vectors$\theta_{f\Delta w1}$ and $\theta_{g\Delta w1}$ composed of the elements of w_{f}^{1} and w_{g}^{1} respectively into the sets Ω_{wf} and Ω_{wg}, and $\theta_{f\Delta w1}^{(i)} = \theta_{f\Delta}^{(i+2m)}$, $\theta_{g\Delta w1}^{(i)} = \theta_{g\Delta}^{(i+2m)}$, $1\le i\le m^{2}$. Other adjustable parameters in $\theta_{f\Delta\sigma y}$ and $\theta_{g\Delta\sigma y}$ have clear physical meaning, their reasonable ranges are determined respectively according their practical ranges and the corresponding modified algorithm is adopted to prevent them from drifting respectively, where $\theta_{f\Delta\sigma y}^{(i)} = \theta_{f\Delta}^{(i)}$, $\theta_{g\Delta\sigma y}^{(i)} = \theta_{g\Delta}^{(i)}$, $1\le i\le 2m$.

For $\theta_{f\Delta w1}$, consider $\Omega_{wf}=\{\theta_{f\Delta w1}: \mid\theta_{f\Delta w1}\mid\le M_{wf}\}$

$$\dot{\theta}_{f\Delta w1} = \begin{cases} -\gamma_{f\Delta}E^{T}PB\dfrac{\partial \hat{f}_{\Delta}}{\partial \theta_{f\Delta w1}} \\[4pt] \quad \text{if } \mid\theta_{f\Delta w1}\mid < M_{wf} \text{ or } \mid\theta_{f\Delta w1}\mid = M_{wf} \text{ and } E^{T}PB\dfrac{\partial \hat{f}_{\Delta}}{\partial \theta_{f\Delta w1}} \ge 0 \\[10pt] -\gamma_{f\Delta}E^{T}PB\dfrac{\partial \hat{f}_{\Delta}}{\partial \theta_{f\Delta w1}} + \gamma_{f\Delta}\dfrac{E^{T}PB\cdot\theta_{f\Delta w1}^{T}}{\mid\theta_{f\Delta w1}\mid M_{wf}}\dfrac{\partial \hat{f}_{\Delta}}{\partial \theta_{f\Delta w1}}\theta_{f\Delta w1} \\[10pt] \quad \text{if } \mid\theta_{f\Delta w1}\mid = M_{wf} \text{ and } E^{T}PB\dfrac{\partial \hat{f}_{\Delta}}{\partial \theta_{f\Delta w1}} < 0 \end{cases} \tag{16}$$

where $\gamma_{f\Delta}$ is the adaptive gain for $\theta_{f\Delta w1}$ and $\Gamma_{f\Delta}^{ii} = \gamma_{f\Delta}$, $2m+1\le i\le 2m+m^{2}$.

For $\theta_{g\Delta w1}$, consider $\Omega_{wg} = \{\theta_{g\Delta w1} : |\theta_{g\Delta w1}| \le M_{wg}\}$

$$
\dot{\theta}_{g\Delta w1} = \begin{cases}
-\gamma_{g\Delta} E^{\mathrm{T}} PB \dfrac{\partial \hat{g}_{\Delta}}{\partial \theta_{g\Delta w1}} u_c \\
\quad \text{if } |\theta_{g\Delta w1}| < M_{wg} \text{ or } |\theta_{g\Delta w1}| = M_{wg} \text{ and } E^{\mathrm{T}} PB \dfrac{\partial \hat{g}_{\Delta}}{\partial \theta_{g\Delta w1}} u_c \ge 0 \\[4mm]
-\gamma_{g\Delta} E^{\mathrm{T}} PB \dfrac{\partial \hat{g}_{\Delta}}{\partial \theta_{g\Delta w1}} u_c + \gamma_{g\Delta} \dfrac{E^{\mathrm{T}} PB \cdot \theta_{g\Delta w1}^{\mathrm{T}}}{|\theta_{g\Delta w1}| M_{wg}} \dfrac{\partial \hat{g}_{\Delta}}{\partial \theta_{g\Delta w1}} \theta_{g\Delta w1} u_c \\
\quad \text{if } |\theta_{g\Delta w1}| = M_{wg} \text{ and } E^{\mathrm{T}} PB \dfrac{\partial \hat{g}_{\Delta}}{\partial \theta_{g\Delta w1}} u_c < 0
\end{cases} \tag{17}
$$

where $\gamma_{g\Delta}$ is the adaptive gain for $\theta_{g\Delta w1}$, and $\Gamma_{g\Delta}^{ii} = \gamma_{g\Delta}$, $2m+1 \le i \le 2m+m^2$.

For $\theta_{f\Delta\sigma y}$, consider $\Omega_{f\Delta} = \{\theta_{f\Delta\sigma y} : b_{f\Delta}^i - \delta_{f\Delta}^i \le \theta_{f\Delta\sigma y}^i \le c_{f\Delta}^i + \delta_{f\Delta}^i\}$, $1 \le i \le 2m$, $b_{f\Delta}^i$ and $c_{f\Delta}^i$ are points having distances $\delta_{f\Delta}^i$ from the low and upper limit of the adjustable parameters, $\delta_{f\Delta}^i$ is design parameters, and their relations are similar with the case shown in Fig.2, in which # stands for $f\Delta$. Define $\Psi_{f\Delta} \equiv E^{\mathrm{T}} PB \dfrac{\partial \hat{f}_{\Delta}}{\partial \theta_{f\Delta\sigma y}}$, $\psi_{f\Delta}^i$ is the ith component of $\Psi_{f\Delta}$, $\overline{\psi}_{f\Delta}^i \equiv [1 + (c_{f\Delta}^i - \theta_{f\Delta\sigma y}^i)/\delta_{f\Delta}^i] \psi_{f\Delta}^i$, $\breve{\psi}_{f\Delta}^i \equiv [1 + (\theta_{f\Delta\sigma y}^i - b_{f\Delta}^i)/\delta_{f\Delta}^i] \psi_{f\Delta}^i$.

Then the modified algorithm for preventing $\theta_{f\Delta\sigma y}$ from drifting is

$$
\dot{\theta}_{f\Delta\sigma y}^i = \begin{cases}
-\Gamma_{f\Delta}^{ii} \overline{\psi}_{f\Delta}^i & \text{if } \theta_{f\Delta\sigma y}^i > c_{f\Delta}^i \text{ and } \psi_{f\Delta}^i > 0 \\
-\Gamma_{f\Delta}^{ii} \breve{\psi}_{f\Delta}^i & \text{if } \theta_{f\Delta\sigma y}^i < b_{f\Delta}^i \text{ and } \psi_{f\Delta}^i < 0 \\
-\Gamma_{f\Delta}^{ii} \psi_{f\Delta}^i & \text{others}
\end{cases} \tag{18}
$$

where $\Gamma_{f\Delta}^{ii}$ is the adaptive gain for $\theta_{f\Delta\sigma y}^i$, $1 \le i \le 2m$.

For $\theta_{g\Delta\sigma y}$, $\Omega_{g\Delta} = \{\theta_{g\Delta\sigma y} : b_{g\Delta}^i - \delta_{g\Delta}^i \le \theta_{g\Delta\sigma y}^i \le c_{g\Delta}^i + \delta_{g\Delta}^i\}$, $1 \le i \le 2m$, $b_{g\Delta}^i$ and $c_{g\Delta}^i$ are the points having distances $\delta_{g\Delta}^i$ away from the adjustable parameters' low and upper limit and $\delta_{g\Delta}^i$ is design parameters and their relations are similar with the case shown in Fig.2, in which # stands for $g\Delta$. and their relations are similar with the case in Fig.2, in which # stands for $f\Delta$. Define $\Psi_{g\Delta} \equiv E^{\mathrm{T}} PB \dfrac{\partial \hat{g}_{\Delta}}{\partial \theta_{g\Delta\sigma y}} u_c$, $\psi_{g\Delta}^i$ is the ith component of $\Psi_{g\Delta}$, $\overline{\psi}_{g\Delta}^i \equiv [1 + (c_{g\Delta}^i - \theta_{g\Delta\sigma y}^i)/\delta_{g\Delta}^i] \psi_{g\Delta}^i$, $\breve{\psi}_{g\Delta}^i \equiv [1 + (\theta_{g\Delta\sigma y}^i - b_{g\Delta}^i)/\delta_{g\Delta}^i] \psi_{g\Delta}^i$. Then the modified algorithm preventing $\theta_{g\Delta\sigma y}$ from drifting is

$$
\dot{\theta}_{g\Delta\sigma y}^i = \begin{cases}
-\Gamma_{g\Delta}^{ii} \overline{\psi}_{g\Delta}^i & \text{if } \theta_{g\Delta\sigma y}^i > c_{g\Delta}^i \text{ and } \psi_{g\Delta}^i > 0 \\
-\Gamma_{g\Delta}^{ii} \breve{\psi}_{g\Delta}^i & \text{if } \theta_{g\Delta i\sigma y} < b_{g\Delta}^i \text{ and } \psi_{g\Delta}^i < 0 \\
-\Gamma_{g\Delta}^{ii} \psi_{g\Delta}^i & \text{others}
\end{cases} \tag{19}
$$

where $\Gamma_{g\Delta}^{ii}$ is the adaptive gain for $\theta_{g\Delta\sigma y}^i$, $1 \le i \le 2m$.

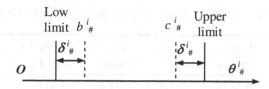

Fig. 2. Relations between $b_\#^i, c_\#^i$ and $\delta_\#^i$, in which # stands for u_{ad}

Modified algorithm preventing $\hat{K}_{vsc}$ from drifting is

$$\dot{\hat{K}}_{vsc} = \Gamma_{Kvsc} \mid E^T PB \mid \varphi - \sigma_{Kvsc} \hat{K}_{vsc} \tag{20}$$

4 Analysis on Experiment Results

Experiment studies on the EHPTS employed by [15] were carried out to verify the effectiveness of the proposed algorithm.

The desired trajectory is selected as $y_d(t)=0.15+0.1\sin(0.1\pi t)$ m in experiment by indirect ADRFNNC, and the initial point is $x(0)=[0,0,0]^T$. The position detector used in experiment system is incremental inductosyn, so a limit end of the cylinder was selected as the measurement original to position the system easily. But the original for modeling the valve controlled system is the middle of the cylinder, the input variable x_1 of ADRFNN should be obtained by subtracting 0.15m from the practical position of the load car, and the desired trajectory $y_d(t)$ is dealt with in the same way. Then the membership function's centre values are selected as $\bar{x}_1(0) = \bar{x}_{d1}(0) =[-0.2,-0.1,0,$ $0.1,0.2]$. Fig.1 shows that ADRFNN become TAFNN if the weights in the structural layer are set to be zero, so the initial values of all the elements of $w_{uad}^1, w_{f\Delta}^1$ and $w_{g\Delta}^1$ can be set to be zero. The states x_2 and x_3 used in the indirect TAFNNC were obtained by differentiating the state x_1 in experiment.

4.1 Experiment Results by Indirect ADRFNNC

The relevant variables for estimating the parameters σ and $\bar{y}_\#^l$ of ADRFNN are listed in table 1. Other parameters are $m=5$, $\mu=12$, $k=[200,50, 6]^T$, $Q=diag(100,100, 100)$. $\beta=g_0(x)=1.1476\times10^6$, $f_0(x)=[0,-1.42\times10^5,-16.92]x$. The parameters related to the gain of VSC are $\sigma_{Kvsc}=100$, $\hat{K}_{vsc}(0)=[1.6\times10^4,10^4]^T$, $\Gamma_{Kvsc}=diag(6\times10^4,6\times10^4)$. $M_{wf}=10$, M_{wg} $=5$, $\gamma_{f\Delta}= 20$, $\gamma_{g\Delta} =10$, The results of the indirect ADRFNNC under the condition of different source pressure and load force are shown in Fig.3. To compare the effect of the identification accuracy of ADRFNN and TAFNN on the chattering of control effort, the result by indirect TAFNN is shown in Fig.4a. Position tracking response by ADRFNNC with constant gain VSC is shown in Fig.4b to investigate the effectiveness of the GAVSC. The relevant steady errors is shown in Fig.5.

Table 1. Variables for parameter estimating of indirect ADRFNN

Estimated variable	Upper limit $c_\#$	Lower limit $b_\#$	Initial value	Adaptive rate $\Gamma_\#^{ii}$	$\delta_\#$
$\sigma_{f\Delta}^j$	0.1058	0.0522	0.079	0.01	0.02
$\sigma_{g\Delta}^j$	0.1058	0.0522	0.079	0.05	0.02
$\bar{y}_{f\Delta}^l$	10^5	-10^5	0	6×10^5	100
$\bar{y}_{g\Delta}^l$	10^7	0	10^6	10^6	100

With $i=j=l=1,2,...,m$, # stands for $f\Delta$ or $g\Delta$.

4.2 Discussions on Experiment Results

4.2.1 Analysis on System's Robustness

Fig.3-Fig.5 show the cylinder has sinusoidal motion with 0.15 m as its center, but the control effort u is asymmetrical to the 0 V line, it results from the compensation of the integrated adaptive function for the valve spool's error caused during manufacturing and assemblage processes. Fig.3a and Fig.3b show that the load force F_L has no effect on system's tracking accuracy, but the curve of the control effort move up wholly, it

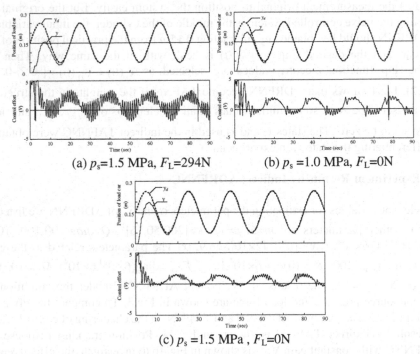

(a) p_s=1.5 MPa, F_L=294N   (b) p_s =1.0 MPa, F_L=0N

(c) p_s =1.5 MPa , F_L=0N

Fig. 3. Position tracking response of the experiment system and its control effort by indirect ADRFNNC with GAVSC

results from the fact that stronger control effort needed in the drag stroke and weaker control effort needed in the pull stroke. Fig.3b and Fig.3c show that the amplitude of the control effort become smaller when the pressure of the oil source increases, the reason is that the gain of the system increases with the increment of oil source pressure and smaller control effort u can obtain corresponding flow. Even so, the system's tracking accuracy is unaffected. These cases fully verify the proposed indirect ADRFNNC can make the system possess strong robustness.

4.2.2 Chattering of the Control Effort

Fig.3~Fig.4 show that the system's control effort by indirect ADRFNNC has smaller amplitude of chattering than that by indirect TAFNNC, reason is that the system by indirect ADRFNNC has smaller secondary uncertainties, so VSC's correction control gain determined by it is smaller, and it makes the amplitude of the chattering smaller. Fig.3~Fig.4 show that if the VSC's correction gain is constant, the amplitude of the chattering holds constant. If GAVSC is adopted, the amplitude of the chattering becomes smaller after adjustment for some time in the starting phase. This fact verifies the proposed GAVSC can auto-adjust the VSC's correction gain according to the bound of system's secondary uncertainty and suppress the chattering of control effort.

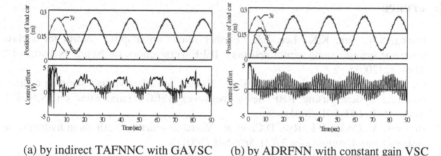

    (a) by indirect TAFNNC with GAVSC   (b) by ADRFNN with constant gain VSC

Fig. 4. Position tracking response of the experiment system and its control effort

4.2.3 Analysis on the System's Steady Error

Fig.5 shows the load car's steady errors (30 seconds later from the start). It shows the steady accuracy by indirect ADRFNNC is better than that by indirect TAFNNC

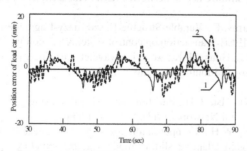

1—By indirect ADRFNNC   2—By indirect TAFNNC

Fig. 5. Steady position error $e_y = y - y_d$ of the load car

5 Conclusion

From the theoretical analyzes and experimental results some properties of the proposed indirect ADRFNNC for the control of hydraulic position tracking system can be concluded as follows: 1) ADRFNN is adopted to identify the nonlinear system, only the measurable variable can be selected as its input, the shortcoming of the structural expansion by larger number of inputs is overcome; 2) The identification accuracy of ADRFNN possessing inner dynamic characteristics is higher than the TAFNN taking all variables as its inputs, so the chattering of the control effort and the steady error of the system's output are improved obviously; 3) The adaptive function integrated in the proposed algorithm make the system have the ability of adaptive compensation for the uncertainty of the system parameters and load disturbance, so the EHTPS with the proposed algorithms have strong robustness and better tracking performance; 4) The gain of the VSC's crrection term for the identification errors is determined online according to the bound of the secondary uncertainties, so the system can obtain the same robustness by smaller control effort.

Reference

1. Huang, S.N., Tan, K.K., Lee, T.H.: Further results on adaptive control for a class of nonlinear systems suing neural networks. IEEE Transactions on Neural Networks 14(3), 719–722 (2003)
2. Li, Y., Qiang, S., Zhung, X., Kaynak, O.: Robust and adaptive backstepping control for nonlinear systems using RBF neural networks. IEEE Transactions on Neural Networks 15(3), 693–701 (2004)
3. Bonchis, A., Corke, P.I., Rye, D.C., et al.: Variable structure methods in hydraulic servo systems control. Automatica 37(4), 589–595 (2001)
4. Tsai, C.H., Chung, H.Y., Yu, F.M.: Neural-sliding mode control with its application to seesaw systems. IEEE Transactions on Neural Networks 15(1), 124–134 (2004)
5. Park, J.H., Park, G.T.: Robust adaptive fuzzy controller for nonlinear system using estimation of bounds for approximation errors. Fuzzy Sets and System 133(1), 19–36 (2003)
6. Tsai, C.H., Chung, H.Y., Yu, F.M.: Neural-sliding mode control with its application to seesaw systems. IEEE Transactions on Neural Networks 15(1), 124–134 (2004)
7. Park, J.H., Huh, S.H., Kim, S.H., et al.: Direct adaptive controller for nonaffine nonlinear systems using self-struture neural networks. IEEE Transactions on Neural Networks 16(2), 414–422 (2005)
8. Elshafei, A.L., Karray, F.: Varable-Structue-Based fuzzy-Logic identification of a class of nonlinear system. IEEE Transaction on control systems technology 13(4), 646–653 (2005)
9. Lin, F.J., Shieh, H.J., Huang, P.K.: Adaptive wavelet neural network control with hysteresis estimation for piezo-positioning mechanism. IEEE Transactions on Neural Networks 17(2), 432–444 (2006)
10. Wu, J.M., Lin, Z.H., Hsu, P.H.: Function approximation using generalized adalines. IEEE Transactions on Neural Networks 17(3), 541–557 (2006)
11. Zhang, Y.W., Gui, W.H.: Compensation for secondary uncertainty in electro-hydraulic servo system by gain adaptive sliding mode variable structure control. J. Cent. South Univ. 15(2), 256–263 (2008)

Logistics Distribution Center Location Evaluation Based on Genetic Algorithm and Fuzzy Neural Network

Yuxiang Shao[1], Qing Chen[2], and Zhenhua Wei[1]

[1] China University of Geosciences, No.388 Lumo Road Wuhan, P.R. China
syxcq@163.com
[2] Wuhan Institute of Technology, Wuhan, Hubei, P.R. China
chenqing@mail.wit.edu.cn

Abstract. Logistics distribution center location evaluation is a dynamic, fuzzy, open and complicated nonlinear system, which makes it difficult to evaluate the distribution center location by the traditional analysis method. The paper proposes a distribution center location evaluation system which uses the fuzzy neural network combined with the genetic algorithm. In this model, the neural network is adopted to construct the fuzzy system. By using the genetic algorithm, the parameters of the neural network are optimized and trained so as to improve the fuzzy system's abilities of self-study and self-adaptation. At last, the sampled data are trained and tested by Matlab software. The simulation results indicate that the proposed identification model has very small errors.

Keywords: logistics distribution center location, fuzzy neural network, genetic algorithm, evaluation.

1 Introduction

Reasonable logistics distribution center location can save costs, speed up the flow of goods, increase logistics companies revenue, so the decision-making of the logistics distribution center location is a very important problem for optimizing the entire logistics system[1].

In recent years, many new decision-making methods of logistics distribution center location are presented, such as fuzzy comprehensive evaluation method, AHP hierarchy analytical process and fuzzy ranking method combined with AHP hierarchy analytical process[2]. However, these methods have some shortcomings such as the weights of membership function have subjective, the target weights are difficult to determine, man-made factors are overweight, the elements of target structure system are mutual independence and so on.

This paper optimizes fuzzy neural network with genetic algorithm(GA) and presents the model which is applied in the logistics distribution center location. Using Matlab train and test sample data, simulation results show that fuzzy neural networks model optimized by GA has high prediction precision and good generalization ability so that it is effective for logistics distribution center location evaluation.

Z. Cai et al. (Eds.): ISICA 2009, CCIS 51, pp. 305–312, 2009.

2   Fuzzy Neural Networks Structure of Logistics Distribution Center Location

2.1   Description of Fuzzy Neural Network

Fuzzy neural network is a concept that integrates some features of the fuzzy logic and the artificial neural networks (ANN) theory. It based on the integration of two complementary theories. Purpose of the integration is to compensate weaknesses of one theory with advantages of the other. Fuzzy logic and neural networks are complementary technologies[3-4]. ANN extracts information from systems to be learned or controlled, while fuzzy logic techniques most often use verbal and linguistic information from experts. A promising approach to obtain the benefits of both fuzzy systems and ANN and solve their respective problems is to combine them into an integrated system. FNN techniques have several features that make them well suited to a wide range of knowledge engineering applications[5-7]. These strengths include fast and accurate learning, good generalization capabilities, excellent explanation facilities in the form of semantically meaningful fuzzy rules, and the ability to accommodate both data and existing expert knowledge about the problem under consideration.

2.2   Network Design of Logistics Distribution Center Location

The principles of Logistics distribution center site choice include reducing costs, improving economic efficiency and customer service levels. Under the guidance of the these principles, pre-select a number of programs, compare these programs through a variety of methods, and ultimately select one program as new center address.

There are many factors impacting distribution center location and select some important factors as decision-making target. In these targets, quantitative factors include candidate land value, transport distance and candidate land area. Here they all choose Gaussian membership function.

Qualitative factors need quantify through expert advice method and expert scoring method, and then make use of relevant membership function to determine membership degree. Qualitative factors include customer distribution, supplier distribution, geological condition, communication condition, road infrastructure. Firstly qualitative factors are described in different categories separately, and then convert the evaluation of natural language to the corresponding membership degree. The membership functions of qualitative factors are shown in Table 1.

Table 1. Membership functions of qualitative factors

target	categories describe	fuzzy constraint set	membership
customer distribution	muster, common, scatter	customer distribution A1	A1={1,0.5,0}
suppliers distribution	muster, common, scatter	suppliers distribution A2	A2={1,0.5,0}
geological conditions	very good, good, common, bad, very bad	geological conditions A3	A3={1.0,0.8,0.5,0.2,0}
communication conditions	very good, good, common, bad, very bad	communication conditions A4	A3={1.0,0.8,0.5,0.2,0}

2.3 Model Construction

The network structure is divided into four layers, i.e. the input layer, the fuzzy layer, the rule layer and the output layer.

The first layer is input layer. Each node of this layer transfers the input to the next layer directly.

$$I_i^{(1)} = x_i^{(1)} \qquad O_i^{(1)} = I_i^{(1)} \tag{1}$$

Here, $x_i^{(1)}$, $I_i^{(1)}$, $O_i^{(1)}$ represent for the input, neat input and output of the i-th node respectively.

The second layer is fuzzy layer, each node of which calculates a degree of membership function. Here we apply Gauss function as the degree of membership function. The j-th fuzzy node that corresponds to the i-th input node has the following degree of membership function :

$$I_j^{(2)} = -\frac{\left(x_i^{(2)} - m_{ij}\right)^2}{\sigma_{ij}^2} \qquad O_j^{(2)} = \exp\left(I_j^{(2)}\right) \tag{2}$$

Here, m_{ij} and σ_{ij} represent the central value and width of the degree of membership function respectively.

The third layer is rule layer. This layer implements the function of fuzzy rule consequence condition, and prescribes that each language variable has only one language value connecting with certain regular node. For the K-th regular node:

$$I_k^{(3)} = \prod_i x_i^{(3)} \qquad O_k^{(3)} = I_k^{(3)} \tag{3}$$

The output of this layer is also called stimulation intensity of rule, which indicates the corresponding degree of the K-th fuzzy regular condition.

The 4th layer is output layer. This layer implements the fuzzy process by calculating the sum of weightings of all regular excitation intensities to realize fuzzy process.

$$I_o^{(4)} = \sum_k w_k^{(4)} x_k^{(4)} \qquad O_o^{(4)} = I_o^{(4)} \tag{4}$$

Here, $w_k^{(4)}$ represents the weight from the rule layer to output layer.

3 Fuzzy Neural Networks Optimized by GA

3.1 Basic Idea

Fuzzy neural network learned by BP algorithm is a good method to set up and adjust the fuzzy inference control system, but this method learns on the basis of error back propagation algorithm of gradient descent, and has slow network training speed and tends to yield minimal local results. The convergence of BP algorithm depends on the choice of initial state.

Genetic algorithms are a kind of auto-adapted global optimization searching algorithm of simulation biological evolution, and reduce the impact of the initial state through crossover and mutation operation. Genetic algorithms can optimize the parameters and structure of fuzzy neural inference system. GA can be used to optimize the fuzzy inference rules by amend the membership function and network nodes.

In order to exert the strengths of GA and BP algorithm, this paper used BP algorithm adjust and optimize the local parameters, used genetic algorithm optimize the overall parameters and network structure. That is using GA train off-line fuzzy neural network, using BP algorithm adjust neural network online local parameters. The integrated use of two kind algorithms can greatly improve fuzzy-neural network self-learning performance and generalization ability.

3.2 Training Algorithm

Because the number of fuzzy neural network layers is relatively fixed, the adjustable parameters are the center value m and width σ of fuzzy control membership function as well as the connection weights ω. Among them, the center value m and width σ are global parameters which can adjust and optimize by GA, while the connection weights ω can regulate by BP algorithm.

(1)coding and decoding

Using genetic algorithm train neural network parameters must firstly encode parameters. This paper adopts simple coding ways and all network parameters arrange in a certain order. So each parameter length is L of the binary number. The method is: if the parameters change in the range of $[\alpha_{min}, \alpha_{max}]$ with L-bit binary number, then

$$\alpha = \alpha_{min} + \frac{B}{2^L}(\alpha_{max} - \alpha_{min}) \tag{5}$$

(2)Determine the fitness function

There are many ways to determine the fitness function. This paper adopts the inverse objective function as fitness function

$$F = 1/_J \qquad J = \frac{1}{2}\sum_{i=1}^{n}(y_i - y_i^*)^2 \tag{6}$$

Here y_i and y_i^* are the expectation export and the actual export respectively of the i-th sample.

(3) Selection strategy

Fitness-proportionate selection strategy often cause early convergence and stagnation. The model adopts ranking selection strategy. Firstly arrange every individual with its fitness degressively, distribute every individual chosen possibility P_k according to its order in population, and at last adopt roulette wheel selection with P_k. P_k is defined as follows:

$$P_k = \begin{cases} q(1-q)^{i-1}, & i = 1,2,...,M-1 \\ (1-q)^{M-1}, & i = M \end{cases} \tag{7}$$

q is a constant which stands for the best individual chosen possibility.

(4) Crossover operators

If there is only through selection operation, the cluster neither generate new individual, nor search new area, thus it is important to adopt crossover operators. The astringency of GA is mainly lie on the astringency of crossover operators. Crossover operators adopt single node cross. Crossover operating is with the possibility P_c. Cross the individual $X_A = (x_A^1, x_A^2, \cdots, x_A^s)$ and $X_B = (x_B^1, x_B^2, \cdots, x_B^s)$ after the k-th vector, crossover operators are designed as follows:

$$X_A^* = \left(x_A^1, \cdots, x_A^k, \alpha_{k+1}x_A^{k+1} + (1 - \alpha_{k+1})x_B^{k+1}, \cdots, \alpha_s x_A^s + (1 - \alpha_s)x_B^s\right) \tag{8}$$

$$X_B^* = \left(x_B^1, \cdots, x_B^k, \alpha_{k+1}x_B^{k+1} + (1 - \alpha_{k+1})x_A^{k+1}, \cdots, \alpha_s x_B^s + (1 - \alpha_s)x_A^s\right) \tag{9}$$

$\alpha_{k+1}, \alpha_{k+2}, \cdots, \alpha_s$ are random values more than 0 and less than 1.

(5) Mutation operators

Using mutation operators can improve GA local search ability and maintain the diversity of cluster.

Mutate the vector x_k in the individual $X = (x_1, x_2, \cdots, x_s)$ to x_k', then

$$x_k' = x_k(1 - r) \tag{10}$$

r is a random value between 0 and 1.

In the genetic algorithm, the choice of M, P_c and P_m greatly affect the genetic algorithm performance. Generally P_c is chosen between 0.5 and 1, P_m is chosen between 0.005 and 0.1. The specific values need determined through a lot of experiments.

When the optimized individual fitness and population average fitness are no longer increase meaningfully, use BP algorithm train networks to improve convergence speed.

4 Application Example

Input the membership indicators into the network, make the experts expect value as network output, the initial weights are random values between 0 and1, learning factor is 0.4, the mean square error is 10^{-3}. After quantification and fuzzy treatment, obtain the experimental training data membership degree which is partly shown in table 2.

After several times iterative training, the obtained weight matrix is considered as the best matrix to select and evaluate distribution center site. Make the optimal matrix as the initial matrix, input the quantitative target into the trained network, the output is all programs' accord degree, that is programs' evaluation value.

The initially selected experimental data and programs' evaluation results and ranking are shown in table 3. From the table, we know that the best prediction sample number is 3, the worst forecast sample number is 5. This result is the same as the expert evaluation and this system is suit to logistics distribution center location evaluation.

Table 2. Studied samples used for training

Sample number	Customer distribution	suppliers distribution	geological conditions	communication conditions	candidate land value	transport distance	candidate land area	road establishment	expert evaluation
1	1.0	1.0	1.0	1.0	1.0	1.0	1.0	1.0	1.0
2	0.87	0.80	0.82	0.84	0.75	0.78	0.65	0.66	0.80
3	0.60	0.60	0.56	0.66	0.49	0.60	0.58	0.56	0.58
4	0.91	0.95	0.90	1.0	0.98	1.0	1.0	0.99	0.98
5	1.0	0.72	0.89	0.82	0.80	0.80	0.89	0.75	0.83
6	0.47	0.41	0.44	0.40	0.49	0.35	0.47	0.44	0.51
7	0.80	0.72	0.78	0.78	0.66	0.80	0.75	0.75	0.75
8	0.72	0.67	0.67	0.66	0.67	0.49	0.60	0.66	0.69
9	1.0	0.67	0.93	0.80	0.75	0.49	0.66	0.22	0.74
10	1.0	0.92	0.80	1.0	0.89	0.89	0.89	0.80	0.81

Table 3. Tested sample and evaluation results

Sample number	Customer distribution	suppliers distribution	geological conditions	communication conditions	candidate land value	transport distance	candidate land area	road establishment	evaluation result	ranking
1	0.08	0.93	0.56	0.92	0.89	0.60	0.24	0.33	0.61	3
2	0.45	0.52	0.40	0.33	0.66	0.80	0.50	0.60	0.56	4
3	0.67	0.89	0.82	1.0	0.80	0.73	0.75	0.85	0.85	1
4	0.87	0.72	0.89	0.92	0.89	0.40	0.49	0.29	0.72	2
5	0.40	0.40	0.33	0.33	0.33	0.40	0.49	0.35	0.43	5

The training curve for fuzzy neural networks optimized by GA is shown in Fig.1. From figure 1, we can learn that the fuzzy neural networks system which is optimized by GA not only speed the training process, but also ensure the training stability.

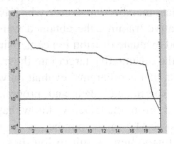

Fig. 1. Training curve for FNN optimized by GA

5 Comparative Analysis of Algorithm

The fuzzy neural networks and fuzzy neural networks optimized by GA are applied to logistics distribution center location above for training and evaluating. The comparative result of algorithm for evaluation result is shown in table 4.

Table 4. Algorithm comparison

sample number	expert evaluation	FNN evaluation result	FNN optimized by GA evaluation result
1	0.62	0.53	0.61
2	0.59	0.55	0.56
3	0.86	0.82	0.85
4	0.71	0.69	0.72
5	0.45	0.35	0.43

From table 4, we know that the evaluation result by fuzzy neural networks system which is optimized by GA is closer to expert evaluation than the evaluation result by fuzzy neural networks model.

6 Conclusion

A study on the establishment of logistics distribution center location evaluation model by using fuzzy neural networks and genetic algorithm is carried out in the study. The following results were obtained based on this investigation.

1)It is successful to establish the fuzzy neural network by introducing the genetic algorithm to optimize the overall parameters and network structure, BP algorithm adjust and optimize the local parameters, improving effectively the convergence velocity and precision.

2)The evaluation model of logistics distribution center location by applying the GA and fuzzy neural network algorithm is established. The method solves the modeling problem of the logistics distribution center location evaluation as a non-linear system, which is difficult to accomplish with a mathematical method.

Acknowledgement

This work is supported by the 863 Program of China (No. 2008AA121602).

References

1. Ge, Z., Sun, Z.: The Neural Network Theory and Matlab Application, pp. 324–327. Publishing House of Electronics Industry, Beijing (2008)
2. Kuo, R.J., Xue, K.C.: Fuzzy Neural Networks with Application to Sales Forecasting. Fuzzy Sets and Systems 108(4), 123–143 (1999)

3. Bagnoli, C., Smith, H.C.: The Theory of Fuzzy Logic and It's Application to Real Estate Prediction. Journal of Real Estate Research 16(2), 169–199 (1998)
4. Lin, C.T., Lee, C.S.G. (eds.): Neural fuzzy systems: A Neural-fuzzy Synergism to Intelligent Systems. Prentice-Hall, Inc., USA (1996)
5. Wolverton, M.L., Senteza, J.: Hedonic Estimates of Regional Constant Quality House Prices. Journal of Real Estate Research 19(3), 235–253 (2000)
6. Huang, Y., Zhou, C.: Recognizing the Taste Signals Using the Clustering-Based Fuzzy Neural Network. Chinese Journal of Electronics 14(1), 21–25 (2005)
7. Liu, X., Cao, L., Wang, X.: The Distribution Center Selection Based on the Fuzzy Neural Network Model. Computer Applications and Software 24(3), 15–17 (2007)

Mean-VaR Models and Algorithms for Fuzzy Portfolio Selection

Wen Dong and Jin Peng

Institute of Uncertain Systems
Huanggang Normal University, Hubei 438000
College of Mathematics and Science
Shanghai Normal University, Shanghai 200234
peng@hgnu.edu.cn

Abstract. In this paper, value-at-risk (VaR for short) is used as the measure of risk. Based on the concept of VaR, a fuzzy mean-VaR model is proposed. Firstly, we recall some definitions and results of value-at-risk in credibilistic risk analysis. Secondly, we propose the fuzzy mean-VaR model of fuzzy programming, or more precisely, credibilistic programming. Thirdly, a hybrid intelligent algorithm is provided to give a general solution of the optimization problem. Finally, numerical examples are also presented to illustrate the effectiveness of the proposed algorithm.

Keywords: risk analysis, credibilistic value-at-risk, mean-VaR model, hybrid intelligent algorithm.

1 Introduction

Classical portfolio theory [14] can be traced back to the pioneering works of Markowitz in the 1950s. The variance could be regarded as risk measure in his mean-variance models. The fact that variance operator is not linear means that the risk of a portfolio, as measured by the variance, is not equal to the weighted sum of risks of the individual assets. Morgan [15] proposed value at risk to evaluate and manage financial risk. A number of authors have used the VaR measure to describe the risk value in risk analysis([2,5,7]). VaR measures are used to estimate a portfolio of assets losing more than a specified amount over a specified time period due to adverse movements in the underlying market factors of a portfolio. For example, VaR is 1 million dollars at the 95% level of confidence implies that the probability of the all losses would exceed 1 million dollars is only 5%.

The traditional portfolio selection models in a stochastic environment was established as one of the most useful tools of probability. Numerous models have been developed based on variance such as models proposed in [3]. Meanwhile, portfolio selection environment often subject to fuzziness and thus the assumptions of only deterministic parameters or stochastic parameters, could no longer be applied.

Z. Cai et al. (Eds.): ISICA 2009, CCIS 51, pp. 313–319, 2009.

Fuzziness is a type of subjective uncertainty. In order to describe fuzzy phenomena, possibility theory has been proposed by Zadeh. Generally speaking, possibility measure is not self-dual. As an alternative measure of a fuzzy event, Liu and Liu [11] presented a self-dual credibility measure. Therefore fuzzy risk analysis based on credibility theory is needed. It is natural to extend VaR technique in fuzzy environment. Peng [16] introduced the concepts of credibilistic VaR.

Fuzzy programming is a powerful tool for handling optimization problems with fuzzy variable parameters [10]. Numerous papers are devoted to introducing and developing fuzzy programming techniques to fuzzy portfolio selection problems [6]. Dong and Peng [4] presented a hybrid intelligent algorithm for solving the proposed credibilistic VaR model.

Mean-VaR model is a very important issue in decision making [1,8]. This paper introduces a fuzzy mean-VaR model of credibilistic programming. For this purpose, we organize this paper as follows. Section 2 recalls some useful definitions for fuzzy risk analysis within the framework of credibility theory, which will be used in the following discussion. In Section 3, we give the Mean-VaR models. In order to solve the models, some hybrid intelligent algorithms and examples are given in Section 4 and Section 5, respectively. Finally, some remarks are made in the last section.

2 Preliminaries

Let ξ be a fuzzy variable with membership function μ. For any $B \subset \Re$, the credibility measure of fuzzy event $\{\xi \in B\}$ was defined by Liu and Liu [11] as

$$\mathrm{Cr}\{\xi \in B\} = \frac{1}{2}\left(\sup_{x \in B} \mu(x) + 1 - \sup_{x \in B^c} \mu(x)\right). \tag{1}$$

The credibility distribution $\Phi \colon \Re \to [0,1]$ of a fuzzy variable ξ was defined by Liu [9] as

$$\Phi(x) = \mathrm{Cr}\{\theta \in \Theta \mid \xi(\theta) \le x\}.$$

The expected value of fuzzy variable ξ was defined by Liu and Liu[11] as

$$E[\xi] = \int_0^{+\infty} \mathrm{Cr}\{\xi \ge r\}\mathrm{d}r - \int_{-\infty}^0 \mathrm{Cr}\{\xi \le r\}\mathrm{d}r \tag{2}$$

provided that at least one of the two integrals is finite. Furthermore, the variance is defined by Liu and Liu [11] as

$$V[\xi] = E[(\xi - E[\xi])^2]. \tag{3}$$

Liu and Gao [13] introduce the independence concept of fuzzy variables. The fuzzy variables $\xi_1, \xi_2, \cdots, \xi_m$ are independent if and only if

$$\mathrm{Cr}\left\{\bigcap_{i=1}^m \{\xi_i \in B_i\}\right\} = \min_{1 \le i \le m} \mathrm{Cr}\{\xi_i \in B_i\}. \tag{4}$$

for any sets $B_1, B_2, \cdots, B_m$ of $\Re$.

The credibilistic VaR of ξ, defined by Peng [16], is the function $\xi_{\mathrm{VaR}}: (0, 1] \to \Re$ such that

$$\xi_{\mathrm{VaR}}(\alpha) = -\inf\{x | \mathrm{Cr}\{\xi \leq x\} \geq \alpha\}. \tag{5}$$

3   Credibilistic Mean-VaR Model

Let $\eta = (\xi_1, \xi_2, \cdots, \xi_n)$ be a vector of fuzzy return asset categories $1, 2, \cdots, n$. Let $X = (x_1, x_2, \cdots, x_n)$ be the weighting factor in these categories respectively. Without loss of generality, we assume that the total is 1. In most cases, the fuzzy portfolio return, which is usually the share-weighted sum of the fuzzy returns for the assets included in the portfolio, are given by

$$f(x, \xi) = \sum_{i=1}^{n} x_i \xi_i.$$

If the return asset categories are independent, then it follows that the portfolio expected return can be calculated by the following equations

$$E[\sum_{i=1}^{n} x_i \xi_i] = \sum_{i=1}^{n} x_i E[\xi_i].$$

Now we consider the following multi-objective mean-VaR model:

$$\begin{cases} \max \; E[f(x, \xi)] \\[2mm] \min \; \xi_{\mathrm{VaR}}(\alpha) \\[2mm] s.t. \; \mathrm{Cr}\{\sum_{i=1}^{n} x_i \xi_i \leq \xi_{\mathrm{VaR}}(\alpha)\} \geq \alpha \\[2mm] \sum_{i=1}^{n} x_i = 1 \\[2mm] x_i \geq 0, \quad i = 1, \cdots, n \end{cases} \tag{6}$$

where α is referred to as the confidence level provided as an appropriate safety margin by the decision-maker. Generally, the objectives are in conflict, and there is no optimal solution that simultaneously maximizes all the objective functions.

If the investors want to minimize the VaR with the given lowest expected return, then the mean-VaR model can be given as follows,

$$\begin{cases} \min \; \xi_{\mathrm{VaR}}(\alpha) \\[2mm] s.t. \; \mathrm{Cr}\{\sum_{i=1}^{n} x_i \xi_i \leq \xi_{\mathrm{VaR}}(\alpha)\} \geq \alpha \\[2mm] E[\sum_{i=1}^{n} x_i \xi_i] \geq r \\[2mm] \sum_{i=1}^{n} x_i = 1 \\[2mm] x_i \geq 0, \quad i = 1, \cdots, n \end{cases} \tag{7}$$

where r is a specified return level, and α is referred to as the confidence level.

If the investors want to maximize the expected return at the given risk level, then the mean-VaR model can be given as follows,

$$
\begin{cases}
\max \ E[\sum_{i=1}^{n} x_i \xi_i] \\
s.t. \ \mathrm{Cr}\{\sum_{i=1}^{n} x_i \xi_i \leq \xi_{\mathrm{VaR}}(\alpha)\} \geq \alpha \\
\sum_{i=1}^{n} x_i = 1 \\
x_i \geq 0, \quad i = 1, \cdots, n
\end{cases}
\tag{8}
$$

where α is referred to as the confidence level.

4 Hybrid Intelligent Algorithm for Solving Mean-VaR Model

In this section, we present a hybrid intelligent algorithm for solving the Mean-VaR Model.

Hybrid Intelligent Algorithm

Step 1. In order to compute the uncertain function

$$
\mathcal{U}(x, \alpha) = \xi_{\mathrm{VaR}}(\alpha) = \inf\{\beta \mid \mathrm{Cr}\{\sum_{i=1}^{n} x_i \xi_i \leq \beta\} \geq \alpha\},
$$

we randomly generate θ_k from the credibility space $(\Theta, \mathcal{P}, \mathrm{Cr})$. Write $v_k = (2\mathrm{Cr}\{\theta_k\}) \wedge 1$ and produce $\xi_k = \xi(\theta_k), k = 1, 2, \cdots, N$, respectively. Equivalently, we randomly generate θ_k and write $v_k = \mu(\theta_k)$ for $k = 1, 2, \cdots, N$, where μ is the membership function of ξ. For any number r, we set

$$
L(r) = \frac{1}{2}(\max_{1 \leq k \leq N}\{v_k \mid f(x, \xi_k) \geq r\} + \min_{1 \leq k \leq N}\{1 - v_k \mid f(x, \xi_k) < r\}).
$$

It follows from monotonicity that we may employ bisection search to find the minimize value r such that $L(r) \geq \alpha$.

Step 2. Train a neural network to approximate the uncertain functions according to the generated training input-output data.

Step 3. Initialize pop-size chromosomes whose feasibility may be checked by the trained neural network.

Step 4. Update the chromosomes by crossover and mutation operations and the trained neural network may be employed to check the feasibility of offsprings.

Step 5. Calculate the objective values for all chromosomes by the trained neural network.

Step 6. Compute the fitness of each chromosome by rank-based evaluation function based on the objective values.

Step 7. Select the chromosomes by spinning the roulette wheel.

Step 8. Repeat the fourth to seventh steps a given number of cycles.

Step 9. Report the best chromosome as the optimal solution.

5 Examples

In order to illustrate its effectiveness, here we give some numerical examples which are all performed on a personal computer with the following parameters: the population size is 30, the probability of crossover Pc is 0.3, the probability of mutation Pm is 0.2, and the parameter a in the rank-based evaluation function is 0.05.

Example 5.1:

$$\begin{cases} \min \ \xi_{\text{VaR}}(0.95) \\[2mm] s.t. \ \text{Cr}\{x_1\xi_1 + x_2\xi_2 + x_3\xi_3 \le \xi_{\text{VaR}}(0.95)\} \ge 0.95 \\[2mm] \quad E[x_1\xi_1 + x_2\xi_2 + x_3\xi_3] \ge 3 \\[2mm] \quad x_1 + x_2 + x_3 = 1 \\[2mm] \quad x_i \ge 0, i = 1, \cdots, 3. \end{cases}$$

where ξ_1, ξ_2, and ξ_3 are assumed to triangular fuzzy variables $(1, 2, 3)$, $(2, 3, 4)$, $(3, 4, 5)$, respectively. We set the level of confidence $\alpha = 0.95$, and the return level $r = 3$.

We train an NN (3 input neurons, 6 hidden neurons, 2 output neurons) to approximate the uncertain function.

Finally, we integrate the trained NN and GA to produce a hybrid intelligent algorithm. A run of the hybrid intelligent algorithm (6000 cycles in simulation, 2000 training data in NN, 1500 generations in GA) shows that the optimal solution is

$$(x_1, x_2, x_3) = (0.1788, 0.5650, 0.2562)$$

with objective value $\xi_{\text{VaR}}(0.95) \approx 3.89$.

Example 5.2:

$$\begin{cases} \min \ \xi_{\text{VaR}}(0.95) \\[2mm] s.t. \ \text{Cr}\{x_1\xi_1 + x_2\xi_2 + x_3\xi_3 \le \xi_{\text{VaR}}(0.95)\} \ge 0.95 \\[2mm] \quad E[x_1\xi_1 + x_2\xi_2 + x_3\xi_3] \ge 2 \\[2mm] \quad x_1 + x_2 + x_3 = 1 \\[2mm] \quad x_i \ge 0, i = 1, \cdots, 3 \end{cases}$$

where ξ_1 is a normally distributed fuzzy variable with expected value 2 and variance 0.3, ξ_2 is an exponential fuzzy variable with moment 2, ξ_3 is an equipossible fuzzy variable on $(2,4)$. We set the level of confidence $\alpha = 0.95$, and the return level $r = 2$.

For this case, we can not calculate the objective value by credibilistic VaR function. We integrate the trained NN and GA to produce a hybrid intelligent algorithm. A run of the hybrid intelligent algorithm (6000 cycles in simulation, 2000 training data in NN, 1500 generations in GA) shows that the optimal solution is

$$(x_1, x_2, x_3) = (0.9168, 0.0670, 0.0161)$$

with objective value $\xi_{VaR}(0.95) \approx 2.82$.

6 Conclusions

In this paper, value-at-risk is used as the measure of risk and the new credibilistic mean-VaR models in fuzzy environment are proposed based on credibility theory. Furthermore, a kind of hybrid intelligent algorithm is given to show how to solve the credibilistic mean-VaR model. Finally, some numerical experiments are provided to illustrate the effectiveness of the proposed algorithm.

Acknowledgements

This work is supported by the National Natural Science Foundation (Grant No.70671050), the major research program (Grant No.Z20082701) of Hubei Provincial Department of Education, China.

References

1. Alexander, G.J., Baptista, A.M.: Economic implications of using a mean-VaR model for portfolio selection: A comparison with mean-variance analysis. Journal of Economic Dynamic & Control 26, 1159–1193 (2002)
2. Choudhry, M.: An Introduction to Value-at-Risk, 4th edn. John Wiley, Chichester (2006)
3. Deng, X.T., Li, X.F., Wang, S.Y.: A minimax portfolio selection strategy with equilibrium. European Journal of Operational Research 166, 278–292 (2005)
4. Dong, W., Peng, J.: Credibilistic Risk Optimization Models and Algorithms. In: Proceedings of 2009 International Conference on Computational Intelligence and Natural Computing(CINC 2009), Wuhan, China, June 6-7, pp. 378–384 (2009)
5. Duffie, D., Pan, J.: An overview of value at risk. Journal of Derivatives 4, 7–49 (1997)
6. Huang, X.X.: Fuzzy chance-constrained portfolio selection. Applied Mathematics and Computation 177, 500–507 (2006)
7. Kaplanski, G., Kroll, Y.: VaR risk measures vs traditional risk measures: An analysis and survey. Journal of Derivatives 4, 7–49 (1997)
8. Kast, R., Luciano, E.; Peccati, L.: VaR and Optimization. In: 2nd International Workshop on Preferences and Decisions, Trento (1998)
9. Liu, B.: Uncertainty Theory, 2nd edn. Springer, Berlin (2007)

10. Liu, B.: Theory and Practice of Uncertain Programming. Springer, Berlin (2008)
11. Liu, B., Liu, Y.K.: Expected value of fuzzy variable and fuzzy expected value models. IEEE Transactions on Fuzzy Systems 10(4), 445–450 (2002)
12. Liu, B.: Minimax chance constrained programming models for fuzzy decision systems. Information Sciences 112(1-4), 25–38 (1998)
13. Liu, Y.K., Gao, J.: The independence of fuzzy variables in credibility theory and its applications. International Journal of Uncertainty, Fuzziness & Knowledge-Based Systems 19, 1–19 (2007)
14. Markovitz, H.: Portfolio selection. Journal of Finance 8, 77–91 (1952)
15. Morgan, J.P.: RiskMetricsTM–Technical Document, 4th edn. Morgan Guaranty Trust Companies, Inc., New York (1996)
16. Peng, J.: Measuring fuzzy risk with credibilistic value at risk. In: Proceedings of the Third International Conference on Innovative Computing, Information and Control (ICICIC 2008), Dalian, China, pp. 718–721 (2008)
17. Peng, J., Liu, B.: Some properties of optimistic and pessimistic values of fuzzy variables. In: Proceedings of the Tenth IEEE International Conference on Fuzzy Systems, vol. 2, pp. 292–295 (2004)
18. Zadeh, L.A.: Fuzzy sets as a basis for a theory of possibility. Fuzzy Sets and Systems 1, 3–28 (1978)

MOEA-Based Fuzzy Control for Seismically Excited Structures

Xiang-liang Ning[1], Ping Tan[2], and Fu-lin Zhou[2]

[1] Harbin Institute of Technology Shenzhen Graduate School, Shenzhen 518055, china
[2] Guangdong Key Laboratory of Earthquake Engineering & Applied Technique,
Guangzhou 510405, china

Abstract. To guarantee the safety and functionality of structures simultaneously at different levels of seismic loadings, this paper proposes a multi-objective switching fuzzy control (MOSFC) strategy. MOSFC functions as a trigger with two control states considered. When the structure is at the state of linear, the main objection of control is the peak acceleration. On the other hand, once the nonlinear appears, the control of peak inter-storey drift is the main objection. Multi-objective genetic algorithm, NSGA-II, is employed for optimizing the fuzzy control rules. A scaled model of a six-storey building with two MR dampers installed at the two bottom floors is simulated here. Linear and Nonlinear numerical simulations demonstrate the effectiveness and robustness.

Keywords: Multi-objective genetic algorithm; fuzzy control; robustness.

1 Introduction

In recent years, genetic algorithm (GA) has been adopted in optimizing the fuzzy controller (FC) to determine the commanded voltage of MR dampers, in which the control performances are related to the objective function of GA, through operations of selection, crossover and mutation, the objective function will be stable after several runs, and then the global optimal fuzzy controller is obtained [1, 2]. In terms of control performance, displacement (relative to the ground), inter-storey drift and acceleration are most often considered. Displacement and inter-storey drift present the safety of the structure when large earthquake occurs. Acceleration is also important for occupant comfort and reducing non-structural damage when wind and small earthquake occurs. Then how to provide a reasonable balance of reduction for all considered performances under different loading levels is worth studying.

In this paper, an approach for a multi-objective optimal design of fuzzy controller is discussed. Three performances indices are considered synchronously to optimize the control rules of fuzzy controller and voltage applied on MR dampers, which necessitates employment of a multi-objective optimization algorithm-NSGA-II proposed by Srinivas and Deb et al [3, 4]. The procedure has been tested for a six-storey scaled model with MR dampers developed by Jansen and Dyke [5].

Z. Cai et al. (Eds.): ISICA 2009, CCIS 51, pp. 320–328, 2009.

2 Integration of Fuzzy Controller and NSGA-II

2.1 Definition of Control Performance Indices

Three performance indices are taken into account herein, which are defined as follows:

$$J_1 = \max_j \left\{ \frac{\max_t |x_{j,controlled}|}{\max_t |x_{uncontrolled}|} \right\} \tag{1}$$

$$J_2 = \max_j \left\{ \frac{\max_t |\ddot{x}_{j,controlled}|}{\max_t |\ddot{x}_{uncontrolled}|} \right\} \tag{2}$$

$$J_3 = \max_j \left\{ \frac{\max_t |D_{j,controlled}|}{\max_t |D_{uncontrolled}|} \right\} \tag{3}$$

where $\max_t |x_{j,controlled}|$, $\max_t |\ddot{x}_{j,controlled}|$ and $\max_t |D_{j,controlled}|$ are the maximum relative displacement, absolute acceleration and inter-storey drift of the jth floor over the entire response, respectively. $\max_t |x_{uncontrolled}|$, $\max_t |\ddot{x}_{uncontrolled}|$ and $\max_t |D_{uncontrolled}|$ denote the uncontrolled maximum relative displacement, absolute acceleration and inter-storey drift of the structure, respectively. The problem of minimizing the objective function vector (J_1, J_2, J_3) simultaneously (i.e., $\min(J_1, J_2, J_3)$) are turned into employ a multi-objective optimization procedure NSGA-II.

2.2 Multi-Objective Switching Fuzzy Control Strategy

To describe the MOSFC strategy concisely for the selected scaled model, Fig. 1 is employed. Only absolute accelerations of the top two floors are chosen as inputs of the MOSFC. To get the displacement and acceleration of every floor, the prediction module of MOSFC is used to predict the information including input exciting and responses of the structure, and neural network can deal with this problem successfully [6], but this is not the main topic here.

The judge the responses module acts as a trigger: when the prediction seismic loadings and responses are both small, the best control performance is that the safety and the functionality should be satisfied simultaneously, then we should select the fuzzy controller that satisfies this control performance from pareto optimal set; once the magnitude of seismic is large, we have to switch the control rules and voltage to insure the safety of the structure at first, then minimize other objectives. We simplify those switching rules to two levels as follows:

If $\max_{Prediction} |D_{controlled}| < D_c$, the structure is linear, we choose the rules that satisfy $J_1 < 1, J_3 < 1$ and J_2 the minimum.

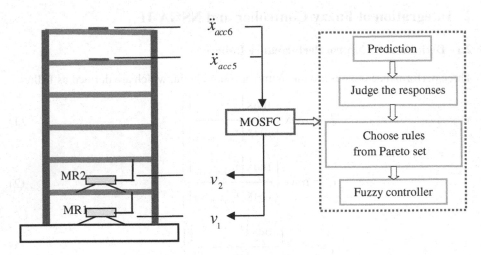

Fig. 1. Illustration of model and controller

Once $\max\limits_{\Pr ediction} \left|D_{controlled}\right| >= D_c$, nonlinear behavior of structure appears, we choose the rules that satisfy $J_1 < 1$, $J_2 < 1$ and J_3 the minimum.

in which $\max\limits_{\Pr ediction} \left|D_{controlled}\right|$ is the prediction value of the peak inter-storey drift. D_c is the critical value of the peak inter-storey drift which insure the structure is linear.

The FC has been designed using five membership functions for each of the input variable (accelerations of 5th and 6th floor) and seven membership functions for the output variable (voltage applied on the two MR dampers). The normal membership functions of input and output variables have been shown in Fig. 2.

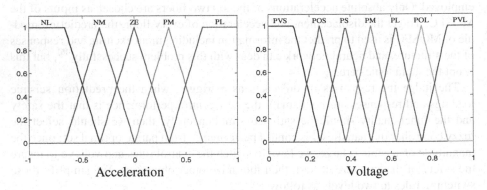

Fig. 2. Membership functions of input and output

2.3 Multi-Objective Optimization Algorithm-NSGA-II

In the current study, a non-dominated sorting genetic algorithm (NSGA-II) is employed to produce a pareto optimal set or pareto optimal front, with which three objectives described by Eq.(1)~(3) can be considered simultaneously and more choice are provided for the decision maker.

The flow chart of NSGA-II is shown in Fig. 3. At the beginning, the population is initialized as usual GA. The initialized population with N individuals is sorted based on non-domination into each front according to the values of objection. The first front being completely non-dominant set in the current population and the second front being dominated by the individuals in the first front only and other fronts are determined in the same way. Individuals in first front are given a fitness value of 1 and individuals in second are assigned fitness value as 2 and so on, as shown in Fig. 4. In addition to fitness value, a new parameter called crowding distance is calculated for each individual. The crowding distance is a measure of how close an individual is to its neighbors. Large average crowding distance will result in better diversity in the population. An individual is selected in the rank is lesser than the other or if crowding distance is greater than the other, this is the main difference between the conventional GA and NSGA-II. Parents are selected from the population by using a binary tournament selection based on the rank and crowding distance. The selected population generates offspring from crossover

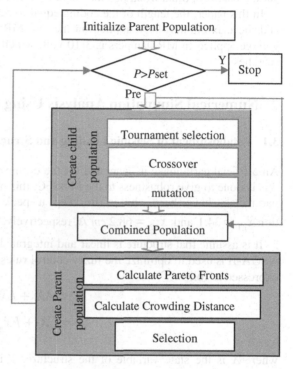

Fig. 3. Flow chart of NSGA-II

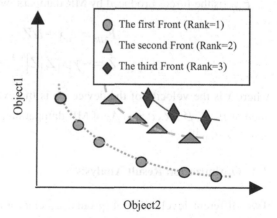

Fig. 4. Pareto curve with sorted rank

and mutation operators. Then the population with the current population and current offspring (called combined population in Fig. 3) is sorted again based on non-domination and only the best N individuals are selected based on the rank and crowding distance. While the number of calculated generation P is larger than the critical number Pset, the search is terminated. The final purpose of this procedure is to get the pareto-optimal front, i.e., the curve with Rank=1 shown in Fig.4.

In this paper, the length of the coding equal to 52, including 50 fuzzy control rules and the maximum voltage applied on the two MR dampers. Assuming the range of voltage applied in MR dampers is 3-10 volt, which is different from the previous researches.

3   Numerical Simulation Analysis Using Optimization Method

3.1   Establishment of Seismic Loading and Structure-Damper Model

An artificial earthquake is generated for the optimization of MOSFC using NSGA-II, this is done to give robustness to the MOSFC, this process is described in [7]. And the parameters have been chosen to keep a peak value of the ground acceleration $\ddot{x}_{g1} = 34.1$ and $\ddot{x}_{g2} = 68.2 \; cm^2/s$, respectively.

It is assume that structure is linear and integrated with nonlinear MR damper when NSGA-II is used to optimize the fuzzy control rules and voltage. The state equation is expressed as follow:

$$\dot{X} = AX + E\ddot{x}_g + BF_{MR}$$
$$Y = CX + F\ddot{x}_g + DF_{MR}$$

(4)

where X is the state variable of the structure, Y is the regulated output, $\ddot{x}_g$ is the seismic loading. A,E,B,C,F,D are matrices with proper dimensions.

F_{MR} is the forces produced by MR dampers, which can be expressed as follow [8]:

$$F_{MR} = c_0\dot{x} + \alpha Z$$
$$\dot{Z} = -\gamma|\dot{x}|Z|Z|^{n-1} - \beta\dot{x}|z|^n + A_0\dot{x}$$

(5)

where $\dot{x}$ is the velocity of the device; z is the evolutionary variable. The parameters such as $n, \gamma, \beta, \alpha, c_0$ and A_0 of MR dampers and the parameters of structure are the same as Yan [1].

3.2   Optimization Result Analysis

Two different levels of peak ground accelerations, $\ddot{x}_{g2} = 34.1 \; cm/s^2$ (named case1) and $\ddot{x}_{g2} = 68.2 \; cm/s^2$ (named case2) are selected in this paper. Then two different optimization results are obtained with respect to these two levels because of the nonlinear behavior of MR dampers and fuzzy controller. The first three ranks of the solutions are plotted in Fig. 5, which shows well distributed solutions in the feasible space.

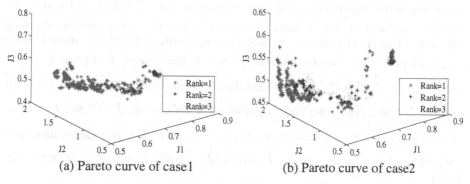

(a) Pareto curve of case1   (b) Pareto curve of case2

Fig. 5. The first three rank of the optimization result

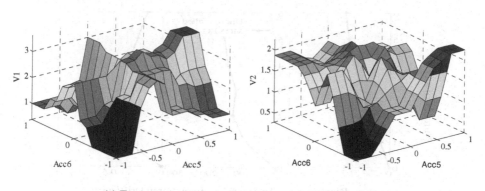

(a) Fuzzy control rule surfaces of case1 for MR1 and MR2

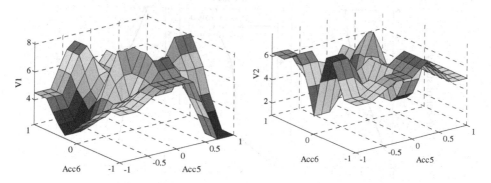

(b) Fuzzy control rule surfaces of case2 for MR1 and MR2

Fig. 6. Rule surface of FC

Fig. 6(a) show the fuzzy control rule surfaces of FIS(fuzzy inference system) chosen from Fig. 5(a) according to the acquirement of MOSFC (linear state, $J_1 < 1, J_3 < 1$ and J_2 the minimum) when $\ddot{x}_{g1} = 34.1\,cm/s^2$; Similarly, when $\ddot{x}_{g2} = 68.2\,cm/s^2$, according to the acquirement of MOSFC (nonlinear state, $J_1 < 1, J_2 < 1$ and J_3 the minimum), the final fuzzy control rule surfaces chosen from Fig. 5(b) are shown in Fig. 6(b). The envelop curves of peak response with and without MOSFC when $\ddot{x}_{g1} = 34.1\,cm^2/s$ are shown Fig.7(a), in which the control performance indices are $J_1 = 0.55$, $J_2 = 0.77$, $J_3 = 0.47$ and the maximum voltages V1=4volt, V2=3volt. When $\ddot{x}_{g2} = 68.2\,cm/s^2$, the control performance indices are $J_1 = 0.50$, $J_2 = 0.79$, $J_3 = 0.44$ and V1=9 volt, V2=10 volt(see Fig.7(b)). MOSFC performances better than the traditional passive on control ($J_1 = 0.73$, $J_2 = 0.89$, $J_3 = 0.65$) with V1=4 volt, V2=3 volt.

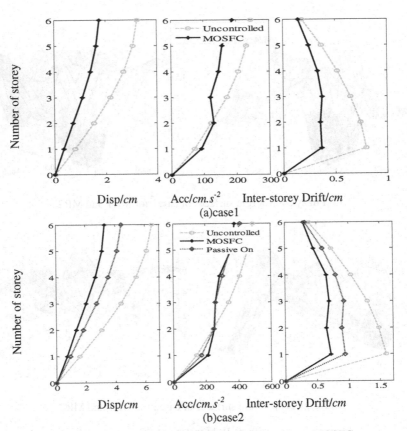

Fig. 7. Peak response of each floor with and without MOSFC

4 Robustness Test with Nonlinear Numerical Simulation

The simulation results presented above based on the assumption that the structure is linear, however, nonlinearities may occur when strong earthquake occurs, to simulate this process to some extent, nonlinear behavior of the structure should be considered. Four real earthquake ground motions with peak value $\ddot{x}_g = 68.2 \; cm/s^2$ are chosen for robustness test. The simulation results are shown in Table 1.

Comparing the results of the linear analysis with artificial wave in previous section, the control performances indices increase when nonlinear behavior of structure is taken into account, but MOSFC still decrease the peak responses significantly. The hysteresis loops of bottom two floors in the case of Chichi is shown in Fig. 8, it shows that the damage of the structure is mitigated significantly.

Table 1. Nonlinear numerical simulation results of robustness test

Earthquake	Control performance index		
	J_1	J_2	J_3
Artificial wave	0.75	0.91	0.80
N. Palm Springs	0.56	0.94	0.73
Chichi	0.68	1.10	0.74
El Centro	0.63	0.99	0.75
Kobe	0.68	0.87	0.71

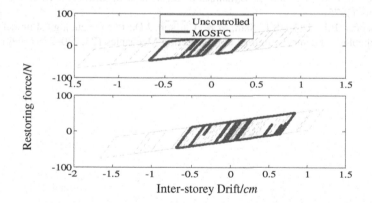

Fig. 8. Hysteresis loops with and without MOSFC

5 Conclusions

The numerical simulation results show that the multi-objective optimization tool, NSGA-II, which gives flexibility in the balance of all control performances (safety and functionality). The pareto optimal sets provide a reasonable balance of reduction for all control performances (peak displacement, inter-storey drift and acceleration) under different earthquake levels. Linear and Nonlinear numerical simulations demonstrate the effectiveness and robustness of MOSFC.

The shortcoming of this optimization process is time-consuming based on time-domain analysis, a fast and reliable method using NSGA-II should be further studied.

Acknowledgments. This research is supported by National Natural Science Foundation of China (Grant No. 50608021).

References

1. Yan, G., Zhou, L.: Integrated fuzzy and genetic algorithm for multi-objective control of structures using MR dampers. Journal of sound and vibration 296, 368–382 (2006)
2. David, A.S., Paul, N.R., Lin, P., et al.: GA-optimized fuzzy control of a large-scale building for seismic loads. Engineering structures 30, 436–449 (2007)
3. Srinivas, N., Deb, K.: Multi-objective optimization using non-dominated sorting in genetic algorithms. Evolutionary Computation 2, 221–248 (1994)
4. Deb, K., Pratap, A., Agarwal, S., Meyarivan, T.: A Fast Elitist Multi-objective Genetic Algorithm: NSGA-II. IEEE Transactions on Evolutionary Computation 6, 182–197 (2002)
5. Jansen, L.M., Dyke, S.J.: Semi-active control strategies for MR dampers: comparative study. Journal of Engineering Mechanics 126, 795–803 (2000)
6. Tani, A., Kawamura, H., Ryu, S.: Intelligent fuzzy control of building structure. Engineering Structures 20, 184–192 (1997)
7. Clough, R.W., Penzien, J.: Dynamics of Structures. McGraw-Hill Book Company, New York (1975)
8. Spencer, B.F., Dyke, S.J., Sain, M.K., Carlson, J.D.: Phenomenological model for magnetorheologcial dampers. Journal of Engineering Mechanics 123, 230–238 (1997)

A Hybrid E-Institution Model for VOs

Youming Zhou[1,2] and Ji Gao[1,*]

[1] Zhejiang University, Department of Artificial Intelligence, Hangzhou, 310027, China
[2] Huzhou Vocational Technical College, Department of computer science, Huzhou, 313000
monitorstudent@126.com, gaoji1@zju.edu.cn

Abstract. In order to pursue their objectives, the groups of agents seem to be well organized according to predefined structures and unambiguously defined concepts. At the same time, the interaction presents some dynamic aspects, that is, the virtual organizations (VO) undergo a life cycle from the objectives formation to the task division, task allocation, plans formation, negotiations, contracts formation, and the final VO dissolvement or evolvement under exceptions. Although E-institutions provide facilitation to the former issues, the facilitation of VO in different stages is still blurred. Hence, this paper proposes a hybrid E-institution model including the static organization structure aspect and the dynamic aspect, provide assistance to the agent interactions. On the one hand, the E-institutions are modelled statically to make the agent cooperation trustable and predictable in terms of ontologies, behavior norms, and organization structure. On the other hand, the E-institutions keep repositories of instantiated (dynamic) information, provide services to facilitate the dynamic VO in different stages. Also, this paper presents explicitly formal descriptions of the static organization structure, dynamic information and institutional services to different VO stages.

1 Introduction

Organisation-oriented approaches to the formation of multi-agent systems assume that a community of agents form a Virtual Organisation. Its purpose is to facilitate resource sharing and problem solving among software and/or human agents [1], [2]. A careful study will show there are some kinds of relations between agents while they interact. In order to pursue their objectives, the groups of agents seem to be well organized according to predefined structures and unambiguously defined concepts. At the same time, the interaction presents some dynamic aspects, that is, the VOs undergo a life cycle from the objectives formation to the task division, task allocation, plans formation, negotiations, contracts formation, and the final VO dissolvement or evolvement under exceptions. E-institutions should provide facilitation to the former issues in different VO stages. But how E-institutions facilitate the VO in different stages is still

* Youming Zhou, born in 1972, doctoral student of Zhejiang University, major in norm oriented regulation in MAS and automatic VO; Ji Gao, born in 1946, doctoral tutor of Zhejiang University, major in artificial intelligence. This subject is Supported by National Natural Science Foundation of China (60775029), 863 project(2007AA01Z187), 973 project(2003CB317005).

Z. Cai et al. (Eds.): ISICA 2009, CCIS 51, pp. 329–343, 2009.

blurred. To do that, E-institutions, We believe, should comprise these elements: (1) Ontologies that define the semantic of the elements of E-institutions; (2) roles that enable to abstract from the specific individuals; (3) Organization structures that define the relation between roles; (4) norms that regulate the interaction; (5)institutional role services, which facilitate the interaction, and domain role services, which are the external agents' capabilities to pursue the system goals; (6) dynamic information, produced by the formation, operation and evolvement of VO, which in return guides and facilitates the formation, operation and evolvement. Hence, a hybrid model for E-institutions is proposed in this paper to facilitate the VOs. We believe that a hybrid model should comprise meta-information, that is, not instantiated information as well as instantiated information. Meta-information is responsible for the static structure of multi-agent system (MAS), whereas instantiated information is responsible for dynamic nature of MAS. Meta-information includes such elements as contract templates, procedure templates, meta-norms, ontologies, roles. Instantiated information includes such elements as instantiated contracts, instantiated norms, and instantiated procedure templates, common goals, agents. Meta-information conceptualizes the more general framework of an Electronic Institution, providing a system of reference which the instantiated information can base on. The operation of MAS produces the instantiated information and the instantiated information, in return, guides and facilitates the operation. This paper presents explicitly formal descriptions of the static organization structure, dynamic information and institutional services to different VO stages.

2   The Hybrid Model

The purpose of the E-institution is to facilitate the agents' interaction, and to facilitate the system goal achievement while agents pursue their respective interests. The descriptions of the E-institutions should include the static elements, the dynamic elements, and institutional services and domain services. Under the internet environment, different domain-dependent vocabulary may be used by different business entities (heterogeneous agents), and as such, a common institutional ontology must be used. As in human society, roles contribute to the global goal of the system, and as such, each role should be marked with certain capabilities, burdened with certain norms, engage in certain interactions, have relations with other roles. As far as capabilities are concerned, roles should be marked with abstract services (role services). The reason we use abstract services is that they should be abstract from specific services realized by the individual agents. Procedure templates are roles' abstract interaction procedures from which the individual concrete interaction plans can be derived. E-institutions are the virtual places to provide trust among parties in terms of norms when they know very little about each other. The Meta-norms deal with roles and procedure templates, instantiated norms deal with agents and their concrete interaction plans. The communication acts (CA), shared communication primitives of the agent communication languages, are used by roles to give supports to the Procedure templates, individual agents use message, instantiated CAs, to communicate to support concrete interaction plans. Thus, the hybrid institution model can be defined as a tuple:

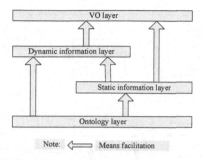

Fig. 1. E-institution architecture

- EI = < Ontology, Domainknowledge, Nego-proco, AuthFrole, MatchFrole, Ar-bitrFrole, MoniFrole, Domain-roles, Meta-norms, Concepts, FacilitateRservices, DomainRservices, Tasks, Proc-templs, Contract-templs, CAs, Repu-Info, History, Report, instan-Domainknow, Nego-proc, AuthFagent, MatchFagent, ArbitrFagent, MoniFagent, Domain-agents, instan-norms, instan-Concepts, FacilitateAservices, DomainAservices, Motivations, Proc-plan, Concrete-contract, Message, in-stan-RepuInfo, instan-History, instan-Report, Initiating, Role-relating, Referring, Regulating, Supporting, Negotiating, Registering >.

In this tuple, Ontology, the semantic layer, is the set of definitions and relations of the elements in the static layer including Domainknowledge, Nego-proco, role (AuthFrole, MatchFrole, ArbitrFrole, MoniFrole, Domain-roles), Meta-norms, Con-cepts, roleservice (FacilitateRservices, DomainRservices), Tasks, Proc-templs, Con-tract-templs and CAs, Repu-Info, History, and Report, see Figure 2 for the relations of the elements in the static layer (note: we do not mean to design these elements in UML, but do express the relation of these elements in UML). And instan-Domainknow, Nego-proc, AuthFagent, MatchFagent, ArbitrFagent, MoniFagent, Domain-agents, instan-norms, instan-Concepts, FacilitateAservices, DomainAservices, motivations, Proc-plan, Concrete-contract and Message, instan-RepuInfo, instan-History, in-stan-Report, which are in the dynamic layer, are the instantiations of Domainknowl-edge, Nego-proco, AuthFrole, MatchFrole, ArbitrFrole, MoniFrole, Domain-roles, Meta-norms, Concepts, FacilitateRservices, DomainRservices, Tasks, Proc-templs, Contract-templs, CAs, Repu-Info, History, and Report, respectively. Thus, the archi-tecture of E-institution can be depicted in Figure 1.

In this tuple, Initiating, Role-relating, Referring, Regulating, Supporting, Negoti-ating, registering can be defined as:

- Initiating: Domainknowledge → instan-Domainknow, F-roles → F-agents, Tasks → Motivations where → means 'result of instantiation', F-roles include AuthFrole, MatchFrole, ArbitrFrole, and MoniFrole, F-agents include AuthFagent, MatchFagent, ArbitrFagent, and MoniFagent,

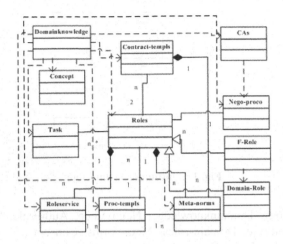

Fig. 2. The relations of some EI static elements

- Role-relating: Facilitating (F–roles, domain-roles) ∪ Tasks (domain-roles) ∪ Proc-templs(domain-roles) where domain-roles is a sub set of Domain-roles, Facilitating (F–roles, domain-roles) means F– roles facilitate the domain- roles, Tasks (domain- roles) means through task decompositions domain-roles take on sub tasks, contributing to the whole task, Proc-templs(domain-roles) means domain-roles participate in one or more procedure templates to finish one or more tasks,
- Referring: relating (Task, subtasks, Proc-templs) which means the task decomposer should refer to the ready Proc-templs, making the best of the ready role relations, while decomposing asks into subtasks,
- Referring: relating (Task, subtasks, Proc-templs) which means the task decomposer should refer to the ready Proc-templs, making the best of the ready role relations, while decomposing asks into subtasks,
- Supporting: Support(Message, Proc-plan) ∪ Support(CAs, Proc-templs) which means agents send Message to fulfill their interacting Proc-plan, roles use the communication acts to support their interacting Proc-templs,
- Negotiating: Proc-templs→Proc-plan, Contract-templs→ Concrete-contracts which means the interacting agents use Proc-templs to form interaction Proc-plan, use Contract-templs to sign Concrete-contracts while negotiating,
- Registering: Domain-agents × Authority × Domain-roles → R-contracts ⊆ Concrete-contract which means domain agents apply for domain roles under the approval of the Authority, sign registering contracts, which are in a subset of Concrete-contract, to take up domain roles.

Domainknowledge in this tuple is used by roles (or agents) to fulfill their tasks or to make necessary inferences. Instan-Domainknow, instantiated domainknowledge, is used by agents. Domainknowledge comprises formulas and terms. Definition 1 and definition 2 are the definitions of formulas and terms respectively. Instan-Domainknow also comprises formulas and terms, but of which some formulas and terms are ground in the process of EI initiation or in the process of agent interaction. That is, there are no free valuables in some formulas and some terms.

- Definition 1 given function symbols Fun_D, identifier symbols Id_D (also called constants), and a countably infinite set of variables Var_D in domain D, $Term_D$ denotes the set of terms, terms are defined inductively on the functions, identifiers and variables, as: $\forall i \in Id_D, i \in Term_D, \forall x \in Var_D, x \in Term_D. \forall t_1, ..., t_n \in Term_D, \forall f \in Func_D, f(t_1,...,t_n) \in Term_D.$
- Definition 2 given predicate symbols $Pred_D$, function symbols Fun_D, identifier symbols Id_D (also called constants), and a countably infinite set of variables Var_D in domain D, the formulas set F_D can be defined inductively, as: If $p \in Pred_D$ of arity n, and $t_1, ..., t_n \in Term_D$, then $p(t_1, ..., t_n) \in F_D$, if $t_1, t_2 \in Term_D$, then $t_1 = t_2 \in F_D$, if $p \in F_D$, then $\neg p \in F_D$, if $p, q \in F_D$, then $p \wedge q \in F_D$, if $p \in F_D$, then $\forall x(p) \in F_D$.

Nego-proco in this tuple is the kinds of negotiation protocols supported by CAs, Nego- proc is the kinds of concrete negotiation processes supported by Message sent by agents. Take the contract net protocol (CNP) for example, CNP can be defined as a tuple:

- CNP= < INVITEBIDDING, BIDDING, SUCCESSFULLBIDDING, CONTRACTING > where INVITEBIDDING is defined as: the auctioneer contacts the participants using CAs, BIDDING is defined as: the participants bid for the auction, SUCCESSFULLBIDDING is defined as: only one participant successfully bids for the auction, CONTRACTING is defined as: the successful participant and the auctioneer sign contracts after the successful bidding.

Role (in this tuple includes AuthFrole, MatchFrole, ArbitrFrole, MoniFrole, Domain-roles) is defined as a tuple:

- Role= < Rid, Roleserviceset, Rolenormset > where Rid is the role identification, Roleserviceset is role service set, if the role is Domain-roles, this element is DomainRservices, else this element is FacilitateRservices, Rolenormset is the Meta-norms, the normative burdens on the role.

AuthFrole, MatchFrole, ArbitrFrole, MoniFrole are the Authority facilitation role, Matchmaker facilitation role, Arbitrator facilitation role, Monitor facilitation role respectively. And AuthFagent, MatchFagent, ArbitrFagent, MoniFagent are the corresponding agents.

Meta-norms are defined as: Meta-norms= $OB_{Rid}(\rho \leq \delta \mid \sigma)$| $FB_{Rid}(\rho \leq \delta \mid \sigma)$| $PM_{Rid}(\rho \leq \delta \mid \sigma)$ where Rid is the role identification, OB is the obligation, FB is the forbiding, PM is the permit, σ is the triggering conditions, δ is the deadline, and ρ is the goal states.

Instan-norms have the same form as that of Meta-norms, but have a slight difference in that Aid, agent identification, replaces the Rid, ρ, δ, and σ are ground whereas in Meta-norms, they are not, instan-norms are instant, that is, as long as ρ and δ are true, instan-norms are no longer valid, whereas Meta-norms are not, they are stable.

Different domain concepts are related through the concept taxonomy. The definitions of concepts and the concept taxonomy are:

ConceptTaxonomy = 'ConceptTaxonomy (' **ConceptTaxonomyN {concept}**⁺ **TOntologyAlias** ')'

concept= 'concept ('**conceptN {superconcept}**⁺ **constraincondition { Synony-mousTerm }**⁺ ')' where ConceptTaxonomyN is the name of concept taxonomy system. TontologyAlias is the alias of the concept taxonomy system. Superconcept is the super class of the concept. SynonymousTerm is the synonymous term for this concept. conceptN is the name of this concept.

Instan-Concepts have the same form as that of concepts, but have a slight difference in that some sockets defined in constraincondition are instantiated with some values.

Role services (in this tuple include FacilitateRservices and DomainRservices) are defined as:

- Roleservices = { 'service ('name parameter output precondition postcondition context ')' }⁺

  parameter = { 'parameter ('**name type constraint** ')'}⁺

  output = { 'output ('name type constraint ')'}⁺

  context = { **contextaspect**}⁺

  contextaspect = 'contextaspect('contextaspectN classificationmethodN categoryN ')'

  contextaspectN = GeopoliticalRegion | BusinessCategory | ProvisionCategory

where parameter is the service parameter, Constraint is the constraint of parameters, classificationmethodN is the classification method name, categoryN is the category name, output is the output type of the service, precondition, formulas defined in Do-mainknowledge, is conditions before using this service, postcondition, formulas de-fined in Domainknowledge, is the goal states after using the service.

The specific agent service has the same form as that of the role service, but with the parameter and precondition ground.

Tasks in this tuple are the problems to be solved. To solve a task, one role service or several role services (defined as Proc-templs) are needed. Tasks are defined as:

- Tasks = 'task ('role parameter output precondition postcondition ')'

  parameter = { 'parameter (' **name type constraint** ')'}⁺

  output = { 'output (' **name type constraint** ')'}⁺

where parameter is the task parameter, Constraint is the constraint of parameters, output is the output type of the task, precondition, formulas defined in Do-mainknowledge, is conditions before solving this task, postcondition, formulas defined in Domainknowledge, is the goal states after solving this task, role, depending on others to solve the tasks, is the liable for the task.

Motivations, created by agents or by users, in this tuple are VO opportunities that motivate the VO formation. Motivations have the same form as that of the tasks, but with the parameter and precondition ground.

Proc-templs are compound role services used to solve the tasks that a single role service can not solve. The compound role services can be provided by one or several roles. Proc-templs can be defined as:

- Proc-templs = < precondition, postcondition, roles, roleservices, Sequence, Con-currence, input, output, Meta-norms, Rawplan > where precondition, formulas defined in Domainknowledge, is conditions before using this compound service, postcondition, formulas defined in Domainknowledge, is the goal states after the using the compound service, roleservices and roles are the sub services of this service and the corresponding providers respectively, Sequence, Concurrence are choreography operators used to sequently, or concurrently schedule the roleservices, input, output are the input, output parameters for the compound role service, Meta-norms are used to regulate the compound role service, the Rawplan is the raw scheduling of the compound service.

Proc-plan is the specific scheduling of the Proc-templs. Proc-plan can be defined as:

- < Proc-plan >::={<Plan-Steps>|(Loop<Plan-Steps>)}$^+$

  <Plan-Steps>::={(←Return<Condition>)|(←<Service-Set>[<Condition>])|

  (or{(←<Service-Set>[<Condition>])}$^+$)}$^+$

  <Service-Set>::=<agentService>|(({Sequence|Concurrence}{(←<agentService>

  [<Condition>])}$^+$)

  <Condition>::=<Conditionexpression>

  <agentService>::=(<name>{<parametervalues>}*)

where agentService is provided by the corresponding agent taking up the corresponding role(s) of the corresponding procedure template.

Contracts are formalizations of business commitments among a group of agents, which make the agents interaction behaviors foreseeable, and comprise a set of applicable norms. In order to formalize the formation of contracts, a set of contract templates, Contract-templs, are needed. The contract templates include the contract header, and the contract body. The contract header includes such information as contract type, which is optional, who sign the contract, when the contract is signed, the contract type related contract information, the contract ending situation, which is a set of formulas, and the contract body may include one or more Meta-norms. The contract templates can be defined as:

- < contract-template >::= < contract-header > < contract- body >

  < contract-header >::= < contract- type > < type- info > < when > < who >

  <ending- situation >

  < contract-body >::= {< Meta-norm >}$^+$

The form of Concrete- contract has the same form as that of Contract- templs, but after negotiation, it includes specific elements including, in contract header, the specific contract type, the specific type- info, the specific time, the specific agents, the specific ending situation, and in contract body, the specific instan-norms.

The CAs are communication acts, the communication primitives, which are building blocks of agent communication languages. The CAs are defined as:

- CA (Rid$_1$, Rid$_2$, content) where Rid$_1$, Rid$_2$ are sending role id and the receiving role id respectively, content is the information to be sent, which is a formula. The basic communication acts include request, commit, inform, and declare.

Message has the same form as that of CAs, but has differences in that Aid, agent identification replaces the Rid, the content in Message is ground whereas, in CAs, it is not.

Repu-Info is the individual reputation information, and can be defined as:

- Repu-Info='Repu-Info ('**Who Reputationdeg**')'
  Reputationdeg=' Reputationdeg ('**best|good|general|bad**')'

where Who means the subject whose reputation is to be concerned, Reputationdeg is the reputation degree.

Instan-RepuInfo is the instantiated reputation information.

Report is the contract performance information including Succfulstate, contracts successfully performed, and Violatingstate, contracts violated, and can be defined as:

- Report=' Report(' **Contract Who State** ')"
  State=' State ('Succfulstate| Violatingstate')'

where Contract is the contract that is violated, Who is the subject who violate the contract.

Instan-Report is the instantiated report.

History is the contract performance history information, can be defined as:

- History=' History ('**Time Contract Who State** ')' where Time is the time when Who perform the Contract.
  Instan-History is the instantiated history.

3 Facilitation to VO

VOs are interesting topics in academic circles. VOs consist of consortiums defining cooperation efforts between agents, and involve specific interactions during a certain time frame. VO agreements and their operation are formalized through contracts. In a VO setting, agents may represent different business units or enterprises, which come together to address new market opportunities by combining skills, resources, risks and finances no partner can alone fulfill. The E-institutions, VO environments, should provide facilitation for VOs in: (1) VO formation and operation (2) VO evolvement.

The VO formation and operation includes several stages: (1) motivation formation, (2) goal decomposition and allocation, (3) raw VO planning, (4) partners search and selection, (5) negotiation, (6) specific VO planning, (7) contracting, (8) VO operation. Thus, E-institutions should provide facilitation for the VO formation and operation in different stages. See Figure 3.

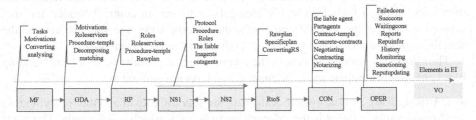

Fig. 3. The VO formation and operation

The first stage is defined as: mf=< Tasks, motivations, converting, analysing >. In this tuple, the motivations motivate the VO formation and are generated in several ways. First, the motivations, designed by the system designer as the system goal, may come from the E-institution initialization. Second, the user can present tasks, which are converted to motivations, to the system using an interface. Third, agents in the system can generate motivations using their knowledge. In this tuple, the E-institution provides static information Tasks, stores dynamic information motivations, provides the institutional services converting by the institutional role matchmaker to convert the tasks to motivations according to the requirements of the liable of the tasks, and provides institutional service feasibility analysing by the matchmaker to analyse the feasibility of the tasks.

The second stage can be defined as: gda=< motivations, subgoals, roleservices, Proc-templs, serviceset, $mapping_1$, $mapping_2$, $mapping_3$, decomposing > where

- $mapping_1$: motivations→roleservices, if the motivation in the set motivations can be found one roleservice in the set roleservices through the matching service of the matchmaker,
- $mapping_2$: motivations→Proc-templs, if the motivation in the set motivations can be found one procedure template in the set Proc-templs through the matching service of the matchmaker,
- decomposing: motivations→subgoals, provided by the matchmaker, that is, if the motivation can not be found a single roleservice or procedure template, the motivation is decomposed into subgoals,
- $mapping_3$: motivations(subgoals) →serviceset($2^{roleservices \cup Proc\text{-}templs}$), after motivation decomposition, the motivation can be found several roleservices or procedure templates through the matching.

The third stage is to roughly design the role level scheduling plan. The raw plan is based on the motivations or the relation of the subgoals of the motivations. This stage can be defined as a tuple: rp=< Roles, Roleservices, Proctempls, Rplans > where Roleservices and Roles are the services and the corresponding providers respectively, Proctempls are the procedure templates, Plans are raw plans.

According to $mapping_1$, the raw plan can be designed as:

- < raw-plan>::=←< Role, Roleservice><Precondition> where Role is responsible for the realization of the motivation through the using of its Roleservice, the definition of Precondition is the same as that of role service.

According to $mapping_2$, the raw plan can be designed as:

- < raw-plan >::={<Plan-Steps>|(Loop<Plan-Steps>)}$^+$
  <Plan-Steps>::={ (←<Service-Set>[<Condition>])|(or{(←<Service-Set> [<Condition>])}$^+$)}$^+$
  <Service-Set>::=<Role, Roleservice >|(({Sequence| Concurrence } {(← < Role, Roleservice > [< Condition>])}$^+$)
  <Condition>::=<Conditionexpression>

where each Role participates in the procedure template.

According to mapping$_3$, the raw plan can be designed as:

- < raw-plan >::={<Plan-Steps>|(Loop<Plan-Steps>)}$^+$
  <Plan-Steps>::={ (←<Service-Set>[<Condition>])|
    (or{(←<Service-Set>[<Condition>])}$^+$)}$^+$
  <Service-Set>::=<service >|(({Sequence| Concurrence }
    {(← < service > [< Condition>])}$^+$)
  <Condition>::=<Conditionexpression>
  <service >::= <Role, Roleservice >|< Proc-templs>

where Proc-templs is defined in E-institutions.

In the third stage, the motivations or subgoals have dispatched to the roles. In our view, a role may be taken up by several agents during the process of the E-institution register phase. The liable agent M for the initial motivation should negotiate with these agents role by role and select the best partner for each role. M can also recruit specific agents outside the E-institution to take up a certain role. Thus, stage 4 and 5 can be depicted as a tuple:

- Ns=< M, Protocol, Procedure, Policy, Roles, inagents, outagents, bestagents > where M is the liable for the motivation, Protocol is the select protocol for the negotiation, Procedure is the specific negotiation procedure selected for negotiation, based on Protocol selected, Policy is the negotiation policy, Roles are participating roles for the motivation, inagents are the agents, each take up a certain role of Roles, outagents are the recruited agents, bestagents are the final selected agents, each is responsible for a certain role. The focus of attention is the Policy, which is part of the Protocol. Take CNP for example, Policy includes the bidding policy, which decides which agents are permitted to receive the bidding document, the policy of submitting a bid, which decides whether to submit a bid or not, successful bid policy, through which the liable considers the submitter's credibility, capability etc.

After the stages 4 and 5, specific agents are selected for the motivation or subgoals. Then the specific VO planning, stage 6, can be defined as: RtoS=<Rawp, Specificp, ConvertingRS> where Rawp is the raw plans, Specificp is the specific plans, ConvertingRS: Rawp ×AuthFrole →Specificp which means the AuthFrole converts Rawp to Specificp. According to mapping$_1$, mapping$_2$, mapping$_3$,the specific plan including specific-plan$_1$, specific-plan$_2$, specific-plan$_3$, can be designed as:

- <specific-plan$_1$>::=←< agent, agentervice><Precondition> where the agent is responsible for the realization of the motivation through the using of its service, agentervice, the definition of Precondition is the same as that of role service, but are ground.

According to mapping$_2$, the specific plan can be designed as:

- < specific – plan$_2$ >::={<Plan-Steps>|(Loop<Plan-Steps>)}$^+$
  <Plan-Steps>::={ (←<Service-Set>[<Condition>])|
    (or{(←<Service-Set>[<Condition>])}$^+$)}$^+$
  <Service-Set>::=< agent, agent service >|(({Sequence| Concurrence }
    {(← < agent, agentservice > [< Condition>])}$^+$)
  <Condition>::=<Conditionexpression>

where agentService is provided by the corresponding agent taking up the corresponding role(s) of the corresponding procedure template.

According to mapping$_3$, the specific plan can be designed as:

- < specific– plan$_3$ >::={<Plan-Steps>|(Loop<Plan-Steps>)}$^+$
  <Plan-Steps>::={ (←<Service-Set>[<Condition>])|
  (or{(←<Service-Set> [<Condition>])}$^+$)}$^+$
  <Service-Set>::=<service >|(({Sequence| Concurrence }
  {(← < service > [< Condition>])}$^+$)
  <Condition>::=<Conditionexpression>
  <service >::= < agent, agentservice >|< Proc-plan >

where Pro-plan has the same definition of E-institution.

After stage6, each pair of the liable and the partner signs a contract. The signed contracts form a contract set. Each contract should be negotiated according to the corresponding contract template. The stage can be defined as:

- Con=< M, Partagents, Contract-templs, Concrete-contracts, Partialorder, Negotiating, Contracting, Notarizing > where M is the liable agent, Partagents are the agents participating in the contracting, Contract-templs are the contract templates used for contracting, Concrete- contracts are the specific contracts signed, Partialorder are the partial performance order of the Concrete-contracts, Negotiating are contract item negotiation such as price, deadline negotiation, Contracting: M × Partagents × Contract-templs → Concrete-contracts which means each pair of the liable and the partner signs a contract, using a certain kind of contract template, notarizing: Arbitrator × Concrete-contracts → Concrete-contracts which means under the Arbitrator's notarization, the Concrete-contracts become effective.

The last stage is the VO operation. After the contracts are signed, agents perform the contract clauses. The stage can be defined as:

- Oper=< Concrete-contracts, Failedcons, Succcons, Waitingcons, Inperformingcons, Succfulstate, Violatingstate, Reports, Repuinfor, History, Monitoring, Sanctioning, Reputupdating, Evolving > where Concrete-contracts are the concrete contracts burdened on the participants, Failedcons (possibly empty, ⊆ Concrete-contracts) are the contracts which are violated by the participants and at that time all the preceding contracts are successfully performed, the preceding contracts are the contracts that are performed prior to the current contracts, Succcons (⊆ Concrete-contracts) are the contracts which are successfully performed, Waitingcons (⊆ Concrete-contracts) are contracts waiting to perform, for part of the preceding contracts are being performed, or violated, Inperformingcons (⊆ Concrete-contracts) are contracts which are being performed, Succfulstate, part of Reports, is the state representing the successful performance of the contract, Violatingstate, part of Reports, is the state representing the violating performance of the contract, Reports include information such as Succfulstate, Violatingstate etc, as defined in E-institution, History is the individual history information, as defined in E-institution, Repuinfor is the individual reputation information, as defined in E-institution, and Monitoring, Sanctioning, Reputupdating, Evolving can be defined as:

- Monitoring: Concrete-contracts × Monitor →Succcons ×Reports (Succfulstate) | Failedcons ×Reports (Violatingstate), which means the Monitor is responsible to monitor the individual Concrete contract, generates the Reports,
- Sanctioning: Failedcons ×Reports (Violatingstate) ×Arbitrator → Instan-norms (∈ Concrete-contracts), which means the Arbitrator is responsible to enforce Instan-norms (sanctioning norms) on each violating agent due to Failedcons,
- Reputupdating: Reports × Arbitrator →Repuinfor × History, which means the Arbitrator is responsible to update the individual Repuinfor and History information, according to the Reports generated,
- Evolving deals with how the VO proceeds when violations occur.

The VO evolvement includes several stages: (1) find out which contracts are violated, (2)if there are some corresponding waiting contracts, m negotiates with the corresponding partner of each waiting contract about whether to continue the cooperation, (3) if the partners of the waiting contracts agree to continue the cooperation, then, the waiting contracts should continue the VO stages 5, 6, 7, 8, and to deal with violated contracts, m repeats the partner selection to select the cooperation partners (including the violating agents), after m's negotiation with cooperation partners, the violated contracts should continue the VO stages 6, 7, 8, (4) if the partners of the waiting contracts do not agree to continue the cooperation or if there are no corresponding waiting contracts, m can dissolve the VO. See figure 4.

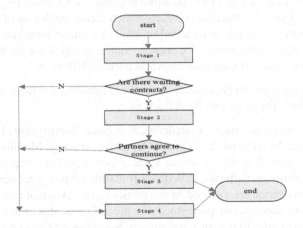

Fig. 4. The VO evolvement

The Monitor is responsible for the analysis of the violation, and responsible for telling m and m's cooperation partners the Violatingstate and the violated contracts. Thus this stage can be defined as:

- Fo=< Concrete-contracts, violated-contracts, Violatingstate, telling > where Concrete-contracts are all the contracts signed, violated-contracts are all the contracts violated, Violatingstate are the Violating state recording the Violating reasons, possible severities, telling is that Monitor tells m and m's cooperation partners the Violatingstate and the violated contracts.

The stage 2 can be defined as:

- mNEp=< Violatingstate, Violated-contracts, Negotiation, Result > where Violatingstate, Violated- contracts are the Violating state and the contracts violated, Negotiation is m negotiates with the corresponding partner of each waiting contract, Result (true, false) is the result of negotiation, where true means continuing cooperation, false means ending cooperation.

The stage 3 can be defined as:

- Con=< Result, Pselection, negotiation, spVOplanning, contracting, Vooperation > where Result is defined in the stage 2, Pselection is the partner selection in violated contracts, negotiation the m's negotiation with the cooperation partners about the such items as price, deadline in the violated or waiting contracts, spVOplanning, contracting, Vooperation are specific VO planning, contracting, VO operation respectively, as defined in VO formation and operation.

The stage 4 can be defined as:

- Ending= <Result, Repealing, Dissolving> where Result are defined in the stage 2, Repealing is Authority repeals all the contracts signed in the VO, Dissolving is the Authority dissolves the VO.

4 Comparison and Conclusion

We have presented an electronic institution framework, the VO environment, which incorporates both the static infrastructure and dynamic infrastructure. In our approach, the EI is seen as a means to facilitate the VO formation, operation and evolvement.

As with any recent discipline, however, differences exist between the conceptual views of the "institutional environment". Some authors advocate a norm approach. Through this approach, Some authors [3] advocate a restrictive "rules of the game" method, where the EI fixes what agents are permitted and forbidden to do and under what circumstances. In this case norms are a set of interaction conventions that agents are willing to conform to. And through this approach, other researchers [4] take a different standpoint, considering the institution as an external entity that ascribes institutional powers and normative positions, while admitting norm violations by prescribing appropriate sanctions. Instead of the norm approach, others still [5] focus on the creation of institutional reality from speech acts, regarding an agent communication language as a set of conventions to act on a fragment of that reality.

As far as the norm approach is concerned, as in [6], [7], [8], the EI is designed with norms, however, norms are just one component of social reality; other components, which also seem to us to be important for the specification of open distributed systems, have been largely neglected by most proposals concerning electronic institutions. In norm approach, the EI is designed without the organization structure to reflect the relation of the different entities, and without the dynamic information to reflect the dynamic interaction. In this approach, without templates, the weakness of the VO creation is the lack of agility.

In [9], [10], in an institutional reality approach, an institution has been defined only through several services, norms and contracts to guide the VO, and VO formation is roughly designed, without the EI multiple layers (the static, the dynamic, and the semantic) to support the formation, also without the operation, evolvement of VO. Compared with theirs, our work present a multiple layer E-institution to support the VO formation, operation, and evolvement, expressing explicitly which EI elements including the semantic, the static, and the dynamic, which services are needed in different VO stages.

In [11], artificial institutions have been defined in terms of social reality. The static elements are mentioned including norms, ontologies, institutional actions and their relation are also mentioned. However E-institutions are designed only with static elements, without the dynamic elements to shorten the gap between the EI and the VO. In our approach, a multiple layer E-institution including the static, the dynamic, and the semantic is designed to support the VO formation, operation, and evolvement.

In brief, we have given explicit description of the EI, including the static, the dynamic, and the semantic elements, and also given explicit description of VO stages, in which the required institution elements are explicitly depicted. We believe only in this institution environment can agents interactions be predictable, trustable, and can the system goals be achievable.

References

[1] Foster, I., Kesselman, C., Tuecke, S.: The Anatomy of the Grid: Enabling Scalable Virtual Organizations. Int'. J. Supercomputer Applications 15, 209–235 (2001)

[2] Norman, T., Preece, A., Chalmers, S., Jennings, N., Luck, M., Dang, V., Nguyen, T., Deora, V., Shao, J., Gray, W., Fiddian, N.: Agent-based Formation of Virtual Organisations. Knowledge Based Systems 17, 103–111 (2004)

[3] Arcos, J.L., Esteva, M., Noriega, P., Rodríguez-Aguilar, J.A., Sierra, C.: Environment engineering for multiagent systems. Engineering Applications of Artificial Intelligence 18, 191–204 (2005)

[4] Artikis, A., Pitt, J., Sergot, M.: Animated specifications of computational societies. In: Castelfranchi, C., Johnson, W.L. (eds.) International Joint Conference on Autonomous Agents and Multi-Agent Systems, pp. 1053–1062. Association for Computing Machinery, New York (2002)

[5] Fornara, N., Viganò, F., Colombetti, M.: Agent Communication and Institutional Reality. In: van Eijk, R.M., Huget, M.-P., Dignum, F.P.M. (eds.) AC 2004. LNCS (LNAI), vol. 3396, pp. 1–17. Springer, Heidelberg (2005)

[6] Cardoso, H.L., Oliveira, E.: A Contract Model for Electronic Institutions. In: Sichman, J.S., Padget, J., Ossowski, S., Noriega, P. (eds.) COIN 2007. LNCS (LNAI), vol. 4870, pp. 27–40. Springer, Heidelberg (2008)

[7] García-Camino, A., Rodríguez-Aguilar, J.A., Sierra, C., Vasconcelos, W.: A Distributed Architecture for Norm-Aware Agent Societies. In: Baldoni, M., Endriss, U., Omicini, A., Torroni, P. (eds.) DALT 2005. LNCS (LNAI), vol. 3904, pp. 89–105. Springer, Heidelberg (2006)

[8] Vázquez-Salceda, J., Aldewereld, H., Grossi, D., Dignum, F.: From human regulations to regulated software agents' behavior. Artificial Intelligence and Law 16, 73–87 (2008)

[9]   Cardoso, H.L., Malucelli, A., Rocha, A.P., Oliveira, E.: Institutional Services for Dynamic Virtual Organizations. IFIP International Federation for Information Processing 186, 521–528 (2005)

[10] Cardoso, H.L., Oliveira, E.: Virtual Enterprise Normative Framework within Electronic Institutions. In: Gleizes, M.-P., Omicini, A., Zambonelli, F. (eds.) ESAW 2004. LNCS (LNAI), vol. 3451, pp. 14–32. Springer, Heidelberg (2005)

[11] Fornara, N., Viganò, F., Verdicchio, M., Colombetti, M.: Artificial institutions: a model of institutional reality for open multiagent systems. Artificial Intelligence and Law 16, 89–105 (2008)

An Optimal Class Association Rule Algorithm

Turiho Jean Claude[1,*], Yang Sheng[1], Li Chuang[1], and Xie Kaia[1,2]

[1] School of Computer and Communication, Hunan University, 410082, Changsha, China
[2] The Methodist Hospital Research Institute, Cornell University, 77030, Houston, TX, USA
tulije@yahoo.fr

Abstract. Classification and association rule mining algorithms are two important aspects of data mining. Class association rule mining algorithm is a promising approach for it involves the use of association rule mining algorithm to discover classification rules. This paper introduces an optimal class association rule mining algorithm known as OCARA. It uses optimal association rule mining algorithm and the rule set is sorted by priority of rules resulting into a more accurate classifier. It outperforms the C4.5, CBA, RMR on UCI eight data sets, which is proved by experimental results.

Keywords: class association rule; association rule; classification; data mining.

1 Introduction

Classification [1], which classifies the objects of dataset by using rules, is one important aspect of data mining. In general, a classifier is composition of a classification rule sets. Sometimes, it is called prediction rules set. The datasets are used to study and build models, which are called training datasets. And, the datasets are used to test the quality of the models, also known as testing data sets. Association rule is another important field in data mining [2]. It finds the relationships between each item in a transaction database. The relationships are represented as simple rules, that is A->C, where A is the antecedent, and C is the consequence. Rules can conduct the products market and sales promotion. It is obvious that classification rules and association rules are distinct in the following aspects. a) Classification rules always have pre-specified consequences that never appear in the antecedent of a classification rule, whereas association rules usually have no pre-specified consequences and the consequence of an association rule may be in the antecedent of another rule. b) The goal of classification rule mining is to obtain a simple and accurate rules set, whereas the goal of association rule mining is to find all rules satisfying some thresholds.

Usually, the classification technology includes covering and reducing algorithms [1,3]. Sometimes, a rule relates to several classes. These algorithms pick up one class that has the biggest correlativity with the rule and discard the rest of all classes. During model training, as soon as a rule is obtained, all objects relating to the rule will be deleted. One object relates to only one rule, so the classifier is smaller. In recent years,

---

* Corresponding author.

Z. Cai et al. (Eds.): ISICA 2009, CCIS 51, pp. 344–350, 2009.

using algorithms of association rules to build classifier was becoming popular [4, 5, 6]. It is necessary to pre-specify the attributes which represent the classes before using algorithms of association rules to mine classification rules. In order to distinguish general association rules, the mixed method in this paper is called classification association rules. The classifier based on classification association rules has higher accuracy than the classifier based on traditional classification algorithm C4.5 [8] as proved in [4, 6].

Generally, association rule algorithm that obtains many rules has low efficiency. Nonredundant association rules algorithm [7] has improved the efficiency and reduced the scale of the rules. In addition, the optimal association rules algorithm [2] has done the job further. Using the optimal association rules algorithms to build the classifier compares with using the general classification association rules algorithms [4, 6]: firstly, the former is faster than the latter in lower support threshold. Secondly, the accuracy of the former is higher than that of the latter [9] making the former more efficient than the latter.

In this paper, we use optimal association rules algorithm [2] to mine classification rules. Then, it sorts the rules by the priority to obtain a classifier. This algorithm is called the optimal classification association rules algorithm--OCARA. This paper is organized as follows: Section 2 describes the concepts and theory, whereas section 3 gives the new classification rules algorithm, followed by the experimental results in section 4. And the paper is ended by a brief conclusion in section 5.

2 Basic Concept and Theory

Classification association rules mining algorithms have to pre-specify the classification attributes. Assuming $U =(C,D)$, where U is the training data set, C is the testing data set, and D is the classification attributes. The definitions and the theorems are used to prune rules in the OCARA as follows:

Definition 1. If the support and interestingness of a rule are not less than given thresholds, this rule is called a strong implication.

Definition 2. Given two rules $P->d$ and $Q->d$ $(d \in D)$, if $P \subset Q$, $Q \subseteq C$, then Q is regarded as more specific than P, and P is regarded as more general than Q.

Definition 3. A rule set is optimal with respect to an interestingness metric if it contains all rules except those with no greater interestingness than one of its more general rules.

Theorem 1. If supp($PX\neg d$)=supp($P\neg d$), then rule $PX->d$ and all its more-specific rules will not occur in an optimal rule set defined by any interestingness.

Corollary 1. If supp(P) = supp(PX), then rule $PX ->d$ for any d and all its more specific rules do not occur in an optimal rule set defined by any interestingness.

Theorem 2. An optimal rule set is a subset of a nonredundant rule set.

Corollary 2. If supp($PX\neg d$) = 0, then all more-specific rules of the rule $P->d$ do not occur in an optimal rule set defined by any interestingness.

In above theorems and corollaries, $P \subseteq C, X \subseteq C, d \in D$, "$PX$" is "$P \cup X$", supp($P\neg d$) is support of $P\neg d$, and $\neg d$ is the negative of d. Since these theorems and corollaries are similar to the theorems in ORD, the proof can refer to paper [2].

Definition 4. A pair of pattern and target set is called a rule set of candidates, denoted by (P, Y) where $P \subseteq C$ and $Y \subseteq D$.

If a class is simply removed from the target set, a candidate rule is removed. If the target set is empty, the candidate stands for no rules. The existence of a candidate relies on two conditions: 1) Pattern P is frequent, and 2) target set Y is not empty. In addition, if we remove d from (P, D), we may lose rule P->d according to Corollary 2, termination statue of target d is defined as follows:

Definition 5. Target $d \in D$ is terminated in candidate (P,D) if supp $(P\neg d) = 0$.

3 OCARA Algorithm

OCARA algorithm (Optimal Class Association Rule Algorithm), according to the definitions and theorems of section 2, prunes the rules (reference: Prune(l+1). The OCARA is described as follows: OCARA algorithm:

Input. training data set U, testing data set T, support σ and confidence θ

Output. classifier, accuracy *accut*

The first stage.

> At this stage, OCARA obtains the optimal rules set by running MORS algorithm as below.
> 1. Scanning the training data set and then finding out frequency itemsets.
> 2. Pruning itemsets, then discovering the optimal rules set ORS. (The main function for pruning is Prune (l+1))

The second stage.

> 1. Sorting the optimal rules set, then building the classifier. (According to: confidence, support, etc)

The third stage.

> Using the classifier to classify the training data set, and computing accuracy.

3.1 Discovering the Optimal Rules Set

Here, the MORS algorithm is given. For MORS, confidence is selected as interestingness metric. In addition, the support is local support in this algorithm. The candidate generation and pruning function of MORS are given.

Function. Candidate_gen

1) for each pair of candidates $(P_{l-1}s, D_s)$ and $(P_{l-1}t, D_t)$ in an *l*-candidate set.

{

> insert candidate (P_{l+1}, D) in the $(l+1)$-candidate set
>
> where $P_{l+1} = P_{l-1}st$ and $D = D_s \cap D_t$

for all $P_l \subset P_{l+1}$
{
      if candidate(P_l, D_l) does not exist
    then remove candidate (P_{l+1}, D) and return
    else $D = D \cap D_t$
    }
}
2) if the target set of (P_{l+1}, D) is empty
    then remove the candidate

The Candidate_gen function has a pruning process. The more pruning is given according to Theorem 1 and its corollary. σ is the minimum support in the following function.

Function. Prune($l+1$)
  for each candidate(P, D) in ($l+1$)-candidate set
{
1) for each $d \in D$
    {
        if supp(Pd)/supp(d) $\leq \sigma$ then remove d from D
        //test the frequency
        else if supp($P\neg d$) = 0 then mark d terminated
    }
2) if D is empty then remove candidate(P, D) and return
3) for each l-level subset $P' \subset P$
    {
        if supp(P) =supp(P') then empty D //test Corollary 1
        else if $(P\neg d)$=supp($P'\neg d$) then //test Theorem 1
        remove d from D
    }
4) if D is empty then remove candidate(P,D)
    }

After describing the Candidate_gen function and pruning function, the MORS is given as follows:

Name. MORS
Input. S, the minimum local support σ and the minimum interestingness θ, condition attributes set C and classification attributes set D in U
Output. an optimal rule set ORS defined by θ
Function.
    1) let $ORS = \Phi$
    2) count support of one-pattern by array
    3) build one-candidate sets
    4) form and add rules to ORS with σ and θ
    5) generate two-candidate sets

6) while new candidate set is not empty
  {
          count support of patterns for new candidates
          prune candidates in the new candidate set
          form rules and add optimal rules to *ORS*
          generate next-level candidate set
  }
7) return the rule set *ORS*

3.2 Sorting Rules

At present, most algorithms that use classification association rule algorithms to mine rules are sorted by descent. They refer to the support when the confidence is the same.

The order of rules will greatly affect the match of rules when it is testing. Moreover, it will affect the accuracy of prediction. Thus, it has to confirm sorting methods of rules. It is defined as follows:

Definition 6. Given two rules $R1$ and $R2$, $R1 \succ R2$ (also called $R1$ precedes $R2$ or $R1$ has a higher precedence than $R2$) if:

1. The confidence of $R1$ is greater than that of $R2$, or
2. The confidence values of $R1$ and $R2$ are the same, but the support of $R1$ is greater than that of $R2$, or
3. Confidence and support values of $R1$ and $R2$ are the same, but $R1$ has fewer conditions attributes in than that of $R2$, or
4. The confidence, support and condition attributes cardinality values of $R1$ and $R2$ are the same, but $R1$ is associated with more frequent classification attributes than that of $R2$, or
5. All above criteria of $R1$ and $R2$ are the same, but $R1$ was generated earlier than $R2$.

Generally, the support is global support, in order to avoid generating rules too many in the most frequent classes and gaining rules too few in the least frequent classes, the local support is introduced. The local support is defined as follows:

Definition 7. Assuming supp(Pd) is the global support of P->d, in that way, supp(Pd)/supp(d) is local support.

3.3 Matching Rules

Assuming ORS is the optimal rules set by using definition 6 to sort, T is the training data sets. The idea of classification prediction is: using the rules in ORS to predict the class of data objects in T. The rule in ORS, which matches the condition attributes of testing data object first time, is the rule to predict the testing data object. The prediction is right when the consequence of rule is as same as the classification attribute values of testing data object.

The definition of match is given as follows:

Definition 8. Assuming Ct is the condition attributes set of one testing data object, Cr is the condition attributes set of one prediction rule, if $Cr \subseteq Ct$, then the testing data object match the condition attributes of the rule.

4 Experimental Results

Eight different data sets of UCI are used in this experiment. OCARA is compared with other three popular classification algorithms (RMR[4], CBA[6], C4.5[8]).

All these experiments run in Pentium IV 3.0GHz and win2003. It was proved that the support threshold was greatly influenced by the rule accuracy and the rule number [6]. If the support threshold is between 0.02 and 0.03, the accuracy will be much better, as discussed in [6]. The support threshold was set as 0.02, and the confidence was set as 0.30 in this paper.

Table 1. The prediction accuracy of four algorithms

DATASET	SIZE	ACCURACY (%)			
		C 4.5	CBA	RMR	OCARA
BALANCE	625	64.31	67.24	77.00	66.80
GLASS	214	66.47	69.23	70.89	76.18
IRIS	150	96.00	93.25	93.80	96.50
BREAST	699	94.66	98.71	95.92	98.85
VOTE	435	88.25	86.92	88.70	92.56
PIMA	768	72.28	75.36	77.76	79.68
ZOO	101	93.01	95.40	95.12	92.29
DIABETES	768	85.12	75.25	78.36	77.84
AVERAGE		82.51	82.68	84.69	85.09

Table 1 shows the classification accuracy of C4.5, CBA, RMR, OCARA for 8 different data sets. The results shown in table 1 indicate that the classification accuracy of OCARA is higher than RMR in 5 different data sets, and the average accuracy of OCARA is 0.4 percent higher than RMR. RMR prunes the rules through heuristic methods and general classification association rules algorithms, which will miss some strong rules and reduce the accuracy rate. The accuracy rate of OCARA is higher than that of RMR. However, the RMR run in covering method, which will obtain smaller rules set.

5 Conclusion

OCARA uses optimal association rule mining algorithm, and the rule set is sorted by rule priority. It is an accurate classifier. This algorithm is compared with C4.5, CBA, and RMR in UCI data sets. Experimental results show that it has better performance, but the rule number of OCARA is obviously more than RMR when the support is lower.

References

1. Quinlan: Induction of Decision Trees. Machine Learning (1), 81–106 (1986)
2. Li, J.: On Optimal Rule Discovery. IEEE Trans. on Knowledge and Data Engineering 18(4), 460–471 (2006)

3. Cendrowska, J.: PRISM: an algorithm for inducing modular rules. Int. J. Man-Mach. Stud. 27(4), 349–370 (1987)
4. Thabtah, F.A., Cowling, P.I.: A greedy classification algorithm based on association rule. Applied Soft Computing 7, 1102–1111 (2007)
5. Coenen, F., Leng, P.: The effect of threshold values on association rule based classification accuracy. Data & Knowledge Engineering 60, 345–360 (2007)
6. Liu, B., Hsu, W., Ma, Y.: Integrating classification and association rule mining. In: Proceeding of The KDD, New York, pp. 80–86 (1998)
7. Zaki, M.J., Charm, C.J.H.: An Efficient Algorithm for Closed Association Rule Mining. In: Proc. SIAM Int. Conf. Data Mining (2002)
8. Quinlan, J.R.: C4.5: Programs for Machine Learning. Moregan Kaufmann, San Mateo (1993)
9. Hu, H., Li, J.: Using Association Rules to Make Rule-Based Classifiers Robust. In: Proc. 16th Australasian Database Conf. (ADC), pp. 47–52 (2005)

Multiple Sequence Alignment Based on Chaotic PSO

Xiu-juan Lei, Jing-jing Sun, and Qian-zhi Ma

School of Computer Science, Shaanxi Normal University, Xi'an 710062, China
{xjlei168,jjsun1116,zhihui312}@163.com

Abstract. This paper introduces a new improved algorithm called chaotic PSO (CPSO) based on the thought of chaos optimization to solve multiple sequence alignment. For one thing, the chaotic variables are generated between 0 and 1 when initializing the population so that the particles are distributed uniformly in the solution space. For another thing, the chaotic sequences are generated using the Logistic mapping function in order to make chaotic search and strengthen the diversity of the population. The simulation results of several benchmark data sets of BAliBase show that the improved algorithm is effective and has good performances for the data sets with different similarity.

Keywords: Chaos., particle swarm optimization, Multiple sequence alignment.

1 Introduction

As one of the most basic tasks of the biological sequence analysis, multiple sequence alignment (MSA) is widely applied in sequence assembly, sequence annotation, the prediction of gene and protein's structure and function, phylogeny and evolutionary analysis and so on. It is one of the hot topics in the current biological information sciences. Multiple sequence alignment is a NP-complete problem in the sense of the sum-of-pairs scoring (SPS).

At present, the existing MSA algorithms were roughly divided into four kinds. They are exact alignment algorithm, evolutionary alignment algorithm, the algorithm based on graph theory and the iterative alignment algorithm. The exact alignment algorithm is completely based on the dynamic programming. The most classical exact algorithm is the Needlman-Wunsch algorithm [1], whose feasible calculation dimension is only 3-D. The evolutionary alignment algorithm was originally proposed by Hogeweg [2] and perfected further by Feng and Taylor. Now the software package CLUSTALW based evolutionary alignment is widely used. The main representative of the alignment algorithm based on graphical model is partial order alignment [3] (POA). In recent years, the iterative alignment algorithms have been increasingly used to solve the problem of multiple sequence alignment. This method is based on the algorithm which can produce alignment, and can improve the multiple sequence alignment through a series of iterations until the results don't become better any longer. There are a lot of algorithms based on this method, such as, simulated annealing algorithm (SA) [4], genetic algorithm (GA) [5], hidden Markov model (HMM) and so on. The most influential software package SAGA [6] (sequence alignment by genetic algorithm) is constructed based on genetic algorithm. The SAGA is designed by twenty-two

Z. Cai et al. (Eds.): ISICA 2009, CCIS 51, pp. 351–360, 2009.

different kinds of genetic operators and applied the dynamic scheduling strategy to control the use of them.

The genetic algorithm and its application in multiple sequence alignment has been relatively mature, but the design of genetic operators and the choice of the parameters are rather complex. While the particle swarm optimization (PSO) algorithm [7] which was originally presented by Kennedy and Eberhart in 1995 is becoming very popular due to its simplicity of implementation, few parameters to adjust and quick convergence to a reasonably good solution. But it still suffers from premature convergence, tending to trap in local minima. In view of its disadvantages, improving the PSO algorithm to solve the multiple sequence alignment problem is a hot spot at present.

On the basis of the study about the standard particle swarm optimization algorithm's application in multiple sequence alignment [8], a novel improved PSO applied in multiple sequence alignment is proposed in this paper. The improved PSO introduces the thought of chaos optimization, which overcomes the premature convergence problem effectively. In view of the SP optimization model of multiple sequence alignment, the Chaotic Particle Swarm Optimization [9] (CPSO) is applied in multiple sequence alignment. The approach is examined by using a set of standard instances taken from the benchmark alignment database, BAliBase. The results show that the proposed algorithm improves the alignment precision and ability.

2   Description of the Problem

2.1   Multiple Sequence Alignment (MSA)

Multiple sequence alignment reflects the evolutionary relationship among the given sequences. Its abstract mathematical model is that add the different numbers of gaps to each sequence of the sequence group so that each sequence has the same length and has a good similarity ultimately.

MSA can be formulated mathematically as follows: A biological sequence is a string composed of l characters. The characters are taken from a finite alphabet Σ. For DNA sequence, Σ includes 4 letters-A, C, G, T, which respectively expresses 4 different nucleotides. For protein sequences, Σ includes 20 different letters, which respectively expresses 20 different amino acids. These letters are collectively referred to as residues. Given a sequence group consisting of n ($n \geq 2$) sequences $S = (s_1, s_2, \cdots s_n)$, where $s_i = s_{i1}s_{i2} \cdots s_{il_i} (1 \leq i \leq n)$, $s_{ij} \in \Sigma (1 \leq j \leq l_i)$, l_i is defined as the length of the i-th sequence. Then the multiple sequence alignment about S can be expressed as a matrix $S' = (s'_{ij})$, in which $1 \leq i \leq n, 1 \leq j \leq l$, $\max(l_i) \leq l \leq \sum_{i=1}^{n} l_i$. The matrix needs to meet the following characteristics.

① Each sequence s'_i is an extension of s_i and it is defined as $s'_{ij} \in \Sigma \cup \{-\}$. The symbol " $-$ " denotes a gap. The deletion of gaps from s'_i, leaves s_i ;

② For all i, j : length(s'_i)=length(s'_j);

③ There is not any column composed of only " $-$ " in S'.

2.2 The Standard for Judging Multiple Sequence Alignment

For multiple sequence alignment, there are some different objective functions. Such as such-of-pairs (SP) function [10], hidden Markov model (HMM) and COFFEE function. In this paper, the SP function is used as the objective function.

Suppose the length of each sequence is L. The j-th character of the i-th sequence is denoted as $c_{ij} (1 \leq j \leq L)$. Then, for all other sequences, the sum-of-pairs score of all the j-th character is defined as $SP - Score(j)$.

$$SP - Score(j) = \sum_{i=1}^{N-1} \sum_{k=i+1}^{N} p(c_{ij}, c_{kj}) \qquad (1)$$

In the above equation, $p(c_{ij}, c_{kj})$ denotes the sum-of-pairs score of the characters c_{ij} and c_{kj}. A formalization representation on $p(c_{ij}, c_{kj})$ is shown below.

$$p(c_{ij}, c_{kj}) = \begin{cases} +2 \ (c_{ij} = c_{kj} \ and \ c_{ij}, c_{kj} \in \Sigma) \\ -1 \ (c_{ij} \neq c_{kj} \ and \ c_{ij}, c_{kj} \in \Sigma) \\ -2 \ (c_{ij} = '-' or \, c_{kj} = '-') \\ 0 \ (c_{ij} = '-' and \, c_{kj} = '-') \end{cases} \qquad (2)$$

Then the score of all characters in the sequence group is:

$$SUM(S')_{align} = \sum_{j=1}^{L} SP - Score(j) \qquad (3)$$

If the input data is taken from the benchmark alignment database-BAliBase, there will be a standard alignment result. We can calculate a relative SP-Score which is called SPS.

$$SPS = SUM(S')_{align} / SUM(S^*)_{align} \qquad (4)$$

If there is no benchmark alignment database, SPS is defined as

$$SPS = SUM(S')_{align} / (L \times N \times (N-1) / 2) \qquad (5)$$

In equations (4) and (5), $SUM(S')$ is the result of one algorithm which we proposed, while $SUM(S^*)$ is the result of the benchmark alignment database. Obviously, SPS reflects the ratio of the accurate alignment. Normally, the higher the value of SPS is, the more accurate the alignment is. The algorithm is more able to reflect the biological characteristics of sequences.

3   Chaotic Particle Swarm Optimization

3.1   Particle Swarm Optimization and Its Premature to Determine

Particle Swarm Optimization [7] is a random algorithm. It is initialized with a population of individuals placed in the search space randomly and searching for optimal solution by updating individual with iteration. The movement of the particles is influenced by two factors, one is the best solution *pbest* which is found by the particle itself, the other is the best solution *gbest* which is found by all particles. Particles update themselves by tracking the two extreme. Then the velocity of particle and its new position will be assigned according to the following equations.

$$v(t+1) = wv(t) + c_1 r_1 (pbest(t) - x(t)) + c_2 r_2 (gbest(t) - x(t)) \tag{6}$$

$$x(t+1) = x(t) + v(t+1) \tag{7}$$

w is inertia weight which controls the memory of the PSO. c_1, c_2 are acceleration constants which determine the relative influence of the *pbest* and *gbest*. r_1, r_2 are generated randomly between 0 and 1. $x(t), v(t)$ denote the location and velocity at the t-th iteration respectively.

Through the analysis of equations (6) and (7), we can found that when some particles get close to *gbest*, the update of velocity will be determined by $w*v(t)$. Obviously, $w < 1$. So the velocity of these particles become less and less, even close to 0. With the iteration, other particles will be congregated around these "inert" particles so that the algorithm terminates and appears premature convergence.

The basis of judging the premature convergence [11] is as follows. Firstly, two threshold values α and β are predefined. If the average distance of the particles meets $Dis < \alpha$ and the variance of the fitness meets $\sigma^2 < \beta$, the particle will be judged premature.

The average distance of the particles *Dis* represents the discrete extent of the population.

$$Dis = \frac{1}{PopSize \cdot L} \cdot \sum_{i=1}^{PopSize} \sqrt{\sum_{d=1}^{D} (p_{id} - p_d)^2} \tag{8}$$

L is the maximal diagonal length of the searching space, D is the dimension of the solution space, p_{id} denotes the i-th particle's coordinate in the d-th dimension, p_d denotes the average of all particles' d-th dimension coordinate. Obviously, the less *Dis* is, the more concentrative the population is; the larger *Dis* is, the more scattered the population is.

The variance of the population's fitness σ^2 is defined as

$$\sigma^2 = \sum_{i=1}^{PopSize} \left(\frac{f_i - f_{avg}}{f} \right)^2 \tag{9}$$

f_i denotes the fitness of the i-th particle, f_{avg} is the average of the fitness of all particles. f is a normalized calibration factor, which is defined as:

$$f = \begin{cases} \max_{1 \le i \le PopSize} |f_i - f_{avg}|, & \max |f_i - f_{avg}| > 1 \\ 1, & otherwise \end{cases} \tag{10}$$

The variance of all particles' fitness σ^2 reflects the assembled degree of the population. The less σ^2 is, the more collective the population is. With the iteration, the fitness of each particle will be closer and closer. When $\sigma^2 < \beta$, the algorithm is easy to fall into a local optimum, and appears premature convergence.

3.2 Chaos and Chaotic Particle Swarm Optimization

Chaos is a universal nonlinear phenomenon, whose behavior is complex and similarly random, but it is very regular. Due to the ergodicity of chaos, searching by chaotic variables has more superiority than searching disorderly and blindly. That can avoid the shortcomings of evolutionary algorithms which are easily getting into a local optimization. The unique nature of chaos is as follows: ①Randomness, that is, chaos has a immethodical behave like random variables. ②Ergodicity, it can go through a range of all states and not repeat. ③Regularity, chaos is generated by a determined function. ④Sensitivity, that is, small changes of the initial value can cause a great change in output after a period.

In view of the ergodicity of chaos and insensitivity of the initial value, the chaotic initialization can be used to overcome the puzzle that the particles of standard PSO distribute in the solution space non-uniformly because of the random election of initial value.

To enrich the search behavior, chaotic dynamics is incorporated into the PSO (CPSO).The logistic map is usually employed for constructing CPSO. Logistic mapping

$$z_{n+1} = \mu z_n (1 - z_n) \tag{11}$$

is a typical chaotic system, when $\mu = 4$, it is completely in a chaotic state. A minute difference in the initial value of the chaotic variable would result in a considerable difference in its longtime behavior. The track if chaotic variable can travel ergodically over the whole search space. Then map the chaotic sequence from the chaotic interval $[0,1]$ to the variable interval $[a,b]$ by equation (12).

$$P_{i,n} = a + (b - a) p_{i,n} \tag{12}$$

In this paper, when PSO appears premature convergence, the chaotic search is used to update the particle of the current population as follows. When the particle traps in the local optimum, firstly, the initial chaotic variables are generated between 0 and 1. Then generate a new chaotic sequence by the Logistic mapping as equation (11), and transfer the span of variables from optimization to chaos as equation (12). Calculate the fitness of each sequence and record the best fitness until the current iteration meets the maximum iteration. At last, compare the best particle of the chaotic population with the best one of the current population. If the former is better than latter, replace the latter with the former, otherwise, randomly chose a particle from the current population and replace it with the best chaotic sequence.

4 Multiple Sequence Alignment Based on Chaotic PSO

4.1 Relevant Definition

In order to make use of PSO to solve multiple sequence alignment, several definitions are redefined as follows.

Definitions 1: A residue sequence $s(a_1, a_2, \cdots a_n)$ is given. $sk(i_k), (1 \leq k \leq n)$ denotes the collection of the locations where insert the gaps into the sequence s. Then $s' = s + sk(i_k)$ is the new sequence according to the $sk(i_k)$ operator. Here, "+" is given different meaning.

E.g.1: s='svynpgnygpylq'+$sk(0,3,7)$='_svy_npgn_ygpylq', where "_" is the gap insereted.

Definitions 2: "$-$" is defined as the subtraction operator. It is used to remove the elements from the previous collection if the posterior collection includes them.

E.g.2: A=$sk(2,3,6,8,10) - sk(0,2,5,6,7,9) = sk(3,8,10)$.

Definition 3: "$\oplus$" is defined as the union operator. It is used to unite the collections and reduce the iterant elements.

E.g.3: A=$sk(2,3,6,8,10) \oplus sk(0,2,5,6,7,9) = sk(0,2,3,5,6,7,8,9,10)$
With the redefinition of subtraction and addition, equation (6) becomes applicable for multiple sequence alignment.

$$v(t+1) = wv(t) \oplus \alpha(pbest(t) - x(t)) \oplus \beta(gbest(t) - x(t)) \tag{13}$$

$$x(t+1) = x(t) + v(t+1) \tag{14}$$

α, β, ω are generated randomly between 0 and 1. Considering the multiple sequence alignment, α, β need to be larger than ω for gaining a better result. Because the collections $(pbest(t) - x(t))$ and $(gbest(t) - x(t))$ contain the gaps inserted to the *pbest* and *gbest*. The information is hoped to be saved for the next generation.

4.2 Several Problems to Be Solved

Problem 1: Initialization. It is considered that there are k sequences to be aligned, and these sequences are generated with various lengths, say, from l_1 to l_k. Parent alignments are presented as matrix where each sequence is encoded as a row with the considered alphabet set. The length of each row in the initialized matrix is from l_{max} to $\alpha * l_{max}$, where $l_{max} = \max(l_1, l_2, \cdots l_n)$. Here, α is chosen as 1.2 according to the analysis of the simulation results [12]. The number of the gaps is always less than 20% of the current sequence's length.

Problem 2: Individual encoding. In view of the characteristics of multiple sequence alignment, two-dimensional encoding method is used. It is simple and intuitive, easy to operate. However, this method always takes up a lot of memory space.

E.g.4: There are three sequences s_1=ydgeilyqskrf, s_2=adesvynpgn and s_3= ydetp ikqser. The encoded result can be shown as Figure1.

```
y_dgeil_yqsk_rf
_ad_esv_yn_pg_n
y_d_etpi_kqs_er
```

Fig. 1. Encoded result

Problem 3: In consideration of the introduction of chaotic search mechanism, the chaotic sequences are produced by Logistic mapping. The mapped results will be non-integer. However, the chaotic sequences in this multiple sequence alignment algorithm express the location of the inserted gaps, which must be integer. The solution is that: firstly, int the values of sequences after Logistic mapping. Then judge whether the location where the gap will be inserted has existed. If it hasn't appeared, the gap will be inserted into this location. Otherwise, the gap will be inserted into a random location from the rest locations.

4.3   The Specific Steps of the Algorithm

The steps of the algorithm are described in detail as follows.

Step1: According to the chaos, initialize the locations of the population. The lengths are between l_{max} and $1.2 * l_{max}$, where $l_{max} = \max(l_1, l_2, \cdots l_n)$ .The initial velocity is generated randomly. Its length is also between l_{max} and $1.2 * l_{max}$. Generate the locations of the gaps randomly and make sure that there is no column which is composed of no other than " – ";

Step 2: Calculate each particle's fitness according to the objective function, that is equation (2);

Step 3: Update *pbest* and *gbest* ;

Step 4: Calculate the variance of all particles' fitness. Then judge whether PSO is premature convergence according to the variance and the predefined threshold value. If it is, go Step 5, otherwise, go Step 6;

Step 5: Make a chaotic search for the population in accordance with the idea of 3.2. Specifically, generate a chaotic population based on the best particle of the current population. Then replace a particle randomly with the best particle of the chaotic population;

Step 6: Update the particles' location and velocity according to the equation (13) and (14);

Step 7: Jump out the circulation if it meets the terminated condition, and output the best particle and its fitness, otherwise, go Step 2 and begin the next iteration.

5 Simulation and Results

The algorithm is implemented using the Matlab 7.0. The machine used for this research is a personal computer with a 1.86GHz processor. The main memory is 1GHz.

The parameters are set as follows: $popsize = 30$, $\alpha = 0.8$, $\beta = 0.8$, $\omega_{end} = 0.4$, $\omega_{start} = 0.9$, $Maxiter = 500$, the threshold value of variance is 10. ω declines linearly from ω_{start} to ω_{end}. The test data sets used in the experiments are from benchmark alignment database, BAliBase. In this experiment, each test data is run for 30 times. Then calculate the average SPS, the maximum SPS and minimum SPS. The results obtained by the proposed CPSO algorithm are shown in table 1.

Table 1. The results of CPSO for solving MSA problems with different identities

Identity	Sequence	Average	Maximum	Minimum
< 25%	SH3	0.5971	0.9461	0.4559
	twitchin	0.4721	0.5248	0.4215
20% ~ 40%	SH2	0.6235	0.6807	0.5723
	Cytochrome c	0.5346	0.5731	0.4822
> 35%	Ribonuclease	0.8256	0.8761	0.7778
	immunophilin	0.5146	0.5739	0.4611

Table 1 shows that for the sequence Ribonuclease, the result of chaotic PSO is closer to the benchmark result. The novel algorithm has good performance. The difference between the maximum and minimum is less. That shows the algorithm is stronger and has better robustness. For the sequence SH3, comparing with the SPS value of reference [13], the result of our algorithm 0.5971 is larger than that 0.537. It testifies the validity of the new algorithm. For other sequences, the results of chaotic PSO still have some distance with that of benchmark alignment. The reason may lie in the reasonable setting of the parameters and the sequence itself.

```
s₁: saeytCGSTCYWSSDVSAA-KAKgyslyesgd-tiddYPHEYHDYEGFDFpvsG
s₂: attCGSTNYSASQVRAAA--NAacqyyqnddtasstY-PHTYNNYEGFDFpvdG
s₃: acmyiCGSVCYSSSAISAALNKgysyyedgatagsssYPHRYNNYEGF-DFpta
s₄: tCGKV-FYSASAVSAASNAacn-y-vrag-staggstYPHVYNNYEGFRFkgls
s₅: -CGGTYYSSTQVNR-AINNaks-gqy-sstgY--PHTY-NNYEGFDFsdycd-G

-TYYEYPIMSDYDVYTGGSPGAD-RVIFNGDDELAGVITHTGASGDDFVAC
PY-QEFPIKSG-GVYTGGSPGADRVVINTNBE-YAGAITHTGASGNNFVGA
KPWYEFPILSSGRVYTGGSPGAD-RVIFDSHGNLDMLITHNGASGNNFVAC
KPFYEFPILSSGKTYTGGSPGADRVVINGQCS-IAGIITHTGASGNAFVAC
PYKEYPLKTS-SSGYTGGSPGADRVVYDSNDGTFCGAITHTGASGNNFVQC
```

Fig. 2. The alignment result for Ribonuclease

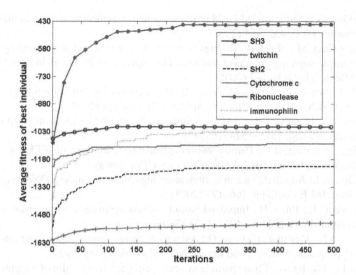

Fig. 3. The score of all characters for each sequence group with iteration

The six problems' alignment results are all described respectively. Here, the matched result of Ribonuclease is shown as figure 2. It is clear that there are many columns which are matched precisely. That approves the validity of the improved algorithm effectively. Figure 3 shows the evolution of the score of all characters for each sequence group.

6 Conclusions

In this paper, we present an improved algorithm chaotic particle swarm optimization (CPSO) for multiple sequence alignment. In the proposed CPSO algorithm, the chaos is introduced to PSO. From simulation results, it is shown that the proposed algorithm is effective, can improve search performance for some sequences. The new method can provide different viewpoint for related research. Furthermore, we will improve our algorithm so that it doesn't depend on the sequences themselves and the parameters can adjust adaptively.

Acknowledgements. The authors would like to thank all scholars' previous researches and the hard work from every member of our team.

References

1. Needleman, S.B., Wunsch, C.D.: A general method applicable to the search for similarities in the amino acid sequence of two proteins. Journal of Molecular Biology 48(3), 443–453 (1970)
2. Hogeweg, P., Hesper, B.: The alignment of sets of sequences and the construction of phylogenetic trees: An integrated meth-od. Journal of Molecular Evolution 20(2), 175–186 (1984)

3. Lee, C., Grasso, C., Sharlow, M.F.: Multiple sequence alignment using partial order graphs. Bioinformatics 18(3), 452–464 (2002)
4. Hernández-Guía, M., Mulet, R., Rodríguez-Pérez, S.: A new simulated annealing algorithm for the multiple sequence alignment problem: The approach of polymers in a random media. Physical Review E 72(3), 1–7 (2005)
5. Horng, J.-T., Wu, L.-C., Lin, C.-M., Yang, B.-H.: A genetic algorithm for multiple sequence alignment. LNCS, vol. 9, pp. 407–420. Springer, Heidelberg (2005)
6. Notredame, C., Higgins, D.G.: SAGA: Sequence alignment by genetic algorithm. Nucleic Acids Research 24(8), 1515–1524 (1996)
7. Kennedy, J., Eberhart, R.C.: Particle swarm optimization. In: Proc. of IEEE Int'l. Conf. on Neural Networks, IV, pp. 1942–1948. IEEE Press, Piscataway (1995)
8. Lei, C., Ruan, J.: A particle swarm optimization algorithm for finding DNA sequence motifs. In: Proc. IEEE Conf., pp. 166–173 (2008)
9. Liu, B., Wang, L., Jin, Y.H.: Improved particle swarm optimization combined with chaos. Chaos, Solitons Fractals 25(5), 1261–1271 (2005)
10. Thompson, J.D., Plewniak, F., Poch, O.: A comprehensive comparison of multiple sequence alignment programs. Nucleic Acid Research 27(13), 2682–2690 (1999)
11. Jun-min, L., Yue-lin, G.: Chaos particle swarm optimization algorithm. Computer applications 28(2), 322–325 (2008)
12. Lee, Z.-J., Su, S.-F., Chuang, C.-C., Liu, K.-H.: Genetic algorithm with ant colony optimization (GA-ACO) for multiple sequence alignment. Applied Soft Computing, 55–78 (2008)
13. Wei-li, X., Zhen-cing, W., Bao-guo, X.: Application of the PSO algorithm with mutation operator to multiple sequence alignment. Control Engineering of China 15(4), 357–368 (2008)

Model Checking Algorithm Based on Ant Colony Swarm Intelligence

Xiangning Wu*, Chengyu Hu[1], and Yuan Wang[2]

[1] School of Computer, China University Of Geosciences, Hubei Wuhan 430074
{wxning,huchengyu}@cug.edu.cn
[2] Computer institute, National University Of Defense Technology, Hunan Changsha 410073
wxningwy@gmail.com

Abstract. This paper proposes a novel model checking algorithm. This algorithm distributes mobile agents, artificial ants modeled natural ants, on control flow graph and states graph of the programs. While the ants reversely track correct traces and error traces, and deposit two kinds of pheromone representing respectively correct traces and error traces along the travel between vertexes of the control flow graph. According to pheromone deposited on traces by ants, causes of the specific errors can be automatically located. Furthermore, the independent and synchronous performance of ants makes it possbile to track different correct traces and error traces at the same time, and locate multiple causes of different errors synchronously. The results of the experiments on medium and small size programs show that the algorithm is effective.

Keywords: Model checking, Automated software testing, Ant colony swarm intelligence, Pheromone.

1 Introduction

How to ensure the correctness of the systems has become of the biggest challenges faced by designers of the hardware and software. Many researchers proposed different methods of detecting the defects of systems, among them, the most notable ones are *Formal Methods*. In a large number of formal methods, *Model Checking* was successfully used in verification of hardware and software as an important technology of the automated validation[1]. For example : the SPIN project developed by Bell Labs [2] was used as model checker for synchronized parallel systems .Microsoft's SLAM project [3] has been widely used in driver testing of the Windows operating system.

The process of the software model checking usually begin with abstracting the model of the system from the source code, and check if the model satisfy the specified attributes, if the system is incorrect, a error trace at the source level is returned. Programmers can track the error trace to discover the causes and correct them.

---

* This work was partially supported by the National Science Fund of China under grant No.60274014, the National Science Fund of Hubei Province under grant No.12003ABA043, and the Research Foundation for Outstanding Young Teachers, China University of Geosciences (Wuhan) under grant No.CUGQNL0617.

Z. Cai et al. (Eds.): ISICA 2009, CCIS 51, pp. 361–368, 2009.
© Springer-Verlag Berlin Heidelberg 2009

However, many error traces are so long that programmers have to spent considerable time to inspect them. Further more, the model checkers only report one error trace per run, the efficiency is relatively low.

This paper presents a novel model checking algorithm based on the ant colony swarm intelligence, the algorithm distribute artificial ants in the model, who can reversely track correct traces and error traces, and deposit pheromone on traces. Comparing pheromone on correct traces with those on error traces we can locate causes.

1.1 Model Checking and Testing

Model Checking is a method of the formal validation used in finite-state system, which check if the system satisfies some properties by exhaustively exploring the reachable state space of a model. That is, given a program P and the formal specification ψ, and model M abstracted from P, if M satisfy ψ then P is correct, otherwise, a counterexample is returned. Figure 1 is the process of the model checking

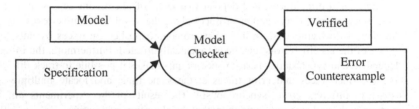

Fig. 1. The Process of the Model Checking

A models is always represented in form of *Control Flow Graph* and *States Transition Graph*[4], the statements of the source program are mapped to *vertexes* of the control flow graph.

The control flow graph of the program P is a directed graph $G^* = (V^*, E^*, e_{main}, x)$ with vertexes set V^*, edges set E^*, entry vertex e_{main} and exit vertexes set x. G^* has single entry vertex and no less than one exit vertexes.

A *state* Ω at a vertex v represents one of the combinations of the value of the variables (before the execution of the statement associated with v). States(v) represents the set of reachable states of v, that is, if there is a trace that ends with (v,Ω), then $\Omega \in$ States(v). Let Θ denote the set of all states.

Each vertex $v \in V^*$ has an associated *transfer function* $\delta(v, \Omega)$ that maps a state to another. For example, if the statement at v is executed in state Ω then the resultant state is $\delta(v, \Omega)$.

Transition means the conversion from one state to another, A transition is denoted by a directed pair $(v_1, \Omega_1) \rightarrow (v_2, \Omega_2)$ such that $(v_1, v_2) \in E^*$ and $(v_2, \Omega_2) \in \delta(v_1, \Omega_1)$. A sequence $\{(v_1, \Omega_1), (v_2, \Omega_2), ..., (v_k, \Omega_k)\}$ denotes a trace, here $v_1 = e_{main}$, and $(v_i, \Omega_i) \rightarrow (v_{i+1}, \Omega_{i+1})$ for $0 < i < k$.

Validation function f can check the validity of the states. if there is a state Ω at vertex v make $f(\Omega) = $ false, then an error trace T_{error} ending with (v, Ω) exists.

1.2 Ant Colony Swarm Intelligence

Ant Colony Optimization (ACO) draws inspiration from problem-solving activities of social insects – ants[5]. Collectively a colony of ants can perform complex social tasks such as searching for food, building and carrying large items, and emigrating of a colony. Ants in nature achieve indirect communication by laying a chemical substance called pheromone that induces changes in the environment which can be sensed by other ants. In ACO, a colony of biological ants is modeled as a society of artificial ants - mobile agents, who can travel between vertexes, deposit pheromone and collect information of transitions between vertexes. all mobile agents cooperate and exhibit collectively intelligent behavior such as tracking correct or error traces which are impossible achieved by single agent.

2 Proposed Algorithm

2.1 Architecture and Assumptions

The entire control flow graph can be seen as network composed of a lot of ant nests, as well as the links between these nests, each vertex in control flow graph is a nest, and transitions became links between the nests. The nests can generate and issue new ants, each nest has a pheromone table, in which the ants passing by the nest deposit pheromone. The most important nest is $v_1 = e_{main}$, which is the starting point of all traces. Figure 2 shows an ant nests network.

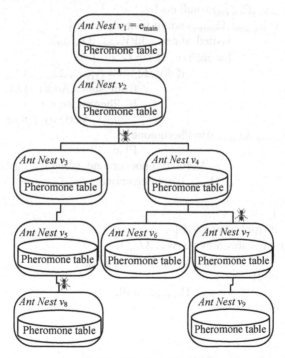

Fig. 2. Ant nests network

2.2 The Artificial Ants Deposit Pheromone on Traces

Each vertex v_i has a pheromone table, a $(m+n)$-by-k matrix, m and n is the number of the correct traces and error traces across v_i respectively, k is the number of the transitions issued from v_i. The entry of pheromone table, pheromone_table $(T(v, \Omega),((v_i, \Omega_i),(v_{next}, \Omega_{next})))$, is value of the pheromone, means that the transition $((v_i, \Omega_i) \rightarrow (v_{next}, \Omega_{next}))$ is a section of the trace $T(v, \Omega)$, $T(v, \Omega)$ is a correct or error trace ended with (v, Ω), if $T(v, \Omega)$ is a correct path, the pheromone value is positive(eg +1), else if $T(v, \Omega)$ is an error trace, the pheromone value is negative (eg -1).

When a state (v, Ω) is verified as an error state, $f(\Omega) = $ false, a error ant Ant_{error} will be generated and issued from (v,Ω). Ant_{error} reversely tracks the error trace until it reached the entry vertex v_1, and deposits error pheromone while passing through vertexes. When Ant_{error} reached v_1, the information of the error trace will be recorded and uniquely identifies by $T_{error}(v, \Omega)$, then Ant_{error} die out automatically.

We can generate a correct ant $Ant_{correct}$ for every verified correct state (v_x, Ω_x) at the exit vertex v_x, here $f(\Omega_x) = $ true. Each $Ant_{correct}$ tracks the correct trace until it reached the entry vertex v_1, and deposits correct pheromone while passing through vertexes.

```
Procedure TrackTraces (G*, δ, v, Ω, f){
    int Pheromone = (f(Ω)?1:-1) ;
    state (v_current ,Ω_current)=(v, Ω);
        set_of_states front_states = Ø;
        set_of_states visited_states = Ø;
        while (v_current ,Ω_current)≠null do {
                if (v_current ,Ω_current) not in visited_states {
                        visited_states .add(v_current ,Ω_current);
                        for each (v_i, Ω_i) in G* do {
                                if δ(v_i, Ω_i) = = (v_current ,Ω_current) {
                                        front_states.Add(v_i, Ω_i);
                                        If Pheromone <0
                                                Vertex(v_i).pheromone_table(T_erro
r(v, Ω),((v_i, Ω_i),(v_current ,Ω_current)))= Pheromone;
                                        Else
                                        Vertex(v_i).pheromone_table(T_correct(v, Ω),((v_i, Ω_i),(v_curre
nt ,Ω_current)))= Pheromone;
                                }
                }
                if front_states≠Ø {
                front_states.remove (v_fore ,Ω_fore);
                        (v_current ,Ω_current)=( v_fore ,Ω_fore);
                else{
                        (v_current ,Ω_current)=null;
                }
        }
    }
}
```

Fig. 3. Algorithm for ants tracking traces

When Ant$_{correct}$ reached v_1, it will die out automatically, and the correct trace will be uniquely identifies by T$_{correct}$(v_x, Ω_x).

Multiple ants can tracking different correct traces and error traces at the same time.

Figure 3 presents the high-level description of the algorithm in procedure *Track-Traces*. The parameters of the algorithm are:

- a control flow graph G^*
- a transfer function $\delta : (V^*,\Theta) \rightarrow (V^*,\Theta)$
- a specified vertex $v \in V^*$ and one of its reachable state $\Omega \in$ States(v)
  a "correctness" validating function $f : \Theta \rightarrow$ bool.

2.3 Locating Causes of the Errors According to Pheromone

When all of the error ants and correct ants reached the entrance vertex v_1, searching causes ants will be generated and issued from v_1, one searching causes ant correspond to one error trace, for example, an searching causes ant Ant$_{search}$(v, Ω) is sending out from the initial state (v_1, Ω_1) of the error trace T$_{error}$(v, Ω), it goes forward along the error trace and search the causes of error by examining pheromone tables at the vertexes passing through. If the edge to which the next transition of the error trace belong has correct pheromone and error pheromone at the same time, the edge is not the cause of the error because it overlaps with the edge of some correct traces, so the ant go forward and keep searching until it find out one edge which only have error pheromone and don't has any correct pheromone, this edge is a branch point of the error trace and correct traces, the end point of the edge is the likely cause of the error.

All of the vertexes of the error trace behind the branch point may be the causes of the error, so the ant must find them out one by one. The ant die out automatically after reaching the end point of the error trace. The searching causes ants can work independently and synchronously too. Figure 4 presents the high-level description of the algorithm in procedure *Locating*, the algorithm takes the control flow graph G^* and the error trace T$_{error}$(v, Ω) as its parameters, and save returned result – causes of the error into the set Causes(T$_{error}$(v, Ω)).

```
procedure Locating(G*, Terror(v, Ω)){
      state (vcurrent ,Ωcurrent)= Terror (v, Ω).Gethead();
      state (vnext ,Ωnext)= Terror (v, Ω).GetNextTransition(vcurrent ,Ωcurrent);
      while (vcurrent ,Ωcurrent)!=( v, Ω) do{
             if not exist Vertex(vcurrent).pheromone_table(Tcorrect (v', Ω'),(( vcurrent ,
Ωcurrent'),( vnext, Ωnext')))>0
             {
                    Causes(Terror(v, Ω)).AddCause(vnext);
             }
             (vcurrent ,Ωcurrent) = (vnext ,Ωnext);
             (vnext ,Ωnext) = Terror (v, Ω). GetNextTransition (vcurrent ,Ωcurrent);
      }
}
```

Fig. 4. Error cause locating algorithm

2.4 Illustrating the Algorithm by Serving an Example

The source program in Figure 5(a) use functions Lock() and UnLock() to acquire and release resource. The resource must be locked and unlocked in strict alternation. In order to facilitate the analysis, the program can be transformed into the program in Figure 5(b), where the value of L will be true after locking, and false after unlocking. Repeated locking or repeated unlocking will lead to failure in assertion.

```
                                      main() {
                                        assume(!L)
         main() {                  1    assert(!L); L := true;
  1           Lock();              2    if (...)
  2           if (...)             3    {assert(L); L := false;}
  3               UnLock();             else
              else                 4    ...;
  4               ...;             5    assert(!L); L := true;
  5           Lock();              6    if (...)
  6           if (...)             7    {assert(L); L := false;}
  7               UnLock();             else
              else                 8    ...
  8               ...;             9    assert(!L);
  9           return;                 }
          }

              (a)                            (b)
```

Fig. 5. Example program with improper lock and unlock

Figure 6 presents the control flow graph and states graph of the program in Figure 5(b), there are two error states failed in assertion, (5,L=T) and (9,L=T). The error ants dispatched from these two states tracked out following two error traces:

$T_{error}(5, L=T) = \{(1, L=F), (2, L=T), (4, L=T), (5, L=T)\}$
$T_{error}(9, L=T) = \{(1, L=F), (2, L=T), (3, L=T), (5, L=F), (6, L=T), (8, L=T), (9, L=T)\}$

The exit vertex of the program is vertex 9, state (9,L=T) is asserted correct, the correct ant dispatched from this state tracked out following correct trace:

$T_{correct}(9, L=F) = \{(1, L=F), (2, L=T), (3, L=T), (5, L=F), (6, L=T), (7, L=T), (9, L=F)\}$

The error traces and correct trace can be simplified as:

$T_{error}(5, L=T) = \{1, 2, 4, 5\}$
$T_{error}(9, L=T) = \{1, 2, 3, 5, 6, 8, 9\}$
$T_{correct}(9, L=F) = \{(1, 2, 3, 5, 6, 7, 9\}$

In Figure 6, the correct traces and error traces are denoted by real lines and dashed lines respectively. They are revealed by the pheromone in pheromone tables. The pheromone tables of every vertex shown in Table 1.

In vertex 5, the edge (5, 6) has correct pheromone and error pheromone, the edge (6,8) only has error pheromone, so he edge (6,8) became the branch point of the

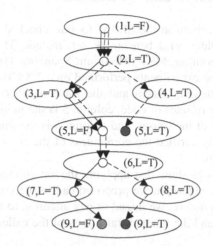

Fig. 6. Control flow graph and states graph for the program

Table 1. Pheromone tables of vertexes(ant nests)

Vertex 1	((1, L=F), (2, L=T))	
Terror(9, L=T)	-1	
Terror(5, L=T)	-1	
Tcorrect(9, L=F)	1	
Vertex 2	((2, L=T), (3, L=T))	((2, L=T), (4, L=T))
Terror(9, L=T)	-1	
Terror(5, L=T)		-1
Tcorrect(9, L=F)	1	
Vertex 3	((3, L=T), (5, L=F))	
Terror(9, L=T)	-1	
Tcorrect(9, L=F)	1	
Vertex 4	((4, L=T), (5, L=T))	
Terror(5, L=T)	-1	
Vertex 5	((5, L=F), (6, L=T))	
Terror(9, L=T)	-1	
Tcorrect(9, L=F)	1	
Vertex 6	((6, L=T), (7, L=T))	((6, L=T), (8, L=T))
Terror(9, L=T)		-1
Tcorrect(9, L=F)	1	
Vertex 7	((7, L=T), (9, L=F))	
Tcorrect(9, L=F)	1	
Vertex 8	((8, L=T), (9, L=T))	
Terror(9, L=T)	-1	

error trace $T_{error}(9, L=T)$ and the correct trace $T_{correct}(9, L=F)$, the end point of the edge (6,8), {8}, is the cause of $T_{error}(9, L=T)$. Likewise, {4} is the cause of $T_{error}(5, L=T)$.

3   Experimental Results and Conclusions

We have tested our algorithm in the SLAM toolkit, checked several C source programs belong to the Olden v1.0 benchmark set, include TSP(Traveling Salesman Problem), Perimeter algorithm, MST (Minimum Spanning Tree algorithm). Table 2 presents the results of the experiments performed on a 2.8 GHz Pentium PC with 1.5 GB RAM. There are 20 error traces and the same number of causes discovered. Column 2 is the number of lines of code, column 3 is the number of the error traces, column 4 is the number of the causes, and column 5 is the running time of the algorithm. We have manually verified the correctness of the error traces and causes discovered by our algorithm.

The experimental results show that applying the ant colony intelligence to model checking is feasible, the algorithm we proposed can locate errors and causes in programs effectively. In the future, we intend to pay attention to the transitions between the callers and callees, and the internal transitions of the callees, so as to further improve our algorithm.

Table 2. Experimental Results

Program	Number of lines of code	Number of error traces	Number of causes	Running Time(Sec)
TSP	565	4	4	138
Perimeter	395	3	3	82
MST	582	13	13	103

References

1. Clarke, E.M., Grumberg, O., Peled, D.A.: Model Checking. MIT Press, Cambridge (2000)
2. Holznmnn, G.J.: The model checker SPIN. IEEE Transactions on Software Engineering 23(5), 279–295 (1997)
3. Ball, T., Rajamani, S.K.: The SLAM project, Debugging System Software Via static Analysis. In: Proc. POPL, pp. 1–3. ACM, New York (2002)
4. Reps, T., Horwitz, S., Sagiv, M.: Precise interprocedural dataflow analysis via graph reachability. In: POPL 1995: Principles of Programming Languages, pp. 49–61. ACM, New York (1995)
5. Bonabeau, E., Dorigo, M., Theraulaz, G.: Inspiration for optimization from social insect behavior. Nature 406(6), 39–42 (2000)

QPSO-MD: A Quantum Behaved Particle Swarm Optimization for Consensus Pattern Identification

Souham Meshoul and Tasneem Al-Owaisheq

Information Technology Department, College of Computer and Information Sciences
King Saud University Riyadh,
Kingdom of Saudi Arabia
meshoul@ccis.edu.sa, tasneem.ksu@gmail.com

Abstract. Particle Swarm Optimization (PSO) has been successfully applied to a wide range of fields. The recent introduction of quantum mechanics principles into PSO has given rise to a Quantum behaviour PSO (QPSO) algorithm. This paper investigates its application into motif discovery, a challenging task in bioinformatics and molecular biology. Given a set of input DNA sequences, the proposed framework acts as a search process where a population of particles is depicted by a quantum behavior. Each particle represents a set of regulatory patterns from which a consensus pattern or motif model is derived. The corresponding fitness function is related to the total number of pairwise matches between nucleotides in the input sequences. Experiment results on synthetic and real data are very promising and prove the effectiveness of the proposed framework.

Keywords: Particle Swarm Optimization, Quantum behaved PSO, Motif Discovery, Sequence Analysis, Consensus Pattern.

1 Introduction

This paper describes an application of Quantum particle Swarm Optimization (QPSO) that consists in finding motif patterns across DNA sequences which is one of the major challenges in Bioinformatics [1]. The original particle Swarm Optimization algorithm was introduced by Kennedy and Eberhart in 1995 [2]. Like genetic algorithms, PSO is a population based evolutionary algorithm. It is inspired by the social behavior of birds' flock and fish' school. Such behavior helps the swarm to find food and escape from local danger. When an individual finds food, it informs the other individuals so they gradually fly towards the same food source. This collective intelligence where each individual within a group contributes with its experience to the group in a manner that makes the group stronger to face danger or to find food is the essence of PSO.

PSO can be abstracted as a global continuous optimization algorithm devoted to solve problems where a solution can be encoded in terms a parameters' vector. It uses a population of particles (a swarm) to explore the search space (parameters space) to find optimal or good quality solutions. Each particle is defined using a position vector

Z. Cai et al. (Eds.): ISICA 2009, CCIS 51, pp. 369–378, 2009.
© Springer-Verlag Berlin Heidelberg 2009

and a velocity vector. The first one represents a potential solution to the problem at hand whereas the second one serves to monitor the change in position during the search process. This latter is governed by two main iterative equations showing how velocities and positions are updated. These equations are given by:

$$v_i(t+1) = w.v_i(t) + c_1.rand(0,1).\left[P_{selfbest}(t) - P_i(t)\right] + c_2.rand(0,1)\left[P_{globalbest} - P_i(t)\right] \quad (1)$$

$$P_i(t+1) = P_i(t) + v_i(t+1) \quad (2)$$

Where v_i and P_i stand for velocity and position vectors respectively. w, c_1 and c_2 denote respectively the inertia weight, the cognitive and social components. They refer to the degree of belief of the particle in itself, its experience and its neighbors. $P_{selfbest}$ and $P_{globalbest}$ refer to the best self performance for each particle and the global best within the swarm.

Since the original PSO algorithm, several variants have been proposed and applied to a variety of problems. The aim is either to improve the search capabilities of the algorithm like more diversity to prevent getting stuck in local optimum or to extend its use to other kind of problems like discrete optimization problems. Recently, quantum principles have been introduced into PSO by Sun et al. [3] resulting in a new algorithm called Quantum Particle Swarm Optimization (QPSO) and improved in [4]. The key idea is to define particles' motion in the field of quantum mechanics instead of the classical Newtonian mechanics where particles are depicted by position and velocity. According to quantum mechanics positions and velocities cannot be determined simultaneously. Therefore, in QPSO each particle is depicted by a wave function whose probability density function helps in learning the probability a particle is in a given position. QPSO focuses on positions only without velocities and suggest the use of the following key rule to update positions:

If $k \geq 0.5$ then $$P_i(t+1) = p + \beta.|Mbest - P_i(t)|.\ln(1/u) \quad (3)$$

Else $$P_i(t+1) = p - \beta.|Mbest - P_i(t)|.\ln(1/u) \quad (4)$$

Where k and u are random numbers distributed uniformly on [0..1], P_i represents the particle position vector, β is the only one tunable parameter used in QPSO called the contraction expansion coefficient, $Mbest$ is the mean best position or Mainstream Thought Point corresponding to the center of gravity of the self best position of the particle swarm. It is expressed as shown in equation (5) below where M and D denote respectively the swarm size and the particle vector dimension.

$$Mbest = 1/M \sum_{i=1}^{M} Pselfbest_i = \left(1/M \sum_{i=1}^{M} Pselfbest_{i1}, 1/M \sum_{i=1}^{M} Pselfbest_{i2}, ..., 1/M \sum_{i=1}^{M} Pselfbest_{iD}\right) \quad (5)$$

Finally, p is a variable that represents the coordinates of the local point to which particles converge. It is given by equation 6 below where φ_1 is a randomly chosen number in [0..1].

$$p = \varphi_1 Pselfbest_i + (1 - \varphi_1) Pgbest) \quad (6)$$

This paper focuses on the use of QPSO to solve motif discovery problem. The rest of the paper is organized as follows. Section 2 presents motif discovery and related concepts and methods. In section 3, a formulation of the tackled problem is given. The proposed method is described in section 4. Section 5 reports on the conducted experiments and the obtained results. Finally conclusions and perspectives are drawn.

2 DNA Motif Discovery

The high throughput sequencing methods and microarray technology with the completion of the human genome project has opened up major challenges in modeling, analyzing, comparing and simulating the biological information embedded in the huge amount of data provided by the on-line databases. Motif discovery is one of the challenging issues in bioinformatics [1] that emerged from the need in sequence analysis to understand gene function and gene regulatory networks. It is mainly concerned with the task of finding transcription factor binding sites in genomic information in order to decipher the mechanisms that regulate gene expression. A gene is a fundamental unit or section of inherited information in DNA that codes for a specific function/protein. It conveys the information needed to produce a protein which is the essence of gene expression. This latter begins with binding of multiple protein factors known as transcription factors to promoter sequences.

A DNA motif can be viewed as a short DNA segment, i.e. a nucleic acid sequence pattern for which acting as a transcription factor binding site is the biological significance. A motif occurs in different genes or several times within a gene. Therefore, motif discovery can be simply defined as the process of depicting an unknown pattern that occurs frequently (over-represented) across a set of sequences.

Although much effort has been spent to cope with motif discovery, it still remains an open problem. No method has been found to be the best for all cases. Methods for motif discovery can be viewed as combinations of the following choices: 1- motif model, 2- motif assessment function and 3- search strategy. The motif model identifies the type of the model used like spaced dyad and palindromic motifs [5]. The second choice also known as objective function helps quantifying the motif significance. It is a critical issue in designing a motif discovery problem as it should assign the best score to the true binding sites. The search strategy deals with the framework that describes the way search is performed to find motifs. Motif discovery methods can be classified in different ways using different criteria. Depending on the background DNA sequence information used [5], a method can deal with either 1-Promoter sequences of coregulated genes from a single genome, 2- Orthologous promoter sequences of a single gene from multiple species 3- Phylogenetic footprinting or 4- Promoter sequences of coregulated genes as well as phylogenetic footprinting. If the search strategy criterion is considered, methods for motif discovery fall into two broad categories: string based and stochastic methods. String based methods also called enumeration methods are based on exhaustive search. Therefore they are rigorous and exact but limited to predict short motifs with highly conserved core across simple patterns. Examples of such methods include [6,7]. The second category of methods rely on the use of probabilistic models and/or machine learning techniques [5]. Within this category, Multiple Expectation Maximization Estimation (MEME) has been introduced by Baily et al. [8] as an extension of the Expectation Maximization (EM) algorithm proposed by Lawrence et al. [9] to identify motifs in unaligned biopolymer sequences. Another series of algorithms based on Gibbs Sampling have been suggested [10]. In [11] a Markov Chain Monte Carlo approach has been adopted. Roth et al. developed AlignACE to align nucleic acid conserved elements using a higher order Markov Chain background model and a probability distribution to estimate the number of copies of the motif in a sequence [12]. Other algorithms of this class include Motif sampler [13] which is a modification of the original Gibbs sampling algorithm and BioProspector [14] used for promoter sequences of coregulated genes. Population based algorithms have been also used to carry out search in the motifs' space in quest of finding appropriate motifs. Examples include FMGA algorithm [15] that uses a genetic algorithm with a specific purpose mutation operator and fitness function. Recently, Particle Swarm Optimisation has been tailored to motif discovery and resulted in some proposals like in [16] for protein and in [17] for DNA motif finding. In the latter, a word dissimilarity graph has been used to cast the motif discovery problem as a continuous integer optimization one and a modification of the original PSO has been adopted to escape from local minima. Surveys on motif discovery can be found in [5,18]. Assessments of these methods can be found in [18,19].

3   Problem Definition

As described before, finding motifs arises from the need to investigate a set of biological sequences that appear to be regulated in a similar manner. Despite the great amount of work that has been devoted to motif discovery, it still remains a challenging task for many reasons among which its complexity that becomes even more critical with the number of sequences, their length as well as the length of the motif to be discovered. Informally, motif discovery problem can be simply described as the task of finding a pattern or substring that occurs frequently across a set of sequences. In a more formal way, it consists in [20]:

Given a set of N sequences $S=\{s_i\}$ $i=1..N$ defined over an alphabet $\sum$ with $|s_i| = m$ and l, d within $0 \leq d < l < m$, we define the (l, d) motif discovery problem as finding a substring x with $|x| = l$ such that each s_i has a substring x_i of length l such that x_i differs from x in at most d places.

Obviously, the problem is combinatorial in nature. Therefore, it requires optimization techniques to be solved. In our work, we focus on DNA sequences although the framework can be applied to protein sequences. We suggest the use of a quantum inspired PSO. In the following, we describe the developed framework which is named QPSO-MD (Quantum Particle Swarm Optimization for Motif Discovery).

4   QPSO-MD: The Proposed Framework

To apply successfully Quantum Particle Swarm Optimization to the tackled problem, we need to define:

1. A representation scheme that allows to express problem solutions in terms of particles (that is, particle encoding).
2. The fitness of each particle which is related to the quality of the solution and.
3. The general dynamic that helps evolving the swarm towards good quality solutions.

The task to be handled by the proposed framework can be illustrated as shown in figure 1. Given a set of DNA sequences, QPSO-MD explores the motifs' space in order to find out the regulatory elements that are short words in the input sequences from which a motif model or consensus pattern can be derived as explained by the example shown in figure 2. Therefore, the consensus pattern is not exactly the same in each sequence because point mutations may occur in the sequences. We assume that the motif length is known.

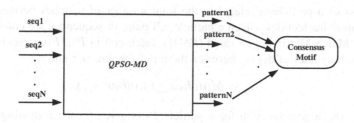

Fig. 1. General specification of QPSO-MD

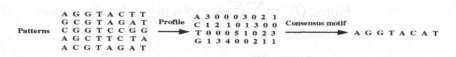

Fig. 2. Deriving consensus motif from patterns

4.1 Particle Encoding

We adopt a simple encoding in which each particle is represented by a vector containing the starting positions of patterns in the input sequences. Figure 3 illustrates such encoding.

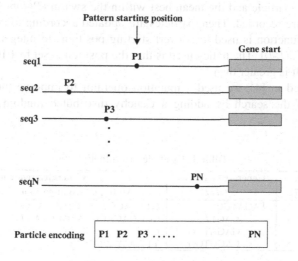

Fig. 3. Particle encoding

During the evolution of the search process, a repair function is used to restrict the values of the positions to the interval $[1..(L - l)]$, where L is the length of sequences and l the length of the motif. Although positions are integer values, the algorithm deals with them as if they are continuous values. Repair function handles conversion of continuous values to integer ones.

4.2 Fitness Function

The fitness of a particle is related to the total number of matches between pairs of same location nucleotides. Given a particle, all pairs of sequences are considered and a Particle Match Matrix is generated (*PMM*). Each cell in *PMM* represents the number of matching nucleotides w_{ij} between the input sequences s_i and s_j.

$$w_{ij} = Matches\_number(s_i, s_j) \tag{7}$$

Therefore, the fitness function for a particle P_k is given by the following score that records the total number of matches through all pairs of sequences.

$$Fitness(P_k) = \sum_{i=1}^{N} \sum_{j=1}^{i-1} w_{ij} \quad : N \text{ is the number of sequences} \tag{8}$$

4.3 Overall Dynamic of QPSO-MD

The objective of the algorithm is to maximize the fitness function described above in equation 8. Informally, the dynamic of the search process can be defined as follows. Initially, a set of particles is generated by randomly selecting motif positions. Then the swarm of particles undergoes an evolutionary process during which the following tasks are performed. First a match matrix is computed for each particle in order to record its fitness value and update its self best performance (*Pselfbest*). Second, the the global best particle and the mean best within the swarm (*Pglobalbest* and *Mbest* respectively) are recorded. Then, particles are updated according to equations (5) and (6). A repair function is used to convert starting positions to integer values lying in the interval $[1 ..(L-l)]$. The policy used is that the position is set to 1 if it is less than 1 and to $(L-l)$ if it is greater than L.

As suggested in [4], we used a mutation operator to improve the diversification capabilities of the search by adding a Cauchy distributed random value to *Mbest* elements.

Table 1. Example of synthetic data

Consensus pattern (*l*=7)	Generated patterns (*d*=2)	Generated sequences Motif planted at positions 23, 24,3 and 14
CAGATGG	TAGATGG CAGTTGG GAGATGG CAGGTGG	GTTCAGCTTCCCTGCCAGGCTGTAGATGGA GCGCACAGCTAAACCTAGTGTACCAGTTGG CAGAGATGGTCCGCGCCCAGCGCTGCCACG TTTCCAACGTCGCCAGGTGGCCCGGTCAAA

Input: Set of N sequences, Motif length l

Initialize a population of M particles $P(t_0)$ with random motif positions

Repeat
    β decreases linearly with iterations
    For *(k = 1 to population size M)*
        Compute matching matrix for each particle P_k
        Evaluate each particle's fitness $f(P_k)$ using eq.(8)
        If $f(P_k) > f(P_{selfbest})$ *// Record $P_{selfbest}$*
            $P_{selfbest} = P_k$
        If $f(P_k) > f(P_{globalbest})$ *// Record $P_{globalbest}$*
            $P_{globalbest} = P_k$
    EndFor

    Calculate Mbest using equation (5)

    For *(k = 1 to population size M)*
        For *(d = 1 to dimension D=N)*
            $\varphi_1 = rand(0,1)$
            $p = \varphi_1 * P_{selfbest}(d) + (1 - \varphi_1) * P_{globalbest}(d)$
            $u = rand(0,1)$
            If $rand(0,1) > 0.5$
                $P_{kd} = p - \beta * | mbest_d - x_{kd} | * ln(1/u)$ eq.(3)
                else
                $P_{kd} = p + \beta * | mbest_d - x_{kd} | * ln(1/u)$ eq.(4)
        EndFor
        Repair (P_k)
    EndFor
Until *Maximum number of iterations reached*
    Output: Motif model

---

5   Experimental Results

Both synthetic and real data have been used to assess the performance of the proposed technique. Synthetic data have been generated using a reverse process to the one shown in figure 1. In another way, a consensus pattern has been generated randomly. From this one, several patterns have been derived by altering d positions randomly. Then each of the derived patterns has been planted at a random position in a background sequence generated randomly. The resulting sequences are then used as input sequences to *QPSO-MD* searcher. Several runs have been executed and the success rate has been recorded. The algorithm succeeded in identifying the right patterns and therefore the initial generated consensus motif. The success rate was about 100% when the background sequences are highly mismatched and about 97% otherwise. Table 1 shows an example of synthetic data used in our experiments. Figure 4 show the behavior of the fitness function with and without using Cauchy based mutation. Obviously, the use of the mutation improves the performance and helps achieving better quality solutions.

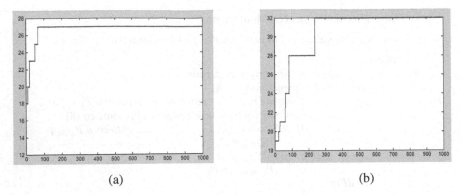

(a)   (b)

Fig. 4. Fitness function through iterations (a) Without (b) with mutation

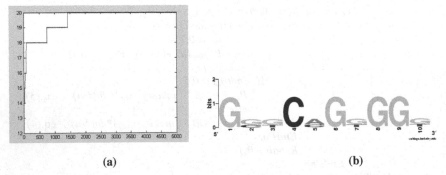

(a)   (b)

Fig. 5. Fitness behavior using mouse data(a) and corresponding sequence logo(b)

For experiments on real data, benchmark data sets available at [21] have been used. In figure 5 we show the behavior of the fitness function with mutation using mouse data (mus06g) with the sequence logo of the corresponding identified patterns.

6 Conclusion

In this paper, we proposed a new framework for DNA motif discovery that suggests the use of a particle swarm optimization approach with a quantum based dynamic. Particles are encoded in a way to identify starting positions of regulatory patterns in the input sequences. The advantage of QPSO is that only one tunable parameter decreasing linearly with iterations is required unlike the original PSO and other population based algorithms such as genetic algorithms that involve several control parameters. Experimental results are very promising and show the effectiveness of the proposed framework using both synthetic and real data sets. As ongoing work, we propose investigating other fitness functions, extending the framework to other type of sequences and improving further the search capabilities of the algorithm.

Acknowledgment

This work was supported by the Research Center of Women Students Medical Studies & Sciences Sections at King Saud University, Riyadh under grant N° 6-A-30.

References

1. Bergeron, B.: Bioinformatics Computing. Prentice Hall, Englewood Cliffs (2002)
2. Kennedy, J., Eberhart, R.: Particle swarm optimization. In: IEEE Int. Conf. on Neural Network, pp. 1942–1948 (1995)
3. Sun, J., Jun, X.W., Feng, B.: A Global Search Strategy of Quantum-Behaved Particle Swarm Optimization. In: IEEE Conference on Cybernetics and Intelligent Systems, pp. 111–115 (2004)
4. Liu, J., Sun, J., Xu, W.: Quantum-Behaved Particle Swarm Optimization with Adaptive Mutation Operator. In: Jiao, L., Wang, L., Gao, X.-b., Liu, J., Wu, F. (eds.) ICNC 2006. LNCS, vol. 4221, pp. 959–967. Springer, Heidelberg (2006)
5. Das, M.K., Dai, H.-K.: A survey of DNA motif finding algorithms. BMC Bioinformatics 8(Suppl. 7), 21 (2007)
6. Tompa, M.: An exact method for finding short motifs in sequences, with application to the ribosome binding site problem. In: Seventh International Conference on Intelligent Systems on Molecular Biology, pp. 262–271 (1999)
7. Van Helden, J., Andre, B., Collado-Vides, J.: Extracting Regulatory Sites from the upstream region of yeast genes by computational analysis of oligonucleotides frequencies. Journal of Molecular Biology 28I, 827–842 (1998)
8. Bailey, T., Elkan, C.: Unsupervised learning of multiple motifs in biopolmers using expectation maximisation. Machine learning 21, 51–80 (1995)
9. Lawrence, C.E., Reilly, A.A.: An expectation maximization (EM) algorithm for the identification and characterization of common sites in unaligned biopolymer sequences. Proteins 7, 41–51 (1990)
10. Lawrence, C.E., Altschul, S.F., Boguski, M.S., Liu, J.S., Neuwald, A.F., Wootton, J.C.: Detecting subtle sequence signnals: a Gibbs sampling strategy for multiple alignment. Science 262, 208–214 (1993)
11. Hertz, G.Z., Hartzell, G.W., Stormo, G.D.: Identification of consensus patternsin unaligned DNA sequences known to be functionally related, comput. Appl. Biosci. 6, 81–92 (1990)
12. Roth, F.P., Hughes, J.D., Estep, P.W., Church, G.M.: Finding DNA regulatory motifs within unaligned noncoding sequences clustered by whole-genome mRNA quantitation. Nature Biotechnology 16, 939–945 (1998)
13. Thijs, G., Marchal, K., Moreau, Y.: A Gibbs sampling method to detect over-represented motifs in upstream regions of co-expressed gene. RECOMB 5, 305–312 (2001)
14. Liu, X., Brutlag, D.L., Liu, J.S.: BioProspector: Discovering conserved DNA motifs in upstream regulatory regions of coexpressed genes. In: Sixth Pacific Symposium on Biocomputing, pp. 127–138 (2001)
15. Liu, F.F.M., Jeffrey, J.P.T., Chen, R.M., Chen, S.N., Shih, S.H.: FMGA: Finding Motifs by Genetic Algorithm. In: Fourth IEEE Symposium on Bioinformatics and Bioengineering, p. 459 (2004)
16. Chang, B.C., Ratnaweera, A., Halgamuge, S., Watson, H.: Particle Swarm Optimisation for Protein Motif Discovery. Genetic Programming and Evolvable Machines Journal 2(5), 203–214 (2004)

17. Lei, C., Ruan, J.: Particle Swarm Optimisation for Finding DNA Sequence Motifs. In: BIBMW 2008, pp. 166–173 (2008)
18. Tompa, M., Li, N., Bailey, T., Church, G., De Moor, B., Eskin, E., Favorov, A., Frith, M., Fu, Y., Kent, W., Makeev, V., Mironov, A., Noble, W., Pavesi, G., Pesole, G., Rgnier, M., Simonis, N., Sinha, S., Thijs, G., Van Helden, J., Vandenbogaert, M., Weng, Z., Workman, C., Ye, C., Zhu, Z.: Assessing computational tools for the discovery of transcription factor binding site. Nat. biotechnology 23, 137–144 (2005)
19. Hu, J., Li, B., Kihara, D.: Limitations and potentials of current motif discovery algorithm. Nucleic Acids Research 15(33), 4899–4913 (2005)
20. Davila, J., Balla, S., Rajasekaran, S.: Fast and Practical Algorithms for Planted (l, d) Motif Search. IEEE/ACM Trans. Comput. Biol. Bioinformatics, 544–552 (2007)
21. http://bio.cs.washington.edu/assessment/download.html

Prediction of Hydrocarbon Reservoir Parameter Using a GA-RBF Neural Network

Jing Chen[1,2], Zhenhua Li[2], and Dan Zhao[2]

[1] Faculty of Resource, China University of Geosciences, China
[2] School of Computer, China University of Geosciences, China

Abstract. Prediction of hydrocarbon reservoir characteristics using seismic attributes is a very complicated problem with much nonlinear relation. The traditional BP neural network with a gradient decent approach may lead to local minima problem, resulting in the production of unstable and non-convergent solutions. To solve these problems and improve the precision, this paper introduces a GA-based optimized method of RBF neural network. A case study shows that the GA-RBF algorithm not only works with high predicting precision comparable to real measured data in oil reservoir thickness, but also is superior to that of tradition BP neural network.

Keywords: reservoir parameter prediction, RBF network, genetic algorithm, structure optimization.

1 Introduction

Reservoir characterization is a critical step in reservoir development and future production management. Knowing the details of a reservoir allows the simulation of different scenarios. The problem, however, is to define an accurate and suitable reservoir model including small-scale heterogeneity. Currently, the most abundant data about the reservoir, which is the seismic data, do not have enough resolution. The typical resolution of seismic data is on the order of 100 feet or more, which does not give enough detail of reservoir properties. In contrast, well log data, which are collected by inserting sensing devices into an exploratory well, give an excellent description of the well at scales ranging from centimeters to hundreds of meters. However, due to its high cost, only a few well locations have log data. This scarce information is usually not sufficient to build a reservoir model that includes the small scale variations. In between wells, reservoir parameter needs to be estimated[1]. However, predicting reservoir parameter from seismic attributes data in heterogeneous reservoirs is a complex problem.

Alternatively, neural networks have been increasingly applied to predict reservoir properties using seismic attributes data. Moreover previous investigations indicated that artificial neural networks, due to their excellent ability of non-linear mapping, generalization, self-organization and self-learning, have been proved to be of widespread utility in reservoir parameter prediction from geophysical seismic attributes data with good accuracy in heterogeneous reservoirs. However, neural network

Z. Cai et al. (Eds.): ISICA 2009, CCIS 51, pp. 379–386, 2009.

training with extensive data still remains to be time consuming. The back propagation (BP) neural network usually trained by back propagation of errors is perhaps the most popular network architecture in use today[2]. But the back propagation training algorithm with a gradient decent approach may suffer from local minima problem, resulting in the production of unstable and non-convergent solutions.

This article proposes a optimize method of radical basis function (RBF) neural network based on genetic algorithm (GA) for minimizing the time and improving the accuracy of reservoir parameter prediction. Moreover, this method is applied successfully to reservoir thickness predicting and obtains better effect in case study. In this method, it focuses on optimizing the basis function center parameters and restricting width using GA to find the optimal architecture and parameter of the RBF neural network.

2   GA-RBF Neural Network

In this section, we adopt a GA-RBF neural network.

The RBF network considered here consists of n input nodes, one output node and a hidden layer of m nodes. The structure of the RBF neural network is shown in Fig.1.

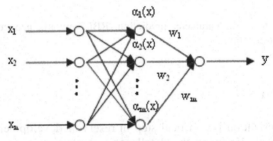

Input layer Hidden layer Output layer

Fig. 1. Structure of RBF Neural Network

Mathematically the network output is expressed as:

$$y = \sum_{i=1}^{m} w_i \alpha_i(x) \qquad (1)$$

where x is the data of samples, y is the predicted output, w_i is the output weight from the hidden node to the output node, and the basis function $\alpha_i(x)$ is chosen to be the Gaussian function, it is given by

$$\alpha_i(x) = \exp[\frac{-\left\| X - c_i \right\|^2}{2\sigma_i^2}] \qquad i = 1,2,\cdots,m \qquad (2)$$

where $X = (x_1, x_2, \cdots, x_n)^T$ $c_i = (c_{i1}, c_{i2}, \cdots, c_{in})^T$ is the center of the ith RBF hidden unit, and σ_i is the width of the ith RBF hidden unit.

A main advantage on using an RBF network in reservoir parameter predicting using seismic samples is that the weights w_i can be determined using a linear square method which makes this calibration method suitable for quickly processing. Learning algorithm of the neural network weight between output y and the hidden layer $\alpha_i(x)$ is

$$w_i(l+1) = w_i(l) + \beta[y^d - y(l)]\alpha_i(x)/\alpha_i^T(x) \tag{3}$$

where y^d is the desired output, l is the iterative times, $0 < \beta < 2$ is learning rate.

The errors are measured by mean square-error (MSE) as defined:

$$MSE = \frac{\sum_{i=1}^{n}(O_i - T_i)^2}{n} \tag{4}$$

where O_i is the desired output for the training data, T_i is the network output for the training data, and n is the number of data in the training data set[7][8].

However, the other parameters cannot be determined using a linear optimization method. In order to obtain the optimal network topology, we have proposed a training scheme by combining GA and RBF network.

2.1 Encode

In order to reduce the search space, one can search for a subset of training set to provide optimal basis function centers and restrict width σ:

$$\sigma \in (0, \sigma_{max}] \tag{5}$$

The width is represented by a binary string with k bits:

$$width = [b_k b_{k-1} \cdots b_2 b_1] \tag{6}$$

The following formula may be used to decode it:

$$\sigma = (\sum_{i=1}^{k} b_i 2^{i-1} + 1)\frac{\sigma_{max}}{2^k} \tag{7}$$

2.2 Evaluation Function

The fitness of a chromosome is evaluated via objective function. RMSE criterion is given by

$$RMSE = \sqrt{\sum_{i=1}^{N} \frac{(C_{NIRi} - C_{REFi})^2}{N}} \tag{8}$$

where N is the number of samples, C_{NIR} is the predicted concentration of the sample and C_{REF} is the concentration of the sample by the standard referenced method.

The objective function is evaluated over the training set and the monitoring set to avoid over fitting the training set and to improve the generalization performance.

2.3 RBF Neural Network Model Based on GA

The algorithm describes as follows:

```
begin
    t = 0;   // t: generation number
    initialize P(t) by encoding routine;
    // P(t):population of chromosomes
    fintness eval(P) by decoding routine;
    while (not termination condition) do
        crossover P(t) to yield C(t);   // C(t):offspring
        mutation P(t) to yield C(t);
        fitness eval(C) by decoding routine;
        select P(t+1) from P(t) and C(t);
        t = t+1;
    end
    RBF neural network iterative. Training RBF neural
network that deals parameter with GA, when the whole
neural network error reaches the appointed degree, the
training ends.
end.
```

3 Case Study

In the case study, we considered a simulation study to predict the thickness of oil reservoir based on the seismic information using GA-RBF model.

3.1 Network Input and Sample

The major tool to predict the thickness of oil reservoir is the seismic information. More than 55 seismic attributes derived from seismic data could be gotten. Not all of them have definite corresponding relationship with the thickness of reservoir. Obviously, the infinite increase of the number of attributes brings bad effects on reservoir prediction. In this article, we extract 10 seismic attributes as network input neurons which are max amplitude, mean amplitude, min amplitude, arc length, average energy, energy half-time, instantaneous frequency, instantaneous phase, average magnitude, ratio of pos to neg sample. Table 1 and Table 2 present the sample and

Table 1. Sample and seismic feature parameters[4]

Oil Well	Max amplitude	Mean amplitude	Min amplitude	Arc length	Average energy	Energy half-time
1	0.13	-0.1	-0.31	1.15	0.03	0.02
2	0.11	-0.60	-1.35	1.12	0.63	0.01
3	0.33	-0.26	-1.07	1.05	0.31	0.02
4	0.01	-053	-1.49	1.22	0.53	0.01
5	0.01	-0.60	-1.59	1.08	0.70	0.01
6*	0.00	-0.40	-1.05	1.21	0.25	0.01
7	0.00	-0.32	-0.89	1.08	0.20	0.01
8*	0.11	-0.63	-1.80	1.15	0.87	0.01
9	0.12	-0.32	-0.89	1.08	0.23	0.02
10*	0.15	-0.71	-1.87	1.15	1.05	0.01
11	0.03	-0.45	-1.64	1.16	0.50	0.02
12*	0.12	-0.67	-1.76	1.13	0.94	0.01
13	0.02	-0.58	-1.51	1.10	0.63	0.01

Table 2. Sample and seismic feature parameters[4]

Oil Well	Instantaneous frequency	Instantaneous phase	Average magnitude	Ratio of pos to neg sample
1	91.25	0.04	1.24	46.15
2	40.39	-0.50	1.84	27.78
3	37.32	0.12	1.45	66.67
4	37.97	0.68	2.15	17.65
5	37.54	0.23	1.48	37.50
6*	45.39	-0.90	1.68	10.53
7	35.19	-0.44	1.27	11.11
8*	39.01	-0.02	2.03	50.00
9	40.15	0.57	1.24	53.33
10*	37.95	0.11	2.07	57.14
11	42.88	0.57	1.35	26.32
12*	37.98	0.11	2.03	37.50
13	38.67	0.19	2.05	17.75

seismic feature parameters. Select 9 of the 13 wells as the sample training network, and 4 wells marked '*' as the testing sample.

3.2 Comparative Researches on Neural Network Prediction

According to the model designed in Section 2, when the training reaches the precision, all the seismic attributes are recognized and reservoir thickness is predicted. Prediction diagram of sandstone thickness is shown in Fig.2.

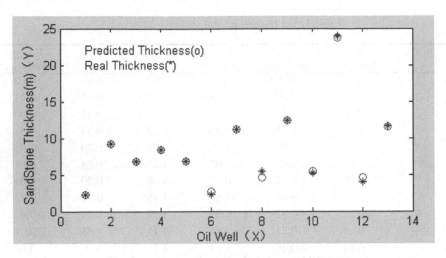

Fig. 2. Prediction diagram of sandstone thickness

And do a comparative research between GA-RBF network model and BP model. Compare data of drill statistical and prediction by GA-RBF and BP are listed in Table 3 and shown in Fig.3. We can see the result that GA-RBF model has better precision than BP model.

Table 3. Comparative table of drill statistical and prediction by GA-RBF and BP

Oil Well	Real thickness (m)	GA-RBF algorithm			BP algorithm		
		predictive value (m)	Abs. E (m)	relative error (RE) (%)	predictive value (m)	Abs. E (m)	relative error (RE) (%)
1	2.20	2.20	0	0	2.37	0.17	7.73
2	9.20	9.20	0	0	8.96	-0. 24	2.61
3	6.80	6.82	-0.02	0.29	6.70	-0.10	1.47
4	8.30	8.40	0.10	1.20	8.64	0.34	4.10
5	2.20	2.26	0.06	2.72	2.66	0.46	20.91
6*	6.80	6.36	-0.44	6.40	6.28	-0.52	7.65
7	11.20	11.14	-0.06	0.54	10.80	-0.4	3.57
8*	5.40	5.08	-0.32	5.93	4.82	-0.58	10.74
9	12.40	12.44	0.04	0.32	12.61	0.21	1.69
10*	5.20	5.48	0.28	5.38	5.47	0.27	5.19
11	24.00	24.05	0.05	0.21	23.61	-0.39	1.63
12*	4.00	4.37	0.37	9.25	4.81	0.81	20.25
13	11.60	11.44	-0.16	1.38	11.42	-0.18	1.55

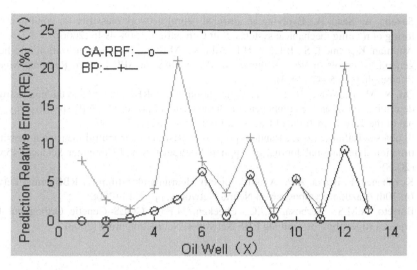

Fig. 3. Comparative diagram of drill statistical and prediction by GA-RBF and BP

4 Conclusions

In this paper, we have presented a new method (GA-RBF) for prediction of hydrocarbon reservoir parameter, which used GA optimizing basis function centers and restricting width to determine the optimal structure of the RBF neural network.

It was shown that this proposed neural network was able to predict oil reservoir thickness with accuracy comparable to real measured data only using available sample and seismic feature parameters of finitely discrete oil wells.

Moreover, a comparison of the prediction performance efficiency of GA-RBF model and BP model was demonstrated through a case study. The result showed that GA-RBF algorithm this paper proposed achieved smaller prediction errors compared with traditional BP algorithm.

References

1. Ahmad, M., Saem, M., Asghari, K.: Estimation of the Reservoir Permeability by Petrophysical Information Using Intelligent Systems. Petroleum Science and Technology, 1656–1667 (2008)
2. Saemi, M., Ahmadi, M., Varjani, A.Y.: Design of neural networks using genetic algorithm for the permeability estimation of the reservoir. Journal of Petroleum Science and Engineering, 97–105 (2007)
3. Li, S., Li, Y.: A GA-based NN approach for makespan estimation. Applied Mathematics and Computation, 1003–1014 (2007)
4. Yu, S., Zhu, K., Diao, F.: A dynamic all parameters adaptive BP neural networks model and its application on oil reservoir prediction. Applied Mathematics and Computation, 66–75 (2008)

5. Saxena. A., Saad. A.: Evolving an artificial neural network classifier for condition monitoring of rotating mechanical systems. Soft Computing, 1568–4946 (2006)
6. Aminian, K., Ameri, S., Bilgesu, H.I., Alla, V., Mustafa, R.: Characterization of a heterogeneous reservoir in West Virginia. In: Proceedings of SPE Eastern Regional Meeting, Pittsburgh, pp. 35–47 (2003)
7. Qu, N., Mi, H., Wang, B., Ren, Y.: Application of GA-RBF networks to the nondestructive determination of active component in pharmaceutical powder by NIR spectroscopy. Journal of the Taiwan Institute of Chemical Engineers, 162–167 (2009)
8. Skubalska-Rafajowicz, E.: Random projection RBF nets for multidimensional density estimation. International Journal of Applied Mathematics and Computer Science, 455–464 (2008)
9. Kokshenev, I., Braga, A.P.: A multi-objective learning algorithm for RBF neural network. In: 10th Brazilian Symposium on Neural Networks, pp. 9–14 (2008)
10. Barreto, A.M.S., Barbosa, H.J.C., Ebecken, N.F.F.: GOLS–Genetic Orthogonal Least Squares Algorithm for Training RBF Networks. Neurocomputing (2006)

Qualitative Simulation of Teachers Group Behaviors Based on BP Neural Network

Tianyin Liu[1,2] and Bin Hu[1,*]

[1] School of Management, HuaZhong University of Science and Technology,
Wuhan, Hubei, 430074, P.R.C
bin_hu@mail.hust.edu.cn
[2] School of Computer Science, Huangshi Institute of Technology,
Huangshi, Hubei, 435003, P.R.C
tianyin_L@163.com

Abstract. This paper discusses the development of the conceptual model of oscillation-equilibrium qualitative simulation(OEQS) for teachers group behaviors and the integration of the approaches of QSIM and Qualitative Reasoning. Teachers group behaviors oscillate between social field gravitation and cost gravitation, and regress gradually to reach an equilibrium. MATLAB 7.0 is used to code BP neural network for describing the two gravitations. Based on the model of OEQS, qualitative simulation engine drives the runs of description method, transition rules and filter theory. Visual Basic 2005 is used to code interval transition rule and graphics of group behaviors. Also, the paper illustrates the application to teachers group management. Simulation results show that OEQS model can serve as a virtual experiment tool for decision making in university management.

Keywords: qualitative simulation, group behavior, neural network, QSIM.

1 Introduction

Psychological modeling of group behavior is first developed by Lewin[1], who forms the famous *group dynamics*. Since then *group dynamics* has become thoroughly embedded within many other branches of the social sciences[2]. Till now, a large interdisciplinary literature has accumulated in the study of group behavior in theory, research and applications. There are a number of theoretical assumptions about the nature of human beings[3]. From the assumptions we can summarize two basic natures: economic nature and social nature. This is the core reason of group behavior's oscillation.

Traditional computer simulation is probability and statistics theory based. The simulated system can be described by mathematical models with probability distribution functions. However, most systems within management field are called complex systems, which are not able to be described by mathematical models. In 1984 and 1986, a series of qualitative simulation approaches for physical system are pub-

---

[*] Corresponding author.

Z. Cai et al. (Eds.): ISICA 2009, CCIS 51, pp. 387–397, 2009.

lished[4,5,6,7]. QSIM (Qualitative SIMulation) has been accepted extensively, and many other methods were published, such as Q2, Q3, fuzzy qualitative simulation, parallel QSIM[8,9,10,11] etc. So far, researches on QSIM have not been paused.

Qualitative reasoning (QR) was derived from *Causality Ordering* proposed by Simon H. A. in 1950. After that, Iwasaki and Simon[7] utilized QR in analyzing behaviors of physical system. Iwasaki[12] improved this method to simulate hybrid system with static and dynamic behaviors simultaneously. Salvaneschi, Cadei and Lazzari[13] integrated quantitative information with QR to simulate and explain the behaviors of physical system.

In this paper we integrate description method of QSIM with qualitative reasoning. Qualitative simulation for complex behaviors of "humans" is the first problem to be solved. Properties of teachers group are as follows: smooth-abrupt change property, causality property, system property and oscillation-equilibrium property. Especially, the change process of teachers behavior runs with evaluating the value between the two gravitations. Then the oscillation happens as Fig. 1.

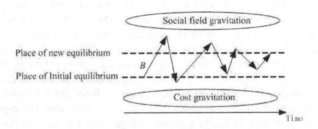

Fig. 1. Behavior change process of teachers group

Both gravitations of social field and economic field, are evaluated and quantified by BP(Back Propagation) neural network coded by MATLAB 7.0 introduced in Section 2. Then, we have developed the conceptual model of oscillation-equilibrium qualitative simulation (OEQS) for teachers group behavior in section 3. Further, qualitative simulation methods are described in Section 4. In addition, an application to teachers group management is performed in Section 5. Finally, conclusions are drawn in section 6.

2 Description of Gravitation

Both gravitations of social field and cost pictured in Fig. 1 are fuzzy concepts. In this paper, BP(Back Propagation) neural network is used to evaluate and quantify them.

2.1 Describing Gravitation Using BP Neural Network

The mapping relationship between social field and its gravitation can be viewed as a type of function shown as Fig. 2(1). This function can be learned by BP neural network represented in Fig. 2(2).

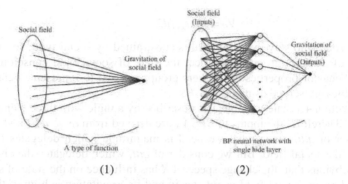

Fig. 2. (1) The mapping relationship between social field and its gravitation. (2) BP neural network learning the mapping relationship between Social field and its gravitation.

After BP neural network is trained in convergence, it is named as *BPS*. It then substitutes the function, i.e. the mapping relationship between social field and its gravitation. When the social field has a change, input the changed social field into BP neural network, the output is then the new gravitation of social field.

In the same way, the mapping relationship between the sensed cost and its gravitation is also a type of mathematical function. After the function is learned by BP neural network, it is named as *BPC*. The changed cost C is inputted into BP neural network, the output is then the corresponding navigation of the sensed cost.

2.2 Obtaining Inputs of BP Neural Network

Let V_C be inputs to *BPC*. Then the value of V_C is illustrated in Fig. 3. Where, x-axis delegates $qval$, y-axis delegates the value of V_C.

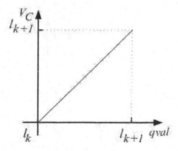

Fig. 3. Value of V_C

From Fig. 3 we know that, when $qval= l_k$ or l_{k+1}, correspondingly the value of V_C is:

$$V_C = l_k \text{ or } l_{k+1} \tag{1}$$

When $qval = (l_k, l_{k+1})$, calculating V_C is given below.

See V_C as stochastic variable which is subjected to uniform distribution on $[l_k, l_{k+1}]$. Then the value of V_C is expectation value of this uniform distribution, i.e.

$$V_C = (l_k + l_{k+1})/2 \tag{2}$$

Teachers group who stay in social field is constrained by social field, so the behavior properties of teachers group may reflect the state of social field consciously. In this paper the behavior properties of teachers group are used to represent social field, i.e. state variables are served as inputs to *BPS*.

In Subsection 4.1 state variable X is described by a tuple with three elements *<qval, qdir, qdt>*. Therefore, the inputs to *BPS* V_X are derived from *qval*, *qdir* and *qdt*. We do not consider of *qdir* since what we need is magnitude which delegates the place X locating at the social field. But we consider of *qdt*, which delegates the change speed of X. It is obvious that, the change speed of X has influence on the state of social field. High speed means social field is not steady and its gravitation is high to the teachers group. Whereas, slow speed means social field is in relative steady state and its gravitation is not much high to the teachers group.

Therefore, calculating the value of V_X is designed as Fig. 4 and 5.

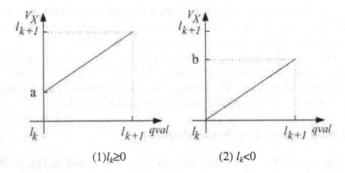

Fig. 4. Value of V_X when *qdt*=1

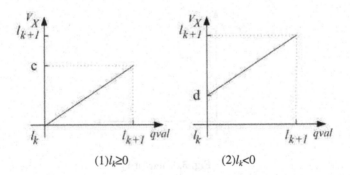

Fig. 5. Value of V_X when *qdt*=2

In Fig. 4(1), a is at 1/3 point from l_k to l_{k+1}. In Fig. 4(2), b is at 2/3 point from l_k to l_{k+1}. In Fig. 5(1), c is at 2/3 point from l_k to l_{k+1}. In Fig. 5(2), d is at 1/3 point from l_k to l_{k+1}.

According to theory of Equation 1 and 2, the value of V_X is calculated as follows.

- When $qdt=1$ and $l_k \geq 0$:

$$V_X = \begin{cases} a, & (qval = l_k); \\ l_{k+1}, & (qval = l_{k+1}); \\ (a + l_{k+1})/2, & (qval = (l_k, l_{k+1})). \end{cases} \tag{3}$$

- When $qdt=1$ and $l_k < 0$:

$$V_X = \begin{cases} l_k, & (qval = l_k); \\ b, & (qval = l_{k+1}); \\ (l_k + b)/2, & (qval = (l_k, l_{k+1})). \end{cases} \tag{4}$$

- When $qdt=2$ and $l_k \geq 0$:

$$V_X = \begin{cases} l_k, & (qval = l_k); \\ c, & (qval = l_{k+1}); \\ (l_k + c)/2, & (qval = (l_k, l_{k+1})). \end{cases} \tag{5}$$

- When $qdt=2$ and $l_k < 0$:

$$V_X = \begin{cases} d, & (qval = l_k); \\ l_{k+1}, & (qval = l_{k+1}); \\ (d + l_{k+1})/2, & (qval = (l_k, l_{k+1})). \end{cases} \tag{6}$$

Fig. 6 and 7 show the structure of *BPS* and *BPC*. Where $|M_X|$ is the gravitation of social field, $|M_C|$ is the gravitation of the sensed cost.

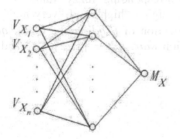
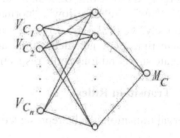

Fig. 6. Schematic structure of *BPS*   **Fig. 7.** Schematic structure of *BPC*

3 The Model

We develop the conceptual model of oscillation-equilibrium qualitative simulation(OEQS) for teachers group behavior, which is shown as Fig. 8.

Description method is the first component. After External environment and Management actions are input, the second component, Transition rules, start to work. Next, the third component, Filter theory, runs to yield the outputs, i.e. Teachers behaviors. The fourth component, Qualitative simulation engine, drives the runs of other three components.

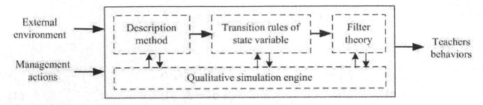

Fig. 8. Conceptual model of Oscillation-Equilibrium Qualitative Simulation(OEQS)

4   Qualitative Simulation Methods

4.1   Variables and Their Description

The variables in this paper are classified as environment variable, decision variable, state variable and cost variables. Suppose E is environment variable set. $E= \{e_1, e_2, ..., e_n\}$. D is decision variable set. $D=\{d_1, d_2, ..., d_m\}$. X is state variable set. $X=\{x_1, x_2, ..., x_p\}$. C is the corresponding cost variable set. $C=\{c_1, c_2, ..., c_q\}$.

State variable of physical system is described by a tuple with two elements in QSIM[6]. According to human behavior's property, for state variable X, QS is designed as a tuple with three elements **<qval, qdir, qdt>**. *qval* is the magnitude of f, which is defined as:

$$qval= \begin{cases} l_k & f(t) = l_k \\ (l_k, l_{k+1}) & f(t) = (l_k, l_{k+1}) \end{cases} \qquad (7)$$

Where $l_k \in \{-0.9, -0.6, -0.3, 0, 0.3, 0.6, 0.9\}$. The corresponding fuzzy value is "very low", "low", "relative low", "normal", "relative high", "high" and "very high", respectively. $k \in \{1,2,3,4,5,6,7\}$. *qdir* is change direction of f. $qdir = \{-, 0, +\}$. *qdt* is change time of f, i.e., delay time at the direction *qdir*. $qdt = \{1, 2\}$. "1" and "2" delegate short and long time, respectively.

4.2   Transition Rules

Interval transition can be represented as:

$$QS(X, t_i) =<qval_1, 0, 0> \rightarrow QS(X, t_i, t_{i+1}) =<qval_2, qdir_2, qdat_2>$$

Where, $qval_1$ is defined in this Section, $qdat_2=\{1,2\}$, i.e., both of quick change and slow change are possible. There are two types of Interval transitions. Ones are those happen at initial time point when E or D has changes. Others are those happen in oscillation mode because of gravitations of social field and cost. In the first type of Interval transitions, the calculators of $qdir_2$ and $qval_2$ are shown in Table 1 and 2. Where, $A \in \{E, D\}$.

Table 1. Calculator of $qdir_2$

W \ QS(A,t_i)	<->	<0>	<+>
-	+	0	-
0	0	0	0
+	-	0	+

Table 2. Calculator of $qval_2$

$qdir_2$ \ $qval_1$	l_1	l_k	l_7
-	l_1	(l_{k-1}, l_k)	(l_6, l_7)
0	l_1	l_k	l_7
+	(l_1, l_2)	(l_k, l_{k+1})	l_7

In the second type of Interval transitions, calculator of $qdir_2$ is:

$$\frac{d(qdir_2)}{dt} = |M_X| - |M_C| \tag{8}$$

Since $qdir_2$ is the discrete variable and $qdir_2 = \{-, 0, +\}$, from Equation 2 we can know that, when $|M_X|-|M_C|<0$, $qdir_2=$"-". When $|M_X|-|M_C|=0$, $qdir_2=$"0". when $|M_X|-|M_C|>0$, $qdir_2=$"+".

When $qval_1 = l_k$, calculators of $qval_2$ are shown in Table 2. When $qval_1 = (l_k, l_{k+1})$, suppose $qval_1 = l^*$, then calculators of $qval_2$ are shown in Table 3.

Table 3. Calculator of $qval_2$

$qdir_2$	-	0	+
$qval_2$	(l_k, l^*)	l^*	(l^*, l_k)

Point transition is represented as:

$$QS(X, t_i, t_{i+1}) = <qval_1, qdir_1, qdat_1> \rightarrow QS(X, t_{i+1}) = <qval_2, 0, 0>$$

Where $qdat_1=\{1,2\}$. Calculators of $qval_2$ are shown in Table 4, where $1 < k < 7$.

Table 4. Calculator of $qval_2$

$qdir_1$ \ $qval_1$	l_1	l_k	l_7	(l_k, l_{k+1})
-	l_1	l_{k-1}	l_6	l_k
0	l_1	l_k	l_7	(l_k, l_{k+1})
+	l_2	l_{k+1}	l_7	l_{k+1}

For transition of C, suppose influence interaction between X and C is $w`$, change direction of X is $qdir$, the transition of C is represented as:

$$QS(C, t_i) = <qval_1> \xrightarrow{r} QS(C, t_i, t_{i+1}) = <qval'>$$

Then, calculators of r and $qval_2$ are shown in Table 5 and 6. Let $QS(C, t_{i+1}) = QS(C, t_i, t_{i+1})$.

Table 5. Calculator of r

w \ $qdir$	<->	<0>	<+>
-	+	0	-
0	0	0	0
+	-	0	+

Table 6. Calculator of $qval_2$

r \ $qval_1$	l_1	l_k	l_7
-	l_1	l_{k-1}	l_6
0	l_1	l_k	l_7
+	l_2	l_{k+1}	l_7

4.3 Filter Theory

At initial time point t_0, E or D has change. Through state transitions of X and C, successor states of X are formed as s numbers of combination, i.e., teachers has s types of work behaviors. It is obvious that transition of C also have s numbers of combination. Take s numbers of combination of X as inputs to BPX_0, s numbers of output can be obtained as $M_{X1}, M_{X2}, ..., M_{XS}$. Take s numbers of combination of C as inputs to BPC_0, s numbers of output can be obtained as $M_{C1}, M_{C2}, ..., M_{CS}$. Let DM_j be the magnitude of difference of M_{Xj} and M_{Cj}, calculator of DM_j is:

$$DM_j = |M_{Xj}| - |M_{Cj}| \qquad (9)$$

Where $j = 1, 2, ..., s$. Seek $\min\{|DM_j|\}$. Then the combination of X, which corresponds to $\min\{|DM_j|\}$, is the most possible successor behavior teachers choose. The other combinations of X can be pruned.

4.4 Qualitative Simulation Engine

For an teachers group of an enterprise, suppose that E or D has a change. So at initial time point $t=t_0$, $QS(E, t_0) \neq <0>$ or $QS(D, t_0) \neq <0>$. For $X=\{x_1, x_2, ..., x_p\}$, $QS(X, t_0) = \{qval, 0, 0\}$. Then the simulation engine is designed as follows:

Let $u=0$, $i=0$.

Step 1: According to $QS(X, t_i)$, train BP neural network to obtain BPX_u and BPC_u.

Step 2: Trigger Interval transition of X to obtain $QS(X, t_i, t_{i+1})$. Trigger transition of C to obtain $QS(C, t_i, t_{i+1})$.

Step 3: Trigger filter theory to obtain the optimal combination of X, and prune the others.

Step 4: Trigger Point transition of X, let $i = i + 1$, $QS(X, t_i)$ is obtained. If $QS(X, t_i)$ and $QS(X, t_{i-2})$ are repeated, stop simulation, $QS(X, t_{i-1}, t_i)$ is the new equilibrium; otherwise, continue.

Step 5: Let $u = u + 1$, go to Step 1.

5 Applications

The behavior of teachers group will tend to have awful change. For example, the loyalty degree of teachers to enterprise x_1, or degree of work endeavor x_2, or cohesion degree of teachers group x_3, or all of them may have changes to become low.

There are two different methods. One is to use social methods, for example, to strengthen culture training for teachers, i.e. $QS(d_1, t)=<+>$. Another is to use economic methods, for example, to increase the salary of teachers, i.e. $QS(d_2, t)=<+>$.

Therefore, we suppose there are two alternatives of management scenarios:

- Alternative 1: $QS(d_1, t_1)=<+>$, $QS(d_2, t_2)=<+>$
- Alternative 2: $QS(d_2, t_1)=<+>$, $QS(d_1, t_2)=<+>$

To compare the simulation results of Alternative 1 with Alternative 2, we analyze the three state variables separately in pairs. Simulation result of x_3 under Alternative 1 is illustrated in Fig. 9. While, Fig. 10 illustrates simulation result of x_3 under Alternative 2.

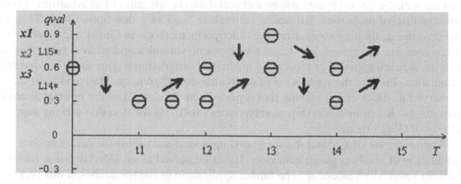

Fig. 9. Change processes of x_3 under Alternative 1

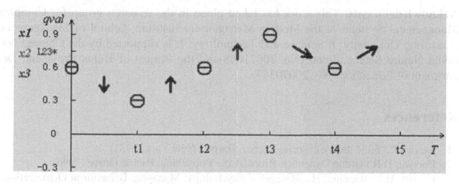

Fig. 10. Change processes of x_3 under Alternative 2

The trend of change processes of x_3 is identical to that of x_2. In Alternative 1, at time stage t_1 influence of social method on x_3 is not heavy. It leads to x_3 have two types of little change at time stage (t_1, t_2). After that x_3 may stay at both "high" states and "low" states. Whereas, in Alternative 2, x_3 is always at "high" states compared with Alternative 1.

Simulation results of x_1 and x_2 are like that of x_3. Therefore, with the above analysis by comparing the experiments of two alternatives, we can draw the conclusion that Alternative 2 is better than Alternative 1. If there is enough finance aid of enterprise, mangers should choose economic method as early as possible. The social method is chosen afterward to support the effect of economic method and to keep teachers group behaviors at the good states.

6 Conclusion

We have developed a conceptual model of OEQS in this paper to research the simulation of teachers group behaviors. Firstly, the generic phenomenon in management field and properties of teachers group behaviors are analyzed and summarized. Especially, the oscillation-equilibrium property is proposed from the perspective of two human natures, i.e. economic nature and social nature. Because of gravitations' fuzzy and qualitative properties, BP neural network is used as a description tool. Then to achieve the qualitative simulation, the description methods in QSIM and Qualitative Reasoning are integrated. We define four types of variables and address two types of transition rules, apply filter theory and qualitative simulation engine to design and run simulation. Finally, the application of oscillation-equilibrium qualitative simulation to be served as the decision making tool is performed. The result of the optimal alternative that is chosen by leadership of universities illustrates the decision making support ability of OEQS model.

The model of OEQS and the integrated approach are useful for researches on the simulation of teachers group behaviors. It can be served as an aided decision making tool for university leadership. The further application of the researches in this paper is to aid decision making in the field of complex management systems.

Acknowledgements. This work has taken place in the research group for Complex Management Systems at the Modern Management Institute, School of Management, Huazhong University of Science and Technology. It is supported by the Chinese National Nature Science Fund (No. 70671048)and the Project of Hubei Provincial Department of Education (No. 20070347).

References

1. Lewin, K.: Field theory in social science. Harper, New York (1951)
2. Forsyth, D.R.: Group Dynamics. Brooks/Cole Publishing, Pacific Grove (1990)
3. Leavitt, H.J., Bahrami, H.: Managerial Psychology: Managing Behavior in Organizations. The University of Chicago Press, Chicago (1998)
4. Kleer, J.D., Brown, J.S.: A Qualitative Physicals Based on Confluences. Artificial Intelligence 24, 7–83 (1984)
5. Forbus, K.D.: Qualitative Process Theory. Artificial Intelligence 24, 85–168 (1984)
6. Kuipers, B.J.: Qualitative Simulation. Artificial Intelligence 29, 289–338 (1986)
7. Iwasaki, Y., Simon, H.A.: Causality in design behavior. Artificial Intelligence 29, 3–32 (1986)
8. Kuipers, B.J.: Qualitative Simulation: Then and Now. Artificial Intelligence 59, 1133–1140 (1993)
9. Kuipers, B.J.: Reasoning with qualitative models. Artificial Intelligence 59, 125–132 (1993)

10. Clancy, D.J., Kuipers, B.J.: Qualitative Simulation as a Temporally - extended Constraint Satisfaction Problem. In: Proceedings of the Fifteenth National Conference on Artificial Intelligence(AAAI 1998). AAAI/MIT Press (1998)
11. Platzner, M., Rinner, B.: Toward Embedded Qualitative Simulation: A Specialized Computer Architecture for QSIM. IEEE Intelligent System, 62–68 (March/April 2000)
12. Iwasaki, Y.: Causal Ordering in a Mixed Structure. In: Proceedings of the Seventh National Conference on Artificial Intelligence(AAAI 1988), St Paul, Minnesota, pp. 313–318 (1988)
13. Salvaneschi, P., Cadei, M., Lazzari, M.: A Causal Modelling Framework for the Simulation and Explanation of the Behavior of Structure. Artificial Intelligence in Engineering 11, 205–216 (1997)

Stabilization of Switched Dynamic Neural Networks with Discrete Delays

Shiping Wen[1] and Zhigang Zeng[2]

[1] School of Automation, Wuhan University of Technology,
Wuhan, Hubei, 430070, China
[2] Control Science and Engineering, Huazhong University of Science and Technology,
Wuhan, Hubei, 430074, China
zgzeng@gmail.com

Abstract. With the rapid development of intelligent control, switched systems have attracted great attention. This paper introduces the idea of the switched systems into the field of dynamic neural networks. First, a mathematical model of the switched dynamic neural networks is established , in which a set of dynamic neural networks are used as the subsystems. Secondly, a scalar function is constructed to develop a new methodology for stabilization of switched dynamic neural networks. This design guarantees the switched dynamic neural networks to be globally asymptotically stable and inverse optimality with respect to a meaningful cost functional. Finally, a numerical example is given to illustrate the results.

Keywords: Dynamic neural networks, Switched systems, Stabilization.

1 Introduction

Neural networks have attracted huge attention and been studied widely [1], [2]. Among the different proposed neural networks, dynamic neural networks have become an important methodology to various scientific areas, such as pattern recognition, system identification and control, and combinatorial optimization. Especially, with the rapid development of intelligent control, hybrid systems [3],[4] have been studied. Some works have been done about the switched systems [5]-[7]. Some methodology for the stabilization of the dynamic neural networks and approaches about the inverse optimal control technique for dynamic neural networks control have been proposed in [8]-[12], and the problem of stabilization of the switched systems has been studied by several works [3],[7].

In this letter, we will study a class of switched dynamic neural networks by integrating the theory of switched systems with neural networks and the subsystems of the switched dynamic neural networks are a set of dynamic neural networks. This paper is organized as follows: In Section 2, the mathematical model formation and some preliminaries are given. The main results are stated in Section 3. An illustrative example is given to illustrate the conclusion in Section 4. Finally, concluding remarks are made in Section 5.

Z. Cai et al. (Eds.): ISICA 2009, CCIS 51, pp. 398–405, 2009.
© Springer-Verlag Berlin Heidelberg 2009

2 Preliminaries

A dynamic neural network model is described by the following equation [8]:

$$\dot{x}(t) = Ax(t) + B\sigma(x(t)) + DF(x(t - \varsigma)) + u, \tag{1}$$

where $A = -\lambda I$, is the state matrix, I is a $n \times n$ matrix, $B \in \Re^{n \times n}$ is the nonlinear feedback matrix, $D \in \Re^{n \times n}$ is the discretely delayed connection matrix, $u \in \Re$ is the input, $x \in \Re^n$ is the neural network state, $\varsigma \in \Re^+$ is the time delay, $\sigma(x(t)) \in \Re^n$, $F(x(t - \varsigma)) \in \Re^n$, and

$$\sigma(x(t)) = \big(\sigma_1(x(t)), \sigma_2(x(t)), \cdots, \sigma_n(x(t))\big)^T,$$

$$F(x(t - \varsigma)) = \big(F_1(x(t - \varsigma)), F_2(x(t - \varsigma)), \cdots, F_n(x(t - \varsigma))\big)^T.$$

Assumption: $\sigma(x(t)), F(x(t))$ are nonlinear Lipschitz continuous functions, and $\sigma(0) = F(0) = 0$, so when $u = 0$, $x = 0$ is an equilibrium point of (1), and there exist

$$\begin{cases} l^- x \le \sigma(x(t)) \le l^+ x(t), \\ f^- x(t) \le F(x(t)) \le f^+ x(t), \end{cases} \tag{2}$$

where

$$l^- = diag\{l_{11}^-, l_{22}^-, \cdots, l_{nn}^-\}, l^+ = diag\{l_{11}^+, l_{22}^+, \cdots, l_{nn}^+\},$$

$$f^- = diag\{f_{11}^-, f_{22}^-, \cdots, f_{nn}^-\}, f^+ = diag\{f_{11}^+, f_{22}^+, \cdots, f_{nn}^+\}.$$

Switched dynamic neural networks can be described as follows

$$\dot{x}(t) = \sum_{i=1}^{N} a_i \Big[A_i x(t) + B_i \sigma_i(x(t)) + D_i F_i(x(t - \varsigma)) + u\Big], \tag{3}$$

where $a_i \ge 0$, $i = 1, 2, \cdots, N$, N is the number of subsystems and $\sum_{i=1}^{N} a_i = 1$. To prove our theorem, the following lemma is also proposed in this letter.

Lemma 1 [1]: Let X, Y be any n-dimensional real column vectors, and let P be an $n \times n$ symmetric positive definite matrix. Then, the following matrix inequality holds:

$$2X^T PY \le X^T PX + Y^T PY.$$

If $P = I$, then we can get:

$$2X^T Y \le X^T X + Y^T Y$$

$$X^T Y \le \frac{1}{2}(\|X\|^2 + \|Y\|^2). \tag{4}$$

3   Main Results

In this section, we will establish and prove our main results. In order to establish the stability conditions, we use the following Lyapunov function:

$$V(x(t)) = \frac{1}{2}x^{\mathrm{T}}(t)x(t) + \sum_{i=1}^{N} a_i \int_{t-\varsigma_i}^{t} \Big(D_i F_i(x(s))\Big)^{\mathrm{T}} \Big(D_i F_i(x(s))\Big) ds, \quad (5)$$

Theorem 1: For the system of switched dynamic neural networks (3), if

$$u^* = -\sum_{i=1}^{N} a_i (2 + \|l_i^+\|^2 \|B_i\|^2 + 2\|f_i^+\|^2 \|D_i\|^2)x, \quad (6)$$

then the system is global asymptotically stable.

Prove: Take the time derivative of $V(x(t))$ along the trajectory of (3)

$$\dot{V}(x(t)) = x^{\mathrm{T}}(t)\dot{x}(t) + \sum_{i=1}^{N} a_i \Big(D_i F_i(x(t))\Big)^{\mathrm{T}} \Big(D_i F_i(x(t))\Big)$$

$$- \sum_{i=1}^{N} a_i \Big(D_i F_i(x(t-\varsigma))\Big)^{\mathrm{T}} \Big(D_i F_i(x(t-\varsigma))\Big)$$

$$= x^{\mathrm{T}}(t) \sum_{i=1}^{N} a_i \Big[A_i x(t) + B_i \sigma_i(x(t)) + D_i F_i(x(t-\varsigma)) + u\Big]$$

$$+ \sum_{i=1}^{N} a_i \Big(D_i F_i(x(t))\Big)^{\mathrm{T}} \Big(D_i F_i(x(t))\Big)$$

$$- \sum_{i=1}^{N} a_i \Big(D_i F_i(x(t-\varsigma))\Big)^{\mathrm{T}} \Big(D_i F_i(x(t-\varsigma))\Big). \quad (7)$$

For the second right-hand side (RHS) terms of (7), using *Lemma 1*, we have

$$x^{\mathrm{T}}(t)B_i\sigma_i(x(t)) \leq \frac{1}{2}x^{\mathrm{T}}(t)x(t) + \frac{1}{2}\sigma_i(x(t))^{\mathrm{T}}B_i^{\mathrm{T}}B_i\sigma_i(x(t))$$

$$\leq \frac{1}{2}x^{\mathrm{T}}(t)\Big(1 + (l_i^+)^{\mathrm{T}}(B_i)^{\mathrm{T}}(B_i)(l_i^+)\Big)x(t)$$

$$\leq \frac{1}{2}\Big(1 + \|l_i^+\|^2\|B_i\|^2\Big)\|x(t)\|^2. \quad (8)$$

For the second right-hand side (RHS) terms of (7), using *Lemma 1*, we have

$$x^{\mathrm{T}}(t)D_i F_i(x(t-\varsigma_i)) \leq \frac{1}{2}x^{\mathrm{T}}(t)x(t) + \frac{1}{2}\Big(D_i F_i(x(t-\varsigma_i))\Big)^{\mathrm{T}} \Big(D_i F_i(x(t-\varsigma_i))\Big) \quad (9)$$

Substituting (6), (8), (9) into (7), we have :

$$\dot{V}(t) \leq \sum_{i=1}^{N} a_i \Big[-\lambda_i \|x(t)\|^2 + \frac{1}{2}\Big(2 + \|l_i^+\|^2 \|B_i\|^2\Big)\|x(t)\|^2 + x(t)^{\mathrm{T}} u$$

$$+ \frac{1}{2}\Big(D_i F_i(x(t-\varsigma_i))\Big)^{\mathrm{T}}\Big(D_i F_i(x(t-\varsigma_i))\Big) + \Big(D_i F_i(x(t))\Big)^{\mathrm{T}}\Big(D_i F_i(x(t))\Big)$$

$$- \Big(D_i F_i(x(t-\varsigma_i))\Big)^{\mathrm{T}}\Big(D_i F_i(x(t-\varsigma_i))\Big)\Big]$$

$$\leq \sum_{i=1}^{N} a_i \Big[-\lambda_i \|x(t)\|^2 + \frac{1}{2}\Big(2 + \|l_i^+\|^2 \|B_i\|^2\Big)\|x(t)\|^2 + x(t)^{\mathrm{T}} u$$

$$+ \Big(D_i F_i(x(t))\Big)^{\mathrm{T}}\Big(D_i F_i(x(t))\Big)\Big]$$

$$\leq \sum_{i=1}^{N} a_i \Big[-\lambda_i \|x(t)\|^2 + \frac{1}{2}\Big(2 + \|l_i^+\|^2 \|B_i\|^2\Big)\|x(t)\|^2 + x(t)^{\mathrm{T}} u$$

$$\|f_i^+\|^2 \|D_i\|^2 \|x(t)\|^2\Big]$$

$$\leq -\sum_{i=1}^{N} a_i \Big[\lambda_i + 1 + \frac{1}{2}\|l_i^+\|^2 \|B_i\|^2 + \|f_i^+\|^2 \|D_i\|^2\Big]\|x(t)\|^2$$

$$\leq 0. \tag{10}$$

Hence system (3) is global asymptotically stable.

Then we continue to do further research about the global inverse optimality with respect to a meaningful cost functional of this system.

For the following kind of nonlinear system

$$\dot{x}(t) = f(x(t)) + g(x(t))u, \tag{11}$$

then

$$\dot{V}(x(t)) = x^{\mathrm{T}}(t)\dot{x}(t) + \sum_{i=1}^{N} a_i \Big(D_i F_i(x(t))\Big)^{\mathrm{T}}\Big(D_i F_i(x(t))\Big)$$

$$- \sum_{i=1}^{N} a_i \Big(D_i F_i(x(t-\varsigma_i))\Big)^{\mathrm{T}}\Big(D_i F_i(x(t-\varsigma_i))\Big)$$

$$= x^{\mathrm{T}}(t)\sum_{i=1}^{N} a_i \Big[A_i x(t) + B_i \sigma_i(x(t)) + D_i F_i(x(t-\varsigma_i)) + u\Big]$$

$$+ \sum_{i=1}^{N} a_i \Big(D_i F_i(x(t))\Big)^{\mathrm{T}}\Big(D_i F_i(x(t))\Big) - \sum_{i=1}^{N} a_i \Big(D_i F_i(x(t-\varsigma_i))\Big)^{\mathrm{T}}\Big(D_i F_i(x(t-\varsigma_i))\Big)$$

$$= V_{x(t)} f(x(t)) + V_{x(t)} g(x(t))u + \Psi, \tag{12}$$

where

$$V_{x(t)} f(x(t)) = x^{\mathrm{T}}(t)\sum_{i=1}^{N} a_i [A_i x(t) + B_i \sigma_i(x(t)) + D_i F_i(x(t-\varsigma_i))],$$

$$V_{x(t)}g(x(t)) = \sum_{i=1}^{N} a_i x(t)^{\mathrm{T}} = x(t)^{\mathrm{T}},$$

$$\Psi = \sum_{i=1}^{N} a_i \Big(D_i F_i(x(t))\Big)^{\mathrm{T}} \Big(D_i F_i(x(t))\Big) - \sum_{i=1}^{N} a_i \Big(D_i F_i(x(t-\varsigma_i))\Big)^{\mathrm{T}} \Big(D_i F_i(x(t-\varsigma_i))\Big).$$

We know

$$u = -\sum_{i=1}^{N} a_i \Big(2 + \|l_i^+\|^2 \|B_i\|^2 + 2\|f_i^+\|^2 \|D_i\|^2\Big) x$$

$$= -\eta \big(R(x(t))\big)^{-1} \big(V_{x(t)g(x(t))}\big)^{\mathrm{T}}, \tag{13}$$

where

$$\eta \big(R(x(t))\big)^{-1} = \sum_{i=1}^{N} a_i (2 + \|l_i^+\|^2 \|B_i\|^2 + 2\|f_i^+\|^2 \|D_i\|^2),$$

$$\big(V_{x(t)}g(x(t))\big)^{\mathrm{T}} = x,$$

with η a positive definite constant.

Theorem 2: A positive-definite function $q(x(t))$ and a strictly positive-function $R(x(t))$ exist, when the feedback control law (6) applied to the system (3), the system can achieve global asymptotically stable, and globally inverse optimality with respect to the following meaning cost functional

$$J = \lim_{t \to \infty} \{2\eta V(x(t)) + \int_0^t q(x(\tau)) + u(x(\tau))^{\mathrm{T}} R(x(\tau)) u(x(\tau)) d\tau\}, \tag{14}$$

where

$$q(x(t)) = -2\eta V_{x(t)}g(x(t)) + \eta^2 (V_{x(t)}g(x(t)))(R(x(t)))^{-1}(V_{x(t)}g(x(t)))^{\mathrm{T}}$$

$$- 2\eta \sum_{i=1}^{N} a_i \big(D_i F_i(x(t))\big)^{\mathrm{T}} \big(D_i F_i(x(t))\big)$$

$$+ 2\eta \sum_{i=1}^{N} a_i \big(D_i F_i(x(t-\varsigma))\big)^{\mathrm{T}} \big(D_i F_i(x(t-\varsigma_i))\big)$$

$$= -2\eta \Big(\dot{V}(x(t)) - x(t)^{\mathrm{T}} u\Big) - \eta x(t)^{\mathrm{T}} u$$

$$= \eta \big(-2\dot{V}(x(t)) + x(t)^{\mathrm{T}} u\big),$$

$$\geq \eta \sum_{i=1}^{N} a_i \Big(2\Big[\lambda_i + 1 + \frac{1}{2}\|l_i^+\|^2\|B_i\|^2 + \|f_i^+\|^2\|D_i\|^2\Big]\|x(t)\|^2$$

$$- \Big[2 + \|l_i^+\|^2\|B_i\|^2 + 2\|f_i^+\|^2\|D_i\|^2\Big]\|x(t)\|^2\Big)$$

$$= \eta \sum_{i=1}^{N} a_i \Big(2\lambda_i \|x(t)\|^2\Big)$$

$$\geq 0, \tag{15}$$

and

$$R(x(t)) = \left(\eta^{-1} \sum_{i=1}^{N} a_i (2 + \|l_i^+\|^2 \|B_i\|^2 + 2\|f_i^+\|^2 \|D_i\|^2) \right)^{-1}$$
$$> 0. \tag{16}$$

We can get

$$u(x(t))^T R(x(t))u(x(t)) = -\eta x(t)^T u, \tag{17}$$

then

$$q(x(t)) + u(x(t))^T R(x(t))u(x(t)) = \eta\big(-2\dot{V}(x(t)) + x(t)^T u \big) - \eta x(t)^T u$$
$$= -2\eta \dot{V}(x(t)), \tag{18}$$

so

$$J = \lim_{t\to\infty} \{2\eta V(x(t)) + \int_0^t q(x(\tau)) + u(x(\tau))^T R(x(\tau))u(x(\tau))dt\}$$
$$= 2\eta V(x(0)), \tag{19}$$

which is the minimum of the cost functional.

From above, we can obtain the following remarks:

Corollary 1: If $i = 1$, and $B = 0$ then (3) can be used to stabilize delayed neural networks in [4].

Corollary 2: If $i = 1$, and $D = 0$ the (3) can be used to stabilize dynamic neural networks in [9].

Corollary 3: If we consider the switched property of this system, (3) can be used to solve the problem about stabilization of the above systems that with switched character as well as discrete delay.

4   Numerical Example

In order to illustrate the effectiveness of the methodology proposed in this letter, we consider the following example. The switched dynamic neural Network is given as (3), with $\lambda_1 = \lambda_2 = 1$, $a_1 = 0.3$, $a_2 = 0.7$,

$$B_1 = \begin{pmatrix} 2 & 5 \\ 7 & -3 \end{pmatrix}, \quad B_2 = \begin{pmatrix} -1 & 4 \\ 3 & 2 \end{pmatrix}, \quad D_1 = \begin{pmatrix} 4 & -1 \\ -1 & 4 \end{pmatrix}, \quad D_2 = \begin{pmatrix} -5 & 2 \\ 4 & 6 \end{pmatrix},$$

$$\sigma_1(x(t)) = \begin{pmatrix} \tanh(2x_1(t)) \\ \tanh(3x_2(t)) \end{pmatrix}, \quad \sigma_2(x(t)) = \begin{pmatrix} \tanh(x_1(t)) \\ \tanh(5x_2(t)) \end{pmatrix},$$

$$F_1(x(t-\varsigma_1)) = \begin{pmatrix} \tanh(3x_1(t-\varsigma_1)) \\ \tanh(5x_2(t-\varsigma_1)) \end{pmatrix}, \quad F_2(x(t-\varsigma_2)) = \begin{pmatrix} \tanh(x_1(t-\varsigma_2)) \\ \tanh(6x_2(t-\varsigma_2)) \end{pmatrix},$$

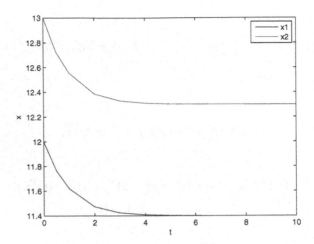

Fig. 1. Phase plane (t, x1, x2) while $(u = 0)$

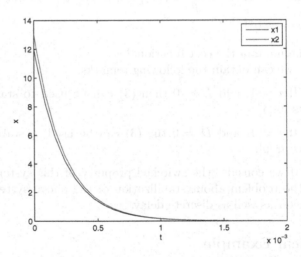

Fig. 2. Phase plane (t, x1, x2) while $(u = u^*)$

$\varsigma_1 = 1$ second, $\varsigma_2 = 10$ seconds, $u = u^*$, where u^* is calculated using (6). If $u = 0$, As can be seen in Fig.1. The neural network is not globally asymptotically stable. If $u = u^*$, corresponding simulated results are shown in Fig.2. It is easy to know the system can achieve global asymptotically stable, and illustrate Theorem 1 and Theorem 2.

5   Conclusions

In this letter, an approach to stabilize the switched dynamic neural networks, has been proposed by combining the theory of switched systems and dynamic neural networks . And the design is based on the technique of nonlinear inverse optimality with respect to a meaningful cost function. The new result would be helpful for the control of nonlinear systems by dynamic neural networks.

Acknowledgments. This work was supported by the Natural Science Foundation of China under Grant 60774051, Program for New Century Excellent Talents in Universities of China under Grant NCET-06-0658, the Fok Ying Tung Education Foundation under Grant 111068 and Major State Basic Research Development Program of China under Grant 2007CB311000.

References

1. Liu, Y., Wang, Z.D., Liu, X.H.: Global Exponential Stability of Generalized Recurrent Neural Networks with Discrete and Distributed Delays. Neural Networks 19, 667–675 (2006)
2. Zeng, Z.G., Wang, J., Liao, X.X.: Global Exponential Stability of A General Class of Recurrent Neural Networks with Time-varying Delays. IEEE Trans. Circuits and Systems I 50, 1353–1358 (2003)
3. Zhai, G., Kondo, H.: Hybrid Static Output Feedback Stabilization of Two-dimensional LTI Systems: Geometric Method. International Journal of Control 79, 982–990 (2006)
4. Sanchez, E.N., Perez, J.P., Perez, J.: Stabilization of Delayed Neural Networks. In: IEEE Internation Conference on Systems, Man and Cybernetics, vol. 3, pp. 2156–2160. IEEE press, New York (2005)
5. Liberzon, D., Morse, A.S.: Basic Problems in Stability and Design of Switched Systems. IEEE Cont. Sys. Mag. 19, 59–70 (1999)
6. Sun, Z.D.: Combined Stabililizing Strategies for Switched Linear Systems. IEEE Trans. Automatic Control 51, 666–674 (2006)
7. Li, Z.G., Wen, C.Y., Soh, Y.C.: Stabilization of a Class of Switched Systems via Designing Laws. IEEE Trans. Automatic Control 46, 665–670 (2001)
8. Sanchez, E.N., Perez, J.P.: Input-to-State Stability(ISS) Analysis for Dynamic Neural networks. IEEE Trans. Circuits and Systems-I 46, 1395–1398 (1999)
9. Sanchez, E.N., Perez, J.P.: Input-to-State Stabilization of Dynamic Neural networks. IEEE Trans. Systems, Man and Cybernetic, Part A 33, 532–536 (2003)
10. Liu, Z.Q., Shih, S.C., Wang, Q.J.: Global Robust Stabilizing Control for a Dynamic Neural Network System. IEEE Trans. Systems, Man and Cybernetic, Part A 39, 426–436 (2009)
11. Liu, Z.Q., Torres, R.E., Patel, N., Wang, Q.J.: Further Development of Input-to-state Stabilizing Control for Dynamic Neural Network systems. IEEE Trans. Systems, Man and Cybernetic, Part A 38, 1425–1433 (2008)
12. Liu, Z.Q., Wang, Q.J.: Further Result on Input-to-State Stabilization of Dynamic Neural Network Systems. In: Proceedings of the American Control Conference Marriott Marquis Hotel at Times Square, pp. 4798–4803. IEEE Press, New York (2007)

ANN Designing Based on Co-evolutionary Genetic Algorithm with Degeneration

Xianshan Zhou[1], Bing Luo[2], and Bing Fu[1]

[1] School of Computer Science, Yangtze University, Jingzhou Hubei 434023, China
[2] School of Information, WuYi University, Jiangmen Guangdong 529020, China
xszhou@yangtzeu.edu.cn, luobing8888@163.com,
fubing@yangtzeu.edu.cn

Abstract. Artificial neural network design is always trouble-causing without systematic rules and local optimum is usually connected with conventional grads based parameters optimization. This paper studies the optimization of neural networks design including structure and parameters based on co-evolutionary genetic algorithm with degeneration. The ANN parameters are coded as genes co-evolving with control genes controlling degeneration. The value of control gene means the damaged rate of the corresponding gene coded for a parameter. Two kinds of genes influence mutually during evolution progress and the degeneration of a gene means the connection of the ANN can be eliminated accordingly. Experiments results show that this approach can get simpler ANN structure, better parameters and quicker training convergence.

Keywords: genetic algorithm; co-evolution; degeneration; neural networks; optimization.

1 Introduction

After McCulloch and Pitts proposed neuron model in 1943, research on artificial neural networks was not always smooth. Till 1980s some new neural networks models and training algorithms were presented as well as the advancements in VLSI technology, interests in ANN were aroused again and application progress had been made in many fields where traditional methods were hard to deal with, such as nonlinear controlling, pattern recognition and associated memory etc[1].

However, the ANN designing for a certain application has not yet established a designing framework; experience of designers and experiments are still the main dependence. Though many machine learning methods have been proposed, ANN structure designing and parameters optimization remain a hard work, whose complexities and difficulties include:

Every ANN is correlated with a certain application problem, and is hard to generalize or reuse.

The size of ANN nodes and weighted connections is infinite, so it is impossible to do enumerative search for a problem. Too large scale ANN usually leads to over-fitting and poor generalization ability whereas too small scale ANN is bad in accuracy.

Z. Cai et al. (Eds.): ISICA 2009, CCIS 51, pp. 406–412, 2009.

The knowledge an ANN learned lies in its hidden layer or layers, but no reasonable explanation about the hidden layer(s) structure and performance can be achieved, which leads to being hard to select the ANN structure for a certain purpose.

Tiny change in an ANN parameter whose effect is not continuous may lead to completely different ANN output performance. With disperse numbers of nodes and connections, parameter space is nonconvex but multi peaks. So local optimum of parameters is inevitable by conventional training methods and gets worse with larger scale of ANN[2].

To solve this problem, ANN training process must be optimized for not only connection weights, but also networks structure, where unnecessary nodes and connections can be eliminated while accuracy and performance maintained.

ANN structure optimization methods can be divided into four types: choosing, removing, constructing and simplifying[3]. The choosing method is based on experience and some criteria. For removing and constructing methods, ANN parameters training and ANN structure optimization are processed respectively with huge computation cost because tiny changing in ANN structure may lead to completely different performance. Whereas, for the simplifying method, ANN structure optimization is combined with parameters training, so computation cost is reduced[4].

During the recent ten years, many studies have been done on ANN structure simplification based on genetic algorithm. Takahama and Sakai proposed binary coded genetic algorithm with mutant genes(MGGA)[5]. Leumg et al proposed real number coded algorithm with damaged gene(DGGA)[6] and genetic algorithm with degeneration(GAD)[7]. These approaches have reduced unnecessary connections by restraining the genes that have little affections for individual surviving. However, because of huge searching space and genetic algorithm's limitation, these approaches still cost vast computation and degeneration degree is uncontrollable. Too rapid degeneration leads to bad ANN performance, whereas slow degeneration leads to no optimization effect and bad ANN generalization ability[8].

In this paper, a co-evolutionary idea is introduced to genetic algorithm with degeneration and applied to ANN optimization, where degeneration can be controlled. To accelerate evolving, uniform crossover is adopted for quickening local searching.

2 Degeneration and Co-evolutionary Genetic Algorithm

Degeneration that some unnecessary organs disappeared during evolving is a very common phenomenon in nature. It is directly caused by damaged gene, with which the individuals and offspring are more fit for survival[8]. If we treat every ANN connection as an organ, ANN structure can be optimized just as creature evolving, connection is reduced as organ degeneration.

A damaged gene is an abnormal gene brought by mutation including substitution, insertion and deletion etc. In genetic algorithm with degeneration, a normal individual's genes are coded for ANN parameters and another type of controlling individual's genes are coded for damaged rate which stands for parameter genes' degeneration degree. Damaged rate values from 0 to 1, where 0 means for normal gene and 1 for completely damaged gene.

As in GA, an individual is represented by a chromosome, which holds genetic information. The chromosome is represented by an array of genes $G = g1g2...Gl$, where L is the chromosome length. The mapping function from genotype to phenotype is h and the fitness function of the individual is $f(h(G))$.

Controlling of degeneration degree and speed is a troublesome problem. To control the degeneration adequately, we adopt the co-evolutionary idea.

In nature, all kinds of creatures maintain various feedbacks to influence each other, such as food chain and commensal etc. Different species' restraint and stimulation have influenced their evolution. This kind of evolutionary phenomenon based on food chain or commensal is called co-evolution, which can be also considered as a positive feedback in evolution kinetics[8][10]. In 1990, Hillis applied this kind of co-evolution to searching optimization for the first time and proposed co-evolutionary genetic algorithm(CGA)[11]. In CGA, there are two types of co-evolving individuals that co-operate or compete. The robust CGA that becomes a kind of fine-grained algorithm has successfully applied in sorting and restriction problems etc with more quickly evolving speed than conventional GA.

3   Gene Coding for ANN and Fitness Function

To apply CGA in ANN designing, individual setting and gene coding is the first step. Here two types of individuals are set: one coded for ANN parameters, and the other for controlling.

All chromosomes of the individuals have the same length. The chromosome of a parameter individual is coded for ANN parameters and that of a controlling individual is coded as damaged rate of the corresponding parameter gene. Through evolving, ANN should get the simplest structure and allowed output error. All chromosomes take real data coding and the evolving includes choosing, crossover, mutation and degeneration based on fitness.

A controlling individual coded for damaged rate controls the degeneration of a parameter individual that has the same gene length. Damaged rate values from 0 to 1, where 0 means a normal gene and 1 a completely damaged gene. The damaged rate changes according to fitness of the corresponding parameter individual. After the parameter individual evolved, namely, some parameters had been changed, fitness should be calculated again. If the fitness increases, the damaged rate of the evolving gene increases too and vice versa. When the damaged rate has exceeded a threshold, the corresponding gene degenerated, namely, the connection can be eliminated from the ANN.

Fig. 1 shows two types of co-evolution individuals. The 3rd and 4th genes in the parameter individual can be degenerated, for their damaged rates have been 1 already.

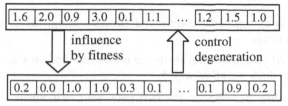

Fig. 1. Two types of co-evolving individuals

An individual coded for parameters of an ANN is composed of an array of genes Gd which are coded for all connections and thresholds of activation functions of every neuron of every layer of the ANN:

$$G^d = L^2 L^3 \cdots L^m \tag{1}$$

$$L^k = N_1^k N_2^k \cdots N_n^k \tag{2}$$

$$N_i^k = \left(\omega_{i1}^k d_{i1}^k \right) \left(\omega_{i2}^k d_{i2}^k \right) \cdots \left(\omega_{in}^k d_{in}^k \right) \left(\theta_i^k d_{i\theta}^k \right) \tag{3}$$

Here, Lk means the kth layer of the ANN, N_i^k means the ith neuron of layer k, n is the number of neurons in the layer, $\left(\omega_{ij}^k d_{ij}^k \right)$ stands for the connection weight between neuron i of layer k and neuron j of layer k-1, and $\left(\theta_i^k d_{i\theta}^k \right)$ stands for the threshold of activation function of neuron i of layer k.

The neuron output corresponding to input IP is:

$$O_i^k(I^P) = f\left(\sum_j \omega_{ij}^k O_j^{k-1}(I^P) - \theta_i^k \right) \tag{4}$$

$$f(x) = \frac{1}{1 + \exp(-x)} \tag{5}$$

Here, O_i^k is the output of neuron i of layer k, f(x) is the activation function of the neuron. The Mean Square Error between the output of the ANN and the teaching signal is taken as the fitness function for evolving:

$$MSE = \frac{1}{P} \sum_P \sum_i \left(\hat{O}_i^P - O_i^m(I^P) \right)^2 \tag{6}$$

P is the number of samples for ANN training, $\hat{O}_i^P$ is the No.i teaching signal data of sample p for input IP.

4   ANN Training Based on CGA

After individuals chromosome coding and fitness setting, the co-evolution can be implemented as below:

Initialization: 100 parameter individuals are initialized randomly as a population, and controlling individuals are all set as 0.5.

Selection: according to fitness, some best parameter individuals and corresponding controlling individuals are duplicated as offspring.

Crossover: parent generation individuals partner for crossover in probability Pc. To accelerate evolving, uniform crossover is taken here[9].

Mutation: parent generation individuals coded for ANN parameters mutate in probability Pm; damaged rates of the mutated genes mutate according to fitness of the mutated individual. The crossover rate Pc and the mutation rate Pm are chosen by experience. Conventionally Pm is from 0.001 to 0.1 and Pc is from 0.1 to 0.8.

   Mutation of parameter individuals influenced by co-evolution: if the damaged rate of a controlling individual exceeds the threshold, the corresponding gene of the parameter individual degenerates, namely the connection in the ANN can be eliminated.

   Mutation of controlling individuals: according to fitness, those genes of the controlling individuals corresponding to mutated or crossovered genes of the parameter individuals mutate: better is fitness, or output error is in allowance, bigger are the damaged rates of these genes and vice versa.

   Recycle to step selection.

   The evolution terminates in specified generations or gets the allowed output error.

5   Experiments and Results

A sorting problem solved by an ANN is designed to testify the co-evolution approach. As shown in Fig. 2, points in a 2-dimensional coordinates ranged from (-1,-1) to (1,1) are sorted to a class of four according to their coordinates. There are 1000 random samples for ANN training and 300 for testing.

   The ANN is initially designed as a perception whose hidden layer has 10 neurons, the input layer has 2 neurons for x-y coordinates input and the output layer has 4 neurons for 4 classes. The input data are the sample's x and y coordinates and the

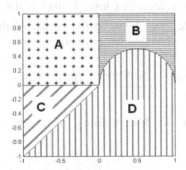

Fig. 2. A sorting problem in 2-dimensional space

output data is 1 standing for belonging to this class or 0 for no relation. The Sigmoid function is taken as activation function for every neuron. Then the individuals are coded for the ANN connection weights and activation function thresholds. Co-evolution genetic algorithm is implemented according to part 3 of this paper and fitness is calculated by formula (6).

The ANN is also trained in conventional genetic algorithm[12] as a contrast. The output accuracy of the ANN is set as 75% to 95% respectively. Table 1 shows the necessary generations for ANN training till reaching the output accuracy in two ways and average convergence output accuracy:

Table 1. Comparison of the ANN training convergence generations

Accuracy	>75%	>80%	>85%	>90%	>95%	average accuracy
GA	43	92	158	231	617	93.1%
CGA^d	16	30	49	72	188	97.5%

Table 2 shows 300 testing samples output accuracy by ANN trained by CGA^d and GA respectively. The evolving generations for ANN training are from 50 to 200:

Table 2. Comparison of the ANN training accuracy

Generations	50	100	150	200
GA	76.1%	82.4%	84.5%	87.2%
CGA^d	85.8%	91.6%	93.0%	95.9%

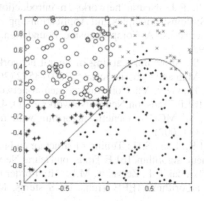

Fig. 3. 300 samples testing result

The experimental results show that the calculating cost in CGA^d is greatly decreased than that in conventional GA. For example, to get 90% output accuracy, the evolving generations needed by CGA^d is only 1/3 of that by GA. Also the accuracy of the trained ANN in CGA^d is 9% better than in GA in the same evolving generations. As shown in Fig. 3, 300 random testing samples are sorted by the ANN trained by CGA^d. In simplified structure optimization,The CGA^d Algorithm can simplify it to

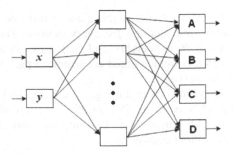

Fig. 4. ANN structure with simplification and optimization

meet the 3-storey structure, 1 hidden layer, 6 neurons in the hidden layer,and some connections can be omitted at the request of the 95 % of classification accuracy.

6 Conclusion

ANN designing based on co-evolution genetic algorithm can effectively optimize ANN parameters as well as its structure. The training speed is greatly quicker than conventional genetic algorithm and local optimum can be avoided. So evolving computation is a new way for ANN designing.

References

1. Bishop, J.M., Mitchell, R.J.: Neural networks-an introduction. In: IEE Colloquium on Neural Networks for Systems: Principles and Applications, pp. 1–3 (1991)
2. Haykin, S.: Neural Networks: A Comprehensive Foundation, pp. 78–97. Prentice Hall, Englewood Cliffs (1992)
3. Takahama, T., Sakai, S.: Structural learning of neural networks. In: Proc. of 2004 IEEE Int. Conf. on Systems, Man and Cybernetics, pp. 3507–3512 (2004)
4. Parekh, R., Yang, J., Honavar, V.: Constructive neural-network learning algorithms for pattern classification. IEEE Trans. on Neural Networks 11(1), 436–451 (2000)
5. Takahama, T., Sakai, S.: MGGA: Genetic algorithm with mutant genes. Systems and Computer 33(14), 23–33 (2002)
6. Frank, H.F., Leumg, H.K., Lam, S.H.: Tuning of structure and parameters of neural network using an improved genetic algorithm. IEEE Trans. on Neural Networks 14(1), 79–88 (2003)
7. Rovithakis, G.A., Chalkiadakis, I., Zervakis, M.E.: High-order neural network structure selection using genetic algorithms. IEEE Trans. on Systems, Man and Cybernetics 34(1), 150–158 (2004)
8. Wang, X., Cao, X.: Genetic Algorithm, pp. 153–156. Xi'an Jiaotong University Press, Xi'an (2002)
9. Liu, H.: Single-object and multi-object optimization based on genetic algorithm, doctor dissertation, pp. 21–24. South China University of Technology, Guangzhou (2002)
10. Paredis, J.: Coevolutionary computation. Artificial Life 2(4), 355–375 (1995)
11. Daniel Hillis, W.: Co-evolving parasites improve simulated evolution as an optimization procedure. Physica D: Nonlinear Phenomena 42(1-3), 228–234 (1990)
12. Yan, P., Zhang, C.: Artificial neural networks and simulating evolving computation, pp. 416–419. Tsinghua University Press, Beijing (2000)

Research on ACA-BP Neural Network Model

Qing Chen[1], Yuxiang Shao[2], and Zhifeng Liu[2]

[1] Wuhan Institute of Technology, Wuhan, Hubei, P.R. China
chenqing@mail.wit.edu.cn
[2] China University of Geosciences, No.388 Lumo Road Wuhan, P.R. China
syxcq@163.com

Abstract. This paper proposes a new model called ACA-BP network. This network combines ant colony algorithm (ACA) with neural network and adopts ant colony algorithm to train authority value and threshold value of BP nerve network. It not only has the extensive mapping ability of neural network, but also has the advantages of high efficiency, rapid global convergence and distributed computation of ant system. The experiment result indicates the ACA-BP neural network outperforms the BP neural network.

Keywords: Ant Colony Algorithm (ACA), BP Neural Network, Optimize.

1 Introduction

As a kind of feed-forward neural networks widely used in many areas, BP neural network self-adaptively obtains high degree and non-linear mapping relation from input to output through training a large number of samples. But in practice application, there are some problems with the traditional BP algorithm such as slow in convergence pace, easy to run into the local optimization and take place the oscillation effect, uncertain hidden nodes' number and initialization value[1].

Ant colony Algorithm(ACA) is a global heuristic algorithm based on the research of ant group behaviors in the natural world, which has characteristics of positive feedback, parallel computing, robustness and easy to combine with other algorithms[2][3]. In recent years, some scholars put forward the max-min ant colony system (MMAC) and ant colony optimization (ACO) which open up new areas for ant colony system theoretical study[4][5].

In this paper, ACA is adopted to train authority value and threshold value of BP nerve network. As a result, an ACA-BP neural network model is developed. Then, two experiments are used to validate the new model. The result shows that the ACA-BP neural network model has higher prediction precision and better generalization ability than BP neural network.

2 ACA-BP Network Model

2.1 Basic Principle

ACA-BP network adopts ant colony algorithm to train authority value and threshold value of BP nerve network, achieves the purpose of the intelligent optimization.

Z. Cai et al. (Eds.): ISICA 2009, CCIS 51, pp. 413–418, 2009.

The basic idea of ACA-BP network can be described as follows[6][7]:

Assuming the network has m parameters, includes all the authority value and threshold value. Firstly, sort these neural network parameters, for each parameter $P_i(1 \leq i \leq m)$, set it to N random nonzero values, take all possible values into a congregation I_{pi}; Secondly, define the number of ants as h, ants depart from the nest to the food source, each ant chooses values according to the amount of pheromone and the probability of moving in congregation I_{pi}. When the ant chooses the values of all congregations, it reaches the food source, and selects a set of network parameters. Then the ant returns to its nest along the walked path, updates the amount of pheromone. Repeat this process until all ants converge on the same path or reach a given number of iterations. Record the best authority value and threshold value obtained at the end, of which BP neural networks will make use.

2.2 Algorithm Realization

(1) initialization

Initial time t and the number of cycles N_c to zero, set the maximum cycle times N_{cmax}. Set the number of ants as h, $\tau_j(I_{pi})$ is the pheromone of the j-th element $p_j(I_{pi})$ in congregation $I_{pi}(1 \leq i \leq m)$, the pheromone $\tau_j(I_{pi})$ in every congregation is τ_0, and $\Delta\tau_j(I_{pi})$ is 0, and all ants are placed in the nest.

(2) Each ant travels along these m congregations, and selects an element from N elements of each set according to the formula (1), and the m elements make up a set of network parameters. Selected rule can be described as follows: for congregation I_{pi}, the probability of select the j-th element of the k-th(k =1, 2, ..., h) ant randomly according to the formula (1):

$$P_r\left(\tau_j^k(I_{pi})\right) = \frac{\tau_j^k(I_{pi})}{\sum\limits_{g=1}^{N}\tau_g^k(I_{pi})} \tag{1}$$

(3) Repeat step (2), until all the ants reach the food source.

(4) Assuming all ants from nest to the food source take m units of time, make $t = t + m$, $N_c = N_c + 1$. Use authority value and threshold value chosen by the ants to calculate training samples' output value and output error of BP neural network, record the optimal solution of current parameters, update the amount of pheromone according to the formula (2):

$$\tau_j\left(I_{pi}\right)(t+m) = (1-\rho)\tau_j\left(I_{pi}\right)(t) + \Delta\tau_j\left(I_{pi}\right) \tag{2}$$

where ρ is a number ranging between 0 and 1 and represents the volatility of the pheromone.

$$\Delta \tau_j \left(I_{pi} \right) = \sum_{k=1}^{h} \Delta \tau_j^k \left(I_{pi} \right) \tag{3}$$

$\Delta \tau_j^k \left(I_{pi} \right)$ is the pheromone trail on the j-th element in collection I_{pi} by the k-th ant, which is computed by

$$\Delta \tau_j^k \left(I_{pi} \right) = \begin{cases} \dfrac{Q}{e^k}, & if \ the \ k\text{-th ant selects} \ P_j \left(I_{pi} \right) \\ 0, & otherwise \end{cases} \tag{4}$$

where Q is a constant called pheromone intensity, which regulates the pheromone adjustment speed. e^k is the maximum output error of the training samples using the authority value and threshold value of the k-th ant chooses, defined as $e^k = \max_{n=1}^{s} |y - d|$. In the formula, s is the number of samples, y is actual output and d is expectation output of neural network. Error e^k is smaller, the corresponding pheromone increases more.

In addition, pheromone of every congregation is restricted between $\left[\tau_{min}, \tau_{max} \right]$ to avoid too fast converge on the local optimal solution. When the pheromone is more than the value τ_{max}, it is taken by τ_{max}. If the pheromone is less than τ_{min}, it is taken by τ_{min}.

In order to extend the ant colony search space, eventually find the optimum solution, this model also introduces smoothing technology, which reduces the difference of pheromone in every congregation as far as possible. The formula is

$$\tau_j^* (I_{pi})(t) = \tau_j (I_{pi})(t) + \delta(\tau_{max}(t) - \tau_j (I_{pi})(t)) \tag{5}$$

where $\delta \in [0,1]$, called smooth intensity. if δ is 0, smooth function will not play a role. If δ is 1, the value of pheromone is $\tau_{max}(t)$, which means that all pheromone are set to the initial value and eliminate the pheromone difference caused by current search. The introduction of smoothing technology can significantly enhance the algorithm solving efficiency.

(5) If all ants convergence to a path or the number of cycle $N_c \geq N_{cmax}$, cycle is end, the best path is obtained, otherwise, goes to step (2).

The flow chart of ACA-NN algorithm is shown in Figure 1.

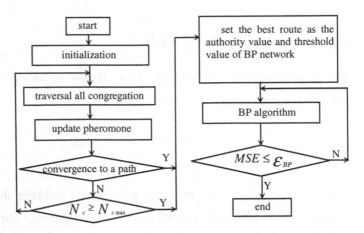

Fig. 1. Flow chart of ACA-NN algorithm

3   Simulation

In this section, we will use two different examples to validate the new model. We do experiment with two different algorithms, BP algorithm and the ACA-BP algorithm. For the two algorithms, we adopt same initialization conditions.

Example 1: simulation of 1-dimensional function

$$y = \sin(5x) + \cos(8x), x \in [0, 2.5]$$

There are 51 learning sample, the structure of network includes three layers, in hidden layer we adopt 10 neurons. From the concrete simulation we obtain Figure 2 to Figure 5.

Example 2: simulation of 2-dimensional function

$$z = \frac{\sin\pi y}{2 + \sin 2\pi x}, 0 \le x \le 1, 0 \le y \le 1$$

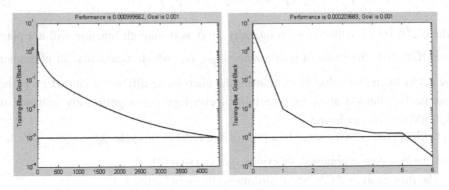

Fig. 2. Training curve for BP-NN   **Fig. 3.** Training curve for ACA-BP

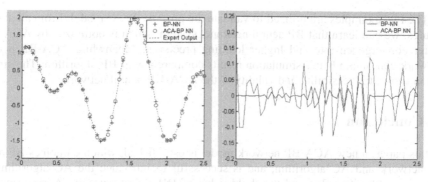

Fig. 4. Simulation result

Fig. 5. Error curve

Choose training samples as

$$x(i) = 0.02 \times i (i = 0,1,\cdots,50)$$
$$y(i) = 0.02 \times i (i = 0,1,\cdots,50)$$

The network includes 3 layers, in hidden layer we adopt 20 neurons. From the concrete simulation we obtain Figure 6 to Figure 9.

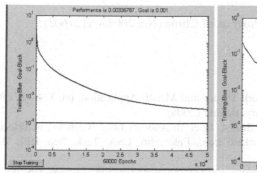

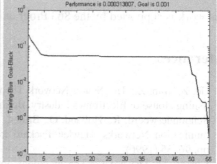

Fig. 6. Training curve for BP-NN

Fig. 7. Training curve for ACA-BP NN

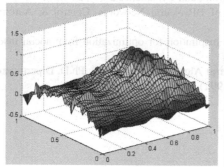

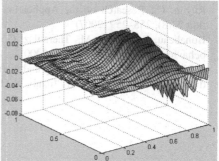

Fig. 8. Error surface for BP-NN

Fig. 9. Error surface for ACA-BP

The two examples are utilized to validate the proposed new model. From all above figures, we can learn that BP neural networks system which is optimized by ACA has better convergence rate and higher learning precision. Meanwhile ACA-BP neural network can obtain better simulation results compared with BP algorithm. The simulation shows the feasibility and validity of the ACA-BP neural network.

5 Conclusion

In this paper, a new ACA-BP network model is established, which combines BP neural network and AC algorithm, and is successful to introduce the AC algorithm to optimize authority value and threshold value of BP neural network. A performance comparison is emphasized on the ACA-BP network with the most commonly used BP network. The numerical results show that the ACA-BP network has a better training performance, faster convergence rate, as well as a better predicting ability than the BP network to the selected cases. It is worth to mention that the current study is very preliminary for the ACA-BP neural networks approach, and there are many works need to be carried on further.

Acknowledgement

This work is supported by the 863 Program of China (No. 2008AA121602)

References

1. Ge, Z., Sun, Z.: The Neural Network Theory and Matlab Application, pp. 324–327. Publishing House of Electronics Industry, Beijing (2008)
2. Schoonderwoerd, R., Holland, O., Bruten, J., et al: Ants for Load Balancing in Telecommunication Networks. Hewlett Packard Lab., Palo Alto, USA, Tech. Rep. HPL 1996, pp. 96–35 (1996)
3. Dorigo, M., Di Caro, G.: The ant colony optimization meta-heuristic, London, UK, pp. 11–32. McGraw Hill, New York (1982)
4. Dorigo, M., Maniezzo, V., Colorni, A.: Ant system: optimization by a colony of cooperating agent. IEEE Transactions on Systerns, Man, and Cybemetics 26(1), 29–41 (1996)
5. Ruyun, C.: Research on the Application of BP Neural Networks. Control & Automation 23(8), 258–259 (2007)
6. Bonabeau, E., Dorigo, M., Theraulaz, G.: Inspiration for optimization from aocial insect behavior. Nature 406(6), 39–42 (2000)
7. Dorig, M.: Optimiztion, Learning and Natural Algorithma (in Italian). Ph.D. Dipartimento di Electronica, Politecnico di Milano, IT (1992)

A Text-Independent Speaker Verification System Based on Cross Entropy

Xiaochun Lu[1,2] and Junxun Yin[1]

[1] School of Electronic and Information Engineering
South China University of Technology
Guangzhou, China
[2] College of computer and Information technology
Guangxi Normal University
Guilin, China
xchun_lu@163.com, eejyin@scut.edu.cn

Abstract. This paper presents a method based on information theory to estimate the distortion between the enrolled speaker's model and the test utterance in speaker verification system. It uses the cross entropy (CE) to compute the distance between two parametric models (such as GMMs). Different from the traditional average log-likelihood method, it considers the symmetry between the test utterance and the referenced model. In the verification phase, the zt - norm is used to compensate the session variability. Experiment results based on the TIMIT database show that the proposed method can efficiently reduce error rates over the standard log-likelihood scoring.

Keywords: speaker verification; GMM score; cross entropy; Gaussian mixture model; normalization.

1 Introduction

Speaker recognition is the process of validating a claimed identity by evaluating the extent to which a test utterance matches the claimant's model. In the text-independent speaker recognition, Gaussian mixture model-Universal Background Model (GMM-UBM) [1] have proven extremely successful and most popularly used for many years. In state-of-the-art system, speaker-dependent GMMs are derived from a speaker-independent universal background model (UBM) by adapting the UBM components with maximum a posteriori (MAP) adaptation using speakers' personal training data.

Speaker recognition can be classified into speaker identification (SI) and speaker verification (SV) [2]. This work focuses on speaker verification systems. The task for a SV system is to reject or accept a claimed identity by analysis a speaker's voice on a test utterance. Two phases are necessary for the system to be able to accomplish this task. The first is design phase which the SV system uses training utterances to estimate statistical models of each of the speakers, and a world model. The second is verification phase, the system analyses a test utterance pronounced by the claimed identity and the world model to compute a verification score.

Z. Cai et al. (Eds.): ISICA 2009, CCIS 51, pp. 419–426, 2009.

In the speaker verification system, we need a verification score and a threshold to decide whether to accept or reject a claimed speaker. Usually, we compute the posterior probability of the test utterance against the claimant speaker's model and the world model as a verification score based on Bayesian rule, which is called the Log Likelihood Ratio (LLR). Computing of the average log-likelihood of the test utterance feature vectors based on assuming frame independence. Previous literature has suggested a variety of methods of GMM scoring. In [3], cross likelihood ratio was calculated between the GMM representing a target speaker and a GMM representing a test utterance. This was done by switching the roles of the training and test utterances and averaging the likelihood of the test utterance given the GMM parameterization of the training utterance given the GMM parameterization of the test utterance, but the inherent asymmetry of the GMM scoring remained. Parameterization of both training and test utterances in a symmetric framework was done in [4], where both target speakers and test utterances were treated symmetrically by being modeled by a covariance matrix. The distance between a target speaker and a test utterance was defined as a symmetric function of the target model and the test utterance model. But a covariance matrix lacks the modeling power of a GMM, which results in low accuracy. The GMM-simulation algorithm described in [5] has speeded up dramatically the speaker retrieval task compared to classical GMM. In this paper, we use Gaussian mixture modeling (GMM) for representing both train and test sessions, and introduce the information entropy to estimate the GMM score instead of the standard method of GMM scoring.

In SV, before making the decision, the system needs to operate a score normalization because of the difference of the distributions of output scores for different speakers' GMMs, which leads to speaker-dependent biases in the client score distribution. And in the real application, it is necessarily to need a global speaker-independent threshold for all of the test utterances. In current SV system, the most frequently used score normalization techniques are the z-Norm [1] and the t-Norm[6] or a combination of both: zt-norm, which performs z-normalization followed by t-normalization, was originally proposed to compensate for both effects [7].

This paper is organized as follows. In Section 2, we provide a brief overview of speaker verification. In Section 3, we discuss CE method for speaker verification system. Finally, experiments and conclusions are described in Sections 4 and 5.

2   Speaker Verification System

2.1   Baseline System

Most state-of-the-art text-independent speaker verification system use GMMs to represent a statistical model of each speaker. The GMM for a speaker s is defined as:

$$P^s\left(x_t \mid \lambda\right) = \sum_{i=1}^{M} \omega_i N_i\left(x_t; \mu_i^s, \Sigma_i^s\right) \tag{1}$$

i.e., $P^s\left(x_t \mid \lambda\right)$ is a weighted sum of Gaussian distributions $N_i\left(x_t; \mu_i^s, \Sigma_i^s\right)$, where μ_i is the mean and Σ_i is the covariance matrix of the i-th Gaussian mixture, and ω_i

is the weight of the i-th Gaussian mixture, M is the number of Gaussian mixture components, and where $\{x_t\}_{t=1}^T$ is a D-dimensional feature vectors, T is the frame number of feature vectors. The complete Gaussian mixture model is parameterized by the mean vectors, covariance matrices and mixture weights from all component densities. These parameters are collectively represented by the notation: $\lambda = \{\omega_i, \mu_i, \Sigma_i\}, i = 1, \cdots, M$. GMM parameters are estimated using the standard Expectation Maximization (EM) algorithm. Each speaker has a unique model, describing the particular features of his/her voice. In the verification phase, for a sequence of T test vectors $\{x_t\}_{t=1}^T$, the resulting GMMs are then used to compute the log-likelihood (LL) of the test utterance vectors can be written in equation (2):

$$\log P^s (X \mid \lambda) = \frac{1}{T} \sum_{t=1}^T \log P^s (x_t \mid \lambda) \tag{2}$$

In a GMM-UBM based speaker verification system, a likelihood ratio score between claimed speaker's model likelihood score and the average likelihood score of a background set is used [8]:

$$LLR(X \mid s) = \log P^s (X \mid \lambda_T) - \log P(X \mid \lambda_U) \tag{3}$$

Where λ_T represents the target speaker model, λ_U is the UBM model parameters.

Then, the standard approach is to normalize $LLR(X \mid s)$ and compare it with a threshold. If it exceeds the threshold, the claimed speaker is accepted, if not, it is rejected. In our work, we use the text-independent speaker verification GMM-UBM system as our baseline system.

2.2 Score Normalization

The use of score normalization techniques has become important in GMM-based speaker verification systems for reducing the effects of the many sources of statistical variability associated with log likelihood ratio scores [6].

For a given target speaker s, the corresponding speaker specific supervector S and test utterance x_{test} speaker normalization is applied to the log likelihood ratio score $LLR(x_{test} \mid s)$. The definition of the score itself and its use in forming the decision rule for accepting or rejecting the claimed identity of speaker s is provided. It is generally assumed that $LLR(x_{test} \mid s)$ is Gaussian distributed when evaluated over utterances that represent a range of the possible sources of variability. Two well-known score normalization techniques, the z-norm and t-norm, form a normalized LLR score by obtaining estimates of the mean μ and standard deviation σ and normalizing as:

$$LLR\left(x_{test} \mid s\right)_{norm} = \frac{LLR\left(x_{test} \mid s\right) - \mu}{\sigma} \tag{4}$$

The z-norm and t-norm differ in how these normalization parameters are computed. In the z-norm, the parameters μ and σ are estimated as the sample mean and standard deviation of a set of log likelihood ratio scores $LLR\left(x_i \mid s\right)$, $i = 1, \ldots, N_{imp}$, where s is the target speaker providing a speaker-specific posterior distribution of supervector s and $x_i, i = 1, \ldots, N_{imp}$, is a set of N_{imp} impostor speaker utterances. This represents an average of scores obtained by scoring the target speaker model against a set of impostor utterances.

In the t-norm, the parameters μ and σ are estimated as the sample mean and standard deviation of a set of log likelihood ratio scores $LLR\left(x_{test} \mid s_j\right)$, $j = 1, \ldots, M_{imp}$, where $s_j, j = 1, \ldots, M_{imp}$, is a set of M_{imp} impostor speakers providing M_{imp} different posterior distributions of s. This represents an average of scores obtained by scoring a set of impostor speaker models against the test utterance.

The zt-norm, which performs z-normalization followed by t-normalization, was originally proposed to compensate for both effects [7]. The form of the zt-norm is similar to the t-norm; however, both the test score $LLR\left(x_{test} \mid s\right)$ and impostor score $LLR\left(x_{test} \mid s_j\right), j = 1, \ldots, M_{imp}$ used in computing the t-norm distribution are first normalized using the z-norm prior to implementing the t-norm. In this paper, we use the zt-norm for the score normalization process.

3   Approximated Cross Entropy (ACE)

In the field of information theory, the KL-divergence, also known as the relative entropy, also called cross entropy (CE), between two probability density functions $f(x)$ and $g(x)$ is defined in equation (5):

$$D\left(f \parallel g\right) = \int f\left(x\right) \log \frac{f\left(x\right)}{g\left(x\right)} dx \tag{5}$$

It is commonly used in statistics as a measure of similarity between two density distributions. The KL divergence was used in speech recognition as determining if two acoustic models are similar [9]. In our work, we use the CE to calculate the similarity between the target speaker model and the test utterance model. If the value of CE is smaller than a pre-decided threshold, indicating that the test utterance is similar to the target speaker, then could be accepted; Otherwise, the value is larger than the threshold, indicating that the less similarity between the test utterance and target speaker, so could be rejected.

Direct computation of the CE should become impossible with multi-dimensional data and complex statistical laws $f(x)$ and $g(x)$, which is the case in SV. Aronowitz *et al* [10] have proven that the average log-likelihood of a test utterance can be approximatively equate to the negative cross entropy of the target GMM and the true model for the test utterance. Therefore, by calculating the log-likelihood of a test utterance, we can try to estimate the negative cross entropy between the target GMM and the true model for the test utterance. In our work, we use the approximated cross entropy (ACE) [10] technique to compute the cross entropy.

Assuming that the target speaker GMM model is denoted by Q, and the true model that generated the test utterance vectors is a GMM denoted by P. The average log-likelihood of an utterance $X = x_1, \cdots, x_n$ of asymptotically infinite length n drawn from model P, is as following:

$$\frac{1}{n}LL(X \mid Q) = \frac{1}{n}\sum_{i=1}^{n}\log\left(\Pr(x_i \mid Q)\right)$$

$$\xrightarrow[n \to \infty]{} \int_x \Pr(x \mid P)\log\left(\Pr(x \mid Q)\right)dx \qquad (6)$$

$$= -H(P, Q)$$

where $H(P, Q)$ is the cross entropy between GMMs P and Q. Equation (6) follows by an assumed ergodicity of the speech frame sequence and the law of large number.

There are two approaches of estimating the ACE [10]. In this paper, after comparison on experiments results, we use the approach, expected ACE (E-ACE), is to calculate the expected negative cross entropy conditioned on the observed test data X as follows:

$$Ep \int_x \Pr(x \mid P)\log\left(\Pr(x \mid Q)\right)dx$$

$$\cong \sum_{g=1}^{n_g^P} \hat{\omega}_g^P \max_j \left\{ \begin{array}{c} \log \omega_j^Q - \dfrac{1}{2}\left(\tilde{\mu}_g^P - \mu_j^Q\right)^T \Sigma_j^{-1}\left(\tilde{\mu}_g^P - \mu_j^Q\right) \\[2mm] -\dfrac{1}{2}\log\det\Sigma_j - \dfrac{D/2}{n\hat{\omega}_g^P + r} - \dfrac{D}{2}\left(\log 2\pi + 1\right) \end{array} \right\} \qquad (7)$$

Where ω_j^Q, μ_j^Q, Σ_j denotes the weight, mean vectors and covariance matrix of

Gaussian j of GMM Q respectively. And $\tilde{\mu}_g^P = \left(n\hat{\omega}_g^P \hat{\mu}_g^P + r\mu_g^{UBM}\right)\Big/\left(n\hat{\omega}_g^P + r\right),$

where $\hat{\omega}_g^P$ denotes the maximum-likelihood (ML) estimated weight of Gaussian g of GMM P from the test utterance, and $\hat{\mu}_g^P$ denotes the corresponding ML estimated mean. In our work, we use fixed diagonal covariance matrices GMMs, i.e., diagonal covariance matrices which are trained for the UBM and are not retrained for each speaker. So the Σ_j is identical of the Σ_j^{UBM}.

4 Experiments

This section presents the experimental evaluation based on the GMM-UBM system for text-independent speaker verification.

4.1 Database

The experiments were conducted using TIMIT database [11]. TIMIT database totally includes 630 speakers, including 438 male and 192 female speakers. Each speaker has ten different sentence utterances. The speech was sampled at 16kHz. In this paper, we randomly select 90 male speakers as a gender-dependent UBM training set. Among the remaining male speakers, 200 speakers are used for selecting the cohort sets for a impostor speakers set and 50 speakers are used for the target speakers set. MAP adaptation is performed with a fixed relevance factor of 16 for all speaker models. The training and test speech data of each target speaker were randomly selected and concatenated from the original TIMIT database, with no train/test data overlap and initial/trailing silence removed (3 utterances were for training data and the remaining were used as test utterances). This gives 350 true tests (50×7) and 2000 impostor trials (200×10) per person.

4.2 Evaluation Measure

The performance of a speaker verification system is usually represented in terms of false acceptance rate (FAR), which is the number of false acceptances divided by the number of impostor accesses, and false rejection rate (FRR), which is the number of false rejection divided by the number of client accesses. A summary of these two values is often given by the equal error rate (EER), which is the point where FAR is equal to FRR. We also used the detection cost function (DCF) defined in [12]:

$$DCF = C_{miss} E_{miss} P_{t\arg et} + C_{fa} E_{fa} \left(1 - P_{t\arg et}\right) \tag{8}$$

where $P_{t\arg et}$ is the a priori probability of the target tests with $P_{t\arg et} = 0.01$ and the specific cost factors $C_{miss} = 10$ and $C_{fa} = 1$.

4.3 System Description

The baseline system is essentially a GMM-UBM based text-indepentent speaker verification system. For feature extraction, an energy-based speech detector is applied to remove the silence segment with low-energy frames and zero crossing rate of the signal. The remaining signals were pre-emphasized by a filter with transfer function $1-0.97z^{-1}$. And then a 12-dimensional MFCC vector is from pre-emphasized speech every 10ms using a 25 ms Hamming window. Delta-cepstral coefficients are computed over a +2 frame span and appended to the cepstral producing a 24 dimensional feature vectors.

The universal background model (UBM) trained with the data from the development set. The UBM used in the experiment is in fact Gaussian mixture models (GMMs) with 512 mixtures constructed through EM estimation. Given the UBM, the target speaker models are then derived using MAP adaptation. For the systems used in the experiment, the means vectors and the weights of the mixture components are adapted.

In our work, zt-norm is also used for a score-based normalization approach to partly compensate the session variability. A set of N_{imp} =120 impostor speaker utterances were used for all of the z-norm results given. A set of M_{imp} =46 impostor speakers models were used for computing the t -norm results.

Both the baseline system and the E-ACE based system are under the same experimental condition such as described above.

4.4 Experimental Results

Table 1 shows a comparison between the baseline system and the system based-proposed scoring method in text-independent speaker verification. In the baseline system, there was no any score normalization technique which is described in section 2.1.

From the results in table 1 showed, it is obviously that the performance of based-ACE system outperforms the baseline system. In comparison with the baseline system, the ACE system achieves relative EER reductions of 23.5%. However the performance of the ACE-system and the baseline+(zt -norm) system was closely. ACE+ zt -norm system has improved significantly over the system of baseline+ zt -norm, with the EER reductions of 29.2% and the Min.DCF reductions of 38.9% respectively. We choose the ACE+ zt -norm as our eventual system.

Table 1. Performance compare with proposed method and baseline

system	EER(%)	Min.DCF
Baseline	12.61	0.0644
Baseline+ zt -norm	10.34	0.0349
ACE	9.65	0.0368
ACE+ zt -norm	7.32	0.0215

Table 2. FAR and FRR for different duration of test utterances

Time of test (second)	FAR(%)	FRR(%)
5s	13.61	11.23
30s	8.22	7.57
50s	6.56	6.11

However, based on ACE GMMs scoring is affected by the length of test speech signal. Table 2 compares the FAR and FRR of the ACE+ zt-norm system with variability of the duration of test utterance. According to the results, with the length of test utterances increasing, the reductions of the FAR and FRR is obviously.

5 Conclusion

In this paper, we introduce the cross entropy to estimate the information distortion between two GMMs in the speaker verification system, contrary to the standard GMM scoring which is based on Bayesian rule, this approach applying the assumption on the test utterances, the assumption is that a GMM extracts the entire speaker information from an utterance as the same in the train stage, i.e., the GMM parameters comprise a sufficient statistic for estimating the identity of the speaker. Both parameterization of training and test utterances could make use of the symmetry. At the same time, the proposed approach may be beneficial for improving the robustness and complexity, because according to the approach, a GMM is fitted for a test utterance, the verification score is calculated by using only the GMM of target speaker and the GMM of the test utterance.

References

1. Reynold, D.A., Quatieri, T.F., Dunn, R.: Speaker verification using adapted Gaussian mixture models. Digtal Signal Processing 10, 19–41 (2000)
2. Bruce, S.F.: Recent advances in speaker recognition. In: Proc. ICASSP, pp. 429–440 (1989)
3. Tsai, W.H., Chang, W.W., Chu, Y.C., Huang, C.S.: Explicit exploitation of stochastic characteristics of test utterance for text-independent speaker identification. In: Proc. Eurospeech, pp. 771–774 (2001)
4. Schmidt, M., Gish, H., Mielke, A.: Covariance estimation methods for channel robust text-independent speaker identification. In: Proc. ICASSP, pp. 333–336 (1995)
5. Aronowitz, H., Burshtein, D., Amir, A.: Speaker indexing in audio archives using gaussian mixture scoring simulation. In: Bengio, S., Bourlard, H. (eds.) MLMI 2004. LNCS, vol. 3361, pp. 243–252. Springer, Heidelberg (2005)
6. Auckenthaler, R., Carey, M., Lloyd-Thomas, H.: Score normalization for text-independent speaker verification system. Digital Signal Process 10, 42–54 (2000)
7. Vogt, R., Baker, B., Sridharan, S.: Modeling session vari- ability in text-independent speaker verification. In: Proc. Eurospeech, Lisbon, Portugal, September 2005, pp. 3117–3120 (2005)
8. Higgins, A., Bahler, L., Porter, J.: Speaker verification using randomized phrase prompting. Digital Signal Processing 1, 89–106 (1991)
9. Olsen, P., Dharanipragada, S.: An efficient integrated gender detection scheme and time mediated averaging of gender dependent acoustic models. In: Proc. Eurospeech, Geneva, Switzerland, September 1-4, vol. 4, pp. 2509–2512 (2003)
10. Aronowitz, H., Burshtein, D.: Efficient Speaker Recognition Using Approximated Cross Entropy (ACE). IEEE Transactions, Speech, and Langauge Processing 15, 2033–2043 (2007)
11. Garofolo, J.S., Lamel, L.F., Fisher, W.M., et al.: TIMIT acoustic-phonetic continuous speech corpus DB/CD (2007), http://www.ldc.upenn.edu/Catalog/
12. The 2000 NIST Speaker recognition evaluation, http://www.nist.gov/speech/tests/spk/2000/index.htm

An Improved Algorithm of Apriori

Binhua Liao

The College of Mathematics and Statistics, Huazhong Normal University
liaobinhua@mail.ccnu.edu.cn

Abstract. This paper puts forward a kind of improved algorithm after analyzing the classical Apriori algorithm. Through scanning database only once, all transactions are transformed into components of a two-dimensional array. The algorithm becomes more practical by introducing weight. Moreover, the unnecessary data are deleted in time, and the joining and pruning steps become simple. This, therefore, improves the efficiency of Apriori algorithm.

Keywords: Data Mining; Association Rule; Apriori.

1 Introduction

Association Rule Mining [1] is proposed by R.Agrawal, et al. first of all in 1993, which has become an important data mining task and a focused theme in data mining research. Association Rule Mining leads to the discovery of associations and correlations among items in large transactional or relational data sets and the discovery of interesting and valuable correlation relationship among huge amounts of transaction records. The object of Association Rule Mining is to find the rule that the occurrence of one event can lead to another incident happened. The APriori[2] algorithm is the most classic association rule mining algorithm. APriori is a seminal algorithm proposed by R.Agrawal and R.Srikant in 1994 for mining frequent itemsets for Boolean association rules. As we have seen, the APriori significantly reduces the size of candidate sets leading to good performance gain. However, it also suffers from two nontrivial costs: it may need to generate a huge number of candidate sets and it may need to repeatedly scan the database and check a large set of candidates by pattern matching. Many variations of APriori algorithm have been proposed that focus on improving the efficiency of the original algorithm. Several of these variations are summarized as follows: Hash-based algorithm, Transaction-reduction-based algorithm [5], Partitioning-based algorithm [6], sampling-based algorithm, dynamic- itemset-counting-based algorithm, array-based algorithm, and so on. But there are many deficiencies: the different itemset and different item of itemset are referred as the same in the variations of APriori algorithm, in fact, they are different. So, this paper puts forward a kind of improved algorithm. Through scanning database only once, all transactions are transformed to be components of array, and the algorithm becomes more practical by introducing weight .At the same time, the unnecessary data is deleted in time, the steps of join and prune become simple, and the efficiency of Apriori algorithm is improved.

Z. Cai et al. (Eds.): ISICA 2009, CCIS 51, pp. 427–432, 2009.
© Springer-Verlag Berlin Heidelberg 2009

2 Definition of Association Rule Mining

2.1 Association Rule

Let $I=\{I_1, I_2, ..., I_m\}$ be a set of item, we call an itemset. An itemset that contains k items is a k-itemset. Let A be a set of items. A transaction T is said to contain A if and only if $A \subseteq D$. An Association Rule is an implication of the form $A \subseteq B$, where $A \subset I$, $B \subset I$, and $A \cap B = \phi$.

Rule *support* and *confidence* are two measures of rule interestingness. They respectively reflect the usefulness and certainty of discovered rules.

2.2 *Support* of Association Rule

The rule $A \Rightarrow B$ holds in the transaction set D with *support* s, where s is the percentage of transactions in D that contain $A \cup B$ (i.e., the union of sets A and B, or say, both A and B). This is taken to be the probability, $P(A \cup B)$. That is,

$$support \ (A \Rightarrow B) = P(A \cup B). \tag{1}$$

2.3 *Confidence* of Association Rule

The rule $A \Rightarrow B$ has *confidence* c in the transaction set D, where c is the percentage of transactions in D containing A that also contain B. This is taken to be the conditional probability; $P(B | A)$. That is,

$$confidence(A \Rightarrow B) = P(B | A) = \frac{support(A \cup B)}{support(A)} = \frac{support\_count(A \cup B)}{support\_count(A)} \tag{2}$$

2.4 *Strong* Association Rule, Minimum Support Threshold, Minimum ConfidenceThreshold

A Minimum Support Threshold and a Minimum Confidence Threshold can be set by users or domain experts. Rules that satisfy both a minimum support threshold (min_sup) and minimum confidence threshold (min_conf) are called *strong*.

The objection of association rule mining is to find rules that satisfy both a minimum support threshold (min_sup) and minimum confidence threshold (min_conf) .Thus the problem of mining association rules can be reduced to that of mining frequent itemsets. In general, association rule mining can be viewed as a two-step process:

1. Find all frequent itemsets.
2. Generate strong association rules from the frequent itemsets.

Because the second step is much less costly than the first, the overall performance of mining association rules if determined by the first step.

3 Synopsis and Property of Apriori Algorithm

3.1 Basic Idea of Apriori Algorithm

Apriori algorithm uses *prior knowledge* of frequent itemset properties. Apriori employs an iterative approach known as a level-wise search, where k-itemsets are used to explore (k+1)-itemsets. First, the set of frequent 1-itemsets is found by scanning the database to accumulate the count for each item,and collecting those items that satisfy both min_sup and min_conf. The resulting set is denoted L_1. Next,L_1 is used to find L_2,the set of frequent 2-itemsets,which is used to find L_3,and so on, until no more frequent k-itemsets can be found. The founding of each L_k requires one full scan of the database. To improve the efficiency of the generation of frequent itemsets, an Apriori property that all nonempty subsets of a frequent itemset must also be frequent is used to reduce the search space.

3.2 Deficiency of Apriori Algorithm

Although the performance of Apriori algorithm is improved, there are many deficiencies in it.

1. It may need to generate a huge number of candidate sets. If there are 10^4 frequent 1-itemsets, the Apriori algorithm will need to generate more than 10^7 candidate 2-itemsets.Moreover, to discover pattern of size 100, it has to generate at least 10^{30} candidates in total.
2. It may need to repeatedly scan the database and check a large set of candidates by pattern matching.
3. Any given itemset or any item of the itemset has the same important in Apriori algorithm. In fact, there are many different among itemsets. Thus, the rules obtained may not be really interest.

4 Improvement of Apriori Algorithm

4.1 Improvement of Apriori Algorithm

Several variations are proposed in this paper, which are summarized as follows:

1. Only one scan of database by using array, thus, the time of I/O operation is reduced. First the database is scanned, the item in each transaction is denoted as '1' in array, or which is denoted as '0'.So, all the items are saved in array. At the same time, the number of occurrences of each item is counted by scanning the database, and is stored to the first column of array, A [i, 0]. Thereby, the item can be accessed directly in array in memory of unnecessarily accessing database frequently.
2. The support count of each candidate itemset can be accumulated directly by array, which is the sum of each column in array, thus, the set of frequent 1-itemsets, L_1, can then be determined.
3. The concept of weight is introduced for the different item and the different itemset having different role. The user can judge if a given itemset or an item of the itemset is important and give them different weight value w_{ij}. So, the new support count of

itemsets needs to be calculated again with the weight value w_{ij}. The itemsets that the new support count is less than min_up must be removed from array. Thus, the meaning of frequent itemsets is changed and the former frequent itemset is not frequent.

4. The size of candidate itemsets is reduced by prune with deep degree. When (k-1)-itemsets are used to explore k-itemsets according to original Apriori Algorithm, we check the first column of array to find if the value less than k. If the value is less than or equal to k, the row of array is marked deleted, the next scan will skip it. Thus, the size of array is reduced, the efficiency of algorithm is improved.

4.2 Improved Algorithm

The pseudo-code for the improved Apriori algorithm and its related procedures are shows as follows:

```
Algorithm: im_Apriori.
Input:
D:a databse of transaction
min_sup:the minimum support count threshold
W[i,j]:the weight of the item of transaction
Output:
L:frequent itemsets in D
Method:
Initializing array A[n,m];
//n is the number of transaction, m is number of item.
L₁=find_frequent_1_itemsets(A);
//find frequent-1-itemset
// k-itemsets are used to explore (k+1)-itemsets
for(k=2;Lₖ₋₁≠∅;k++)
{Cₖ= apriori_gen (Lₖ₋₁);
For each transaction a∈A{//scan A for counts
Cₐ=subset(Cₖ,a);
//get the subsets of t that are candidates
For each candidate c∈Cₐ
c.count++;
}
c.count =c.count*Wᵢⱼ
Lₖ={c∈Cₖ|c.count≥min_sup}
}
Return L=∪ₖLₖ;

Procedure apriori_gen(Lₖ₋₁:frequent(k-1)-itemsets)
For each transaction a∈A
if a[i0]<k then
delete a[i];
else{
For each itemset l₁∈Lₖ₋₁
For each itemset l₂∈Lₖ₋₁
```

```
If(l₁[1]=l₂[1]∧l₁[2]=l₂[2]∧…∧l₁[k-2]=l₂[k-2]∧l₁[k-
1]=l₂[k-1]then {
C=l₁⋈l₂;// join step:generate candidates
If has_infrequent_subset(c,L_{k-1})then
Delete c;//prune step:remove unfruitful candidate
Else add c to C_k;
}
}
return C_k;

procedure has_infrequent_subset(c:candidate k-itemset;
L_{k-1}: frequent (k-1)-itemsets);//use prior knowledge
For each (k-1)-subset s of c
If s∉L_{k-1}then
return true;
return false;
```

4.3 Experiments and Result

In order to validate the effect of the improvement algorithm, I do some experiments. In my experiment data, the number of item in a transaction is less than 10, and the average number is 5. After experimenting, I can get the following table to analyze the effect of the Algorithm.

Table 1. Experiment data and experiment result

Experiment data	the number of the transactions	The performing time of Apriori algorithm (Unit: Second)	the performing time of improvement algorithm (Unit: Second)
Test1	587	0.34	0.28
Test2	5465	3.23	2.12
Test3	78663	34.23	29.23
Test4	234332	234.56	189.78

From the result of experiment, we find that the improvement algorithm is more practical and effective than normal Apriori algorithm.

5 Conclusions

Association Rule Mining is an important data mining task and a focused theme in data mining research. This paper puts forward a kind of improved algorithm after analyzing the classical Apriori algorithm. Through scanning database only once, all transactions are transformed to be components of array, and the algorithm becomes more practical and effective by introducing weight .At the same time, the unnecessary data is erased in time, the steps of join and prune become simple, the cost of computing is reduced, and the efficiency of algorithm is improved.

References

1. Agrawal, R., Imielinski, T., Swami, A.: Mining Association Rules Between Sets of Items in Large Databases. In: Proceedings of the ACM SIGMOD International Conference on Management of Data, Washington, USA, pp. 207–216. ACM Press, New York (1993)
2. Agrawal, R., Srikant, R.: Fast algorithm of mining association rules. In: Proceedings of the 20th International Conference on VLDB, Santigao, pp. 487–499 (1994)
3. Han, J., Kamber, M.: Data Mining: Concepts and Techniques, 2nd edn., p. 4. China Machine Press, Beijing (2006)
4. Qian, X.-z., Kong, F.: Research of Apriori algorithm in mining association rules. Computer Engineering and Applications 44(17), 138–140 (2008)
5. Han, J., Fu, Y.: Discovery of Multiple-level Association Rules from Large Databases. In: 1995 International Conference Very Large Data Bases, Zurich (1995)
6. Savasere, A., Omiecinski, E., Navathe, S.: An Efficient Algorithm for Mining Association Rules in Large Databases. In: 1995 International Conference Very Large Data Bases, Zurich (1995)

An Incremental Clustering with Attribute Unbalance Considered for Categorical Data

Jize Chen[1], Zhimin Yang[2,*], Jian Yin[1], Xiaobo Yang[2], and Li Huang[2]

[1] School of Information Science and Technology, Sun Yat-sen University,
Guangzhou, 510275, China
gjazz@163.com, issjyin@mail.sysu.edu.cn
[2] The 2nd Affiliated Hospital, Guangzhou University of Chinese Medicine,
Guangzhou, 510120, China
yangyo@163.net, yangxiaobomd@163.com, liea1981@126.com

Abstract. Clustering analysis is an important technique used in many fields. But traditional clustering algorithms generally deal with numeric data. While clustering categorical data have always attracted researchers' attentions because of their prevalence in real life. This paper analyses limitations of the categorical clustering algorithms proposed. Based on two observations, a new similarity measure is proposed for categorical data which considers the unbalance of attributes. As the data are getting much larger and more dynamic, incremental is an important quality of good clustering algorithms. The clustering algorithm present is an incremental with linear computing complexity. The experiment results indicate that it outperforms other categorical clustering algorithms referred in the paper.

Keywords: incremental clustering, attribute unbalance, categorical data.

1 Introduction

Clustering analysis is such an important data mining technique that is widely used in many application fields, such as image segmentation, network intrusion detection, and financial fraud detection [1], [6]. Clustering is partitioning objects into clusters or groups, so that objects in the same cluster are more similar than in other clusters.

Nowadays, large amounts of data can be accumulated for various purposes. And data would be inserted or removed over time. Traditional clustering algorithms focus on static data sets, where data points are kept unchanged after being processed. When the data set is modified, they have to re-clustering the whole data set from scratch. However, re-clustering the whole data sets from scratch is time-consuming and even infeasible when the out-of-server time is limited. Clustering algorithms should be incremental which only update the clusters affected by the changed data. Here, we propose such an incremental clustering algorithm that only requires one scan of the whole data set, where clusters are incrementally updated on the new incoming data.

---

* Corresponding author.

Z. Cai et al. (Eds.): ISICA 2009, CCIS 51, pp. 433–442, 2009.

Categorical data is prevalent in real life. Many fields, from statistics to psychology, deal with categorical data. Unlike numeric data, there is no explicit distance meaning in categorical data. For example, assumes the domain of color is {red, green, blue}. We cannot tell how far or near between two different colors. So, the traditional distance-based clustering algorithms like K-Means are not suitable for categorical data. Recently clustering categorical data has attracted many researchers' attentions and many methods have been proposed [7], [2], [5], [3], [4]. However, as we discuss in Section 2, the similarity measures for categorical data proposed by these methods have their own shortcomings.

Here, we would like to introduce our two observations. Firstly, A good clustering result should achieve data points in the same cluster have high intra-cluster similarity, and low inter-cluster similarity in others. For categorical data clusters, we expect that each attribute value predominates in one cluster and rarely occurs in other clusters. Secondly, in real-life data sets, attributes are unequal. They usually don't have the equal contribution to the final decision. Based on these two observations, in this paper, we propose a new similarity measure between cluster and data point which will be described in Section 3.

For solving above problems, in this paper, we provide an Incremental Clustering algorithm which considers the Unbalance of Attribute value distribution for Categorical data, short for ICUAC.

The rest of the paper is organized as follows: In Section 2, we discuss the related works in this literature. In Section 3, we formulate the problem and describe our proposed algorithm, ICUAC. And experimental results are presented in Section 4. Finally, we summarize some conclusions and future works in Section 5.

2 Related Works

Traditional clustering algorithms can be divided into partitional and hierarchical clustering algorithms [1]. Since data turn to be larger, incremental clustering has attracted many studies recently. The BIRCH algorithm [11] is an incremental clustering method with early study, which using CF tree to summary clusters. However, it's originally designed for numeric data. Here, we review recent clustering algorithms for categorical data.

The K-Modes algorithm [7] is traditional partitional clustering method which extends K-Means method for clustering categorical data, replacing the mean of cluster with mode and placing data point to a cluster whose mode shares the most common attribute values with it and updating the mode. However, choosing only one attribute value for each attribute to represent a cluster can cause problems. Suppose that a gender attribute in a cluster is 51% male and 49% female. Only choosing the male for the mode of it will lose the information from female, which is almost a half in it.

The ROCK algorithm [2] is a hierarchical clustering algorithm which treats each record (data point) as one market-basket transaction and computes distances between two records using Jaccard coefficient. Two records are said to be neighbors when their distance below the pre-specified threshold. A link between two records exists when they share a neighbor. Records are grouped based on the links between them in an agglomerative way. However, the threshold is difficult to set in practice. And its links estimation function $f(\theta)$ depends on data sets. Moreover, the time complexity of ROCK is high and not suitable for large data and incremental clustering process.

The COOLCAT method [5] is an incremental clustering algorithm based on weighing entropy of clusters. It places data points from one cluster to another several times till obtaining the lowest entropy of the whole clusters. Hence, the computing time is considerable. What is more, when computing the entropy of clusters, the method assumes the attributes are independent, which is not true in real data set.

The Squeezer algorithm [3] is an incremental clustering method which introduces a "support" conception (actually, attribute value frequency) to measure the similarity between cluster and data point. The similarity between a cluster and a point is the sum of the frequency of the point's attribute value in that cluster. This clustering method places each new coming data point one by one to a cluster with maximal similarity if the value above pre-specified threshold, else the data point to be a new cluster. Like ROCK, the similarity threshold is hard to set. Moreover, it is order-sensitive (data input order affects clustering result).

The FAVC algorithm [4] first partitions all the tuples (records) into k clusters randomly, and then repeats re-assigning each tuple to the cluster with maximal similarity until the expected entropy of clustering result below pre-defined threshold. It defines the similarity between one cluster and a tuple as the sum of all the $2^n - 1$ combinations of n attribute values (of the record) frequencies in that cluster. The computing time complexity as pointed out by the authors is increasing at geometric series. Hence, when n is large, the computing time is very considerable.

Above all, all the clustering algorithm mentioned above do not consider the unbalance of attribute value distribution in real-life data sets. [8] presents a fuzzy clustering method with feature weighted, in which the weights are computed on the whole data set before clustering. But computing weight on the whole data set is impossible when using incremental method for clustering dynamic increased data.

3 Our Algorithm

In this section, we present our ICUAC algorithm that is based on the conditional probability of an attribute value in one cluster and its weight attained after considering its distribution over all the clusters. We formulate the problem in Section 3.1 and present our ICUAC algorithm in Section 3.2.

3.1 Problem Formulation

The clustering problem we try to solve can be formulated as follows. Given a data set D of n points, $D = \{P_1, P_2, \cdots, P_n\}^T$ where each point is a multidimensional vector of m categorical attributes, $Pi = [P_{i1}, P_{i2}, \cdots, P_{im}]$, $i = 1, 2, \cdots, n$. Define the domain of attribute A_u as $Dom(A_u) = \bigcup_{i=1}^{n}(P_{iu})$, $u = 1, 2, \cdots, m$. This definition denotes that the domain of an attribute can be changed when the data set has been modified. Given an integer k, we would like to partition the points into k clusters $C_1, C_2, \cdots, C_k$. The clustering result is $C = \{C_1, C_2, \cdots, C_k\}$, where $C_r = \{P_1, P_2, \cdots, P_s\}$, $r = 1, 2, \cdots, k$, $|C_r| = s^r$, $|D| = |C| = \sum_{r=1}^{k} s^r$.

Definition 1. The similarity between point P_i and point P_j is a Jaccard coefficient like measure, defined as follow:

$$J(P_i, P_j) = \frac{1}{m} \sum_{u=1}^{m} \phi(P_{iu}, P_{ju}) \qquad \text{where} \quad \phi(x, y) = \begin{cases} 1, x = y \\ 0, x \neq y \end{cases}. \tag{1}$$

Definition 2. The similarity between cluster C_r and point P_i is defined as follow:

$$Sim(C_r, P_i) = \sum_{u=1}^{m} \Pr(A_u = P_{iu} \mid C_r) * W_u(A_u = P_{iu}) \tag{2}$$

where

$$W_u(A_u = P_{iu}) = \frac{W_u^{'}(A_u = P_{iu})}{\sum_{u=1}^{m} W_u^{'}(A_u = P_{iu})} \tag{3}$$

$\Pr(A_u = P_{iu} \mid C_r)$ is the conditional probability of attribute value P_{iu} given cluster C_r, and $W_u(A_u = P_{iu})$ is the weight of attribute value $A_u = P_{iu}$, which has been normalized. $W_u^{'}(A_u = P_{iu})$ is defined by Definition 3. It's not difficult to figure out that the similarity value belongs to [0, 1].

According to our first observation, if the attribute-values of a point have high probability occurring in one cluster, the point is much similar with this cluster. And according to our second observation, attribute value distributions are unbalanced. If one attribute value predominates in only a few clusters, then it should have higher weight; otherwise, if it's prevalent over all clusters, then its weight should be lower. Obviously, Equation 2 can achieve both qualities, which promises that if one point shares more import attribute-values of one cluster, then it can be more similar with that cluster.

Definition 3. The weight of an attribute value is defined as follow:

$$W_u^{'}(A_u = P_{iu}) = 1 - \frac{-1}{\log k} \sum_{r=1}^{k} \Pr^{'}(A_u = P_{iu} \mid C_r) * \log \Pr^{'}(A_u = P_{iu} \mid C_r) \tag{4}$$

where

$$\Pr^{'}(A_u = P_{iu} \mid C_r) = \frac{\Pr(A_u = P_{iu} \mid C_r)}{\sum_{r=1}^{k} \Pr(A_u = P_{iu} \mid C_r)} \tag{5}$$

Equation 4 is very similar with the entropy equation, which can tell how chaos of a system. We divide the entropy by $\log k$ for normalizing the weight in [0, 1] and also treat equation 5 with the same principle. Assumes some attribute value spreads over all clusters, that is to say, its conditional probabilities in clusters are almost the same, and then the Equation 4 gives very low weight for this attribute value. Otherwise, assume one attribute value's conditional probability in one cluster is 1, while the others is 0, then Equation 4 will get this attribute value a weight of 1. That makes sense, because such attribute value is just an important feature of that cluster and it is worthy of high weight.

Table 1. Initialization Steps

---

1. Given w (<=buffer-size) points $P = \{P_1, P_2, \cdots, P_w\}$ and k empty clusters $C = \{C_1, C_2, \cdots, C_k\}$, where k is the desired number of clusters, let $B = \varnothing$

2. For each point P_i in P, compute $SJ_i = \sum_{P_j \in P, j \neq i} J(P_i, P_j)$

3. Place P_t in C_1, satisfying $P_t = \arg\max_{P_i \in P}\{SJ_i\}$, $B = B \cup \{P_t\}$

4. Place P_r in C_2, satisfying $P_r = \arg\max_{P_i \in P-B}\{(1 - J(P_i, P_t)) * SJ_i\}$, $B = B \cup \{P_r\}$, $d = 2$

5. While $d < k$ do

    a) For each P_i in $P - B$, compute $\min_{P_q \in B}\{(1 - J(P_i, P_q)) * SJ_i\}$

    b) Place P_s in C_{d+1}, which satisfies $P_s = \arg\max_{P_i \in P-B}\{\min_{P_q \in B}\{(1 - J(P_i, P_q)) * SJ_i\}\}$,

       $B = B \cup \{P_s\}$, $d = d + 1$

6. End While

7. For each P_i in $P - B$

    a) Assign P_i to C_r in C which satisfies $C_r = \arg\max_{C_s \in C}\{Sim(C_s, P_i)\}$,

       update C_r, where $Sim(C_s, P_i)$ is defined in Definition 2.

8. Repeat:

    a) for each point P_i in P, where P_i has assigned to C_r

       i.   re-compute each $Sim(C_s, P_i)$ where C_s in C

       ii.   if $t \neq r$ where $C_t = \arg\max_{C_s \in C}\{Sim(C_s, P_i)\}$, then re-assign P_i from

             C_r to C_t, update C_r and C_t

9. Until no P_i has changed its assigned cluster, or reach the pre-specified iterations

---

3.2 ICUAC Algorithm

Our ICUAC algorithm consists of two parts: initialization steps and incremental steps. Initialization is very important for many clustering algorithm, especially for partitional clustering algorithm whose clustering result affected by the number of clusters and k initial seeds (centers of clusters). [9].

Here, we propose a simple initialization way which will supply good initial clusters for incremental steps in that important attribute value most occurs in its own cluster. The detailed initialization steps have been shown in Table 1. Preparation is done by step 1, where k is user-defined parameter and m is number of points for initialization which is less than the size of buffer (e.g. 500). Step2 and Step 3 aim at finding a point as the first cluster that has most similarity with others. Step 4 is finding the second point as the second cluster that not only has similarity with others but also is dissimilar with the first point. The function we use in Step 4 is exactly based on this idea. The following Step 5 is almost the same, which finding k-2 points as k-2 clusters which have most similarity with others but dissimilar with the existing points as cluster. The remaining points are assigned to their proper clusters in Step 7. Step 8 is a refining process which repeats until no points changing their proper clusters (convergence) or reaching the iterations (e.g. 100 times).

Incremental steps of our algorithm are shown in Table 2. Step 1 and Step 2 are preparation steps, where n is the number of data points read in buffer which is less than the size of buffer (e.g. 500). Step 3 is assigning the n data points to their proper clusters according to its maximal similarity with that cluster. Step 4 and Step 5 are also a refining processing step. The process is terminated when it converges or reaching the iterations.

Table 2. Incremental Steps

---

1. Given an initial set of k clusters $C = \{C_1, C_2, \cdots, C_k\}$

2. Read new coming n (<= buffer-size) points $P = \{P_1, P_2, \cdots, P_n\}$ to memory

3. For each point P_i in P

     b)   compute each $Sim(C_s, P_i)$ where C_s in $C = \{C_1, C_2, \cdots, C_k\}$

     c)   assign P_i to C_r in C satisfying $C_r = \arg\max_{C_s \in C}\{Sim(C_s, P_i)\}$, update C_r

4. Repeat:

     d)   for each point P_i in P, where P_i has assigned to C_r

        i.   re-compute each $Sim(C_s, p_i)$ where C_s in C

        ii.   if $t \neq r$ where $C_t = \arg\max_{C_s \in C}\{Sim(C_s, P_i)\}$, then re-assign P_i from C_r

            to C_t, update C_r and C_t

5. Until no P_i has changed its assigned cluster, or reach the pre-specified iterations

6. Terminate if no new points come, otherwise go to Step 2

---

4 Experiments

In this section, we first give two widely used methods for evaluating clustering result in Section 4.1. And we used two kinds of data sets – real data sets and synthetic data sets, one for evaluating the quality of our algorithm and the other for testing the scalability of our algorithm in Section 4.2 and Section 4.3.

We implemented our algorithm in Java. And experiments were conducted on a machine equipped with Intel Pentium-R processor running at 2.00GHz and 512MB of main memory, running Microsoft Windows XP Professional operating system.

4.1 Evaluation of Clustering Result

The first measure of clustering quality is expected entropy defined as follow:

$$E(C) = \sum_{r=1}^{k} \frac{|C_r|}{|D|} E(C_r) \qquad \text{where} \quad E(C_r) = \sum_j P(L = V_j) \log P(L = V_j) \qquad (6)$$

Here, L is a class attribute which did not participate in the clustering. And V_j is one value of attribute L. The smaller the value of $E(C)$, the better clustering results.

The second measure for evaluating clustering is the category utility function which attempts to attempts to maximize both the probability that two points in the same cluster have attribute values in common, and the probability that points from different clusters have different attributes [5]. The CU function is shown in Equation 7,

$$CU = \sum_{r=1}^{k} \frac{|C_r|}{|D|} \sum_i \sum_j [P(A_i = V_{ij} | C_r)^2 - P(A_i = V_{ij})^2] \qquad (7)$$

where $P(A_i = V_{ij} | C_r)$ is the conditional probability that the attribute A_i has the value V_{ij} given cluster C_r, and the $P(A_i = V_{ij})$ is the overall probability that the attribute A_i having the value V_{ij} in the entire data set. Hence, the higher the value of CU, the better clustering results.

4.2 Real Data Sets and Results

We used three real data sets all from UCI Machine Learning Repository [10] for evaluating clustering quality.

The "Soybean" data set has 47 records and 35 attributes. Among the 35 attributes, there is one class (or label) attribute which has four values each representing one disease. Except for one disease which has 17 records, all other diseases have 10 records. And the class attribute is not used for clustering. 14 attributes of the 35 attributes have only one category, which were not deleted but retained in our experiment.

The "Mushroom" data set have 8124 records and 23 attributes (include label attribute). The poisonous/edible attribute is a label attribute not used for clustering. Each record represents a mushroom. And 4208 records are edible mushrooms and 3916 records are poisonous mushrooms.

The "Congressional Voting" data set contains 435 records: 267 for Democrats and 168 for Republicans and 17 attributes (include label attribute). All attributes except the label attribute are Boolean with either yes or no. However, the data set has missing values and "Mushroom" data set also has such problem. Here, we simply treat them as a new ordinary value.

The clustering results of "Soybean" data set using the three algorithms have been shown in Table 3. We set the user-input similarity threshold S to 26 for Squeezer. And we set the desired number of clusters K for K-Mode and ICUAC to 4. For ICUAC, we set its buffer size to 500, maximal iterations to 100 (usually converged after several times in our experiments), which was also the same for the following data sets. Each algorithm was executed 10 times and the input records were disorder randomly for each time (The following experiments used the same method). For

Squeezer, we only retained the clustering results when total number of clusters found by it is 4. Table 3 shows that our ICUAC algorithm can get the best clustering result each time. In the best case, Squeezer and K-Mode also can find the good clustering result, but bad in the worst case. One reason can be explained by the efficiency of the initialization steps of our ICUAC, which is not so sensitive to data input order. Another reason is our ICUAC algorithm considering the unbalance of attributes. Actually, there are many attributes have only one category in "Soybean" data set as we pointed out before.

Table 3. Clustering results of ICUAC, Squeezer and K-Mode using Soybean data set ("Entr" short for entropy)

	Worst Case		Best Case		Average	
	CU	Entr	CU	Entr	CU	Entr
ICUAC	7.7357	0	7.7357	0	7.7357	0
Squeezer	6.9044	0.3619	7.7357	0	7.2269	0.2363
K-Mode	4.8748	0.7099	7.7357	0	6.2756	0.3556

The clustering results of "Congressional Vote" data set using the four algorithms (For the difficulty of setting the similarity threshold exactly, Squeezer was not taken for comparison any more) have been shown in Table 4. We set the desired number of clusters to 2 for all. And for FAVC and COOLCAT, the sample size is 40%. The CU value of ICUAC is almost the same with FAVC and COOLCAT, but its running time is smaller.

Table 4. Clustering results of ICUAC, K-Mode, FAVC and COOLCAT using Congressional Vote data set

	CU	Entropy	Time (Sec.)
ICUAC	2.9241	0.4954	0.234
K-Mode	2.8948	0.504	0.142
FAVC	2.92	N/A	1.83
COOLCAT	2.9	N/A	0.33

The clustering results of "Mushroom" data set by the four algorithms present in Table 5. We set the desired number of clusters to 20 for all. The sample size is 40% for FAVC and COOLCAT. As shown in Table 5, the CU value of ICUAC is the highest and also with smaller running time.

Table 5. Clustering results of ICUAC, K-Mode, FAVC and COOLCAT using Mushroom data set

	CU	Entropy	Time (Sec.)
ICUAC	9.5464	0.0344	3.78
K-Mode	7.8000	0.2079	3.25
FAVC	6.5	N/A	828
COOLCAT	6.5	N/A	2175

4.3 Synthetic Data Sets and Results

For testing the scalability of ICUAC, we would like to use a synthetic data generator [12] to generate data sets with different numbers of tuples (from 1k to 1000k) and attributes (from 5 to 50) using 3 rules. As shown in Figure 1, the running time (excluding I/O time) of ICUAC is linear regarding the number of attributes and the size of the data set.

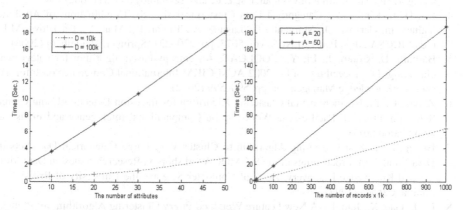

Fig. 1. Running times of ICUAC for synthetic data sets, where D is the data size and A is the number of attributes

5 Conclusions

In this paper, we propose a new similarity measure for categorical data which considers the unbalance between attributes. The clustering algorithm ICUAC we present is incremental with linear computing complexity. And the experiments have proved that ICUAC outperforms proposed clustering algorithms, which work well on many data sets with less order-sensitivity and smaller computing time. In the future works, we would like to extend our new similarity measure for mixed data type. And apply our algorithm for streaming data or intrusion detection.

Acknowledgments

This work is supported by the National Natural Science Foundation of China (60773198, 60703111), Natural Science Foundation of Guangdong Province (06104916, 8151027501000021,7300272), Program for New Century Excellent Talents in University of China(NCET-06-0727), Research Foundation of Science and Technology Plan Project in Guangdong Province (2007B031403003), National Key Technology R&D Program in the 11th Five year Plan of China (2006BAI13B02).

References

1. Jain, A.K., Murty, M.N., Flynn, P.J.: Data Clustering: A Review. ACM Computing Survey 31(3), 264–323 (1999)
2. Guha, S., Rastogi, R., Shim, K.: ROCK: A Robust Clustering Algorithm for Categorical Attributes. In: Proc. 15th Int'l. Conf. Data Eng., ICDE (1999)
3. Zengyou, H., Xiaofei, X., Shengchun, D.: Squeezer: An Efficient Algorithm for Clustering Categorical Data. Journal of Computer Science and Technology 17(5) (2002)
4. Do, H.-J., Kim, J.-Y.: Categorical Data Clustering Using the Combinations of Attribute Values. In: Gervasi, O., Murgante, B., Laganà, A., Taniar, D., Mun, Y., Gavrilova, M.L. (eds.) ICCSA 2008, Part II. LNCS, vol. 5073, pp. 220–231. Springer, Heidelberg (2008)
5. Barbara, D., Couto, J., Li, Y.: COOLCAT: An entropy-based algorithm for categorical clustering. In: Proceedings of the 2002 ACM CIKM International Conference on Information and Knowledge Management, pp. 590–599 (2002)
6. Zhong, C., Li, N.: Incremental Clustering Algorithm for Intrusion Detection Using Clonal Selection. In: IEEE Pacific-Asia Workshop on Computational Intelligence and Industrial Application (2008)
7. Huang, Z.: A Fast Clustering Algorithm to Cluster Very Large Categorical Data Sets in Data Mining. In: Proceedings of the SIGMOD Workshop on Research Issues on Data Mining and Knowledge Discovery, Dept. of Computer Science, the University of British Columbia, Canada (1997)
8. Li, J., Gao, X., Jiao, L.: A New Feature Weighted Fuzzy Clustering Algorithm. In: Pfahler, P., Kastens, U. (eds.) CC 1992. LNCS (LNAI), vol. 641, pp. 412–420. Springer, Heidelberg (1992)
9. Cao, F., Liang, J., Bai, L.: A New Initialization Method for categorical data clustering. Expert Systems with Applications (2009), doi:10.1016/j.eswa.2009.01.060
10. UCI machine Learning Repository,
    http://www.ics.uci.edu/~mlearn/MLRepository.html
11. Zhang, T., Ramakrishnan, R., Livny, M.: BIRCH: an efficient data clustering method for very large databases. In: Proceedings of SIGMOD, Canada (1996)
12. Dataset Generator (DatGen), http://www.datasetgenerator.com

Decision Tree Classifier for Classification of Plant and Animal Micro RNA's

Bhasker Pant[1], Kumud Pant[1], and K.R. Pardasani[2]

[1] Department of Bioinformatics, MANIT, Bhopal, India
pantbhaskar2@gmail.com, pant.kumud@gmail.com
[2] Department of Mathematics, MANIT, Bhopal, India
kamalrajp@rediffmail.com

Abstract. Gene expression is regulated by miRNAs or micro RNAs which can be 21-23 nucleotide in length. They are non coding RNAs which control gene expression either by translation repression or mRNA degradation. Plants and animals both contain miRNAs which have been classified by wet lab techniques. These techniques are highly expensive, labour intensive and time consuming. Hence faster and economical computational approaches are needed. In view of above a machine learning model has been developed for classification of plant and animal miRNAs using decision tree classifier. The model has been tested on available data and it gives results with 91% accuracy.

Keywords: Micro RNA's, Decision Tree, Classification, Cross validation.

1 Introduction

A thorough understanding of the basic process of miRNA functioning is important because miRNAs have wide application in development of biotech products, diagnostics, drug development, agro industry and therapeutics for example .miRNA based drugs[4]. The miRNAs in animals besides controlling regulatory functions have role in diseases like cancer, heart ailments, neurological disorders and aging. In plants they play specific role in plant development, including the regulation of flowering time and floral organ identity, leaf polarity and morphology. In Agro Biology they can play a major role in enhancing crop productivity and increasing the resistance towards major pests and diseases. There is a growing interest in identifying miRNA and determining their role in skeletal muscle and adipose tissue development in cattle. Also the miR motifs are associated with feed efficiency which is an important factors that represent greater than 50% of the total cost in most livestock production systems[5]. Hence correct identification of miR that regulate cellular processes and impact economically important traits is the need of the industry.

The information of classification is useful in diverse areas like evolutionary studies. The miRNAs belonging to one specie show conservation with other species e.g. those conserved in *Arabidopsis* show conservation with rice (*Oryza sativa*). This shows evolutionary decent. Hence through classification information their evolutionary conservation can be predicted. This classification of various features has

Z. Cai et al. (Eds.): ISICA 2009, CCIS 51, pp. 443–451, 2009.
© Springer-Verlag Berlin Heidelberg 2009

application in forensic sciences as well where the miRNA belonging to the organism can be identified. The miRNA classified can be shown to have relationship with the sequence, structure and function of the genes lying nearby. The upstream and down-stream genomic region can be identified with miRNA classification and signature [1]. By correlating their functions with the mRNA they control, the specific role they play in organism and hence the resultant functions of genes they control can be of great use in systems biology.   Recently it has been shown that the miRNA precursor stem–loops structures exhibit greater mutational robustness in comparison with random RNA sequences with similar stem–loop structures. This is attributed not to base composition bias or thermodynamic stability but towards direct evolutionary pressure towards increased mutational robustness [17]. This requires better understanding of characteristics of miRNAs which can be done by understanding the differences between miRNA's of different organisms.   In various laboratories throughout the world novel miRNAs in various species of plants, animals and other organisms are routinely attempted to be discovered using both in-vivo and in-silico techniques. A comprehensive literature survey reveals that no attempt has been made so far to develop computational approaches for classification of plant and animal miRNAs. Thus there is a need to develop newer algorithms which are robust, fast and economical considering the financial and time constraint which it poses on existing lab techniques.

Plant and animal miRNA system show basic similarity in their function, both play fundamental role in development and control regulatory genes. They both post transcriptionally regulate gene expression by interacting with their target mRNA which are often genes involved with regulation of key developmental processes. Despite these similarities both plant and animal miRNAs exert their control in fundamentally different ways. In plants the first step of miRNA biogenesis involves DCL1 whereas Drosha in animals is key regulator of this feature [1], [15]. Most of the miRNA's in plants are derived from single primary transcripts from loci found in the intergenic regions of the chromosomes but few from introns. Plant miRNAs mainly regulate their targets by cleaving the coding regions of the RNA whereas animal miRNAs mainly operate by translation repression [9], [10], [11]. But there is almost always an exception that breaks the rule. Here the above characteristics which are most suitable are combined to give an accurate classification. Rests of the parameters which do not contribute to the accuracy of the classifier are omitted.

2   Materials and Methods

Decision tree induction is the learning of decision trees from class-labeled training tuples. A decision tree is a flowchart-like tree structure, where each internal node (non leaf node) denotes a test on an attribute, each branch represents an outcome of the test, and each leaf node (or terminal node) holds a class label. The topmost node in a tree is the root node. Internal nodes are denoted by rectangles, and leaf nodes are denoted by ovals. Some decision tree algorithms produce only binary trees (where each internal node branches to exactly two other nodes), whereas others can produce non binary trees [6],[13]. Decision trees can easily be converted to classification rules.

The construction of decision tree classifiers does not require any domain knowledge or parameter setting, and therefore is appropriate for exploratory knowledge discovery. Decision trees can handle high dimensional data. Their representation of acquired knowledge in tree form is intuitive and generally easy to assimilate by humans. In general, decision tree classifiers have good accuracy. Decision tree induction algorithms have been used for classification in many application areas, such as medicine, manufacturing and production, financial analysis, astronomy, and molecular biology. Decision trees are the basis of several commercial rule induction systems. During tree construction, attribute selection measures are used to select the attribute that best partitions the tuples into distinct classes. A model is developed to classify animal and plant miRNA on the basis of physical characteristics only. It exploits features already available in databases, like size of fold back loop, presence of miRNA in clusters, number of binding sites and complementariness and combines them into a J48 decision tree classifier to obtain the classification of animal and plant miRNA. These features are given in Table 1.

Table 1. Features of Animal and Plant miRNAs [1]

Characteristics	Plants	Animals
Number of miRNA genes present.	**100-200**	**100-500**
Location within genome	**Predominantly intergenic region**	**Intergenic region intron**
Presence of miRNA clusters	**Uncommon**	**Common**
Micro RNA bio synthesis	**Dicer like**	**Drosha , Dicer**
Number of miRNA binding sites within target genes	**Generally one**	**Generally multiple**
Location of miRNA binding motifs within target genes	**Predominantly the open reading frame**	**Predominantly the 3'-UTR**

2.1 Software

The miRNA target registry software is used to extract the properties of the animal and plant miRNA. The Weka Data Mining Java script 3.6 was used for training and testing the J48 (a variant of the C4.5 decision tree) classifier and for the comparison to other learning algorithm.

2.2 Classifier

All the algorithms used were taken from the Weka suite [8]. In addition to the J48 (a variant of the C4.5 decision tree) the other classifiers used were: Adaboost Ml method, Alternating Decision Tree (AD Tree), Lazy Bayesian Rules Classifier (LBR),

Logistic Model Trees (LMT), Naive Bayes tree (NB Tree), One Rule classifier (1R classifier), PART decision list, Ridge Logistic Regression and Ripple Down Rule learner (Ridor).

2.3 Evaluation

The standard way of predicting the error rate of a learning technique given a single, fixed sample of data is to use stratified 10 fold cross validation. All evaluation parameters are calculated with a ten times, tenfold cross-evaluation. The method uses nine tenths of the data for training the system while the remaining tenth is set aside as a test set (control) for estimating the various evaluation parameters, like the success rate. The data is randomized and the procedure is repeated 10 times to estimate the average value for each parameter [12], [13], [14], [15]. Extensive tests on numerous datasets with different learning techniques have shown that 10 is about the right number of folds to get the best estimate of error.

In the two class case with classes yes and no, a single prediction has the four different possible outcomes (where TP = true positive, FP = false positive, TN = true negative and FN = false negative). The true positive and true negatives are correct classification. A false positive occurs when the outcome is incorrectly predicted. A false negative occurs when the outcome is incorrectly predicted as negative when it is actually positive. The true positive rate is divided by the total number of positives which is TP+FN, the false positive rate is FP divided by the total number of negatives FP+TN. The overall success rate is the number of correct classification divided by the total number of classification.

$$\frac{TP + TN}{TP + TN + FP + FN}$$

Finally the error rate is one minus success rate.

Graphical descriptions of various attributes used in the classifier are shown in figure 1, 2, 3 &4. Each and every attribute is checked with the given class and their frequency is plotted in the form of graph.

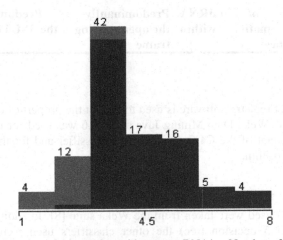

Fig. 1. Number of mismatches with target mRNA/vs. Number of miRNA

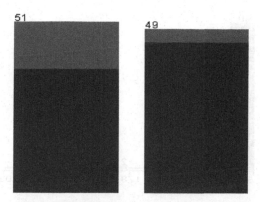

Fig. 2. Presence of clusters/vs. Number of miRNA

Figure 1 shows the number of mismatches with mRNA. The red graph indicates data for plants, majority of which are found to have zero or less than or equal to three mismatches, very few have four. For animals the blue graphs indicate number of mismatches which can be as many as 8. None of the miRNAs in animals have 0 mismatches.

Figure 2 shows presence of clusters. They are found maximally in animals, in comparison to plants where very few clusters are found. This feature is not included in the classification as it stands at the extreme ends with either yes or no values with very less exceptions. Hence it is less suitable for classification.

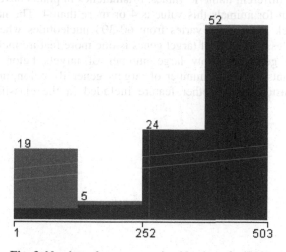

Fig. 3. Number of target genes/vs. Number of miRNA

Figure 3 shows that number of target genes in case of plants is less, whereas for animals the number of target genes exceeds as much as 503. Exceptional cases in plants are very few where number of target genes exceeds the value reported for plants.

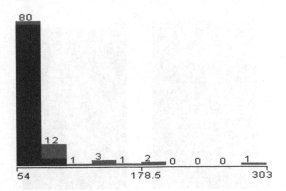

Fig. 4. Size of fold back loop/vs. Number of miRNA

Figure 4 shows the size of fold back loop. For animal the variation in loop is lesser whereas for plants the loop size varies as much as 303.

3   Training Set

For the classification purpose the dissimilarity between the animal and plant miRNAs were taken into account. Features like number of mismatches in animals and plants have different numeric values. Mismatches in plants have values less than or equal to 3 but for animals this value is 4 or more than 4. The next feature is the size of fold back loop which varies from 60-303 nucleotides whereas for animals the variation is less. Number of target genes is one more feature included in the classifier. Animals generally show large number of targets belonging to different families but plants have less number of targets generally belonging to one family. Presence of clusters was another feature included in the classifier. Clusters are

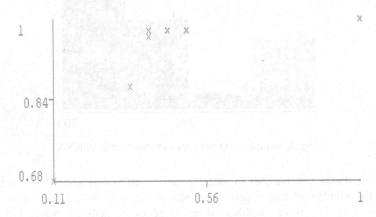

Graph. 1. R.O.C. Curve for Plant and Animal

generally found in animals whereas very few plants contain them [18]. With these characteristics we have trained the weka classifier and the values we get are given in the table 2.

4   Results and Discussion

A set of attributes was collected and the corresponding attribute values were fed to the classifier for each transcript of all plant and animal miRNA genes. Not all attributes, however, are fit for use in a classifier. First, some attributes are clearly not independent and do not provide any additional advantage when evaluated together. For example complementarity is a feature which is dependent on number of mismatches with the target. The results show 91% classified instances and 9% unclassified instances. The detailed characteristics of the classification are given in table2 which uses decision tree.

ROC curves depict the performance of a classifier without regard to class distribution or error costs. The horizontal axis represents false positive and vertical axis represents true positive. The value of ROC curve for this data set comes out to be 0.863 which represents these values in the true positive region.

Table 2. Detailed accuracy by class

Correctly Classified Instances	91	91	%
Incorrectly Classified Instances	9	9	%
Kappa statistic		0.6581	
Mean absolute error		0.097	
Root mean squared error		0.2998	
Relative absolute error		32.3459 %	
Root relative squared error		77.9374 %	
Total Number of Instances		100	

ROC Area	TP Rate Class	FP Rate	Precision	Recall	F-Measure
0.863	0.976 Animal	0.389	0.92	0.976	0.947
0.863	0.611 Plant	0.024	0.846	0.611	0.71
0.863	0.91 Weighted Avg.	0.323	0.906	0.91	0.904

Confusion Matrix
 a b <-- classified as
80 2 | a = Animal
 7 11 | b = Plant

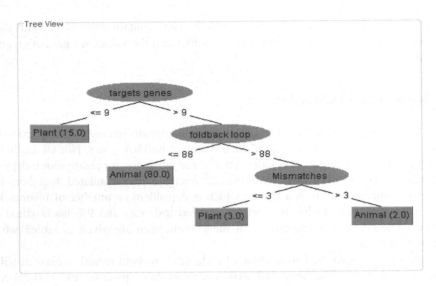

Fig. 5. Decision Tree Classifier

5 Conclusion

Both plant and animal miRNA systems share similarities but dissimilarities exist to a greater extent. A rule based model like this can be validated with more and more results being tested and checked. The amount and quality of data input to the model will determine the accuracy and reliability of the results. Exceptional cases can also be checked and verified using the above approach and further validation can be achieved through wet lab experiments. Various probabilistic combinations can provide new insight for wet lab experiments. The decision tree developed above does not considers presence of clusters as one of the attributes for classification since majority of the values stand at extreme ends (i.e. present or absent) and hence does not improve the accuracy of the classifier. We have been able to develop a computational approach to discover if a miRNA is animal or plant using simple features of that miRNA and its surroundings. This is made possible by the integration of different attributes operated by the J48 (a variant of the C4.5 decision tree), which are available in literature. The information generated by this classifier can be of great help in understanding and formulating various association rules, clustering algorithms and other data mining activities for both plant and animal miRNAs which the author intends to carry out in future.

The characteristics (number of mismatches with target mRNA, number of target genes and size of fold back loop) used in the model to develop the classifier give us fairly good accuracy in results i.e. 91% accuracy. Here we infer that these characteristics are very important and must be included in any classifier of plant and animal miRNA's. The inclusion of other characteristics like presence of clusters does not brings any improvement in the classifier. Other characteristics like size of miRNA family and number of binding sites within target genes etc can be included in the classification models to improve the performance and efficiency of the classifier but the limitation is that sufficient information is not available about these additional characteristics in the literature at present. However as soon as sufficient information about more additional characteristics becomes available in the literature, the authors intend to include the same in the above classifier in future to improve its performance and accuracy. The authors also wish to extend the classification for all the organisms and their miRNA's listed in the mirBASE registry [18].

References

1. Anthony, A.M., Peter, M.W.: Plant and animal microRNAs: similarities and differences. SpringerLink Funct Integr Genomics 5, 129–135 (2005)
2. Pierre, B., Soren, B.: Bioinformatics the Machine Learning Approach, 2nd edn. (2001)
3. Aagaard, L., Rossi, J.J.: RNAi Therapeutics: Principles, Prospects and Challenges. Elsevier Science, Amsterdam (2007)
4. McDaneld, T.G., Wiedmann, R.T., Miles, J.R., Cushman, R., Vallet, R., Smith, T.P.L.: NE microRNA technology in livestock: expression profiling of bovine oocyte and developmental stages of porcine skeletal muscle. USDA/ARS U.S (2007)
5. Witten, I.H., Frank, E.: Data Mining – Practical machine learning tools and techniques with Java implementations. Morgan Kaufmann, San Francisco (2005)
6. De, F.L.: Mining housekeeping genes with a Naive Bayes classifier. BMC Genomics 7, 277 (2006)
7. Weka Data Mining Java Software, http://www.cs.waikato.ac.nz/~ml/weka/
8. Jones-Rhoades, M.W., Bartel, D.P.: Computational identification of plant microRNAs and their targets, including a stress-induced miRNA. Mol. Cell 14, 787–799 (2004)
9. Meyerowitz, E.M.: Plants compared to animals: the broadest comparative study of development. Science 295, 1482–1485 (2002)
10. Floyd, S.F., Bowman, J.L.: Ancient microRNA target sequences in plants. Nature 428, 485–486 (2004)
11. Ambros, V.: The functions of animal microRNAs. Nature 431, 244–350 (2004)
12. Langley, P., Sage, S.: Elements of machine learning. Morgan Kaufmann, San Francisco (1994)
13. Han, J., Kamber, M.: Data Mining: Concepts and Techniques. Morgan Kaufmann, San Francisco (2001)
14. Heckerman, D., Geiger, D., Chickering, D.M.: Learning Bayesian network: The combination of knowledge and statistical data. Machine Learning 20(3), 197–243 (1995)
15. Holte, R.C.: Very simple classification rules perform well on most commonly used datasets. Machine Learning 11, 63–91 (1993)
16. Borenstein, E., Eytan, R.: Direct evolution of genetic robustness in microRNA. PNAS 103, 6593–6598 (2006)
17. Micro RNARegistry, http://micrornasanger.ac.uk

Embedded Classification Learning for Feature Selection Based on K-Gravity Clustering

Weizhao Guo[1], Jize Chen[1], Zhimin Yang[2,*], Jian Yin[1], Xiaobo Yang[2], and Li Huang[2]

[1] School of Information Science and Technology, Sun Yat-sen University,
Guangzhou, 510275, China
weizhao1758@126.com, gjazz@139.com, issjyin@mail.sysu.edu.cn
[2] The 2nd Affiliated Hospital, Guangzhou University of Chinese Medicine,
Guangzhou, 510120, China
yangyo@163.net, yangxiaobomd@163.com, liea1981@126.com

Abstract. Conventional feature selection methods based on clustering have been developed and optimized to focus on samples-based clustering, but less work has been done for features-based clustering. Especially, it is impossible to achieve prefect prediction results for the relatively small number of samples in high dimensional data, such as gene expression data. To overcome this problem, this paper proposes an efficient algorithm, K-Gravity, that groups interdependent features into clusters. Each feature cluster is treated as a single entity for classification evaluation. Unlike previous work that selects a subset of top feature groups from each cluster or top feature groups from all clusters to make up feature pools in final classification, a new classification evaluation method, Embedded Classification Learning (**ECL**) picks up some top feature groups and builds a classifier on each selected feature groups. The experiment results present that the proposed methods can achieve better feature clustering in final classification than conventional samples-based methods, such as K-Means clustering. Also the proposed evaluation methods, Embedded Classification Learning (**ECL**), can pay more attention to diversity between different feature groups and improve final classification accuracy further.

Keywords: K-Gravity, Gravitational Attraction, Embedded Classification Learning, Kernel Density Estimation.

1 Introduction

The presence of the relatively small number of samples in high dimensional data, such as the colon-cancer data set [3] [6] and the prostate data set [3], has been more and more abundant in classification problems and results in severe degradation of classification accuracy. Hence feature selection algorithms [1] [3] have been developed and optimized to overcome this problem by identifying the minimum subset of relevant features for best predictive accuracy and removing the irrelevant, redundant, or least useful features.

---

* Corresponding author.

Z. Cai et al. (Eds.): ISICA 2009, CCIS 51, pp. 452–460, 2009.
© Springer-Verlag Berlin Heidelberg 2009

Also, feature selection algorithms based on clustering have been paid more and more attention to and group different features into several clusters based on similarity. The features within a cluster are highly similar to each other and the ones without the same cluster are much dissimilar. K-Means [2] [7], one of the well-known clustering algorithms, supposes that there are k centroids in the given data and partitions the data into k independent clusters based on distance measures, such as Euclidean distance and Person's correlation coefficient. Maybe K-Means algorithm is simple and fast, but K-Means algorithm always acquires favorable performance for samples-based clustering and may be sensitive to noise [2]. In this paper, we propose a new cluster criterion Gravitational Attraction to evaluate the interdependent of different features and group relatively relevant features into groups. The proposed method, K-Gravity, is inspired by a key observation of Newton's Law of Universal Gravitation and can cluster relevant features into groups better and can be scale to the number of features in the data set.

In this paper, the next key problem is how to evaluate the performance of the clustering results in final classification. Two conventional evaluations for the feature clustering are as follows. One method is to select the top features from each of the clusters respectively and treat each feature as an entity for evaluation and classification, such as [8]. The other method is to identify each feature group as an entity and pick up the top feature groups from all generated feature groups. For an example, Yu etc. [3] assumed the dense core regions are stable with respect to sampling of the dimensions and selected the top k representative feature groups from all feature groups. Unlike the proposed methods above, we introduce a new evaluation method Embedded Classification Learning (ECL) in final classification. We can treat each feature group as an entity for classification and build a classifier in each selected feature groups. This can pay more attentions to diversity between different feature groups.

Here, we first attempt to estimate the density of each feature in a data set by applying the kernel density estimator [3] [4]. Then a new measurement, Gravitational Attraction, is proposed to evaluate the interdependence between different features and groups the relevant features into clusters. Next, a commonly statistical measurement, Kappa Statistical, is used to identify the feature groups and select the top K feature groups. Finally, we introduce a new evaluation method ECL to build a classifier in each selected feature group and obtain final classification result by Majority Rule, which improves the classification accuracy further.

The rest of this paper is organized as follows. In Section 2, we review the related work about feature selection algorithms based on clustering. In Section 3, a new algorithm based on features clustering K-Gravity is proposed to select the top relevant feature groups from all generated feature groups. Also, we introduce ECL to improve the final classification accuracy. The experiment results are presented in Section 4. Finally, we draw a conclusion of our work in Section 5.

In this section, we introduce some background knowledge about our work. In Section 2.1, feature selection approaches based on clustering are presented and two commonly evaluation methods for the performance of feature selection algorithm are introduced currently. Then a commonly method, kernel density estimation (Parzen Window) [3] [4], for estimating the density of each feature in a data set is introduced in Section 2.2.

2 Related Work

In this section, we introduce some background knowledge about our work. In Section 2.1, feature selection approaches based on clustering are presented and two commonly evaluation methods for the performance of feature selection algorithm are introduced currently. Then a commonly method, kernel density estimation (Parzen Window) [3] [4], for estimating the density of each feature in a data set is introduced in Section 2.2.

2.1 Feature Selection Based on Clustering

Clustering algorithms always seeks to partition given data objects into several disjoint groups. Intuitively, the objects in a cluster are more correlated than ones between different clusters. Based on this intuition, many existing clustering algorithms are applied to feature selection, For example, K-Means algorithm [2] [7] always finds k disjoint clusters which optimize the objective function (1), so that features in a cluster is highly relevant. Assume that there are k clusters $\{C_1, C_2, ..., C_k\}$ and Feature A_{ij} means the j-th feature of Cluster C_i, so the optimum object function is defined as follows:

$$D = \min(\sum_{i=1}^{k} \sum_{A_{ij} \in C_i} |A_{ij} - O_i|) \tag{1}$$

where O_i is the centroid of Cluster C_i.

However, a weakness of using K-Means algorithms is that K-Means may be powerful in samples-based clustering, but not features-based clustering. The reason is that K-Means algorithm only considers the similarity between different features, but doesn't take account of the distribution of all feature spaces. In Section 3, we will introduce a new partition criterion Gravitational Attraction to overcome this drawback and it can obtain good performances in features-based clustering.

After features are grouped into several disjoint subsets, the next key problem is how to select suitable features from all generated feature groups in final classification. There are two commonly used methods to solve it. One is to select k representative features from each feature group to make up feature pools. For example, R. Butterworth [8] made use of dendrogram of the resulting cluster hierarchy to select the top relevant features from each of the feature groups. The other is that assume each feature group is an stable entity for evaluation and classification and we can pick up the representative feature groups from all generated clusters, such as [3]. However, in this paper we pay more attention to the discrimination between different feature groups and attempt to improve classification accuracy further. Intuitively, if feature groups are strictly independent from each other, we can build a classifier on each selected feature group and the classification accuracy will increase further. Owing to this idea, we propose a new method, Embedded Classification Learning (**ECL**) to gain better predication results. In Section 3, we will give the detail description about **ECL**.

2.2 Feature Density Estimation

Kernel density estimation is applied to estimate the density of each feature in a data set by Yu etc. [3]. The features with larger value of density estimation are denser than ones with smaller value of density estimation. The low-density feature is usually no interest for feature selection. In fact, feature clustering based on kernel density estimation is applied in many fields as the established technique [3] [10]. Suppose that there are n samples with d dimensions in a data set, and then the density estimator for feature x will be represented as formula (2).

$$\rho(x) = \frac{1}{nh^d} \sum_{i=1}^{n} K(\frac{x - x_i}{h}) \tag{2}$$

where h is the bandwidth parameter which is used to control the scope convergence. The choice of the bandwidth parameter is an intractable problem and there are many feasible methods to estimate it, such as [3] [9].

There are many choices for kernel function and one of the most commonly used kernel functions is Gaussian kernel. Generally, we assume that the samples with d dimensions satisfy the Gaussian distribution and the Gaussian kernel function is given as follow.

$$K(x) = (2\pi)^{-d/2} \exp(-\frac{1}{2}\|x\|^2) \tag{3}$$

In next section, we apply kernel density estimation function to estimate the density of each feature, and then a new measurement Gravitational Attraction will be presented in details.

3 Proposed Methods

In Section 3.1, we first propose a new clustering algorithm, K-Gravity, to cluster the relevant features into the same feature group. In Section 3.2, a new evaluation method Embedded Classification Learning (**ECL**) will be introduced.

3.1 K-Gravity Clustering

K-Means algorithm partitions data objects into K disjoint subsets simply and fast, but it doesn't considering the distribution of all the data objects and always doesn't give the suitable partitions for the data objects. In this paper, we will propose a new partition criterion Gravitational Attraction, which considers the distribution of the data objects and presents more suitable clustering. Firstly, because our proposed algorithm, K-Gravity, is features-based clustering, so we should transpose the data matrix representing the data set, so that features serves as data objects to be clustered, while samples are treated as features. Secondly, K-Gravity is motivated by Newton's law of Universal Gravitation which describes the gravitational attraction between different entities.

Definition 1. Any entity attracts every other entity by a force pointing along the line intersecting both entities. Assume that m_1 is the mass of the entity A, m_2 is the mass of the entity B and d is the distance between A and B. So the gravitational force between A and B is defined as:

$$F(A,B) = G\frac{m_1 m_2}{d^2} \tag{4}$$

where G is the gravitational constant.

In our work, a key observation is that each feature in the data set is treated as an entity and the mass of the entity can be estimated by kernel density estimation (Parzen window), which has been described detailedly in Section 2.2. Also, this paper gives a hypothesis that features in each dimension follow the Gaussian distribution in this paper, so kernel density estimation based on the Gaussian distribution is used to estimate the distribution of all features. Let us suppose that there are p features, which is represented as $A_1, ..., A_p$.

Definition 2. The Gravitational Attraction between Feature A_i and Feature A_j is defined as:

$$F(A_i, A_j) = \frac{\rho(A_i)\rho(A_j)}{d^{p-1} + \varepsilon} \tag{5}$$

where d is the Euclidean distance between A_i and A_j. $\rho(A_i)$ is the density of Feature A_i by calculating Formula (2). ε represents a small constant used to avoid a zero denominator.

$F(A_i, A_j)$ reflects the magnitude of the Gravitational Attraction between A_i and A_j. Moreover, Gravitational Attraction considers the distribution of all features by introducing the kernel density estimation so that features can be grouped into clusters more accurately.

Definition 3. Suppose that there are m features $\{A_1, ..., A_m\}$, so Total Gravitational Attraction of Feature A_i in a cluster is defined as:

$$TGA(A_i) = \sum_{j=1}^{m} F(A_i, A_j) \tag{6}$$

In this paper, the feature with the maximum TGA plays the role of gravity in a cluster. When we assign certain feature L to one of the clusters, the Gravitation Attraction $F(L, G_i)$ between feature L and the gravity G_i is calculated, where G_i means the gravity of the i-th cluster and $i \in \{1, ..., k\}$. If $F(L, G_j)$ has the maximum Gravitation Attraction for all $j \in \{1, ..., k\}$, and then feature L is assigned to the j-th Cluster. Based on the analysis above, K-Gravity algorithm is formulated in details as follows.

Table 1. Algorithm K-Gravity Clustering

Input:	p features { A_1, ..., A_p }, K
Output:	feature groups { C_1, ..., C_k }

1. Calculate the density $\rho(A_i)$ of Feature A_i, where $i \in$ { 1, ..., p}

2. Select k features as initial gravities {G1, ..., G_k } randomly.

3. Repeat

4. For each feature A_i, $i \in$ {1, ..., p}, if $F(A_i, G_s) \geq F(A_i, G_r)$ for all $r \in$ {1, ..., k}, then A_i is assigned to G_s.

5. For each cluster C_r, $r \in$ {1, ..., k}, if $TGA(A_i) \geq TGA(A_j)$ for all j $\in$ {1, ..., k} and all $A_i, A_j \in C_r$, then A_i is selected as the gravity of C_r.

6. If the gravities {G1, ..., G_k } for all clusters still change, Go to 3;
Else Go to 7.

7. Return features groups { C_1, ..., C_k }

K-Means clustering often partitions the data objects into clusters by similarity measurement, such as Euclidean distance and Pearson's correlation coefficient, but it doesn't take the distribution of all the data objects into account. The proposed algorithm, K-Gravity Clustering, gives an evident description of the distribution of all features by computing Formula (5) and presents more accurate partitions for all features. In Section 4, our experiment results will validate the rationality of our proposed algorithms for feature selection, which outperforms K-Means in terms of the improvement of classification accuracy.

3.2 Embedded Classification Learning

In this section, our work will address the problem how to select features for feature selection in final classification. Two Conventional methods are given as follows. One is that we choose a subset of top features from each feature group to make up feature pools, but it often causes the instability of feature selection algorithms. The other is that a feature group can be regarded as a stable entity and we can choose some of feature groups to constitute feature pools, such as Yu's DRAGS [3]. However, previous work doesn't give their attention to the discrimination between different feature groups. If some of feature groups are selected to build up feature pools and just one classifier is built on this feature pools, it often depresses the classification accuracy.

Based on the consideration above, our proposed framework, Embedded Classification Learning (ECL), is presented expressly as Table 2. After features are clustered into groups, we build a classifier on each feature group. And then the feature groups are ranked according to relevance measures. A popularly statistical measure, Kappa Statistic, is selected as relevance measures for feature groups in this paper. Finally, the top s feature groups are picked up and certain test instance θ is tested by the classifiers built on κ selected feature groups, so we obtain the final prediction label for θ by Majority Rule. Here to validate the correctness of our proposed framework more simply, κ is set as 3 in our experiment.

Table 2. Algorithm ECL

Input: test instance θ, feature groups $\{C_1, ..., C_k\}$
Output: prediction label for θ

1. Build a classifier on each feature group C_i, $i \in \{1, ..., k\}$
2. Rank $C_1, ..., C_k$ according to Kappa Statistic
3. Select top $\mathcal{K}$ feature groups.
4. Test θ on the classifiers of s selected feature groups respectively and acquire the final prediction label for θ by Majority Rule.
5. Return prediction label for θ

Unlike other frameworks, ECL doesn't put all the selected features together to make up a feature pool simply, but pays more attention to the discrimination between different feature groups. Moreover, ECL proposes a framework that builds a classifier on each selected feature group respectively, it's more efficient to reflect the quality of feature selection algorithms. In Section 4, we evaluate the validity of feature selection algorithm by applying our proposed framework ECL in our experiment.

4   Experimental Results

In this section, we evaluate the performance of our proposed algorithm K-Gravity in the framework ECL. One public microarray data set, Colon data set [3] [6], which is listed in Table 3, are applied in our experiments. It is worth to note that features in these data sets are continuous, so before the experiment results are presented and discussed, we should normalized all features vectors so that each feature vector is standardized with the standard deviation one and zero mean.

Table 3. Data Sets Used in Our Experiments

Data	No. of Features	No. of Samples	No. of Class
Colon	2000	62	2

To validate the classification performance, leave-one-out cross-validation, a widely used process for gene expression data classification [11], is introduced in our experiments. Assume that there are n samples in the data set; the first sample serves as the test instance and the remaining n-1 samples as the training instances. Repeating continuously from the first sample to the n-th sample, final classification accuracy is obtained. Our experiment employs NaiveBayes algorithm and RBFNetwork algorithm to build classifiers on selected top feature groups. The experiment results present that our proposed algorithm K-Gravity outperforms K-Means algorithm in terms of the improvement of classification accuracy and we will give the detailed experiment results about Colon data set as below.

In this study, the Colon data set is the well-known gene expression data set which consists of 62 samples and 2000 features. Because our work aims at feature selection on features-based clustering, so features are treated as data objects and samples play the role of features. That is, Colon data set is represented by a 2000×62 data matrix so that we can make clusters to features. Table 4 shows the classification results with all 2000 features. It is found that classification accuracy for NaïveBayes methods is 56.45% and one for RBFNetwork methods 70.97%.

Table 4. Classification Accuracy on the Colon data set. (%)

Classifier	Accuracy
NaiveBayes	56.45
RBFNetwork	70.97

Table 5 compares the classification accuracy (leave-one-out cross validation) on the Colon data set for NaïveBayes method and RBFNetwork method under a wide range of k. Here k denotes the number of feature groups for K-Gravity or K-Means and is assigned as 5, 7, 9, 11, 13, 15, and 17. When we used Naïve Bayes method to build a classifier on feature groups, it is discovered that the average classification accuracy with K-Gravity is 79.72%, higher than one with K-Means 69.58%. Meanwhile, when RBFNetwork method is employed to build a classifier on feature groups, the average classification accuracy with K-Gravity is 80.88% and the average classification accuracy with K-Means 75.35%.

Experimental result shows the validity of our proposed method. Moreover, K-Gravity algorithm for feature selection is more effective than K-Means algorithm. If k is selected appropriately, the classification accuracy may be higher.

Table 5. Classification Accuracy after Feature Selection on the Colon data set (%)

k	NaiveBayes		RBFNetwork	
	K-Means	K-Gravity	K-Means	K-Gravity
5	59.68	74.19	64.52	79.03
7	58.06	77.42	74.19	80.65
9	69.35	75.81	74.19	79.03
11	72.58	77.42	77.42	82.26
13	74.19	83.87	77.42	82.26
15	74.19	83.87	80.65	82.26
17	79.03	85.48	79.03	80.65
Avg.	**69.58**	**79.72**	**75.35**	**80.88**

5 Conclusion and Future Work

Firstly, this paper shows a new algorithm K-Gravity to cluster the relevant features into groups. Also, K-Gravity algorithm takes account of the distribution of all features by introducing Gravitational Attraction measurement and gives more reasonable clusters. The experiment results validate the correctness and validity of our proposed algorithm. Secondly, unlike other frameworks, Embedded Classification Learning

(ELC) doesn't consider the discrimination between different feature groups; but also presents more accurate classification by building a classifier on each selected feature group and obtaining the final classification result by Majority Rule.

It is worth to note for us that ELC is not a specific algorithm, but it is a general framework used to evaluate the validity of the feature selection algorithms. In the future work, we will verify our proposed algorithm using more classification algorithm, such as SVM, Decision Tree, Self-organizing maps.

Acknowledgments

This work is supported by the National Natural Science Foundation of China (60773198, 60703111), Natural Science Foundation of Guangdong Province (06104916, 8151027501000021,7300272), Program for New Century Excellent Talents in University of China(NCET-06-0727), Research Foundation of Science and Technology Plan Project in Guangdong Province (2007B031403003), National Key Technology R&D Program in the 11th Five year Plan of China (2006BAI13B02).

References

1. Yan, J., Zhang, B., Liu, N., et al.: Effective and Efficient Dimensionality Reduction for Large-Scale and Streaming Data Preprocessing. IEEE Transactions on Knowledge and Data Engineering 18(3), 320–333 (2006)
2. Jiang, D., Tang, C., Zhang, A.: Cluster Analysis for Gene Expression Data: A Survey. IEEE Transactions on Knowledge and Data Engineering 16(11), 1370–1380 (2004)
3. Yu, L., Ding, C., Loscalzo, S.: Stable Feature Selection via Dense Feature Groups. In: KDD, pp. 803–811 (2008)
4. Denton, A.: Kernel-Density-Based Clustering of Time Series Subsequences Using a continuous Random-Walk Noise Model. In: ICDM, pp. 122–129 (2005)
5. Wand, M.P., Jones, M.C.: Kernel Smoothing. Chapman and Hall, Boca Raton (1995)
6. Alon, U., Barkai, N., Notterman, D.A., Gish, K., Ybarra, S., Mack, D., Levine, A.J.: Broad Patterns of Gene Expression Revealed by Clustering Analysis of Tumor and Normal Colon Tissues Probed by Oligonucleotide Arrays. Proceedings of the National Academy of Sciences of the United States of America 96(12), 6745–6750 (1999)
7. Tavazoie, S., Hughes, J.D., Campbell, M.J., et al.: Systematic determination of genetic network architecture. Nature Genetics, 281–285 (1999)
8. Butterworth, R., Piatesky-Shapiro, G., Simovici, D.A.: On Feature Selection through Clustering. In: ICDM, pp. 581–584 (2005)
9. Turlach, B.A.: Bandwidth Selection in Kernel Density Estimation: A Review (1993)
10. Comaniciu, D., Meer, P.: Mean shift: a robust approach toward feature space analysis. IEEE Transactions on Pattern Analysis and Machine Intelligence 24(5), 603–619 (2002)
11. Simon, R.: Supervised Analysis when the Number of Candidate Features (p) Greatly Exceeds the Number of Cases(n). SIGKDD Explorations 5(2), 31–36 (2003)

Evaluation Measures of the Classification Performance of Imbalanced Data Sets

Qiong Gu[1,2], Li Zhu [2], and Zhihua Cai[2]

[1] Faculty of Mathematics & Computer Science, Xiangfan University, Xiangfan, Hubei, 441053, China
[2] School of Computer, China University of Geosciences, Wuhan, Hubei, 430074, China
gujone@163.com, cugzhuli@163.com, zhcai@cug.edu.cn

Abstract. Discriminant Measures for Classification Performance play a critical role in guiding the design of classifiers, assessment methods and evaluation measures are at least as important as algorithm and are the first key stage to a successful data mining. We systematically summarized the evaluation measures of Imbalanced Data Sets (IDS). Several different type measures, such as commonly performance evaluation measures and visualizing classifier performance measures have been analyzed and compared. The problems of these measures towards IDS may lead to misunderstanding of classification results and even wrong strategy decision. Beside that, a series of complex numerical evaluation measures were also investigated which can also serve for evaluating classification performance of IDS.

Keywords: Evaluation, classification performance, imbalanced data sets.

1 Introduction

The purpose of evaluation in Machine Learning is to determine the usefulness of our learned classifiers or of our learning algorithms on various collections of data sets. Most measures in use today focus on a classifier's ability to identify classes correctly. Assessment methods and evaluation measures of classification performance play a critical role in guiding the design of classifiers. Even the most widely used methods such as measuring accuracy or error rate on a test set has severe limitations. Thus the modification of classification algorithms in some extent equals the improvement of criterions. Many efforts have been conducted to design/develop more advanced algorithms to solve the classification problems. In fact, the assessment methods and evaluation measures are at least as important as algorithm and is the first key stage to a successful data mining.

The purpose of this paper is to give the reader an intuitive idea of what could go wrong with our commonly used evaluation methods. In particular, we show, through examples, that since evaluation metrics summarize the system's performance, they can, at times, obscure important behaviors of the hypotheses or algorithms under consideration. Since the purpose of evaluation is to offer simple and convenient ways to judge the performance of a learning system and/or to compare it to others, evaluation methods can be seen as summaries of the systems' performance.

Z. Cai et al. (Eds.): ISICA 2009, CCIS 51, pp. 461–471, 2009.

The outline of the paper is as follows. Several different types commonly performance evaluation measures, such as numeric measure and visualizing classifier performance measure, have been analyzed and compared in section 2, Section 3 focuses on the issue of performance metrics. More specifically, it demonstrates, through a number of examples the shortcomings of Accuracy, Precision/Recall and ROC. Beside that, a series of complex numerical evaluation measures were also investigated which can also serve for evaluating classification performance of IDS in section 4. Finally, the conclusion is drawn in Section 5.

2   Commonly Performance Evaluation Measures

Methods for evaluating the performance of classifiers fall into two broad categories: numerical and graphical. Numerical evaluations produce a single number summarizing a classifier's performance, whereas graphical methods depict performance in a plot that typically has just two or three dimensions so that it can be easily inspected by humans. Examples of numerical performance measures are accuracy, precision, recall⁺, recall⁻ and AUC. Examples of graphical performance evaluations are Lift chart, ROC curve[1, 2], precision-recall curve[3], cost curve[4],et al.

2.1   Numerical Value Performance Measure

Most of the studies in IDS mainly concentrate on two-class problem as multi-class problem can be simplified to two-class problem. By convention, the class label of the minority class is positive, and the class label of the majority class is negative. Table 1 illustrates a confusion matrix of a two-class problem. The first column of the table is the actual class label of the examples, and the first row presents their predicted class label. TP and TN denote the number of positive and negative examples that are classified correctly, while FN and FP denote the number of misclassified positive and negative examples respectively.

Table 1. A confusion matrix for a two-class classification

Recognized Actually Class	Predicted as Positive Class	Predicted as Negative Class
Actually Positive class	True Positive(TP)	False Negative(FN)
Actually Negative class	False Positive(FP)	True Negative(TN)

Based on Table 1, the performance metrics are defined as:

$$Accuracy = \frac{TP + TN}{TP + TN + FP + FN}$$

$$True\ Positive\ Rate(Acc^+) = \frac{TP}{TP + FN} = Recall^+ = Sensitivity$$

$$True\ Negative\ Rate(Acc-) = \frac{TN}{TN + FP} = Recall- = Specificity$$

$$Positive\ Predictive\ Value = \frac{TP}{TP + FP} = Precision$$

Traditionally, accuracy is the most commonly used measure for these purposes. However, for classification with the class imbalance problem, accuracy is no longer a proper measure since the rare class has very little impact on accuracy as compared to the prevalent class[5]. this measurement is meaningless to some applications where the learning concern is the identification of the rare cases. Accuracy does not distinguish between the numbers of correct labels of different classes. For any classifier, there is always a trade off between true positive rate and true negative rate; and the same applies for recall and precision. In the case of learning extremely imbalanced data, quite often the rare class is of great interest. In many cases, it is desirable to have a classifier that gives high prediction accuracy over the minority class ($Acc+$), while maintaining reasonable accuracy for the majority class ($Acc-$).

2.2 Graphical Performance Analysis with Probabilistic Classifiers

Graphical methods are especially useful when there is uncertainty about the misclassification costs or the class distribution that will occur when the classifier is deployed. In this setting, graphical measures can present a classifier's actual performance for a wide variety of different operating points (combinations of costs and class distributions), whereas the best a numerical measure can do is to represent the average performance across a set of operating points.

2.2.1 Lift Chart

The lift chart is a standard detection evaluation method to validate machine learning algorithms. The lift chart represents an effective measure for the validation of the detection process and on whether a given attack classification is valid or not. The x-axis represents the number of examples of the test set that were selected according to the probabilistic ranking generated by the classifier. The y-axis represents the percentage of positive examples in the subset of selected examples. This percentage is calculated over the total number of examples in the test set.

$$x = \text{Yrate}(t) = \frac{TP(t) + FP(t)}{P + N}, \, y = \text{TP}(t) \tag{1}$$

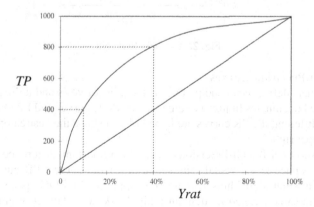

Fig. 1. A hypothetical lift chart

Figure 1 shows the lift chart for the attack type parameter upsweep. Normally, we'd like to be in a lift chart is near the upper left-hand corner, at the very best, the further to the northwest the better. The upper lift point (0,1000) denotes the ideal case for accurate detection with minimum cost. Lift curve also indicates how far the detector model is effective from the point of view of reducing the false alarms.

2.2.2 ROC Curves

ROC curve[6] is one of the popular metrics to evaluate the learners for IDS. It is a two-dimensional graph in which TP_{rate} is plotted on the y-axis and FP_{rate} is plotted on the x-axis. ROC curve depicts relative trade-offs between benefits (TP_{rate}) and costs (FP_{rate}). Consider that the minority class, whose performance will be analyzed, is the positive class. Some classifiers have parameter for which different settings produce different ROC points. Figure 2 shows a ROC curve, Typically this is a discrete set of points, including (0,0) and (1,1), which are connected by line segments. The lower left point (0,0) represents a strategy that classifies every example as belonging to the negative class. The upper right point represents a strategy that classifies every example as belonging to the positive class. The point (0,1) represents the perfect classification, and the line x = y represents the strategy of random guessing the class. The ideal model is one that obtains 1 True Positive Rate and 0 False Positive Rate (1,0). A ROC curve gives a good summary of the performance of a classification model. To compare several classification models by comparing ROC curves, it is hard to claim a winner unless one curve clearly dominates the others over the entire space[7].

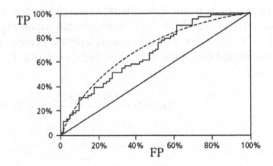

Fig. 2. A sample ROC curve

2.2.3 Recall-Precision Curves

Some researchers define recall and precision, and a list of yes's and no's represent a ranking of retrieved documents.In just the same way as ROC curves and lift charts, except that the axes are different, the PR curves are hyperbolic in shape,the desired operating point is toward the upper right.

Figure 3 shows a Recall-Precision curve. An important difference between ROC space and PR space is the visual representation of the curves. PR curves can expose differences between algorithms that are not apparent in ROC space. These curves, taken from the same learned models on a highly-skewed dataset, highlight the visual difference between these spaces. The goal in ROC space is to be in the upper-left-hand corner, and when one looks at the ROC curves they appear to be fairly close to optimal. In PR space the goal is to be in the upper-right-hand corner and the PR curves show that there is still vast room for improvement. Each dataset contains a fixed number of positive and negative examples. It is revealed in the study that there exists a sound relationship between ROC and PR spaces. For a given dataset of positive and negative examples, there exists a one-to-one correspondence between a curve in ROC space and a curve in PR space, such that the curves contain exactly the same confusion matrices, if Recall $\neq 0$. For a fixed number of positive and negative examples, one curve dominates a second curve in ROC space if and only if the first dominates the second in PR space.

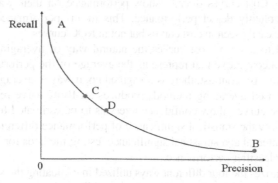

Fig. 3. Recall-Precision curve

2.2.4 Cost Curves

Cost curves are a different kind of display on which a single classifier corresponds to a straight line that shows how the performance varies as the class distribution changes. Cost curves are perhaps the ideal graphical method in this setting because they directly show performance as a function of the misclassification costs and class distribution. Figure 4 shows ROC Curve and corresponding Cost Curve.

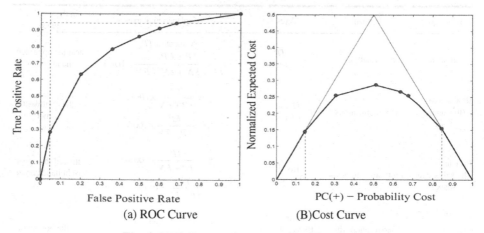

(a) ROC Curve   (B)Cost Curve

Fig. 4. ROC Curve and corresponding Cost Curve

In particular, the x-axis and y-axis of a cost curve plot are defined as follows. The x-axis of a cost curve plot is defined by combining the two misclassification costs and the class distribution-represented by p(+), the probability that a given instance is positive-into a single value, PC(+), using the following formula:

$$PCF(+) = \frac{p(+)*C(-|+)}{p(+)*C(-|+)+p(-)*C(+|-)} \qquad (2)$$

where C(-|+)is the cost of a false negative and C(+|-)is the cost of a false positive. Classifier performance, the y-axis of a cost curve plot, is normalized expected cost(NEC), NEC ranges between 0 and 1. Cost curves directly show performance on their y-axis, whereas ROC curves do not explicitly depict performance. This means performance and performance differences can be easily seen in cost curves but not in ROC curves.

When applied to a set of cost curves the natural way of averaging two-dimensional curves produces a cost curve that represents the average of the performances represented by the given curves. By contrast, there is no agreed upon way to average ROC curves, and none of the proposed averaging methods produces an ROC curve representing average performance. Cost curves allow confidence intervals to be estimated for a classifier's performance, and allow the statistical significance of performance differences to be assessed. The confidence interval and statistical significance testing methods for ROC curves do not relate directly to classifier performance.

Table 2 summarizes the four different ways utilized in evaluating the same basic trade off. Either the proportion can be increased by using a smaller coverage, or the coverage can be increased at the expense of the proportion. Different techniques can be plotted as different lines on any of these graphical charts. Each point on a lift chart, ROC curve, or recall–precision curve represents a classifier, typically obtained using different threshold values for a method. Cost curves represent each classifier using a straight line, and a suite of classifiers will sweep out a curved envelope whose lower limit shows how well that type of classifier

Table 2. Different Measures Used to Evaluate the False Positive versus the False Negative Trade Off

Technique	Domain	Axes	Explanation of axes	at the very best place
Lift chart	marketing	TP subset size	Number of TP $$\frac{TP+FP}{TP+FN+TN+FN}\times 100\%$$	near the upper left-hand corner
ROC curve (the jagged line)	communications	TP rate FP rate	$tp = \dfrac{TP}{TP+FN}\times 100\%$ $fp = \dfrac{FP}{FP+TN}\times 100\%$	the northwest corner
PR Curve (hyperbolic in shape)	Information retrieval	Recall Precision	$tp = \dfrac{TP}{TP+FN}\times 100\%$ $\dfrac{TP}{TP+FP}\times 100\%$	toward the upper right hand corner
Cost curve	Classification with known error costs.	Normalized Expected Cost Probability Cost Function	$FN\times Pc(+)+FP\times(1-Pc(+))$ $PC(+)=\dfrac{p(+)*C(+|-)}{p(+)*C(+|-)+p(-)*C(-|+)}$	at the bottom of graphics

can do if the parameter is well chosen. Although such measures may be useful if costs and class distributions are unknown, one method must be chosen to handle all situations. ROC curves are a very useful tool for visualizing and evaluating classifiers.

3 Shortcomings of Some Performance Metrics

In this section, we consider the three most commonly metrics in Machine Learning: Accuracy, Precision/Recall and ROC Analysis. In each case, we begin by stating the advantages of these methods, continue by explaining the shortcomings they each have.

3.1 Shortcomings of Accuracy

Accuracy is the simplest, most intuitive evaluation measure for classifiers, but in learning extremely imbalanced data; the accuracy is often not an appropriate measure of performance. It is worth noting that Accuracy does not distinguish between the types of errors it makes..

We illustrate the problem more specifically with the following example: Consider two classifiers represented by the two confusion matrices of Table 3. These two classifiers behave quite differently. The one symbolized by the confusion matrix on left does not classify positive examples very well, getting only 200 out of 600 right. On the other hand, it does not do a terrible job on the negative data, getting 500 out of 600 well classified. The classifier represented by the confusion matrix on the right does the exact opposite, classifying the positive class better than the negative class with 500 out of 600 versus 200 out of 600. It is clear that these classifiers exhibit quite different strengths and weaknesses and shouldn't be used blindly on a data set. Yet, both classifiers exhibit the same accuracy of 58.3%.

Table 3. The trouble with Accuracy: Two confusion matrices yielding the same accuracy despite serious differences

Prediction Class	Algorithm A		Algorithm B	
True class	Positive	Negative	Positive	Negative
Positive P=600	200	400	500	100
Negative N=600	100	500	400	200

3.2 Shortcomings of Precision/Recall

Precision and Recall still have a relatively straightforward interpretation,Precision assesses to what extent the classifier was correct in classifying examples as positives, while Recall assesses to what extent all the examples that needed to be classified as positive were so. Precision and Recall have the advantage of not falling into the problem encountered by Accuracy. Indeed, considering, again, the two confusion matrices of Table 3, we can compute the values for Precision and Recall and obtain the following results:

Precision = 66.7% and Recall = 33.3% in the left case, and
Precision = 55.6% and Recall = 83.3% in the right

These results, indeed, reflect the strength of the right classifier on the positive data, with respect to the left classifier. This is a great advantage over accuracy.

More specifically, consider, as an extreme situation, the confusion matrices of table 4. The matrix on left is the same as the left matrix of Table 3, whereas the one on the right represents a new classifier tested on a different data set. Although both classifiers have the same Precision and Recall of 66.7% and 33.3%, respectively, it is clear that the classifier represented by the confusion matrix on the right presents a much more severe shortcoming than the one on left since it is incapable of classifying true negative examples as negative. This suggests that Precision and Recall are quite blind, in a certain respect, and might be more useful when combined with accuracy or when applied to both the positive and the negative class.

Table 4. The trouble with Precision and Recall: Two confusion matrices with the same values of precision and recall, but very different behaviors

| Prediction Class | Data set A | | Data set B | |
True class	Positive	Negative	Positive	Negative
Positive	200	400	200	400
Negative	100	500	100	0

3.3 Shortcomings of ROC

ROC Analysis has intuitive appeal. We only consider ROC Analysis: the performance measure it uses. The great advantage of this performance measure is that it separates the algorithm's performance over the positive class from its performance over the negative class. As a result, it does not suffer from either of the two problems we considered before. Indeed, in the case of Table 3, the left classifier is represented by ROC graph point (0.167, 0.333) while the right classifier is represented by point (0.667, 0.833). This clearly shows the tradeoff between the two approaches: although the left classifier makes fewer errors on the negative class than the right one, the right one achieves much greater performance on the positive class than the left one. It is, thus clear that ROC Analysis has great advantages over Accuracy, Precision and Recall. Nonetheless, there are reasons why ROC analysis is not an end in itself, either. This is illustrated numerically in the following example. Consider the two confusion matrices of Table 5. The classifier represented by the confusion matrix on the right generates a point in ROC space that is on the same vertical line as the point generated by the classifier represented by the confusion matrix on left ($x = $ FP rate $= 0.25\%$), but that is substantially higher (by 22.25%, [recall_left= 40%; recall_right = 62.5%]) than the one on left. This suggests that the classifier on the right is a better choice than the one on the left, yet, when viewed in terms of precision, we see that the classifier on left is much more precise, with a precision of 95.24% than the one on the right, with a precision of 33.3%. Ironically, this problem is caused by the fact that ROC Analysis nicely separates the performance of the two classes, thus staying away from the previous problems encountered by Accuracy and Precision/Recall.

Table 5. Two confusion matrices representing the same point in ROC space, but with very different precisions

Prediction Class True class	Algorithm A		Algorithm B	
	Positive	Negative	Positive	Negative
Positive	200	300	500	300
Negative	10	4000	1000	400000

4 Complex Numerical Evaluation Measures

Some measures that caught our attention have been used in medical diagnosis to analyze tests. They combine sensitivity and specificity and their complements.

4.1 F-Measure

F-measure is a popular evaluation metric for imbalance problem[8]. It is a kind of combination of recall and precision, which are effective metrics for information retrieval community where the imbalance problem exists. F-measure also depends on the β factor, which is a parameter that takes values from 0 to infinity and is used to control the influence of recall and precision separately. It can be shown that when $\beta=0$ then F-measure reduces to precision and conversely when $\beta \rightarrow \infty$ then F-measure approaches recall.

$$F\text{-measure} = \frac{(1+\beta)*Precision*Recall}{\beta*Precision+Recall} \tag{3}$$

When $\beta = 1$ then F-measure is suggested to integrate these two measures as an average, In principle, F-measure represents a harmonic mean between recall and precision.

$$F\text{-measure} = \frac{2*Precision*Recall}{Precision+Recall} \tag{4}$$

The harmonic mean of two numbers tends to be closer to the smaller of the two. Hence, a high F-measure value ensures that both recall and precision are reasonably high.

4.2 G-Mean

When the performance of both classes is concerned, both True Positive Rate (TP_{rate}) and True Negative Rate (TN_{rate}) are expected to be high simultaneously. Kubat et al[9] suggested the G-mean defined as:

$$G\text{-mean} = \sqrt{TP_{rate} \cdot TN_{rate}} \tag{5}$$

G-mean measures the balanced performance of a learning algorithm between these two classes. The comparison among harmonic, geometric, and arithmetic means are illustrated in[8].This measure tries to maximize accuracy in order to balance both classes at the same time. It is an evaluation measure that allows to simultaneously maximizing the accuracy in positive and negative examples with a good trade-off.

4.3 Youden's Index

The avoidance of failure complements accuracy, or the ability to correctly label examples. Youden's index $\gamma^{[10]}$evaluates the algorithm's ability to avoid failure-equally weights its performance on positive and negative examples:

$$\gamma = \text{sensitivity} + \text{specificity} - 1 \qquad (6)$$

Youden's index has been traditionally used to compare diagnostic abilities of two tests[11]. It summarizes sensitivity and specificity and has linear correspondence balanced accuracy (a higher value of γ means better ability to avoid failure):

$$\gamma = 2\text{AUC}_b - 1 \qquad (7)$$

4.4 Likelihoods

If a measure accommodates both sensitivity and specificity, but treats them separately, then we can evaluate the classifier's performance to finer degree with respect to both classes. The following measure combining positive and negative likelihoods allows us to do just that[11]:

$$\text{Positive Likelihood Ratio, } LR^+ = TPR/FPR = Sensitivity/(1 - Specificity) \qquad (8)$$

$$\text{Negative Likelihood Ratio, } LR- = (1 - TPR)/(1 - FPR) = (1 - Sensitivity)/\ Specificity \qquad (9)$$

A higher positive and a lower negative likelihood mean better performance on positive and negative classes respectively. If an algorithm does not satisfy this condition, then "positive" and "negative" likelihood values should be swapped.Relations depicted show that the likelihoods are an easy-to-understand measure that gives a comprehensive evaluation of the algorithm's performance.

4.5 Discriminatory Power

Another measure summarizes sensitivity and specificity is Discriminatory power (DP) [12]:

$$DP = \frac{\sqrt{3}}{\pi}(\log(Sensitivity/(1 - Sensitivity)) + \log(Specificity/(1 - Specificity))) \qquad (10)$$

To the best of our knowledge, until now DP has been mostly used in ML for feature selection. The algorithm is a poor discriminate if DP< 1, limited if DP< 2, fair if DP< 3, good – in other cases.

5   Conclusions

In general, there is no a generalized evaluation measure for various kind of classification problems. A good strategy to identify a proper evaluation measure should largely depend upon specific application requirement. Choose appropriate evaluation measure according to different background can help people make correct judgment to the algorithm classification performance. We hope that this very simple review of some of the problems surrounding evaluation will sensitize Machine Learning and Data Mining researchers to the issue and encourage us to think twice, prior to selecting and applying an evaluation method.

References

1. Pepe, M.S.: Receiver Operating Characteristic Methodology. Journal of the American Statistical Association 95, 308–311 (2000)
2. Fawcett, T.: ROC graphs: Notes and practical considerations for researchers. Machine learning 31 (2004)
3. Davis, J., Goadrich, M.: The relationship between precision-recall and ROC curves. In: The 23rd International Conference on Machine Learning (ICML 2006), pp. 233–240. ACM, New York (2006)
4. Drummond, C., Holte, R.C.: Cost curves: An improved method for visualizing classifier performance. Machine learning 65, 95–130 (2006)
5. Weiss, G.M.: Mining with rarity: a unifying framework. Newsletter of the ACM Special Interest Group on Knowledge Discovery and Data Mining 6, 7–19 (2004)
6. Bradley, A.P.: The use of the area under the ROC curve in the evaluation of machine learning algorithms. Pattern Recognition 30, 1145–1159 (1997)
7. Provost, F., Fawcett, T.: Analysis and Visualization of Classifier Performance: Comparison under Imprecise Class and Cost Distributions. In: The 3rd International Conference on Knowledge Discovery and Data Mining, pp. 43–48 (1997)
8. van Rijsbergen, C.J.: Information Retrieval. Butterworths, London (1979)
9. Kubat, M., Holte, R.C., Matwin, S.: Machine Learning for the Detection of Oil Spills in Satellite Radar Images. Machine Learning 30, 195–215 (1998)
10. Youden, W.J.: Index for rating diagnostic tests. Cancer 3, 32–35 (1950)
11. Biggersta, B.J.: Comparing diagnostic tests: a simple graphic using likelihood ratios. Statistics in Medicine 19, 649–663 (2000)
12. Blakeley, D.D., Oddone, E.Z., Hasselblad, V., Simel, D.L., Matchar, D.B.: Noninvasive carotid artery testing: a meta-analytic review. Am. Coll. Physicians 122, 360–367 (1995)

Hybrid Classification of Pulmonary Nodules

S.L.A. Lee[1], A.Z. Kouzani[1], and E.J. Hu[2]

[1] School of Engineering, Deakin University, Waurn Ponds,
VIC, 3217 Australia
[2] School of Mechanical Engineering, Adelaide University
SA 5005, Australia
{slale,kouzani}@deakin.edu.au, eric.hu@adelaide.edu.au

Abstract. Automated classification of lung nodules is challenging because of the variation in shape and size of lung nodules, as well as their associated differences in their images. Ensemble based learners have demonstrated the potentialof good performance. Random forests are employed for pulmonary nodule classification where each tree in the forest produces a classification decision, and an integrated output is calculated. A classification aided by clustering approach is proposed to improve the lung nodule classification performance. Three experiments are performed using the LIDC lung image database of 32 cases. The classification performance and execution times are presented and discussed.

Keywords: nodule, detection, lung images, classification, classification aided by clustering, ensemble learning, random forest.

1 Introduction

According to [1], early detection of lung cancer allows on-time therapeutic intervention and can thus increase the survival rate of the patient. With the evolution of spiral (helical) CT imaging technology, lung cancer screening with low-dose CT has become preferable due to its sensitivity in detecting lung nodules [2]. Conventional chest x-ray is of limited usage because it can only visualise large lung nodules [3]. Magnetic resonance imaging (MRI) is also used for preliminary lung cancer analysis. Further diagnosis through biopsy is conducted when there are suspicious findings in the preliminary analysis. CT imaging is more suitable for examining the lung tissue. Although MRI provides resolution with better contrast compared to CT, it produces less image slices than that of CT [4]. Therefore, CT is more popular for preliminary analysis of nodules which can be malignant.

With the constant improvement in the CT imaging technology, the amount of data per subject increases continuously. Whilst the additional data benefits the accuracy of nodule visualisation, it also increases the complexity of inspection and interpretation, and may affect the evaluation judgment by expert radiologists. Currently, nodules are mainly detected by one or multiple expert radiologists inspecting the captured CT images of the patient's lung through an image visualisation tool. Recent research however shows that there may exist inter-reader variability in the detection of nodules by expert radiologists [5]. An automated diagnostic system can thus provide initial

Z. Cai et al. (Eds.): ISICA 2009, CCIS 51, pp. 472–481, 2009.
© Springer-Verlag Berlin Heidelberg 2009

nodule detection which may help expert radiologists in their decision making. This automated approach could improve the precision of lung nodule detection.

Based on the review article by Li [3], the performance of a typical nodule detection from chest radiography recorded 70-75% sensitivity with 1.5 to 3 false positives per image. For thick-section CT images, the performance showed to increase to 80-90% sensitivity with only 1-2 false positives per image. Using thin-section CT scans, the performance of the system demonstrated to achieve 80 to 100% sensitivity with less than 1-2 false positive per image. The results only provide a rough indication and could not be directly compared with other existing work due to the difference in the size of the database, evaluation methods, and characteristics of the nodule. Sluimer *et al.* [6] elucidated that there are four steps included in a typical nodule detection system. The steps are pre-processing, nodule candidate scheme, false positive reduction, and classification. In this paper, the authors are interested in classification based lung nodule detection.

Ozekes *et al.* [7] implemented genetic cellular neural network to select the initial candidate nodules, classification of region of interest is performed by applying 3D template matching algorithm to locate nodule-like structures from the candidate nodules and fuzzy rule-based threshold is employed to effectively detect the true nodules. 16 cases with 425 slices from the LIDC database [8] is tested and 214 false positives (FP) and 100% sensitivity were recorded. Also, classification through 3D template matching is realised in Osman *et al.* [9] system where the nodule-like shapes are strengthen and the non-nodule shapes are suppressed. The test image consists of 160 slices from LIDC with 6 cases resulted 100% sensitivity and 0.46 FP per slice for nodule thickness $\geq$ 5.625mm.

Quantised convergence index filter is depicted by Matsumoto *et al.* [10] system to enhance the nodule-like lesion in the image slices. The intermediate nodule is classify by linear discriminant analysis with eight features and the system is evaluated using 5 datasets containing 50 nodules which recorded 90% sensitivity and 1.67 FP per slice. Utilisation of convergence index is reported in Nie *et al.* [11] system to calculate the nodule features of the region of interest. Mean shift clustering is used to group the feature vector sets to relevant nodule clusters and 39 nodules samples is tested with the best accuracy of 89% is obtained.

Fast marching algorithm is employed by Guo *et al.* [12] to solve the boundary leakage problem in lung lobes. Combining fast marching algorithm with support vector machine (SVM) based classifier demonstrated to outperforms watershed and conventional fast marching algorithm.

Ensemble classification [13] combines the decisions of multiple classifiers to form an integrated output has emerged as an effective classification method. It also refers to the algorithms that produce collections or ensembles of classifiers which learn to classify by training individual learners and fused their predictions. Multi-scale and multi-oriented filter bank responses produced invariant features used in multi-layer perceptrons (MLP) to train different data was proposed by Pereira *et al.* [14]. For 19 different classifiers in the MLP, the mean of 77.71% sensitivity and 87.18% specificity on the 154 nodules images are recorded. Another trend is the appearance of ensemble learners which utilized a large amount of weak classifiers with boosting. Ochs *et al.* [15] illustrated a method for voxel-by-voxel classification of airways, fissures, nodules, and vessels from CT images. The AdaBoost algorithm was implemented on the 29 cases. The area under the curve, A_z for nodule classification is 0.945.

Referring to the lung nodule detection review, it is evident that there is still room to improve the performance of automated nodule classification. The current systems have a tradeoff between sensitivity and specificity for the particular nodule size/class.

2 Existing Clustering-Based Classification Approaches

One of the techniques to improve image classification is through clustering [16] approach. Fig. 1 shows the common architecture for clustering which involves feature selection/extraction, inter-pattern similarity, and grouping. There exist well-established and popular clustering algorithms such as k-means, expectation maximization, fuzzy c-means, iterative self-organizing data analysis, and so on.

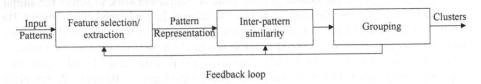

Fig. 1. Common architecture for clustering [17]

Classification aided by clustering has been applied across various research areas such as text [18], traffic [19], protein [20], medical [21], semantic role labelling [22], remote sensing [23], and spam filtering [24]. In the above research areas, employing the clustering method into classification has proven to improve the classification accuracies.

Kawata *et al.* [25] proposed a linear discriminant classification boosted by k-means clustering using malignant and benign pulmonary nodules datasets based on topological histogram features. The k-means clustering procedure in this context improves the homogeneity of the sample distribution by clustering the different properties according to the CT density value. Class I represents classes with high mean CT density value in the nodule pattern and Class II represents the lower mean value. Each class used an individual linear discriminant classifier which is trained using CT density value and curvature features extracted for the particular class and then, the classifier discriminate either benign or malignant pattern accordingly. The A_z value under the receiver operating characteristic (ROC) curve of the hybrid approach (k-means cluster with linear discriminant classifier) was recorded to be higher than the single linear discriminant classifier. Anatomical model is elucidate by Antonelli *et al.* [26] to distinguish the chest wall, trachea, and two lung lobes. A set of routines consisting of thresholding, region growing, and border detection are used to segment the 3D image. Fuzzy c-means algorithm is applied to cluster the 3D region of interest to either nodules or vessels. Fuzzy based neural network is trained to classify the nodules or non-nodules according to the 2D and 3D features. The system tested on 20 cases (contained 29 juxta-pleural nodules, 70 micro-nodules and 12 nodules) resulted sensitivity of 86.21% juxta-pleural, 82.86% micro-nodules, and 100% nodule with 1.4 false positives per slice.

According to Ozgencil et al. [22], implementation of k-means clustering to partition the data through the subset of features and multi-label SVM classifiers is then trained individually on each clusters using automatic feature selection improved the overall system classification accuracies by approximately 2% on validation data and 1.5 % for test data. For the argument identifier module, the pruning technique and the cluster based classification improved the testing performance from 84.67% achieved by a single SVM with pruning to 86.66%. Based on the argument labelling module, an accuracy of 89.77% was recorded when the cluster aided classification was employed comparing with 88.37% using single SVM classifier.

According to the literature, it is clear that classification aided by clustering (CAC) has proven to improve the classification accuracy.

3   Proposed Random Forest Classification Aided by EM Clustering on Pulmonary Nodules

In this section, the authors propose the architecture for a random forests (RF) CAC (see Fig. 2). It consists of training and test stages. The training stage consists of the nodule and non-nodule parts that are separated. Each part is clustered into M clusters. M could be made different for the nodule and non-nodule parts. Using the original labels of the training set instances, $2 \times M$ groups are formed named $N1$, $N2$, ...NM for nodules, and $NN1$, $NN2$, ..., NNM for non-nodules. A multi-class classifier consisting of $2 \times M$ classes is trained. In the test stage, on the other hand, the test set instances are presented to the developed classifier and then classified into $2 \times M$ classes.

The randomly selected training data consists of nodule and non-nodule is separately clustered using EM algorithm. After clustering the nodule and non-nodule patterns into two clusters each, the classifiers RF, SVM, and DT are trained on the four clusters produced previously with nodule and non-nodule class identified. For testing phase, the randomly selected nodule and non-nodule patterns not used in training phase is combined and presented to the cluster model (previously trained in the training phase). The results from the cluster model identify the instances which belong to each class. The relevant classifier's model (RF, SVM, and DT) are tested based on the instances present in each class.

To study the influence of the train and test dataset size on the performance of the systems, three randomly selected sets of training and test datasets are constructed, 20-80, 50-50, and 80-20. Details of the experimental procedure could be obtained from [27]. The parameters used in EM are as follows: maximum iterations=100, minimum standard deviation=1×10^{-6}, number of clusters=2, and seed=100.

We obtained 32 scans of different subjects from the LIDC database contained a total of 5721 image files. All images were of the size 512×512. For nodule patterns that could fit within a 30×30 region, we extracted from the image such a region surrounding the nodule pattern. On the other hand, for nodule patterns that could not fit within a 30×30 region, we extracted the entire nodule pattern first, and then resized it into a 30×30 region. In total, we created 1203 30×30 nodule files. In addition, we developed

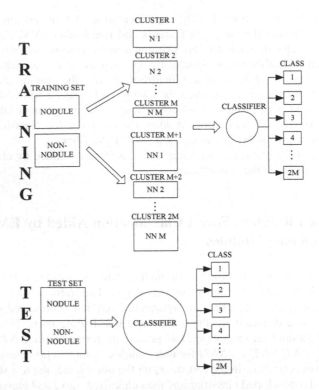

Fig. 2. Architecture for the proposed classification aided by clustering system

a program that searched through all 5721 image files and randomly captured 1203 30×30 regions that did not contain any nodule patterns. Thus, we formed a two-class dataset consisting of 1203 30×30 nodule and 1203 30×30 non-nodule patterns.

In the three experiments below, the parameters for each classifier are identified based on the consistency of the classifiers' performance. For RF parameters, the no-of-trees-grown is set to 100 and no-of-variables at each split is set to 25. The cost and gamma parameters of the SVM are set to $2^{4.5}$ and 2^{-29} respectively. Pruning confidence parameter and minimum number of instances per leaf of the decision tree (DT) is set to 0.25 and 2 accordingly.

In each experiment, the following parameters are calculated and presented: true positive rate (TPR), false positive rate (FPR), specificity (SPC), and accuracy (ACC).

3.1 Experiment I

In this experiment, 20% of the images of each of the nodule and non-nodule classes were used to form the training set, and the other 80% of the images were used to form the test set. The gray-level values were directly used as features for classification. The number of training and test images, and features were 482 (240

Table 1. Non-CAC and CAC Performances

Non-CAC Performances					
Classifier	TPR	FPR	SPC	ACC	Execution Time (sec)
DT	90.55	13.01	86.99	88.77	10.43
SVM	90.55	10.82	89.18	89.86	7.25
RF	94.50	11.55	88.45	91.48	6.97
CAC Performances					
Classifier	TPR	FPR	SPC	ACC	Execution Time (sec)
DT	92.32	14.67	85.33	88.83	70.14
SVM	91.17	11.24	88.76	89.97	65.43
RF	95.12	10.93	89.07	92.10	66.78

nodules and 242 non-nodule patterns), 1924 (963 nodules and 961 non-nodule patterns), and 900, respectively. Table 1 presented the result for single classification and CAC.

3.2 Experiment II

In this experiment, 50% of the images of each class were used to form the training set, and the other 50% of the images were used to form the test set. Therefore, the number of training and test images, and features were 1203 (601 nodules and 602 non-nodule patterns), 1203 (602 nodules and 601 non-nodule patterns), and 900, respectively. Table 2 presented the result for single classification and CAC.

Table 2. Non-CAC and CAC Performances

Non-CAC Performances					
Classifier	TPR	FPR	SPC	ACC	Execution Time (sec)
DT	90.70	8.99	91.01	90.86	15.29
SVM	89.70	5.66	94.34	92.01	10.86
RF	94.68	5.99	94.01	94.34	9.05
CAC Performances					
Classifier	TPR	FPR	SPC	ACC	Execution Time (sec)
DT	90.37	8.15	91.85	91.11	94.29
SVM	91.03	6.82	93.18	92.10	89.91
RF	95.02	5.99	94.01	94.51	90.13

3.3 Experiment III

In this experiment, 80% of the images of each class were used to form the training set, and the other 20% of the images were used to form the test set. Therefore, the number of training and test images, and features were 1924 (963 nodules and 961 non-nodule patterns), 482 (240 nodules and 242 non-nodule patterns), and 900, respectively. Table 3 presented the result for single classification and CAC.

Table 3. Non-CAC and CAC Performances

Non-CAC Performances					
Classifier	TPR	FPR	SPC	ACC	Execution Time (sec)
DT	91.67	9.92	90.08	90.87	65.68
SVM	90.00	4.96	95.04	92.53	41.27
RF	95.00	3.72	96.28	95.64	45.42
CAC Performances					
Classifier	TPR	FPR	SPC	ACC	Execution Time (sec)
DT	92.92	9.09	90.91	91.29	131.79
SVM	92.50	2.89	97.11	94.81	120.33
RF	96.67	3.72	96.28	96.47	119.47

4   Discussions

This study was motivated by the emergence of ensemble-based classification approaches, and also the importance of CAC approach. Three experiments were carried out on single classifiers, each using a different set of train and test datasets. The implemented systems were trained and tested on an Intel Xeon CPU 5130 @2.00GHz on-board of a Dell Precision Workstation 490. The total average execution time of both the training and the test operations were recorded.

As can be seen, the results demonstrate that the single RF based system performs better than the SVM as well as the DT in all experiments. The highest classification accuracy of 95.64%, sensitivity of 95.00%, specificity of 96.28%, and false positive rate of only 3.72% was produced by the RF based system where the training set contained 80% of images and the test set consisted of the remaining 20%. The highest classification accuracy achieved by the tested SVM and the DT classifiers were 92.53% and 91.29% for the same training and test sets, respectively. Considering the results in the three experiments, it can be stated that the RF classifier performed better where larger training set was used to train it.

Comparing the CAC performance (see in Fig. 3), RF CAC performs better than SVM and DT CAC. It recorded the highest classification accuracy of 96.47% with 80-20 dataset size. The other classifiers only achieved 94.81% and 91.29% accuracy each on the same dataset size. Overall, the proposed RF CAC improved the performance of lung nodule classification.

Clearly, the execution time recorded by CAC is higher than that of single classifier. This is due to the complexity of the CAC structure where training the EM algorithm and the classifier increase the execution time. For single classifier architecture, SVM classifier recorded an average of 19.79 seconds, which was slightly less than that of RF of 20.48 seconds for the three experiments. Also, SVM based CAC presented the lowest execution time for all the three dataset sizes, with an average of 91.54 seconds. The RF based CAC's execution time for the three different dataset sizes are slightly higher than SVM based classifier with an average of 92.13 seconds. It can be concluded that for the three classifiers, the RF CAC performs the best.

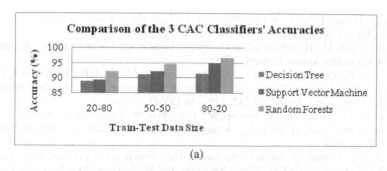

(a)

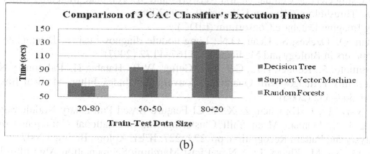

(b)

Fig. 3. (a) Accuracies results. (b) Execution times results

5 Conclusion

A random forest based classification aided by EM algorithm was developed. Its performance was compared against that of the support vector machine and the decision tree methods. Three different set of training and test datasets were devised to study the influence of the data sizes against the classification performance. The highest accuracy of 96.47% was produced by the proposed random forest-based CAC. The total average execution time of both the training and the test operations for this classifier was 92.13 seconds. The highest classification accuracy produced by the tested support vector machine and the decision tree classifiers were 92.53% and 91.29% for the same training and test sets, respectively. The proposed CAC is also compared against each individual classifier. Comparing the individual classifier against the CAC approach, an accuracy improvement ranging from 0.09% to 2.28% was recorded. Therefore, RF proved to be an accurate classifier and performed well when incorporating with the CAC approach for the lung nodule detection problem.

References

1. Mittinen, O.S.: Screening for lung cancer. Radiol. Clinics North Am. 38, 479–496 (2000)
2. Swensen, S.J., Jett, J.R., Hartman, T.E., Midthun, D.E., Sloan, J.A., Sykes, A.M., Aughenbaugh, G.L., Clemens, M.A.: Lung cancer screening with CT: Mayo Clinic experience. Radiology 226, 756–761 (2003)

3. Li, Q.: Recent Progress in Computer-Aided Diagnosis of Lung Nodules on Thin-Section CT. Comput. Med. Imaging Graph 31, 248–257 (2007)
4. Karthikeyan, D.: High-Resolution Computed Tomography of the Lungs - A Pattern Approach. Hodder Arnold, London (2005)
5. Armato III, S.G., McLennan, G., McNitt-Gray, M.F., Meyer, C.R., Yankelevitz, D., et al.: Lung Image Database Consortium Developing a Resource for the Medical Imaging Research Community. Radiology 232, 739–748 (2004)
6. Sluimer, I.C., Schilham, A., Prokop, M., Ginneken, B.: Computer Analysis of Computed Tomography Scans of the Lung: A Survey. IEEE Transactions on Medical Imaging 25, 385–405 (2006)
7. Ozekes, S., Osman, O., Ucan, O.N.: Nodule Detection in a Lung Region that's Segmented with Using Genetic Cellular Neural Networks and 3D Template Matching with Fuzzy Rule Based Thresholding. Korean J. Radiol. 9, 1–9 (2008)
8. Lung Imaging Database Consortium (LIDC)
9. Osman, O., Ozekes, S., Ucan, O.N.: Lung nodule diagnosis using 3D template matching. Computers in Biology and Medicine 37, 1167–1172 (2007)
10. Matsumoto, S., Kundel, H.L., Gee, J.C., Gefter, W.B., Hatabu, H.: Pulmonary Nodule Detection in CT Images with Quantized Convergence Index Filter. Medical Image Analysis 10, 343–352 (2006)
11. Nie, S.-D., Li, L.-H., Chen, Z.-X.: A CI Feature-Based Pulmonary Nodule Segmentation Using Three-Domain Mean Shift Clustering. In: International Conference on Wavelet Analysis and Pattern Recognition, pp. 223–227. IEEE Xplore, Beijing (2007)
12. Guo, Q., Xu, M., Zhang, J.: A Novel Fast Marching Segmentation Algorithm for Pulmonary Nodules in Chest Radiographs. In: Peng, Y., Weng, X. (eds.) 7th Asian-Pacific Conference on Medical and Biological Engineering (APCMBE), vol. 19, pp. 225–228. Springer, Heidelberg (2008)
13. Lu, J., Plataniotis, K.N., Venetsanopoulos, A.N., Li, S.Z.: Ensemble-based discriminant learning with boosting for face recognition. IEEE Trans. on Neural Networks 17, 166–178 (2006)
14. Pereira, C.S., Alexandre, L.A., Mendonça, A.M., Campilho, A.: A Multiclassifier Approach for Lung Nodule Classification. In: Campilho, A., Kamel, M.S. (eds.) ICIAR 2006. LNCS, vol. 4142, pp. 612–623. Springer, Heidelberg (2006)
15. Ochs, R.A., Goldin, J.G., Fereidoun, A., Kim, H.J., Brown, K., Batra, P., Roback, D., McNitt-Graya, M.F., Brown, M.S.: Automated classification of lung bronchovascular anatomy in CT using AdaBoost. Medical Image Analysis 11, 315–324 (2007)
16. Lu, D., Weng, Q.: A Survey of Image Classification Methods and Techniques for Improving Classification Performance. International Journal of Remote Sensing 28, 823–870 (2007)
17. Jain, A.K., Murty, M.N., Flynn, P.J.: Data Clustering: A Review. ACM Computing Surveys 31, 264–323 (1999)
18. Kyriakopoulou, A.: Text Classification Aided by Clustering: a Literature Review. In: Tools in Artificial Intelligence, pp. 233–252. I-Tech Education and Publishing KG, Vienna (2008)
19. Erman, J., Arlitt, M., Mahanti, A.: Traffic Classification Using Clustering Algorithms. In: Joint International Conference on Measurement and Modeling of Computer Systems (SIGCOMM), pp. 281–286. ACM, Pisa (2006)
20. Weston, J., Leslie, C., Zhou, D.Y., Elisseeff, A., Noble, W.S.: Semi-supervised protein classification using cluster kernels. Bioinformatics 21, 3241–3247 (2005)
21. Wang, S., Zhou, M., Gen, G.: Application of Fuzzy Cluster Analysis for Medical Image Data Mining. In: Proceedings of the IEEE International Conference on Mechatronics & Automation, pp. 631–636. IEEE Xplore, Niagara Falls (2005)

22. Ozgencil, N.E., McCracken, N., Mehrotra, K.: A Cluster-Based Classification Approach to Semantic Role Labeling. In: Nguyen, N.T., Borzemski, L., Grzech, A., Ali, M. (eds.) IEA/AIE 2008. LNCS (LNAI), vol. 5027, pp. 265–275. Springer, Heidelberg (2008)
23. Droj, G.: The Applicability of Fuzzy Theory in Remote Sensing Image Classification. Informatica L II, 89–96 (2007)
24. Neumayer, R.: Clustering Based Ensemble Classification for Spam Filtering. In: Proceedings of the 6th Workshop on Data Analysis, pp. 11–22. Elfa Academic Press, London (2006)
25. Kawata, Y., Niki, N., Ohmatsu, H., Kusumoto, M., Kakinuma, R., Mori, K., Nishiyama, H., Eguchi, Y., Kaneko, M., Moriyama, M.: Hybrid Classification Approach of Malignant and Benign Pulmonary Nodules Based on Topological and Histogram Features. In: Delp, S.L., DiGoia, A.M., Jaramaz, B. (eds.) MICCAI 2000. LNCS, vol. 1935, pp. 297–306. Springer, Heidelberg (2000)
26. Antonelli, M., Frosini, G., Lazzerini, B., Marcelloni, F.: A CAD System for Lung Nodule Detection based on an Anatomical Model and a Fuzzy Neural Network. North American Fuzzy Information Processing Society, pp. 448–453. IEEE Xplore (2006)
27. Kouzani, A., Lee, S., Hu, E.J.: Lung Nodules Detection by Ensemble Classification. In: Poo, A.-N. (ed.) Proceedings of 2008 IEEE International Conference on Systems, Man, and Cybernetics (SMC 2008), pp. 324–329. IEEE Xplore, Singapore (2008)

Erratum to: Evaluation Measures of the Classification Performance of Imbalanced Data Sets

Qiong Gu[1,2], Li Zhu [2], and Zhihua Cai[2]

[1] Faculty of Mathematics & Computer Science, Xiangfan University, Xiangfan, Hubei,
441053, China
[2] School of Computer, China University of Geosciences, Wuhan, Hubei, 430074, China
gujone@163.com, cugzhuli@163.com, zhcai@cug.edu.cn

Z. Cai et al. (Eds.): ISICA 2009, CCIS 51, pp. 461–471, 2009.
© Springer-Verlag Berlin Heidelberg 2009

DOI 10.1007/978-3-642-04962-0_55

The contents of Sections 4.3, 4.4, and 4.5 of the paper "Evaluation Measures of the Classification Performance of Imbalanced Data Sets", by Quiong Gu, appearing on pages 461-471 of this volume, were directly taken and copied from the paper "Beyond Accuracy, F-score and ROC: A Family of Discriminant Measures for Performance Evaluation", by M. Sokolova, N. Japkowicz, and S. Szpakowicz, published in LNCS 4304, pp. 1015-1021.

The original online version for this chapter can be found at
http://dx.doi.org/10.1007/978-3-642-04962-0_53

Author Index

Al-Owaisheq, Tasneem   369

Cai, Zhihua   461, E1
Cao, Jun   207
Chen, Hongwu   1
Chen, Jin   97
Chen, Jing   379
Chen, Jize   433, 452
Chen, Kejuan   16
Chen, Leichen   257
Chen, Peng   25
Chen, Qing   305, 413
Cui, Zhiming   188

Dai, Guangming   45, 247
Dong, Wen   313
Duan, W.   118

Feng, Daming   188
Fu, Bing   406
Fu, Chaojin   162

Galván-López, Edgar   56
Gao, Ji   329
Gao, Junxiang   66
Gao, Zhechao   1
Gao, Zhong-chang   285
Gong, Wenyin   215
Gu, Baolei   104
Gu, Qiong   461, E1
Guo, Weizhao   452

He, Guo-liang   110
He, Min   16
He, Yongxiang   225, 257
Hoai, Nguyen Xuan   56
Hu, Bin   387
Hu, E.J.   472
Hu, Chengyu   361
Huang, Li   433, 452
Huang, Shanzhi   225
Huang, Shiyong   35
Huang, Yuan-feng   295

Jia, Liyuan   215

Kang, Lishan   146, 240
Kang, Shuo   66
Kapsokalivas, L.   138
Kouzani, A.Z.   118, 472

Lee, S.L.A.   472
Lei, Xiu-juan   351
Li, Chuang   344
Li, Huanhuan   76
Li, Lingling   276
Li, Qing   180
Li, Xiang   25, 171
Li, Yuan-xiang   110
Li, Zhenhua   97, 379
Li, Zhigang   276
Liang, Dingwen   1
Liao, Binhua   427
Lim, Y.C.   118
Lin, Guangming   146
Liu, Gang   240
Liu, Jianjuan   88
Liu, Jing   247
Liu, Jinguo   199
Liu, Jingzheng   276
Liu, Kunqi   240
Liu, Tianyin   387
Liu, Xiaoming   1
Liu, Yong   232
Liu, Yu   207
Liu, Zhifeng   413
Lu, Xiaochun   419
Lu, Xin   146
Luo, Bing   406

Ma, Qian-zhi   351
Ma, Zhao   35
Mann, M.   138
McKay, Bob   56
Meshoul, Souham   369
Min, Peng   295
Mo, Li   45

Ning, Xiang-liang   320

O'Neill, Michael   56

Pan, Bowen   1
Pant, Bhasker   443
Pant, Kumud   443
Papageorgiou, Elpiniki I.   266
Pardasani, K.R.   443
Peng, Jin   313

Ren, Wei   35
Rossi, Ryan Anthony   128

Shao, Yuxiang   305, 413
Shi, Zhongzhi   110
Song, Jun   35
Steinhöfel, K.   138
Sun, Jian-ping   207
Sun, Jing-jing   351

Tan, Ping   320
Tian, Yanping   66
Tong, Hengjian   171
Turiho, Jean Claude   344

Ullah, A. Dayem   138
Uy, Nguyen Quang   56

Wang, Feng-hu   207
Wang, Yuan   361
Wei, Wei   180
Wei, Zhenhua   305
Wen, Shiping   398
Wu, Ailong   162
Wu, Hongbin   215
Wu, Jia   1
Wu, Jian   188
Wu, Jing   285
Wu, Song   66
Wu, Xiangning   361

Wu Xiao-yan   285
Wu, Xingxing   199

Xie, Kaia   344
Xu, Jing   188
Xue, Haidong   225, 257

Yang, Sheng   344
Yang, Xiaobo   433, 452
Yang, Zhimin   433, 452
Yao, Hong   156
Ye, Bin   180
Ye, Feng   9
Yin, Jian   433, 452
Yin, Junxun   419
Yu, Da   199
Yu, Linchen   156

Zeng, Sanyou   76
Zeng, Zhigang   398
Zhang, Dongzhi   16
Zhang, Fang   225
Zhang, Jingmin   240
Zhang, Qingbin   66
Zhang, Sifa   9
Zhang, You-wang   295
Zhao, Dan   97, 379
Zhao, Dongdong   76
Zhao, Man   171
Zhao, Yunsheng   97
Zheng, Hao   1
Zhou, Fu-lin   320
Zhou, Jungang   276
Zhou, Xianshan   406
Zhou, Youming   329
Zhu, Jiankai   45
Zhu, Li   25, 225, 257, 461, E1
Zhu, Xiao-dong   207
Zuo, Fengmei   9